Anonymus

Fancy and Practical Knitting

Anonymus

Fancy and Practical Knitting

ISBN/EAN: 9783742866226

Manufactured in Europe, USA, Canada, Australia, Japa

Cover: Foto ©Andreas Hilbeck / pixelio.de

Manufactured and distributed by brebook publishing software (www.brebook.com)

Anonymus

Fancy and Practical Knitting

FANCY AND PRACTICAL

.

KNITTING.

PRICE:

FIFTY CENTS OR TWO SHILLINGS.

PUBLISHED BY

THE BUTTERICK PUBLISHING CO. (LIMITED),

LONDON, AND NEW YORK,

1897.

CONTENTS.

— — —

Fancy and Practical Knitting.

ABBREVIATIONS USED IN KNITTING.

k.—Knit plain.
p.—Purl, or as it is often called, seam.
pl.—Plain knitting.
n.—Narrow.
k 2 to.—Knit 2 together. Same as n.
th o or o.—Throw the thread over the needle.
Make one.—Make a stitch thus: Throw the thread in front of the needle and knit the next stitch in the ordinary manner. (In the next row or round this throw-over, or put-over as it is frequently called, is used as a stitch.) Or, knit one and purl one out of a stitch.
To Knit Crossed.—Insert needle in the back of the stitch and knit as usual.

sl.—Slip a stitch from the left needle to the right needle without knitting it
sl and b.—Slip and bind. Slip one stitch, knit the next; pass the slipped stitch over the knit stitch as in binding off work.
To Bind or Cast Off.—Either slip or knit the first stitch; knit the next; pass the first or slipped stitch over the second, and repeat as far as directed.
Row.—Knitting once across the work when but two needles are used.
Round.—Knitting once around the work when four or more needles are used.
Repeat.—This means to work designated rows, rounds or portions of work as many times as directed.

☞ * Stars or asterisks mean, as mentioned wherever they occur, that the details given between them are to be repeated as many times as directed before going on with those details which follow the next star. As an example: * K 2, p 1, th o, and repeat twice more from * (or last *), means that you are to knit as follows: k 2, p 1, th o] k 2, p 1, th o] k2, p 1, th o, thus repeating the k 2, p 1, th o, twice more after making it the first time, making it three times in all before proceeding with the next part of the direction.

FANCY STITCHES, STRIPES AND OTHER DESIGNS IN KNITTING.

In issuing this book we have purposely omitted, in a majority of instances, giving sizes and numbers of needles and threads or yarn, for the following reasons: The book is prepared for various countries and localities, and in most of them materials and sizes of implements vary owing to different makes, the same as do sizes of gloves, shoes, etc. What we might direct as chosen from our own locality possibly might not be found in hundreds of other cities, though suitable substitutes would probably be there. Quantities are not given owing to the variation in the closeness of the work of knitters.

BALL STITCH.

No. 1.—Use fine needles and ordinary wool. Cast on any number of stitches divisible by 6 and allow 4 extra stitches, 2 for each edge. These edge stitches are always to be knit plain for a selvedge, and to keep the work straight and even.

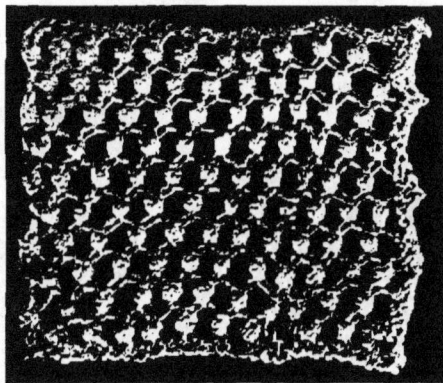

NO. 1.—BALL STITCH.

First row.—Knit the 2 edge stitches plain *, n 5 together and drop; o; then k 1, p 1, k 1, in the next loop; o, repeat the directions from * as many times as will make the desired width; knit two edge stitches plain.

Second row.—K 2, * p 5, o, (or around the needle to make 1 stitch), repeat from * as many times as desired, k 2.

Third row.—K 2, * o; then k 1, p 1, k 1, in loop; o, n 5 together and drop; repeat from * as many times as desired; k 2.

Fourth row.—K 2, * o; p 5, repeat from * as desired; k 2.

To drop:—Draw out the stitch into a long loop, push the spool or ball of thread through the loop, draw down snugly, thus dropping the stitch entirely. The purled rows come on the right side of the work.

This stitch is very pretty when used for fascinators and small shawls, or in silk, for a netting over children's plain silk hoods.

PINE-BURR PATTERN IN KNITTING.

No. 2.—Cast on an odd number of stitches.

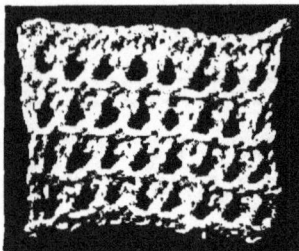

No. 2.—PINE-BURR PATTERN IN KNITTING.

First row.—Knit 1, then knit 2 together, to the end.
Second row.—Knit 1, over twice, knit 1, over twice; repeat to the end.
Third row.—Knit 1; purl 1 and knit 1 in the 2 put overs; repeat from beginning of row.
Fourth row.—Knit 1, * knit 2 together, knit 1; repeat from *. Repeat, beginning with 1st row.

STITCH FOR BABIES' QUILTS, CHAIR-BACKS, ETC.

No. 3.—The pretty stitch illustrated can be knitted in either wide or narrow strips. Use double Berlin or Germantown wool, and two medium-sized needles.
Cast on any number of stitches that may be divided by three.
First row.— Plain knitting.
Second row.— Purl.
Third row.—* Wool over, knit 3 stitches; with the left-hand needle pass the first of these 3 stitches over the other two; repeat from *.
Fourth row.— Purl.

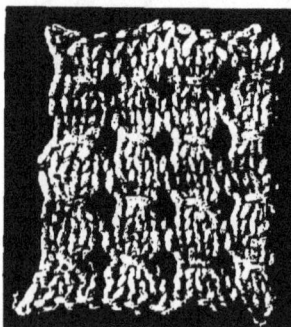

No. 3.—STITCH FOR BABIES' QUILTS, CHAIR-BACKS, ETC.

Repeat these four rows for all the work.
Strips of two prettily contrasting colors may be joined by a third color in single crochet, or by a fancy, over-and-over or cross stitch.

LASSO STITCH.

No. 4.—Cast on any number of stitches. All the rows are knitted in the same manner.
Put the needle in the stitch, and pass the thread entirely around both needles, then around the right-hand needle, and knit as in plain knitting.

The stitch is pretty for shawls, clouds, fascinators, etc., made of any popular yarn, such as Shetland and Ice wools, Saxony, split zephyr, Spanish knitting yarn, etc. White used alone or combined with any dainty tint would be appropriate.

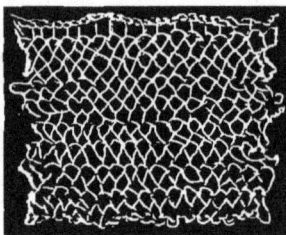

No. 4.—LASSO STITCH.

STITCH FOR LADIES' KNITTED SHAWL.

No. 5.— Use Saxony yarn and large ivory needles. Cast on any number of stitches divisible by three.
First and Second rows.—Knit plain.
Third row.—* Sl 1, n and b to the end of the needle.
Fourth row.—K 3 in every st. by inserting the

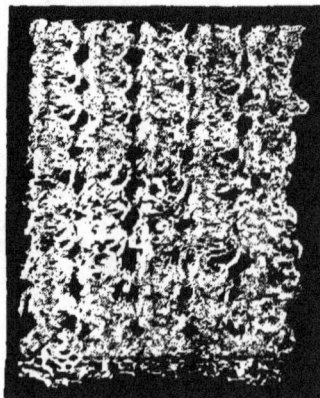

No. 5.—STITCH FOR LADIES' KNITTED SHAWL.

needle first forwards then backwards, then forwards, to the end of the needle.
Fifth and Sixth rows.—Knit plain.
Repeat from *.

SEMI-DOUBLE KNITTING.

No. 6.—Cast on any number of stitches.
First row.—Slip 1; then purl 1 and knit 1 out of every stitch across the row, purling the last stitch.

Second row.—Slip 1; then knit 2 together to end of row, purling the last stitch.
Repeat these two rows for all the work.

SPIDER-WEB DESIGN FOR DOUBLE MITTEN.

No. 7.—Yarn of two colors, red and white, is used. Cast on any number of stitches divisible by 8 and knit around plain with red.
First round.—Knit 3 red, 5 white; repeat all around.
Second round.—1 w, 1 r, * 1 w, 1 r, 3 w, 1 r, 1 w, 1 r; repeat from *.
Third round.—1 w, 1 r, * 2 w, 1 r, 1 w, 1 r, 2 w, 1 r; repeat from *.

No. 7.—SPIDER-WEB DESIGN FOR DOUBLE MITTEN.

Fourth round.—1 w, 1 r, * 3 w, 1 r, 3 w, 1 r; repeat from *.
Fifth round.—Like third.
Sixth round.—Like second.
Seventh round.—Like first.
Eighth round.—Knit plain with red. Repeat.

These directions are simply for the pattern without regard to the shape of the mitten to be knitted.

KNITTED STRIPE FOR AN AFGHAN.

No. 8.—Germantown wool is generally used in making an afghan, and the stripes may be all of one color or of varying shades to suit the taste of the worker.
The stripe illustrated calls for 31 stitches but it may be made wider if desired by casting on 10 stitches for every extra pattern. Use bone needles, medium size.
Cast on 31 stitches by knitting the stitch and then slipping it onto the left needle ; this method of casting on is required in order to make the decided point at the center of each pattern. Knit across plain.
First row.—Knit 1, o, *, k 3, slip 1, n, pass slipped

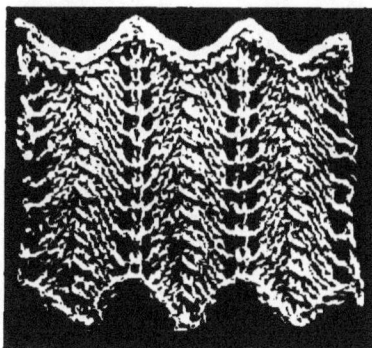

No. 8.—KNITTED STRIPE FOR AN AFGHAN.

stitch over, k 3, o, k 1, o, and repeat from * across the row, and end with o, k 1.
Second row.—Purl.
Repeat these two rows until the stripe is long enough, but at the end, instead of purling back for the last row, knit it, and then bind off ; this will form the points to correspond with the other end.

KNITTED FANCY STRIPE.
(For Illustration see Page 8.)

No. 9.—Cast on 38 stitches.
First row.—K 9 white (or light), 8 dark, 12 white, 6 dark, 3 white.
Second row.—P 3 w, 6 d, 12 w, 8 d, 9 w.
Third row.—K 7 w, 2 d, 2 w, 2 d, 18 w, 4 d, 3 w.
Fourth row.—P 3 w, 4 d, 18 w, 2 d, 2 w, 2d, 7 w.
Fifth row.—K 5 w, 6 d, 20 w, 2 d, 5 w.
Sixth row.—P 5 w, 2 d, 20 w, 6d, 5 w.
Seventh row.—K 3 w, 8 d, 20 w, 2 d, 5 w.
Eighth row.—P 5 w, 2 d, 20 w, 8 d, 3 w.
Ninth row.—K 3 w, 10 d, 16 w, 2 d, 7 w.

Tenth row.—P 7 w, 2 d, 16 w, 10d, 3 w.
Eleventh row.—K 3 w, 12 d, 10 w, 4 d, 9 w.
Twelfth row.—P 9 w, 4 d, 10 w, 12 d, 3 w.
Thirteenth row.—K 3 w, 6 d, 2 w, 6 d, 21 w

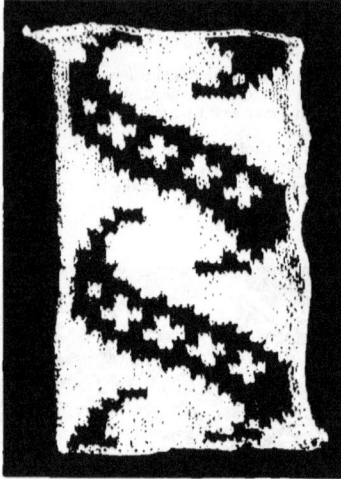

No. 9.—KNITTED FANCY STRIPE.
(For Description see Page 7.)

Fourteenth row.—P 21 w, 6 d, 2 w, 6 d, 3 w.
Fifteenth row.—K 3 w, 4 d, 6 w, 6 d, 19 w.
Sixteenth row.—P 19 w, 6 d, 6 w, 4 d, 3 w.
Seventeenth row.—K 5 w, 4 d, 2 w, 4 d, 2 w, 6 d, 15 w.
Eighteenth row.—P 15 w, 6 d, 2 w, 4 d, 2 w, 4 d, 5 w.
Nineteenth row.—K 7 w, 6 d, 6 w, 8 d, 11 w.
Twentieth row.—P 11 w, 8 d, 6 w, 6 d, 7 w.
Twenty-first row.—K 9 w, 6 d, 2 w, 4 d, 2 w, 6 d, 9 w.
Twenty-second row.—P 9 w, 6 d, 2 w, 4 d, 2 w, 6 d, 9 w.
Twenty-third row.—K 11 w, 8 d, 6 w, 6 d, 7 w.
Twenty-fourth row.—P 7 w, 6 d, 6 w, 8 d, 11 w.
Twenty-fifth row.—K 15 w, 6 d, 2 w, 4 d, 2 w, 4 d, 5 w.
Twenty-sixth row.—P 5 w, 4 d, 2 w, 4 d, 2 w, 6 d, 15 w.
Twenty-seventh row.—K 17 w, 8 d, 6 w, 4 d, 3 w.
Twenty-eighth row.—P 3 w, 4 d, 6 w, 8d, 17 w.
Twenty-ninth row.—K 21 w, 6 d, 2 w, 6 d, 3 w.
Thirtieth row.—P 3 w, 6 d, 2 w, 6 d, 21 w.
Thirty-first row.—K 25 w, 6 d, 2 w, 2 d, 3 w.
Thirty-second row.—P 3 w, 2 d, 2 w, 6 d, 25 w.
Thirty-third row.—K 27 w, 8 d, 3 w.
Thirty-fourth row.—P 3 w, 8 d, 27 w.
This completes the design. Begin again at the first row and repeat for each row.

PRINCE OF WALES' FEATHER DESIGN.

No. 10.—This is an old pattern and is said to have been very popular at the time the Prince of Wales was married, from its resemblance to the coat of arms used by Albert Edward—a plume of three white ostrich feathers. .
Knitted with any kind of wool and large needles, it makes a pretty shawl or skirt pattern. Cast on 50 stitches; knit across plain.
First row.—Knit 1, n 4 times; then th o and k 1, 8 times; n 8 times; th o and k 1, 8 times; n 4 times, k 1.
Second row.—Purl across. Repeat from these two rows. This forms one whole pattern and two half-patterns. The design can be made any size desired, but the half pattern must always be at each side.

FANCY STRIPE IN CHECK DESIGN.

(For Illustration see Page 9.)

No. 11.—This stripe is knitted with two contrasting colors, which may be in cotton, wool or silk, as preferred; and for convenience, l. (light) and d. (dark) are used to designate them.
Cast on 30 stitches. Three stitches are always knitted on each side with the light, and they will not be further mentioned in the directions.
First row.—K 3 d, 12 l, 3 d, 3 l, 3 d.
Second row.—Purl each color over itself.
Third row.—Like 1st row.
Fourth row.—P 3 l, 3 d, 6 l, 3 d, 3 l, 3 d, 3 l.
Fifth row.—Knit each color over itself.
Sixth row.—Like 4th row.
Seventh row.—K 6 l, 3 d, 6 l, 3 d, 3 l, 3 d.

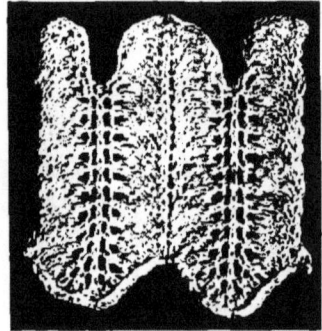

10.—PRINCE OF WALES' FEATHER DESIGN.

Eighth row.—Purl each color over itself.
Ninth row.—Like 7th row.
Tenth row.—P 12 l, 3 d, 3 l, 3 d, 3 l.
Eleventh row.—Knit each color over itself.
Twelfth row.—Like 10th row.

Thirteenth row.—K 12 l, 3 d, 3 l, 3 d, 3 l.

Fourteenth row.—Purl, working each color over itself.

Fifteenth row.—K 12 l, 3 d, 3 l, 3 d, 3 l.

Sixteenth row.—P 6 l, 3 d, 6 l, 3 d, 3 l, 3 d.

Seventeenth row.—Knit, working each color over itself.

Eighteenth row.—Like 16th.

Nineteenth row.—K 3 l, 3 d, 6 l, 3 d, 3 l, 3 d, 3 l.

Twentieth row.—Like 14th.

Twenty-first row.—Like 19th.

Twenty-second row.—P 3 d, 12 l, 3 d, 3 l, 3 d.

Twenty-third row.—Like 17th.

Twenty-fourth row.—Like 22nd.

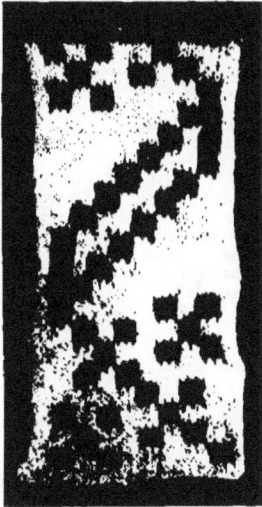

No. 11.—FANCY STRIPE IN CHECK DESIGN.
(For Description see Page 8.)

Twenty-fifth row.—K 18 l, 6 d.

Twenty-sixth row.—Purl each color over itself.

Twenty-seventh row.—Like 25th row.

Twenty-eighth row.—P 3 d, 3 l, 3 d, 15 l.

Twenty-ninth row.—K each color over itself.

Thirtieth row.—Like 28th row.

Thirty-first row.—K 12 l, 3 d, 6 l, 3 d.

Thirty-second row.—Like 26th row.

Thirty-third row.—Like 31st row.

Thirty-fourth row.—P 3 l, 3 d, 6 l, 3 d, 9 l.

Thirty-fifth row.—Knit each color over itself.

Thirty-sixth row.—Like 34th.

Thirty-seventh row.—K 6 l, 3 d, 6 l, 3 d, 6 l.

Thirty-eighth row.—Purl each color over itself.

Thirty-ninth row.—Like 37th row.

Fortieth row.—P 9 l, 3 d, 6 l, 3 d, 3 l.

Forty-first row.—Knit each color over itself.

Forty-second row.—Like 40th.

Forty-third row.—K 3 d, 6 l, 3 d, 12 l.

Forty-fourth row.—Purl each color over itself.

Forty-fifth row.—Like 43d row.

Forty-sixth row.—P 15 l, 3 d, 3 l, 3 d.

Forty-seventh row.—Knit each color over itself.

Forty-eighth row.—Like 46th row.

Forty-ninth row.—K 6 d, 18 l.

Fiftieth row.—Purl each color over itself.

Fifty-first row.—Like 49th row.

Repeat from 1st row.

GRECIAN STRIPE.

No. 12.—This stripe is knitted with two colors or shades of wool, silk, cotton or whatever material is desired, according to the use to which the stripe will be put. For convenience we use the terms light and dark, to distinguish the colors.

Cast on 27 stitches; 3 of these on each side are used for the edge and are always knitted with the light; therefore, they will not be further mentioned.

First row.—Knit 21 dark.

Second row.—Purl 21 d.

Third row.—Like first row.

Fourth row.—Purl 18 light, 3 d.

Fifth row.—Knit 3 d, 18 l.

Sixth row.—Like fourth row.

Seventh row.—Knit 3 d, 3 l, 15 d.

Eighth row.—Purl 15 d, 3 l, 3 d.

Ninth row.—Like seventh row.

Tenth row.—Purl 3 d, 9 l, 3 d, 3 l, 3 d.

Eleventh row.—Knit 3 d, 3 l, 3 d, 9 l, 3 l.

Twelfth row.—Like tenth row.

Thirteenth row.—K 3 d, 3 l, 9 d, 3 l, 3 d.

Fourteenth row.—Purl, working each color over itself.

Fifteenth row.—Like thirteenth row.

Sixteenth row.—P 3 d, 3 l, 3 d, 9 l, 3 d.

Seventeenth row.—Knit each color over itself.

Eighteenth row.—Like sixteenth row.

Nineteenth row.—K 15 d, 3 l, 3 d.

Twentieth row.—Purl each color over itself.

No. 12.—GRECIAN STRIPE.

Twenty-first row.—Like nineteenth row.

Twenty-second row.—P 3 d, 18 l.

Twenty-third row.—Knit each color over itself.

Twenty-fourth row.—Like twenty-second row.

Repeat from first row.

STRIPE-DESIGN FOR A KNITTED SKIRT.

No. 13.—Cast on 252 stitches, which will make just one-half the skirt for a grown person. In

No. 13.—STRIPE-DESIGN FOR A KNITTED SKIRT.

knitting the second half cast on 126 stitches and knit a piece as deep as you wish the placket to be ; then knit another piece exactly like it ; now put all the stitches of both pieces onto one needle, and proceed the same as with the first half. When you have knit the section to the desired length, bind off at the third row, and if you wish, crochet a narrow edge along the scollop.

First row.—*K 2, o, k 1, o, k 1, o, k 1, o, k 1, o, k 1, o, k 1, o, k 1, o, k 2, p 3, take off the next 2 stitches onto another needle, k 2, and put the 2 stitches back onto the first needle and knit them, p 3 and repeat from*.

Second row.—*Knit 3, p 4, k 3, p 19, and repeat from *.

Third row.—* K 1, sl and b, k 13, n, k 1, p 3, k 4, p 3, and repeat from *.

Fourth row.—* K 3, p 4, k 3, p 1, p 2 to., p 11, p to., p 1, and repeat from *.

Fifth row.—* K 1, sl and b, k 9, n, k 1, p 3, k 4, p 3, and repeat from *.

Sixth row.—* K 3, p 4, k 3, p 1, p 2 to., p 7, p 2 to., p 1 and repeat from *.

Repeat from first row for all the work.

FLUTED DESIGN FOR A KNITTED PETTICOAT.

No. 14.—To make the petticoat, a section of which is here illustrated, use soft knitting yarn, four-thread Saxony, Germantown or any preferred wool, and two rather coarse needles. Cast on 120 stitches for each side section, 140 for the front and 160 for the back ; or, if preferred,

the 540 stitches may be equally divided and the skirt knit in two pieces instead of four. After the pieces are knitted, sew them together "over-and-over." The pattern-design calls for 10 stitches ; therefore, if a larger or smaller skirt be desired, use any number of stitches divisible by 10 that are necessary to make the desired width.

First row.—P 9, k 1, and repeat across the row.

Second row.—P 2, k 8, and repeat across the row.

Third row.—P 7, k 3, and repeat.
Fourth row.—P 4, k 6 ; repeat.
Fifth row.—P 5, k 5 ; repeat.
Sixth row.—P 6, k 4 ; repeat.
Seventh row.—P 3, k 7 ; repeat.
Eighth row.—P 8, k 2 ; repeat.
Ninth row.—P 1, k 9 ; repeat.
Tenth row.—The same as last row.
Eleventh row.—Like 8th.
Twelfth row.—Like 7th.
Thirteenth row.—Like 6th.
Fourteenth row.—Like 5th.
Fifteenth. row.—Like 4th.
Sixteenth row.—Like 3rd.
Seventeenth row.—Like 2nd.
Eighteenth and Nineteenth rows.—Like 1st row.
Repeat from 2nd row until the section is a little more than half the length required, then narrow twice every 10 stitches. Now knit the remainder in rib fashion, thus : k 2, p 2 across the row, and,

No. 14.—FLUTED DESIGN FOR A KNITTED PETTICOAT.

in working back, be careful to knit the purled, and purl the knitted stitches of last row. If a child's skirt be desired. use only three instead of four widths.

KNITTING PATTERN FOR SHAWLS, CRADLE
COVERS, COUNTERPANES, ETC.

No. 15.—This pattern worked in Shetland or in
Germantown wool is suitable for shawls; in coarse
wool or knitting cotton, for cradle covers and
counterpanes. Cast on any number of stitches
divisible by 27, and allow 1 stitch at the beginning
and 5 stitches at the end, the latter for the open-
work stitches that close each stripe, and work as
follows:

First row.—Sl 1 st. * k 2, th o, k 2 together
crossed, k 5, k 2 to., th o, k 6, th o, k 2 together
crossed, * * k 1, k 2 to., th o, k 3, th o, k 2 to.
crossed; repeat from *; on the last 5, k 2, th o, k 2
to. crossed, k 1.

Second row.—Sl 1, p 2, th o, p 2 to., * p 10,
th o, p 2 to., p 13, th o, p 2 to.; repeat from *;
k 1.

Third row.—Sl 1, k 2, * th o, k 4, k 2 to.
crossed, k 4, k 2 to., th o, k 7, th o, k 2 to.
crossed, * * k 2 to., th o, k 5, th o, k 2 to. crossed,
k 1; repeat from *; finally, th o, k 2 to. crossed,
k 1.

Fourth row.—Work as in the 2nd row; all
the other even rows are to be worked in the
same manner, and therefore require no further
mention.

Fifth row.—Sl 1, k 2, * th o, k 2 to. crossed,
k 3, k 2 to., .th o, k 8, th o, k 2 to. crossed, * *
k 2, th o, k 2 to. crossed, k 1, k 2 to., th o, k 3;
repeat from *; at the end, th o, k 2 to. crossed,
k 1.

Seventh row.—Sl 1, k 2, * th o, k 2 to. crossed, k
1, th o, k 2 to. crossed, k 4, th o, k 2 to. crossed, k
4, th o, k 2 to. crossed, * * k 3, th o, n 2 st. (to do
so, sl the next st., k the following 2 together, and
over the resulting st., cast off the slipped st.), th o,
k 4; repeat from *; at the end of the round th o, k
2 to. crossed, k 1.

Ninth row.—Sl 1, k 2, * th o, k 2 to. crossed, k 2,
th o, k 2 to. crossed, k 4, th o, k 2 to. crossed, k 3;
th o, k 2, th o, k 2 to. crossed.

Eleventh row.—Sl 1, k 2, * th o, k 2 to. crossed,

knitting the next even row, repeat the 1st to 12th
rows as previously described.

Thirteenth row.—Like 1st half of the 1st row
to * * and last half from * * of 5th row.

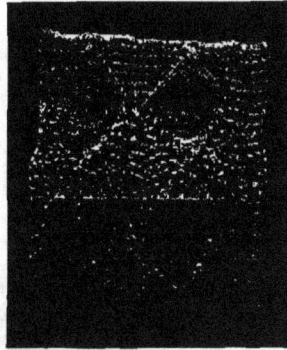

No. 16.—KNITTED STRIPE FOR COUNTERPANE OR AFGHAN.

Fifteenth row.—Like 1st half of 3rd row to * *
and like last half from * * of 7th row.

Seventeenth row.—Like 1st half to * * of 5th row,
and last half from * * of 9th row which is the same
as last half of 1st row.

Nineteenth row.—Like 1st half to * * of 7th row
and last half from * * of 11th row which corresponds with 3rd row.

Twenty-first row.—Like 1st of 9th row to * * and
last half from * * of 5th row.

Twenty-third row.—Like 1st half to * * of 11th
row, and last half from * * of 7th row.

This makes 3 complete diamonds and now you
repeat from the beginning and work as described
for last 3 for remainder of work.

KNITTED STRIPE FOR COUNTER-
PANE OR AFGHAN.

No. 16.—Cast on 33 stitches.

First row.—Slip 1, k 3, sl 1, k 1,
pass slipped stitch over, k 5, o, k 1,
o, k 5, sl 1, n, pass slipped stitch
over, k 5, o, k 1, o, k 5, sl 1, k 1,
pass slipped stitch over.

Second row.—Sl 1, k 5, p 3, k 11,
p 3 k 10.

Third row.—Sl 1, k 3, sl 1, k 1,
pass slipped stitch over, k 4, o, k 3,
o, k 4, sl 1, n, pass slipped stitch
over, k 4, o, k 3, o, k 4, sl 1, k 1, pass slipped stitch
over.

Fourth row.—Sl 1, k 4, p 5, k 9, p 5, k 9.

Fifth row.—Sl 1, k 3, sl 1, k 1, pass slipped stitch

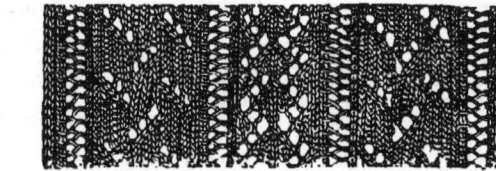

No. 15.—KNITTING PATTERN FOR SHAWLS, CRADLE COVERS, COUNTERPANES, ETC.

k 3, th o, k 2 to. crossed, k 4, th o, k 2 to. crossed,
k 2; then, in accordance with the preceding ex-
planation, work on the rest of the st. in the pattern
as in the corresponding part of the 3rd row; after

over, k 3, o, k 5, o, k 3, sl 1, n, pass slipped stitch over, k 3, o, k 5, o, k 3, sl 1, k 1, pass slipped stitch over.

Sixth row.—Sl 1, k 3, p 7, k 7, p 7. k 8.

Seventh row.—Sl 1, k 3, sl 1, k 1, pass slipped stitch over, k 2, o, k 7, o, k 2, sl 1, n, pass slipped stitch over, k 2, o, k 7, o, k 2, sl 1, k 1, pass slipped stitch over.

Eighth row.—Sl 1, k 2, p 9, k 5, p 9, k 7.

Ninth row.—Sl 1, k 3, sl 1, k 1, pass slipped stitch over, k 1, o, k 9, o, k 1, sl 1, n, pass slipped stitch over, k 1, o, k 9, o, k 1, slip 1, k 1, pass slipped stitch over.

Tenth row.—Sl 1, k 1, p 11, k 3, p 11, k 6.

Eleventh row.—Sl 1, k 3, sl 1, k 1, pass slipped stitch over, o, k 11, o, sl 1, n, pass slipped stitch over, o, k 11, o, slip 1, k 1, pass slipped stitch over.

Twelfth row.—Sl 1, p 13, k 1, p 13, k 5.

Thirteenth row.—Sl 1, k 4, o, k 5, sl 1, n, pass slipped stitch over, k 5, o, k 1, o, k 5, sl 1, n, pass slipped stitch over, k 5, o, k 1.

Fourteenth row. —Sl 1, k 1, p 11, k 3, p 11, k 6.

Fifteenth row. —Sl 1, k 5, o, k 4, sl 1, n, pass slipped stitch over, k 4, o, k 3, o, k 4, sl 1, n, pass slipped stitch over, k 4, o, k 2.

Sixteenth row. —Sl 1, k 2, p 9, k 5, p 9, k 7.

Seventeenth row.—Sl 1, k 6, o, k 3, sl 1, n, pass slipped stitch over, k 3, o, k 5, o, k 3, sl 1, n, pass slipped stitch over, k 3, o, k 3.

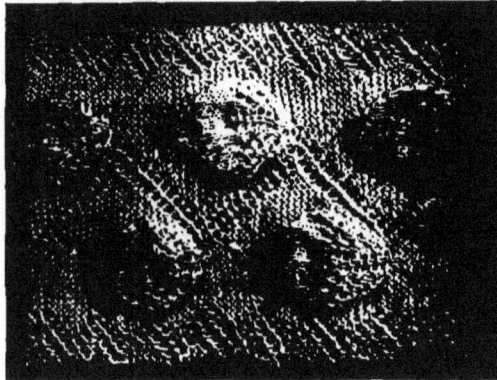

No. 17.—STRIPE FOR KNITTED BED-SPREAD.

First row.—Sl 1, k 14, o, k 1, o, k 16, sl 1, k 1, pass slipped stitch over, k 7, n, k 15.

Second row.—Sl 1, o, n, o, n, k 10, p 9, k 12, o, n, o, n, p 3, k 11, o, n, o, n.

Third row.—Sl 1, k 15, o, k 1, o, k 17, sl 1, k 1, pass slipped stitch over, k 5, n, k 15.

Fourth row.—Sl 1, k 1, o, n, o, n, k 9, p 7, k 11, o, n, o, n, k 1, p 5, k 10, o, n, o, n, k 1.

Fifth row.—Sl 1, k 16, o, k 1, o, k 18, sl 1, k 1, pass slipped stitch over, k 3, n, k 15.

Sixth row.—Sl 1, k 2, o, n, o, n, k 8, p 5, k 10, o, n, o, n, k 2, p 7, k 9, o, n, o, n, k 2.

Seventh row.—Sl 1, k 15, o, n, o, k 1, o, n, o, k 17, sl 1, k 1, pass slipped stitch over, k 1, n, k 15.

Eighth row.—Sl 1, k 3, o, n, o, n, k 7, p 3, k 9, o, n, o, n, k 3, p 9, k 8, o, n, o, n, k 3.

Ninth row.—Sl 1, k 15, o, n, k 1, o, k 1, o, k 1 n, o, k 17, sl 1, n, pass slipped stitch over, k 15.

Tenth row.— Sl 1, k 4, o, n, o, n, k 15, o, n, o, n, k 4, p 11, k 7, o, n, o, n, k 4.

Eleventh row. —Sl 1, k 15, o, n, o, n, o, n, k 1, o, n, o, n, o, k 33.

Twelfth row.— Sl 1, k 5, o, n, o, n, k 13, o, n, o, n, k 5, p 13, k 6, o, n, o, n, k 5.

Thirteenth row. —Sl 1, k 15, o, n, o, n, k 1, o, k 1, o, n, o, n, k 33.

Fourteenth row. —Sl 1, k 4, o, n, o, n, k 13, o, n, o, n, k 6, p 15, k 7, o, n, o, n, k 4.

Fifteenth row. —Sl 1, k 15, o, n, o, n, o, n, o, k 1, o, n, o, n, o, n, o, k 33.

Eighteenth row.—Sl 1, k 3, p 7, k 7, p 7, k 8.

Nineteenth row.—Sl 1, k 7, o, k 2, sl 1, n, pass slipped stitch over, k 2, o, k 7, o, k 2, sl 1, n, pass slipped stitch over, k 2, o, k 4.

Twentieth row.—Sl 1, k 4, p 5, k 9, p 5, k 9.

Twenty-first row.—Sl 1, k 8, o, k 1, sl 1, n, pass slipped stitch over, k 1, o, k 9, o, k 1, sl 1, n, pass slipped stitch over, k 1, o, k 4.

Twenty-second row.—Sl 1, k 5, p 3, k 11, p 3, k 10.

Twenty-third row.—Sl 1, k 9, o, sl 1, n, pass slipped stitch over, o, k 11, o, sl 1, n, pass slipped stitch over, o, k 6.

Twenty-fourth row.—Sl 1, k 6, p 1, k 13, p 1, k 11. Repeat from 1st row.

STRIPE FOR KNITTED BED-SPREAD.

No. 17.—Use No. 12 knitting needles and No. 12 four-strand knitting cotton. Cast on 58 stitches and knit across plain.

Sixteenth row.—Sl 1, k 3, o, n, o, n, k 13, o, n, o. n, k 7, p 17, k 8, o, n, o, n, k 3.

Seventeenth row.—Sl 1, k 15, o, n, o, n, o, n, k 1, o, k 1, o, k 1, n, o, n, o, n, o, n, o, k 33.

Eighteenth row.—Sl 1, k 2, o, n, o, n, k 13, o, n, o, n, k 8, p 19, k 9, o, n, o, n, k 2.

Nineteenth row.—Sl 1, k 14, sl 1, k 1, pass slipped stitch over, k 15, n, k 32.

Twentieth row.—Sl 1, k 1, o, n, o, n, k 13, o, n, o, n, k 9, p 17, k 10, o, n, o, n, k 1.

Twenty-first row.—Sl 1, k 14, sl 1, k 1, pass slipped stitch over, k 13, n, k 32.

Twenty-second row.—Sl 1, o, n, o, n, o, n, k 13, o, n, o, n, k 10, p 15, k 11, o, n, o, n.

Twenty-third row.—Sl 1, k 14, sl 1, k 1, pass slipped stitch over, k 11, n, k 32.

Twenty-fourth row.—Sl 1, k 1, o, n, o, n, k 11, o, n, o, n, k 11, p 13, k 10, o, n, o, k 1.

Twenty-fifth row.—Sl 1, k 14, sl 1, k 1, pass slipped stitch over, k 9, n, k 32.

Twenty-sixth row.—Sl 1, k 2, o, n, o, n, k 9, o, n, o, n, k 12, p 11, k 9, o, n, o, n, k 2.

Twenty-seventh row.—Sl 1, k 14, sl 1, k 1, pass slipped stitch over, k 7, n, k 16, o, k 1, o, k 15.

Twenty-eighth row.—Sl 1, k 3, o, n, o, n, k 7, p 3, k 1, o, n, o, n, k 11, p 9, k 8, o, n, o, n, k 3.

Twenty-ninth row.—Sl 1, k 14, sl 1, k 1, pass slipped stitch over, k 5, n, k 17, o, k 1, o, k 16.

Thirtieth row.—Sl 1, k 4, o, n, o, n, k 6, p 5, k 2, o, n, o, n, k 10, p 7, k 7, o, n, o, n, k 4.

Thirty-first row.—Sl 1, k 14, sl 1, k 1, pass slipped stitch over, k 3, n, k 18, o, k 1, o, k 17.

Thirty-second row.—Sl 1, k 3, o, n, o, n, k 7, p 7, k 3, o, n, o, n, k 9, p 5, k 8, o, n, o, n, k 3.

Thirty-third row.—Sl 1, k 14, sl 1, k 1, pass slipped stitch over, k 1, n, k 17, o, n, o, k 1, o, n, o, k 16.

Thirty-fourth row.—Sl 1, k 2, o, n, o, n, k 8, p 9, k 4, o, n, o, n, k 8, p 3, k 9, o, n, o, n, k 2.

Thirty-fifth row.—Sl 1, k 14, sl 1, n, pass slipped stitch over, k 17, o, n, k 1, o, k 1, o, k 1, o, k 1, n, o, k 16.

Thirty-sixth row.—Sl 1, k 1, o, n, o, n, k 9, p 11, k 5, o, n, o, n, k 18, o, n, o, n, k 1.

Thirty-seventh row.—Sl 1, k 32, o, n, o, n, o, n, k 1, o, n, o, n, o, k 16.

Thirty-eighth row.—Sl 1, o, n, o, n, k 10, p 13, k 6, o, n, o, n, k 18, o, n, o, n.

Thirty-ninth row.—Sl 1, k 32, o, n, o, n, k 1, o, k 1, o, k 1, n, o, n, o, k 16.

Fortieth row.—Sl 1, k 1, o, n, o, n, k 9, p 15, k 7, o, n, o, n, k 16, o, n, o, n, k 1.

Forty-first row.—Sl 1, k 32, o, n, o, n, o, n, o, k 1, o, n, o, n, o, n, o, k 16.

Forty-second row.—Sl 1, k 2, o, n, o, n, k 8, p 17, k 8, o, n, o, n, k 14, o, n, o, n, k 2.

Forty-third row.—Sl 1, k 32, o, n, o, n, o, n, k 1, o, k 1, o, k 1, n, o, n, o, n, o, k 16.

Forty-fourth row.—Sl 1, k 3, o, n, o, n, k 7, p 19, k 9, o, n, o, n, k 12, o, n, o, n, k 3.

Forty-fifth row.—Sl 1, k 31, sl 1, k 1, pass slipped stitch over, k 15, n, k 15.

Forty-six row.—Sl 1, k 4, o, n, o, n, k 6, p 17, k 10, o, n, o, n, k 10, o, n, o, n, k 4.

Forty-seventh row.—Sl 1, k 31, sl 1, k 1, pass slipped stitch over, k 13, n, k 15.

Forty-eighth row.—Sl 1, k 3, o, n, o. n, k 7, p 15, k 11, o, n, o, n, k 10, o, n, o, n, k 3.

Forty-ninth row.—Sl 1, k 31, sl 1, k 1, pass slipped stitch over, k 11, n, k 15.

Fiftieth row.—Sl 1, k 2, o, n, o, n, k 8, p 13, k 12, o, n, o, n, k 10, o, n, o, n, k 2.

Fifty-first row.—Sl 1, k 31, sl 1, k 1, pass slipped stitch over, k 9, n, k 15.

Fifty-second row.—Sl 1, k 1, o, n, o, n, k 9, p 11, k 13, o, n, o, n, k 10, o, n, o, n, k 1.

Fifty-third row.—Repeat from 1st row.

In beginning this stripe the half-berry formed by the directions may be omitted in order to produce a straight end to the stripe.

KNITTED STRIPE FOR SPREAD OR AFGHAN.

No. 18.—Cast on 58 stitches and knit across plain.

First row.—K 1, * p 2, k 1, n, k 6, p 2, th o, k 1, th o twice * (except after the last repetition, when you put it over once) ; repeat between stars across the row, k 1.

Second row.—K 1, * p 3, k 2, p 5, p 2 together, p 1, k 2 * ; repeat between stars to edge ; k 1.

Third row.—K 1, * p 2, k 1, n, k 4, p 2, k 1, th o, k 1, th o, k 1, * ; repeat between stars to edge ; k 1.

Fourth row.—K 1, * p 5, k 2, p 3, p 2 together, p 1, k 2, * ; repeat between stars to edge ; k 1.

Fifth row.—K 1, * p 2, k 1, n, k 2, p 2, k 2, th o, k 1, th o, k 2, * ; repeat between stars ; k 1.

Sixth row.—K 1, * p 7, k 2, p 1, p 2 together, p 1, k 2, * ; repeat between stars ; k 1.

Seventh row.—K 1, * p 2, k 1, n, p 2, k 3, th o, k 1, th o, k 3, * ; repeat between stars ; k 1.

Eighth row.—K 1, * p 9, k 2, n, k 2 * ; repeat between stars ; k 1.

Ninth row.—K 1, * p 2, th o, k 1, th o twice, p 2, k 1, n, k 6, * ; repeat between stars ; k 1.

Tenth row.—K 1, * p 5, p 2 together, p 1, k 2, p 3, k 2, * ; repeat between the stars ; k 1.

Eleventh row.—K 1, * p 2, k 1, th o, k 1, th o, k 1, p 2, k 1, n, k 4, * ; repeat between stars, k 1.

Twelfth row.—K 1, * p 3, p 2 together, p 1, k 2, p 5, k 2, * ; repeat between stars ; k 1.

Thirteenth row.—K 1, * p 2, k 2, th o, k 1, th o, k 2, p 2, k 1, n, k 2, * ; repeat between stars ; k 1.

Fourteenth row.—K 1, * p 1, p 2 together, p 1, k 2, p 7, k 2, * ; repeat between stars ; k 1.

Fifteenth row.—K 1, * p 2, k 3, th o, k 1, th o, k 3, p 2, k 1, n, * ; repeat between stars ; k 1.

Sixteenth row.—K 1, * p 2 together, k 2, p 9, k 2, * repeat between stars ; k 1.

Repeat from 1st row.

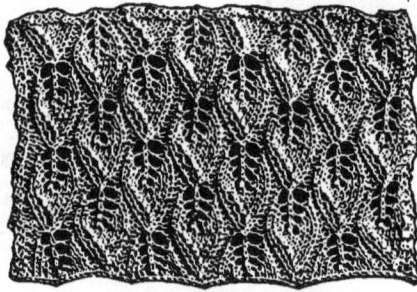

No. 18.—KNITTED STRIPE FOR SPREAD OR AFGHAN.

KNITTED EDGINGS, INSERTIONS AND FRINGES.

HEART AND DIAMOND EDGING.

No. 1.—Cast on 29 stitches, knit across plain twice.

First row.—K 3, o twice, p 2 to. twice, o, k 1,

No. 1.—HEART AND DIAMOND EDGING.

n, o twice, n twice, o twice, n, k 3, n, o, n, o, k 1, o, n, o, n, k 1.

Second row.—K 15, p 1, k 3, p 1, knit rest plain.

Third row.—K 3, o twice, p 2 to. twice, o, k 3, n, o twice, n, k 4, n, o, n, o, k 3, o, n, o, k 2.

Fourth row.—K 18, p 1. Knit rest plain.

Fifth row.—K 3, o twice, p 2 to. twice, o, k 10, n, o, n, o, k 5, o, n, o, k 2.

Sixth row.—Knit this and every even row up to the 42nd row inclusive, plain.

Seventh row.—K 3, o twice, p 2 to. twice, o, k 9, n, o, n, o, k 7, o, n, o, k 2.

Ninth row.—K 3, o twice, p 2 to. twice, o, k 8, n, o, k 1, o, n, o, n, k 3, n, o, n, o, n, k 1.

Eleventh row.—K 3, o twice, p 2 to. twice, o, k 7, n, o, n, o, k 1, o, n, o, n, k 1, n, o, n, o, n, k 1.

Thirteenth row.—K 3, o twice, p 2 to. twice, o, k 6, n, o, n, o, k 3, o, n, o, k 3 to., o, n, o, n, k 1.

Fifteenth row.—K 3, o twice, p 2 to. twice, o, k 5, n, o, n, o, k 13.

Seventeenth row.—K 3, o twice, p 2 to. twice, o, k 4, n, o, n, o, k 4, n, o, n, o, k 1, o, n, o, n, k 1.

Nineteenth row.—K 3, o twice, p 2 to. twice, o, k 3, n, o, n, o, k 4, n, o, n, o, k 3, o, n, o, k 2.

Twenty-first row.—K 3, o twice, p 2 to. twice, o, k 2, n, o, n, o, k 4, n, o, n, o, k 5, o, n, o, k 2.

Twenty-third row.—K 3, o, twice, p 2 to. twice, o k 1 n. o, n, o, k 4, n, o, n, o, k 7, o, n, o, k 2.

Twenty-fifth row.—K 3, o twice, p 2 to. twice, o, k 3, o, n, o, n, k 4, o, n, o, n, k 3, n, o, n, o, n, k 1.

Twenty-seventh row.—K 3, o twice. p 2 to. twice, o, k 4, o, n, o, n, k 4, o. n, o, n, k 1, n, o, n, o, n, k 1.

Twenty-ninth row.—K 3, o twice, p 2 to. twice, o, k 5, o, n, o, n, k 4, o, n, o, k 3 to., o, n, o, n, k 1.

Thirty-first row.—K 3, o twice, p 2 to. twice, o, k 6, o, n, o, n, k 12.

Thirty-third row.—K 3, o twice, p 2 to. twice, o, k 7, o, n, o, n, k 1, n, o, n, o, k 1, o, n, o, n, k 1.

Thirty-fifth row.—K 3, o twice, p 2 to. twice, o, k 8, o, n, o, k 3 to., o, n, o, n, k 3, o, n, o, k 2.

Thirty-seventh row.—K 3, o twice, p 2 to. twice, o, k 9, o, k 3 to., o, n, o, k 5, o, n, o, k 2.

Thirty-ninth row.—K 3 o, twice, p 2 to. twice, o, k 9, n, o, n, o, k 7, o, n, o, k 2.

Forty-first row.—K 3, o twice, p 2 to. twice, o, k 11, o, n, o, n, k 3, n, o, o, o, n, k 1.

Forty-third row—K 3, o twice, p 2 to. twice, o, k 3, n, o twice, n, k 5, o, n, o, n, k 1, n, o, n, o, n, k 1.

Forty-fourth row.—K 18, p 1, k 11.

Forty-fifth row.—K 3, o twice, p 2 to. twice, o, k 1, n, o twice, n twice, o twice, n, k 4, o, n, o, k 3 to., o, n, o, n, k 1.

Forty-sixth row.—K 15, p 1, k 3, p 1, k 9.

Forty-seventh row.—K 3, o twice, p 2 to. twice, o, k 3, n, o twice, n, k 15.

Forty-eighth row.—K 17, p 1, k 11.

Repeat from 1st row.

KNITTED HAMBURG INSERTION.

No. 2.—Cast on 18 stitches and knit across plain.

First row.—Th o twice, p 2 to., o, p 2 to., k 1, o

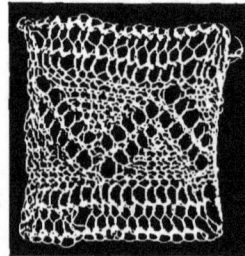

NO. 2.—KNITTED HAMBURG INSERTION.

twice, p 2 to., o, p 2 to., k 5, o twice, p 2 to., o, p 2 together.

Second row.—Th o twice, p 2 to., o, p 2 to k 10, o twice, p 2 to., o, p 2 to., drop last st.

Third row.—Th o twice, p 2 to., o, p 2 to., k 2, o twice, p 2 to., o, p 2 to., k 4, o twice, p 2 to., o, p 2 to., drop last st. in each row.

Fourth row.—Th o twice, p 2 to., o, p 2 to., k 10, o twice, p 2 to., o, p 2 together.

Fifth row.—Th o twice, p 2 to., o, p 2 to., k 3, o twice, p 2 to., o, p 2 to., k 3, o twice, p 2 to., o, p 2 together.

Sixth row.—Th o twice, p 2 to., o, p 2 to., k 10, o twice, p 2 to., o, p 2 together.

Seventh row.—Th o twice, p 2 to., o, p 2 to., k 4, o twice, p 2 to., o, p 2 to., k 2, o twice, p 2 to., o, p 2 together.

Eighth row.—Th o twice, p 2 to., o, p 2 to., k 10, o twice, p 2 to., o, p 2 together.

Ninth row.—Th o twice, p 2 to., o, p 2 to., k 5, o twice, p 2 to., o, p 2 to., k 1, o twice, p 2 to., o, p 2 together.

Tenth row.—Th o twice, p 2 to., o, p 2 to., k 10, o twice, p 2 to., o, p 2 together.

Eleventh row.—Th o twice, p 2 to., o, p 2 to., k 6, o twice, p 2 to., o, p 2 to., o, p 2 together.

Twelfth row.—Th o twice, p 2 to., o, p 2 to., k 10, o twice, p 2 to., o, p 2 together.

Thirteenth row.—Th o twice, p 2 to., o, p 2 to., k 10, o twice, p 2 to., o, p 2 to. Repeat from first row.

TRAILING FERN LACE.

No. 3.—Cast on 35 stitches and knit across plain.

First row.—K 3, o, n, o, n, n, k 5, o, k 1, o, k 1, o, k 1, o, k 5, n, k 1, o, n, o, n, o twice, n, k 1, o twice, n, k 1.

Second row.—K 3, p 1, k 3, p 1, k 1, o, n, o, n, p, 2 to., p 15, p 2 to., k 1, o, n, o, n, k 2

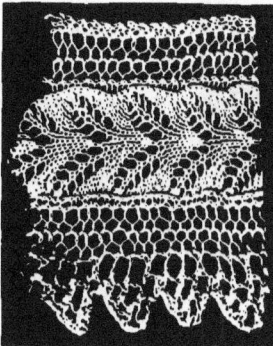

Third row.—K 3, o, n, o, n, n, k 4, o, k 1, o, k 3, o, k 1, o, k 4, n, k 1, o, n, o, n, o twice, n, k 6.

Fourth row.—K 2, o twice, n, o twice, n, k 2, p

1, k 1, o, n, o, n, p 2 to., p 15, p 2 to., k 1, o, n, o, n, k 2.

Fifth row.—K 3, o, n, o, n, n, k 3, o, k 1, o, k 5, o, k 1, o, k 3, n, k 1, o, n, o, n, o twice, n, k, 3, p 1, k 2, p 1, k 2.

Sixth row.—K 11, p 1, k 1, o, n, o, n, p 2 to., p 15, p 2 to., k 1, o, n, o, n, k 2.

Seventh row.—K 3, o, n, o, n, n, k 2, o, k 1, o, k 7, o, k 1, o, k 2, n, k 1, o, n, o, n, o twice, n, k 1, o twice, n, o twice, n, o twice, n, o twice, n, k 1.

Eighth row.—K 3, p 1, k 2, p 1, k 2, p 1, k 2, p 1, k 3, p 1, k 1, o, n, o, n, p 2 to., p 15, p 2 to., k 1, o, n, o, n, k 2.

Ninth row.—K 3, o, n, o, n, n, k 1, o, k 1, o, k 9, o, k 1, o, k 1, n, k 1, o, n, o, n, o twice, n, k 15.

Tenth row.—Bind off 12 stitches, k 4, p 1,

k 1, o, n, o, n, p 2 to., p 15, p 2 to., k 1, o, n, o, n, k 2. Repeat from first row.

PILLOW-CASE LACE.

No. 4.—Cast on 33 stitches; knit across plain.

First row.—K 2, th o twice, p 2 to., k 1, th o twice, p 2 to., k 1, * th o twice, k 3 to.; repeat from star 7 times, and k 1.

Second row.—K 3, p 1, k 2, p 1, k 2, p 1, k 2, p 1, k 2, p 1, k 2, p 1, k 2, p 1, k 2, p 1, k 1, th o twice, p 2 to., k 1, th o twice, p 2 to., k 2.

Third row.—K 2, th o twice, p 2 to., k 1, th o twice, p 2 to., k 26.

Fourth row.—K 26, th o twice, p 2 to., k 1, th o twice, p 2 to., k 2.

Fifth row.—K 2, th o twice, p 2 to., k 1, th o twice, p 2 to., k 1, th o twice, n, th o twice, n, th o twice, n, k 1.

Sixth row.—K 3, p 1, k 2, p 1, k 2, p 1, k 2, p 1, k 17, th o twice, p 2 to., k 1, th o twice, p 2 to., k 2.

Seventh row.—K 2, th o twice, p 2 to., k 1, th o twice, p 2 to., k 30.

Eighth row.—K 30, th o twice, p 2 to., k 1, th o twice, p 2 to., k 2.

Ninth row.—K 2, th o twice, p 2 to., k 1, th o twice, p 2 to., k 1, th o twice, k 3 to., th o twice, k 3 to., th o twice, n, k 12, th o twice, n, th o twice, n, th o twice, n, th o twice, n, k 1.

Tenth row.—K 3, p 1, k 2, p 1, k 2, p 1, k 2, p 1, k 14, p 1, k 2, p 1, k 2, p 1, k 1, th o twice, p 2 to., k 1, th o twice, p 2 to., k 2.

Eleventh row.—K 2, th o twice, p 2 to., k 1, th o twice, p 2 to., k 35.

Twelfth row.—K 35, th o twice, p 2 to., k 1, th o twice, p 2 to., k 2.

Thirteenth row.—K 2, th o twice, p 2 to., k 1, th o twice, p 2 to., k 26, * th o twice, n, repeat 3 times from *, k 1.

Fourteenth row.—K 3, p 1, k 2, p 1, k 2, p 1, k 2, p 1, k 26, th o twice p 2 to., k 1, th o twice, p 2 to., k 2.

Fifteenth row.—K 2, th o twice, p 2 to., k 1, th o twice, p 2 to., k 39.

Sixteenth row.—Bind off 13, knit 25, th o twice, p 2 to., k 1, th o twice, p 2 to., k 2.

KNITTED LACE FRINGE.

No. 5.—Cast on 66 stitches.

First row.—Sl 1, k 2, o, n, o, n, o, n, k 16, n, o,n, k 3, n, o twice, n, k 6, n, o twice, n, k 6, n, o twice, n, k 3, n, n, o, k 3.

Second row.—Over, n, rest plain, except over twice in previous rows, where you k 1, p 1. Knit all even rows the same.

Third row.—Sl 1, k 23, n, o, k 1, o, k 2, n, o twice, n, n, o twice, n, k 2, n, o twice, n, n, o twice, n, k 2, n, o twice, n, n, o twice, n, k 1, n, o, k 1, o, k 3.

Fifth row.—Sl 1, k 2, o, n, o, n, o, n, k 14, n, o, k 3, o, n, k 2, n, o twice, n, k 6, n, o twice, n, k 6, n, o twice, n, k 2, n, o, k 3, o, k 3.

Seventh row.—Sl 1, k 21, n, o, k 5, o, n, k 26, n, o, k 5, o, k 3.

Ninth row.—Sl 1, k 2, o, n, o, n, o, n, k 12, n, o, k 2, n, o, k 3, o, n, k 24, n, o, k 2, n, o, k 3, o, k 3.

Eleventh row.—Sl 1, k 19, n, o, k 2, n, o, k 1, o, n, k 2, o, n, k 22, n, o, k 2, n, o, k 1, o, n, k 2, o, k 3.

Thirteenth row.—Sl 1, k 2, o, n, c, n, o, n, k 10, n, o. k 2, n, o, k 3, o, n, k 2, o, n, k 20, n, o, k 2, n, o, k 3, o, n, k 2, o, k 3.

Fifteenth row.—Sl 1, k 17, n, o, < 2, n, o, k 5, o, n, k 2, o, n, k 7, n, o twice, n, k 7, n, o, k 2. n, o, k 5, o, n, k 2, o, k 3.

Seventeenth row.—Sl 1, k 2, o, n, o, n, o, n, k 8, n, o, k 2, n, o, k 2, n, o, k 3, o, n, k 2, o, n, k 4, n, o twice, n, n, o twice, n, k 4, n, o, k 2, n, o, k 3, o, n, k 2, o, n, k 2, o, k 3.

Nineteenth row.—Sl 1, k 15, n, o, k 2, n, o, k 2, n, o, k 1, o, n, k 2, o, n, k 2, o, n, k 5, n, o twice, n, k 5, n, o, k 2, n, o, k 2, n, o, k 1, o, n, k 2, o, n, k 2, o, k 3.

Twenty-first row.—Sl 1, k 2, o, n, o, n, o, n, n. k 6, n, o, k 2, n, o, k 2, n, o, k 3, o, n, k 2, o, n, k 2, o, n, k 2, n, o twice, n, k 2, n, o, k 2, n, o, k 2, n, o, k 3, o, n, k 2, o, n, k 2, o, k 3.

Twenty-third row.—Sl 1, k 13, n, o, k 2, n, o, k 2, n, o, k 5, o, n, k 2, o, n. k 2, o, n, k 3, n, o twice, n, k 3, n, o, k 2, n, o, k 2, n, o, k 5, o, n, k 2, o, n, k 2, o, k 3.

Twenty-fifth row.—Sl 1, k 2, o, n, o, n, o, n, k 4, n, o, k 2, n, o, k 2, n, o, k 2, n, o, k 3, o, n, k 2, o, n, k 2, o, n, k 8, n, o, k 2, n, o, k 2, n, o, k 2, n, o, k 3, o, k 2, n, o, k 3.

Twenty-seventh row.—Sl 1, k 11, n, o, k 2, n, o, k 2, n, o, k 2, n, o, k 1, o, n, k 2, o, n, k 2, o, n, k 2, o, n, k 6, n, o, k 2, n, o, k 2, n, o, k 2, n, o, k 1, o, n, k 2, o, n, k 2, o, n, k 2, o, k 3.

Twenty-ninth row.—Sl 1, k 2, o, n, o, n, o, n, k 2, *n, o, k 2, n, o, k 2, n, o, k 2, n, o, k 3, o, n, k 2, o, n, k 2, o, n, k 2, * o, n, k 4, repeat between stars; o, k 3.

Thirty-first row.—Sl 1, k 9, n, o, k 2, n, o,· k 2, n, o, k 2, n, o, k 5, o, n, k 2, o, n, k 2, o, n, k 2, o, n, k 2, n, o, k 2, n, o, k 2, n, o, k 2, n, o, k 2, n, o, k 2, n, o, k 5, o, n, k 2, o, n, k 2, o, n, k 2, o, k 3.

Thirty-third row.—Sl 1, k 2, o, n, o, n, o, n, n, o, k 2, n, o, k 2, n, o, k 2, n, o, k 2, n, o, k 2, n, o, k 3, o, n, k 2, n, o, k 2, n, o, k 2, n, o, k 2, n, o, k 2, n, o, k 2, n, o, k 3, o, n, k 2, o, n, k 2, o, n, k 2, o, n, k 2, o, n, k 2, o, n, k 2, o, k 3.

Thirty-fifth row.—Sl 1, k 10, o, n, k 2, o, n, k 2, o, n, k 2, o, n, k 3, n, o, k 2, n, o, k 2, n, o, k 2, n, o, k 4, o, n, k 2, o, n, k 2, o, n, k 2, o, n, k 3, n, o, k 2, n, o, k 2, n, o, k 2, n, o, k 2, n, o, k 2.

Thirty-seventh row.—Sl 1, k 2, o, n, o, n, o, n, k 3, o, n, k 2, o, n, k 2, o, n, k 2, o, n, k 1, n, o, k 2, n, o, k 2, n, o, k 2, n, o, k 6, o, n, k 2, o, n, k 2, o, n, k 2, o, n, k 1, n, o, k 2, n, o, k 2, n, o, k 2, n, o, n, k 2.

NO. 5.—KNITTED LACE FRINGE.

Thirty-ninth row.—Sl 1, k 12. 0, n, k 2, 0, n, k 2, 0, n, k 2, 0, k 3 together, 0, k 2, n, 0, k 2, n, 0, k 2, n, 0, k 8, 0, n, k 2, 0, n, k 2, 0, n, k 2, 0, k 3 together, 0, k 2, n, 0, k 2, n, 0, k 2, n, 0, n, k 2.

Forty-first row.—Sl 1, k 2, 0, n, 0, n, 0, n, k 5, 0, n, k 2, 0, n, k 2, 0, n, k 5, n, 0, k 2, n, 0, k 2, n, 0, k 3, n, 0 twice, n, k 3, 0, n, k 2, 0, n, k 2, 0, n, k 5, n, 0, k 2, n, 0, k 2, n, 0, n, k 2.

Forty-third row.—Sl 1, k 14, 0, n, k 2, 0, n, k 2, 0, n, k 3, n, 0, k 2, n, 0, k 2, n, 0, k 2, n, 0 twice, n, n, 0 twice, n, k 2, 0, n, k 2, 0, n, k 2, 0, n, k 3, n, 0, k 2, n, 0, k 2, n, 0, n, k 2.

Forty-fifth row.—Sl 1, k 2, 0, n, 0, n, 0, n, k 7, 0, n, k 2, 0, n, k 2, 0, n, k 1, n, 0, k 2, n, 0, k 2, n, 0, k 5, n, 0 twice, n, k 5, 0, n, k 2, 0, n, k 2, 0, n, k 1, n, 0, k 2, n, 0, k 2, n, 0, n, k 2.

Forty-seventh row.—Sl 1, k 16, 0, n, k 2, 0, n, k 2, 0, k 3 together. 0, k 2, n, 0, k 2, n, 0, k 4, n, 0 twice, n, n, 0 twice, n, k 4, 0, n, k 2, 0, n, k 2, 0, k 3 together, 0, k 2, n, 0, k 2, n, 0, n, k 2.

Forty-ninth row.—Sl 1, k 2, 0, n, 0, n, 0, n, k 9, 0, n, k 2, 0, n, k 5, n, 0, k 2, n, 0, k 7, n, 0 twice, n, k 7, 0, n, k 2, 0, n, k 5, n, 0, k 2, n, 0, n, k 2.

Fifty-first row.—Sl 1, k 18, 0, n, k 2, 0, n, k 3, n, 0, k 2, n, 0, k 20, 0, n, k 2, 0, n, k 3, n, 0, k 2, n, 0, n, k 2.

Fifty-third row.—Sl 1, k 2, 0, n, 0, n, 0, n, k 11, 0, n, k 2, 0, n, k 1, n, 0, k 2, n, 0, k 22, 0, n, k 2, 0, n, k 1, n, 0, k 2, n, 0, n, k 2.

Fifty-fifth row.—Sl 1, k 20, 0, n, k 2, 0, k 3 together, 0, k 2, n, 0, k 24, 0, n, k 2, 0, k 3 together, 0, k 2, n, 0, n, k 2.

Fifty-seventh row.—Sl 1, k 2, 0, n, 0, n, 0, n, k 13, 0, n, k 5, n, 0, k 26, 0, n, k 5, n, 0, n, k 2.

Fifty-ninth row.—Sl 1, k 22, 0, n, k 3, n, 0, k 28, 0, n, k 3, n, 0, n, k 2.

Sixty-first row.—Sl 1, k 2, 0, n, 0, n, 0, n, k 15. 0, n, k 1, n, 0, k 3, n, 0 twice, n, k 6, n, 0 twice, n, k 6, n, 0 twice, n, k 3, 0, n, k 1, n, 0, n, k 2.

Sixty-third row.—Sl 1, k 24, 0, k 3 together, 0, k 2, n, 0 twice, n, n, 0 twice, n, k 2, n, 0 twice, n, n, 0 twice, n, k 2, n, 0 twice, n, n, 0 twice, n, k 2, 0, k 3 together, 0, n, k 2. Repeat from first row.

The fringe may be of any desired depth; it is tied in each loop on the edge.

KNITTED FRINGE.

No. 6. — Cut fringe the desired length from Germantown yarn. Cast on 14 stitches, knit across plain.

First row.—Slip off 1st stitch, knit 2nd stitch, then lay three strands of the fringe so that the middle of the strands come between 2nd and 3rd stitches. Knit 3rd and 4th stitches, then bring the three strands of fringe at the back of your work to the front, between 4th and 5th stitches. Knit 5th and 6th stitches, then lay all the strands of fringe together between 6th and 7th stitches, which puts the strands at the back of work. Knit 7th and 8th stitches, and bring the strands (or fringe) to the front between 8th and 9th stitches. Knit 9th and 10th stitches; again put the fringe to the back of work between 10th and 11th stitches; knit 11th and 12th stitches, bring fringe to the front between 12th and 13th stitches. Knit 13th and 14th stitches.

Second row.—Knit across plain.

Third row.—Like 1st row, and 4th row like 2nd, and so on to the end.

DOUBLE APPLE LEAF LACE.

(For Illustration see Page 18.)

No. 7.—This lace, together with the accompanying insertion would decorate aprons or pillow-cases very effectively. Cast on 31 stitches, and purl across once.

First row.—Sl 1, k 3, p 1, p 2 to., 0, k 1, 0, k 1, 0, k 1, p 2, k 1, 0, k 1, 0, k 1, o twice, p 2 to., p 1, k 6, 0, n, 0, n, 0, n, k 1.

Second row.—P 2; k 1, p 1 in loop; p 3; k 1, p 1, in loop; p 6, k 2, p 6, k 2, p 6, k 2, p 4.

Third row.—Sl 1, k 3, p 1, p 2 to., 0, k 2, 0, k 1, 0, k 2, p 2, k 2, 0, k 1, 0, k 2, o twice, p 2 to., p 1, k 8, 0, n, 0, n, 0, n, k 1.

Fourth row.—P 2; k 1, p 1 in loop; p 3; k 1, p 1, in loop; p 8, k 2, p 8, k 2, p 8, k 2, p 4.

Fifth row.—Sl 1, k 3, p 1, p 2 to., 0, k 3, 0, k 1,

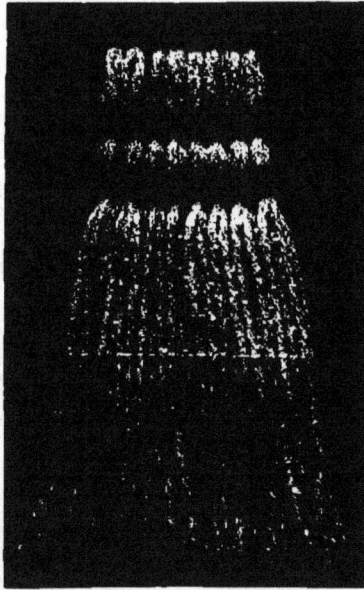

No. 6.—KNITTED FRINGE.

o, k 3, p 2, k 3, o, k 1, o, k 3, o twice, p 2 to., p 1, k 10, o, n, o, n, o, n, k 1.

Sixth row.—P 2 ; k 1, p 1 in loop ; p 3 ; k 1, p 1, in loop ; p 10, k 2, p 10, k 2, p 10, k 2, p 4.

NO. 7.—DOUBLE APPLE LEAF LACE.
(For Description see Page 17.)

Seventh row.—Sl 1, k 3, p 1, p 2 to., o, k 4, o, k 1, o, k 4, p 2, k 4, o, k 1, o, k 4, o twice, p 2 to., p 1, k 12, o, n, o, n, o, n, k 1.

Eighth row.—P 2 ; k 1, p 1, in loop ; p 3 ; k 1, p 1, in loop ; p 12, k 2, p 12, k 2, p 12, k 2, p 4.

Ninth row.—Sl 1, k 3, p 1, p 2 to., o, k 5, o, k 1, o, k 5, p 2, k 5, o, k 1, o, k 5, o twice, p 2 to., p 1, k 21.

Tenth row.—Bind off 8 stitches, p 12, k 2, p 14, k 2, p 14, k 2, p 4.

Eleventh row.—Sl 1, k 3, p 1, p 2 to., o, sl and b., k 9, n, p 2, sl and b., k 9, n, o twice, p 2 to., p 1, k, 6, o, n, o, n, o, n, k 1.

Twelfth row.—P 2 ; k 1, p 1, in loop ; p 3 ; k 1, p 1, in loop ; p 6, k 2, p 12, k 2, p 12, k 2, p 4.

Thirteenth row.—Sl 1, k 3, p 1, p 2 to., o, sl and b., k 7, n, o twice, p 2, o, sl and b., k 7, n, o twice, p 2 to., p 1, k 8, o, n, o, n, o, n, k 1.

Fourteenth row.—P 2 ; k 1, p 1, in loop ; p 3 ; k 1, p 1, in loop ; p 8, k 2, p 10, k 4, p 10, k 2, p 4.

Fifteenth row.—Sl 1, k 3, p 1, p 2 to., o, sl and b., k 5, n, p 2, o, p 2, sl and b., k 5, n, o twice, p 2 to., p 1, k 10, o, n, o, n, o, n, k 1.

Sixteenth row.—P 2 ; k 1, p 1, in loop ; p 3 ; k 1, p 1, in loop ; p 10, k 2, p 8, k 2, p 8, k 2, p 4.

Seventeenth row.—Sl 1, k 3, p 1, p 2 to., o, sl and b., k 3, n, p 2, o, k 1, o twice, p 2, sl and b., k 3, n, o twice, p 2 to., p 1, k 12, o, n, o, n, o, n, k 1.

Eighteenth row.—P 2 ; k 1, p 1, in loop ; p 3 ; k 1, p 1, in loop ; p 12, k 2, p 6, k 2, p 3, k 2, p 6, k 2, p 4.

Nineteenth row.—Sl 1, k 3, p 1, p 2 to., o, sl and b., k 1, n, p 2, o, k 1, o twice, p 1, k 1 in next, o, k 1, o twice, p 2, sl and b., k 1, n, o twice, p 2 to., p 1, k 21.

Twentieth row.—Bind off 8 stitches, p 12, k 2, p 4, k 2, p 3, k 2, p 3, k 2, p 4, k 2, p 4.

Twenty-first row.—Sl 1, k 3, p 1, p 2 to., o, k 3 to., p 2, o, k 1, o, k 1, o, k 1, p 2, k 1, o, k 1, o, k 1, o twice, p 2, k 3 to , o twice, p 2 to., p 1, k 6, o, n, o, n, o, n, k 1.

Twenty-second row.—P 2 ; k 1, p 1, in loop ; p 3 ; k 1, p 1, in loop ; p 6, k 2, n, k 2, p 6, k 2, p 6, k 2, n, k 2, p 4.

Twenty-third row.—Sl 1, k 3, p 4, p 2 to., o, k 2, o, k 1, o, k 2, p 2, k 2, o, k 1, o, k 2, o twice, p 2 to., p 4, k 8, o, n, o, n, o, n, k 1.

Twenty-fourth row.—P 2 ; k 1, p 1, in loop ; p 3 ; k 1, p 1, in loop ; p 8, k 1, n, k 2, p 8, k 2, p 8, k 2, n, k 1, p 4.

Twenty-fifth row.—Sl 1, k 3, p 3, p 2 to., o, k 3, o, k 1, o, k 3, p 2, k 3, o, k 1, o, k 3, o twice, p 2 to., p 3, k 10, o, n, o, n, o, n, k 1.

Twenty-sixth row.—P 2 ; k 1, p 1, in loop ; p 3 ; k 1, p 1, in loop ; p 10, n, n, p 10, k 2, p 10, n, n, p 4.

Repeat from 7th row.

Made in wool this is a very pretty border for a counterpane, spread or afghan.

DOUBLE APPLE LEAF INSERTION.

No. 8.—This insertion is made to match the edging just given. It will also form very pretty stripes, knitted in wool, for afghans, etc.

Cast on 22 stitches and purl across once.

First row.—Sl 1, k 3, p 1, p 2 to., o, k 1, o, k 1, o, k 1, p 2, k 1, o, k 1, o, k 1, o twice, p 2 to., p 1, k 4.

Second row.—Sl 1, p 3, k 2, p 6, k 2, p 6, k 2, p 4.

Third row.—Sl 1, k 3, p 1, p 2 to., o, k 2, o, k 1, o, k 2, p 2, k 2, o, k 1, o, k 2, o twice, p 2 to., p 1, k 4.

Fourth row.—Sl 1, p 3, k 2, p 8, k 2, p 8, k 2, p 4.

Fifth row.—Sl 1, k 3, p 1, p 2 to., o, k 3, o, k 1, o, k 3, p 2, k 3, o, k 1, o, k 3, o twice, p 2 to., p 1, k 4.

Sixth row.—Sl 1, p 3, k 2, p 10, k 2, p 10, k 2, p 4.

Seventh row.—Sl 1, k 3, p 1, p 2 to., o, k 4, o, k 1, o, k 4, p 2, k 4, o, k 1, o, k 4, o twice, p 2 to., p 1, k 4.

Eighth row.—Sl 1, p 3, k 2, p 12, k 2, p 12, k 2, p 4.

Ninth row.—Sl 1, k 3, p 1, p 2 to., o, k 5, o, k 1, o, k 5, p 2, k 5, o, k 1, o, k 5, o twice, p 2 to., p 1, k 4.

Tenth row.—Sl 1, p 3, k 2, p 14, k 2, p 14, k 2, p 4.

Eleventh row.—Sl 1, k 3, p 1, p 2 to., o, slip and bind, k 9, n, p 2, s and b., k 9, n, o twice, p 2 to., p 1, k 4.

Twelfth row.—Sl 1, p 3, k 2, p 12, k 2, p 12, k 2, p 4.

FIGURE NO. 8.—DOUBLE APPLE LEAF INSERTION.

Thirteenth row.—Sl 1, k 3, p 1, p 2 to., o, s and b., k 7, n, o twice, p 2, o, s and b., k 7, n, o twice, p 2 to., p 1, k 4.

Fourteenth row.—Sl 1, p 3, k 2, p 10, k 4, p 10, k 2, p 4.

Fifteenth row.—Sl 1, k 3, p 1, p 2 to., o, s. and

b., k 5, n, p 2, o, p 2, s. and b., k 5, n, o twice, p 2 to., p 1, k 4.

Sixteenth row.—Sl 1, p 3. k 2, p 8, k 2, p 1, k 2, p 8, k 2, p 4.

Seventeenth row.—Sl 1, k 3, p 1, p 2 to., o, s and b., k 3, n, p 2, o, k 1, o twice, p 2, s and b., k 3, n, o twice, p 2 to., p 1, k 4.

Eighteenth row.—Sl 1, p 3, k 2, p 6, k 2, p 3, k 2, p 6, k 2, p 4.

Nineteenth row.—Sl 1, k 3, p 1, p 2 to., o, s and b., k 1, n, p 2, o, k 1, o twice ; p 1 and k 1 in next stitch ; o, k 1, o twice, p 2, s and b., k 1, n, o twice, p 2 to., p 1, k 4.

Twentieth row.—Sl 1, p 3, k 2, p 4, k 2, p 3, k 2, p 3, k 2, p 4, k 2, p 4.

Twenty-first row.—Sl 1, k 3, p 1, p 2 to., o, k 3 to., p 2, o, k 1, o, k 1, o, k 1, p 2, k 1, o, k 1, o, k 1, o twice, p 2, k 3 to., o twice, p 2 to., p 1, k 4.

Twenty-second row.—Sl 1, p 3, k 2, n, k 2, p 6, k 2, p 6, k 2, n, k 2, p 4.

Twenty-third row.—Sl 1, k 3, p 4, p 2 to., o, k 2, o, k 1, o, k 2, p 2, k 2, o, k 1, o, k 2, o twice, p 2 to., p 4, k 4.

Twenty-fourth row.—Sl 1, p 3, k 1, n, k 2, p 8, k 2, p 8, k 2, n, k 1, p 4.

Twenty-fifth row.—Sl 1, k 3, p 3, p 2 to., o, k 3, o, k 1, o, k 3, p 2, k 3, o, k 1, o, k 3, o twice, p 2 to., p 3, k 4.

Twenty-sixth row.—Sl 1, p 3, n, n, p 10, k 2, p 10, n, n, p 4. Repeat from 7th row.

DIAMOND INSERTION.

No. 9.—Cast on 23 stitches and knit across plain.

First row.—Sl 1, k 1, o twice, p 2 to., k 15, o twice, p 2 to., k 2.

Second row.—Sl 1, k 1, o twice, p 2 to., k 1, o,

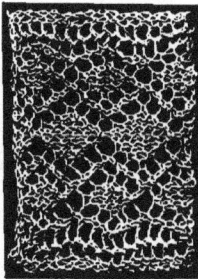

No. 9.—DIAMOND INSERTION.

k 1, o, n, o, n, k 3, n, o, n, o, k 1, o, k 1, o twice, p 2 to., k 2.

Third row.—Sl 1, k 1, o twice, p 2 to., k 17, o twice, p 2 to., k 2.

Fourth row.—Sl 1, k 1, o twice, p 2 to., k 1, o, k 3, o, n, o, n, k 1, n, o, n, o, k 3, o, k 1, o twice, p 2 to., k 2.

Fifth row.—Sl 1, k 1, o twice, p 2 to., k 19, o twice, p 2 to., k 2.

Sixth row.—Sl 1, k 1, o twice, p 2 to., k 1, o, k 5, o, n, o, k 3 to., o, n, o, k 5, o, k 1, o twice, p 2 to., k 2.

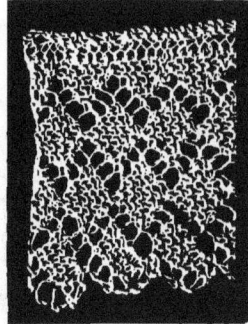

No. 10.—DIAMOND LACE.

Seventh row.—Sl 1, k 1, o twice, p 2 to., k 21, o twice, p 2 to., k 2.

Eighth row.—Sl 1, k 1, o twice, p 2 to., n, o, n, k 1, n, o, n, o, k 3, o, n, o, n, k 1, n, o, n, o twice, p 2 to., k 2.

Ninth row.—Like fifth.

Tenth row.—Sl 1, k 1, o twice, p 2 to., n, o, k 3 to., o, n, o, k 5, o, n, o, k 3 to., o, n, o twice, p 2 to., k 2.

Eleventh row.—Like third row.

Twelfth row.—Sl 1, k 1, o twice, p 2 to., n, o, k 3 to., o, k 7, o, k 3 to., o, n, o twice, p 2 to., k 2. Repeat.

DIAMOND LACE.

No. 10.—Cast on 20 stitches.

First row.—Knit across plain.

Second row.—Sl 1, k 1, th o, n, k 2, n, (by slipping the needle through the back part of the sts.) th o, k 3, th o, n, k 3, n (as before), th o, k 1, th o, k 1. Then work as follows :

Third and all odd rows.—Knit plain until there are but 3 stitches left ; th o, n, k 1.

Fourth row.—Sl 1, k 1, th o, n, k 1, n (under as before directed), th o, k 5, th o, n, k 1, n, th o, k 3 th o, k 1.

Sixth row.—Sl 1, k 1, th o, n, n (as before), th o, k 7, th o, narrow 3 stitches together, th o, k 5, th o, k 1.

Eighth row.—Sl 1, k 1, th o, n, k 2, th o, n, k 3, n (as before), th o, k 3, th o, n, k 4, th o, k 1.

Tenth row.—Sl 1, k 1, th o, n, k 3, th o, n, k 1, n (as before), th o, k 5, th o, n, k 4, th o, k 1.

Twelfth row.—Sl 1, k 1, th o, n, k 4, th o, n 3 stitches together, th o, k 7 ; slip the last 6 stitches on the needle over the next stitch, th o, and knit the one you slipped the stitches over.

Repeat from second row for the next scollop.

OAK LEAF AND ACORN LACE.

No. 11.—Cast on 31 stitches and knit across plain.

First row.—Th o, n, k 7, o, k 3, n, p 1,

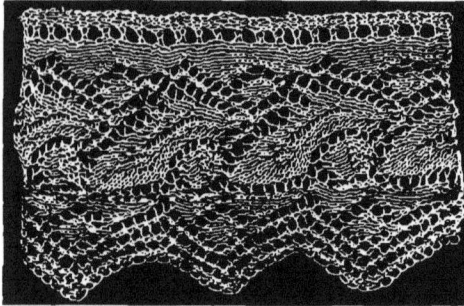

No. 11.—OAK LEAF AND ACORN LACE.

n, k 3; o and narrow twice; k 3, o, n, k 2.

Second row.—K 4, p 11, k 1, p 8; o, and narrow twice; o, k 1, p 1.

Third row.—Th o, n, k 8, o, k 2 in next stitch, o, k 2, n, p 1, n, k 2; o and n twice; k 7.

Fourth row.—K 4, p 10, k 1, p 11; o and n twice; o, k 1, p 1+.

Fifth row.—Th o, n, k 9, o, k 2 in each of next 3 stitches, o, k 4, n, p 1, n, k 3, o, n, o, k 3, o, n, k 2.

Sixth row.—K 4, p 10, k 1, p 16; o and n twice; o, k 1, p 1.

Seventh row.—Th o, n, k 9, n, o, k 6, o, k 2, n, p 1, n, k 3; o and n twice; k 1, o, n, k 2.

Eighth row.—K 4, p 9, k 1, p 14, p 2 together, o, p 1; over and narrow twice; o, k 1, p 1.

Ninth row.—Th o, n, k 10, n, o, k 6, o, k 2, n, p 1, n, k 2, o, n, o, k 7.

Tenth row.—K 4, p 9, k 1, p 4, k 2 in each of next 6 stitches, p 3, p 2 together, o, p 3, o and n twice; o, k 1, p 1.

Eleventh row.—Th o, n, k 11, n, o, p 12, o, k 2, n, p 1, n, k 1, o, n, o, k 4, o, n, k 2.

Twelfth row.—K 4, p 9, k 1, p 4, n 6 times, p 2, purl 2 together, o, p 5; o and n twice; o, k 1, p 1.

Thirteenth row.—Th o, n, k 12, n, o, p 6, o, k 2, n, p 1, k 2, o, n, o, k 9.

Fourteenth row.—K 4, p 10, k 1, p 4, n 3 times, p 4, o, p 2 together, p 1, p 2 together, o and n 3 times, p 1.

Fifteenth row.—Th o, n, k 12, o, k 1, o, p 3 together, o, k 2, n, p 1, k 2, o, n, o, k 6, o, n, k 2.

Sixteenth row.—K 4, p 11, k 1, p 12, o, p 3 together; o and n 3 times; purl 1.

Seventeenth row.—Th o, n, k 11, o, k 3, o, n, o, k 1, n, p 1, k 2, o, n, o, k 11.

Eighteenth row.—K 4, p 13, k 1, p 14, p 2 together; o and n twice; purl 1.

Nineteenth row.—Th o, n, k 10, o, k 5; o and n twice; purl 1, n, o, n, o, k 1, o, n, k 5, o, n, k 2.

Twentieth row.—K 4, p 12, k 1, p 13, p 2 together; o and n 3 times, p 1.

Twenty-first row.—Th o, r, k 9, o, k 7, o, n, o, k 3 together, o, n, o, k 3, o, n, k 8.

Twenty-second row.—K 4, p 26, p 2 together, o, n 3 times, p 1.

Twenty-third row.—Th o, n, k 8, o, k 4, p 1, k 4, over, sl 1, k 1, bind, sl 1, n, bind, pass the first slipped stitch over the last, o, k 5, o, n, k 3, o, n, k 2.

Twenty-fourth row.—K 4, p 17, k 1, p 8; o and n 3 times; p 1.

Twenty-fifth row.—Th o, n, k 8, o, k 3, n, p 1, n, k 3; o and n twice; k 1, n, o, n, k 7.

Twenty-sixth row.—K 4, p 15, k 1, p 6, p 2 together; o and n 3 times; p 1.

Twenty-seventh row.—Th o, n, k 7, o, k 3, n, p 1, n, k 3, o, n, o, k 3, together, o, k 5, o, n, k 2.

Twenty-eighth row.—K 4, p 14, k 1, p 5, p 2 together; o and n 3 times; p 1.

Twenty-ninth row.—Th o, n, k 6, o, k 3, n, p 1, n, k 3; o and n twice; k 9.

Thirtieth row.—K 4, p 12, k 1, p 7; o and n 3 times; p 1.

KNITTED LACE.

No. 12.—Use No. 90 linen thread, and steel needles No. 20 for this lace. Cast on 20 stitches and knit across plain.

First row.—Sl 1, k 3, o, n, k 1, o twice, k 6, o, n, k 1, o twice, n, o, n, p 1 in same stitch before slipping it off the needle.

Second row.—N, o, n, k 1, p 1, k 2, o, n, k 6, p 1, k 2, o, n, k 3.

Third row.—Sl 1, k 3, o, narrow 3 times, k 1, o

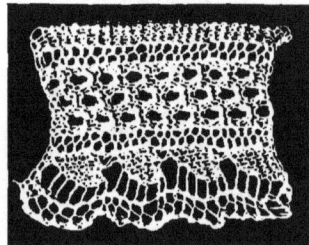

No. 12.—KNITTED LACE.

twice, k 4, o, n, k 2, o twice, n, o, n, p 1 in same stitch.

Fourth row.—N, o, n, k 1, p 1, k 3, o, n, k 4, p 1, k 4, o, n, k 3.

Fifth row.—Sl 1, k 3, o, n, k 2, n, n, k 1, o twice, k 2, o, n, k 3, o twice, n, o, n, p 1.

Sixth row.—N, o, n, k 1, p 1, k 4, o, n, k 2, p 1, k 6, o, n, k 3.

Seventh row.—Sl 1, k 3, o, n, k 1, o twice, k 3, n, n, k 1, o, n, k 4, o twice, n, o, n, p 1.

Eighth row.—N, o, n, k 1, p 1, k 5, o, n, k 6, p 1, k 2, o, n, k 3.

Ninth row.—Sl 1, k 3, o, narrow 3 times, k 1, o twice, k 4, o, n, k 5, o twice, n, o, n, p 1.

Tenth row.—N, o, n, k 1, p 1, k 6, o, n, k 4, p 1, k 4, o, n, k 3.

Eleventh row.—Sl 1, k 3, o, n, k 2, n, n, k 1, o, twice, k 2, o, n, k 6, o twice, n, o, n, p 1.

Twelfth row.—N, o, n, k 1, p 1, n, pass purled stitch over, n, pass last st. over, n, pass stitch over, k 1, o, n, k 2, p 1, k 6, o, n, k 3.

Thirteenth row.—Sl 1, k 3, o, n, k 1, o twice, k 3, n, n, k 1, o, n, k 1, o twice, n, o n, p 1.

Repeat from 2nd row.

NARROW KNITTED LACE.

No. 13.—Cast on 14 stitches.

First row.—Sl 1, k 1, o, n, k 1, o, n, o, n, o, n, o, n, k 1.

Second row.—Th o, k rest plain.

Third row.—Sl 1, k 1, o, n, k 2, o, n, o, n, o, n, o, n, k 1.

Fourth row.—Same as second row.

Fifth row.—Sl 1, k 1, o, n, k 3, o, n, o, n, o, n, o, n, k 1.

Sixth row.—Same as second row.

Seventh row.—Sl 1, k 1, o, n, k 4, o, n, o, n, o, n, o, n, k 1.

Eighth row.—Same as second row.

Ninth row.—Sl 1, k 1, o, n, k 5, o, n, o, n, o, n, o, n, k 1.

Tenth row.—Same as second row.

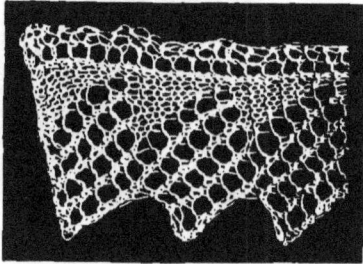

No. 13.—NARROW KNITTED LACE.

Eleventh row.—Sl 1, k 1, o, n, k 6, o, n, o, n, o, n, o, n, k 1.

Twelfth row.—Cast off 5 stitches, leaving 13 on the left hand needle; knit rest plain.

KNITTED EDGING.

No. 14.—Cast on 20 stitches and knit across plain.

First row.—Sl 1, k 1, o twice, p 2 to., k 1, * k 2, bind, k 1, bind, k 1, bind, k 5 stitches in next

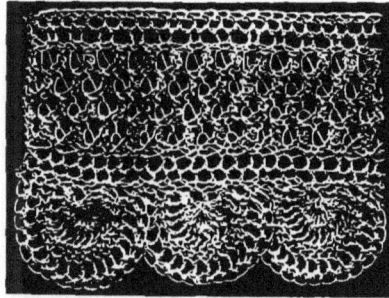

No. 14.—KNITTED EDGING.

stitch thus : k 1, p 1, k 1, p 1 ; repeat from * k 1, o twice, p 2 to., k 2.

Second row.—Sl 1, k 1, o twice, p 2 to., k 12, o twice, p 2 to., k 2.

Third row.—Sl 1, k 1, o twice, p 2 to., k 1, * k 4 in next st., k 2, bind, k 1, bind, k 1, bind ; repeat from *, k 1, o twice, p 2 to., k 2.

Fourth and Sixth rows.—Like second.

Fifth row.—Like first row.

Seventh row.—Like third row.

Eighth row.—With the empty needle take up three loops on the side, or along the lower edge that has just been knit, throw thread round needle to make a stitch, p 1, k 2 sts. in next st. thus : p 1, k 1, o twice, 1.

Ninth row.—O twice, p 2 to., k 2, o twice, p 2 to., turn, letting the 20 sts. remain on needle ; knit the six stitches back and forth like 9th row until the strip has 15 loops on the side. Drop the last loop at the outer edge each time across.

Tenth row.—Take up 14 loops on the needle that has 20 sts. along the edge where the 6 stitches were just knit back and forth ; k 1, sl. this st. on left needle, and turn 13 loops off on this st., draw thread up close, k 2 to., k 1, o twice, p 2 to., k 12 o twice, p 2 to., k 2.

Eleventh row.—Like first row to 20th st., then k 3 to., and turn.

Twelfth row.—Knit back, like second row, except sl 1, k 2, then o twice, etc.

Thirteenth row.—Like third row to 20th st., k 2 to., turn.

Fourteenth row.—Knit back, like twelfth row.

Fifteenth row.—Like first row to 20th st, k 2 to., turn.

Sixteenth row.—Knit back, like twelfth row.

Seventeenth row.—Like third row to 20th st., k 2 to., drop last stitch.

Eighteenth row.—Like second row, except sl 1, n, then, o twice, etc. Repeat from first row.

DEEP KNITTED LACE.

No. 15.—The materials required are : Barbour's flax thread No. 100, 3-cord, 200-yard spools and two knitting needles No. 19.

Cast on 47 stitches.

First row.—O twice, p 3 to., o twice, n, k 1 ; o,

No. 15.—DEEP KNITTED LACE.

n 19 times ; o twice, k 1, o twice, p 2 to. Drop last loop in every row.

Second row.—O twice, p 3 to., k 1, p 1, k 41, p 1, o twice, p 2 to.

Third row.—O twice, p 3 to., o twice, n ; o, n 6 times ; k 2 ; o, n 5 times, k 2 ; o, n 5 times ; k 2, o, n, o twice, k 1, o twice, p 2 to., drop last loop.

Fourth row.—O twice, p 3 to., k 1, p 1, k 42, p 1, thread around the needle once, p 2 to.

Fifth row.—O twice, p 3 to., o twice, n, k 1 ; o, n 6 times ; k 2 ; o, n 5 times ; k 2 ; o, n 5 times ; k 2 ; o, n, o twice, k 1, o twice, p 2 to.

Sixth row.—O twice, p 3 to., k 1, p 1, k 43, p 1, o, p 2 to.

Seventh row.—O twice, p 3 to., o twice, n ; o, n 5 times ; k 2, o, n, k 2 ; o, n 3 times ; k 2, o, n, k 2 ; o, n 3 times ; k 2, o, n, k 2, o, n, over twice, k 1, o twice, p 2 to.

Eighth row.—O twice, p 3 to., k 1, p 1, k 44, p 1, o, p 2 to.

Ninth row.—O twice, p 3 to., o twice, n, k 1 ; o, n 5 times ; k 2, o, n, k 2 ; o, n 3 times ; k 2, o, n, k 2 ; o, n 3 times ; k 2, o, n, k 2, o, n, o twice, k 1, o twice, p 2 to.

Tenth row.—O twice, p 3 to., k 1, p 1, k 45, p 1, o, p 2 to.

Eleventh row.—O twice, p 3 to., o twice, n ; o, n 4 times ; k 2, o, n, k 6, o, n, k 2, o, n, k 6, o, n, k 2, o, n, k 6, o, n, o twice, k 1, o twice, p 2 to.

Twelfth row.—O twice, p 3 to., k 1, p 1, k 46, p 1, o, p 2 to.

Thirteenth row.—O twice, p 3 to., o twice, n, k 1 ; o, n 4 times ; k 2, o, n, k 6, o, n, k 2, o, n, k 6, o, n, k 2, o, n, k 6, o, n, o twice, k 1, o twice, p 2 to.

Fourteenth row.—O twice, p 3 to., k 1, p 1, k 47, p 1, o, p 2 to.

Fifteenth row.—O twice, p 3 to., o twice, n ; o, n 5 times : k 10, o, n, k 10, o, n, k 10, o, n, o twice, k 1, o twice, p 2 to.

Sixteenth row.—O twice, p 3 to., k 1, p 1, k 48, p 1, o, p 2 to.

Seventeenth row.—O twice, p 3 to., o twice, n, k 1 ; o, n, 5 times ; k 10, o, n, k 10, o, n, k 10, o, n, o twice, k 1, o twice, p 2 to.

Eighteenth row.—O twice, p 3 to., k 1, p 1, k 49, p 1, o, p 2 to.

Nineteenth row.—O twice, p 3 to., o twice, n ; o, n 6 times ; k 10, o, n, k 10, o, n, k 10, o, n, o twice, k 1, o twice, p 2 to.

Twentieth row.—O twice, p 3 to., k 1, p 1, k 50, p 1, o, p 2 to.

Twenty-first row.—O twice, p 3 to., o twice, n, n ; o, n 4 times ; * o, k 10, n, and repeat twice more from *, o, k 3 to., o twice, k 1, o twice, p 2 to.

Twenty-second row.—O twice, p 3 to., k 1, p 1, k 49, p 1, o, p 2 to.

Twenty-third row.—O twice, p 3 to., o twice, n 3 to.; o, n 4 times ; * o, k 10, n, repeat from * twice more, o, k 3 to., o twice, k 1, o twice, p 2 to.

Twenty-fourth row.—O twice, p 3 to., k 1, p 1, k 48, p 1, o, p 2 to.

Twenty-fifth row.—O twice, p 3 to., o twice, n, n ; o, n 3 times ; * o, k 2, n, o, k 6, n, twice more from * ; o, k 3 to., o twice, k 1, o twice, p 2 to.

Twenty-sixth row.—O twice, p 3 to., k 1, p 1, k 47, p 1, o, p 2 to.

Twenty-seventh row.—O twice, p 3 to., o twice, k 3 to.; o, n 3 times ; * o, k 2, n, o, k 6, n ; repeat twice more from * ; o, k 3 to., o twice, k 1, o twice, p 2 to.

Twenty-eighth row.—O twice, p 3 to., k 1, p 1, k 46, p 1, o, p 2 to.

Twenty-ninth row.—O twice, p 3 to., o twice, n, n ; o n 4 times ; o, k 2, n, twice ; o, n twice ; o, k 2, n, twice ; and o, n, twice ; o k 2, n, twice ; o, k 3 to., o twice, k 1 o twice, p 2 to.

Thirtieth row.—O twice, p 3 to., k 1, p 1, k 45, p 1, o, p 2 to.

No. 16.—INSERTION TO MATCH DEEP KNITTED LACE.

(For Description see Page 23.)

Thirty-first row.—O twice, p 3 to., o twice, n 3 to.; o, n 4 times ; o, k 2, n, twice ; o, n twice ; o, k 2, n, twice ; o, n twice ; o, k 2, n, twice ; o, k 3 to., o twice, k 1, o twice, p 2 to.

Thirty-second row.—O twice, p 3 to., k 1, p 1, k 44, p 1, o, p 2 to.

Thirty-third row.—O twice, p 3 to., o twice, n, n ; o, n, 5 times ; o, k 2, n; o, n, 4 times ; o, k 2, n; o, n, 4 times ; o, k 2, n, o, k 3 to., o twice, k 1, o twice, p 2 to.

Thirty-fourth row.—O twice, p 3 to., k 1, p 1, k 43 ; p 1, o, p 2 to.

Thirty-fifth row.—O twice, p 3 to., o twice, n 3 to.; o, n 5 times: o, k 2, n, o, n, 4 times; o, k 2, n, o, k 3 to., o twice, k 1, o twice, p 2 to.

Thirty-sixth row.—O twice, p 3 to., k 1, p 1, k 42, p 1, o, p 2 to.

Thirty-seventh row.—O twice, p 3 to., o twice, n, n; o, n 18 times; o, k 3 to., o twice, k 1, o twice, p 2 to.

Thirty-eighth row.—O twice, p 3 to., k 1, p 1, k 41, p 1, o, p 2 to.

Thirty-ninth row.—O twice, p 3 to., o twice, n 3 to., k 36, o, k 3 to., o twice, k 1, o twice, p 2 to.

Fortieth row.—O twice, p 3 to., k 1, p 1, k 40, p 1, o, p 2 to.

Repeat from first row.

INSERTION TO MATCH DEEP, KNITTED LACE.

(For Illustration see Page 22.)

No. 16.—Cast on 33 stitches and knit across plain.

First row.—O twice, p 3 to., leave thread forward, o twice, (this makes 2 stitches), n; o, n, 4 times, k 2, o, k 3 to., o, k 2; n, o, 4 times ; k 2, p 1, o, p 2 to. Drop last loop in every row.

Second row.—O twice, p 3 to., o twice, n, k 25, p 1, o, p 2 to.

Third row.—O twice, p 3 to., o twice, n, k 1 ; o, n twice ; k 2, o, n, k 5, n, o, k 2, n, o, n, o, k 3, p 1, o, p, 2 to.

Fourth row.—This and all even rows same as 2nd.

Fifth row.—O twice, p 3 to., o twice, n; o, n 3 times; k 2, o, n, k 3, n, o, k 2; n, o 3 times; k 2, p 1, o, p 2 to.

Seventh row.—O twice, p 3 to., o twice, n, k 1, o, n, k 2, o, n, k 9, n, o, k 2, n, o, k 3, p 1, o, p 2 to.

Ninth row.—O twice, p 3 to., o twice, n ; o, n twice ; k 2, o, n. k 7, n, o, k 2, n, o, n, o, k 2, p 1, o, p 2 to.

Eleventh row.—O twice, p 3 to., o twice, n, k 1 ; o, n twice ; k 13; n, o, twice; k 3, p 1, o, p 2 to.

Thirteenth row.—O twice, p 3 to., o twice, n ; o, n 3 times; k 11; n, o, 3 times; k 2, p 1, o, p 2 to.

Fifteenth row.—O twice, p 3 to., o twice, n, k 1 ; o, n, 3 times ; k 9 ; n, o, 3 times; k 3, p 1, o, p 2 to.

Seventeenth row.—O twice, p 3 to., o twice, n, o, n 4 ; times; k 7 ; n, o, 4 times ; k 2, p 1, o, p 2 to.

Nineteenth row.—O twice, p 3 to., o twice, n, k 1; o, n, 4 times; k 5; n, o, 4 times; k 3, p 1, o, p 2 to.

Twenty-first row.—O twice, p 3 to., o twice, n ; o, n, 5 times; k 3 ; n, o, 5 times; k 2, p 1, o, p 2 to.

Twenty-third row.—O twice, p 3 to., o, n, k 1 ;

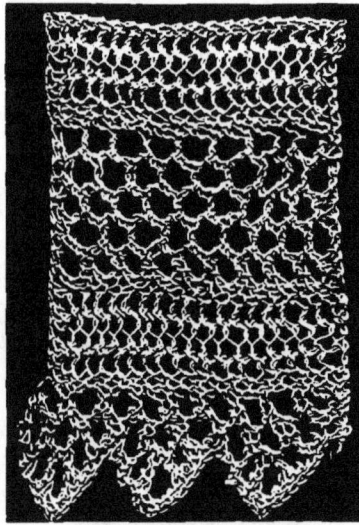

No. 17.—KNITTED LACE.

o, n 3 times ; k 2, o, n, k 1, n, o, k 2 ; n, o, 3 times; k 3, p 1, o, p 2 to.

Knit 24th like 2nd, and then repeat from 1st row.

KNITTED LACE.

No. 17.—Cast on 30 stitches and knit across plain.

First row.—Sl 1, k 1, o twice, p 2 together, o (to make a stitch), p 2 together, k 1, n, o twice, n, n, o twice, n, n, o twice, n, k 1, o twice, p 2 together, o, p 2 together, k 2, o twice, n, o twice, n.

Second row.—Knit 2, p 1 k 2, p 1, k 2, o twice, p 2 together, o, p 2 together, k 3, p 1, k 3, p 1, k 3, p 1, k 2, o twice, p 2 together, o, p 2 together, k 2.

Third row.—Slip 1, k 1, o twice, p 2 together, th o, p 2 together k 3, n, o twice, n, n, o twice, n, k 3, o twice, p 2 together, o, p 2 together, k 8.

Fourth row.—Knit 8, o twice, p 2 together, o, p 2 together, k 5, p 1, k 3, p 1, k 4, o twice, p 2 together, o, p 2 together, k 2.

Fifth row.—Slip 1, k 1, o twice, p 2 together, o, p 2 together, k 1, n, o twice, n, n, o twice, n, n, o twice, n, k 1, o twice, p 2 together, o, p 2 together, k 2, o twice, n, o twice, n, o twice n.

Sixth row.—Knit 2, p 1, k 2, p 1, k 2, p 1, k 2, o twice, p 2 together, o, p 2 together, k 3, p 1, k 3, p 1, k 3, p 1, k 2, o twice, p 2 together, o, p 2 together, k 2.

Seventh row.—Slip 1, k 1, o twice, p 2 together, o, p 2 together, k 3, n, o twice, n, n, o twice, n, k 3, o twice, p 2 together, o, p 2 together, k 11.

Eighth row.—Knit 11, o twice, p 2 together, o, p 2 together, k 5. p 1, k 3, p 1, k 4, o twice, p 2 together, o, p 2 together, k 2.

Ninth row.—Slip 1, k 1, o twice, p 2 together, o, p 2 together, k 1, n, o twice, n, n, o twice. n, n, o twice, n, k 1, o twice, p 2 together, o, p 2 together, k 2, * o twice, n, repeat from * three times, k 1.

Tenth row.—Knit 3, p 1, k 2, p 1, k 2, p 1, k 2, p 1, k 2, o twice, p 2 together, o, p 2 together, k 3, p 1, k 3, p 1, k 3, p 1, k 2, o twice, p 2 together, o, p 2 together, k 2.

Eleventh row.—Slip 1, k 1, o twice, p 2 together, o, p 2 together, k 3, n, o twice, n, n, o twice, n, k 3, o twice, p 2 together, o, p 2 together, k 15.

Twelfth row.—Bind off 10 stitches, (counting the first knitted stitch one) k 5, o twice, p 2 together, o, p 2 together, k 5, p 1, k 3, p 1, k 4, o twice, p 2 together, o, p 2 together, k 2.

Repeat from first row.

DOTTED LACE. (TWO SQUARES.)

No. 18.—Cast on 28 stitches and knit across plain.

First row.—Sl 1, k 2, o, n, k 4, n, o, k 3, o, n, k 5, n, o, k 3, o, k 2.

Second row.—O, n, k 23, o, n, k 2.

Third row.—Sl 1, k 2, o, n, k 3, n, o, k 5, o, n, k 3, n, o, k 5, o, k 2.

Fourth row.—O, n, k 24, o, n, k 2.

Fifth row.—Sl 1, k 2, o, n, k 2, n, o, k 7, o, n, k 1, n, o, k 7, o, k 2.

Sixth row.—O, n, k 25, o, n, k 2.

Seventh row.—Sl 1, k 2, o, n, k 1, n, o, k 3, n, o twice, n, k 2, o, n 3 to., o, k 3, n, o twice, n, k 2, o, k 2.

Eighth row.—O, n, k 5, p 1, k 11, p 1, k 8, o, n, k 2.

Ninth row.—Sl 1, k 2, o, n, k 3, o, n, k 5, n, o, k 3, o, n, k 5, n, o, n, k 1.

Tenth row.—Repeat 6th row.

Eleventh row.—Sl 1, k 2, o, n, k 4, o, n, k 3, n, o, k 5, o, n, k 3, n, o, n, k 1.

Twelfth row.—Repeat 4th row.

Thirteenth row.—Sl 1, k 2, o, n, k 5, o, n, k 1, n, o, k 7, o, n, k 1, n, o, n, k 1.

Fourteenth row.—Repeat second row.

Fifteenth row.—Sl 1, k 2, o, n, k 6, o, n 3 tog., o, k 3, n, o twice, n, k 2, o, n 3 to., o, n, k 1.

Sixteenth row.—O, n, k 7, p 1, k 14, o, n, k 2. Repeat from 1st row.

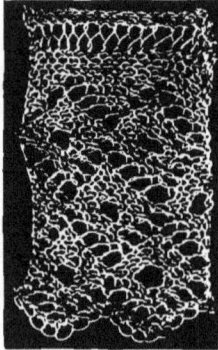

No. 18.—DOTTED LACE. (TWO SQUARES.)

DOTTED INSERTION.

No. 19.—Cast on 36 stitches and knit across plain.

First row.—Sl 1, k 2, o, n, k 4, n, o, k 3, o, n, k 5, n, o, k 3, o, n, k 4, o, n, k 2.

Second row.—Sl 1, k 2, o, n, k 27, o, n, k 2.

Third row.—Sl 1, k 2, o, n, k 3, n, o, k 5, o, n, k 3, n, o, k 5, o, n, k 3, o, n, k 2.

Fourth and Sixth rows like Second.

Fifth row.—Sl 1, k 2, o, n, k 2, n, o, k 7, o, n, k 1, n, o, k 7, o, n, k 2, o, n, k 2.

Seventh row.—Sl 1, k 2, o, n, k 1, n, o, k 3, n, o twice, n, k 2, o, n 3 to., o, k 3, n, o twice, n, k 2, o, k 1, o, n, k 2.

Eighth row.—Sl 1, k 2, o, n, k 6, p 1, k 11, p 1, k 8, o, n, k 2.

Ninth row.—Sl 1, k 2, o, n, k 3, o, n, k 5, n, o, k 3, o, n, k 5, n, o, k 2.

Tenth, Twelfth and Fourteenth rows like Second rows.

Eleventh row.—Sl 1, k 2, o, n, k 4, o, n, k 3, n, o, k 5, o, n, k 3, n, o, k 4, o, n, k 2.

Thirteenth row.—Sl 1, k 2, o, n, k 5, o, n, k 1, n, o, k 7, o, n, k 1, n, o, k 5, o, n, k 2.

Fifteenth row.—Sl 1, k 2, o, n, k 6, o, n 3 to., o, k 3, n, o twice, n, k 2, o, n 3 to., o, k 6, o, n, k 2.

Sixteenth row.—Sl 1, k 2, o, n, k 12, p 1, k 13, o, n, k 2.

Repeat from first row.

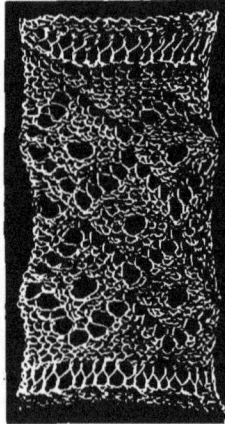

NO. 19.—DOTTED INSERTION.

DOTTED LACE. (ONE SQUARE.)

No. 20.—Cast on 14 stitches and knit across plain.

First row.—Sl 1, k 1, o, n, k 3, n, o, k 3, o, k 2.

Second row.—O, n, k 10, o, n, k 1.

Third row.—Sl 1, k 1, o, n, k 2, n, o, k 5, o, k 2.

Fourth row.—O, n, k 11, o, n, k 1.

Fifth row.—Sl 1, k 1, o, n, k 1, n, o, k 7, o, k 2.

Sixth row.—O, n, k 12, o, n, k 1.

Seventh row.—Sl 1, k 1, o, n, n, o, k 3, n, o twice, n, k 2, o, k 2.

Eighth row.—O, n, k 5, p 1, k 7, o, n, k 1.

Ninth row.—Sl 1, k 1, o, n, k 2, o, n, k 5, n, o, n, k 1.

Tenth row.—Repeat 6th row.

Eleventh row.—Sl 1, k 1, o, n, k 3, o, n, k 3, n, o, n, k 1.

Twelfth row.—Repeat the 4th row.

Thirteenth row.—Sl 1, k 1, o, n, k 4, o, n, k 1, n, o, n, k 1.

Fourteenth row.—Repeat 2nd row.

Fifteenth row.—Sl 1, k 1, o, n, k 5, o, n 3 to., o, n, k 1.

Sixteenth row.—O, n, k 9, o, n, k 1.

Seventeenth row.—Repeat from 1st row.

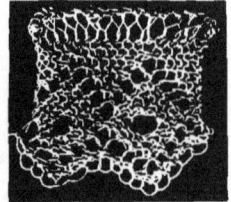

NO. 20.—DOTTED LACE. (ONE SQUARE.)

FRENCH LACE.

No. 21.—Cast on 13 stitches.
First row.—K 3, o, n, k 2, o, n, k 4.
Second row.—K 2, o 3 times, k 2, o, n, k 2, o, n, k 3.
Third row.—K 5, o, n, k 2, o, n; p 1, k 1; p 1 and k 1 out of the last of the 3 put-overs; k 2.
Fourth row.—K 8, o, n, k 2, o, n, k 3.
Fifth row.—K 5, o, n, k 2, o, n, k 6.
Sixth row.—K 10, o, n, k 2, o, n, k 1.
Seventh row.—K 3, o, n, k 2, o, n, k 8.
Eighth row.—Bind off 4, k 12.
Repeat from 1st row.

BLOCK INSERTION.

No. 22.—Cast on 19 stitches.
First row.—K 2, th o twice, p 2 to., k 1, n, o twice, n, k 1, n, o twice, n, k 1, o twice, p 2 to., k 2.
Second row.—K 2, o twice, p 2 to., k 3, p 1, k 4, p 1, k 2, o twice, p 2 to., k 2.
Third row.—K 2, o twice, p 2 to., k 2, o, n, k 3, n, o, k 2, o twice, p 2 to., k 2.
Fourth, Fifth, Sixth, Seventh and Ninth rows.—K 2, o twice, p 2 to., k 11, o twice, p 2 to., k 2.
Eighth row.—K 2, o twice, p 2 to., k 2, o, n, k 3, n, o, k 2, o twice, p 2 to., k 2.
Tenth row.—K 2, o twice, p 2 to., k 1, n, o twice, n, k 1, n, o twice, n, k 1, o tw., p 2 to., k 2.
Eleventh row.—K 2, o twice, p 2 to., k 3, p 1, k 4, p 1, k 2, o twice, p 2 to., k 2.
Twelfth row.—K 2, o twice, p 2 to., k 1, n, o three times, n, k 3 to., sl 1st stitch over 2nd, o three times, n, k 1, o twice, p 2 to., k 2.
Thirteenth row.—K 2, o

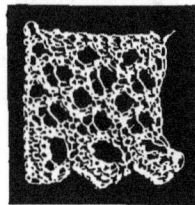

No. 21.—FRENCH LACE.

twice, p 2 to., k 3, p 1, k 3, p 1, k 3, o twice, p 2 to., k 2. Repeat from first row.

BLOCK LACE.

No. 23.—Cast on 29 stitches.
First row.—K 3, o twice, p 2 to., k 1, n, o twice, n, k 1, n, o twice, n, k 1, o twice, p 2 to., k 3, n, o twice, k 4, o twice, p 2 to.
Second row.—Th o twice, p 2 to., k 5, p 1, k 4, o twice, p 2 to., k 3, p 1, k 4, p 1, k 2, o twice, p 2 to., k 3.

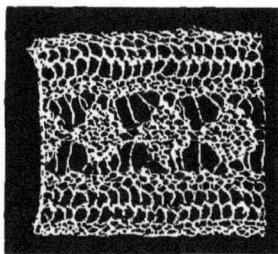

No. 22.—BLOCK INSERTION.

Third row.—K 3, o twice, p 2 to., k 2, o, n, k 3, n, o, k 2, o twice, p 2 to., k 1, n, o twice, n, n, o twice, k 3, o twice, p 2 to. Drop the last stitch.
Fourth row.—Th o twice, p 2 to., k 4, p 1, k 3, p 1, k 2, o twice, p 2 to., k 11, o twice, p 2 to., k 3.
Fifth row.—K 3, o twice, p 2 to., k 11, o twice, p 2 to., k 3, n, o twice, k 6, o twice, p 2 to. Drop the last stitch.
Sixth row.—Th o twice, p 2 to., k 7, p 1, k 4, o twice, p 2 to., k 11,

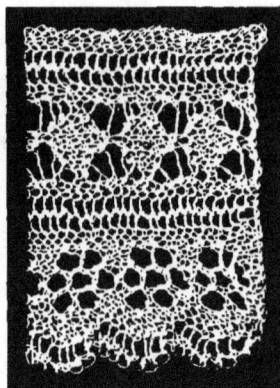

No. 23.—BLOCK LACE.

over twice, purl 2 to., knit 3.
Seventh row.—K 3, o twice, p 2 to., k 11, o twice, p 2 to., k 1, n, o twice, n, n, o twice, k 5, o twice, p 2 to. Drop the last stitch.
Eighth row.—Th o twice, p 2 to., k 6, p 1, k 3, p 1, k 2, o twice, p 2 to., k 11, o twice, p 2 to., k 3.
Ninth row.—K 3, o twice, p 2 to., k 2, o, n, k 3, n, o, k 2, o twice, p 2 to., k 3, n, o twice, k 6, n, o twice, p 2 to. Drop the last stitch.
Tenth row.—Th o twice, p 2 to., k 8, p 1, k 4, o twice, p 2 to., k 11, o twice, p 2 to., k 3.
Eleventh row.—K 3, o twice, p 2 to., k 1, n, o twice, n, k 1, n, o twice, n, k 1, o twice, p 2 to., k 11, n, o twice, p 2 to. Drop the last stitch.
Twelfth row.—Th o twice, p 2 to., k 3, p 1, k 12, o twice, p 2 to., k 3, p 1, k 4, p 1, k 2, o twice, p 2 to., k 3.
Thirteenth row.—K 3, o twice, p 2 to., k 1, n, o three times, n, k 3 to., slip 1st narrowed stitch over the last, o three times, n, k 1, o twice, p 2 to., k 10, n, o twice, p 2 to. Drop the last stitch.
Fourteenth row.—Th o twice, p 2 to., k 1, slip the 2 stitches over the last, k 10, o twice, p 2 to., k 3, p 1, k 3, p 1, k 3, o twice, p 2 to., k 3. Repeat from first row.

LACE FOR PILLOW-CASE.

No. 24.—Cast on 25 stitches, knit across plain.
First row.—K 3, o twice, p 2 together, n, o twice, n, k 9, o twice, p 2 together, k 2, o twice, n, k 1.
Second row.—K 3, purl loop. k 2, o twice, p 2

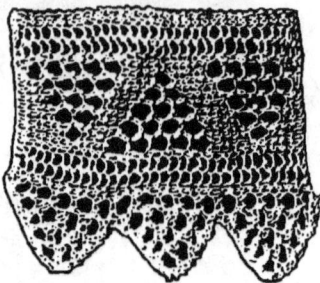

No. 24.—LACE FOR PILLOW-CASE.

together, k 11, purl loop, k 1, o twice, p 2 together, k 3.
Third row.—K 3, o twice, p 2 together, k 2, n, o twice, n, k 7, o twice, p 2 together, k 6.
Fourth row.—K 6, o twice, p 2 together, k 9, purl loop, k 3, o twice, p 2 together, k 3.
Fifth row.—K 3, o twice, p 2 together, n, o twice, n, n, o twice, n, k 5, o twice, p 2 together, k 2, o twice, n, o twice, k 2.
Sixth row.—K 3, purl loop, k 2, purl loop, k 2, o twice, p 2 together, k 7, purl loop, k 3, purl loop, k 1, o twice, p 2 together, k 3.
Seventh row.—K 3, o twice, p 2 together, k 2, n, o twice, n, n, o twice, n, k 3, o twice, p 2 together, k 9.
Eighth row.—K 9, o twice, p 2 together, k 5, p loop, k 3, p loop, k 3, o twice, p 2 together, k 3.
Ninth row.—K 3, o twice, p 2 together, n, o twice, n, n, o twice, n, k 1, o twice, p 2 together, k 2, o twice, n, o twice, n, o twice, n, k 1.
Tenth row.—K 3, p loop, k 2, p loop, k 2, p loop, k 2, o twice, p 2 together, k 3, p loop, k 3, p loop, k 3, p loop, k 1, o twice, p 2 together, k 3.
Eleventh row.—K 3, o twice, p 2 together, k 2, n, o twice, n, n, o twice, n, k 3, o twice, p 2 together, k 12.
Twelfth row.—K 3, n, k 7, o twice, p 2 together, k 5, p loop, k 3, p loop, k 3, o twice, p 2 together, k 3.
Thirteenth row.—K 3, o twice, p 2 together, n, o twice, n, n, o twice, n, k 5, o twice, p 2 together, k 2, o twice, n, o twice, n, o twice, n, k 1.
Fourteenth row.—K 3, p loop, k 2, p loop, k 2, p loop, k 2, p loop, k 2, o twice, p 2 together, k 7, p loop, k 3, p loop k 1, o twice, p 2 together, k 3.
Fifteenth row.—K 3, o twice, p 2 together, k 2, n o twice, n, k 7, o twice, p 2 to., k 15.
Sixteenth row.—K 3, n, k 3, n, k 5, o twice, p 2 together, k 9, p loop, k 3, o twice, p 2 together, k 3.

Seventeenth row.—K 3, o twice, p 2 together, n, o twice, n, k 9, o twice, p 2 together, k 2, o twice, n, o twice, n, o twice, n, o twice, n, k 1.
Eighteenth row.—K 3, p loop, k 2, p loop, k 2, p loop, k 2, p loop, k 2, p loop, k 2, o twice, p 2 together, k 11, p loop, k 1, o twice, p 2 together, k 3.
Nineteenth row.—K 3, o twice, p 2 together, k 13, o twice, p 2 together, k 18.
Twentieth row.—Bind off 13, after slipping the 1st stitch, k 4, o twice, p 2 together, n, o twice, n, k 9, o twice, p 2 together, k 3.
Twenty-first row.—K 3, o twice, p 2 together, k 11, p loop, k 1, o twice, p 2 together, k 2, o twice, n, k 1.
Twenty-second row.—K 3, p loop, k 2, o twice, p 2 together, k 2, n, o twice, n, k 7, o twice, p 2 together, k 3.
Twenty-third row.—K 3, o twice, p 2 together, k 9, p loop, k 3, o twice, p 2 together, k 6.
Twenty-fourth row.—K 6, o twice, p 2 together, n, o twice, n, n, o twice, n, k 5, o twice, p 2 together k 3.
Twenty-fifth row.—K 3, o twice, p 2 together, k 7, p loop, k 3, p loop, k 1, o twice, p 2 together, k 2, o twice, n, o twice, k 2.
Twenty-sixth row.—K 3, p loop, k 2, p loop, k 2, o twice, p 2 together, k 2, n, o twice, n, n, o twice, n, k 3, o twice, p 2 together, k 3.
Twenty-seventh row.—K 3, o twice, p 2 together, k 5, p loop, k 3, p loop, k 3, o twice, p 2 together, k 9.
Twenty-eighth row.—K 9, o twice, p 2 together, n, o twice, n, n, o twice, n, n, o twice, n, k 1, o twice, p 2 together, k 3.
Twenty-ninth row.—K 3, o twice, p 2 together, k 3, p loop, k 3, p loop, k 3, p loop, k 1, o twice, p 2 together, k 2, o twice, n, o twice, n, o twice, n, k 1.
Thirtieth row.—K 3, p loop, k 2, p loop, k 2, p loop, k 2, o twice, p 2 together, k 2, n, o twice, n, n, o, twice, n, k 3, o twice, p 2 together, k 3.

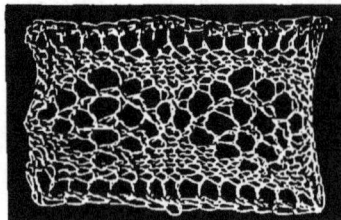

No. 25.—KNITTED INSERTION.
(For Description see Page 27.)

Thirty-first row.—K 3, o twice, p 2 together, k 5, p loop, k 3, p loop, k 3, o twice, p 2 together, k 12.
Thirty-second row.—K 3, n, k 7, o twice, p 2 together, n, o twice, n, n, o twice, n, k 5, o twice, p 2 together, k 3.

Thirty-third row.—K 3, o twice, p 2 together, k 7, p loop, k 3, p loop, k 1, o twice, p 2 together, k 2, o twice, n, o twice, n, o twice, n, o twice, n, k 1. ·

Thirty-fourth row. - K 3, p loop, k 2, p loop, k 2, p loop, k 2, p loop, k 2, o twice, p 2 together, k 2, n, o twice, n, k 7, o twice, p 2 together, k 3.

Thirty-fifth row.—K 3, o twice, p 2 together, k 9, p loop, k 3, o twice, p 2 together, k 15.

Thirty-sixth row.—K 3, n, k 3, n, k 5, o twice, p 2 together, n, o twice, n, k 9, o twice, p 2 together, k 3.

Thirty-seventh row.—K 3, o twice, p 2 together, k 11, p loop, k 1, o twice, p 2 together, k 2, o twice, n, o twice, n, o twice, n, o twice, n, k 1.

Thirty-eighth row.—K 3, p loop, k 2, p loop, k 2, p loop, k 2, p loop, k 2, p loop, k 2, o twice, p 2 together, k 13, o twice, p 2 together, k 3.

Thirty-ninth row.—K 3, o twice, p 2 together, k 13, o twice, p 2 together, k 18.

Fortieth row.—Bind off 13, after slipping the 1st st, k 4, o twice, p 2 together k 13, o twice, p 2 together, k 3. Begin again at 1st row.

KNITTED INSERTION.
(For Illustration see Page 28.)

No. 25.—Cast on 15 stitches and knit across plain.

First row.—Th o twice, p 2 to., k 5, th o twice. k 2 to., k 4, o twice, p 2 to.

Second row.—Th o twice, p 2 to., k 11, dropping the second half of the put over, th o twice, p 2 to ; drop the last stitch.

Third row.—Th o twice, p 2 to., k 4, th o 3 times, p 2 to., th o twice, k 2 to., k 3, th o twice, p 2 to.

Fourth, Sixth and Eighth rows.—Make these rows like the second.

Fifth row.—Th o twice, p 2 to., k 3, th o 3 times, p 2 to., th o 3 times, p 2 to., th o twice, k 2 to., k 2, th o twice, p 2 to.

Seventh row.—Th o twice, p 2 to., k 2, th o 3 times, p 2 to., th o 3 times, p 2 to., th o 3 times, p 2 to., th o twice, k 2 to., k 1, th o twice, p 2 to.

Ninth row.—Like eighth row, but there will

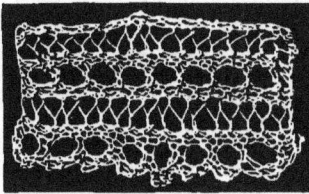

No. 26.—NARROW LACE. (To be Used for Beading.)

be no put-overs to drop in middle of row.

Tenth row.—Th o twice, p 2 to., k 3, th o twice, k 2 to., th o twice, k 2 to., th o twice, k 2 to., k 2, th o twice, p 2 to.

Eleventh row.—Th o twice, p 2 to., k 11, dropping

the extra put-overs, th o twice, p 2 to.

Twelfth row.—Th o twice, p 2 to., k 4, th o twice, k 2 to., th o twice, k 2 to., k 3, th o twice, p 2 to.

Thirteenth row.—Th o twice, p 2 to., k 11, th o twice, p 2 to.

Fourteenth row.—Th o twice, p 2 to., k 5,

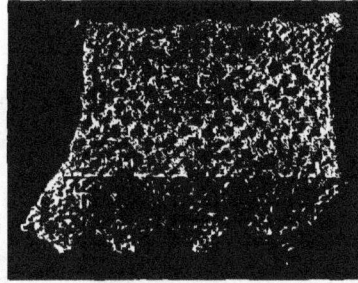

No. 27.—KNITTED LACE WITH SOLID POINT.

th o twice, k 2 to., k 4, th o twice, p 2 to.

Fifteenth row.—Th o twice, p 2 to., k 11, th o twice, p 2 to.

Sixteenth row.—Like ninth.

Repeat from first row.

NARROW LACE. (To be Used for Beading.)

No. 26.—Cast on 12 stitches and knit across plain.

First row.—Knit 4, th o, n, k 3, o, n, k 1.

Second row.—Slip 1, k 1, o, n, k 1, o twice, k 2, o, n, k 1, o twice, k 2.

Third row.—Knit 3, p 1, k 2, o, n, k 2, p 1, k 2, o, n, k 1.

Fourth row.—Slip 1, k 1, o, n, k 5, o, n, k 5.

Fifth row.—Bind off 2, k 3, o, n, n, n, k 1, o, n, k 1.

Sixth row.—Slip 1, k 1, o, n, k 1, o twice, k 2, o, n, k 1, o twice, knit 2, and repeat from 3rd row.

KNITTED LACE WITH SOLID POINT.

No. 27.—Cast on 21 stitches and knit across plain.

First row.—Knit 3, o, n 4 times, o, k 10.

Second row.—Knit plain.

Third row.—Knit 4, o, n 4 times, o, k 10.

Fourth row.—Knit plain.

Fifth row.—Knit 5, o, n 4 times, o, k 10.

Sixth row.—Knit plain.

Seventh row.—Knit 6, o, n 4 times, o, k 10.

Eighth row.—Knit plain.

Ninth row.—Knit 7, o, n 4 times, o, k 10.

Tenth row.—Knit 8, o, n 4 times, o, k 10.

Eleventh row.—Bind off all but 21 stitches, counting on both needles, and knit plain.

The first scallop is now formed. Proceed as from the 1st row.

KNITTED LACE.

No. 28.—This lace is worked in fine cotton or

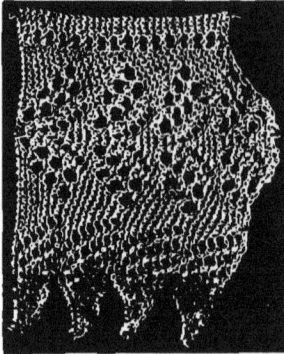

No. 28.

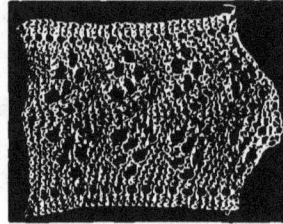

No. 29.

Nos. 28 AND 29.—KNITTED LACE AND INSERTION TO MATCH.

linen, and with the insertion makes a pretty trimming for underclothing.

Use needles to correspond with the size of the thread selected, and cast on 43 stitches. Then knit across plain.

First row.—Sl 1, k 3, o twice, n, k 1, n, o twice, n, o twice, n, n, o, n, k 6, n, o, n, n, o twice, n, o twice, n, k 2, o, n, o, n, o, n, o, k 2.

Second row.—Thread over needle and k the row plain, all excepting the o twice; out of each of these make 2 st., thus: k 1, p 1.

Third row.—Sl 1, k 14, n, o, n, k 4, n, o, n, k 10, o, n, o, n, o, n, o, k 3.

Fourth and each alternate row.—Like second row.

Fifth row.—Sl 1, k 3, o twice, n, k 3, n, o twice, n, o twice, n, n, o, n, k 2, n, o, n, n, o twice, n, o twice, n, k 5, o, n, o, n, o, n, o, k 4.

Seventh row.—Sl 1, k 16, n, o, n, n, o, n, k 13, o, n, o, n, o, n, o, k 5.

Ninth row.—Sl 1, k 3, o twice, n, k 5, n, o twice, n, o twice, n, n, o, n, o, n, n, o twice, n, o twice, n, k 8, o, n, o, n, o, n, o, k 6.

Eleventh row.—Sl 1, k 18, n, o, n, k 17, o, n, o, n, o, n, o, k 7.

Thirteenth row.—Sl 1, k 3, o twice, n, k 9, n, o twice, n, n, n, n, o twice, n, k 13, o, n, o, n, o, n, o, k 8.

Fifteenth row.—Sl 1, k 18, n, n, k 32.

Sixteenth row.—Bind off 10 stitches and knit the remainder plain. Repeat from first row.

KNITTED INSERTION.

No. 29.—Cast on 32 stitches and knit across once plain.

First row.—Sl 1, k 3, n, o twice, n, o twice, n, n, o, n, k 4, n, o, n, n, o twice, n, o twice, n, k 4.

Second row.—Sl 1, and k the remainder plain, excepting the o twice ; in each of these knit 1 and purl 1.

Third row.—Sl 1, k 2, o, k 8, n, o, n, k 2, n, o, n, k 8, o, k 3.

Fourth row, and each alternate row.—Like second.

Fifth row.—Sl 1, k 5, n, o twice, n, o twice, n, n, o, n, o, n, n, o twice, n, o twice, n, k 6.

Seventh row.—Sl 1, k 2, o, k 10, n, o, n, o, n, k 10, o, k 3.

Ninth row.—Sl 1, k 9, n, o twice, n, n, o, n, k 1, n, o twice, n, k 10.

Eleventh row.—Sl 1, k 2, o, k 11, n, n, k 11, o, k 3.

Thirteenth row.—Sl 1, knit remainder plain.

Fifteenth row.—Sl 1, k 2, o, k 11, n, n, k 11, o, k 3.

Sixteenth row.—Sl 1, knit remainder plain. Repeat from first row.

KNITTED LEAF LACE.

No. 30.—Cast on 25 stitches.
First row.—Purl.
Second row.—Th o, k 1, o, k 2, n twice, k 2, o, k 1, o, k 2, n twice, k 2, o, n, o, n, o, n, o, n, k 1.
Third, Fifth, Seventh and Ninth rows.—Purl.
Fourth row.—Th o, k 3, o, k 1, n twice, k 1, o, k 3, o, k 1, n twice, k 1, o, n, o, n, n, k 1.

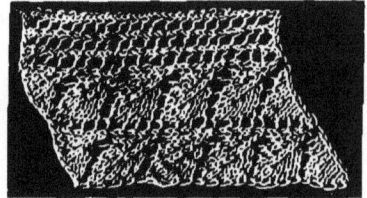

No. 30.—KNITTED LEAF LACE.

Sixth row.—Th o, k 5, o, n twice, o, k 5, o, n twice, o, n, o, n, o, n, k 1.
Eighth row.—Th o, k 3, n, k 2, o, n, o, k 3, n, k 2, o, n, o, n, o, n, o, n, k 1.
Begin at the 2nd row for the next leaf.

NORMANDY INSERTION.

No. 31.—Cast on 17 stitches.

First row.—Slip 1, k 4, n, o, k 3, o, n, k 4, k 1 twist stitch. (To knit a twist stitch, insert needle in the back part of stitch and knit as usual.)

Second row.—Sl 1, k 3, n, o, k 5, o, n, k 3, k 1 twist.

Third row.—Sl 1, k 2, n, o, k 1, n, o, k 1, o, n, k 1, o, n, k 2, k 1 twist.

Fourth row.—Sl 1, k 1, n, o. k 1, n, o, k 3, o, n, k 1, o, n, k 1, k 1 twist.

Fifth row.—Sl 1, n, o, k 1, n, o, k 5, o, n, k 1, o, n, k 1 twist.

Sixth row.—N, o, k 1, n, o, k 3, o, n, k 2, o, n, k 1, o, n.

Seventh row.—Sl 1, o, n, k 1, o, n, k 3, n, o, k 1, n, o, k 2, k 1 twist.

Eighth row.—Sl 1, k 2, o, n, k 1, o, n, k 1, n, o, k 1, n, o, k 2, k 1 twist.

Ninth row.—Sl 1, k 3, o, n, k 1, o, sl 1, n, pass slipped stitch over, o, k 1, n, o, k 3, k 1 twist.

Tenth row.—Sl 1, k 4, o, n, k 3, n, o, k 4, k 1 twist.

Eleventh row.—Sl 1, k 5, o, n, k 1, n, o, k 5, k 1 twist.

Twelfth row.—Sl 1, k 6, o, k 3, to., o, k 6, k 1 twist. Repeat from first row for all the work.

KNITTED EDGING.

No. 32.—Cast on 12 stitches.

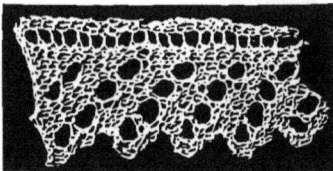

NO. 32.—KNITTED EDGING.

First row.—K 2, o, n, k 1, o twice, n, k 2, o twice, n, k 1.

Second row.—K 3, p 1, k 4, p 1, k the rest plain.

Third row.—K 2, o, n, k the rest.

Fourth row.—Knit.

Fifth row.—K 2, o, n, k 3, o twice, n, k 2, o twice, n k 1.

Sixth row.—K 3, p 1, k 4, p 1, k the rest plain.

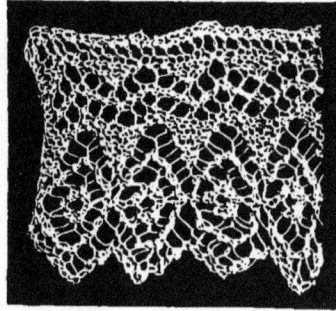

NO. 33.—NORMANDY LACE.

Seventh row.—K 2, o, n, k the rest plain.

Eighth row.—Bind off 4, k the rest plain, and repeat from first row.

NORMANDY LACE.

No. 33.—Cast on 20 stitches and knit across plain.

First row.—K 13, k 2 to., o, k 3, o, k 2.

Second row.—K 2, o, k 5, o, k 2 to., k 3, o, k 2 to., o, k 2 to., k 2, o, k 2 to., k 1.

Third row.—K 11, k 2 to., o, k 1, k 2 to., o, k 1, o, k 2 to., k 1, o, k 2.

Fourth row.—K 2, o, k 1, k 2 to., o, k 3, o, k 2 to., k 1, o, k 2 to., k 2, o, k 2 to., o, k 2 to., k 1, o, k 2, to., k 1.

Fifth row.—K 9, k 2 to., o, k 1, k 2 to., o, k 5, o, k 2 to., k 1, o, k 2.

Sixth row.—K 2, o, k 1, k 2 to., o, k 3, o, k 2 to., k 2, o, k 2 to., k 1, o, k 2 to., o, k 2 to., o, k 2 to., k 1, o, k 2 to., k 1.

Seventh row.—K 10, o, k 2 to., k 1, o, k 2 to., k 3, k 2 to., o, k 1, k 2 to., o, k 1, k 2 to.

Eighth row.—Cast off 1, k 1, o, k 2 to., k 1, o, k 2 to., k 1, k 2 to., o, k 1, k 2 to., o, k 8, o, k 2 to., k 1.

Ninth row.—K 5, o, k 2 to., o, k 2 to., k 3, o, k 2 to., k 1, slip 1, k 2 to., pass slipped stitch over, o, k 1, k 2 to., o, k 1, k 2 to.

Tenth row.—K 2, o, k 2 to., k 3, k 2 to., o, k 10, o, k 2 to., k 1.

Eleventh row.—K 6, o, k 2 to., o, k 2 to., k 4, o k 2 to., k 1, k 2 to., o, k 3.

Twelfth row.—Cast off 2, k 1, o, k 3 to., o, k 12, o, k 2 to., k 1. Repeat from first row.

Fan Lace.

No. 34.—Cast on 39 stitches, and knit across plain.

First row.—K 2, o twice, p 2 to., k 2, o twice, n, k 17, o twice, p 2 together, k 2, o twice, n, k 6, o twice, p 2 together.

Second row.—Th o twice, p 2 to., k 8, p 1, k 2, o twice, p 2 to., k 2, o twice, n, k 15, p 1, k 2, o twice, p 2 to., k 2.

Third row.—K 2, o twice, p 2 to., k 20, p 1, k 2, o twice, p 2 to., k 11, o twice, p 2 to., drop last stitch.

Fourth row.—Th o twice, p 2 to., k 11, o twice, p 2 to., k 23, o twice, p 2 to., k 2.

Fifth row.—K 2, o twice, p 2 to., k 2, o twice, n, o twice, n, k 17, o twice, p 2 to., k 2, o twice, n, o twice, n, k 5, o twice, p 2 to., drop the last stitch.

Sixth row.—Th o twice, p 2 to., k 7, p 1, k 2, p 1, k 2, o twice, p 2 to., k 2, o twice, n, o twice, n, k 13, p 1, k 2, p 1, k 2, o twice, p 2 to., k 2.

Seventh row.—K 2, o twice, p 2 to., k 2 1, p 1, k 2, p 1, k 2, o twice, p 2 to., k 13, o twice, p 2 to., drop the last stitch.

Eighth row.—Th o twice, p 2 to., k 13, o twice, p 2 to., k 27, o twice, p 2 to., k 2.

Ninth row.—K 2, o twice, p 2 to., k 2, o twice, n, o twice, n, o twice, n, k 19, o twice, p 2 to., k 2, o twice, n, o twice, n, o twice, n, k 5, o twice, p 2 to., drop the last stitch.

Tenth row.—Th o twice, p 2 to., k 7, p 1, k 2, p 1, k 2, o twice, n, o twice, n, o twice, n, k 13, p 1, k 2, p 1, k 2, o twice, p 2 to., k 2.

Eleventh row.—K 2, o twice, p 2 to., k 24, p 1, k 2, p 1, k 2, p 1, k 2, o twice, p 2 to., k 16, o twice, p 2 to., drop the last stitch.

Twelfth row.—Th o twice, p 2 to., k 16, o twice, p 2 to., k 33, o twice, p 2 to., k 2.

Thirteenth row.—K 2, o twice, p 2 to., k 2, o twice, n, k 6, pass 12 stitches over the next one, o twice, p 2 to., k 9, o twice, p 2 to., k 2, o twice, n, k 6, pass 6 stitches over same as before, o twice, p 2 to., drop the last stitch. Repeat from 2nd row.

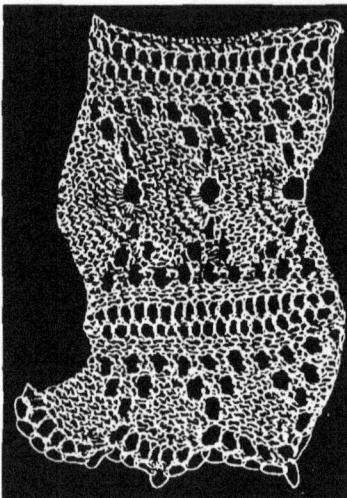

No. 34.—Fan Lace.

Fan Insertion.

No. 35.—Cast on 29 stitches, and then knit across plain.

First row.—K 2, th o twice, p 2 to., k 2, o twice, n, k 17, o twice, p 2 to., k 2.

Second row.—K 2, o twice, p 2 to., k 2, th o twice, n, k 15, p 1, k 2, o twice, p 2 to., k 2.

Third row.—K 2, o twice, p 2 to., k 20, p 1, k 2, o twice, p 2 to., k 2.

Fourth row.—K 2, o twice, p 2 to., k 23, o twice, p 2 to., k 2.

Fifth row.—K 2, o twice, p 2 to., k 2, o twice, n, o twice, n, k 17, o twice, p 2 to., k 2.

Sixth row.—K 2, o twice, p 2 to., k 2, o twice, n, o twice, n, k 13, p 1, k 2, p 1, k 2, o twice, p 2 to., k 2.

Seventh row.—K 2, o twice, p 2 to., k 21, p 1, k 2, p 1, k 2, o twice, p 2 to., k 2.

Eighth row.—K 2, o twice, p 2 to., k 27, o twice, p 2 to., k 2.

Ninth row.—K 2, o twice, p 2 to., k 2, o twice, n, o twice, n, k 19, o twice, p 2 to., k 2.

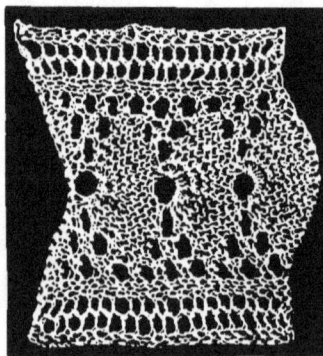

No. 35.—Fan Insertion.

Tenth row.—K 2, o twice, p 2 to., k 2, o twice, n, o twice, n, o twice, n, k 13, p 1, k 2, p 1, k 2, p 1, k 2, o twice, p 2 to., k 2.

Eleventh row—K 2, o twice, p 2 to., k 24, p 1, k 2, p 1, k 2, p 1, k 2, o twice, p 2 to., k 2.

Twelfth row.—K 2, o twice, p 2 to., k 33, o twice, p 2 to., k 2.

Thirteenth row.—K 2, o twice, p 2 to., k 2, o twice, n, k 6, pass 12 stitches over the next stitch, o twice, p 2 to., k 9, o twice, p 2 to., k 2. Repeat from 2nd row and always be careful to k 1, and p 1 out of every 2 put-overs as directed.

DAISY LACE.

No. 36.—Cast on 26 stitches and knit across plain.

First row.—Sl 1, k 2, th o twice, p 2 to., k 5, n, th o twice, n, k 3, th o twice, n, th o twice, n, th o, n, k 3.

Second row.—Knit 4, th o, n, k 1, p 1, k 2, p 1, k 5, p 1, k 6, th o twice, p 2 to., k 3.

Third row.—Sl 1, k 2, th o twice, p 2 to., k 3, n, th o twice, n, n, th o twice, n, k 7, th o, n, k 3.

Fourth row.—Knit 4, th o, n, k 8, p 1, k 3, p 1, k 4, th o twice, p 2 to., k 3.

Fifth row.—Sl 1, k 2, th o twice, p 2 to., k 5, n, th o twice, n, k 3, th o twice, n, k 4, th o, n, k 3.

Sixth row.—Knit 4, th o, n, k 5, p 1, k 5, p 1, k 6, th o twice, p 2 to., k 3.

Seventh row.—Sl 1, k 2, th o twice, p 2 to., k 3, n, th o twice, n, n, th o twice, n, k 8, th o, n k 3.

Eighth row.—Bind off 3, k 3, th o, n, k 6, p 1, k 3, p 1, k 4, th o twice, p 2 to., k 3.

Ninth row.—Sl 1, k 2, th o twice, p 2 to., k 5, n,

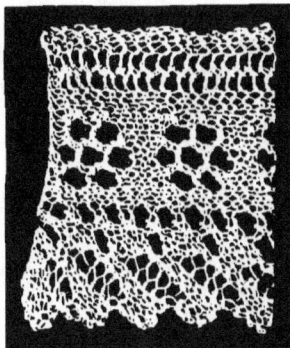

NO. 36.—DAISY LACE.

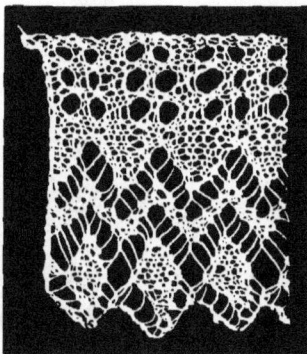

NO. 37.—HAMBURG LACE.

(For Hamburg Insertion see Page 14.)

th o twice, n, k 3, th o twice, n, th o twice, n, th o, n, k 3.

Tenth row.—Knit 4, th o, n, k 1, p 1, k 2, p 1, k 5, p 1, k 6, th o twice, p 2 to., k 3.

Eleventh row.—Sl 1, k 2, th o twice, p2 to., k 18, th o, n, k 3.

Twelfth row.—Knit 4, th o, n, k 17, th o twice, p 2 to., k 3.

Thirteenth row.—Sl 1, k 2, th o twice, p 2 to., k 12, th o twice, n, k 4, th o, n, k 3.

Fourteenth row.—Knit 4, th o, n, k 5, p 1, k 12, th o twice, p 2 to., k 3.

Fifteenth row.—Sl 1, k 2, th o twice, p 2 to., k 19, th o, n, k 3.

Sixteenth row.—Bind off 3, k 3, th o, n, k 15, th o twice, p 2 to., k 3.

HAMBURG LACE.

No. 37.—Cast on 22 stitches and knit across plain.

First row.—Slip 1, k 1, th o, n, th o, n, th o, n, knit 4, n, th o, k 2, n, th o, k 1, th o, k 3 to.

Second row.—Slip 1, th o, k 3, th o, n, k 2, th o, n, k 11.

Third row.—Sl 1, k 9, n, th o, k 2, n, th o, k 5, th o, k 1.

Fourth row.—Sl 1, th o, k 7, th o, n, k 2, th o, n, k 9.

Fifth row.—Sl 1, k 1, th o, n, th o, n, th o, n, n, th o, k 2, n, th o, k 9, th o, k 1.

Sixth row.—K 2 to., th o, n, k 5, n, th o, k 2, n, th o, k 10.

Seventh row.—Sl 1, k 10, th o, n, k 2, th o, n, k 3, n, th o, n.

Eighth row.—N, th o, n, k 1, n, th o, k 2, n, th o, k 12.

Ninth row.—Sl 1, k 1, th o, n, th o, n, th o, n, k 5, th o, n, k 2, th o, k 3 to., th o, n.

Tenth row.—N, th o, k 1, th o, k 2, n, th o, k 14.

Eleventh row.—Sl 1, k 11, n, th o, k 2, n, th o, k 1, th o, k 3 to.

Repeat from 2nd row.

ROSE-LEAF INSERTION.

No. 38.—For this insertion cast on 33 stitches, and knit across once plain.

First row.—Sl 1, k 1, th o twice, p 2 together, k 2, th o, k 3, th o, n, p 1, n, p 1, n, p 1, n, th o, n,

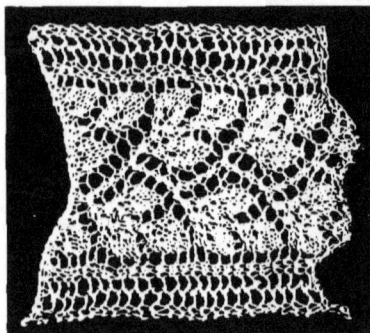

NO. 38.—ROSE-LEAF INSERTION.

th o, k 1, th o, n, p 1, n, th o, k 1, th o, k 2, th o twice, p 2 together, k 2.

Second row.—Sl 1, k 1, th o twice, p 2 together, k 2, p 4, k 1, p 7, k 1, p 1, k 1, p 1, k 1, p 4, k 2, th o twice, p 2 together, k 2.

Third row.—Sl 1, k 1, th o twice, p 2 together, k 2, th o, k 3, th o, sl 1, n, pass slipped stitch over, p 1, sl 1, n, pass slipped stitch over, th o, n, th o, k 3, th o, sl 1, n, pass slipped stitch over, th o, k 3, th o, k 2, th o twice, p 2 together, k 2.

Fourth row.—Sl 1, k 1, th o twice, p 2 together, k 2, p 14, k 1, p 6, k 2, th o twice, p 2 together, k 2 .

Fifth row.—Sl 1, k 1, th o twice, p 2 together, k 2, th o, k 5, th o, sl 1, n, pass slipped stitch over, th o, n, th o, k 5, th o twice, p 1, th o, k 5, th o, k 2, th o twice, p 2 together, k 2.

Sixth row.—Sl 1, k 1, th o twice, p 2 together, k 2, p 7, k 1, p 17, k 2, th o twice, p 2 together, k 2.

Seventh row.—Sl 1, k 1, th o twice, p 2 together, k 2, th o, k 1, n, p 1, n, k 1, th o, sl 1, n, pass slipped stitch over, th o, k 1, n, p 1, n, k 1, p 1, k 1, n, p 1, n, k 1, th o, k 2, th o twice, p 2 together, k 2.

Eighth row.—Sl 1, k 1, th o twice, p 2 together, k 2, p 3, k 1, p 2, k 1, p 2, k 1, p 7, k 1, p 3, k 2, th o twice, p 2 together, k 2.

Ninth row.—Sl 1, k 1, th o twice, p 2 together, k 2, th o, k 1, th o, n, p 1, n, th o, k 1, th o, n, th o, n, p 1, n, p 1, n, p 1, n, th o, k 1, th o, k 2, th o twice, p 2 together, k 2.

Tenth row.—Sl 1, k 1, th o twice, p 2 together, k 2, p 4, k 1, p 1, k 1, p 1, k 1, p 7, k 1, p 4, k 2, th o twice, p 2 together, k 2:

Eleventh row.—Sl 1, k 1, th o twice, p 2 together, k 2, th o, k 3, th o, sl 1, n, pass slipped stitch over, th o, k 3, th o, n, th o, sl 1, n, pass slipped stitch over, p 1, sl 1, n, pass slipped stitch over, th o, k 3, th o, k 2, th o twice, p 2 together, k 2.

Twelfth row.—Sl 1, k 1, th o twice, p 2 together, k 2, p 6, k 1, p 14, k 2, th o twice, p 2 together, k 2.

Thirteenth row.—Sl 1, k 1, th o twice, p 2 together, k 2, th o, k 5, th o twice, p 1, th o, k 5, th o, n, th o, sl 1, n, pass slipped stitch over, th o, k 5, th o, k 2, th o twice, p 2 together, k 2.

Fourteenth row.—Sl 1, k 1, th o twice, p 2 together, k 2, p 17, k 1, p 7, k 2, th o twice, p 2 together, k 2.

Fifteenth row.—Sl 1, k 1, th o twice, p 2 together, k 2, th o, k 1, n, p 1, n, k 1, p 1, k 1, n, p 1, n, k 1, th o, sl 1, n, pass slipped stitch over, th o, k 1, n, p 1, n, k 1, th o, k 2, th o twice, p 2 together, k 2.

Sixteenth row.—Sl 1, k 1, th o twice, p 2 together, k 2, p 3, k 1, p 7, k 1, p 2, k 1, p 2, k 1, p 3, k 2, th o twice, p 2 together, k 2. Repeat from first row.

ROSE-LEAF LACE.

No. 39.—Use No. 30 Coats' spool cotton. Cast on 17 stitches, and knit across plain.

First row.—Th o, n, th o, n, th o, k 1, th o, n, p 1, n, th o, k 1, th o, n, th o, n, th o, k 2.

Second row.—Sl 1, k 1, p 8, k 1, p 8.

Third row.—Th o, n, th o, n, th o, k 3, th o, sl 1, n, pass slipped stitch over, th o, k 3, th o, n, th o, n, th o, k 2.

Fourth row.—Sl 1, k 1, p 19.

Fifth row.—Th o, n, th o, n, th o, k 5, th o twice, p 1, th o, k 5, th o, n, th o, n, th o, k 2.

Sixth row.—Sl 1, k 1, p 11, k 1, p 11.

Seventh row.—Th o, n, th o, n, th o, k 1, n, p 1,

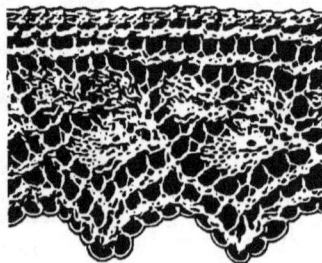

NO. 39.—ROSE-LEAF LACE.

n, k 1, p 1, k 1, n, p 1, n, k 1, th o, n, th o, n, th o, k 2.

Eighth row.—Sl 1, k 1, p 7, k 1, p 2, k 1, p 2, k 1, p 7.

Ninth row.—Th o, k 3 together, th o, n, th o, n,

p 1, n, p 1, n, p 1, n, th o, k 1, th o, n, th o, k 2.

Tenth row.—Sl 1, k 1, p 8, k 1, p 1, k 1, p 1, k 1, p 6.

Eleventh row.—Th o, k 3 together, th o, n, th o, sl 1, n, pass slipped stitch over, p 1, sl 1, n, pass slipped stitch over, th o, k 3, th o, n, th o, n, th o, k 2.

Twelfth row.—Sl 1, k 1, p 10, k 1, p 6.

Thirteenth row.—Th o, k 3 together, th o, n, th o, sl 1, n, pass slipped stitch over, th o, k 5, th o, n, th o, n, th o, k 2.

Fourteenth row.—Sl 1, k 1. Purl all the balance of stitches on needle.

Fifteenth row.—Th o, k 3 together, th o, sl 1, pass slipped stitch over, th o, k 1, n, p 1, n, k 1, th o, n, th o, n, th o, k 2.

Sixteenth row.—Sl 1, k 1, p 7, k 1. Purl all of the stitches left on needle. Begin work at first row again and repeat the pattern until you make the work of the desired length.

SMILAX EDGING.

No. 40.—Cast on 15 stitches.

First row.—Sl 1, k 1, o, n, k 3, n, o, n, o, k 1, o, k 1, o twice, p 2 to., drop the last stitch.

Second row.—Th o twice, p 2 to., then p across the row; make every alternate or even row the same as 2nd.

Third row.—Slip 1, k 2, o, n, k 1, n, o, n, o, k 3, o, k 1, o twice, p 2 to., drop the last stitch.

Fifth row.—Slip 1, k 3, o, sl l, n, pass slipped stitch over, o, n, o, k 5, o, k 1, o twice, p 2 to., drop the last stitch.

Seventh row.—Slip 1, k 4, o, sl 1, n, pass slipped stitch over, o, k 7, o, k 1, o twice, p 2 to., drop the last stitch.

Ninth row.—Slip 1, k 2, n, o, k 1, o, n, o, n, k 3, n, o, n, o twice, p 2 to.

Eleventh row.—Slip 1, k 1, n, o, k 3, o, n, o,

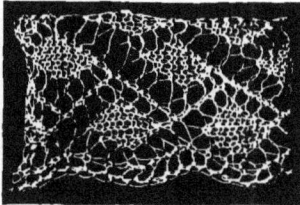

No. 40 —SMILAX EDGING.

n, k 1, n, o, n, o twice, p 2 to., drop the last stitch.

Thirteenth row.—Slip 1, n, o, k 5, o, n, o, sl 1, n, pass slipped stitch over, o, n, o twice, p 2 to., drop the last stitch.

Fifteenth row.—N, o, k 7, o, sl 1, n, pass slipped

3

stitch over, o, n, o twice, p 2 to., drop the last stitch, and repeat from the first row.

MYRTLE LEAF LACE.

No. 41.—Cast on 26 stitches.

First row.—K 2, th o, n, k 1, th o, k 2, sl 1, n,

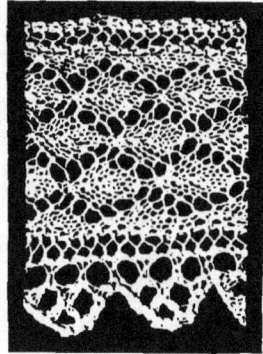

No. 41.—MYRTLE LEAF LACE.

pass slipped stitch over, k 2, th o, k 1, th o, k 2, sl 1, n, pass slipped stitch over, k 2, th o, k 2, th o, n, o twice, k 2.

Second row.—K 3, p 1, k 1, th o, n, p 17, k 1, th o, n, k 1.

Third row.—K 2, th o, n, k 2, th o, k 1, sl 1, n, pass slipped stitch over, k 1, th o, k 3, th o, k 1, sl 1, n, pass slipped stitch over, k 1, th o, k 3, th o, n, k 4.

Fourth row.—K 5, th o, n, p 17, k 1, th o, n, k 1.

Fifth row.—K 2, th o, n, k 3, th o, sl 1, n, pass slipped stitch over, th o, k 5, th o, sl 1, n. pass slipped stitch over, th o, k 4, th o, n, o twice, n, o twice, k 2.

Sixth row.—K 3, p 1, k 2, p 1, k 1, th o, n, p 17. k 1, th o, n, k 1.

Seventh row.—K 2, th o, n, n, k 2, th o, k 1, th o, k 2, sl 1, n, pass slipped stitch over, k 2, th o, k 1, th o, k 2, sl 1, k 1, pass slipped stitch over, k 1, th o, n, k 7.

Eighth row.—K 8, th o, n, p 17, k 1, th o, n, k 1.

Ninth row.—K 2, th o, n, n, k 1, th o, k 3, th o, k 1, sl 1, n, pass slipped stitch over, k 1, th o, k 3, th o, k 1, sl 1, k 1, pass slipped stitch over, k 1, th, o, n, o twice, n, o twice, n, o twice, n, k 1.

Tenth row.—K 3, p 1, k 2, p 1, k 2, p 1, k 1, th o, n, p 17, k 1, th o, n, k 1.

Eleventh row.—K 2, th o, n, n, th o, k 5, th o, sl 1, n, pass slipped stitch over, th o, k 5, th o, sl 1, k 1, pass slipped stitch over, th o, n, k 10.

Twelfth row.—Cast off 8 stitches leaving 25 on the left hand needle, k 2, th o, n, p 17, k 1, th o, n, k 1. Repeat.

HERRING-BONE LACE.

No. 42.—Cast on 35 stitches and knit across twice.

First row.—Sl 1, k 1, o, n, k 11, n, o twice, n, k 11, o, n, k 1, o 3 times, k 2.

Second row.—K 2 ; then k 1, p 1. and k 1 all out

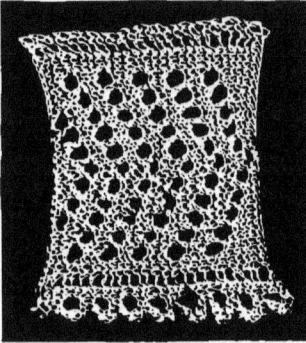

No. 42.—HERRING-BONE LACE.

of the loop formed by putting the th o 3 times ; k 16, p 1, k 16.

Third row.—Sl 1, k 1 o, n, k 9, o twice, n, n, o twice, n, k 9, o, n, k 6.

Fourth row.—Bind off 3, k 15, p 1, k 3, p 1, k 14.

Fifth row.—Sl 1, k 1, o, n, k 7, n, o twice, n, k 4, n, o twice, n, k 7, o, n, k 3.

Sixth row.—K 14, p 1, k 7, p 1, k 12.

Seventh row.—Sl 1, k 1, o, n, k 5, n, o twice, n, k 8, n, o twice, n, k 5, o, n, k 1, o 3 times, k 2.

Eighth row.—K 2 ; then k 1, p k, and k 1 all out of the 3 put-overs ; k 10, p 1, k 11, p 1, k 10.

Ninth row.—Sl 1, k 1, o, n, k 3, n, o twice, n, k 4, n, o twice, n, k 4, n, o twice, n, k 3, o, n, k 6.

Tenth row.—Bind off 3, k 9, p 1, k 7, p 1, k 7, p 1, k 8.

Eleventh row.—Sl 1, k 1, o, n, k 1, n, o twice, n, k 4, n, o twice, n, n, o twice, n, k 4, n, o twice, n, k 1, o, n, k 3.

Twelfth row.—K 8, p 1, k 7, p 1, k 3, p 1, k 7, p 1, k 6.

Thirteenth row.—Like the fifth row to the last narrowing, after which k 1, o 3 times, k 2.

*Fourteenth row—*K 2 ; then k 1, p 1, and k 1 all out of the 3 put-overs ; k 12, p 1, k 7, p 1, k 12.

Fifteenth row,—Like seventh row to the last narrowing, after which k 3.

Sixteenth row.—Bind off 3, k 11, p 1, k 11, p 1, k 10.

Seventeenth row.—Like ninth row to the last narrowing, after which k 3.

Eighteenth row.—K 10, p 1, k 7, p 1, k 7, p 1, k 8.

Nineteenth row.—Like eleventh row to the last narrowing, after which k 1, o 3 times, k 2.

Twentieth row.—K 2 ; then k 1, p 1, and k 1 all out of the 3 put-overs ; k 6, p 1, k 7, p 1, k 3, p 1, k 7, p 1, k 6.

Twenty-first row.—Like fifth row to the last narrowing, after which k 6.

Twenty-second row.—Bind off 3, k 13, p 1, k 7, p 1, k 12.

Twenty-third row.—Like seventh row to the last narrowing, after which k 3.

Twenty-fourth row.—K 12, p 1, k 11, p 1, k 10.

Twenty-fifth row.—Like ninth row to the last narrowing, after which k 1, o 3 times, k 2.

Twenty-sixth row.—K 2 ; then k 1, p 1, and k 1 all out of the 3 put-overs ; k 8, p 1, k 7, p 1, k 7, p 1, k 8.

Twenty-seventh row.—Like the eleventh row to the last narrowing, after which k 6.

Twenty-eighth row.—Bind off 3, k 7, p 1, k 7, p 1, k 3, p 1, k 7, p 1, k 6.

Repeat from fifth row for all the work.

KNITTED EDGING.

No. 43.—Cast on 10 stitches and knit across plain.

First row.—O twice, p 2 to., k 6, o twice, p 2 to.

Second row.—O twice, p 2 to., k 6, o twice, p 2 to., drop last stitch.

Third, Fourth, Fifth, Sixth, Seventh, Eighth and Ninth rows.—Knit like first and second.

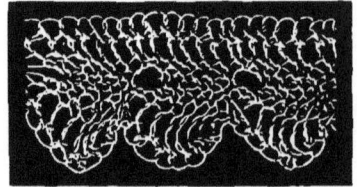

No. 43.—KNITTED EDGING.

Tenth row.—Slip and bind 3, or until there are 6 sts. left ; k 3, o 3 times, k 1, o twice, p 2 to.

Eleventh row.—Begin the second scollop which is knit like the first except that you k, p and k, the 3 put-overs instead of dropping them, and count them as part of the 6 knit stitches.

KNITTED EDGING.

No. 44.—Cast on 10 stitches.

First row.—K 2, thread over twice and n, k remainder plain.

Second row.—K 7, k first loop and p 2nd, k 2.

Third and Fourth rows.—K across plain.

Fifth row.—K 2, thread over twice and narrow, put thread over twice and narrow, k remainder plain.

Sixth row.—K 6, k first loop plain and p 2nd, k 1, k first loop plain and p 2nd, k 2.

Seventh and Eighth rows.—K across plain.

Ninth row.—K 2, thread over twice and n, put thread over twice and n, th o twice and n, k remainder plain.

Tenth row.—K 6, k first loop plain and p 2nd, k 1, k 1st loop plain and p 2nd, k 1, k first loop plain and p 2nd, k 2.

Eleventh row.—K across plain.

Twelfth row.—Bind off 6 stitches. Knit remainder plain.

KNITTED LACE.

No. 45.—Use very fine needles and No. 90 linen. Cast on 41 stitches, knit across plain.

First row.—Sl 1, k 3, o twice, p 2 to., p 27, o, p 2 to., k 2, o twice, n, o, n, p 1 in same stitch.

Second row.—N, o, n, k 1, p 1, k 2, o twice, p 2 to., sl and b, k 5, o, k 1, o, k 1, sl and b, k 5, o, k 1, o, k 1, sl and b, k 5, o, k 1, o, k 1, o twice, p 2 to., k 4.

Third row.—Sl 1, k 3, o twice, p 2 to., p 30, o, p 2 to., k 3, o twice, n, o, n, p 1 in same stitch.

Fourth row.—N, o, n, k 1, p 1, k 3, o twice, p 2 to., sl and b, k 8, sl and b, k 8, sl and b, k 8, o twice, p 2 to., k 4.

Fifth row.—Sl 1, k 3, o twice, p 2 to., p 27, o, p 2 to., k 4, o twice, n, o, n, p 1.

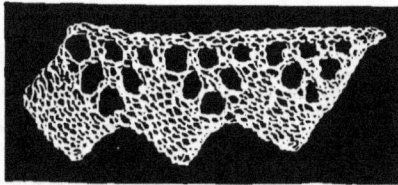

Sixth row.—N, o, n, k 1, p 1, k 4, o twice, p 2 to., sl and b, k 4, o, k 1, o, k 2, sl and b, k 4, o, k 1, o, k 2, sl and b, k 4, o, k 1, o, k 2, o twice, p 2 to., k 4.

Seventh row.—Sl 1, k 3, o twice, p 2 to., p 30, o, p 2 to., k 5, o twice, n, o, n, p 1.

Eighth row.—N, o, n, k 1, p 1, k 5, o twice, p 2 to., sl and b, k 8, sl and b, k 8, sl and b, k 8, o twice, p 2 to., k 4.

Ninth row.—Sl 1, k 3, o twice, p 2 to., p 27, o, p 2 to., k 6, o twice, n, o, n, p 1.

Tenth row.—N, o, n, k 1, p 1, k 6, o twice, p 2 to., sl and b, k 3, o, k 1, o, k 3, sl and b, k 3, o,

No. 45.—KNITTED LACE.

k 1, o, k 3, sl and b, k 3, o, k 1, o, k 3, o twice, p 2 to., k 4.

Eleventh row.—Sl 1, k 3, o twice, p 2 to., p 30, o, p 2 to., k 7, o twice, n, o, n, p 1.

Twelfth row.—N, o, n, k 1, p 1, k 7, o twice, p 2 to., sl and b, k 8, sl and b, k 8, sl and b, k 8, o twice, p 2 to., k 4.

Thirteenth row.—Sl 1, k 3, o twice, p 2 to., p 27, o, p 2 to., k 6, n, o twice, n, o, n, p 1.

Fourteenth row.—N, o, n, k 1, p 1, n, k 5, o twice, p 2 to., sl and b, k 2, o, k 1, o, k 4, sl and b, k 2, o, k 1, o, k 4, sl and b, k 2, o, k 1, o, k 4, o twice, p 2 to., k 4.

Fifteenth row.—Sl 1, k 3, o twice, p 2 to., p 30, o, p 2 to., k 5, n, o twice, n, o, n, p 1.

Sixteenth row.—Sl 1, k 3, o twice, p 2 to., p 27, o, p 2 to., sl and b, k 8, sl and b, k 8, sl and b, k 8, o twice, p 2 to., k 4.

Seventeenth row.—Sl 1, k 3, o twice, p 2 to., p 27, o, p 2 to., k 4, n, o twice, n, o, n, p 1.

Eighteenth row.—N, o, n, k 1, p 1, n, k 3, o twice, p 2 to., sl and b, k 1, o, k 4, sl and b, k 1, o, k 5, sl and b, k 1, o, k 1, o, k 5, o twice, p 2 to., k 4.

Nineteenth row.—Sl 1, k 3, o twice, p 2 to., p 30, o, p 2 to., k 3, n, o twice, n, o, n, p 1.

Twentieth row.—N, o, n, k 1, p 1, n, k 2, o twice, p 2 to., sl and b, k 8, sl and b, k 8, sl and b, k 8, o twice, p 2 to., k 4.

Twenty-first row.—Sl 1, k 3, o twice, p 2 to., p 27, o, p 2 to., k 2, n, o twice, n, o, n, p 1.

Twenty-second row.—N, o, n, k 1, p 1, n, k 1, o twice, p 2 to., sl and b, o, k 1, o, k 6, sl and b, o, k

1, o, k 6, sl and b, o, k 1, o, k 6, o twice, p 2 to., k 4.

Twenty-third row.—Sl 1, k 3, o twice, p 2 to., p 30, o, p 2 to., k 1, n, o twice, n, o, n, p 1.

Twenty-fourth row.—N, o, n, k 1, p 1, n, o twice, p 2 to., sl and b, k 8, sl and b, k 8, sl and b, k 8, o twice, p 2 to., k 4.

Repeat from first row.

WIDE INSERTION.

No. 46.—Cast on 39 stitches.

First row.—K 3, th o, n, k 4, n, o, k 3, o, n, k 1, o, n, k 3, n, o, k 1, n, o, k 1, n, o, k 3, o, n, k 4, n, o, k 3.

Second and all even rows.—Knit plain.

Third row.—K 3, o, n, k 3, n, o, k 5, o, n, k 1, o,

1, n, pass slipped stitch over, o, k 1, n, o, k 5, o, n, k 1, o, sl 1, n, pass slipped stitch over, o, k 1, n, o, k 3, n, o, k 3.

Seventeenth row.—K 3, o, n, k 4, o, n, k 3, n, o, k 1, n, o, k 1, o, n, k 1, o, n, k 3, n, o, k 4, n, o, k 3.

Nineteenth row.—K 3, o, n, k 5, o, n, k 1, n, o, k 1, n, o, k 3, o, n, k 1, o, n, k 1, n, o, k 5, n, o, k 3.

Twenty-first row.—K 3, o, n, k 6, o, sl 1, n, pass slipped stitch over, o, k 1, n, o, k 5, o, n, k 1, o, sl 1, n, pass slipped stitch over, o, k 6, n, o, k 3.

Twenty-third row.—K 3, o, n, k 5, n, o, k 1, o, n, n, o, k 4, n, o, k 1, n, o, k 1, o, n, k 5, n, o, k 3.

Repeat from 1st row.

EDGING TO MATCH WIDE INSERTION.

No 47.—Cast on 31 stitches.

First row.—K 3, th o, k 3, o, n, k 1 o, n,

No. 46.

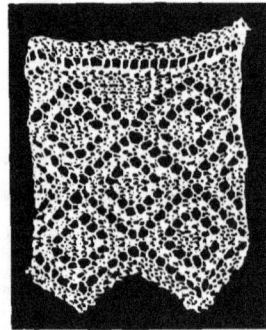

No. 47.

NOS. 46 AND 47.—WIDE INSERTION, WITH EDGING TO MATCH.

sl 1, n, pass slipped stitch over, o, k 1, n, o, k 5, o, n, k 3, n, o, k 3.

Fifth row.—K 3, o, n, k 2, n, o, k 1, n, o, k 1, o, n, k 1, o, n, k 3, n, o, k 1, n, o, k 1, o, n, k 1, o, n, k 2, n, o, k 3.

Seventh row.—K 3, o, n, k 1, n, o, k 1, n, o, k 3, o, n, k 1, o, n, k 1, n, o, k 1, n, o, k 3, o, n, k 1, o, n, k 1, n, o, k 3.

Ninth row.—K 3, o, n, n, o, k 1, n, o, k 5, o, n, k 1, o, sl 1, n, pass slipped stitch over, o, k 1, n, o, k 5, o, n, k 1, o, n, n, o, k 3.

Eleventh row.—K 3, o, n, k 1, o, n, n, o, k 4, n, o, n, k 1, o, k 1, o, n, n, o, k 4, n, o, n, k 1, o, k 1, n, o, k 3.

Thirteenth row.—K 3, o, n, k 2, o, n, k 1, o, n, k 1, n, o, k 1, n, o, k 3, o, n, k 1, o, n, k 1, n, o, k 1, n, o, k 2, n, o, k 3.

Fifteenth row.—K 3, o, n, k 3, o, n, k 1, o, slip

k 1, n, o, k 1, n, o, k 3, o, n, k 4, n, o, k 3.

Second and every even row.—Knit plain.

Third row.—K 3, th o, k 5, o, n, k 1, o, k 3 to., o, k 1, n, o, k 5, o, n, k 3, n, o, k 3.

Fifth row.—K 3, th o, k 1, n, o, k 1, o, n, k 1, o, n, k 3, n, o, k 1, n, o, k 1, o, n, k 1, o, n, k 2, n, o, k 3.

Seventh row.—K 3, o, k 1, n, o, k 3, o, n, k 1, o, n, k 1, n, o, k 1, n, o, k 3, o, n, k 1, o, n, k 1, n, o, k 3.

Ninth row.—K 3, o, k 1, n, o, k 5, o, n, k 1, o, k 3 to., o, k 1, n, o, k 5, o, n, k 1, o, n, n, o, k 3.

Eleventh row.—K 3, o, n, n, o, n, k 1, o, k 1, o, n, n, o, k 4, n, o, n, k 1, o, k 1, n, o, k 3.

Thirteenth row.—Bind off 1, k 2, o, n, k 1, o, n, k 1, n, o, k 1, n, o, k 3, o, n, k 1, o, n, k 1, n, o, k 2, n, o, k 3.

Fifteenth row.—Bind off 1, k 2, th o, n, k 1, o, k 3 to., o, k 1, n, o, k 5, o, n, k 1, o, k 3, to., o, k 1, n, o, k 3, n, o, k 3.
Seventeenth row.—Bind off 1, k 2, o, n, k 3, n, o, k 1, n, o, k 1, o, n, k 1, o, n, k 3, n, o, k 4, n, o, k 3.
Nineteenth row.—Bind off 1, k 2, o, n' k 1, n, o, k 1, n, o, k 3, o, n, k 1, o, n, k 1, n, o, k 5, n, o, k 3.
Twenty-first row.—Bind off 1, k 2, o, k 3 to., o, k 1, n, o, k 5, o, n, k 1, o, k 3 to., o, k 6, n, o, k 3.
Twenty-third row.—Bind off 1, k 2, o, k 1, o, n, n, o, k 4, n, o, k 1, n, o, k 1, o, n, k 5, n, o, k 3. Repeat from 1st row.

SHELL EDGING.

No. 48—Cast on 13 stitches and knit across plain.
First row.—Sl 1, k 12.

the 12 long stitches off onto the right-hand needle, slip them back onto the left-hand needle, and knit all together as 1 stitch. This completes one shell.
Repeat from the 1st row.

SHELL INSERTION.

No. 49—Cast on 17 stitches. Knit across plain.
First row.—Sl 1, k 16.
Second row.—Sl 1, k 2 together, o twice, k 2 together, k 12.
Third row.—Sl 1, k 2 together, o twice, k 2 together, k 9, p 1, k 2.
Fourth row.—Sl 1, k 13, p 1, k 2.
Fifth row.—Sl 1, k 16.
Sixth row.—Sl 1, k 2 together, o twice, k 2 together, k 1, o twice, k 2 together, o twice,

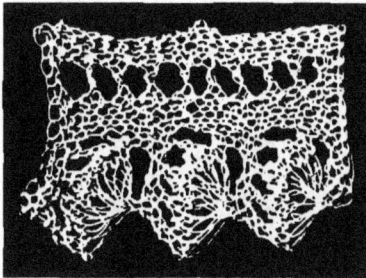

No. 48.

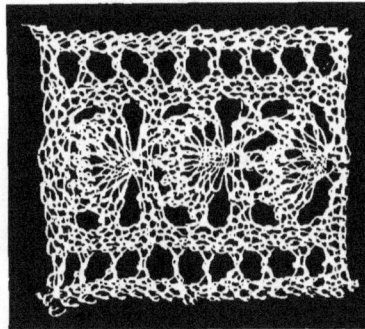

No. 49.

NOS. 48 AND 49.—SHELL EDGING, WITH INSERTION TO MATCH.

Second row.—Sl 1, k 1, k 2 together, o twice, k 2 together, k 7.
Third row.—Sl 1, k 8, p 1, k 3.
Fourth row.—Sl 1, k 12.
Fifth row.—Like the 4th.
Sixth row.—Sl 1, k 1, k 2 together, o twice, k 2 together, k 2, o twice, k 1, o twice, k 1, o twice, k 1, o twice, k 2.
Seventh row.—Sl 1, k 2, p 1, k 2, p 1, k 2, p 1, k 2, p 1, k 4, p 1, k 3.
Eighth row.—Sl 1, k 20.
Ninth row.—Sl 1, k 20.
Tenth row.—Sl 1, k 1, k 2 together, o twice, k 2 together, k 15.
Eleventh row.—Put the needle in the first stitch, as if to knit, thread around the needle 3 times, then knit; repeat for 12 stitches, then thread over 3 times, k 5, p 1, k 3.
Twelfth row.—Sl 1, k 9, p 1, k 1; take each of

knit 1, over twice, knit 2 together, o twice, knit 6.
Seventh row.—Sl 1, k 2 together, o twice, k 2 together, k 2, p 1, k 2, p 1, k 2, p 1, k 2, p 1, k 3, p 1, k 2.
Eighth row.—Sl 1, k 19, p 1, k 2.
Ninth row.—Sl 1, k 22.
Tenth row.—Sl 1, k 2 together, o twice, k 2, together, k 18.
Eleventh row.—Sl 1, k 2 together, o twice, k 2 together, k 1, o twice; put the needle in the next stitch as if to knit; thread around the needle 3 times, then knit, and repeat this for 11 times; then, th o twice, k 3, p 1, k 2.
Twelfth row.—Slip 1, k 6, p 1; take each of the 11 long stitches in the middle, and knit them as 1 stitch, the same as in the edging described at figure No. 2; k 1, p 1, k 3, p 1, k 2. This completes one shell.
Repeat from the first row.

KNITTED WIDE LACE FOR APRONS.

No. 50.—Cast on 50 stitches and knit across plain.

First row.—K 3, th o twice, p 2 together, k 2, th

No. 50.—KNITTED WIDE LACE FOR APRONS.

o, n, o, n, k 6, o twice, p 2 to., k 6, n, o, k 1, o, n, k 6, o twice, p 2 to., k 2, th o twice, n, k 6, o, k 2.

Second row.—K 11, p 1, k 2, th o twice, p 2 to., k 17, o twice, p 2 to., k 12, o twice, p 2 to., k 3.

Third row.—K 3, o twice, p 2 to., k 3, th o, n, o, n, k 5, o twice, p 2 to., k 5, n, o, k 3, o, n, k 5, o twice, p 2 to., k 11, o, n, k 1.

Fourth row.—K 14, o twice, p 2 to., k 17, o twice, p 2 to., k 12, o twice, p 2 to., k 3.

Fifth row.—K 3, o twice, p 2 to., k 4, o, n, o, n, k 4, o twice, p 2 to., k 4, n, o, n, o, k 1, o, n, o, n, k 4, o twice, p 2 to., k 2, o twice, n, o twice, n, k 5, o, n, k 1.

Sixth row.—K 10, p 1, k 2, p 1, k 2, o twice, p 2 to., k 17, o twice, p 2 to., k 12, o twice, p 2 to., k 3.

Seventh row.—K 3, o twice, p 2 to., k 5, o, n, o, n, k 3, o twice, p 2 to., k 3, n, o, n, o, k 3, o, n, o, n, k 3, o twice, p 2 to., k 13, o, n, k 1.

Eighth row.—K 16, o twice, p 2 to., k 17, o twice, p 2 to., k 12, o twice, p 2 to., k 3.

Ninth row.—K 3, o twice, p 2 to., k 6, o, n, o, n, k 2, o twice, p 2 to., k 2, n, o, n, o, k 2, o twice, p 2 to., k 2, o twice, n, o twice, n, o twice, n, k 5, o, n, k 1.

Tenth row.—K 10, p 1, k 2, p 1, k 2, p 1, k 2, o twice, p 2 to., k 17, o twice, p 2 to., k 12, o twice, p 2 to., k 3.

Eleventh row.—K 3, o twice, p 2 to., k 7, o, n, o, n, k 1, o twice, p 2 to., k 1, n, o, n, o, k 7, o, n, o, n, k 1, o twice, p 2 to., k 16, o, n, k 1.

Twelfth row.—Bind off 7, k 11, o twice, p 2 to., k 17, o twice, p 2 to., k 12, o twice, p 2 to., k 3.

Thirteenth row.—K 3, o twice, p 2 to., k 2, o, n, o, n, k 6, o twice, p 2 to., n, o, n, o, k 9, o, n, o, n, o twice, p 2 to., k 2, o twice, n, k 6, o, k 2.

Fourteenth row.—K 11, p 1, k 2, o twice, p 2 to., k 17, o twice, p 2 to., k 12, o twice, p 2 to., k 3.

Fifteenth row.—K 3, o twice, p 2 to., k 3, o, n, o, n, k 5, o twice, p 2 to., k 2, o, n, o, n, k 5, n, o, n, o, k 2, o twice, p 2 to., k 11, o, n, k 1.

Sixteenth row.—K 14, o twice, p 2 to., k 17, o twice, p 2 to., k 12, o twice, p 2 to., k 3.

Seventeenth row.—K 3, o twice, p 2 to., k 4, o, n, o, n, k 4, o twice, p 2 to., k 3, o, n, o, n, k 3, n, o, n, o, k 3, o twice, p 2 to., k 2, o twice, n, o twice, n, k 5, o, n, k 1.

Eighteenth row.—K 10, p 1, k 2, p 1, k 2, o twice, p 2 to., k 17, o twice, p 2 to., k 12, o twice, p 2 to., k 3.

Nineteenth row.—K 3, o twice, p 2 to., k 5, o, n, o, n, k 3, o twice, p 2 to., k 4, o, n, o, n, k 1, n, o, n, o, k 4, o twice, p 2 to., k 13, o, n, k 1.

Twentieth row.—K 16, o twice, p 2 to., k 17, o twice, p 2 to., k 12, o twice, p 2 to., k 3.

Twenty-first row.—K 3, o twice, p 2 to., k 6, o, n, o, n, k 2, o twice, p 2 to., k 5, o, n, o, n, sl 1, n, pass slipped stitch over, o, n, o, k 5, o twice, p 2 to., k 2, o twice, n, o twice, n, o twice, n, k 5, o, n, k 1.

Twenty-second row.—K 10, p 1, k 2, p 1, k 2, p 1, k 2, o twice, p 2 to., k 17, o twice, p 2 to., k 12, o twice, p 2 to., k 3.

Twenty-third row.—K 3, o twice, p 2 to., k 7, o, n, o, n, k 1, o twice, p 2 to., k 6, o, n, k 1, n, o, k 6, o twice, p 2 to., k 16, o, n, k 1.

Twenty-fourth row.—K 19, th o twice, p 2 to., k 17, o twice, p 2 to., k 12, o twice, p 2 to., k 3.

Twenty-fifth row.—K 3, o twice, p 2 to., k

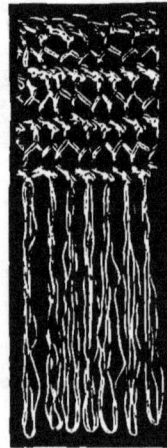

No. 51.—KNITTED FRINGE.
(For Description see Page 39.)

12, o twice, p 2 to., k 7, o, sl 1, n, pass sl st over, o, k 7, o twice, p 2 to., k 16, o, n, k 1.

Twenty-sixth row.—Bind off 7, k 11, o twice, p 2 to., k 17, o twice, p 2 to., k 12, o twice, p 2 to., k 3. Repeat from first row.

KNITTED FRINGE.

(For Illustration see Page 38.)

No. 51.—Cast on 13 stitches, using material *doubled*.

First row.—Knit plain.

Second row.—Thread over, narrow; repeat across the row, knitting last stitch plain.

All rows are like the 2nd row. Continue knitting until the trimming is of the desired length; then bind off all but four stitches, drop these and ravel back to beginning.

KNITTED LACE.

No. 52.—Cast on 40 stitches and knit across plain.

First row.—K 4, n, o, n, o, n, o, k 2, n, k 4, n, k 2, o, k 1, o, n, o, n, o, k 5, o, n, o, n, o three times, n o twice, p 2 to.

Second row.—Th o twice, p 2 to., k 2; p 1 k 1 and p 1 all in the next loop; k 1, p 1, k 1, p 1, k 4, p 24, k 4.

Third row.—K 4, n, o, n, o, n, o, k 2, n, k 2, n, k 2, o, k 3, o, n, o, n, o, k 5, o, n, k 1, o, n, k 4, o twice, p 2 to.; drop the last thread.

Fourth row.—Th o twice, p 2 to., k 5, p 1, k 2, p 1, k 4, p 24, k 4.

Fifth row.—K 4, n, o, n, o, n, o, k 2, n, n, k 2, o, k 5, o, n, o, n, o, k 5, o, n, k 2, o, n, k 3, o twice, p 2 to.; drop the last thread.

Sixth row.—Th o twice, p 2 to., k 4, p 1, k 3, p 1, k 4, p 24, k 4.

Seventh row.—K 5, o, n, o, n, o, n, o, k 1, o, k 2, n, k 4, n, k 2, o, n, o, n, o, n, k 4, o, n, k 3, o, n, k 2, o twice, p 2 to.

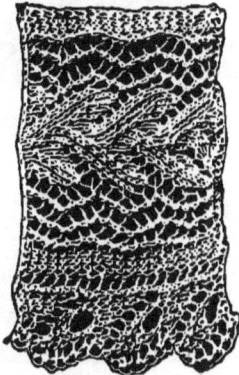

No. 52.—KNITTED LACE.

Eighth row.—Th o twice, p 2 to., k 3, p 1, k 4, p 1, k 4, p 24, k 4.

Ninth row.—K 5, o, n, o, n, o, k 3, o, k 2, n, k 2, n, k 2, o, n, o, n, o, n, k 4, o, n, k 4, o, n, k 1, o twice, p 2 to.

Tenth row.—Th o twice, p 2 to., k 2, p 1, k 5, p 1, k 4, p 24, k 4.

Eleventh row.—K 5, o, n, o, n, o, k 5, o, k 2, n, n, k 2, o, n, o, n, o, n, k 4, o, n, k 5, o, n, o twice, p 2 to.

No. 53.—KNITTED LINEN FRINGE FOR TABLE-COVER.

Twelfth row.—Cast off 3 stitches, then pass the stitch from the right hand needle onto the left one; now, th o twice, p 2 to., k 5, p 1, k 4, p 24, k 4.

KNITTED LINEN FRINGE FOR TABLE-COVER.

No. 53.—From heavy Canton flannel cut a cover half an inch larger on all sides than your table. For the fringe use linen macramé cord the shade of the cover. Cut two pieces of pasteboard six inches in length, one of them three inches and a half in width and the other slightly narrower. Lay the two pieces together; wind the cord smoothly over their width, and when covered cut the cord at one edge of the strips by passing a knife or scissors between them. The fringe is now ready to be used. Two very large steel needles are required to knit the heading. Cast on eleven stitches.

First row.—*Throw thread over, k 2 together*; repeat between stars until there are three stitches on the left-hand needle. Now lay three pieces of the cord you have cut across the work between the needles; knit one stitch, draw the end of the fringe from the under side across the work, so that both ends may turn towards you. Knit one stitch, throw both ends of the fringe across the work to the under side, knit one stitch.

Second row.—Knit 4 stitches; * th o, n, * repeat between stars until you have one stitch left. Knit it. Sew the fringe a quarter of an inch from the edge of the cover. If the table is square, lay a small plait at each corner; if round, draw the fringe tightly as you sew it on.

SPIDER LACE.

No. 54.—Cast on 49 stitches and knit across plain.
First row.—K 2, o, p 2 to., k 3, o, k 1, o, k 3, o,

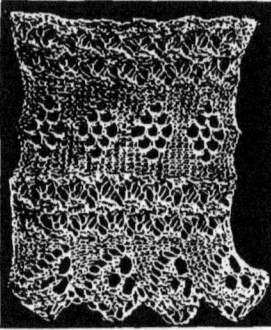

No. 54.—SPIDER LACE.

p 2 to., k 16, o, p 2 to., k 3, o, k 1, o, k 3, o, p 2 to., k 1, o, n, o twice, n, k 2, o twice, p 2 to.

Second row.—O twice, p 2 to., k 3, make 4 sts. out of loop of "over twice," k 3, o, p 2 to., k 2, o, k 3, o, k 2, o, p 2 to., k 16, o, p 2 to., k 2, o, k 3, o, k 2, o, p 2 to., k 2.

Third row.—K 2, o, p 2 to., k 1, o, k 5, o, k 1, o, p 2 to., k 16, o, p 2 to., k 1, o, k 5, o, k 1, o, p 2 to., k 2, o, n, k 4, o twice, n, o twice, p 2 to. Drop last loop.

Fourth row.—O twice, p 2 to., k 1, make 4 sts. of loop, k 8, o, p 2 to., o, k 7, o twice, p 2 to., k 16, o, p 2 to., o, k 7, o twice, p 2 to., k 2.

Fifth row.—K 3, o, k 3, o, p 3 to., k 3, o, k 7, n, o twice, n, k 7, o, k 3, o, p 3 to., k 3, o, k 4, o, n, k 2, o twice, n, k 4, o twice, p 2 to.; drop last loop.

Sixth row.—O twice, p 2 to., k 5, make 4 sts. out of loop, k 9, o, k 2, o, p 3 to., k 2, o, k 10, p 1, k 9, o, k 2, o, p 3 to., k 2, o, k 4.

Seventh row.—K 5, o, k 1, o, p 3 to., k 1, o, k 7, n, o twice, n twice, o twice, n, k 7, o, k 1, o, p 3 to., k 1, o, k 7, o, n, k 8, n, o twice, p 2 to.; drop last loop.

Eighth row.—O twice, p 2 to., k 19, o twice, p 3 to., o, k 10, p 1, k 3, p 1, k 9, o twice, p 3 to., o, k 6.

Ninth row.—K 2, o, p 2 to., k 3, o, k 1, o, k 3, o, p 2 to., k 2, n, o twice, n twice, o twice, o twice, n, k 2, o, p 2 to., k 3, o, k 1, o, k 3, o, p 2 to., k 5, o, n, k 6, n, o twice, p 2 to., drop last loop.

Tenth row.—O twice, p 2 to., k 14, o, p 2 to., k 2, o, k 3, o, k 2, o, p 2 to., k 4, p 1, k 3, p 1 k 3, p 1, k 3, o, p 2 to., k 2, o, k 3, o, k 2, o, p 2 to., k 2.

Eleventh row.—K 2, o, p 2 to., k 1, o, k 5, o, k 1, o, p 2 to., k 4, n, o twice, n twice, o twice, n, k 4, o, p 2 to., k 1, o, k 5, o, k 1, o, p 2 to., k 6, o, n, k 4, n, o twice, p 2 to., drop last loop.

Twelfth row.—O twice, p 2 to., k 13, o, p 2 to., o, k 7, o twice, p 2 to., k 6, p 1, k 3, p 1, k 5, o, p 2 to., o, k 7, o twice, p 2 to., k 2.

Thirteenth row.—K 3, o, k 3, o, p 3 to., k 3, o, k 7, n, o twice, n, k 7, o, k 3, o, p 3 to., k 3, o, k 8, o, n 3 times, o twice, p 2 to., drop last loop.

Fourteenth row.—O twice, p 2 to., k 13, o, k 2, o, p 3 to., k 2, o, k 10, p 1, k 9, o, k 2, o, p 3 to., k 2, o, k 4.

Fifteenth row.—K 5, o, k 1, o, p 3 to., k 1, o, k 22, o, k 1, o, p 3 to., k 1, o, k 11, o twice, p 3 to., n, drop last loop.

Sixteenth row.—O twice, p 3 to., n, k 10, o twice, p 3 to., o, k 24, o twice, p 3 to., o, k 6.

Repeat from first row.

KNITTED LACE.

No. 55.—Cast on 9 stitches.

First row.—Slip 1, k 1, th o twice, p 2 to., k 1, o twice, k 2 to., o twice, p 2 to.

Second row.—Make 1, p 2 to., k 1; k 1 and p 1 out of the same stitch; k 1, th o twice, p 2 to., k 2.

Third row.—Slip 1, k 1, th o twice, p 2 to., k 4, o twice, p 2 to.

Fourth row.—Make 1, p 2 to., k 4, o twice, p 2 to., k 2.

Fifth row.—Slip 1, k 1, o twice, p 2 to., k 1, o twice, k 2 to., o twice, k 1, o twice, p 2 to.

Sixth row.—Make 1, p 2 to., k 1; k 1 and p 1 out of the same stitch; k 1; k 1 and p 1 out of the same stitch; k 1, o twice, p 2 to., k 2.

Seventh row.—Slip 1, k 1, o twice, p 2 to., k 7, o twice, p 2 to.

Eighth row.—Make 1, p 2 to., k 7, o twice, p 2 to., k 2.

Ninth row.—Slip 1, k 1, o twice, p 2 to., k 7, o twice, p 2 to.

Tenth row.—Cast off 4 stitches. K 4, th o

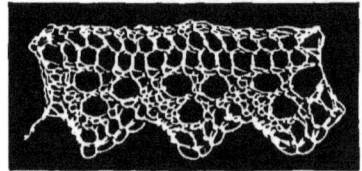

No. 55.—KNITTED LACE.

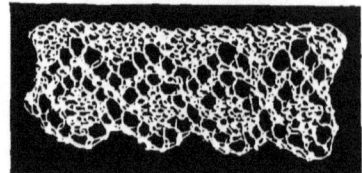

No. 56.—DIAMOND LACE.

twice, purl 2 to., knit 2. Repeat from first row.

DIAMOND LACE.

No. 56.—Cast on 9 stitches. Knit every other row plain.

First row.—K 3, n, o, n, o, k 1, o, k 1.

Third row.—K 2, n, o, n, o, k 3, o, k 1

Fifth row.—K 1, n, o, n, o, k 5, o, k 1.
Seventh row.—K 3, o, n, o, n, k 1, n, o, n.
Ninth row.—K 4, o, n, o, k 3 together, o, n.
Eleventh row.—K 5, o. k 3 together, o, n.
Repeat from first row.

NARROW KNITTED LACE.

No. 57.—Cast on 6 stitches and knit across plain.

First to Tenth rows (inclusive).—Make 1 (by putting the thread over), purl 2 together, make 1, purl 2 together, make 1, purl 2 together.

Eleventh row.—Make 1, slip 1, p 3 to., pass the slipped stitch and the made stitch over, th o 4 times, p 2 to.

Twelfth row.—Make 1, slip 1, k 1, p 1, k 1, make 1, p 2 to.

Thirteenth row.—Make 1, p 2 to., make 1, p 2 to., make 1, p 3 to.

Repeat from the first row.

WHEAT-EAR LACE.

No. 58.—Cast on 5 stitches.

First row.—K 2, th o, k 1, th o twice, p 2 to.
Second row.—Th o twice, p 2 to., k 4.
Third row.—Sl 1, k 2, th o, k 1, th o twice, p 2 to.
Fourth row.—Th o twice, p 2 to., k 5.
Fifth row.—Sl 1, k 3, th o, k 1, th o twice, p 2 to.
Sixth row.—O twice, p 2 to., 6 plain.
Seventh row.—Sl 1, k 5, th o twice, p 2 to.
Eighth row.—Th o twice, p 5 to., k 3. Repeat from 1st row.

FAVORITE LACE.

No. 59.—Cast on 43 stitches, knit across plain twice.

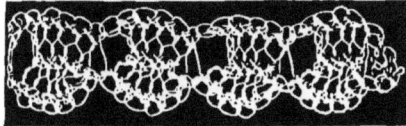

No. 57.—NARROW KNITTED LACE.
(IN IMITATION OF HAIR-PIN LACE.)

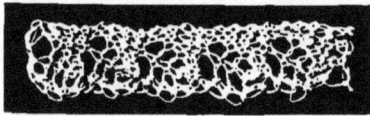

No. 58.—WHEAT-EAR LACE.

First row.—K 2, n, o twice, n, k 2, n, o twice, n, k 1, o, n, k 1, o, n, k 1, o, n, k 8, n, o, n, o, n, o, k 1, n, o twice, n, k 2, o twice, n, k 1.

Second row.—K 3, p 1, k 4, p 1, k 25, p 1, k 5, p 1, k 3.

Third row.—K 10, n, o twice, n, k 2, o, n, o, n, k 6, n, o, k 2, n, o twice, n, k 8.

Fourth row.—K 10, p 1, k 21, p 1, k 11.

Fifth row.—K 2, n, o twice, n, k 6, n, o twice, n, k 3, o, n, k 4, n, o, k 3, n, o twice, n, k 7, o twice, n, k 1.

Sixth row.—K 3, p 1, k 9, p 1, k 17, p 1, k 9, p 1, k 3.

No. 59.—FAVORITE LACE.

Seventh row.—K 14, n, o twice, n, k 2, o, n, k 2, n, o, k 2, n, o twice, n, k 13.

Eighth row.—K 15, p 1, k 13, p 1, k 15.

Ninth row.—K 2, n, o twice, n, k 10, n, o twice, n, k 1, o, n twice, o, k 1, n, o twice, n, k 12, o twice, n, k 1.

Tenth row.—K 3, p 1, k 14, p 1, k 9, p 1, k 13, p 1, k 3.

Eleventh row.—K 18, n, o twice, n, k 2, n, o twice, n, k 15, n, k 1.

Twelfth row.—K 19, p 1, k 5, p 1, k 19.

Thirteenth row.—K 2, n, o twice, n, k 10, n, o twice, n twice, o, k 2, o, n, o twice, o twice, n, k 10, n, o twice, n, k 1.

Fourteenth row.—K 3, p 1, k 13, p 1, k 9, p 1, k 13, p 1, k 3.

Fifteenth row.—K 14, n, o twice, n, k 1, n, o, k 4, o, n, k 1, n, o twice, n, k 10, n, k 1.

Sixteenth row.—K 14, p 1, k 13, p 1, k 15.

Seventeenth row.—K 2, n, o twice, n, k 6, n, o twice, n twice, o, n, o, k 6, o, n, o, n twice, o, twice, n, k 5, n, o twice, n, k 1.

Eighteenth row.—K 3, p 1, k 8, p 1, k 17, p 1, k 9, p 1, k 3.

Nineteenth row.—K 10, n, o twice, n, k 1, n, o, n, o, k 8, o, n, o, n, k 1, n, o twice, n, k 5, n, k 1.

Twentieth row.—K 9, p 1, k 21, p 1, k 11.

Twenty-first row.—*K 2, n, o twice, n ; repeat once from * ; n, o, n, o, n, o, k 10, o, n, o, n, o, n; n, o twice, n twice, o twice, n ; k 1.

Twenty-second row.—K 3, p 1, k 3, p 1, k 25, p 1, k 5, p 1, k 3.

Twenty-third row.—K 6, n, o twice, n, k 1, n, o, n, o, n, o, k 12, o, n, o, n, o, n, k 1, n, o twice, n, k 3.

Twenty-fourth row.—K 5, p 1, k 29, p 1, k 7.
Repeat from first row.

KNITTED LACE.

No. 60.—Cast on 25 stitches. Knit across plain.
First row.—K 3, * pass needle through the next

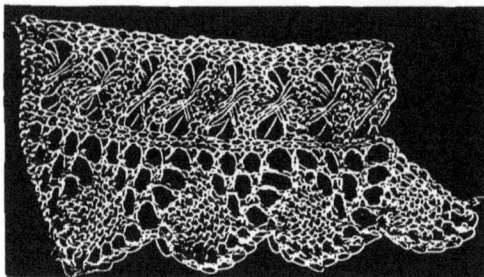

NO. 60.—KNITTED LACE.

stitch, o 4 times, k the stitch, * repeat seven times
more from *, k 2, o twice, n, k 7, o, n, k 1.
Second row.—O, n, k 13, purling the put-over,
slip 8 long stitches on right-hand needle, to unwind
them : then slip the 8 back on left-hand needle, k
the 5th, 6th, 7th and 8th, slipping them over the
first 4 stitches; then k the first 4 stitches, k 3.
Third row.—K 23, o, n, k 1.
Fourth row.—O, n, k 24.
Fifth row.—K 13, o twice, n, o twice, n, k 6, o,
n, k 1.
Sixth row.—O, n, k 26, purl the put-overs.
Seventh row.—K 25, o, n, k 1.
Eighth row.—O, n, k 26.
Ninth row.—K 3, * pass needle through the next
stitch, o 4 times, k the stitch, * repeat 7 times more
from *, k 2, o twice, n, o twice, n, o twice, n, k 6,
o, n, k 1.
Tenth row.—O, n, k 18, purling the put-overs;
remainder like second row from " k 13."
Eleventh row.—K 28, o, n, k 1.
Twelfth row.—O, n, k 29.
Thirteenth row.—K 13, o twice, n, o twice, n, o twice, n, o twice, n, k 7, o, n, k 1.
Fourteenth row.—O, n, k 33, purling the put-overs.
Fifteenth row.—K 24, slip 10 stitches on the left-hand needle
over first stitch, knit stitch.
Sixteenth row.—K 25. Repeat from first row.

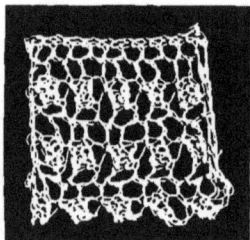

NO. 61.—CREOLE LACE.

CREOLE LACE.

No. 61.—Cast on 11 stitches.
First row.—Sl 1, k 1, th o twice, p 2 to. ; now p
1, k 1, p 1, and knit 1 all out of the next
stitch before slipping it off the needle; th
o twice, p 2 to., make 4 stitches out of the
next stitch in the manner just described,
th o twice, p 2 to., make 4 stitches as
before out of the next stitch.
Second row.—K 4, th o twice, p 2 to.,
and repeat twice more; then k 2.
Third row.—Sl 1, k 1, * th o twice, p 2
to., k 4, and repeat twice more from *.
Fourth row.—Slip 1, bind off 3, th o
twice, p 2 to., repeat twice more and then
k 2. Repeat from the 1st row.

KNITTED LACE.

No. 62.—Cast on 24 stitches.
First row.—Th o, p 2 to., k 2, o twice,
p 2 to.,* o, p 2 to., and repeat 7 times
more from *; o, k 2.
Second row.—K 23, o twice, p 2 to.
Third row.—Th o, p 2 to., k 9, o twice, p 2 to.,* o,

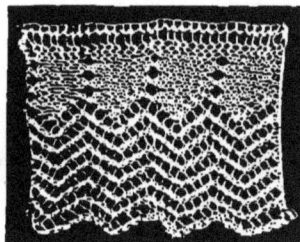

NO. 62.—KNITTED LACE.

p 2 to., and repeat 4 times more from *, o, k 2.
Fourth row.—Knit 24, o twice, p 2 to.
Fifth row.—Th o, p 2 to., k 10, o twice, p 2 to.,
*, o, p 2 to., and repeat 4 times more from *, o, k 2.
Sixth row.—K 25, o twice, p 2 to.
Seventh row.—Th o, p 2 to., k 11, o twice, p 2 to.,
* o, p 2 to., and repeat 4 times more from *, o, k 2.
Eighth row.—K 26, th o twice, p 2 to.
Ninth row.—Th o, p 2 to., k 9, n, o twice, p 2 to.,
* o, p 2 to., and repeat 4 times more from *, o, k 1, n.
Tenth row.—K 25, o twice, p 2 to.
Eleventh row.—Th o, p 2 to., k 8, n, o twice, p 2 to.,
* o, p 2 to., and repeat 4 times more from *, o, k 1, n.
Twelfth row.—Knit 24, o twice, p 2 to.
Thirteenth row.—Th o, p 2 to., k 7, n, o twice, p 2
to., * o, p 2 to., repeat 4 times more from *, o, k1, n.
Fourteenth row.—Knit 23, o twice, p 2 to.
Fifteenth row.—Th o, p 2 to., k 6, n, o twice, p 2
to., *, o, p 2 to., repeat 4 times more from *, o, k 1, n.
Sixteenth row.—Knit 22, o twice, p 2 to. Repeat
from first row.

43

Knitted Lace.

No. 63.—Cast on 20 stitches, knit across plain.
First row.—Sl 1, k 3, o twice, p 2 to., p 3, k 1, o, k 1, o, k 1, p 3, o, p 2 to., k 1, o twice, k 2.
Second row.—K 3, p 1, k 1, o twice, p 2 to., k 3, p 5, k 3, o twice, p 2 to., k 4.
Third row.—Sl 1, k 3, o twice, p 2 to., p 3, k 2, o, k 1, o, k 2, p 3, o, p 2 to., k 5.
Fourth row.—Bind off 2, k 2, o twice, p 2 to., k 3, p 7, k 3, o twice, p 2 to., k 4.
Fifth row.—Sl 1, k 3, o twice, p 2 to., p 3, k 3, o, k 1, o, k 3, p 3, o, p 2 to., k 1, o twice, k 2.
Sixth row.—K 3, p 1, k 1, o twice, p 2 to., k 3, p 9, k 3, o twice, p 2 to., k 4.
Seventh row.—Sl 1, k 3, o twice, p 2 to., p 3, sl 1, k 1, pass sl stitch o, k 5, n, p 3, o, p 2 to., k 5.
Eighth row.—Bind off 2, k 2, o twice, p 2 to., k 3, p 7, k 3, o twice, p 2 to., k 4.
Ninth row.—Sl 1, k 3, o twice, p 2 to., p 3, sl 1, k 1, pass sl stitch o, k 3, n, p 3, o, p 2 to., k 1, o twice, k 2.
Tenth row.—K 3, p 1, k 1, o twice, p 2 to., k 3, p 5, k 3, o twice, p 2 to., k 4.
Eleventh row.—Sl 1, k 3, o twice, p 2 to., p 3, sl 1, k 1, pass sl stitch o, k 1, n, p 3, o, p 2 to., k 5.

No. 63.—Knitted Lace.

Twelfth row.—Bind off 2, k 2, o twice, p 2 to., k 3, p 3, k 3, o twice, p 2 to., k 4. Repeat from first row.

Mikado Insertion.

No. 64.—Cast on 22 stitches and knit across plain.
First row.—K 11, th o twice, k 11.
Second row.—K 3, p 8, then make 6 stitches of the double loop as follows: P 1, k 1, p 1, k 1, p 1, k 1, p 8, k 3.
Third row.—K 3, sl 1, k 1, pass slipped stitch over, k 18, n, k 3.
Fourth row.—K 3, p 20, k 3.
Fifth row.—K 3, sl 1, k 1, pass slipped stitch over, k 5, th o, k 1, th o, k 1, th o, k 1, th o, k 1, th o, k 1, th o, k 6, n, k 3.
Sixth row.—K 3, p 24, k 3.
Seventh row.—K 3, sl 1, k 1, pass slipped stitch over, k 20, n, k 3.
Eighth row.—K 3, p 22, k 3.
Ninth row.—K 3, sl 1, k 1, pass slipped stitch over, k 3, th o, n, th o, n, th o, n, th o, n, th o, n, th o, n, th o, k 3, n, k 3.
Tenth row.—K 3, p 21, k 3.

Eleventh row.—K 3, sl 1, k 1, pass slipped stitch over, k 17, n, k 3.
Twelfth row.—K 3, p 19, k 3.
Thirteenth row.—K 3, sl 1, k 1, pass slipped stitch

No. 64.—Mikado Insertion.

over, th o, n, th o, n, th o, n, th o, n, th o, n, th o, n, th o, n, th o, k 3 together, k 3.
Fourteenth row.—K 3, p 17, k 3.
Fifteenth row.—K 3, p 2 together, p 15, k 3.
Sixteenth row.—K 22. Repeat.

Knitted Fluted Edging.

No. 65.—Use Saxony yarn or knitting silk of any pretty tint desired. The engraving illustrates the lace as only one-half its actual size.
Cast on 21 stitches and knit across plain.
Second row.—Plain, leaving 3 stitches on the left-hand needle. Turn.
Third row.—K 1, then o, n, across the row, knitting last stitch.
Fourth row.—Purl all but last 3, which knit plain.
Fifth row.—Plain.
Sixth row.—Plain, leaving 3 on left-hand needle. Turn.
Seventh row.—Purl.
Eighth row.—Plain.
Ninth row.—K 3 and purl the rest.
Tenth row.—Plain, leaving 3 stitches. Turn.
Eleventh row.—Plain.
Twelfth row.—Purl all except last 3, which knit.
Thirteenth row.—K 4, * o, n; repeat from * 7 times, k 1.
Fourteenth row.—Purl, leaving last 3. Turn.
Fifteenth and Sixteenth rows.—Plain.
Seventeenth row.—K 3, purl the rest.

No. 65.—Knitted Fluted Edging.

Eighteenth row.—Plain, leaving last 3. Turn.
Nineteenth row.—Purl.
Repeat from tenth row.

NORMANDY LACE.

No. 66.—Cast on 36 stitches. Knit across plain.
First row.—K 12, n, o, k 3, o, n, k 10, n, o, k 3, o, k 2.

Second row.—K 2, o, k 5, o, n, k 8, n, o, k 5, o, n, k 11.

Third row.—K 10, n, o, k 1, n, o, k 1, o, n, k 1, o, n, k 6, n, o, k 1, n, o, k 1, o, n, k 1, o, k 2.

Fourth row.—K 2, o, k 1, n, o, k 3, o, n,

No. 66.—NORMANDY LACE.

k 1, o, n, k 4, n, o, k 1, n, o, k 3, o, n, k 1, o, n, k 9.
Fifth row.—K 8, n, o, k 1, n, o, k 5, o, n, k 1, o, n, k 2, n, o, k 1, n, o, k 5, o, n, k 1, o, k 2.
Sixth row.—K 2, o, k 1, n, o, k 3. o, n, k 2, o, n, k 1, o, n, o, n, o, k 1, n, o, k 3, o, n, k 2, o, n, k 1, o, n, k 7.
Seventh row.—K 9, o, n, k 1, o, n, k 3, n, o, k 1, n, o, k 2, n, k 1, o, n, k 1, o, n, k 3, n, o, k 1, n, o, k 1, n.
Eighth row.—K 3, o, n, k 1, o, n, k 1, n, o, k 1, n, o, k 6, o, n, k 1, o, n, k 1, n, o, k 1, n, o, k 10.
Ninth row.—K 11, o, n, k 1, o, slip 1, n, pass the slipped stitch over, o, k 1, n, o, k 8, o, n, k 1, o, slip 1, n, pass slipped stitch over, o, k 1, n, o, k 2, n.
Tenth row.—N, k 2, o, n, k 3, n, o, k 10, o, n, k, 3, n, o, k 12.
Eleventh row.—K 13, o, n, k 1, n, o, k 12, o, n, k 1, n, o, k 2, n.
Twelfth row.—N, n, o, k 3 to, o, k 14, o, k 3 to, o, k 14. Repeat from first row.

TORCHON LACE.

No. 67.—Cast on 14 stitches and knit across plain.
First row.—Sl 1, o, n, k 2, o, n, k 1, n, o, n, o, k 1, o, k 1.
Second and every alternate row.—Knit plain.
Third row.—Sl 1, o, n, k 4, n, o, n, o, k, 3 o, k 1.
Fifth row.—Sl 1, o, n, k 3, n, o, n, o, k 5, o, k 1.

Seventh row.—Sl 1, o, n, k 2, n, o, n, o, k 7, o, k 1.
Ninth row.—Sl 1, o, n, k 1, n, o, n, o, k 4, o, n, k 3, o, k 1.
Eleventh row.—Sl 1, o, n, n, o, n, o, k 4, n, o, n, k 3, o, k 1.
Thirteenth row.—Sl 1, o, n, k 2, o, n, o, n, k 3, o, n, k 3, o, n.
Fifteenth row.—Sl 1, o, n, k 3, o, n, o, n, k 5, n, o, n.
Seventeenth row.—Sl 1, o, n, k 4, o, n, o, n, k 3, n, o, n.
Nineteenth row.—Sl 1, o, n, k 5, o, n, o, n, k 1, n, o, n.
Twenty-first row.—Sl 1, o, n, k 2, o, n, k 2, o, n, o, k 3 to., o, n.
Twenty-third row.—Sl 1, o, n, k 3, o, n, k 2, o, k 3 to., o, n.

KNITTED LACE.

No. 68.—Cast on 15 stitches.
First row.—Slip 1, k 2, o, n, o, n, k 4, o, n, over twice, k 2.

Second row.—Sl 1, k 2, p 1, k 2, o, n, k 6, o, n, k 1.

Third row.—Sl 1, k 2, o, n, k 1, o, n, k 3, o, n, k 4.

Fourth row.—Sl 1, k 5, o, n, k 6, o, n, k 1.

Fifth row.—Sl 1, k 2, o, n, k 2, o, n, k 2, o, n, o twice, n, o twice, k 2.

Sixth row.—Sl 1, k 2, p 1, k 2, p 1, k 2, o, n, k 6, o, n, k 1.

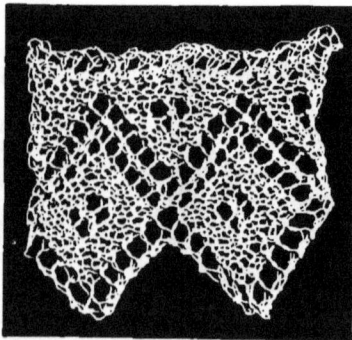

No. 67.—TORCHON LACE.

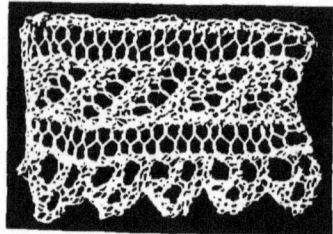

No. 68.—KNITTED LACE.

Seventh row.—Sl 1, k 2, o, n, k 3, o, n, k 1, o, n, k 7.
Eighth row.—Bind off 5, k 3, o, n, k 6, o, n, k 1.
Repeat from first row.

NEWPORT LACE.

No. 69.—This lace may be made from silk, linen or cotton thread, or from Saxony yarn.

Cast on 40 stitches, and knit across once plain.

First row.—K 3, n, k 2, th o, k 1, th o, n, th o, n. th o, k 2, n, k 4, n, k 2, th o, k 1, th o, n, th o, n, th o, k 3, n, k 2, th o, k 1, th o, n, th o, k 1.

Second and all following even rows.—Purl.

Third row.—K 2, n, k 2, th o, k 3, th o, n, th o, n, th o, k 2, n, k 2, n, k 2, th o, k 3, th o o, n, th o, n, th o, k 2, n, k 2, th o, k 3, th o, n, th o, k 1.

Fifth row.—K 1, n, k 2, th o, k 5, th o, n, th o, n, th o, k 2, n, k 2, n, th o, k 5, th o, n, th o, n, th o, k 1, n, k 2, th o, k 5, th o, n, th o, k 1.

Seventh row.—K 6, n, k 2, th o, n, th o, k 1, th o, k 1, th o, k 2, n, k 2, n, k 1, n, k 2, th o, n, th o, n, th o, n, k 5, n, k 2, th o, n, th o, n.

Ninth row.—K 5, n, k 2, th o, n, th o, n, th o, k 3, th o, k 2, n, k 2, n, k 2, th o, n, th o, n, th o, n, k 4, n, k 2, th o, n, th o, n.

Eleventh row.—K 4, n, k 2, th o, n, th o, n, th o, k 5, th o, k 2, n, k 2, n, th o, n, th o, n, th o, n, k 3, n, k 2, th o, n, th o, n.

Repeat from first row.

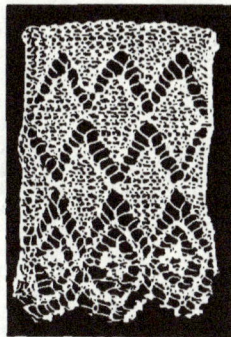

DOTTED DIAMOND LACE.

No. 70.—Cast on 32 stitches and knit across plain.

First row.—Sl 1, k 7, n, th o, k 3, th o, n, k 2, n, th o twice, n, k 3, n, th o, k 3, th o, k 3.

Second row.—Th o, n, k 12, p 1, k 18.

Third row.—Sl 1, k 6, n, th o, k 5, th o, n, k 7, n, th o, k 5, th o, k 3.

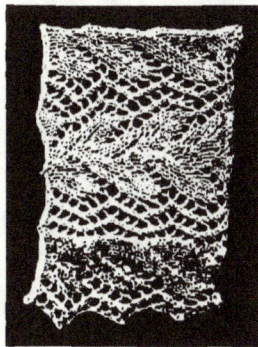

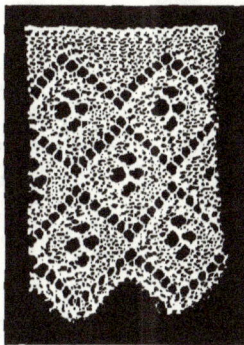

No. 70.—DOTTED DIAMOND LACE.

Fourth row.—Th o, n, k 32.

Fifth row.—Sl 1, k 5, n, th o, k 7, th o, n, k 5, n, th o, k 7, th o, k 3.

Sixth row.—Th o, n, k 33.

Seventh row.—Sl 1, k 4, n, th o, k 9, th o, n, k 3, n, th o, k 9, th o, k 3.

Eighth row.—Th o, n, k 34.

Ninth row.—Sl 1, k 3, n, th o, k 3, n, th o twice, n, k 4, th o, k 3, n, th o twice, n, k 4, th o, k 3.

Tenth row.—Th o, n, k 8, p 1, k 15, p 1, k 10.

No. 69.—NEWPORT LACE.

Eleventh row.—Sl 1, k 2, n, th o, k 2, n, th o twice, n, n, th o twice, n, k 3, th o, k 3 to., th o, k 2, n, th o twice, n, n, th o twice, n, k 3, th o, k 3.

Twelfth row.—Th o, n, k 7, p 1, k 3, p 1, k 11, p 1, k 3, p 1, k 8.

Thirteenth row.—Sl 1, k 4, th o, n, k 2, n, th o twice, n, k 3, n, th o, k 3, th o, n, k 2, n, th o twice, n, k 3, th o, n, k 2.

Fourteenth row.—Th o, n, k 8, p 1, k 15, p 1, k 10.

Fifteenth row.—Sl 1, k 5, th o, n, k 7, n, th o, n, k 7, n, th o, n, k 2.

No. 71.—NORMANDY LACE.

Sixteenth row.—Th o, n, k 34.

Seventeenth row.—Sl 1, k 6, th o, n, k 5, n, th o, k 7, th o, n, k 5, n, th o, n, k 2.

Eighteenth row.—Th o, n, k 33.

Nineteenth row.—Sl 1, k 7, th o, n, k 3, n, th o, k 9, th o, n, k 3, n, th o, n, k 2.

Twentieth row.—Th o, n, k 32.

Twenty-first row.—Sl 1, k 8, th o, n, k 1, n, th o, k 3, n, th o twice, n, k 4, th o, n, k 1, n, th o, n, k 2.

Twenty-second row.—Th o, n, k 12, p 1, k 18.

Twenty-third row.—Sl 1, k 9, th o, k 3 to., th o, k 2, n, th o twice, n, n, th o twice, n, k 3, th o, k 3 to., th o, n, k 2.

Twenty-fourth row.—Th o, n, k 9, p 1, k 3, p 1, k 16.

Repeat from first row.

NORMANDY LACE.

No. 71.—*First row.*—Cast on 31 stitches and and knit across plain.

Second row.—K 8, n, o, k 3, o, n, k 9, n, o, k 3, p 1, o, k 1.

Third row.—K 2, o, k 5, o, n, k 7, n, o, k 5, o, n, k 7.

Fourth row.—K 6, n, o, k 7, o, n, k 5, n, o, k 1, n, o, k 1, o, n, k 1, p 1, o, k 1.

Fifth row.—K 2, o, k 1, n, o, k 3, o, n, k 1, o, n, k 3, n, o, k 9, o, n, k 5.

Sixth row.—K 4, n, o, k 11, o, n, k 1, n, o, k 1, n, o, k 5, o, n, k 1, p 1, o, k 1.

Seventh row.—K 2, o, k 1, n, o, k 3, o, n, k 2, o, n, k 1, o, k 3 to., o, k 13, o, n, k 3.

Eighth row.—K 5, o, n, k 9, n, o, k 3, o, n, k 1, o, n, k 3, n, o, k 1, n, o, k 1, n.

Ninth row.—Bind off 1, k 1, o, n, k 1, o, n, k 1 n, o, k 1, n, o, k 5, o, n, k 7, n, o, k 6.

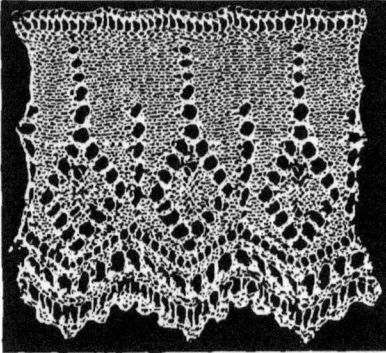

NO. 72.—KNITTED LACE.

Tenth row.—K 7, o, n, k 5, n, o, k 7, o, n, k 1, o, sl 1, n, pass slipped stitch over, o, k 1, n, o, k 1, n.

Eleventh row.—Bind off 1, k 1, o, n, k 3, n, o, k 9, o, n, k 3, n, o, k 8.

Twelfth row.—K 9, o, n, k 1, n, o, k 11, o, n, k 1, n, o, k 1, n.

Thirteenth row.—Bind off 1, k 1, o, k 3 to., o, k 13, o, k 3 to., o, k 10.

KNITTED LACE.

No. 72.—Cast on 42 stitches, and knit across.

First row.—O 2, ("o 2" means o twice) p 2 to., k 12; o twice, sl 1, n; bind 5 times; n, o, n, k 1 o, 3 times, sl 1, k 3 to., bind, k 1, o twice, n, k 1.

Second row.—Sl 1, k 2, p 1, k 3, p 1, k 7, p 1; k 2, p 1 4 times; k 12, o twice, p 2 to.

Third row.—O 2, p 2 to., k 29, o, k 7, o 2, n, k 2.

Fourth row.—Sl 1, k 3, p 1, k 37, o 2, p 2 to.; drop last stitch.

Fifth row.—O 2, p 2 to., k 30, o, k 2, o 3 times, sl 1, k 3 to., b, k 1, o 2, n, k 3.

Sixth row.—Bind off 3, k 1, p 1, k 3, p 1, k 34, o 2, p 2 to.; drop last stitch.

Seventh row.—O 2, p 2 to., k 22, n, o 2, n, k 5, o, k 7, o 2, n, k 1.

Eighth row.—Sl 1, k 2, p 1, k 15, p 1, k 23, o 2, p 2 to.; drop last stitch.

Ninth row.—O 2, p 2 to., k 20, n, o 2, n, n, o 2, n, k 4, o, k 2, o 3 times, sl 1, k 3 to., b, k 1, o 2, n, k 2.

Tenth row.—Sl 1, k 3, p 1, k 3, p 1, k 10, p 1, k 3, p 1, k 21, o 2, p 2 to.; drop last stitch.

Eleventh row.—O 2, p 2 to., k 18, n, o 2, n, k 4, n, o 2, n, k 3, o, k 7, o 2, n, k 3.

Twelfth row.—Bind off 3, k 1, p 1, k 13, p 1, k 7, p 1, k 19, o 2, p 2 to.; drop last stitch.

Thirteenth row.—O 2, p 2 to., k 16, n, o 2, n, k 8; n, o 2, n, k 2, o, k 2, o 3 times, sl 1, k 3 to., b, k 1, o 2, n, k 1.

Fourteenth row.—Sl 1, k 2, p 1, k 3, p 1, k 8, p 1, k 11, p 1, k 17, o 2, p 2 to.; drop last stitch.

Fifteenth row.—O 2, p 2 to., k 3; o, n, 3 times; o 2, sl 1, n, b, o 2, sl 1, k 3 to., b, o 2, n, k 2, * throw thread around needle 4 times; k 1 and repeat 7 times more. from *; k 2, n, o 2, n, k 1, o, k 7, o 2, n, k 2.

Sixteenth row.—Sl 1, k 3, p 1, k 11, p 1, k 3, sl 8 on right hand needle letting off all loops, then back on left hand needle, knit the last 4 loops over the first 4, one at a time, knit the first 4; k 4, p 1, k 2, p 1, k 2, p 1, k 9, o 2, p 2 to.; drop last stitch.

Seventeenth row.—O 2, p 2 to., k 16, n, o 2, n, k 8, n, o 2, n, k 1, n, o, n, k 1, o 3 times, sl 1, k 3 to., b, k 1, o 2, n, k 3.

Eighteenth row.—Bind off 3, k 1, p 1, k 3, p 1, k 8, p 1, k 11, p 1, k 17, o 2, p 2 to.; drop last stitch.

Nineteenth row.—O 2, p 2 to., k 18, n, o 2, n, k 4, n, o 2, n, k 2, n, o, n, k 6, o 2, n, k 1.

Twentieth row.—Sl 1, k 2, p 1, k 13, p 1, k 7, p 1, k 19, o 2, p 2 to.; drop last stitch.

Twenty-first row.—O 2, p 2 to., k 20, n, o 2, n, n, o 2, n, k 3, n, o, n, k 1, o 3 times, sl 1, k 3 to., b, k 1, o 2, n, k 2.

Twenty-second row.—Sl 1, k 3, p 1, k 3, p 1, k 10, p 1, k 3, p 1, k 21, o 2, p 2 to.

Twenty-third row.—O 2, p 2 to., k 22, n, o 2, n, k 4, n, o, n, k 6, o 2, n, k 3.

Twenty-fourth row.—Bind off 3, k 1, p 1, k 15, p 1, k 23, o 2, p 2 to.; drop last stitch.

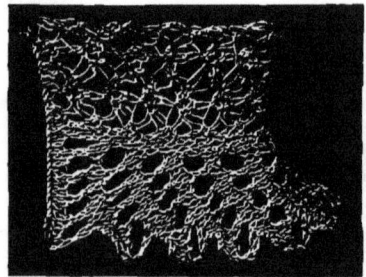

NO. 73.—COBWEB LACE.
(For Description see Page 47.)

Twenty-fifth row.—O 2, p 2 to., k 29, n, o, n, k 1, o 3 times, sl 1, k 3 to., k 1, o 2, n, k 1.

Twenty-sixth row.—Sl 1, k 2, p 1, k 3, p 1, k 34, o 2, p 2 to.; drop last stitch.

Twenty-seventh row.—O 2, p 2 to., k 28, n, o, n, k 6, o 2, n, k 2.

Twenty-eighth row.—Sl 1, k 3, p 1, k 37, o 2, p 2 to.; drop last stitch.

Repeat from first row excepting the small points on edge, which you will have learned in knitting the first scollop.

COBWEB LACE.
(For Illustration see Page 46.)

No. 73.—Cast on 26 stitches, and knit across plain.

First row.—K 4, over, k 1, o, n, k 1, o, n, n, o. n, k 2; o twice and n 5 times.

Second row.—K 2 and p 1 five times; p 2, k 2, o, n, k 1, n, o, k 3, o, n, k 2.

Third row.—K 1, n, o, k 5, o, k 3 to., o, k rest plain.

Fourth row.—P 17, k 4, o, k 1, o, n, k 1, o, n, n, o, n.

Fifth row.—K 2, o, n, k 1, n, o, k 3, o, n, k rest plain.

Sixth row.—Bind off 5, p 12, k 1, n, o, k 5, o, k 3 to., o, k 3.

Repeat from first row.

TORCHON-POINT LACE.

No. 72.—This is a very pretty pattern of knitted lace, which may be made of silk, cotton or wool. Cast on 12 stitches.

First row.—Knit 2, th o, n, th o, n, k 1, th o twice, n, k 3.

Second row.—K 5, p 1, k 2, th o, n, th o, n, k 1.

Third, Seventh, Eleventh and Fifteenth rows.—K 2, th o, n, th o, n, k remainder of row plain.

Fourth row.—K 8, th o, n, th o, n, k 1.

Fifth row.—K 2, th o, n, th o, n, k 1, th o twice, n, th o twice, n, k 2.

Sixth row.—K 4, p 1, k 2, p 1, k 2, th o, n, th o, n, k 1.

Eighth row.—K 10, th o, n, th o, n, k 1.

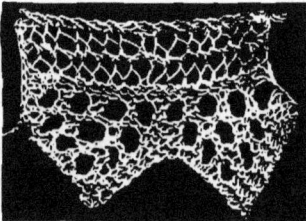

No. 74.—TORCHON-POINT LACE.

Ninth row.—K 2, th o, n, th o, n, k 1, th o twice, n, th o twice, n, th o twice, n, k 2.

Tenth row.—K 4, p 1, k 2, p 1, k 2, p 1, k 2, th o, n, th o, n, k 1.

Twelfth row.—K 13, th o, n, th o, n, k 1.

Thirteenth row.—K 2, th o, n, th o, n, k 1, th o twice, n, th o twice, n, th o twice, n, th o twice, n, k 3.

Fourteenth row.—K 5, p 1, k 2, p 1, k 2,

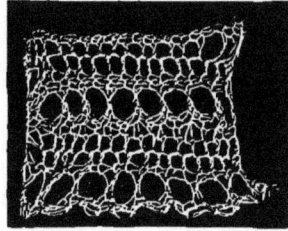

No. 75.—BEADING LACE.

p 1, k 2, p 1, k 2, th o, n, th o, n, k 1.

Sixteenth row.—Bind off 10 (leaving 11 on the left hand needle), k 6, th o, n, th o, n, k 1.

Repeat these details for all the work.

BEADING LACE.

No. 75.—Cast on 13 stitches, and knit across plain.

First row.—Sl 1, k 1, over twice, p 2 to., k 2, o twice, k 2, o twice, p 2 to., k 1, o twice, k 2.

Second row.—K 3, p 1, k 1, o twice, p 2 to., k 3, p 1, k 2 o twice, p 2 to., k 2.

Third row.—Sl 1, k 1, o twice, p 2 to., k 6, o twice, p 2 to., k 5.

Fourth row.—Bind off 2, k 2, o twice, p 2 to., k 1, k 3 to., k 2, o twice, p 2 to., k 2.

Repeat from first row.

WIDE LACE.
(For Illustration see Page 48.)

No. 76.—This lace is nearly a quarter of a yard deep when made of moderately fine thread or knitting cotton. Cast on 61 stitches and knit across plain.

First row.—K 2, o, n, o, o, n, o, n, k 3, o, n, k 1, n, o, k 3, o, n, k 1, n, o, k 2, n, o, k 3, o, n, k 1, n, o, k 3, o, n, o, k 1, n, o, k 3, o, n, o, o, n, o, n, k 3, o, n, o, k 3.

Second row.—K 10, o, n, k 2 (always make but 1 stitch in loop where thread is thrown over twice) o, n, k 39, o, n, k 2, o, n, k 1.

Third row.—K 2, o, n, k 2, o, n, k 4, o, k 3 to., o, k 5, o, k 3 to., o, k 1, o, n, k 2, o, k 3 to., o, k 5, o, k 3 to., o, k 4, o, n, k 2, o, n, k 4, o, n, o, k 3.

Fourth row.—K 11, o, n, k 2, o, n, k 39, o, n, k 2, o, n, k 1.

Fifth row.—K 2, o, n, o, o, n, o, n, k 5, o, k 3 to., k 3, k 3 to., o, k 2, n, o, k 3, o, n, k 2, o, k 3 to., k 3, k 3 to., o, k 5, o, n, o, o, n, o, n, k 5, o, n, o, k 3.

Sixth row.—K 12, 0, n, k 2, 0, n, k 35, 0, n, k 2, o, n, k 1.

Seventh row.—K 2, 0, n, k 2, 0, n, k 6, 0, n, k 1, n, 0, k 2, n, 0, k 5, 0, n, k 2, 0, n, k 1, n, 0, k 6, 0, n, k 2, 0, n, k 6, 0, n, 0, k 3.

Eighth row.—K 13, 0, n, k 2, 0, n, k 35, 0, n, k 2, o, n, k 1.

Ninth row.—K 2, 0, n, 0, 0, n, 0, n, k 7, 0, k 3 to., 0, k 2, n, 0, k 2, n, 0, k 3, 0, n, k 2, 0 k 3 to., 0, k 7, 0, n, 0, 0, n, 0, n, k 4, n, 0, k 1, 0, n, 0, k 3.

Tenth row.—K 14, 0, n, k 2, 0, n, k 35, 0, n, k 2, o, n, k 1.

Eleventh row.—K 2, 0, n, k 2, 0, n, k 8, 0, n, k 1, n, 0, k 2, n, 0, k 1, 0, n, k 2, 0, n, k 2, 0, n, k 7, 0, n, k 2, 0, n, k 4, n, 0, k 2, n, 0, k 3.

Twelfth row.—K 15, 0, n, k 2, 0, n, k 35, 0, n, k 2, 0, n, k 1.

Thirteenth row.—K 2, 0, n, 0, 0, n, 0, n, k 10, n, 0, k 2, n, 0, k 3, 0, n, k 2, 0, n, k 10, 0, n, 0, 0, n, 0, n, k 2, n, 0, k 5, 0, n, 0, k 3.

Fourteenth row.—K 16, 0, n, k 2, 0, n, k 35, 0, n, k 2, o, n, k 1.

Fifteenth row.—K 2, 0, n, k 2, 0, n, k 9, n, 0, k 2, n, 0, k 5, 0, n, k 2, 0, n, k 9, 0, n, k 2, 0, n, k 1, n, 0, k 7, 0, n, 0, k 3.

Sixteenth row.—K 17, 0, n, k 2, 0, n, k 35, 0, n, k 2, 0, n, k 1.

Seventeenth row.—K 2, 0, n, 0, 0, n, 0, n, k 8, n, 0, k 2, n, 0, k 2, n, 0, k 3, 0, n, k 2, 0, n, k 8, 0, n, 0, o, n, 0, n, n, 0, k 3, n, 0, 0, k 4, 0, n, 0, k 3.

Eighteenth row.—K 18, 0, n, k 2, 0, n, k 35, 0, n, k 2, 0, n, k 1.

Nineteenth row.—K 2, 0, n, k 2, 0, n, k 7, n, 0, k 2, n, 0, k 2, n, 0, k 1, 0, n, k 2, 0, n, k 2, 0, n, k 7, 0, n, k 2, 0, n, k 2, 0, n, k 5, n, 0, n, 0, n, k 2.

Twentieth row.—K 17, 0, n, k 2, 0, n, k 35, 0, n, k 2, 0, n, k 1.

Twenty-first row.—K 2, 0, n, 0, 0, n, 0, n, k 6, n, 0, k 2, n, 0, k 2, n, 0, k 3, 0, n, k 2, 0, n, k 2, 0, n, k 6, 0, n, 0, 0, n, 0, n, k 3, 0, n, k 3, n, 0, n, 0, n, k 2.

Twenty-second row.—K 16, 0, n, k 2, 0, n, k 35, 0, n, k 2, 0, n, k 1.

Twenty-third row.—K 2, 0, n, k 2, 0, n, k 5, n, 0, k 2, n, 0, k 2, n, 0, k 5, 0, n, k 2, 0, n, k 2, 0, n, k 5, o, n, k 2, 0, n, k 4, 0, n, k 1, n, 0, n, 0, n, k 2.

Twenty-fourth row.—K 15, 0, n, k 2, 0, n, k 35, 0, n, k 2, 0, n, k 1.

Twenty-fifth row.—K 2, 0, n, 0, 0, n, 0, n, k 4, n, 0, k 2, n, 0, k 2, n, 0, k 2, n, 0, k 3, 0, n, k 2, 0, n, k 2, 0, n, k 4, 0, n, 0, 0, 0, n, 0, n, k 5, 0, k 3, to., 0, n, 0, n, k 2.

Twenty-sixth row.—K 14, 0, n, k 2, 0, n, k 35, 0, n, k 2, 0, n, k 1.

Twenty-seventh row.—K 2, 0, n, k 2, 0, n, k 3, n, 0, k 2, n, 0, k 2, n, 0, k 1, 0, n, 0, k 2, 0, n, k 2, 0, n, k 3, 0, n, k 2, 0, n, k 5, n, 0, n, 0, n, k 2.

Twenty-eighth row.—K 13, 0, n, k 2, 0, n, k 35, 0, n, k 2, 0, n, k 1.

Twenty-ninth row.—K 2, 0, n, 0, 0, n, 0, n, k 2, n, 0, k 2, n, 0, k 2, n, 0, k 3, 0, n, k 2, 0, n, k 2, 0, n, n, k 2, 0, n, k 4, n, 0, k 2, n, 0, n, k 2.

Thirtieth row.—K 12, 0, n, k 2, 0, n, k 35, 0, n, k 2, 0, n, k 1.

Thirty-first row.—K 2, 0, n, k 2, 0, n, k 1, n, 0, k 2, n, 0, k 2, n, 0, k 5, 0, n, k 2, 0, n, k 2, 0, n, k 2, 0, n, k 1, 0, n, k 2, 0, n, k 3, n, 0, n, 0, n, k 2.

Thirty-second row.—K 11, 0, n, k 2, 0, n, k 35, 0, n, k 2, 0, n, k 1.

Thirty-third row.—K 2, 0, n, 0, 0, n, 0, n, 0, k 2, n, 0, k 2, n, 0, k 2, n, 0, k 7, 0, n, k 2, 0, n, k 2, 0, n, 0, 0, n, 0, 0, n, 0, n, k 2, n, 0, n, 0, n, k 2.

Thirty-fourth row.—K 10, 0, n, k 2, 0, n, k 35, 0, n, k 2, 0, n, k 1.

Thirty-fifth row.—K 2, 0, n, k 2, 0, n, k 2, 0, n, k 2, 0, n, k 2 0, n, k 2, 0, n, k 3, n, 0, k 2, n, 0, k 2, n, 0, k 2, n, 0, k 2, 0, n, k 2, 0, n, k 1, n, 0, n, 0, n, k 2.

Thirty-sixth row.—K 9, 0, n, k 2, 0, n, k 35, 0, n, k 2, 0, n, k 1.

Thirty-seventh row.—K 2, 0, n, 0, 0, n, 0, n, k 3, 0, n, k 2, 0, n, k 2, 0, n, k 2, 0, n, k 1, n, 0, k 2, n, 0, k 2, n, 0, k 2, n, 0, k 3, 0, n, 0, 0, n, 0, n, k 3, 0, n, 0, k 3.

Thirty-eighth row.—K 10, 0, n, k 2, 0, n, k 35, 0, n, k 2, 0, n, k 1.

No. 76.—WIDE LACE.

(For Description see Page 47.)

Thirty-ninth row.—K 2, o, n, k 2, o, n, k 4, o, n, k 2, o, n, k 2, o, n, k 2, o, k 3 to., o, k 2, n, o, k 2, n, o, k 2, n, o, k 4, o, n, k 2, o, n, k 4, o, n, o, k 3.

Fortieth row.—K 11, o, n, k 2, o, n, k 35, o, n, k 2, o, n, k 1.

Forty-first row.—K 2, o, n, o, o, n, o, n, k 5, o, n, k 2, o, n, k 2, o, n, k 2, o, n, k 1, n, o, k 2, n, o, k 2, n, o, k 5, o n, o, o, n, o, n, k 5, o, n, o, k 3.

Forty-second row.—K 12, o, n, k 2, o, n, k 35, o, n, k 2, o, n, k 1.

Forty-third row.—K 2, o, n, k 2, o, n, k 6, o, n, k 2, o, n, k 2, o, n, k 2, o, k 3 to., o, k 2, n, o, k 2, n, o, k 6, o, n, k 2, o, n, k 6, o, n, o, k 3.

Forty-fourth row.—K 13, o, n, k 2, o, n, k 35, o, n, k 2, o, n, k 1.

Forty-fifth row.—K 2, o, n, o, o, n, o, n, k 7, o, n, k 2, o, n, k 2, o, n, k 2, o, n, k 1, n, o, k 2, n, o, k 7, o, n, o, o, n, o, n, k 4, n, o, k 1, o, n, o, k 3.

Forty-sixth row.—K 14, o, n, k 2, o, n, k 35, o, n, k 2, o, n, k 1.

Forty-seventh row.—K 2, o, n, k 2, o, n, k 8, o, n, k 2, o, n, k 2, o, n, k 2, o, k 3 to., o, k 2, n, o, k 8, o, n, k 2, o, n, k 3, n, o, k 3, o, n, o, k 3.

Forty-eighth row.—K 15, o, n, k 2, o, n, k 35, o, n, k 2, o, n, k 1.

Forty-ninth row.—K 2, o, n, o, o, n, o, n, k 9, o, n, k 2, o, n, k 2, o, n, k 2, o, n, k 1, n, o, k 9, o, n, o, o, n, o, n, k 2, n, o, k 5, o, n, o, k 3.

Fiftieth row.—K 16, o, n, k 2, o, n, k 35, o, n, k 2, o, n, k 1.

Fifty-first row.—K 2, o, n, k 2, o, n, k 10, o, n, k 2, o, n, k 2, o, n, k 2, o, k 3 to., o, k 10, o, n, k 2, o, n, k 1, n, o, k 7, o, n, o, k 3.

Fifty-second row.—K 17, o, n, k 2, o, n, k 35, o, n, k 2, o, n, k 1.

Fifty-third row.—K 2, o, n, o, o, n, o, n, k 11, o, n, k 2, o, n, k 2, o, n, k 2, o, n, k 10, o, n, o, o, n, o, n, n, o, k 3, n, o, o, k 4, o, n, o, k 3.

Fifty-fourth row.—K 18, o, n, k 2, o, n, k 35, o, n, k 2, o, n, k 1.

Fifty-fifth row.—K 2, o, n, k 2, o, n, k 9, n, o, k 1, o, k 2, n, o, k 2, n, o, k 2, n, o, n, k 9, o, n, k 2, o, n, k 2, o, n, k 5, n, o, n, o, n, k 2.

Fifty-sixth row.—K 17, o, n, k 2, o, n, k 35, o, n, k 2, o, n, k 1.

Fifty-seventh row.—K 2, o, n, o, o, n, o, n, k 8, n, o, k 3, o, n, k 2, o, n, k 2, o, n, k 2, o, n, k 8, o, n, o, o, n, o, n, k 3, o, n, k 3, n, o, n, k 2.

Fifty-eighth row.—K 16, o, n. k 2, o, n, k 35, o, n, k 2, o, n, k 1.

Fifty-ninth row.—K 2, o, n, k 2, o, n, k 7, n, o, k 2, n, o, k 1, o, n, k 2, o, n, k 2, o, n, k 2, o, n, k 7, o, n, k 2, o, n, k 4, o, n, k 1, n, o, n, o, n, k 2.

Sixtieth row.—K 15, o, n, k 2, o, n, k 35, o, n, k 2, o, n, k 1.

Sixty-first row.—K 2, o, n, o, o, n, o, n, k 6, n, o, k 2, n, o, k 3, o, n, k 2, o, n, k 2, o, n, k 2, o, n, k 6, o, n, o, o, n, o, n, k 5, o, k 3 to., o, n, o, n, k 2.

Sixty-second row.—K 14, o, n, k 2, o, n, k 35, o, n, k 2, o, n, k 1.

Sixty-third row.—K 2, o, n, k 2, o, n, k 5, n, o, k 2, n, o, k 2, n, o, k 1, o, n, k 2, o, n, k 2, o, n, k 2, o, n k 5, o, n, k 2, o, n, k 5, n, o, n, o, n, k 2.

Sixty-fourth row.—K 13, o, n, k 2, o, n, k 35, o, n, k 2, o, n, k 1.

Sixty-fifth row.—K 2, o, n, o, o, n, o, n, k 4, n, o, k 2, n, o, k 2, n, o, k 3, o, n, k 2, o, n, k 2, o, n, k 2, o, n, k 4, o, n, o, o, n, o, n, k 4, n, o, n, o, n, k 2.

Sixty-sixth row.—K 12, o, n, k 2, o, n, k 35, o, n, k 2, o, n, k 1.

Sixty-seventh row.—K 2, o, n, k 2, o, n, k 3, n, o, k 2, n, o, k 2, n, o, k 2, n, o, k 1, o, n, k 2, o, n, k 2, o, n, k 2, o, n, k 3, o, n, k 2, o, n, k 3, n, o, n, o, n, k 2.

Sixty-eighth row.—K 11, o, n, k 2, o, n, k 35, o, n, k 2, o, n, k 1.

Sixty-ninth row.—K 2, o, n, o, o, n, o, n, k 2, n, o, k 2, n, o, k 2, n, o, k 2, n, o, k 3, o, n, k 2, o, n, k 2, o, n, o, n, k 2, o, n, k 2, o, n, k 2, n, o, n, o, n, k 2.

Seventieth row.—K 10, o, n, k 2, o, n, k 35, o, n, k 2, o, n, k 1.

Seventy-first row.—K 2, o, n, k 2, o, n, k 1, n, o, k 2, n, o, k 2, n, o, k 2, n, o, k 5, o, n, k 2, o, n, k 2, o, n, k 2, o, n, k 1, o, n, k 2, o, n, k 1, n, o, n, o, n, k 2.

Seventy-second row.—K 9, o, n, k 2, o, n, k 35, o, n, k 2, o, n, k 1.

Seventy-third row.—K 2, o, n, o, o, n, o, n, n, o, k 2, n, o, k 2, n, o, k 2, n, o, k 7, o, n, k 2, o, n, k 2, o, n, k 2, o, n, o, n, o, o, n, o, n, k 3, o, n, o, n, k 3.

Seventy-fourth row.—K 10, o, n, k 2, o, n, k 35, o, n, k 2, o, n, k 1.

Seventy-fifth row.—K 2, o, n, k 2, o, n, k 2, o, n, k 2, o, n, k 2, o, n, k 2, o, n, k 3, n, o, k 2, n, o, k 2, n, o, k 2, n, o, k 2, o, n, k 4, o, n, o, k 3.

Seventy-sixth row.—K 11, o, n, k 2, o, n, k 35, o, n, k 2, o, n, k 1.

Seventy-seventh row.—K 2, o, n, o, o, n, o, n, k 3, o, n, k 2, o, n, k 2, o, n, k 2, o, n, k 1, n, o, k 2, n, o, k 2, n, o, k 2, n, o, k 3, o, n, o, o, n, o, n, k 5, o, n, o, k 3.

Seventy-eighth row.—K 12, o, n, k 2, o, n, k 35, o, n, k 2, o, n, k 1.

Seventy-ninth row.—K 2, o, n, k 2, o, n, k 4, o, n, k 2, o, n, k 2, o, n, k 2, o, k 3 to., o, k 2, n, o, k 2, n, o, k 4, o, n, k 2, o, n, k 6, o, n, o, k 3.

Eightieth row.—K 13, o, n, k 2, o, n, k 35, o, n, k 2, o, n, k 1.

Eighty-first row.—K 2, o, n, o, o, n, o, n, k 5, o, n, k 2, o, n, k 2, o, n, k 2, o, n, k 1, o, n, k 2, n, o, k 2, n, o, k 5, o, n, o, o, n, o, n, k 4, n, o, k 1, o, n, o, k 3.

Eighty-second row.—K 14, o, n, k 2, o, n, k 35, o, n, k 2, o, n, k 1.

Eighty-third row.—K 2, o, n, k 2, o, n, k 6, o, n, k 2, o, n, k 2, o, n, k 3, n, o, k 2, n, o, k 2, n, o, k 6, o, n, k 2, o, n, k 3, n, o, k 3, o, n, o, k 3.

Eighty-fourth row.—K 15, o, n, k 2, o, n, k 35, o, n, k 2, o, n, k 1.

Eighty-fifth row.—K 2, o, n, o, o, n, o, n, k 7, o, n, k 2, o, n, k 2, o, n, k 1, n, o, k 2, n, o, k 2, n, o, k 7, o, n, o, o, n, o, n, k 2, n, o, k 5, o, n, o, k 3.

Eighty-sixth row.—K 16, o, n, k 2 o, n, k 35, o, n, k 2, o, n, k 1.

Eighty-seventh row.—K 2, o, n, k 2, o, n, k 8, o, n, k 2, o, n, k 2, o. k 3 to., o, k 2, n, o, k 2, n, o, k 8, o, n, k 2, o, n, k 1, n, o, k 7, o, n, o, k 3.

Eighty-eighth row.—K 17, o. n. k 2, o, n, k 35, o, n, k 2, o, n, k 1.

Eighty-ninth row.—K 2, o, n, o, o, n, o, n, k 9, o, n, k 2, o, n, k 2, o, n, k 1, n, o, k 2, n, o, k 9, o, n, o, o, n, o, n, n, o, k 3, n, o, o, k 4, o, n, o, k 3.

Ninetieth row.—K 18, o, n, k 2, o, n, k 35 o, n, k 2, o, n, k 1.

Ninety-first row.—K 2, o, n, k 2, o, n, k 10, o, n, k 2, o, n, k 3, n, o, k 2, n, o, k 10, o, o, n, k 2, o, n, k 2, o, n, k 5, n, o, n, o, n, k 2.

Ninety-second row.—K 17, o, n, k 2, o, n, k 35, o, n, k 2, o, n, k 1.

Ninety-third row.—K 2, o, n, o, o, n, o, n, k 11, o, n, k 2, o, n, k 1, n, o, k 2, n, o, k 11, o, n, o, o, n, o, n, k 3, o, n, k 3, n, o, n, o, n, k 2.

Ninety-fourth row.—K 16, o, n, k 2, o, n, k 35, o, n, k 2, o, n, k 1.

Ninety-fifth row.—K 2, o, n, k 2, o, n, k 7, n, o, k 3, o, n, k 2, o, n, k 3 to., o, k 2, n, o, k 3, o, n, k 7, o, n, k 2, o, n, k 4, o, n, k 1, n, o, n, o, n, k 2.

Ninety-sixth row.—K 15, o, n, k 2, o, n, k 35, o, n, k 2, o, n, k 1.

Ninety-seventh row.—K 2, o, n, o, o, n, o, n, k 6, n, o, k 1, o, n, k 2, o, n, k 2, o, n, k 1, n, o, k 2, n, o, k 1, o, n, k 6, o, n, o, o, n, o, n, k 5, o, k 3 to., o, n, o, n, k 2.

Ninety-eighth row.—K 14, o, n, k 2, o, n, k 35, o, n, k 2, o, n, k 1.

Ninety-ninth row.—K 2, o, n, k 2, o, n, k 5, n, o, k 3, o, n, k 2, o, n, k 3, n, o, k 2, n, o, k 3, o, n, k 5, o, n, k 2 o, n, k 5, n, o, n, o, n, k 2.

One Hundredth row.—K 13, o, n, k 2, o, n, k 35, o, n, k 2, o, n, k 1.

One Hundred and First row.—K 2, o, n, o, o, n, o, n, k 4, n, o, k 5, o, n, k 2, o, n, k 1, n, o, k 2, n, o, k 5, o, n, k 4, o, n, o, o, n, o, n, k 4, n o, n, o, n, k 2.

One Hundred and Second row.—K 12, o, n, k 2, o, n, k 35, o, n, k 2, k n, k 1.

One Hundred and Third row.—K 2, o, n, k 2, o, n, k 3, n, o, k 1, o. n, k 1, n, o, k 1, o, n, k 2, o, k 3 to., o, k 2, n, o, k 1, o, n, k 1. n, o, k 1, o, n, k 3, o, n, k 2, o, n, k 3, n, o, n, o, n, k 2.

One Hundred and Fourth row.—K 11, o, n, k 2, o, n, k 35, .o. n. k 2, o, n, k 1.

One Hundred and Fifth row.—K 2, o, n, o, o, n, o, n, k 2, n, o, k 3, o, k 3 to., o, k 3, o, n, k 2, o, n, k 1, n, o, k 3, o, k 3 to., o, k 3, o, n, k 2, o, n, o, o, n, o, n, k 2, n, o, n, o, n, o, n, k 2.

One Hundred and Sixth row.—K 10, o, n, k 2, o, n, k 35, o, n, k 2, o, n, k 1.

One Hundred and Seventh row.—K 2, o, n, k 2, o, n, k 1, n, o, k 5, o, k 1, o, o, k 5, o, n, k 3, n, o, k 5, o, k 1, o, k 5, o, n, k 1, o, n, k 2, o, n, k 1, n, o, n, o, n, k 2.

One Hundred and Eighth row.—K 9, o, n, k 2, o, n, k 39, o, n, k 2, o, n, k 1.

This completes one pattern.

KNITTED INSERTION FOR BEDSPREAD.

No. 77.—Cast on 72 stitches and knit across plain. ("O 2" means over twice.)

First row.—O 2, p 2 to., k 6, n, o 2, n, n, o 2, n, k 12; n 2, n, o. 4 times; k 12, n, o 2, n, n, o 2, n, k 6, o 2, p 2 to.

Second row.—O 2, p 2 to., k 8, p 1, k 3, p 1, k 15, p 1; k 3, p 1 3 times; k 15, p 1, k 3, p 1, k 7, o 2, p 2 to.

Third row.—O 2, p 2 to.. k 4; n, o 2 n, 3 times; k 12; n, o 2 n, 3 times; k 12; n, o 2 n 3 times; k 4, o 2, p 2 to.

Fourth row.—O 2, p 2 to., k 6, p 1; k 3, p 1 twice; k 15, p 1; k 3, p 1 twice; k 5, o 2, p 2 to.

Fifth row.—O 2, p 2 to., k 2; n, o 2, n, 4 times; k 12, n, o 2, n, n, o 2, n, k 12; n, o 2 n, 4 times; k 2, o 2, p 2 to.

Sixth row.—O 2, p 2 to., k 4, p 1; k 3, p 1, 3 times; 1 15, p 1, k 3, p 1, k 15, p 1; k 3, p 1, 3 times; k 3, o 2, p 2 to.

Seventh row.—O 2, p 2 to.; n, o 2, n 5 times; k 12, n, o 2, n, k 12; n, o 2, n, 5 times; o 2, p 2 to.

Eighth row.—O 2, p 2 to., k 2, p 1; k 3, p 1, 4 times; k 15, p 1, k 15, p 1; k 3, p 1, 4 times; k 1, o 2, p 2 to.

Ninth row.—O 2, p 2 to., k 2; n, o 2, n, 5 times; k 8, n, o 2, n, n, o 2, n, k 8; n, o 2, n, 5 times; k 2, o 2, p 2 to.

Tenth row.—O 2, p 2 to., k 4, p 1; k 3, p 1, 4 times; k 11, p 1, k 3, p 1, k 11, p 1; k 3, p 1, 4 times; k 3, o 2, p 2 to.

Eleventh row.—O 2, p 2 to., k 4; n, o 2, n, 5

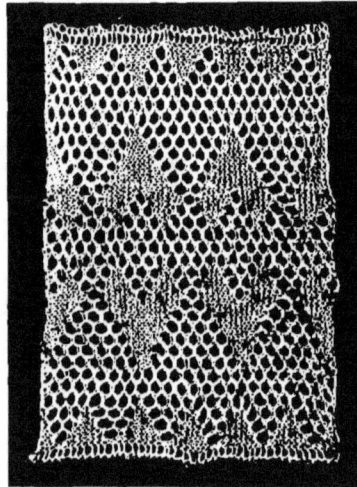

No. 77.—KNITTED INSERTION FOR BEDSPREAD.

times ; k 4 ; n, o 2, n, 3 times ; k 4 ; n, o 2, n, 5 times ; k 4, o 2, p 2 to.

Twelfth row.—O 2, p 2 to., k 6, p 1 ; k 3, p 1, 4 times ; k 7, p 1; k 3, p 1 twice; k 7, p 1; k 3, p 1 4 times; k 5, o 2, p 2 to.

Thirteenth row.—O 2, p 2 to., k 6 ; n, o 2, n 14 times ; k 6. o 2, p 2 to.

Fourteenth row.—O 2, p 2 to., k 8, p 1 ; k 3, p 1, 13 times ; k 7, o 2, p 2 to.

Fifteenth row.—O 2, p 2 to., k 8 ; n, o 2, n, 13 times ; k 8, o 2, p 2 to.

Sixteenth row.—O 2, p 2 to., k 10, p 1 ; k 3, p 1, 12 times ; k 9, o 2, p 2 to.

Seventeenth row.—Like 13th row.
Eighteenth row.—Like 14 row.
Nineteenth row.—Like 11th row.
Twentieth row.—Like 12th row.
Twenty-first row.—Like 9th row.
Twenty-second row.—Like 10th row.
Twenty-third row.—Like 7th row.
Twenty-fourth row.—Like 8th row.
Twenty-fifth row.—Like 5th row.
Twenty-sixth row.—Like 6th row.
Twenty-seventh row.—Like 3rd row.
Twenty-eighth row.—Like 4th row.
Twenty-ninth row.—Like 1st row.
Thirtieth row.—Like 2nd row.
Thirty-first row.—O 2, p 2 to., k 8, n, o 2, n, k 12; n, o 2, n, 5 times; k 12, n, o 2, n, k 8, o 2, p 2 to.

Thirty-second row.—O 2, p 2 to., k 10, p 1, k 15, p 1; k 3, p 1, 4 times; k 15, p 1, k 9, o 2, p 2 to.
Repeat from 1st row.

NO. 78.—KNITTED LACE.

KNITTED LACE.

No. 78.—Cast on 27 stitches and knit across plain.

First row.—K 3, th o, n, k 1, th o, n, k 11, th o, n, k 1, th o twice, n, th o twice, n, k 1.

Second row.—K 3, p 1, k 2, p 1, k 2, th o, n, k 1, th o, n, k 11, th o, n, k 2.

Third row.—K 3, th o, n, k 2, th o, n, k 10, th o, n, k 8.

Fourth row.—K 9, th o, n, k 2, th o, n, k 10, th o, n, k 2.

Fifth row.—K 3, th o, n, k 2, th o, n, k 9, th o, n, k 3, th o twice, n, th o twice, n, k 1.

Sixth row.—K 3, p 1, k 2, p 1, k 4, th o, n, k 3, th o, n, k 9, th o, n, k 2.

Seventh row.—K 3, th o, n, k 4, th o, n, k 8, th o, n, k 10.

Eighth row.—K 11, th o, n, k 4, th o, n, k 8, th o, n, k 2.

Ninth row.—K 3, th o, n, k 5, th o, n, k 7, th o, n, k 5, th o twice, n, th o twice, n, k 1.

Tenth row.—K 3, p 1, k 2, p 1, k 6, th o, n, k 5, th o, n, k 7, th o, n, k 2.

Eleventh row.—K 3, th o, n, k 14, th o, n, k 12.

Twelfth row.—Bind off 6, k 6, th o, n, k 14, th o n, k 2.
Repeat from 1st row.

KNITTED LACE.

No. 79.—Cast on 34 stitches, and knit across plain; knit all even rows plain.

First row.—Slip 1, k 3, * th o, n, k 2, repeat 7 times from *, th o, k 2.

Third row.—Slip 1, k 4, * th o, n, k 2, repeat 7 times from *, th o, k 2.

Fifth row.—Slip 1, k 5, * th o, n, k 2, repeat 7 times from *, th o, k 2.

NO. 79.— KNITTED LACE.

Seventh row.—Slip 1, k 6, * th o, n, k 2, repeat 7 times from *, th o, k 2.

Eighth row.—Bind off 4 stitches; knit rest plain.

KNITTED BORDER FOR PILLOW SHAMS.
(For Illustration see Page 52.)

No. 80.—Cast on 56 stitches and knit across plain. ("O 2" means over twice.)

First row.—O 2, p 2 to., k 3, o 2, sl 1, n, k 24, b, o 2, sl 1, n, b, k 11, k 4 to., k 2, o, k 1, o 2, n, k 1.

Second row.—Sl 1, k 2, p 1, k 18, p 1, k 26, p 1, k 3, o 2, p 2 to.

Third row.—O 2, p 2 to., k 6 ; o 2, sl 1, n, b, 8 times ; k 12, n, o 2, n, k 2, o, k 1, o 2, n, k 2.

Fourth row.—Sl 1, k 3, p 1, k 6, p 1, k 15, p 1 ; k 2, p 1, 7 times; k 6, o 2, p 2 to.

Fifth row.—O 2, p 2 to., k 40, n, o 2, n, n, o 2, k 3, o, k 1, o 2, n, k 3.

Sixth row.—Bind off 3, k 1, p 1, k 6, p 1, k 3, p 1, k 41, o 2, p 2 to.

Seventh row.—O 2, p 2 to., k 6 ; o, n, k 5, 3 times ; o, n, k 9, n, o 2, n, n, o 2, n, n, k 3, o, k 1, o 2, n, k 1.

Eighth row.—Sl 1, k 2, p 1, k 8, p 1, k 3, p 1, k 39, o 2, p 2 to.

Ninth row.—O 2, p 2 to., k 36; n, o 2, n, 3 times; k 3, o, k 1, o 2, n, k 2.

Tenth row.—Sl 1, k 3, p 1, k 7, p 1, k 3, p 1, k 3, p 1, k 39, o 2, p 2 to.

Eleventh row.—O 2, p 2 to., k 7; o, n, k 5, 3 times; o, n, k 4; n, o 2 n, 4 times; k 2, o, k 1, o 2, n, k 3.

Twelfth row.—Bind off 3, k 1, p 1, k 6, p 1; k 3, p 1, 3 times; k 35, o 2, p 2 to.

Thirteenth row.—O 2, p 2 to., k 32; n, o 2 n, 4 times; n, k 3, o, k 1, o 2, n, k 1.

Fourteenth row.—Sl 1, k 2, p 1, k 8, p 1; k 3, p 1, 3 times; k 33, o 2, p 2 to.

Fifteenth row.—O 2, p 2 to., k 8, o, n, k 5, o, n, k 5, o, n, k 6; n, o 2, n, 5 times; k 3, o, k 1, o 2, n, k 2.

Sixteenth row.—Sl 1, k 3, p 1, k 7, p 1; k 3, p 1, 4 times; k 31, o 2, p 2 to.

Seventeenth row.—O 2, p 2 to., k 28; n, o 2, n, 6 times; k 2, o, k 1, o 2, n, k 3.

Eighteenth row.—Bind off 3, k 1, p 1, k 6, p 1; k 3, p 1, 5 times; k 29, o 2, p 2 to.

Nineteenth row.—O 2, p 2 to., k 9, o, n, k 5, o, n, k 3, o 2, sl 1, n, b, o 2, sl 1, k 3 to., b; o 2, n, n, 6 times; k 3, o, k 1, o 2, n, k 1.

Twentieth row.—Sl 1, k 2, p 1, k 8, p 1; k 3, p 1, 5 times; k 2, p 1, k 2, p 1, k 21, o 2, p 2 to.

Twenty-first row.—O 2, p 2 to., k 28; n, o 2, n, 5 times; n, o 2, k 3 to., k 2, o, k 1, o 2, n, k 2.

Twenty-second row.—Sl 1, k 3, p 1, k 6, p 1; k 3, p 1, 5 times; k 29, o 2, p 2 to.

Twenty-third row.—O 2, p 2 to., k 7; n, o, k 5, n, o, k 5, n, o, k 7; n, o 2, n, 5 times; k 3 to., k 2, o, k 1, o 2, n, k 3.

Twenty-fourth row.—Bind off 3, k 1, p 1, k 7, p 1; k 3, p 1, 4 times; k 31, o 2, p 2 to.

Twenty-fifth row.—O 2, p 2 to., k 32; n, o 2 n, 4 times; k 3 to., k 3, o, k 1, o 2, n, k 1.

Twenty-sixth row.—Sl 1, k 2, p 1, k 8, p 1; k 3, p 1, 3 times; k 33, o 2, p 2 to.

Twenty-seventh row.—O 2, p 2 to., k 6; n, o, k 5, 4 times; n, o 2, n, 3 times; n, o 2, k 3 to., k 2, o, k 1, o 2, n, k 2.

Twenty-eighth row.—Sl 1, k 3, p 1, k 6, p 1; k 3, p 1, 3 times; k 35, o 2, p 2 to.

Twenty-ninth row.—O 2, p 2 to., k 36; n, o 2, n, 3 times; k 3 to., k 2, o, k 1, o 2, n, k 3.

Thirtieth row.—Bind off 3, k 1, p 1, k 7, p 1, k 3, p 1, k 3, p 1, k 37, o 2, p 2 to.

Thirty-first row.—O 2, p 2 to.; k 5, n, o, 4 times; k 10, n, o 2, n, n, o 2, n, k 3 to., k 3, o, k 1, o 2, n, k 1.

Thirty-second row.—Sl 1, k 2, p 1, k 8, p 1, k 3, p 1, k 39, o 2, p 2 to.

Thirty-third row.—O 2, p 2 to., k 40, n, o 2, n, n, o 2, k 3 to., k 2, o, k 1, o 2, n, k 2.

Thirty-fourth row.—Sl 1, k 3, p 1, k 6, p 1, k 3, p 1, k 41, o 2, p 2 to.

Thirty-fifth row.—O 2, p 2 to., k 6; o 2, sl 1, n, b, 8 times; k 12, n, o 2, n, k 3 to., k 2, o, k 1, o 2, n, k 3.

Thirty-sixth row.—Bind off 3, k 1, p 1, k 7, p 1, k 15, p 1; k 2, p 1, 7 times; k 6, o 2, p 2 to.

Repeat from 1st row.

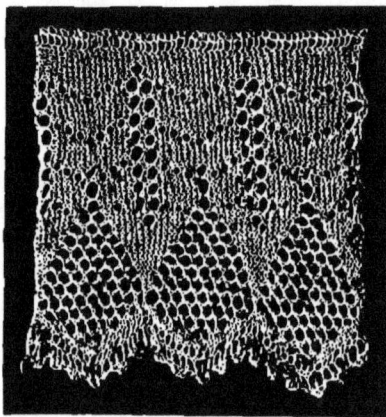

No. 80.—KNITTED BORDER FOR PILLOW SHAMS.

(For Description see Page 51.)

KNITTED BORDER FOR A SCARF.

(For Illustration see Page 53.)

No. 81.—Cast on 51 stitches and knit across plain.

First row.—Sl 1, k 5, o 2, p 2, o, o 2, (make 3 st. of every "o 2" preceding sl 1), sl 1, k 3 to., b, k 4, n, o, k 2, n, o, k 1, o, n, k 2, o, n, k 8, o 2, p 2 to., o 2, sl 1, k 3 to., b, n, o, k 3 to., o 2, k 1, o 2, p 2 to.

Second row.—O 2, p 3 to., k 1, p 1, k 5, p 1, k 1, o 2, p 2 to., o 2, sl 1, k 3 to., b, k 23, p 1, k 1, o 2, p 2 to., o 2, sl 1, k 3 to., b, k 2.

Third row.—Sl 1, k 3, p 1, k 1, o 2, p 2 to., k 11, n, o, k 3, o, n, k 9, p 1, k 1, o 2, p 2 to., k 6, o, n, o 2, k 1, o 2, p 2 to.

Fourth row.—O 2, p 3 to., k 1, p 1, k 8, o 2, p 2 to., k 29, o 2, p 2 to., k 6.

Fifth row.—Sl, k 5, o 2, p 2 to., o 2, sl 1, k 3 to., b, k 6, n, o, n, o, k 1, o, n, o, n, k 10, o 2, p 2 to., o 2, sl 1, k 3 to., b, k 3, o, n, o 2, k 1, o 2, p 2 to.

Sixth row.—O 2, p 3 to., k 1, p 1, k 7, p 1, k 1, o 2, p 2 to., o 2, sl 1, k 3 to., b, k 23, p 1, k 1, o 2, p 2 to., o 2, sl 1, k 3 to., b, k 2.

Seventh row.—Sl 1, k 3, p 1, k 1, o 2, p 2 to., k 9, n, o, n, o, k 3, o, n, o, n, k 7, p 1, k 1, o 2, p 2 to., k 8, o, n, o 2, k 1, o 2, p 2 to.

Eighth row.—O 2, p 3 to., k 1, p 1, k 10, o 2, p 2 to., k 29, o 2, p 2 to., k 6.

Ninth row.—Sl 1, k 5, o 2, p 2 to., o 2, sl 1, k 3 to., b, k 4, n, o, 3 times ; k 1, o, n, 3 times ; k 8, o 2, p 2 to., o 2, sl 1, k 3 to., b, k 2, n, o, k 3 to., o 2, k 1, o 2, p 2 to.

Tenth row.—O 2, p 3 to., k 1, p 1, k 7, p 1, k 1,

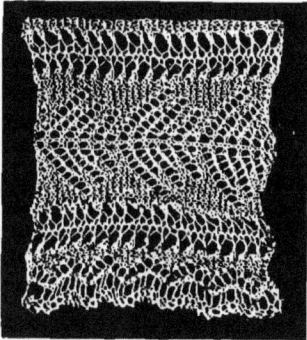

NO. 81.—KNITTED BORDER FOR A SCARF.
(For Description see Page 52.)

o 2, p 2 to., o 2, sl 1, k 3 to., b, k 23, p 1, k 1, o 2, p 2 to., o 2, sl 1, k 3 to., b, k 2.

Eleventh row.—Sl 1, k 3, p 1, k 1, o 2, p 2 to., k 7, n, o, 3 times; k 3, o, n, 3 times; k 5, p 1, k 1, o 2, p 2 to., k 5, n, o, k 3 to., o 2. k 1, o 2, p 2 to.

Twelfth row.—Like 4th row.

Thirteenth row.—Sl 1, k 5, o 2, p 2 to., o 2, sl 1, k 3 to., b, k 2, n, o, 4 times; k 1, o, n, 4 times; k 6, o 2, p 2 to., o 2, sl 1, k 3 to., b, n, o, k 3 to., o 2, k 1, o 2, p 2 to.

Fourteenth row.—O 2, p 3 to., k 1, p 1, k 5, p 1, k 1, o 2, p 2 to., o 2, sl 1, k 3 to., b, k 23, p 1, k 1, o 2, p 2 to., o 2, sl 1, k 3 to. b, k 2.

Fifteenth row.—Sl 1, k 3, p 1, k 1, o 2, p 2 to., k 5, n, o, k 2, n, o, n, o, k 3, o, n, o, n, k 2, o, n, k 3, p 1, k 1, o 2, p 2 to., k 6, o, n, o 2, k 1, o 2, p 2 to.

Sixteenth row.—Like 4th row.

Seventeenth row.—Sl 1, k 5, o 2, p 2 to., o 2, sl 1, k 3 to., b, n, o, k 2, n, o 3 times; k 1, o, n 3 times; k 2, o, n, k 4, o 2, p 2 to., o 2, sl 1, k 3 to., b, k 3. o, n, o 2, k 1, o 2, p 2 to.

Eighteenth row.—O 2, p 3 to., k 1, p 1, k 7, p 1, k 1, o 2, p 2 to., o 2, sl 1, k 3 to., b, k 23, p 1, k 1, o 2, p 2 to., o 2, sl 1, k 3 to., b, k 2.

Nineteenth row.—Sl 1, k 3, p 1, k 1, o 2, p 2 to., k 7, n, o, k 2, n, o, k 3, o, n, k 2, o, n, k 5, p 1, k 1, o 2, p 2 to., k 8, o, n, o 2, k 1, o 2, p 2 to.

Twentieth row.—Like 8th row.

Twenty-first row.—Sl 1, k 5, o 2, p 2 to., o 2, sl

1, k 3 to., b, k 2, n, o, k 2, n, o, n, o, k 1, o, n, o, n, k 2, o, n, k 6, o 2, p 2 to., o 2, sl 1, k 3 to., b, k 2, n, o, k 3 to., o 2, k 1, o 2, p 2 to.

Twenty-second row.—O 2, p 3 to., k 1, p 1, k 7, p 1, k 1, o 2, p 2 to., o 2, sl 1, k 3 to., b, k 23, p 1, k 1, o 2, p 2 to., o 2, sl 1, k 3 to., b, k 2.

Twenty-third row.—Sl 1, k 3, p 1, k 1, o 2, p 2 to., k 9, n, o, k 7, o, n, k 7, p 1, k 1, o 2, p 2 to., k 5, n, o, k 3 to., o 2, k 1, o 2, p 2 to.

Twenty-fourth row.—Like 4th row. Repeat from 1st row.

NARROW KNITTED LACE.

No. 82.—Cast on 11 stitches.

First row.—Sl 1, k 2, n, o, k 1, o, n, k 1, o, k 2.

Second row.—O, n, rest plain; all even rows same.

Third row.—Sl 1, k 1, n, o, k 3, o, n, k 1 o, k 2.

Fifth row.—Sl 1, n, o, k 5, o, n, k 1, o, k 2.

Seventh row.—Sl 1, k 2, o, n, k 1, n, o, n, k 1, o, n, k 1.

Ninth row.—Sl 1, k 3, o, k 3 to., o, n, k 1, o, n, k 1.

Eleventh row.—Sl 1, k 5, n, k 1, o, n, k 1. Repeat.

A FEW SUGGESTIONS.

In making the laces illustrated and described upon this and previous pages, we must leave the matter of sizes of needles, coarseness or fineness

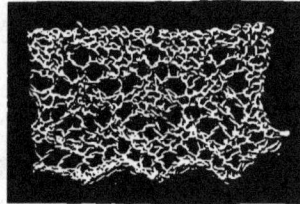

NO. 82.—NARROW KNITTED LACE.

of thread, and whether the latter is to be silk, wool or cotton to the knitter herself. No one knows as well as she how fine or how coarse she wishes the lace to be, and it is not a difficult task for her to experiment with different threads and needles in order to find out.

Steel needles are always used in knitting fine cotton laces or edgings of silk. If wool is to be used for an edging then bone or ivory needles are most appropriate, though coarse steel needles are frequently used for the purpose. Common sense will be able to suggest substitutes for materials and implements where those named are unattainable or undesirable.

DOILEYS, MATS, COUNTERPANES, ETC.

KNITTED ROUND DOILY.

No. 1.—Cast on 57 stitches and knit across plain.
First row.—Sl 1, k 41 ; o, n, 7 times ; o, k 1.
Second row.—Sl 1, k 54, leave 3.
Third row.—Sl 1, k 41 ; o, n, 6 times ; o, k 1.
Fourth row.—Sl 1, k 52, leave 6.
Fifth row.—Sl 1, k 41 ; o, n, 5 times ; o, k 1.
Sixth row.—Sl 1, k 50, leave 9.
Seventh row.—Sl 1, k 49, o, k 1.
Eighth row.—Sl 1, k 48, leave 12.
Ninth row.—Sl 1, k 15, * o 3 times, sl 1, k 3 to, pass the slipped stitch over ; * repeat 7 times between stars, k 5.
Tenth row.—Bind off 4, k 2, p 1 ; k 3, p 1, 6 times ; k 14, leave 15.
Eleventh row.—Sl 1, k 41.
Twelfth row.—Sl 1, k 38, leave 18.
Thirteenth row.—Sl 1, k 23 ; o, n, 7 times; o, k 1.
Fourteenth row.—Sl 1, k 36, leave 21.
Fifteenth row.—Sl 1, k 23 ; o, n, 6 times; o, k 1.
Sixteenth row.—Sl 1, k 34, leave 24.
Seventeenth row.—Sl 1, k 23 ; o, n, 5 times; o, k 1.
Eighteenth row.—Sl 1, k 32, leave 27.
Nineteenth row.—Sl 1, k 31, o, k 1.
Twentieth row.—Sl 1, k 30. leave 30.
Twenty-first row.—Sl 1, k 5, * o 3 times, sl 1, k 3 to., pass slipped stitch over ; * repeat 5 times between the stars ; k 5.
Twenty-second row.—Bind off 4, k 2, p 1 ; k 3, p 1, 4 times ; k 4, leave 33.
Twenty-third row.—Sl 1, k 23.
Twenty-fourth row.—Sl 1, k 56.
Repeat eighteen times.

KNITTED DOILY.
(For Illustration see Page 55.)

No. 2.—Cast on 71 stitches, and knit 2 plain rows. Slip the first stitch of every row to make the edge even. In all rows where the 2 loops (or th o twice) occur knit 1 and drop the second half, thus making only 1 stitch.
First row.—K 35, o twice, n, k 34.
Second row.—Knit plain.
Third and Fourth rows.—K 36, o twice, n, k 33.
Fifth and Sixth rows.—K 37, o twice, n, k 32.
Seventh and Eighth rows.—K 38, o twice, n, k 31.
Ninth row.—K 35, o twice, n, k 2, o twice, n, k 30.
Tenth row.—K 39, o twice, n, k 30.
Eleventh and Twelfth rows.—K 36, o twice, n, k 2, o twice, n k 29.
Thirteenth and Fourteenth rows.—K 37, o twice, n, k 2, o twice, n, k 28.
Fifteenth and Sixteenth rows.—K 38, o twice, n, k 2, o twice, n, k 27.
Seventeenth row.—K 35, o twice, n, k 2, o twice, n, k 2, o twice, n, k 26.
Eighteenth row.—K 39, o twice, n, k 2, o twice, n, k 26.
Nineteenth and Twentieth rows.—K 36, o twice, n, k 2, o twice, n, k 2, o twice, n, k 25.
Twenty-first and Twenty-second rows.—K 37, o twice, n, k 2, o twice, n, k 2, o twice, n, k 24.
Twenty-third and Twenty-fourth rows.—K 38, o twice, n, k 2, o twice, n, k 2, o twice, n, k 23.
Twenty-fifth row.—K 35, o twice, n, k 2, o twice, n, k 2, o twice, n, k 2, o twice, n, k 22.
Twenty-sixth row.—K 39, o twice, n, k 2, o twice, n, k 2, o twice, n, k 22.
Twenty-seventh and Twenty-eighth rows.—K 36, o twice, n, k 2, o twice, n, k 2, o twice, n, k 2, o twice, n, k 21.
Twenty-ninth and Thirtieth rows.—K 37, o twice, n, k 2, o twice, n, k 2, o twice, n, k 2, o twice, n, k 20.
Thirty-first and Thirty-second rows.—K 38, o twice, n, k 2, o twice, n, k 2, o twice, n, k 2, o twice, n, k 19.
Thirty-third and Thirty-fourth rows.—K 39, o twice, n, k 2, o twice, n, k 2, o twice, n, k 2, o twice, n, k 18.

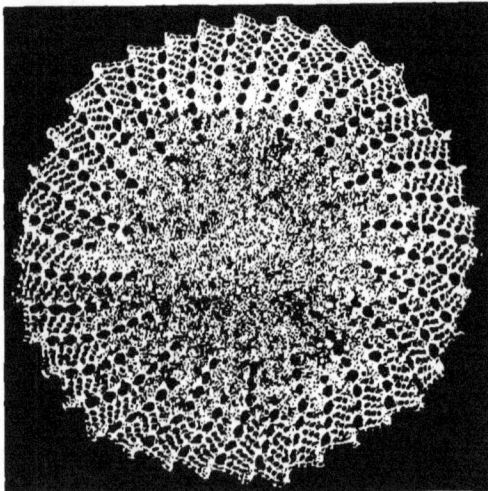

No. 1.—KNITTED ROUND DOILY.

Thirty-fifth and Thirty-sixth rows.—K 40, o twice, n, k 2, o twice, n, k 2, o twice, n, k 2, o twice, n, k 17.
Thirty-seventh and Thirty-eighth rows.—K 41, o twice, n, k 2, o twice, n, k 2, o twice, n, k 2, o twice, n, k 16.
Thirty-ninth and Fortieth rows.—K 42, o twice, n, k 2, o twice, n, k 2, o twice, n, k 2, o twice, n, k 15.
Forty-first and Forty-second rows.—K 43, o twice, n, k 2, o twice, n, k 2, o twice, n, k 2, o twice, n, k 14.
Forty-third and Forty-fourth rows.—K 44, o twice, n, k 2, o twice, n, k 2, o twice, n, k 2, o twice, n, k 13.
Forty-fifth and Forty-sixth rows.—K 45, o twice, n, k 2, o twice, n, k 2, o twice, n, k 2, o twice, n, k 12.
Forty-seventh and Forty-eighth rows.—K 46, o twice, n, k 2, o twice, n, k 2, o twice, n, k 2, o twice, n, k 11.
Forty-ninth and Fiftieth rows—K 47, o twice, n, k 2, o twice, n, k 2, o twice, n, k 2, o twice, n, k 10.
Fifty-first and Fifty-second rows.—K 48, o twice, n, k 2, o twice, n, k 2, o twice, n, k 2, o twice, n k 9.
Fifty-third and Fifty-fourth rows.—K 49, o twice, n, k 2, o twice, n, k 2, o twice, n, k 2, o twice, n, k 8.
Fifty-fifth and Fifty-sixth rows.—K 50, o twice, n, k 2, o twice, n, k 2, o twice, n, k 2, o twice, n, k 7.
Fifty-seventh and Fifty-eighth rows.—K 51, o twice, n, k 2, o twice, n, k 2, o twice, n, k 2, o twice, n, k 6.
Fifty-ninth and Sixtieth rows.—K 52, o twice, n, k 2, o twice, n, k 2, o twice, n, k 2, o twice, n, k 5.
Sixty-first and Sixty-second rows.—K 53, o twice, n, k 2, o twice, n, k 2, o twice, n, k 2, o twice, n, k 4.
Sixty-third and Sixty-fourth rows.—K 54, o twice, n, k 2, o twice, n, k 2, o twice, n, k 2, o twice, n, k 3.
Sixty-fifth and Sixty-sixth rows.—K 55, o twice, n, k 2, o twice, n, k 2, o twice, n, k 2, o twice, n, k 2.
Sixty-seventh row.—Knit plain.
Sixty-eighth and Sixty-ninth rows.—K 3, o twice, n, k 2, o twice, n, k 2, o twice, n, k 2, o twice, n, k 54.
Seventieth and Seventy-first rows.—K 4, o twice, n, k 2, o twice, n, k 2, o twice, n, k 2, o twice, n, k 53.
Seventy-second and Seventy-third rows.—K 5, o

twice, n, k 2, o twice, n, k 2, o twice, n, k 2, o twice, n, k 52.
Seventy-fourth and Seventy-fifth rows.—K 6, o twice, n, k 2, o twice, n, k 2, o twice, n, k 2, o twice, n, k 51.
Seventy-Sixth and Seventy-seventh rows.—K 7, o twice, n, k 2, o twice, n, k 2, o twice, n, k 2, o twice, n, k 50.
Seventy-eighth and Seventy-ninth rows.—K 8, o twice, n, k 2, o twice, n, k 2, o twice, n, k 2, o twice, n, k 49.
Eightieth and Eighty-first rows.—K 9, o twice, n, k 2, o twice, n, k 2, o twice, n, k 2, o twice, n, k 48.
Eighty-second and Eighty-third rows.—K 10, o twice, n, k 2, o twice, n, k 2, o twice, n, k 2, o twice, n, k 47.
Eighty-fourth and Eighty-fifth rows.—K 11, o twice, n, k 2, o twice, n, k 2, o twice, n, k 2, o twice, n, k 46.
Eighty-sixth and Eighty-seventh rows.—K 12, o twice, n, k 2, o twice, n, k 2, o twice, n, k 2, o twice, n, k 45.
Eighty-eighth and Eighty-ninth rows.—K 13, o twice, n, k 2, o twice, n, k 2, o twice, n, k 2, o twice, n, k 44.
Ninetieth and Ninety-first rows.—K 14, o twice, n, k 2, o twice, n, k 2, o twice, n, k 2, o twice, n, k 43.
Ninety-second and Ninety-third rows.—K 15, o twice, n, k 2, o twice, n, k 2, o twice, n, k 2, o twice, n, k 42.
Ninety-fourth and Ninety-fifth rows.—K 16, o twice, n, k 2, o twice, n, k 2, o twice, n, k 41.
Ninety-sixth and Ninety-seventh rows.—K 17, o twice, n, k 2, o twice, n, k 2, o twice, n, k 2, o twice, n, k 40.
Ninety-eighth and Ninety-ninth rows.—K 18, o twice, n, k 2, o twice, n, k 2, o twice, n, k 2, o twice, n, k 39.
One Hundredth and One Hundred and First rows.—K 19, o twice, n, k 2, o twice, n, k 2, o twice, n, k 2, o twice, n, k 38.
One Hundred and Second and One Hundred and Third rows.—K 20, o twice, n, k 2, o twice, n, k 2, o twice, n, k 2, o twice, n, k 37.
One Hundred and Fourth and One Hundred and Fifth rows.—K 21, o twice, n, k 2, o twice, n, k 2, o twice, n, k 2, o twice, n, k 36.

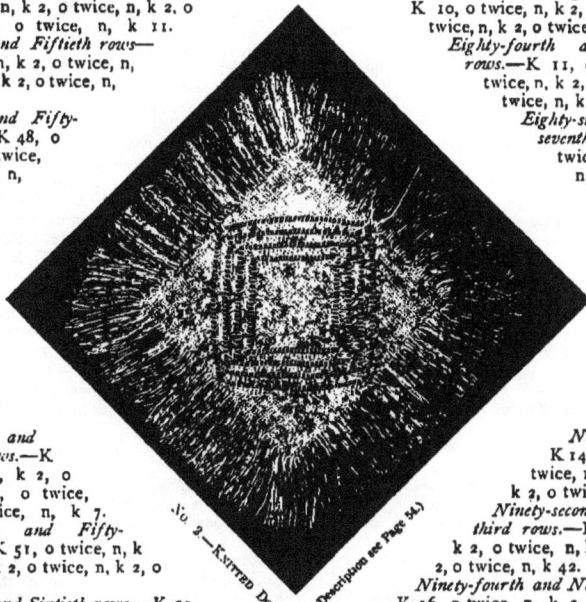

No. 2.—KNITTED DOILY. (For Description see Page 54.)

One Hundred and Sixth and One Hundred and Seventh rows.—K 22, o twice, n, k 2, o twice, n, k 2, o twice, n, k 2, o twice, n, k 35.

One Hundred and Eighth row.—K 23, o twice, n, k 2, o twice, n, k 2, o twice, n, k 2, o twice, n, k 36.

One Hundred and Ninth row.—K 23, o twice, n, k 2, o twice, n, k 2, o twice, n, k 2, o twice, n, k 37.

One Hundred and Tenth and One Hundred and Eleventh rows.—K 24, o twice, n, k 2, o twice, n, k 2, o twice, n, k 39.

One Hundred and Twelfth row.—K 25, o twice, n, k 2, o twice, n, k 2, o twice, n, n, n, k 39.

One Hundred and Thirteenth row.—K 25, o twice, n, k 2, o twice, n, k 2, o twice, n, k 36.

One Hundred and Fourteenth row.—K 26, o twice, n, k 2, o twice, n, k 2, o twice, k 3 to., k 34.

One Hundred and Fifteenth row.—K 26; o twice, n, k 2, o twice, n, k 2, o twice, k 36.

One Hundred and Sixteenth row.—K 27, o twice, n, k 2, o twice, n, k 2, o twice, k 36.

One Hundred and Seventeenth row.—K 27, o twice, n, k 2, o twice, n, k 39.

One Hundred and Eighteenth row.—K 28, o twice, n, k 2, o twice, n, k 38.

One Hundred and Nineteenth row.—K 28, o twice, n, k 2, o twice, n, n, n, k 34.

One Hundred and Twentieth row.—K 29, o twice, n, k 2, o twice, n, k 35.

One Hundred and Twenty-first row.—K 29, o twice, n, k 2, o twice, k 3 to., k 34.

One Hundred and Twenty-second row.—K 30, o twice, n, k 2, o twice, k 35.

One Hundred and Twenty-third row.—K 30, o twice, n, k 2, o twice, k 36.

One Hundred and Twenty-fourth and One Hundred and Twenty-fifth rows.—K 31, o twice, n, k 38.

One Hundred and Twenty-sixth row.—K 32, o twice, n, n, n, k 33.

One Hundred and Twenty-seventh row.—K 32, o twice, n, k 35.

One Hundred and Twenty-eighth and One Hundred and Twenty-ninth rows.—K 33, o twice, n, k 34.

One Hundred and Thirtieth row.—K 34, o twice, k 35.

One Hundred and Thirty-first row.—K 34, o twice, k 30.

One Hundred and Thirty-second and One Hundred and Thirty-third rows.—Knit plain. Bind off.

Should the edge of the doily be a little full, run a fine thread in a needle through the length of it and draw it to the right size. Finish with fringe the desired length. The one illustrated was an inch and a half deep when finished, and 2 threads were used each time.

KNITTED COUNTERPANE—SQUARE.
(For Illustration see Page 57.)

No. 3.—Cast on 2 stitches.
First row.—O, k 2.
Second row.—O, k 1, p 1, k 1.
Third row.—O, k 1, o, k 1, o, k 2.
Fourth row.—O, k 2, p 3, k 2.
Fifth row.—O, k 1, p 1, k 1, o, k 1, o, k 1, p 3.
Sixth row.—O, k 3, p 5, k 3.

Seventh row.—O, k 1, p 2, k 2, o, k 1, o, k 2, p 4.
Eighth row.—O, k 4, p 7, k 4.
Ninth row.—O, k 1, p 3, k 3, o, k 1, o, k 3, p 5.
Tenth row.—O, k 5, p 9, k 5.
Eleventh row.—O, k 1, p 4, k 4, o, k 1, o, k 4, p 6.
Twelfth row.—O, k 6, p 11, k 6.
Thirteenth row.—O, k 1, p 5, k 5, o, k 1, o, k 5, p 7.
Fourteenth row.—O, k 7, p 13, k 7.
Fifteenth row.—O, k 1, p 6, k 2 to. crossed, k 9, n, p 8.
Sixteenth row.—O, k 8, p 11, k 8.
Seventeenth row.—O, k 1, p 7, k 2 to. crossed, k 7, n, k 9.
Eighteenth row.—O, k 9, p 9, k 9.
Nineteenth row.—O, k 1, p 8, k 2 to. crossed, k 5, n, p 10.
Twentieth row.—O, k 10, p 7, k 10.
Twenty-first row.—O, k 1, p 9, k 2 to. crossed, k 3, n, p 11.
Twenty-second row.—O, k 11, p 5, k 11.
Twenty-third row.—O, k 1, p 10, k 2 to. crossed, k 1, n, p 12.
Twenty-fourth row.—O, k 12, p 3, k 12.
Twenty-fifth row.—O, k 1, p 11, sl 1, n, pass slipped st. over, p 13. *Twenty-sixth row.*—O, k 27.
Twenty-seventh row.—O, k 1, p 27. *Twenty-eighth row.*—O, k 29. *Twenty-ninth row.*—O, k 1, p 29.
Thirtieth row.—O, k 1, p 30. *Thirty-first row.*—O, k 33. *Thirty-second row.*—O, k 1, p 32. *Thirty-third row.*—O, k 1, * o, n, repeat 15 times more from * k 1. *Thirty-fourth row.*—O, k 1, p 34. *Thirty-fifth row.*—O, k 36. *Thirty-sixth row.*—O, k 1, p 36. *Thirty-seventh row.*—O, k 38. *Thirty-eighth row.*—O, k 1, p 38. *Thirty-ninth row.*—O, k 1, p 39. *Fortieth row.*—O, k 41. *Forty-first row.*—O, k 1, p 41. *Forty-second row.*—O, k 1, * o, n, and repeat 20 times more from *. *Forty-third row.*—O, k 1, p 43. *Forty-fourth row.*—O, k 45. *Forty-fifth row.*—O, k 1, p 45. *Forty-sixth row.*—O, k 47.
Forty-seventh row.—O, k 1, p 2, cast on 5 stitches thus: Use a crochet hook and make a chain of 5 stitches, beginning by drawing the first one through the last knit stitch on the right hand needle; then pick up the 4 stitches of chain onto the knitting needle, and slip the last loop of chain on it also, holding the wrong side of the chain toward you; this makes the 5 cast-on stitches; * p 4, cast on 5 stitches as before, and repeat 9 times more from * p 5.
Forty-eighth row.—O, k 5, p 5, * k 4, p 5 and repeat 9 times more from *, k 4.
Forty-ninth row.—O, k 1, p 3, k 2 to. crossed, k 1, n, * p 4, k 2 to. crossed, k 1, n, repeat 9 times more from *, p 6.
Fiftieth row.—O, k 6, p 3, * k 4, p 3, repeat 9 times more from *, k 5.
Fifty-first row.—O, k 1, p 4, sl 1, n, pass slipped stitch over, * p 4, sl 1, n, pass slipped stitch over, and repeat 9 times more from *, p 7.
Fifty-second row.—O, k 6, n, * k 3, n, and repeat 9 times more from *, k 6.
Fifty-third row.—O, k 1, p 53.
Fifty-fourth row.—O, k 55.

Fifty-fifth row.—O, k 1, p 4, cast on 5, with the crochet hook * p 4, cast on 5 as before, and repeat 10 times more from *, p 7.

Fifty-sixth row.—O, k 7, p 5, * k 4, p 5, repeat 10 times more from *, k 6.

Fifty-seventh row.—O, k 1, p 5, k 2 to. crossed, k 1, n, * p 4, k 2 to. crossed, k 1, n, repeat 10 times more from *, p 8.

Fifty-eighth row.—O, k 8, p 3, * k 4, p 3; repeat 10 times more from *, k 7.

Fifty-ninth row.—O, k 1, p 6, sl 1, n, pass slipped stitch over, * p 4, sl 1, n, pass slipped stitch over, repeat 10 times more from *, p 9.

Sixtieth row.—O, k 8, n, * k 3, n, repeat 10 times more from *, k 8.

Sixty-first row.—O, k 1, p across.

Sixty-second row.—O, k across (63 stitches).

Sixty-third row.—O, k 1, p 6, cast on 5, with crochet hook *, p 4, cast on 5 as before, and repeat 11 times more from *, p 9.

Sixty-fourth row.—O, k 9, p 5, * k 4, p 5, and repeat 11 times more from *, k 8.

Sixty-fifth row.—O, k 1, p 7, k 2 to. crossed, k 1, n, * p 4, k 2 to. crossed, k 1, n, and repeat 11 times more from *, p 10.

Sixty-sixth row.—O, k 10, p 3, * k 4, p 3, repeat 11 times more from *, k 9.

Sixty-seventh row.—O, k 1, p 8, sl 1, n, pass slipped stitched over, * p 4, sl 1, n, pass slipped stitch over, and repeat 11 times more from *, p 11.

Sixty-eighth row.—O, k 10, n, * k 3, n, and repeat 11 times more from *, k 10.

Sixty-ninth row.—O, k 1, p 69. *Seventieth row.*—O, k 71. *Seventy-first row.*—O, k 1, p 71. *Seventy-second row.*—O, k 1, p 72. *Seventy-third row.*—O, k 73. *Seventy-fourth row.*—O, k 1, * o, n, repeat 35 times more from *. *Seventy-fifth row.*—O, k 75. *Seventy-sixth row.*—O, k 1, p 75. *Seventy-seventh row.*—O, k 77. *Seventy-eighth row.*—O, k 78. *Seventy-ninth row.*—O, k 1, p 78. *Eightieth row.*—O, k 77, n, k 1. *Eighty-first row.*—O, n, k 75, n, k 1. *Eighty-second row.*—O, n, p 73, p 2 to, p 1. *Eighty-third row.*—O, n, k 73, n, k 1. *Eighty-fourth row.*—O, n, repeat 38 times more, k 1. *Eighty-fifth row.*—O, n, k 72, n, k 1. *Eighty-sixth row.*—O, n, p 71, p 2 to., p 1. *Eighty-*

seventh row.—O, n, k 70, n, k 1. *Eighty-eighth row.*—O, n, k 69, n, k 1. *Eighty-ninth row.*—O, n, p 14, * k 1, o, k 1, o, k 1, p 7, repeat 4 times more from *, p 5, p 2 to., p. 1.

Ninetieth row.—O, n, k 11, * p 5, k 7, repeat 4 times more from *, k 6, n, k 1.

Ninety-first row.—O, n, p 13, * k 2, o, k 1, o, k 2 p 7, repeat 4 times more from *, p 3, p 2 to., p 1.

Ninety-second row.—O, n, k 10, * p 7, k 7, and repeat 4 times more from *, k 5, n, k 1.

Ninety-third row.—O, n, p 12, * k 3, o, k 1, o, k 3, p 7, repeat 4 times more from *, p 2, p 2 to., p 1.

Ninety-fourth row.—O, n, k 9, * p 9, k 7, repeat 4 times more from *, k 4, n, k 1.

Ninety-fifth row.—O, n, p 11, * k 4, o, k 1, o, k 4, p 7, repeat 4 times more from *, p 1, p 2 to., p 1.

Ninety-sixth row.—O, n, k 8, * p 11, k 7, repeat 4 times more from *; k 3, n, k 1.

Ninety-seventh row.—O, n, p 10, * k 5, o, k 1, o, k 5, p 7, repeat 4 times more from *, p 2 to., p 1.

Ninety-eighth row.—O, n, k 7, * p 13, k 7, repeat 4 times more from *, k 2, n, k 1.

Ninety-ninth row.—O, n, p 9, k 6, o, k 1, o, k 6, * p 7, k 6, o, k 1, o, k 6 and repeat 3 times more from *, p 5, p 2 to., p 1.

One Hundredth row.—O, n, k 5, * p 15, k 7, repeat 4 times more from *, k 2, n, k 1.

One Hundred and First row.—O, r, p 8, k 2 to. crossed, k 11, n, * p 7, k 2 to. crossed, k 11, n, and repeat 3

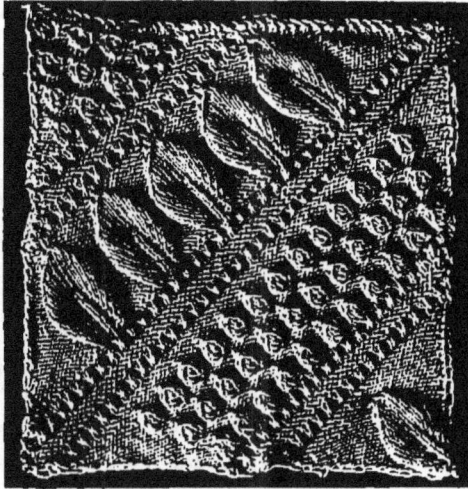

No. 3.—KNITTED COUNTERPANE-SQUARE.
(For Description see Page 56.)

times more from *, p 4, p 2 to., p 1.

One Hundred and Second row.—O, n, k 4, * p 13 k 7, repeat 4 times more from *, n, k 1.

One Hundred and Third row.—O, n, p 7, k 2 to crossed, k 9, n, * p 7, k 2 to. crossed, k 9, n, repeat 3 times more from *, p 3, p 2 to., p 1.

One Hundred and Fourth row.—O, n, k 3, p 11, * k 7, p 11, repeat three times more from *, k 6, n, k 1.

One Hundred and Fifth row.—O, n, p 6, k 2 to. crossed, k 7, n, * p 7, k 2 to. crossed, k 7, n, and repeat 3 times more from *, p 2, p 2 to., p 1.

One Hundred and Sixth row.—O, n, k 2, p 9, * k 7, p 9, and repeat 3 times more from *, k 5, n, k 1.

One Hundred and Seventh row.—O, n, p 5, k 2 to. crossed, k 5, n, * p 7, k 2 to. crossed, k 5, n and repeat 3 times more from *, p 1, p 2 to., p 1.

One Hundred and Eighth row.—O, n, k 1, p 7, * k 7, p 7, and repeat 3 times more from *, k 4, n, k 1.

One Hundred and Ninth row.—O, n, p 4, k 2 to. crossed, k 3, n, * p 7, k 2 to. crossed, k 3, n, and repeat 3 times more from *, n, k 1.

One Hundred and Tenth row.—O, n, p 5, * k 7, p 5, and repeat 3 times more from *, k 3, n, k 1.

One Hundred and Eleventh row.—O, n, p 3, k 2 to. crossed, k 1, n, * p 7, k 2 to. crossed, k 1, n, and repeat 3 times more from *, p 2 to.

One Hundred and Twelfth row.—O, n, k 1, p 3, * k 7, p 3, and repeat 3 times more from *, k 2, n, k 1.

One Hundred and Thirteenth row.—O, n, p 2, slip 1, n, pass slipped stitch o, * p 7, slip 1, n, pass slipped stitch over, and repeat twice more from *, n.

One Hundred and Fourteenth row.—O, n, p 33, p 2 to., p 1.

One Hundred and Fifteenth row.—O, n, k 31, n, k 1.

One Hundred and Sixteenth row.—O, n, p 30, p 2 to., p 1.

One Hundred and Seventeenth row.—O, n, and repeat 16 times more.

One Hundred and Eighteenth row.—O, n, p 29, p 2 to., p 1.

One Hundred and Nineteenth row.—O, n, k 28, n, k 1.

One Hundred and Twentieth row.—O, n, p 27, p 2 to., p 1.

One Hundred and Twenty-first row.—O, n, p 25, p 2 to., p 1.

One Hundred and Twenty-second row.—O, n, k 24, n, k 1.

One Hundred and Twenty-third row.—O, n, p 23, p 2 to., p 1.

One Hundred and Twenty-fourth row.—O, n, p 25.

One Hundred and Twenty-fifth row.—O, n, p 25.

One Hundred and Twenty-sixth row.—O, n, p 25.

One Hundred and Twenty-seventh row.—* O, n, and repeat 12 times more from *, k 1.

One Hundred and Twenty-eighth row.—O, n, p 25.

One Hundred and Twenty-ninth row.—O, n, k 22, n, k 1.

One Hundred and Thirtieth row.—O, n, p 21, n, p 1.

One Hundred and Thirty-first row.—O, n, p 4, * cast on 5 stitches, p 4, and repeat 3 times more from *, p 2 to., p 1.

One Hundred and Thirty-second row.—O, n, * k 4, p 5, repeat 3 times more from *, k 3, n, k 1.

One Hundred and Thirty-third row.—O, n, p 3, * k 2 to. crossed, k 1, n, p 4, repeat twice more from *, k 2 to. crossed, k 1, n, p 3, n, p 1.

One Hundred and Thirty-fourth row.—O, n, k 3, p 3, * k 4, p 3, repeat twice more from *, k 2, n, k 1.

One Hundred and Thirty-fifth row.—O, n, p 2, * slip 1, n, pass sl st o, k 4, repeat twice more from *, sl 1, n, pass sl st o, p 2, p 2 to., p 1.

One Hundred and Thirty-sixth row.—O, n, k 1, * n, k 3, and repeat twice more from *, n, k 1, n, k 1.

One Hundred and Thirty-seventh row.—O, n, p 3, cast on 5, p 4, cast on 5, p 4, cast on 5, p 3, p 2 to., p 1.

One Hundred and Thirty-eighth row.—O, n, k 3, p 5, k 4, p 5, k 4, p 5, k 2, n, k 1.

One Hundred and Thirty-ninth row.—O, n, k 2 to. crossed, k 1, n, p 2, k 2 to. crossed, k 1,

n, p 4, k 2 to. crossed, k 1, n, p 2, p 2 to., p 1.

One Hundred and Fortieth row.—O, n, k 2, p 3, k 4, p 3, k 4, p 3, k 1, n, k 1.

One Hundred and Forty-first row.—O, n, k 1, sl 1, n, pass sl st o, p 4, sl 1, n, pass sl st o, p 4, sl 1, n, pass sl st o, p 1, p 2 to., p 1.

One Hundred and Forty-second row.—O, n, n, k 3, n, k 3, n, n, k 1.

One Hundred and Forty-third row.—O, n, p 2, cast on 5, p 4, cast on 5, p 2, p 2 to., p 1.

One Hundred and Forty-fourth row.—O, n, k 2, p 5, k 4, p 5, k 1, n, k 1.

One Hundred and Forty-fifth row.—O, n, p 1, k 2 to. crossed, k 1, n, p 4, k 2 to. crossed, k 1, n, p 1, p 2 to., p 1.

One Hundred and Forty-sixth row.—O, n, k 1, p 3, k 4, p 3, p 2 to., p 1.

One Hundred and Forty-seventh row.—O, n, sl 1, n, pass slipped st over, p 4, sl 1, n, pass sl st o, p 2 to., p 1.

One Hundred and Forty-eighth row.—O, k 1, n, k 4, n. k 1.

One Hundred and Forty-ninth row.—O, n, p 2, cast on 5 sts. p 2, p 2 to., p 1.

One Hundred and Fiftieth row.—O, n, k 2, p 5, k 2, n.

One Hundred and Fifty-first row.—O, n, k 1, k 2 to. crossed, k 1, n, k 1, n, k 1.

One Hundred and Fifty-second row.—O, n, p 4, p 2 to., p 1.

One Hundred and Fifty-third row.—N, sl 1, n, pass sl st o, n.

One Hundred and Fifty-fourth row.—N twice.

One Hundred and Fifty-fifth row.—Slip one stitch over the other and fasten off.

SHELL FOR COUNTERPANE.
(For Illustration see Page 59.)

No. 4.—Cast on 50 stitches and knit once across plain

Second row.—K 2, th o, n, and repeat across the row.

Third and Fourth rows.—Plain.

Fifth and Sixth rows.—K 4, n ; knit the rest plain.

Seventh row.—K 4, n ; purl all but last 4 stitches, which knit plain.

Eighth and Ninth rows.—K 4, n ; k plain.

Tenth row.—K 4, n ; purl all except last 4, which you knit plain.

Now repeat from the 8th row until only 8 stitches remain ; then slip and bind at the edge 1 stitch in each row, until all the stitches are narrowed off.

Sew the shells together to make squares. Join as many squares as are needed, and add a pretty border, either knitted or crocheted.

KNITTED DOILY.
(For Illustration see Page 60.)

No. 5.—Cast on 71 stitches and knit one row plain. Slip the first stitch of every row to make the edge even. In all rows where the 2 loops (or th o twice occur), knit one in the first half and drop the second half, thus making only one stitch

First row.—K 1 ; o twice and n, 7 times ; k 14 ; o twice and n, 7 times ; k 14 ; o twice and n, 7 times.

Second, Third and Fourth rows.—Knit plain. Repeat the last 4 rows 6 times more.

Twenty-ninth row.—K 15 ; o twice and n, 7

No. 4.—SHELL FOR COUNTERPANE.
(For Description see Page 58.)

times; k 14; o twice and n, 7 times; k 14.

Thirtieth, Thirty-first and Thirty-second rows.—Knit plain. Repeat the last four rows 6 times more.

Fifty-seventh to Eighty-fourth row.—Knit the same as the first 28 rows.

Eighty-fifth to One Hundred and Twelfth row.—Work the same as the second repetition.

One Hundred and Thirteenth to One Hundred and Fortieth row.—Work the same as the first repetition. Bind off.

Should the edge of the doily be a little full, run a fine thread through the length of it and draw to the right side. Finish with a fringe the desired length. The fringe illustrated is an inch and a half long and two strands each cut three inches long are used each time.

KNITTED CENTER-PIECE.
(For Illustration see Page 60.)

No. 6.—Cast on 85 stitches.

First row.—Sl 1, k 23, n, o, k 4, o twice, p 2 to., k 13, n, o, n, o, k 4, o twice, p 2 to., k 11, n, o twice, n, k 10, o twice, p 2 to., k 1, o, k 2.

Second row.—K 4, o twice, p 2 to., k 12, p 1, k 12, o twice, p 2 to., k 21, o twice, p 2 to., k 28, leave 2.

Third row.—Sl 1, k 20, n, o, k 5, o twice, p 2 to., k 12, n, o, n, o, k 5, o twice, p 2 to., k 9, n, o twice, n, n, o twice, n, k 8, o twice, p 2 to., k 2, o, k 2.

Fourth row.—K 5, o twice, p 2 to., k 10, p 1, k 3, p 1, k 10, o twice, p 2 to., k 21, o twice, p 2 to., k 26, leave 4.

Fifth row.—Sl 1, k 17, n, o, k 6, o twice, p 2 to., k 11, n, o, n, o, k 6, o twice, p 2 to., k 7, n, o twice, n, n, o twice, n, n, o twice, n, k 6, o twice, p 2 to., k 3, o, k 2.

Sixth row.—K 6, o twice, p 2 to., k 8, p 1, k 3, p 1, k 3, p 1, k 8, o twice, p 2 to., k 21, o twice, p 2 to., k 24, leave 6.

Seventh row.—Sl 1, k 14, n, o, k 7, o twice, p 2 to., k 10, n, o, n, o, k 7, o twice, p 2 to., k 5, n, o twice, n, n, o twice, n, n, o twice, n, n, o twice, n, k 4, o twice, p 2 to., n, o twice, n, o, k 2.

Eighth row.—K 5, p 1, k 1, o twice, p 2 to., k 6, p 1, k 3, p 1, k 3, p 1, k 3, p 1, k 6, o twice, p 2 to., k 21, o twice, p 2 to., k 22, leave 8.

Ninth row.—Sl 1, k 11, n, o, k 1, n, o, k 1, o, n, k 2, o twice, p 2 to., k 9, n, o, n, o, k 1, n, o, k 1, o, n, k 2, o twice, p 2 to., k 3, n, o twice, n, n, o twice, n, n, o twice, n, n, o twice, n, k 2, o twice, p 2 to., k 7.

Tenth row.—Bind off 4, k 2, o twice, p 2 to., k 4, p 1, k 3, p 1, k 3, p 1, k 3, p 1, k 3, p 1, k 4, o twice, p 2 to., k 21, o twice, p 2 to., k 20, leave 10.

Eleventh row.—Sl 1, k 8, n, o, k 1, n, o, k 3, o, n, k 1, o twice, p 2 to., k 8, n, o, n, o, k 1, n, o, k 3, o, n, k 1, o twice, p 2 to., k 5, n, o twice, n, n, o twice, n, n, o twice, n, k 4, o twice, p 2 to., k 1, o, k 2.

Twelfth row.—K 4, o twice, p 2 to., k 6, p 1, k 3, p 1, k 3, p 1, k 3, p 1, k 6, o twice, p 2 to., k 21, o twice, p 2 to., k 18, leave 12.

Thirteenth row.—Sl 1, k 5, n, o, k 2, n, o, k 3, o, n, k 1, o twice, p 2 to., k 7, n, o, n, o, k 2, n, o, k 3, o, n, k 1, o twice, p 2 to., k 7, n, o twice,

n, n, o, twice, n, n, o twice, n, k 6, o twice, p 2 to., k 2, o, k 2.

Fourteenth row.—K 5, o twice, p 2 to., k 8, p 1, k 3, p 1, k 3, p 1, k 8, o twice, p 2 to., k 21, o twice, p 2 to., k 16, leave 14.

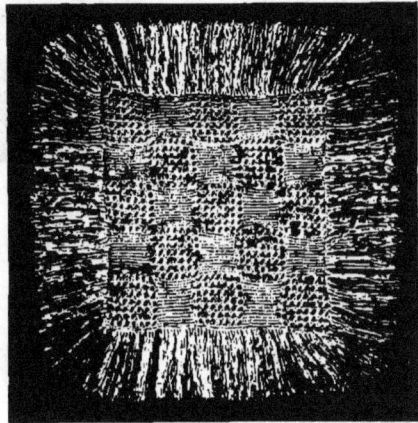

No. 5.—KNITTED DOILY.
(For Description see Page 58.)

Fifteenth row.--Sl 1, k 5, o, n, k 2, o, k 3, to., o, k 3, o twice, p 2 to., k 6, n, o, n, o, k 5, o, k 3 to., o, k 3, o twice, p 2 to., k 9, n, o twice, n, n, o twice, n, k 8, o twice, p 2 to., k 3, o, k 2.

Sixteenth row.--K 6, o twice, p 2 to., k 10, p 1, k 3, p 1, k 10, o twice, p 2 to., k 21, o twice, p 2 to., k 14, leave 16.

Seventeenth row.--Sl 1, k 4, o, n, k 7, o twice, p 2 to., k 5, n, o, n, o, k 12, o twice, p 2 to., k 11, n, o twice, n, k 10, o twice, p 2 to., n, o twice, n, o, k 2.

Eighteenth row.--K 5, p 1, k 1, o twice, p 2 to., k 12, p 1, k 12, o twice, p 2 to., k 21, o twice, p 2 to., k 12, leave 18.

Nineteenth row.--Sl 1, k 3, o, n, k 6, o twice, p 2 to., k 4, n, o, n, o, k 1, n, o, k 1, o, n, k 7, o twice, p 2 to., k 2, n, o twice, n, k 13, n, o twice, n, k 2, o twice, p 2 to., k 7.

Twentieth row.--Bind off 4, k 2, o twice, p 2 to., k 4, p 1, k 16, p 1, k 3, o twice, p 2 to., k 21, o twice, p 2 to., k 10, leave 20.

Twenty-first row.--Sl 1, k 2, o, n, k 5, o twice, p 2 to., k 3, n, o, n, o, k 1, n, o, k 3, o, n, k 6, o twice, p 2 to., k 4, n, o twice, n, k 9, n, o twice, n, k 4, o twice, p 2 to., k 1, o, k 2.

Twenty-second row.--K 4, o twice, p 2 to., k 6, p 1, k 12, p 1, k 5, o twice, p 2 to., k 21, o twice, p 2 to., k 8, leave 22.

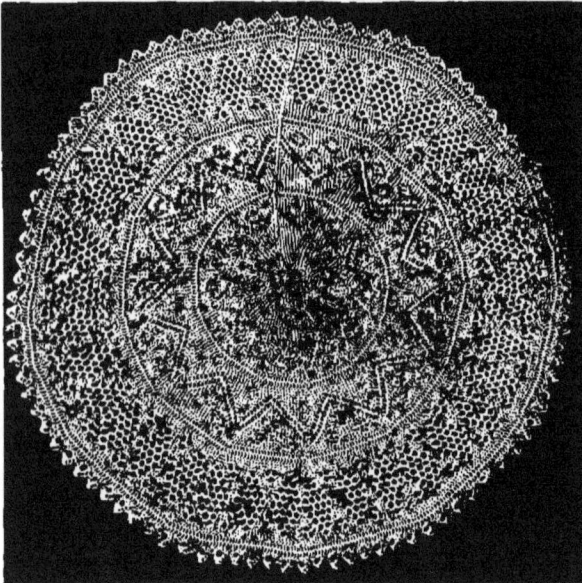

No. 0.--KNITTED CENTER-PIECE.
(For Description see Page 59.)

Twenty-third row.--Sl 1, k 1, o, n, k 4, o twice, p 2 to., k 2, n, o, n, o, k 2, n, o, k 3, o, n, k 6, o twice, p 2 to., k 2, n, o twice, n, k 13, n, o twice, n, k 2, o twice, p 2 to., k 2, o, k 2.

Twenty-fourth row.--K 5, o twice, p 2 to., k 4, p 1, k 16, p 1, k 3, o twice, p 2 to., k 21, o twice, p 2 to., k 6, leave 24.

Twenty-fifth row.--Sl 1, o, n, k 3, o twice, p 2 to., k 4, o, n, o, n, o, k 2, o, k 3 to., o, k 8, o twice, p 2 to., k 11, n, o twice, n, k 10, o twice, p 2 to., k 3, o, k 2.

Twenty-sixth row.--K 6, o twice, p 2 to., k 12, p 1, k 12, o twice, p 2 to., k 21, o twice, p 2 to., k 4, leave 26.

Twenty-seventh row.--Sl 1, k 3, o twice, p 2 to., k 5, o, n, o, n, k 12, o twice, p 2 to., k 9, n, o twice, n, n, o twice, n, k 8, o twice, p 2 to., n, o twice, n, o, k 2.

Twenty-eighth row.--K 5, p 1, k 1, o twice, p 2 to., k 10, p 1, k 3, p 1, k 10, o twice, p 2 to., k 21, o twice, p 2 to., k 2, leave 28.

Twenty-ninth row.--Sl 1, k 1, o twice, p 2 to., k 6, o, n, o, n, k 4, n, o, k 1, o, n, k 2, o twice, p 2 to., k 7, n, o twice, n, n, o twice, n, k 6, o twice, p 2 to., k 7.

Thirtieth row.--Bind off 4, k 2, o twice, p 2 to., k 8, p 1, k 3, p 1, k 3, p 1, k 8, o twice, p 2 to., k 21, o twice, p 2 to., leave 30.

Thirty-first row.--Sl 1, k 8, o, n, o, n, k 2, n, o, k 3, o, n, k 1, o twice, p 2 to., k 5, n, o twice, n, n, o twice, n, n, o twice, n, n, o twice, n, k 4, o twice, p 2 to., k 1, o, k 2.

Thirty-second row.--K 4, o twice, p 2 to., k 6, p 1, k 3, p 1, k 3, p 1, k 3, p 1, k 6, o twice, p 2 to., k 21, leave 32.

Thirty-third row.--Sl 1, k 7, o, n, o, n, k 1, n, o, k 3, o, n, k 1, o twice, p 2 to., k 3, n, o twice, n, n, o twice, n, n, o twice, n, n, o twice, n, k 2, o twice, p 2 to., k 2, o, k 2.

Thirty-fourth row.--K 5, o twice, p 2 to., k 4, p 1, k 3, p 1, k 3, p 1, k 3, p 1, k 4, o twice, p 2 to., k 19, leave 34.

Thirty-fifth row.--Sl 1, k 6, o, n, o, n, k 2, o, k 3 to., o, k 3, o, n, k 5, n, o twice, n, n, o twice, n, n, o twice, n, k 4, o twice, p 2 to., k 3, o, k 2.

Thirty-sixth row.--K 6, o twice, p 2 to., k 6, p 1, k 3, p 1, k 3, p 1, k 6, o twice, p 2 to., k 17, leave 36.

Thirty-seventh row.--Sl 1, k 5, o, n, o, n, k 7, o

twice, p 2 to., k 7, n, o twice, n, n, o twice, n, n, o twice, n, k 6, o twice, p 2 to., n, o twice, n, o, k 2.

Thirty-eighth row.—K 5, p 1, k 1, o twice, p 2 to., k 8, p 1, k 3, p 1, k 3, p 1, k 8, o twice, p 2 to., k 15, leave 38.

Thirty-ninth row.—Sl 1, k 4, o, n, o, n, k 6, o twice, p 2 to., k 9, n, o twice, n, n, o twice, n, k 8, o twice, p 2 to., k 7.

Fortieth row.—Bind off 4, k 2, o twice, p 2 to., k 10, p 1, k 3, p 1, k 10, o twice, p 2 to., k 13, leave 40.

Forty-first row.—Sl 1, k 3, o, n, o, n, k 5, o twice, p 2 to., k 11, n, o twice, n, k 10, o twice, p 2 to., k 1, o, k 2.

Forty-second row.—K 4, o twice, p 2 to., k 12, p 1, k 12, o twice, p 2 to., k 11, leave 42.

Forty-third row.—Sl 1, k 2, o, n, o, n, k 4, o twice, p 2 to., k 2, n, o twice, n, k 13, n, o twice, n, k 2, o twice, p 2 to., k 2, o, k 2.

Forty-fourth row.—K 5, o twice, p 2 to., k 4, p 1, k 16, p 1, k 3, o twice, p 2 to., k 9, leave 44.

Forty-fifth row.—Sl 1, k 1, o, n, o, n, k 3, o twice, p 2, to., k 4, n, o, twice, n, k 9, n, o twice, n, k 4, o twice, p 2 to., k 3, o, k 2.

Forty-sixth row.—K 6, o twice, p 2 to., k 6, p 1, k 12, p 1, k 5, o twice, p 2 to., k 7 leave 46.

Forty-seventh row.—Sl 1, k 6, o twice, p 2 to., k 2, n, o twice, n, k 13, n, o twice, n, k 2, o twice, p 2 to., n, o twice, n, o, k 2.

Forty-eighth row.—K 5, p 1, k 1, o twice, p 2 to., k 4, p 1, k 16, p 1, k 3, o twice, p 2 to., k 5, leave 48.

Forty-ninth row.—Sl 1, k 4, o twice, p 2 to., k 11, n, o twice, n, k 10, o twice, p 2 to., k 7.

Fiftieth row.—Bind off 4, k 2, o twice, p 2 to., k 12, p 1, k 12, o twice, p 2 to., k 3, leave 50.

Fifty-first row.—Sl 1, k 2, o twice, p 2 to., k 9, n, o twice, n, n, o twice, n, k 8, o twice, p 2 to., k 1, o, k 2.

Fifty-second row.—K 4, o twice, p 2 to., k 10, p 1, k 3, p 1, k 10, o twice, p 2 to., k 1, leave 52.

Fifty-third row.—Sl 1, o twice, p 2 to., k 7, n, o twice, n, n, o twice, n, n, o twice, n, k 6, o twice, p 2 to., k 2, o, k 2.

Fifty-fourth row.—K 5, o twice, p 2 to., k 8, p 1, k 3, p 1, k 3, p 1, k 9, leave 54.

Fifty-fifth row.—Sl 1, k 5, n, o twice, n, n, o twice, n, n, o twice, n, n, o twice, n, k 4, o twice, p 2 to., k 3, o, k 2.

Fifty-sixth row.—K 6, o twice, p 2 to., k 6, p 1, k 3, p 1, k 3, p 1, k 3, p 1, k 5, leave 56.

Fifty-seventh row.—Sl 1, k 1, n, o twice, n, n, o twice, n, n, o twice, n, n, o twice, n, n, o twice, n, k 2, o twice, p 2, to., n, o twice, n, o, k 2.

Fifty-eighth row.—K 5, p 1, k 1, o twice, p 2 to., k 4, p 1, k 3, p 1, k 3, p 1, k 3, p 1, k 3, p 1, k 1, leave 58.

Fifty-ninth row.—Sl 1, k 1, n, o twice, n, n, o

twice, n, n, o twice, n, n, o twice, n, k 4, o twice, p 2 to., k 7.

Sixtieth row.—Bind off 4, k 2, o twice, p 2 to., k 6, p 1, k 3, p 1, k 3, p 1, k 3, p 1, k 1, leave 60.

Sixty-first row.—Sl 1, k 1, n, o twice, n, n, o twice, n, n, o twice, n, k 6, o twice, p 2 to., k 1, o, k 2.

Sixty-second row.—K 4, o twice, p 2 to., k 8, p 1, k 3, p 1, k 3, p 1, k 1, leave 62.

Sixty-third row.—Sl 1, k 1, n, o twice, n, n, o twice, n, k 8, o twice, p 2 to., k 2, o, k 2.

Sixty-fourth row.—K 5, o twice, p 2 to., k 10, p 1, k 3, p 1, k 1, leave 64.

Sixty-fifth row.—Sl 1, k 1, n, o twice, n, k 10, o twice, p 2 to., k 3, o, k 2.

Sixty-sixth row.—K 6, o twice, p 2 to., k 12, p 1, k 1, leave 66.

Sixty-seventh row.—Sl 1, k 7, n, o twice, n, k 2, o twice, p 2 to., n, o twice, n, o, k 2.

Sixty-eighth row.—K 5, p 1, k 1, o twice, p 2 to., k 4, p 1, k 7, leave 68.

Sixty-ninth row.—Sl 1, k 3, n, o twice, n, k 4, o twice, p 2 to., k 7.

Seventieth row.—Bind off 4, k 2, o twice, p 2 to., k 6, p 1, k 3, leave 70.

Seventy-first row.—Sl 1, k 3, n, o twice, n, k 2, o twice, p 2 to., k 1, o, k 2.

Seventy-second row.—K 4, o twice, p 2 to., k 4, p 1, k 3, leave 72.

Seventy-third row.—Sl 1, k 7, o twice, p 2 to., k 2, o, k 2.

Seventy-fourth row.—K 5, o twice, p 2 to., k 6, leave 74.

Seventy-fifth row.—Sl 1, k 5, o twice, p 2 to., k 3, o, k 2.

Seventy-sixth row.—K 6, o twice, p 2 to., k 4, leave 76.

Seventy-seventh row.—Sl 1, k 3, o twice, p 2 to., n, o twice, n, o, k 2.

Seventy-eighth row.—K 5, p 1, k 1, o twice, p 2 to., k 2, leave 78.

Seventy-ninth row.—Sl 1, k 1, o twice, p 2 to., k 7.

Eightieth row.—Bind off 4, k 2, o twice, p 2 to., k 80.

Repeat from first row until there are twelve points.

KNITTED OCTAGONAL DOILY WITH CROCHETED EDGE.

(For Illustration see Page 62.)

No. 7.—This doily is made of knitting cotton on medium-sized steel needles. Cotton of any size can be used, but Nos. 12 and 14 are good sizes. Five needles are required. The directions are given for one needle only, as the stitches on each needle are knitted the same.

Cast 2 stitches on each of four needles and knit with a fifth.

First round.—Purl.

Second round.—Th o and k 1, all round.

Third round.—Purl.

Fourth round.—Th o, k 1 and p 1 in the same stitch, th o, k 3, and repeat.

Fifth round.—K 1, p 2, k 1, p 3; repeat.

Sixth round.—Th o, k 1, p 2, k 1, th o, k 3; repeat.

Seventh round.—K 2, p 2, k 2, p 3; repeat.

Eighth round.—Th o, k 2, p 2, k 2, th o twice to make 1 stitch, p 3; repeat.

Ninth round.—P 1, k 2, p 2, k 2, p 4; repeat.

Tenth round.—Th o twice to make 1 stitch, p 1, k 2, p 2, k 2, p 1, th o, k 3; repeat.

Eleventh round.—P 2, k 2, p 2, k 2, p 5; repeat.

Twelfth round.—Th o to make 1 stitch, p 2, k 2, p 2, k 2, p 2, th o, k 3; repeat.

Thirteenth round.—K 1, p 2, k 2, p 2, k 2, p 2, k 1, p 3; repeat.

Fourteenth round.—Th o, k 1, p 2, k 2, p 2, k 2, p 2, k 1, th o, k 3; repeat.

Fifteenth round.—K 2, p 2, k 2, p 2, k 2, p 2, k 2, p 3; repeat.

Sixteenth round.—Th o, k 2, p 2, k 2, p 2, k 2, p 2, k 2, th o, k 3; repeat.

Seventeenth round.—P 1; make the rest like 16th round, except that you purl last 4 stitches.

Eighteenth round.—Th o, to make 1 stitch; rest like 17th row till last 4; then p 1, th o, k 3.

Nineteenth round.—P 2, k 2; repeat till last 5, which you purl.

Twentieth round.—Th o twice; rest like 19th round till last 5; then p 2, k 3; repeat.

Twenty first round.—K 1; rest like 20th round till last 4; then k 1, p 3.

Twenty-second round.—Th o; rest like 21st round till last 3; then, th o, k 3.

Twenty-third round.—K 2; rest like 22nd round till last 5; then k 2, p 3. There should now be 25 stitches on each needle.

Twenty-fourth round. Th o twice, slip and bind; continue to p 2, and k 2 till only 5 remain, then narrow, th o twice, k 3; repeat.

Twenty-fifth round.—P 2 loops, k 1, then p 2, k 2, p till last 6; k 1, p 5; repeat.

Twenty-sixth round.—K 2, th o twice, slip and bind, p 1, k 2, p 2 and repeat till last 7; then n, th o twice, k 5.

Twenty-seventh round.—P 4, k 1, p 1, k 2, p 2, till last 9; then p 1, k 1 p 7.

Twenty-eighth round.—K 4, th o twice, sl and b, k 2, p 2, till last 9; then n, th o twice, k 7.

Twenty-ninth round.—P 6, k 3, p 2, k 2, p 2, k 2, p 2, k 3, p 9.

Thirtieth round.—K 6, th o twice, sl and b, k 1, p 2, k 2, p 2, k 2, p 2, k 1, n, th o twice, k 9.

Thirty-first round.—P 8, k 2, p 2, k 2, p 2, k 2, p 2, k 2, p 11.

Thirty-second round.—K 8, th o twice, sl and b, p 2, k 2, p 2, k 2, p 2, n, th o twice, k 11.

Thirty-third round.—P 10, k 1, p 2, k 2, p 2, k 2, p 2, k 1, p 13.

Thirty-fourth round.—K 10, th o twice, sl and b, p 1, k 2, p 2, k 2, p 1, n, th o twice, k 13.

Thirty-fifth round.—P 12, k 1, p 1, k 2, p 2, k 2, p 1, k 1, p 15.

Thirty-sixth round.—K 12, th o twice, sl and b, k 2, p 2, k 2, n, th o twice, k 15.

Thirty-seventh round.—P 14, k 3, p 2, k 3 p 17.

Thirty-eighth round.—K 14, th o twice, sl and b, k 1, p 2, k 1, n, th o twice, k 17.

Thirty-ninth round.—P 16, k 2, p 2, k 2, p 19.

Fortieth round.—K 16, th o twice, sl and b, p 2, n, th o twice, k 19.

Forty-first round.—P 18, k 1, p 2, k 1, p 21.

Forty-second round.—K 18, th o twice, sl and b, n, k 21.

Forty-third round.—Purl.

No. 7.—KNITTED OCTAGONAL DOILY WITH CROCHETED EDGE.
(For Description see Page 61.)

Forty-fourth round.—Th o, k 1; repeat till last 3 on needle; then th o, k 1, th o, k 1, th o, k 1.

Forty-fifth round.—K plain.

Forty-sixth round.—Purl till last 3, then th o, p 1, th o, p 1, th o, p 1.

Forty-seventh round. — Knit plain and bind off.

For the Crocheted Edge.—Join thread, ch. 3, 1 s. c. in every 3rd stitch, repeat all round.

Second round.—1 s. c., 2 d. c., 1 s. c., over each 3-ch.

Though these directions sound quite elaborate, they are really very simple, as after the pattern is started each round can be knit by the preceding one, with such changes for widening as can be readily seen.

FINGER-BOWL DOILY.

No. 8.—Cast on 35 stitches.

First row.—Sl 1, k 23, n, o, k 4, o twice, p 2 to., k 1, o, k 2.

Second row.—Knit 4, o twice, p 2 to., k 28, leave 2.

Third row.—Sl 1, k 20, n, o, k 5, o twice, p 2 to., k 2, o, k 2.

Fourth row.—Knit 5, o twice, p 2 to., k 26, leave 4.

Fifth row.—Sl 1, k 17, n, o, k 6, o twice, p 2 to., k 3, o, k 2.

Sixth row.—Knit 6, o twice, p 2 to., k 24, leave 6.

Seventh row.—Sl 1, k 14, n, o, k 7, o twice, p 2 to., n, o twice, n, o, k 2.

Eighth row.—Knit 5, p 1, k 1, o twice, p 2 to., k 22, leave 8.

Ninth row.—Sl 1, k 11, n, o, k 1, n, o, k 1, o, n, k 2, o twice, p 2 to., k 7.

Tenth row.—Bind off 4, k 2, o twice, p 2 to., k 20, leave 10.

Eleventh row.—Sl 1, k 8, n, o, k 1, n, o, k 3, o, n, k 1. o twice, p 2 to., k 1, o, k 2.

Twelfth row.—Knit 4, o, twice, p 2 to., k 18, leave 12.

Thirteenth row.—Sl 1, k 5, n, o, k 2, n, o, k 3. o, n, k 1, o twice, p 2 to., k 2, o, k 2.

Fourteenth row.—Knit 5, o twice, p 2 to., k 16, leave 14.

Fifteenth row.—Sl 1, k 5, o, n, k 2, o, k 3 to., o, k 3, o twice, p 2 to., k 3, o, k 2.

Sixteenth row.—Knit 6, o twice, p 2 to., k 14, leave 16.

Seventeenth row.—Sl 1, k 4, o, n, k 7, o twice, p 2 to., n, o twice, n, o, k 2.

Eighteenth row.—Knit 5, p 1, k 1, o twice, p 2 to., k 12, leave 18.

Nineteenth row.—Sl 1, k 3, o, n, k 6, o twice p 2 to., k 7.

Twentieth row.—Bind off 4, k 2, o twice, p 2 to., k 10, leave 20.

Twenty-first row.—Sl 1, k 2, o, n, k 5, o twice, p 2 to., k 1, o, k 2.

Twenty-second row.—Knit 4, o twice, p 2 to., k 8, leave 22.

Twenty-third row.—Sl 1, k 1, o, n, k 4, o twice, p 2 to., k 2, o, k 2.

Twenty-fourth row.—Knit 5, o twice, p 2 to., k 6, leave 24.

Twenty-fifth row.—Sl 1, o, n, k 3, o twice, p 2 to., k 3, o, k 2.

Twenty-sixth row.—Knit 6, o twice, p 2 to., k 4, leave 26.

Twenty-seventh row.—Sl 1, k 3, o twice, p 2 to., n, o twice, n, o, k 2.

Twenty-eighth row.—Knit 5, p 1, k 1, o twice, p 2 to., k 2, leave 28.

Twenty-ninth row.—Sl 1, k 1, o twice, p 2 to., k 7.

Thirtieth row.—Bind off 4, k 2, o twice, p 2 to., k 30.

Repeat until you have twelve points.

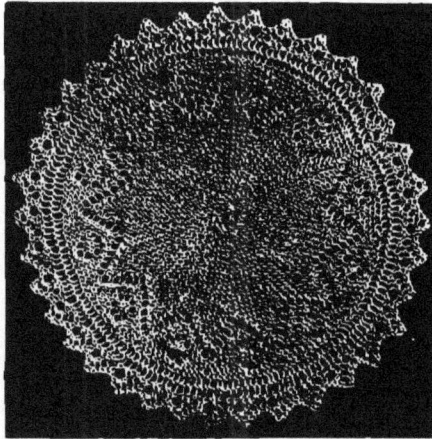

NO. 8.—FINGER-BOWL DOILY.

KNITTED QUILT.

(For Illustration see Page 64.)

NOS. 9, 10 AND 11.—This is an exceedingly pretty pattern for a knitted quilt. The squares are joined together on the right side by a row of single crochet (see figure No. 10); then two rows of scollops are worked, taking up one stitch on each side of previous row of crochet (see figure No. 11). The quilt is then to be lined with any desirable shade of sateen or other goods and a frill of the doubled fabric may be added around the edge or not, as fancy dictates.

Use any kind of knitting cotton preferred, and five steel needles of a size to correspond with the cotton. Cast 2 stitches on each of 4 needles.

First and each alternate round.—Knit plain.

Second round.—* K 1, o, k 1 *; repeat from * to * for the entire round.

Fourth round.—* K 1, o, k 1, o, k 1 *; repeat between the stars all round.

Sixth round.—* K 1, o, k 1, o, k 1, o, k 1, o, k 1 *; repeat as before.

Eighth round.—* K 1, o, k 3, o, k 1, o, k 3, o, k 1 *; repeat.

Tenth round.—* K 1, o, k 5, o, k 1, o, k 5, o, k 1 *; repeat.

Twelfth round.—* K 1, o, k 7, o, k 1, o, k 7, o, k 1 *; repeat.

Fourteenth round.—* K 1, o, k 9, o, k 1, o, k 9, o, k 1 *; repeat.

Sixteenth round.—* K 1, o, slip 1 st., k 1, then pull the slipped st. over the knit one ; k 19, n, o, k 1 *; repeat.

Eighteenth round.—* K 1, o, k 1, o, slip and bind as in the 16th round, k 5, o, k 7, o, k 5, n, o, k 1, o, k 1 *; repeat.

Twentieth round.—* K 1, o, k 1, n, o, sl. and bind, k 2, n, o, k 9, o, sl. and bind, k 2, n, o, sl. and bind, k 1, o, k 1 *; repeat.

Twenty-second round.—* K 1, o, k 2, n, o, sl and b,

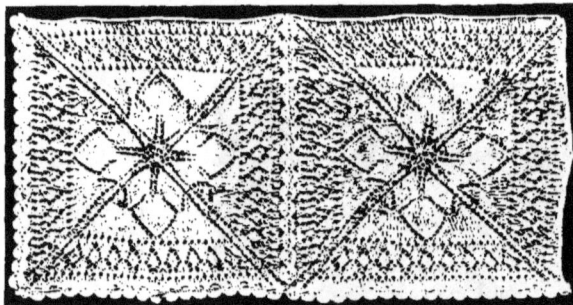

No. 9.

n, o, k 11, o, sl and b, n, o, sl and b, k 2, o, k 1 *; repeat.

Twenty-fourth round.—* K 1, o, k 3, n, o, n, o, k 13, o, n, o, sl. and bind, k 3, o, k 1 *; repeat.

Twenty-sixth round.—* K 1, o, k 8, o, sl. and bind, k 9, n, o, k 8, o, k 1 *;repeat.

Twenty-eighth round.—* K 1, o, k 10, o, sl and bind, k 7, n, o, k 10, o, k 1 *; repeat.

Thirtieth round.—* K 1, o, k 12, o, sl and bind, k 5, n, o, k 12, o, k 1 *; repeat.

Thirty-second round.—* K 1, o, k 14, o, sl. and bind, k 3, n, o, k 14, o, k 1 *; repeat.

Thirty-fourth round.—* K 1, o, k 16, o, sl. and bind, k 1, n, o, k 16, o, k 1 *; repeat.

Thirty-sixth round.—* K 1, o, k 18, o, n 3 to., o, k 18, o, k 1; * repeat.

Thirty-eighth round.—* K 1, o, k 41, o, k 1 *; repeat.

Fortieth round.—(a) K 1, o, k 1, * o, n *; repeat from * to * until only 1 st. remains, then, o, k 1 (a); repeat from (a) to (a) for the entire round.

Forty-second round.—* K 1, o, k 45, o, k 1 *; repeat.

Forty-fourth round.—(b) K 1, o, k 3, * o, n, k 3 *; repeat from * to * until only 5 sts. remain, then, o, n, k 2, o, k 1 (b); repeat from (b) to (b) for the whole round.

Forty-sixth round.—(c) K 1, o, * k 1, n, k 1, o, k 1, o *; repeat from * to * until only 5 sts. remain, then k 1, n, k 1, o, k 1 (c); repeat from (c) to (c).

Forty-eighth round.—(d) K 1, o, k 1, n 3 to., * o, k 3 *; repeat from * to * until only 5 sts. remain, then o, n 3 to., k 1, o, k 1 (d); repeat from (d) to (d) for entire round.

Fiftieth round.—(e) K 2, n, * k 5, n 3 to. *; repeat from * to * until 9 sts. remain, then, k 5, n, k 2 (e); repeat from (e) to (e) for the whole round.

Fifty-first round.—(f) K 1, o, sl. and bind, * o, n, k 1, n, o, k 1 *; repeat from * to * until only 8 sts. remain, then, o, n, k 1, n, o, k, 1 (f); repeat from (f) to (f) for the whole round.

Fifty-second and alternate rounds.—Plain.

Fifty-third round.—(g) K 1, o, * k 3, o, n 3 to., o *; repeat from * to * until only 4 sts. remain, then, k 3, o, k 1 (g); repeat from (g) to (g) for the entire round.

Fifty-fifth round.—(h) K 1, * o, n, k 1, n, o, k 1 *; repeat from * to * until only 6 sts. remain, then, o, n, k 1, n, o, k 1 (h) repeat from (h) to (h) for the whole round.

Fifty-seventh round.—(i) K 1, o, knit plain until there

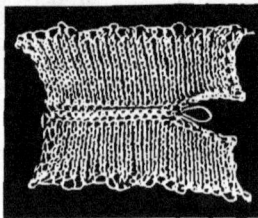

No. 10.

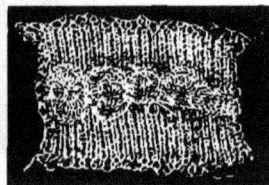

No. 11.

NOS. 9, 10 AND 11.—KNITTED QUILT.

(For Description see Page 63.)

is only 1 stitch left on the needle, then, o, k 1 (i); repeat from (i) to (i) for whole round.

Fifty-ninth round.—(j) K 1, o, k 1, * o, n *; repeat from * to * until only 1 remains, then, o, k 1 (j); repeat from (j) to (j) for the whole round.

Sixty-first round.—(k) K 1, o, knit plain until only 1 remains, then, o, k 1 (k); repeat.

Sixty-third round.—(l) K 1, o, knit plain until only 1 remains, then, o, k 1 (l); repeat.

Sixty-fourth round.—Plain. Bind off loosely.

After knitting the desired number of squares, place the edges of two of them together in such a way that the right side of each will be on the outside, then, with a crochet hook of suitable size, fasten the two squares together, by working a row of single crochet, taking care to catch only the back stitch of the edge of each square (see illustration No. 10). Join squares in this way until the strip is of the desired length. Now fasten the cotton in the back stitch of previous row of crochet (see illustration No. 11), missing two stitches at the edge *; chain 1 st., miss 1, 5 d. c. in next, miss 1, slip st. in next stitch *; repeat from * to * until only 2 stitches remain; break off cotton, and work a row of scollops on the opposite side, taking great care to catch the loop directly opposite to the one taken up in working the scollops on the other side of the row of single crochet.

After working a double row of scollops on each row of single crochet (leaving two sts. at each end of the row of single crochet), break off the cotton. When the desired number of strips are finished, join them together in the same way that the squares are joined. When the strips are crocheted together, work a double row of scollops around the edge—taking up the back stitch of edge for one row and the front stitch for the second row of scollops. When the quilt is ready, line it with a handsome shade of sateen or silk. An extra border of knitted or crocheted lace may be added, if desired.

OPEN-WORK DOILY.

No. 12.—Cast on 27 stitches very loosely.
First round.—P 2 to.; o, p 2 to. 11 times; k 1, o 3 times, k 2.
Second round.—K 3, p 1, k 2, o twice, p 2 to., o, p 2 to.
Third round.—P 2 to., o, p 2 to., k 6.
Fourth round.—K 6, o twice, p 2 to., o, p 2 to., o, p 2 to., o, p 1.
Fifth round.—P 2 to.; o, p 2 to. 3 times; k 6.

Sixth round.—K 6, o twice, p 2 to.; o, p 2 to. 4 times; o, p 1.
Seventh round.—P 2 to.; o, p 2 to. 5 times; k 6.
Eighth round.—Sl and bind 3, k 2, o twice, p 2 to.; o, p 2 to. 6 times; o, p 1.
Ninth round.—P 2 to.; o, p 2 to. 7 times; k 1, o 3 times, k 2.
Tenth round.—K 3, p 1, k 2, o twice, p 2 to.; o, p 2 to. 8 times; o, p 1.
Eleventh round.—P 2 to.; o, p 2 to. 9 times; k 6.
Twelfth round.—K 6, o twice, p 2 to.; o, p 2 to. 10 times; o, p 1.
Thirteenth round.—P 2 to.; o, p 2 to. 11 times; k 6.
Fourteenth round.—K 6, o twice, p 1.
Fifteenth round.—P 2 to., k 6.
Sixteenth round.—Sl and bind 3, k 2, o twice, p 2 to.; o, p 2 to., o, p 1.
Seventeenth round.—P 2 to., o, p 2 to, o, p 2 to., k 1, o 3 times, k 2.
Eighteenth round.—K 3, p 1, k 2, o twice, p 2 to.; o, p 2 to. 3 times; o, p 1.
Nineteenth round.—P 2 to.; o, p 2 to. 4 times; k 6.
Twentieth round.—K 6, o twice, p 2 to.; o, p 2 to. 5 times; o, p 1.
Twenty-first round.—P 2 to.; o, p 2 to. 6 times; k 6.
Twenty-second round.—K 6, o twice, p 2 to.; o, p 2 to. 7 times; o, p 1.
Twenty-third round.—P 2 to.; o, p 2 to. 8 times; k 6.
Twenty-fourth round.—Sl and bind 3, k 2, o twice, p 2 to.; o, p 2 to. 9 times; o, p 1.
Twenty-fifth round.—P 2 to.; o, p 2 to. 10 times; k 1, o 3 times, k 2.
Twenty-sixth round.—K 3, p 1, k 2, o twice, p 2 to.; o, p 2 to. 10 times; o, p 1.
Twenty-seventh round.—P 2 to.; o, p 2 to. 11 times; k 6.
Twenty-eighth round.—K 6, o twice, p 2 to.; o, p 1.
Twenty-ninth round.—P 2 to., o, p 2 to., k 6.

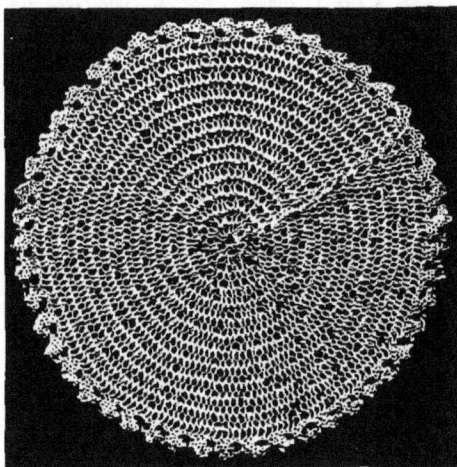

NO. 12.—OPEN-WORK DOILY.

Thirtieth round.—K 6, o twice, p 2 to., o, p 2 to., o, p 2 to.; o, p 1.

Thirty-first round.—P 2 to.; o, p 2 to. 3 times; k 6.

Thirty-second round.—Sl and bind 3, k 2, o twice, p 2 to.; o, p 2 to. 4 times; o, p 1.

Thirty-third round.—P 2 to., o, p 2 to. 5 times; k 1, o 3 times; k 2.

Thirty-fourth round.—K 3, p 1, k 2, o twice, p 2 to.; o, p 2 to. 6 times; o, p 1.

Thirty-fifth round.—P 2 to.; o, p 2 to. 7 times; k 6.

Thirty-sixth round.—K 6, o twice, p 2 to.; o, p 2 to. 8 times; o, p 1.

Thirty-seventh round.—P 2 to.; o, p 2 to. 9 times; k 6.

Thirty-eighth round.—K 6, o twice, p 2 to.; o, p 2 to. 10 times; o, p 1.

Thirty-ninth round.—P 2 to., o, p 2 to. 11 times; k 6.

Fortieth round.—Sl and bind 3, k 2, o twice; p 1.

Forty-first round.—P 2 to., k 1, o 3 times; k 2.

Forty-second round.—K 3, p 1, k 2, o twice, p 2 to.; o, p 2 to.; o, p 1.

Forty-third round.—P 2 to, o, p 2 to., o, p 2 to.; k 6.

Forty-fourth round.—K 6, o twice, p 2 to., o, p 2 to. 3 times; o, p 1.

Forty-fifth round.—P 2 to., o, p 2 to. 4 times; k 6.

Forty-sixth round.—k 6, o twice, p 2 to., o, p 2 to. 5 times; o, p 1.

Forty-seventh round.—P 2 to.; o, p 2 to. 6 times; k 6.

Forty-eighth round.—Sl and bind 3, k 2, o twice; p 2 to., o, p 2 to. 7 times; o, p 1.

Forty-ninth round.—P 2 to.; o, p 2 to. 8 times; k 1, o 3 times; k 2.

Fiftieth round.—K 3, p 1, k 2, o twice, p 2 to., o, p 2 to. 9 times; o, p 1.

Fifty-first round.—P 2 to., o, p 2 to. 10 times; k 6.

Fifty-second round.—K 6, o twice, p 2 to., o, p 2 to. 10 times; o, p 1.

Fifty-third round.—P 2 to.; o, p 2 to. 11 times; k 6.

Fifty-fourth round.—K 6, o twice, p 2 to., o, p 1.

Fifty-fifth round.—P 2 to., o, p 2 to.; k 6.

Fifty-sixth round.—Sl and bind 3, k 2, o twice, p 2 to.; o, p 2 to. 3 times; o, p 1.

Fifty-seventh round.—P 2 to.; o, p 2 to. 4 times; k 1, o 3 times; k 2.

Fifty-eighth round.—K 3, p 1, k 2, o twice, p 2 to.; o, p 2 to. 5 times; o, p 1.

Fifty-ninth round.—P 2 to.; o, p 2 to. 6 times; k 6.

Sixtieth round.—K 6, o twice, p 2 to.; o, p 2 to. 7 times; o, p 1.

Sixty-first round.—P 2 to.; o, p 2 to. 8 times; k 6.

Sixty-second round.—K 6, o twice, p 2 to.; o, p 2 to. 9 times; o, p 1.

Sixty-third round.—P 2 to.; o, p 2 to. 10 times; k 6.

Sixty-fourth round.—Sl and bind 3, k 2, o twice, p 2 to.; o, p 2 to. 10 times; o, p 1.

Sixty-fifth round.—P 2 to.; o, p 2 to. 11 times; k 1, o 3 times, k 2.

Sixty-sixth round.—K 3, p 1, k 2, o twice, p 2 to., o, p 2 to., o, p 1.

Sixty-seventh round.—P 2 to.; o, p 2 to., o, p 2 to.; k 6.

Sixty-eighth round.—K 6, o twice, p 2 to.; o, p 2 to. 4 times; o, p 1.

Sixty-ninth round.—P 2 to.; o, p 2 to. 5 times; k 6.

Seventieth round.—K 6, o twice, p 2 to.; o, p 2 to. 6 times; o, p 1.

Seventy-first round.—P 2 to.; o, p 2 to. 7 times; k 6.

Seventy-second round.—Sl and bind 3, k 2, o twice, p 2 to.; o, p 2 to. 8 times; o, p 1.

Seventy-third round.—P 2 to.; o, p 2 to. 9 times; k 1, o 3 times; k 2.

Seventy-fourth round.—K 3, p 1, k 2, o twice, p 2 to.; o, p 2 to. 10 times; o, p 1.

Seventy-fifth round.—P 2 to.; o, p 2 to. 11 times; k 6.

Seventy-sixth round.—K 6, o twice; p 1.

Seventy-seventh round.—P 2 to.; k 6.

Seventy-eighth round.—K 6, o twice, p 2 to.; o, p 2 to., o, p 2 to., o, p 1.

Seventy-ninth round.—P 2 to.; o, p 2 to. 3 times; k 6.

Eightieth round.—Sl and bind 3, k 2, o twice, p 2 to.; o, p 2 to. 4 times; o, p 1.

Eighty-first round.—P 2 to.; o, p 2 to. 5 times; k 1, o 3 times; k 2.

Eighty-second round.—K 3, p 1, k 2, o twice, p 2 to.; o, p 2 to. 6 times; o, p 1.

Eighty-third round.—P 2 to.; o, p 2 to. 7 times; k 6.

Eighty-fourth round.—K 6, o twice, p 2 to.; o, p 2 to. 8 times; o, p 1.

Eighty-fifth round.—P 2 to.; o, p 2 to. 9 times; k 6.

Eighty-sixth round.—K 6, o twice, p 2 to.; o, p 2 to. 10 times; o, p 1.

Eighty-seventh round.—P 2 to.; o, p 2 to. 11 times; k 6.

Eighty-eighth round.—Sl and bind 3, k 2, o twice, p 2 to.; o, p 1.

Eighty-ninth round.—P 2 to.; o, p 2 to., k 1, o 3 times; k 2.

Ninetieth round.—K 3, p 1, k 2, o twice, p 2 to., o, p 2 to., o, p 2 to., o, p 1.

Ninety-first round.—P 2 to.; o, p 2 to. 3 times; k 6.

Ninety-second round.—K 6, o twice, p 2 to.; o, p 2 to. 4 times; o, p 1.

Ninety-third round.—P 2 to.; o, p 2 to. 5 times; k 6.

Ninety-fourth round.—K 6, o twice, p 2 to.; o, p 2 to. 6 times; o, p 1.

Ninety-fifth round.—P 2 to.; o, p 2 to. 7 times; k 6.

Ninety-sixth round.—Sl and bind 3, k 2, o twice, p 2 to.; o, p 2 to. 10 times; o, p 1.

Repeat the entire direction four times. Break off the thread long enough to sew the edges together. Run the sewing needle through a stitch, take it off the knitting needle and fasten securely to the other edge. Proceed in this way till all the stitches have been taken off the knitting needle and sewn to the opposite edge of the doily.

KNITTED DOILY.

No. 13.—Slip the first st. of every row to make the edge even. In all rows where the 2 loops occur knit one and drop the second half, thus making only one stitch. Cast on 71 stitches and knit 2 plain rows.

First row.—K 3; o twice and n 33 times; k 2.

Second, Third and Fourth rows.—Knit plain.

Fifth row.—K 3; o twice and n 16 times; k 2; o twice and n 16 times; k 2. Next three rows plain.

Ninth row.—K 3, o twice and n 15 times; k 6; o twice and n 15 times; k 2. Next three rows plain.

Thirteenth row.—K 3; o twice and n 14 times; k 10; o twice and n 14 times; k 2. Next three rows plain.

Seventeenth row.—K 3; o twice and n 13 times; k 14; o twice and n 13 times; k 2. Next three rows plain.

Twenty-first row.—K 3; o twice and n 12 times; k 18; o twice and n 12 times; k 2. Next three rows plain.

Twenty-fifth row.—Knit 3; o twice and n 11 times; k 22, o twice and n 11 times; k 2. Next three rows plain.

Twenty-ninth row.—K 3; o twice and n 10 times; k 26; o twice and n 10 times; k 2. Next three rows plain.

Thirty-third row.—K 3; o twice and n 9 times; k 30; o twice and n 9 times; k 2. Next three rows plain.

Thirty-seventh row.—K 3; o twice and n 8 times; k 34; o twice and n 8 times; k 2. Next three rows plain.

Forty-first row.—K 3; o twice and n 7 times; k 18; o twice, n, once, k 18; o twice and n 7 times; k 2. Next three rows plain.

Forty-fifth row.—K 3; o twice and n 6 times; k 18; o twice and n 13 times; k 18; o twice and n 6 times; k 2. Next three rows plain.

Forty-ninth row.—K 3; o twice and n 5 times; k 18; o twice and n 5 times; k 18; o twice and n 5 times; k 2. Next three rows plain.

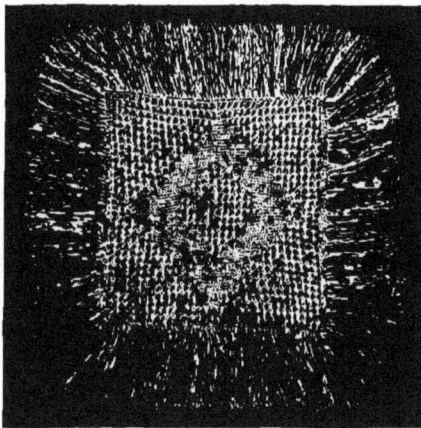

No. 13.—KNITTED DOILY.

Fifty-third row.—K 3; o twice and n 4 times; k 18; o twice and n 7 times; k 18; o twice and n 4 times; k 2. Next three rows plain.

Fifty-seventh row.—K 3; o twice and n 3 times; k 18; o twice and n 9 times; k 18; o twice and n 3 times; k 2. Next three rows plain.

Sixty-first row.—K 3; o twice and n twice; k 18; o twice and n 11 times; k 18; o twice and n twice; k 2. Next three rows plain.

Sixty-fifth row.—K 3; o twice and n once; k 18; o twice and n 13 times; k 18; o twice and n once; k 2. Next three rows plain.

Sixty-ninth row.—K 3; o twice and n twice; k 18; o twice and n 11 times; k 18; o twice, and n twice; k 2. Next three rows plain.

Seventy-third row.—K 3; o twice and n 3 times; k 18; o twice and n 9 times; k 18; o twice and n 3 times; k 2. Next three rows plain.

Seventy-seventh row.—K 3; o twice and n 4 times; k 18; o twice and n 7 times; k 18; o twice and n 4 times; k 2. Next three rows plain.

Eighty-first row.—K 3; o twice and n 5 times; k 18; o twice and n 5 times; k 18; o twice and n 5 times; k 2. Next three rows plain.

Eighty-fifth row.—K 2; o twice and n 6 times; k 18; o twice and n 3 times; k 18; o twice and n 6 times; k 2. Next three rows plain.

Eighty-ninth row.—K 2; o twice and n 7 times; k 18; o twice and n once, k 18; o twice and n 7 times; k 2. Next three rows plain.

Ninety-third row.—K 3; o twice and n 8 times; k 34; o twice and n 8 times; k 2. Next three rows plain.

Ninety-seventh row.—K 3; o twice and n 9 times; k 30; o twice and n 9 times; k 2. Next three rows plain.

One Hundred and First row.—K 3; o twice and n 10 times; k 26; o twice and n 10 times; k 2. Next three rows plain.

One Hundred and Fifth row.—K 3; o twice and n 11 times; k 22 o twice and n 11 times; k 2. Next three rows plain.

One Hundred and Ninth row.—K 3; o twice and

n 12 times; k 18; o twice and n 12 times; k 2. Next three rows plain.

One Hundred and Thirteenth row.—K 3; o twice and n 13 times; k 14; o twice and n 13 times; k 2. Next three rows plain.

One Hundred and Seventeenth row.—K 3; o twice and n 14 times; k 10; o twice and n 14 times; k 2. Next three rows plain.

One Hundred and Twenty-first row.—K 3; o twice and n 15 times; k 6; o twice and n 15 times; k 2. Next three rows plain.

One Hundred and Twenty-fifth row.—K 3; o twice and n 16 times; k 2; o twice and n 16 times; k 2. Next three rows plain.

One Hundred and Twenty-ninth row.—K 3; o twice and n 33 times; k 2. Next three rows plain.

Should the edge of the doily be a little full, run a fine thread through the length of it and draw it to the right size. Finish with a fringe of the desired length. The fringe illustrated was an inch and a half deep and 2 threads were used for each strand.

KNITTED TUMBLER DOILY.

No. 14.—Cast on 25 stitches.

First row.—Sl 1, k 19, th o twice, p 2 to., k 1, o, k 2.

Second row.—K 4, o twice, p 2 to., k 19, leave 1; turn work.

Third row.—Sl 1, k 14, n, o, k 2, o twice, p 2 to., k 2, o, k 2.

Fourth row.—K 5, o twice, p 2 to., k 18, leave 2.

Fifth row.—Sl 1, k 12, n, o, k 3, o twice, p 2 to., k 1, o, k 2, o, k 2.

Sixth row.—K 7, o twice, p 2 to., k 17, leave 3.

Seventh row.—Sl 1, k 10, n, o, k 4, o twice, p 2 to., k 7.

Eighth row.—Bind off 4, k 2, o twice, p 2 to., k 16, leave 4.

Ninth row.—Sl 1, k 8, n, o, k 5, o twice, p 2 to., k 1, o, k 2.

Tenth row.—K 4, o twice, p 2 to., k 15, leave 5.

Eleventh row.—Sl 1, k 6, n, o, n, o, k 1, o, n, k 1, o twice, p 2 to., k 2, o, k 2.

Twelfth row.—K 5, o twice, p 2 to., k 14, leave 6.

Thirteenth row.—Sl 1, k 4, n, o, n, o, k 3, o, n, o twice, p 2 to., k 1, o, k 2, o, k 2.

Fourteenth row.—K 7, o twice, p 2 to., k 13, leave 7.

Fifteenth row.—Sl 1, k 2, n, o, k 1, n, o, k 3, o, n, o twice, p 2 to., k 7.

Sixteenth row.—Bind off 4, k 2, o twice, p 2 to., k 12, leave 8.

Seventeenth row.—Sl 1, k 3, o, n, k 1, o, k 3 to., o, k 2, o twice, p 2 to., k 1, o, k 2.

Eighteenth row.—K 4, o twice, p 2 to, k 11, leave 9.

Nineteenth row.—Sl 1, k 3, o, n, k 5, o twice, p 2 to., k 2, o, k 2.

Twentieth row.—K 5, o twice, p 2 to., k 10, leave 10.

Twenty-first row.—Sl 1, k 3, o, n, k 4, o twice, p 2 to., k 1, o, k 2, o, k 2.

Twenty-second row.—K 7, o twice, p 2 to., k 9, leave 11.

Twenty-third row.—Sl 1, k 3, o, n, k 3, o twice, p 2 to., k 7.

Twenty-fourth row.—Bind off 4, k 2, o twice, p 2 to., k 8, leave 12.

Twenty-fifth row.—Sl 1, k 3, o, n, k 2, o twice, p 2 to., k 1, o, k 2.

Twenty-sixth row.—K 4, o twice, p 2 to., k 7, leave 13.

Twenty-seventh row.—Sl 1, k 3, o, n, k 1, o twice, p 2 to., k 2, o, k 2.

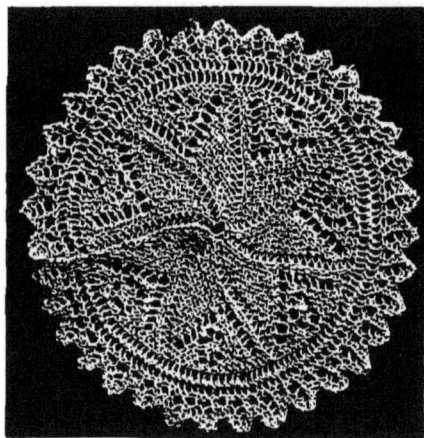

NO. 14.—KNITTED TUMBLER DOILY.

Twenty-eighth row.—K 5, o twice, p 2 to., k 6, leave 14.

Twenty-ninth row.—Sl 1, k 5, o twice, p 2 to., k 1, o, k 2, o, k 2.

Thirtieth row.—K 7, o twice, p 2 to., k 5, leave 15.

Thirty-first row.—Sl 1, k 4, o twice, p 2 to., k 7.

Thirty-second row.—Bind off 4, k 2, o twice, p 2 to., k 4, leave 16.

Thirty-third row.—Sl 1, k 3, o twice, p 2 to., k 1, o, k 2.

Thirty-fourth row.—K 4, o twice, p 2 to., k 3, leave 17.

Thirty-fifth row.—Sl 1, k 2, o twice, p 2 to., k 2, o, k 2.

Thirty-sixth row.—K 5, o twice, p 2 to., k 2, leave 18.

Thirty-seventh row.—Sl 1, k 1, o twice, p 2 to., k 1, o, k 2, o, k 2.

Thirty-eighth row.—K 7, o twice, p 2 to., k 1, leave 19.

Thirty-ninth row.—Sl 1, o twice, p 2 to., k 7.

Fortieth row.—Bind off 4, k 2, o twice, p 2 to., k 20. This completes a point.

KNITTED BLOCK FOR A COUNTERPANE.

No. 15.—Use No. 8 knitting cotton or unbleached carpet warp, and common knitting needles. Widen in every row until the middle of the block is reached, then narrow in each row.

Cast on 3 stitches. Knit back and forth in garter style for 24 rows, widening in each row by slipping the first stitch, throwing the thread over and then knitting across in the manner directed. This completes the plain stripe.

For the Eyelet Stripe.—Knit 1 row, purl 1 row, k 1 row, p 1 row.

Then k 1 row thus: K 1 stitch, * th o, k 1, and repeat across the row from *.

Next row.—P 1 stitch, n, and repeat across the row.

Next row.—Knit.
Next row.—Purl.
Next row.—Knit.
Next row.—Purl. This completes the eyelet stripe.

Now make a plain stripe of 28 rows, and then another eyelet stripe.

Next knit back and forth for 6 rows. This brings you to the basket pattern, which is knit thus:

First row.—K 4, p 4 across the row to form the blocks.

NO. 15.—KNITTED BLOCK FOR COUNTERPANE.

Second row.—K 4, p 4, keeping the order of the blocks.

Third row.—K 4, p 4.
Fourth row.—P 4, k 4.
These four rows form one row of blocks.

Repeat those four rows, making each alternate four so that the knitted blocks will come over the purled ones.

Begin to narrow at the middle of the third row of blocks. At the end of the fifth row knit 6 rows back and forth to correspond with those on the opposite side.

Next make an eyelet stripe, and then 6 more plain rows.

Now knit 7 rows of small squares thus: K 2, p 2 across the row; next row, p 2, k 2, so that the knitted stitches will come over the purled ones of the previous row. These two rows form a row of small blocks.

Next knit back and forth for 6 rows. Then make another eyelet stripe. Now knit plain for 8 rows. This brings the work to the corner and completes the block.

Join the blocks so that the corresponding stripes will meet. The result will be an effect of two varieties of squares, and it is very pretty. A knitted or crocheted border may be added.

KNITTED PLATE DOILY.
(For Illustration see Page 70.)

No. 16.—Cast on 47 stitches.

First row.—Sl 1, k 39, o twice, p 2 to., k 1, o 3 times, n, o, k 2.

Second row.—K 5, p 1, k 2, o twice, p 2 to., k 38, leave 2; turn.

Third row.—Sl 1, k 25, n, o twice, n, k 8, o twice, p 2 to., k 8.

Fourth row.—K 8, o twice, p 2 to., k 10, p 1, k 25, leave 4.

Fifth row.—Sl 1, k 21, * n, o twice, n, * ; repeat once more between stars ; k 6, o twice, p 2 to., k 6, o, k 2.

Sixth row.—K 9, o twice, p 2 to., k 8, p 1, k 3, p 1, k 21, leave 6.

Seventh row.—Sl 1, k 17, * n, o twice, n, * ; repeat twice more between stars ; k 4, o twice, p 2 to., k 9.

Eighth row.—Bind off 4, k 4, o twice, p 2 to., k 6, p 1 ; k 3 and p 1 twice ; k 17, leave 8.

Ninth row.—Sl 1, k 13, * n, o twice, n, * ; repeat 3 times more between stars ; k 2, o twice, p 2 to., k 1, o 3 times, n, o, k 2.

Tenth row.—K 5, p 1, k 2, o twice, p 2 to., k 4 p 1 ; k 3, p 1 3 times ; k 13, leave 10.

Eleventh row.—Sl 1, k 9, * n, o twice, n, * ; repeat 4 times more between stars ; o twice, p 2 to., k 8.

Twelfth row.—K 8, o twice, p 2 to., k 2, p 1 ; k 3 and p 1 4 times ; k 9, leave 12.

Thirteenth row.—Sl 1, k 9, * n, o twice, n, * ; repeat 3 times more between stars ; k 2, o twice, p 2 to., k 6, o, k 2.

Fourteenth row.—K 9, o twice, p 2 to., k 4, p 1 ; k 3 and p 1 3 times ; k 9, leave 14.

Fifteenth row.—Sl 1, k 9, * n, o twice, n, * ; repeat twice more between stars ; k 4, o twice, p 2 to., k 9.

Sixteenth row.—Bind off 4, k 4, o twice, p 2 to., k 6, p 1 ; k 3 and p 1 twice ; k 9, leave 16.

Seventeenth row.—Sl 1, k 9, * n, o twice, n, * ; repeat once more between stars ; k 6, o twice, p 2 to., k 1, o 3 times, n, o, k 2.

Eighteenth row.—K 5, p 1, k 2, o twice, p 2 to., k 8, p 1, k 3, p 1, k 9, leave 18.

Nineteenth row.—Sl 1, k 9, n, o twice, n, k 8, o twice, p 2 to., k 8.

Twentieth row.—K 8, o twice, p 2 to., k 10, p 1, k 9, leave 20.

Twenty-first row.—Sl 1, k 19, o twice, p 2 to., k 6, o, k 2.

Twenty-second row.—K 9, o twice, p 2 to., k 18, leave 22.

Twenty-third row.—Sl 1, k 17, o twice, p 2 to., k 9.

Twenty-fourth row.—Bind off 4, k 4, o twice, p 2 to., k 16, leave 24.

Twenty-fifth row.—Sl 1, k 10, n, o twice, n, k 1, o twice, p 2 to., k 1, o 3 times, n, o, k 2.

Twenty-sixth row.—K 5, p 1, k 2, o twice, p 2 to., k 3, p 1, k 10, leave 26.

Twenty-seventh row.—Sl 1, k 6, n, otwice, n, k 3, o twice, p 2 to., k 8.

Twenty-eighth row.—K 8, o twice, p 2 to., k 5, p 1, k 6, leave 28.

Twenty ninth row.—Sl 1, k 6, n, o twice, n, k 1, o twice, p 2 to., k 6, o, k 2.

Thirtieth row.—K 9, o twice, p 2 to., k 3, p 1, k 6, leave 30.

Thirty-first row.—Sl 1, k 9, o twice, p 2 to., k 9.

Thirty-second row.—Bind off 4, k 4, o twice, p 2 to., k 8, leave 32.

Thirty-third row.—Sl 1, k 7, o twice, p 2 to., k 1, o 3 times, n, o, k 2.

Thirty-fourth row.—K 5, p 1, k 2, o twice, p 2 to., k 6, leave 34.

No. 16.—KNITTED PLATE DOILY.
(For Description see Page 60.)

Thirty-fifth row.—Sl 1, k 5, o twice, p 2 to., k 8.

Thirty-sixth row.—K 8, o twice, p 2 to., k 4, leave 36.

Thirty-seventh row.—Sl 1, k 3, o twice, p 2 to., k 6, o, k 2.

Thirty-eighth row.—K 9, o twice, p 2 to., k 2, leave 38.

Thirty-ninth row.—Sl 1, k 1, o twice, p 2 to., k 9.

Fortieth row.—Bind off 4, k 4, o twice, p 2 to., k 40.

This completes one point, and 12 points are required to form the doily. The stitches should be cast on and bound off very loosely, and the edges sewed together over-hand, and the center drawn together and fastened.

KNITTED DOILY.

No. 17.—Use linen thread No. 90 and two steel needles No. 20. Cast on 50 stitches.

First row.—Knit 4, o, n, k 3, o, n, k 3.

Second row.—Turn the work, sl 1, p 2, k 1, o, n, k 1, o twice, k 2, o, n, k 1, o twice, k 2.

Third row.—Knit 3, p 1, k 2, o, n, k 2, p 1, k 2, o, n, k 6. Turn the work.

Fourth row.—Slip 1, p 5, k 1, o, n, k 5, o, n, k 5.

Fifth row.—Bind off 2, k 3, o, n, n, n, k 1, o, n, k 9. Turn work.

Sixth row.—Slip 1, p 8, k 1, o, n, k 1, o twice, k 2, o, n, k 1, o twice, k 2.

Seventh row.—Knit 3, p 1, k 2, o, n, k 2, p 1, k 2, o, n, k 12. Turn the work.

Eighth row.—Slip 1, p 11, k 1, o, n, k 5, o, n, k 5.

Ninth row.—Bind off 2, k 3, o, n, n, n, k 1, o, n, k 15. Turn the work.

Tenth row.—Slip 1, p 14, k 1, o, n, k 1, o twice, k 2, o, n, k 1, o twice, k 2.

Eleventh row.—K 3, p 1, k 2, o, n, k 2, p 1, k 2, o, n, k 18, Turn the work.

Twelfth row.—Slip 1, p 17, k 1, o, n, k 5, o, n, k 5.

Thirteenth row.—Bind off 2, k 3, o, n, n, n, k 1, o, r, k 21. Turn the work.

Fourteenth row.—Slip 1, p 20, k 1, o, n, k 1, o twice, k 2, o, n, k 1, o twice, k 2.

Fifteenth row.—Knit 3, p 1, k 2, o, n, k 2, p 1, k 2, o, n, k 24. Turn the work.

Sixteenth row.—Slip 1, p 23, k 1, o, n, k 5, o, n, k 5.

Seventeenth row.—Bind off 2, k 3, o, n, n, n, k 1, o, n, k 27. Turn the work.

Eighteenth row.—Slip 1, p 26, k 1, o, n, k 1, o twice, k 2, o, n, k 1, o twice, k 2.

Nineteenth row.—Knit 3 p 1, k 2, o, n, k 2, p 1, k 2, o, n, k 30. Turn the work.

Twentieth row.—Slip 1, p 29, k 1, o, n, k 5, o, n, k 5.

Twenty-first row.—Bind off 2, k 3, o, n, n, n, k 1, o, n, k 33. Turn the work.

Twenty-second row.—Slip 1, p 32, k 1, o, n, k 1, o twice, k 2, o, n, k 1, o twice, k 2.

Twenty-third row.—Knit 3, p 1, k 2, o, n, k 2, p 1, k 2, o, n, k 36. Turn the work.

Twenty-fourth row.—Slip 1, p 35, k 1, o, n, k 5, o, n, k 5.

Twenty-fifth row.—Bind off 2, k 3, o, n, n, n, k 1, o, n, k 39.

Twenty-sixth row.—Slip 1, p 38, k 1, o, n, k 1, o twice, k 2, o, n, k 1, o twice, k 2. This makes one gore or section.

Twenty-seventh row.—Knit 3, p 1, k 2, o, n, k 2, p 1, k 2, o, n, k 2, o, n, p 3. Turn the work.

Twenty-eighth row.—Slip 1, k 3, o, n, k 5, o, n, k 5.

Twenty-ninth row.—Bind off 2, k 3, o, n, n, n, k 1, o, n, p 6.

Thirtieth row.—Slip 1, k 6, o, n, k 1, o twice, k 2, o, n, k 1, o twice, k 2.

Thirty-first row.—K 3, p 1, k 2, o, n. k 2, p 1, k 2, o, n, p 9.

Thirty-second row.—Slip 1, k 9, o, n, k 5, o, n, k 5.

Thirty-third row.—Bind off 2, k 3, o, n, n, n, k 1, o, n, p 12.

Thirty-fourth row.—Slip 1, k 12, o, n, k 1, o twice, k 2, o, n, k 1, o twice, k 2.

Thirty-fifth row.—Knit 3, p 1, k 2, o, n, k 2, p 1, k 2, o, n, p 15.

Thirty-sixth row.—Slip 1, k 15, o, n k 5, o, n, k 5.

Thirty-seventh row.—Bind off 2, k 3, o, n, n, n, k 1, o, n, p 18.

Thirty-eighth row.—Slip 1, k 18, o, n, k 1, o twice, k 2, o, n, k 1, o twice, k 2.

Thirty-ninth row.—Knit 3, p 1, k 2, o, n, k 2, p 1, k 2, o, n, p 21.

Fortieth row.—Slip 1, k 21, o, n, k 5, o, n, k 5.

Forty-first row.—Bind off 2, k 3, o, n, n, n, k 1, o, n, p 24.

Forty-second row.—Slip 1, k 24, o, n, k 1, o twice, k 2, o, n, k 1, o twice, k 2.

Forty-third row.—Knit 3, p 1, k 2, o, n. k 2, p 1, k 2, o, n, p 27.

Forty-fourth row.—Slip 1, k 27, o, n, k 5, o, n, k 5.

Forty-fifth row.—Bind off 2, k 3, o, n, n, n, k 1 o, n, p 30.

Forty-sixth row.—Slip 1, k 30, o, n, k 1, o twice, k 2, o, n, k 1, o twice, k 2.

Forty-seventh row.—Knit 3, p 1, k 2, o, n. k 2, p 1, k 2, o, n, p 33.

Forty-eighth row.—Slip 1, k 33, o, n, k 5, o, n, k 5.

Forty-ninth row.—Bind off 2, k 3, o, n, n, n, k 1, o, n, p 36.

Fiftieth row.—Slip 1, k 36, o, n, k 1, o twice k 2, o, n, k 1, o twice, k 2.

Fifty-first row.—Knit 3, p 1, k 2, o, n, k 2, p 1, k 2, o, n, p 39.

Fifty-second row.—Slip 1, k 39, o, n, k 5, o, n, k 5. This finishes the second section.

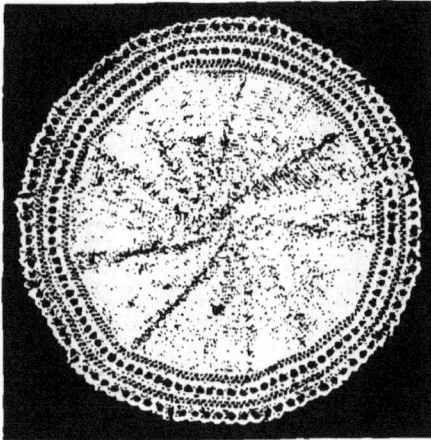

NO. 17.—KNITTED DOILY.

Fifty-third row.—Bind off 2, k 3, o, n, n, n, k 1, o, n, k 3, and proceed to knit like first and second sections alternately until 16 sections are knitted, 8 plain and 8 purled. Bind off, run a thread around the hole in the center and sew the edges or sides together. The doily can be made any size by adding more or less stitches divisible by three.

OVAL DOILY FOR VEGETABLE DISH.

No. 18.—This doily is made of No. 12 knitting cotton and is seven inches long by five and one half wide. Cast on 22 stitches.

First row.—Sl 1, k 2; o, n 9 times; k 1.

Second row.—O, then knit plain; all even rows same.

Third row.—O, k 9, n, o, k 1, o, n, k 9.

Fifth row.—O, k 2; o, n 3 times; o, k 3 to., o, k 3; o, n 5 times; k 1.

Seventh row.—O, k 9, n, o, k 5, o, n, k .9

Ninth row.—O, k 2; o, n 3 times; o, k 3 to., o, k 2, n, o, k 3; o, n 5 times; k 1.

Eleventh row.—O, k 9, n, o, k 2, n, o, k 1, o, n, k 2, o, n, k 9.

Thirteenth row.—O, k 2; o, n 3 times; o, k 3 to., o, k 2, n, o, k 3, o, n, k 2; o, n 5 times; k 1.

Fifteenth row.—O, k 9, n, o, k 2, n, o k, 5, o, n, k 2, o, n, k 9.

Seventeenth row.—O, k 2; o, n 3 times; o, k 3 to., o, k 2, n, o, k 2, n, o, k 3, o, n, k 2; o, n 5 times; k 1. There are now 39 stitches, the required width.

Nineteenth row.—Sl 1, k 8, n, o, k 2, n, o, k 2, n, o, k 1, o, n, k 2, o, n, k 2, o, n, k 9.

Twentieth row.—Sl 1, knit plain, and all even rows same.

Twenty-first row.—Sl 1, k 2, o, n, o, n, o k 3 to., o, k 2, n, o, k 2, n, o, k 3, o, n, k 2, o, n, k 2; o, n 4 times; k 2.

Twenty-third row.—Sl 1, k 6, n, o, k 2, n, o, k 2, n, o, k 5, o, n, k 2, o, n, k 2, o, n, k 7.

Twenty-fifth row.—Sl 1, k 2; o, n 4 times; k 2, o, n, k 2, o, n, k 1, n, o, k 2, n, o, k 2, n, o, k 1; o, n 3 times.

Twenty-seventh row.—Sl 1, k 9, o, n, k 2, o, n, k 2, o, k 3 to., o, k 2, n, o, k 2, n, o, k 10.

Twenty-ninth row.—Sl 1, k 2; o, n 5 times; k 2, o, n, k 5, n, o, k 2, n, o, k 1; o, n 4 times; k 2.

Thirty-first row.—Sl 1, k 11, o, n, k 2, o n, k 3, n, o, k 2, n, o, k 12.

Thirty-third row.—Sl 1, k 2; o, n 6 times; k 2, o, n, k 1, n, o, k 2, n, o, k 1; o, n 5 times; k 2.

Thirty-fifth row.—Sl 1, k 13, o, n, k 2, o, k 3 to., o, k 2, n, o, k 14.

Thirty-seventh row.—Sl 1, k 2; o, n 7 times; k 5, n, o, k 1; o, n 6 times; k 2.

Thirty-ninth row.—Sl 1, k 15, o, n, k 3, n, o, k 16.

Forty-first row.—Sl 1, k 2; o, n 8 times; k 1, n, o, k 1; o, n 7 times; k 2.

Forty-third row.—Sl 1, k 17, o, k 3 to., o, k 18.

Forty-fifth row.—Sl 1, k 2; o, n 6 times; o, k 3 to., o, k 3; o, n 8 times; k 2.

Forty-seventh row.—Sl 1, k 14, n, o, k 5, o, n, k 15.

Forty-ninth row.—Sl 1, k 2; o, n 5 times; o, k 3 to., o, k 2, n, o, k 3; o, n 7 times; k 2.

Fifty-first row.—Sl 1, k 12, n, o, k 2, n, o, k 1, o, n, k 2, o, n, k 13.

Fifty-third row.—Sl 1, k 2; o, n 4 times; o, k 3 to., o, k 2, n, o, k 3, o, n, k 2; o, n 6 times; k 2.

Fifty-fifth row.—Sl 1, k 10, n, o, k 2, n, o, k 5, o, n, k 2, o, n, k 11.

Fifty-seventh row.—Sl 1, k 2; o, n 3 times; o, k 3 to., o, k 2, n, o, k 2, n, o, k 3, o, n, k 2: o, n 5 times; k 2.

Fifty-ninth row.—Like 19th row.

Sixty-first row.—Like 21st row.

Sixty-third row.—Like 23rd row.

Sixty-fifth row.—Like 25th row.

Sixty-seventh row.—Like 27th row.

Sixty-ninth row.—Sl 1, n, k 2; o, n 4 times; k 2, o, n, k 5, n, o, k 2, n, o, k 1; o, n 3 times; k 1, n, k 1.

Seventy-first row.—Sl 1, n, k 8, o, n, k 2, o, n, k 3, n, o, k 2, n, o, k 8, n, k 1.

Seventy-third row.—Sl 1, n; o, n 5 times; k 2, o, n, k 1, o, n, k 2, n, o, k 1; o, n 4 times, n.

Seventy-fifth row.—Sl 1, n, k 8, o, n, k 2, o, k 3 to., o, k 2, n, o, k 8, n, k 1.

Seventy-seventh row.—Sl 1, n; o, n 5 times; k 5; n, o, k 1; o, n 4 times; n.

Seventy-ninth row.—Sl 1, n, k 8, o, n, k 3, n, o, k 8, n, k 1.

Eighty-first row.—Sl 1, n; o, n 5 times; k 1, n, o, k 1; o, n 4 times; n.

Eighty-third row.—Sl 1, n, k 8, o, k 3 to., o, k 8, n, k 1. Bind off loosely.

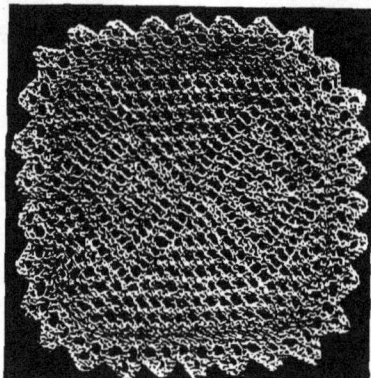

NO. 18.—OVAL DOILY FOR VEGETABLE DISH.

NARROW EDGE FOR DOILY.

Cast on 4 stitches.

First row.—Sl 1, k 1, o 2, k 2.

Second row.—K 3, p 1, k 2.

Third row.—Sl 1, k 5.

Fourth row.—K 6.

Fifth row.—Sl 1, k 1, o twice, n, o twice, k 2.

Sixth row.—K 3, p 1, k 2, p 1, k 2.

Seventh row.—Sl 1, k 8.

Eighth row.—Bind off 5, k 3.

Repeat until there are 30 points, then join and sew around doily.

MAT OR DOILY FOR CUSHION.

No. 19.—Cast on 3 stitches. Thread over, knit plain. Repeat until you have 10 stitches.

First row.—O, k 3, n, o, k 5.

Second row and all even rows.—O, knit plain, but whenever there are 2 put-overs purl the second half so as to make 2 stitches.

Third row.—O, k 3, n, o, k 1, o, n, k 4.

Fifth row.—O, k 3, n, o, k 3, o, n, k 4.

Seventh row.—O, k 3, n, o, k 5, o, n, k 4.

Ninth row.—O, k 3. n, o, k 2, n, o, k 3, o, n, k 4.

Eleventh row.—O, k 3, n, o, k 2, n, o, k 1, o, n, k 2, o, n, k 4.

Thirteenth row.—O, k 3, n, o, k 2, n, o, k 3, o, n, k 2, o, n, k 4.

Fifteenth row.—O, k 3, n, o, k 2, n, o, k 5, o, n, k 2, o, n, k 4.

Seventeenth row.—O, k 3, n, o, k 2, n, o, k 2. n, o, k 3, o, n, k 2, o, n, k 4.

Nineteenth row.—O, k 3, n, o, k 2, n, o, k 2, n, o, k 1, o, n, k 2, o, n, k 2, o, n, k 4.

Twenty-first row.—O, k 3, n, o, k 2, n, o, k 2, n, o, k 3, o, n, k 2, o, n, k 2, o, n, k 4.

Twenty-third row.—O, k 3, n, o, k 2, n, o, k 2, n, o, k 5, o, n, k 2, o, n, k 2, o, n, k 4.

Twenty-fifth row.—O, k 3, n, o, k 2, n, o, k 2, n, o, k7, o, n, k 2, o, n, k 2, o, n, k 4.

Twenty-seventh row.—O, k 3, n, o, k 2, n, o, k 2, n, o. k 3, n, o twice, k 4, o, n, k 2, o, n, k 2, o, n, k 4.

Twenty-ninth row.—O, k 3, n, o, k 2, n, o, k 2, n, o, k 2, n, o twice, n, n, o twice, n, k 2, o, n, k 2, o, n, k 2, o, n, k 4.

Thirty-first row.—O, k 3, n, o, k 2, n, o, k 5, n, o twice, n, k 5, o, n, k 2, o, n, k 2, o, n, k 4.

Thirty-third row.—O, k 3, n, o, k 2, n, o, k 1, o, n, k 2, o, n, k 1, n, o twice, n, n, o twice, n, k 1, n, o, k 2, o, n, k 1, o, n, k 2, o, n, k 4.

Thirty-fifth row.—O, k 3, n, o, k 2, n, o, k 3, o, n, k 2, o, n, k 2, n, o twice, n, k 2, n, o, k 2, n, o, k 3, o, n, k 2, o, n, k 4.

Thirty-seventh row.—O, k 3, n, o, k 2, n, o, k 5, o, n, k 2, o, n, k 6, n, o, k 2, n, o, k 5, o, n, k 2, o, n, k 4.

Thirty-ninth row.—O, k 3, n, o, k 2, n, o, k 2, n,

o, k 3, o, n, k 2, o, n, k 2, o, n, k 4, n, o, k 2, n, o, k 2, n, o, k 3, o, n, k 2, o, n, k 4.

Forty-first row.—O, k 3, n, o, k 2, n, o, k 2, n, o, k 1, o, n, k 2, o, n, k 2, o, n, k 2, n, o, k 2, n, o, k 2, n, o, k 1, o, n, k 2, o, n, k 2, o, n, k 4.

Forty-third row.—O, k 3, n, o, k 2, n, o, k 2, n, o, k 3, o, n, k 2, o, n, k 2, o, n, n, bind 1 over, o, k 2, n, o, k 2, n, o, k 3, o, n, k 2, o, n, k 2, o, n, k 4.

Forty-fifth row.—O, k 3, n, o, k 2, n, o, k 2, n, o, k 5, o, n, k 2, o, n, k 5, n, o, k 2, n, o, k 5, o, n, k 2, o, n, k 2, o, n, k 4.

Forty-seventh row.—O, k 3, n, o, k 2, n, o, k 2, n, o, k 7, o, n, k 2, o, n, k 3, n, o, k 2, n, o, k7, o, n, k 2, o, n, k 2, o, n, k 4.

Forty-ninth row.—O, k 3, n, o, k 2, n, o, k 2, n, o, k 3, n, o twice, k 4, o, n, k 2, o, n, k 1, n, o, k 2, n, o, k 3, n, o twice, k 4, o, n, k 2, o, n, k 2, o, n, k 4.

Fifty-first row.—O, k 3, n, o, k 2, n, o, k 2, n, o, k 2, n, o twice, n, n, o twice, n, k 2, o, n, k 2, o, k 3 to, o, k 2, n, o, k 2, n, o twice, n, n, o twice, n, k 2, o, n, k 2, o, n, k 2, o, n, k 4.

Fifty-third row.—O, k 3, n, o, k 2, n, o, k 2, n, o, k 5, n, o twice, n, k 5, o, n, k 5, n, o, k 5, n, o twice, n, k 5, o, n, k 2, o, n, k 2, o, n, k 4.

There are now 66 stitches. Decrease as follows in even rows: O, n, knit plain.

Fifty-fifth row.—O, n, n, k 2, o, n, k 2, o, n, k 2, o, n, k 2, o, n, k 1, n, o twice, n, n, o twice, n, k 1, n, o, k 2, n, o, k 1, o, n, k 2, o, n, k 1, n, o twice, n, n, o twice, n, k 1, n, o, k 2, n, o, k 2, n, o, n, k 5.

Fifty-seventh row.—O, n, n, k 2, o, n, k 2, o, n. k 2, o, n, k 2, n, o twice, n, k 2, n, o, k 2, n, o, k 3, o, n, k 2, o, n, k 2, n, o twice, n, k 2, n, o, k 2, n, o, k 2, n, o, k 2, n, n, k 1.

Fifty-ninth row.—O, n, n, k 2, o, n, k 2, o, n, k 2, o, n, k 6, n, o, k 2, n, o, k 5, o, n, k 2, o, n, k 6, n, o, k 2, n, o, k 2, n, o, k 2, n, k 2.

Sixty-first row.—O, n, n, k 2, o, n, k 2, o, n, k 2, o, n, k 4, n, o, k 2, n, o, k 2, n, o, k 3, o, n, k 2, o, n, k 4, n, o, k 2, n, o, k 2, n, o, k 2, n, k 2.

Sixty-third row.—O, n, n, k 2, o, n, k 2, o, n, k 2, o, n, k 2, n, o, k 2, n, o, k 2, n, o, k 2, n, o, k 1, o, n, k 2, o, n, k 2, o, n, k 2, n, o, k 2, n, o, k 2, n, o, k 2, n, o, k 2, n, o, k 2, n, o, k 2, n. k 2.

NO. 19.—MAT OR DOILY FOR CUSHION.

Sixty-fifth row.—O, n, n, k 2, o, n, k 2, o, n, k 2, o, n, n, bind 1 over, o, k 2, n, o, k 2, n, o, k 3, o, n, k 2, o, n, k 2, o, n, n, bind 1 over, o, k 2, n, o, k 2, n, o, k 2, n, k 2.

Sixty-seventh row.—O, n, n, k 2, o, n, k 2, o, n, k 5, n, o, k 2, n, o, k 5, o, n, k 2, o, n, k 5, n, o, k 2, n, o, k 2, n, k 2.

Sixty-ninth row.—O, n, n, k 2, o, n, k 2, o, n, k 3, n, o, k 2, n, o, k 7, o, n, k 2, o, n, k 3, n, o, k 2, n, o, k 2, n, k 2.

Seventy-first row.—O, n, n, k 2, o, n, k 2, o, n, k 1, n, o, k 2, n, o, k 3, n, o twice, k 4, o, n, k 2, o, n, k 1, n, o, k 2, n, o, k 2, n, k 2.

Seventy-third row.—O, n, n, k 2, o, n, k 2, o, k 3 to., o, k 2, n, o, k 2, n, o twice, n, n, o twice, n, k 2, o, n, k 2, o, k 3 to., o, k 2, n, o, k 2, n, k 2.

Seventy-fifth row.—O, n, n, k 2, o, n, k 5, n, o, k 5, n, o twice, n, k 5, o, n, k 5, n, o, k 2, n, k 2.

Seventy-seventh row.—O, n, n, k 2, o, n, k 2, o, n, k 2, o, n, k 1, n, o twice, n, n, o twice, n, k 1, n, o, k 2, n, o, k 2, n, o, k 2, n, k 2.

Seventy-ninth row.—O, n, n, k 2, o, n, k 2, o, n, k 2, o, n, k 2, n, o twice, n, k 2, n, o, k 2, n, o, k 2, n, k 2.

Eighty-first row.—O, n, n, k 2, o, n, k 2, o, n, k 6, n, o, k 2, n, o, k 2, n, o, k 2, n, k 2.

Eighty-third row.—O, n, n, k 2, o, n, k 2, o, n, k 2, o, n, k 4, n, o, k 2, n, o, k 2, n, o, k 2, n, k 2.

Eighty-fifth row.—O, n, n, k 2, o, n, k 2, o, n, k 2, o, n, k 2, n, o, k 2, n, o, k 2, n, o, k 2, n, k 2.

Eighty-seventh row.—O, n, n, k 2, o, n, k 2, o, n, k 2, o, n, n, bind 1, o, k 2, n, o, k 2, n, k 2.

Eighty-ninth row.—O, n, n, k 2, o, n, k 2, o, n, k 5, n, o, k 2, n, o, k 2, n, k 2.

Ninety-first row.—O, n, n, k 2, o, n, k 2, o, n, k 3, n, o, k 2, n, o, k 2, n, k 2.

Ninety-third row.—O, n, n, k 2, o, n, k 2, o, n, k 1, n, o, k 2, n, o, k 2, n, k 2.

Ninety-fifth row.—O, n, n, k 2, o, n, k 2, o, k 3 to:, o, k 2, n, o, k 2, n, k 2.

Ninety-seventh row.—O, n, n, k 2, o, n, k 5, n, o, k 2, n, k 2.

Ninety-ninth row.—O, n, n, k 2, o, n, k 3, n, o, k 2, n, k 2.

One Hundred and First row.—O, n, n, k 2, o, n, k 1, n, o, k 2, n, k 2.

One Hundred and Third row.—O, n, n, k 2, o, k 3 to., o, k 2, n, k 2.

One Hundred and Fifth row.—O, n, n, k 5, n, k 2.

One Hundred and Seventh row.—O, n, n, k 3, n, k 2.

One Hundred and Ninth row.—O, n, n, k 1, n, k 2.

One Hundred and Eleventh row.—O, n, n, n, k 1.

One Hundred and Thirteenth row.—O, n, n, k 1.

One Hundred and Fifteenth row.—O, n, n, bind off 2.

EDGE FOR COVER.

Cast on 13 stitches.

First row.—Sl 1, k 2, n, o, k 1, o, n, k 1, o, n, o, k 2.

Second row.—Plain. All even rows same.

Third row.—Sl 1, k 1, n, o, k 3, o, n, k 1, o, n, o, k 2.

Fifth row.—Sl 1, n, o, k 5, o, n, k 1, o, n, o, k 2.

Seventh row.—Sl 1, k 2, o, n, k 1, n, o, k 4, o, n, o, k 2.

Ninth row.—Sl 1, k 3, o, k 3 to., o, k 6, o, n. o, k 2.

Eleventh row.—Plain.

Twelfth row.—Bind off 5, k 12.

Repeat pattern 7 times more.

For Corner.—First row.—*Sl 1, k 8, o, n, o k 2.

Second row.—K 12, leave 2.

Third row.—Sl 1, k 2, n, o twice, n, k 1, o, n, o, k 2.

Fourth row.—K 8, p 1, k 2, leave 4.

Fifth row.—Sl 1, k 6, o, n, o, k 2.

Sixth row.—K 10, leave 6.

Seventh row.—Sl 1, k 5, o, n, o, k 2.

Eighth row.—K 9, leave 8.

Ninth row.—Sl 1, k 4, o, n, o, k 2.

Tenth row.—K 8, leave 10.

Eleventh row.—Sl 1, k 7.

Twelfth row.—Bind off 5, k 12.

Repeat 4 times from *, then from beginning.

KNITTED DOILY.
(For Illustration see Page 78.)

No. 20.—Cast on 51 stitches.

First row.—O twice, p 3 to., k 1, p 1, k 6, turn.

Second row.—Sl 1, n, o, k 1, o, k 3 to., o twice, k 1, o twice, p 2 to.

Third row.—O twice, p 3 to., k 1, p 1, k 7, turn.

Fourth row.—Sl 1, n, o, k 3, o, n, o twice, k 1, o twice, p 2 to.

Fifth row.—O twice, p 3 to., k 1, p 1, k 9, turn.

Sixth row.—Sl 1, n, o, k 5, o, n, o twice, k 1, o twice, p 2 to.

Seventh row.—O twice, p 3 to., k 1, p 1, k 11, turn.

Eighth row.—Sl 1, n, o, n, o twice, k 3 to., o twice, n, o, n, o twice, k 1, o twice, p 2 to.

Ninth row.—O twice, p 3 to., k 1, p 1, k 4, p 1, k twice, p 1, k 5, turn.

Tenth row.—Sl 1, n, o, n, o twice, k 5, o twice, n, o, n, o twice, k 1, o twice, p 2 to.

Eleventh row.—O twice, p 3 to., k 1, p 1, k 4, p 1, k 6, p 1, k 5, turn.

Twelfth row.—Sl 1, k 2, o, k 3 to., o twice, k 3 to., k 1, k 3, o twice, n, o, k 1, o, n, o twice, k 1, o twice, p 2 to.

Thirteenth row.—O twice, p 3 to., k 1, p 1, k 6, p 1, k 4, p 1, k 6, turn.

Fourteenth row.—Sl 1, k 4, o, k 3 to., o twice, k 3 to., o twice, k 3 to., o, k 3, o, n, o twice, k 1, o twice, p 2 to.

Fifteenth row.—O twice, p 3 to., k 1, p 1, k 8, p 1, k 2, p 1, k 8, turn.

Sixteenth row.—Sl 1, k 6, o, n, k 3, n, o, k 5, o, n, o twice, k 1, o twice, p 2 to.

Seventeenth row.—O twice, p 3 to., k 1, p 1, k 22, turn.

Eighteenth row.—Sl 1, k 8, o, n. k 1, n, o, n, o twice, k 3 to., o twice, n, o, n, o twice, k 1, o twice, p 2 to.

Nineteenth row.—O twice, p 3 to., k 1, p 1, k 4, p 1, k 2, p 1, k 16, turn.

Twentieth row.—Sl 1, k 10, o, sl 1, n, b, o, n, o twice, k 5, o twice, n, o, n, o twice, k 1, o twice, p 2 to.

Twenty-first row.—O twice, p 3 to., k 1, p 1, k 4, p 1, k 6, p 1, k 16, turn.

Twenty-second row.—Sl 1, k 10, n, o, k 1, o, k 3 to., o twice, k 3 to., k 1, k 3 to., o twice, k 3 to., o, n, o twice, k 1, o twice, p 2 to.

Twenty-third row.—O twice, p 3 to., k 1, p 1, k 4, p 1, k 4, p 1, k 17, turn.

Twenty-fourth row.—Sl 1, k 10, n, o, k 3, o, k 3 to., o twice, k 3 to., o twice, k 3 to., o, k 3 to., o twice, k 1, o twice, p 2 to.

Twenty-fifth row.—O twice, p 3 to., k 1, p 1, k 4, p 1, k 2, p 1, k 19, turn.

Twenty-sixth row.—Sl 1, k 10, n, o, k 5, o, n, k 3, n, o, k 3 to., o twice, k 1, o twice, p 2 to.

Twenty-seventh row.—O twice, p 3 to., k 1, p 1, k 27, turn.

Twenty-eighth row.—Sl 1, k 10, n, o, n, o twice, k 3 to., o twice, n, o, n, k 1, n, o, k 3 to., o twice, k 1, o twice, p 2 to.

Twenty-ninth row.—O twice, p 3 to., k 1, p 1, k 8, p 1, k 2, p 1, k 15, turn.

Thirtieth row.—Sl 1, k 10, n, o, n, o twice, k 5, o twice, n, o, sl 1, n, b, o, k 3 to., o twice, k 1, o twice, p 2 to.

Thirty-first row.—O twice p 3 to., k 1, p 1, k 6, p 1, k 6, p 1, k 15, turn.

Thirty-second row—Sl 1, k 12, o, k 3 to., o twice, k 3 to., k 1, k 3 to; o twice, k 4 to., o, k 3 to., o twice, k 1, o twice, p 2 to.

Thirty-third row.—O twice, p 3, to., k 1, p 1, k 4, p 1, k 4, p 1, k 16, turn.

Thirty-fourth row.—Sl 1, k 14, o k 3 to., o twice k 3 to., o twice, k 3 to., o, k 3 to., o twice, k 1, o twice, p 2 to.

Thirty-fifth row.—O twice, p 3 to., k 1, p 1, k 4, p 1, k 2, p 1, k 18, turn.

Thirty-sixth row.—Sl 1, k 16, o, n, k 3, n, o, k 3 to., o twice, k 1, o twice, p 2 to.

Thirty-seventh row.—O twice, p 3 to., k 1, p 1, k 26, turn.

Thirty-eighth row.—Sl 1, k 18, o, n, k 1, n, o, k 3 to., o twice, k 1, o twice, p 2 to.

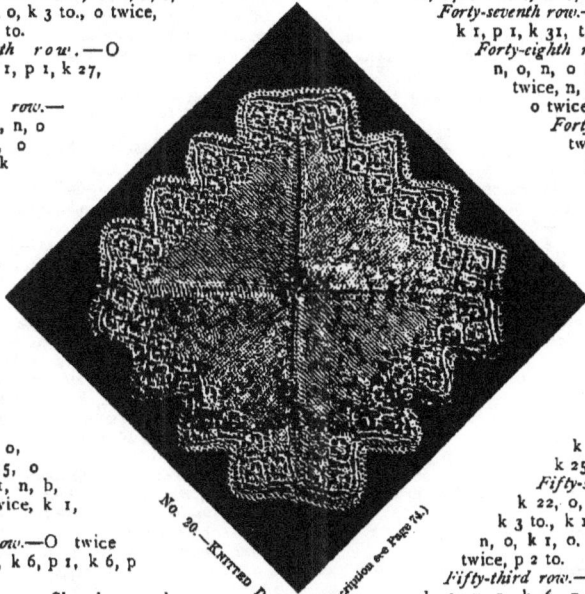

No. 20.—Knitted Doily.—(For Description see Page 74.)

Thirty-ninth row.—O twice, p 3 to., k 1, p 1, k 26, turn.

Fortieth row.—Sl 1, k 20, o, sl 1, n, b, o, k 3 to., o twice, k 1, o twice, p 2 to.

Forty-first row.—O twice, p 3 to., k 1, p 1, k 26, turn.

Forty-second row.—Sl 1, k 20, n, o, k 1, o, k 3 to., o twice, k 1, o twice, p 2 to.

Forty-third row.—O twice, p 3 to., k 1, p 1, k 27, turn.

Forty-fourth row.—Sl 1, k 20, n, o, k 3, o, n, o twice, k 1, o twice, p 2 to.

Forty-fifth row.—O twice, p 3 to., k 1, p 1. k 29, turn.

Forty-sixth row.—Sl 1, k 20, n, o, k 5, o, n, o twice, k 1, o twice, p 2 to.

Forty-seventh row.—O twice, p 3 to., k 1, p 1, k 31, turn.

Forty-eighth row.—Sl 1, k 20, n, o, n, o twice, k 3 to., o twice, n, o, n, o twice, k 1. o twice, p 2 to.

Forty-ninth row.—O twice, p 3 to., k 1, p 1, k 4, p 1, k 2, p 1, k 25, turn.

Fiftieth row.—Sl 1, k 20, n, o, n, o twice, k 5, o twice, n, o, n, o twice, k 1, o twice, p 2 to.

Fifty-first row.—O twice, p 3 to., k 1, p 1, k 4, p 1, k 6, p 1, k 25, turn.

Fifty-second row.—Sl 1, k 22, o, k 3 to., o twice, k 3 to., k 1, k 3 to., o twice, n, o, k 1, o. n, o twice, k 1, o twice, p 2 to.

Fifty-third row.—O twice, p 3 to., k 1, p 1, k 6, p 1, k 4, p 1, k 26, turn.

Fifty-fourth row.—Sl 1, k 24, o, k 3 to., o twice, k 3 to., o twice, k 3 to., o, k 3, o, n, o twice, k 1, o twice, p 2 to.

Fifty-fifth row.—O twice, p 3 to., k 1, p 1, k 8, p 1, k 2, p 1, k 28, turn.

Fifty-sixth row.—Sl 1, k 26, o, n, k 3, n, o, k 5, o, n, o twice, k 1, o twice, p 2 to.

Fifty-seventh row.—O twice, p 3 to., k 1, p 1, k 42, turn.

Fifty-eighth row.—Sl 1, k 28, o, n, k 1, n, o, n, o twice, k 3 to., o twice, n, o, n, o twice, k 1, o twice, p 2 to.

Fifty-ninth row.—O twice, p 3 to., k 1, p 1, k 4, p 1, k 2, p 1, k 36, turn.

Sixtieth row.—Sl 1, k 30, o, sl 1, n. b, o, n, o twice,

k 5, o twice, n, o, n, o twice, k 1, o twice, p 2 to.

Sixty-first row.—O twice, p 3 to., k 1, p 1, k 4, p 1, k 6, p 1, k 36, turn.

Sixty-second row.—Sl 1, k 30, n, o, k 1, o, k 3 to., o twice, k 3 to., k 1, k 3 to., o twice, k 3 to., o, n, o twice, k 1, o twice, p 2 to.

Sixty-third row.—O twice, p 3 to., k 1, p 1, k 4, p 1, k 4, p 1, k 37, turn.

Sixty-fourth row.—Sl 1, k 30, n, o, k 3, o, k 3 to., o twice, k 3 to., o twice, k 3 to., o, k 3 to., o twice, k 1, o twice, p 2 to.

Sixty-fifth row.—O twice, p 3 to., k 1, p 1, k 4, p 1, k 2, p 1, k 39, turn.

Sixty-sixth row.—Sl 1, k 30, n, o, k 5, o, n, k 3, n, o, k 3 to., o twice, k 1, o twice, p 2 to.

Sixty-seventh row.—O twice, p 3 to., k 1, p 1, k 47, turn.

Sixty-eighth row.—Sl 1, k 30, n, o, n, o twice, k 3 to., o twice, n, o, n, k 1, n, o, k 3 to., o twice, k 1, o twice, p 2 to.

Sixty-ninth row.—O twice, p 3 to., k 1, p 1, k 8, p 1, k 2, p 1, k 35, turn.

Seventieth row.—Sl 1, k 30, n, o, n, o twice, k 5, o twice, n, o, sl 1, n, b, o, k 3 to., o twice, k 1, o twice, p 2 to.

Seventy-first row.—O twice, p 3 to., k 1, p 1, k 6, p 1, k 6, p 1, k 35, turn.

Seventy-second row.—Sl 1, k 32, o, k 3 to., o twice, k 3 to., k 1, k 3 to., o twice, k 4 to., o, k 3 to., o twice, k 1, o twice, p 2 to.

Seventy-third row.—O twice, p 3 to., k 1, p 1, k 4, p 1, k 4, p 1, k 36, turn.

Seventy-fourth row.—Sl 1, k 34, o, k 3 to., o twice, k 3 to., o twice, k 3 to., o, k 3 to., o twice, k 1, o twice, p 2 to.

Seventy-fifth row.—O twice, p 3 to., k 1, p 1, k 4, p 1, k 2, p 1, k 38, turn.

Seventy-sixth row.—Sl 1, k 36, o, n, k 3, n, o, k 3 to., o twice, k 1, o twice, p 2 to.

Seventy-seventh row.—O twice, p 3 to., k 1, p 1, k 46, turn.

Seventy-eighth row.—Sl 1, k 38, o, n, k 1, n, o, k 3 to., o twice, k 1, o twice, p 2 to.

Seventy-ninth row.—O twice, p 3 to., k 1, p 1, k 46, turn.

Eightieth row.—Sl 1, k 40, o, sl 1, n, b, o, k 3 to., o twice, k 1, o twice, p 2 to.

Eighty-first row.—O twice, p 3 to., k 1, p 1, k 46, turn.

Eighty-second row.—Sl 1, k 40, n, o, k 1, o, k 3 to., o twice, k 1, o twice, p 2 to.

Eighty-third row.—O twice, p 3 to., k 1, p 1, k 45, leave 1.

Eighty-fourth row.—Sl 1, k 38, n, o, k 3, o, n, o twice, k 1, o twice, p 2 to.

Eighty-fifth row.—O twice, p 3 to., k 1, p 1, k 45, leave 2.

Eighty-sixth row.—Sl 1, k 36, n, o, k 5, o, n, o twice, k 1, o twice, p 2 to.

Eighty-seventh row.—O twice, p 3 to., k 1, p 1, k 45, leave 3.

Eighty-eighth row.—Sl 1, k 34, n, o, n, o twice, k 3 to., o twice, n, o, n, o twice, k 1, o twice, p 2 to.

Eighty-ninth row.—O twice, p 3 to., k 1, p 1, k 4, p 1, k 2, p 1, k 37, leave 4.

Ninetieth row.—Sl 1, k 32, n, o, n, o twice, k 5, o twice, n, o, n, o twice, k 1, o twice, p 2 to.

Ninety-first row.—O twice, p 3 to., k 1, p 1, k 4, p 1, k 6, p 1, k 35, leave 5.

Ninety-second row.—Sl 1, k 32, o, k 3 to., o twice, k 3 to., k 1, k 3 to., o twice, n, o, k 1, o, n, o twice, k 1, o twice, p 2 to.

Ninety-third row.—O twice, p 3 to., k 1, p 1, k 6, p 1, k 4, p 1, k 34, leave 6.

Ninety-fourth row.—Sl 1, k 32, o, k 3 to., o twice, k 3 to., o twice, k 3 to., o, k 3, o, n, o twice, k 1, o twice, p 2 to.

Ninety-fifth row.—O twice, p 3 to., k 1, p 1, k 8, p 1, k 2, p 1, k 34, leave 7.

Ninety-sixth row.—Sl 1, k 32, o, n, k 3, n, o, k 5, o, n, o twice, k 1, o twice, p 2 to.

Ninety-seventh row.—O twice, p 3 to., k 1, p 1, k 46, leave 8.

Ninety-eighth row.—Sl 1, k 32, o, n, k 1, n, o, n, o twice, k 3 to., o twice, n, o, n, o twice, k 1, o twice, p 2 to.

Ninety ninth row.—O twice, p 3 to., k 1, p 1, k 4, p 1, k 2, p 1, k 38, leave 9.

One Hundredth row.—Sl 1, k 32, o, sl 1, n, b, o, n, o twice, k 5, o twice, n, o, n, o twice, k 1, o twice, p 2 to.

One Hundred and First row.—O twice, p 3 to., k 1, p 1, k 4, p 1, k 6, p 1, k 36, leave 10.

One Hundred and Second row.—Sl 1, k 30, n, o, k 1, o, k 3 to., o twice, k 3 to., k 1, k 3 to., o twice, k 3 to., o, n, o twice, k 1, o twice, p 2 to.

One Hundred and Third row.—O twice, p 3 to., k 1, p 1, k 4, p 1, k 4, p 1, k 35, leave 11.

One Hundred and Fourth row.—Sl 1, k 28, n, o, k 3, o, k 3 to., o twice, k 3 to., o twice, k 3 to., o, k 3 to., o twice, k 1, o twice, p 2 to.

One Hundred and Fifth row.—O twice, p 3 to., k 1, p 1, k 4, p 1, k 2, p 1, k 35, leave 12.

One Hundred and Sixth row.—Sl 1, k 26, n, o, k 5, o, n, k 3, n, o, k 3 to., o twice, k 1, o twice, p 2 to.

One Hundred and Seventh row.—O twice, p 3 to., k 1, p 1, k 41, leave 13.

One Hundred and Eighth row.—Sl 1, k 24, n, o, n, o twice, k 3 to., o twice, n, o, n, k 1, n, o, k 3 to., o twice, k 1, o twice, p 2 to.

One Hundred and Ninth row.—O twice, p 3 to., k 1, p 1, k 8, p 1, k 2, p 1, k 27, leave 14.

One Hundred and Tenth row.—Sl 1, k 22, n, o, n, o twice, k 5, o twice, n, o, sl 1, n, b, o, k 3 to., o twice, k 1, o twice, p 2 to.

One Hundred and Eleventh row.—O twice, p 3 to., k 1, p 1, k 6, p 1, k 6, p 1, k 25, leave 15.

One Hundred and Twelfth row.—Sl 1, k 22, o, k 3 to., o twice, k 3 to., k 1, k 3 to., o twice, k 4 to., o, k 3 to., o twice, k 1, o twice, p 2 to.

One Hundred and Thirteenth row.—O twice, p 3 to., k 1, p 1, k 4, p 1, k 4, p 1, k 24, leave 16.

One Hundred and Fourteenth row.—Sl 1, k 22, o, k 3 to., o twice, k 3 to., o twice, k 3 to., o, k 3 to., o twice, k 1, o twice, p 2 to.

One Hundred and Fifteenth row.—O twice, p 3 to., k 1, p 1, k 4, p 1, k 2, p 1, k 24, leave 17.

One Hundred and Sixteenth row.—Sl 1, k 22, o, n, k 3, n, o, k 3 to., o twice, k 1, o twice, p 2 to.

One Hundred and Seventeenth row.—O twice, p 3 to., k 1, p 1, k 30, leave 18.

One Hundred and Eighteenth row.—Sl 1, k 22, o, n, k 1, n, o, k 3 to., o twice, k 1, o twice, p 2 to.

One Hundred and Nineteenth row.—O twice, p 3 to., k 1, p 1, k 28, leave 19.

One Hundred and Twentieth row.—Sl 1, k 22, o, sl 1, n, b, o, k 3 to., o twice, k 1, o twice, p 2 to.

One Hundred and Twenty-first row.—O twice, p 3 to., k 1, p 1, k 26, leave 20.

One Hundred and Twenty-second row.—Sl 1, k 20, n, n, k 1, o, k 3 to., o twice, k 1, o twice, p 2 to.

One Hundred and Twenty-third row.—O twice, p 3 to., k 1, p 1, k 25, leave 21.

One Hundred and Twenty-fourth row.—Sl 1, k 18, n, o, k 3, o, n, o twice, k 1, o twice, p 2 to.

One Hundred and Twenty-fifth row.—O twice, p 3 to., k 1, p 1, k 25, leave 22.

One Hundred and Twenty-sixth row.—Sl 1, k 16, n, o, k 5, o, n, o twice, k 1, o twice, p 2 to.

One Hundred and Twenty-seventh row.—O twice, p 3 to., k 1, p 1, k 25, leave 23.

One Hundred and Twenty-eighth row.—Sl 1, k 14, n, o, n, o twice, k 3 to., o twice, n, o, n, o twice, k 1, o twice, p 2 to.

One Hundred and Twenty-ninth row.—O twice, p 3 to., k 1, p 1, k 4, p 1, k 2, p 1, k 17, leave 24.

One Hundred and Thirtieth row.—Sl 1, k 12, n, o, n, o twice, k 5, o twice, n, o, n, o twice, k 1, o twice, p 2 to.

One Hundred and Thirty-first row.—O twice, p 3 to., k 1, p 1, k 4, p 1, k 6, p 1, k 15, leave 25.

One Hundred and Thirty-second row.—Sl 1, k 12, o, k 3 to., o twice, k 3 to., k 1, k 3 to., o twice, n, o, k 1, o, n, o twice, k 1, o twice, p 2 to.

One Hundred and Thirty-third row.—O twice, p 3 to., k 1, p 1, k 6, p 1, k 4, p 1, k 14, leave 26.

One Hundred and Thirty-fourth row.—Sl 1, k 12, o, k 3 to., o twice, k 3 to., o twice, k 3 to., o, k 3, o, n, o twice, k 1, o twice, p 2 to.

One Hundred and Thirty-fifth row.—O twice, p 3 to., k 1, p 1, k 8, p 1, k 2, p 1, k 14, leave 27.

One Hundred and Thirty-sixth row.—Sl 1, k 12, o, n, k 3, n, o, k 5, o, n, o twice, k 1, o twice, p 2 to.

One Hundred and Thirty-seventh row.—O twice, p 3 to., k 1, p 1, k 36, leave 28.

One Hundred and Thirty-eighth row.—Sl 1, k 12, o, n, k 1, n, o, n, o twice, k 3 to., o twice, n, o, n, o twice, k 1, o twice, p 2 to.

One Hundred and Thirty-ninth row.—O twice, p 3 to., k 1, p 1, k 4, p 1, k 2, p 1, k 18, leave 29.

One Hundred and Fortieth row.—Sl 1, k 12, o, sl 1, n, b, o, n, o twice, k 5, o twice, n, o, n, o twice, k 1, o twice, p 2 to.

One Hundred and Forty-first row.—O twice, p 3 to., k 1, p 1, k 4, p 1, k 6, p 1, k 16, leave 30.

One Hundred and Forty-second row.—Sl 1, k 10, n, o, k 1, o, k 3 to., o twice, k 3 to., k 1, k 3 to., o twice, k 3 to., o, n, o twice, k 1, o twice, p 2 to.

One Hundred and Forty-third row.—O twice, p 3 to., k 1, p 1, k 4, p 1, k 4, p 1, k 15, leave 31.

One Hundred and Forty-fourth row.—Sl 1, k 8, n, o, k 3, o, k 3 to., o twice, k 3 to., o twice, k 3 to., o, k 3 to., o twice, k 1, o twice, p 2 to.

One Hundred and Forty-fifth row.—O twice, p 3 to., k 1, p 1, k 4, p 1, k 2, p 1, k 15, leave 32.

One Hundred and Forty-sixth row.—Sl 1, k 6, n, n, o, k 5, o, n, k 3, n, o, k 3 to., o twice, k 1, o twice, p 2 to.

One Hundred and Forty-seventh row.—O twice, p 3 to., k 1, p 1, k 21, leave 33.

One Hundred and Forty-eighth row.—Sl 1, k 4, n, o, n, o twice, k 3 to., o twice, n, o, n, k 1, n, o, k 3 to., o twice, k 1, o twice, p 2 to.

One Hundred and Forty-ninth row.—O twice, p 3 to., k 1, p 1, k 8, p 1, k 2, p 1, k 7, leave 34.

One Hundred and Fiftieth row.—Sl 1, k 2, n, o, n, o twice, k 5, o twice, n, o, sl 1, n, b, o, k 3 to., o twice, k 1, o twice, p 2 to.

One Hundred and Fifty-first row.—O twice, p 3 to., k 1, p 1, k 6, p 1, k 6, p 1, k 5, leave 35.

One Hundred and Fifty-second row.—Sl 1, k 2, o, k 3 to., o twice, k 3 to., k 1, k 3 to., o twice, k 4 to., o, k 3 to., o twice, k 1, o twice, p 2 to.

One Hundred and Fifty-third row.—O twice, p 3 to., k 1, p 1, k 4, p 1, k 4, p 1, k 4, leave 36.

One Hundred and Fifty-fourth row.—Sl 1, k 2, o, k 3 to., o twice, k 3 to., o twice, k 3 to., o, k 3 to., o twice, k 1, o twice, p 2 to.

One Hundred and Fifty-fifth row.—O twice, p 3 to., k 1, p 1, k 4, p 1, k 2, p 1, k 4, leave 37.

One Hundred and Fifty-sixth row.—Sl 1, k 2, o, n, k 3, n, o, k 3 to., o twice, k 1, o twice, p 2 to.

One Hundred and Fifty-seventh row.—O twice, p 3 to., k 1, p 1, k 10, leave 38.

One Hundred and Fifty-eighth row.—Sl 1, k 2, o, n, k 1, n, o, k 3 to., o twice, k 1, o twice, p 2 to.

One Hundred and Fifty-ninth row.—O twice, p 3 to., k 1, p 1, k 8, leave 39.

One Hundred and Sixtieth row.—Sl 1, k 2, o, sl 1, n, b, o, k 3 to., o twice, k 1, o twice, p 2 to.

Repeat four times.

KNITTED LEAF MAT.

(For Illustration see Page 78.)

No. 21.—This mat is made of écru linen thread and with four needles. Cast 247 stitches very loosely on three fine steel needles.

First and Second rows.—Plain.

Third to Eighth row.—Purl.

Ninth row.—K 5, n; k 22, n, 9 times; k rest plain.

Tenth and Eleventh rows.—Plain.

Twelfth to Seventeenth row.—Purl.

Eighteenth row.—K 10, n; k 21, n, 9 times; k rest plain.

Nineteenth row.—Plain.

Twentieth row.—K 15, n; k 20, n, 9 times; k rest plain.

Twenty-first to Twenty-sixth row.—Purl.

Twenty-seventh row.—N, k 19, 9 times; n, k rest plain.

Twenty-eighth row.—Plain.

Twenty-ninth row.—K 6; n, k 18, 9 times; n, k rest plain. There must be 197 stitches on needles.

Thirtieth row.—O, k 2, p 1, k 2, o, n ; * o, k 3 to.; o, n 8 times ; * repeat between the stars 10 times.

Thirty-first row.—K 3, p 1, k rest plain.

Thirty-second row.—O, n, k 1, p 1, k 2 ; o, n, 6 times ; o, k 1, o, k3 to. ; o, n, 9 times ; o, k 1, o, k 3 to. ; o, n, 11 times ; o, k 1, o, k 3 to. ; o, n, 13 times ; o, k 1 ; o, n, 13 times ; o, k 3 to., o, k 1 ; o, n, 11 times ; o, k 3 to., o, k 1 ; o, n, 9 times ; o, k 3 to., o, k 1 ; o, n, 5 times ; o, k 3 to.

Thirty-third row.—K 3, p 1, k rest.

Thirty-fourth row.—This and many other rows go only part of the way round. O, n, k 1, p 1, n, o, k 3 to. ; o, n, 3 times ; o, k 3 to., o, k 3 ; o, n, 8 times ; o, k 3 to., o, k 3 ; o, n, 10 times ; o, k 3 to., o, k 3 ; o, n, 12 times ; o, k 3 to., o, k 3, o, k 3 to.; o, n, 12 times ; o, k 3, o, k 3 to. ; o, n, 10 times ; o, k 3, o, k 3 to. ; o, n, 8 times ; o, k 3, o, k 3 to. ; o, n, 3 times ; 8 stitches will be left on third needle ; turn and purl back on wrong side of work. Same must be down with all rows which are knitted only part of the way.

Thirty-fifth row. —Sl 1, p all except last 8 stitches on third needle which were left the last time.

Thirty-sixth row. —Sl 1 ; o, n, 3 times ; o, k 5, o, k 3 to. ; o, n, 7 times ; o, k 5, o, k 3 to. ; o, n, 9 times ; o, k 5, o, k 3 to.; o, n, 11 times ; o, k 5 ; o, n, 11 times ; o, k 3 to., o, k 5 ; o, n, 9 times ; o, k 3 to., o, k 5, o, n, o, k 1. Always take care to have the plain 5 stitches over the 3 plain below, then, in the next row the k 3, p 1, k 3, over the 5 plain stitches below ; always keep the purl stitch over purl stitch.

Thirty-seventh row.—Sl 1, p 122.

Thirty-eighth row.—Sl 1, o, k 3, p 1, k 3 ; o, n, 8 times ; o, k 3 to., o, k 3, p 1, k 3 ; o, n, 10 times ; o, k 3 to., o, k 3, p 1, k 3, o, k 3 to. ; o, n 10 times ; o, k 3, p 1, k 3, o, k 3 to. ; o, n, 8 times ; o, k 3, p 1, k 3, o, k 1.

Thirty-ninth row.—Sl 1, p 4, k 1, p 25, k 1, p 29, k 1, p 29, k 1, p 5.

Fortieth row.—Sl 1, o, k 4, p 1, k 4, o, k 3 to. ; o, n, 9 times ; o, k 4, p 1, k 4 ; o, n, 9 times ; o, k 3 to., o, k 4, p 1, k 4, o, k 1.

Forty-first row.—Sl 1, p 5, k 1, p 29, k 1, p 6.

Forty-second row.—Sl 1, o, k 5, p 1, k 5, o, k 3 to. ; o, n, 7 times.

Forty-third row.—Sl 1, p 20, k 1, p 23.

Forty-fourth row.—N, o, 7 times ; k 3 to., o, k 4, n, p 1, n, k 4, o, k 3 to. ; o, n, 7 times ; o, k 5, p 1, k 5 ; o, n, 7 times ; o, k 3 to.

Forty-fifth row.—Sl 1, p 20, k 1, p 28, k 1, p 20.

Forty-sixth row.—Sl 1 ; o, n, 7 times ; o, k 5, p 1, k 5, k 3 to. ; o, n, 7 times ; o, k 6, p 1, k 6 ; o, n, times ; o, k 1.

Forty-seventh row.—Sl 1, p 21, k 1, p 28, k 1, p 22, k 1, p 22, k 1, p 4.

Forty-eighth row.—Sl 1, o, k 3, p 1, k 3 ; o, n, 6 times ; o, k 3 to., o, k 4, p 1, k 4 ; o, n, 7 times ; o, k 4, n, p 1, n, k 4, o, n, 6 times, o, k 3 to., o, k 5, n, p 1, n, k 5, o, k 3 to. ; o, n, 6 times ; o, k 4, p 1, k 4, o, k 3 to. ; o, n, 6 times ; o, k 3 to., o, k 4, p 1, k 4, o, k 3 to. ; o, n, 7 times ; o, k 5, o, k 3 to. ; o, n, 3 times ; this row goes all around.

Forty-ninth row.—Knit all around, purling the purled stitches.

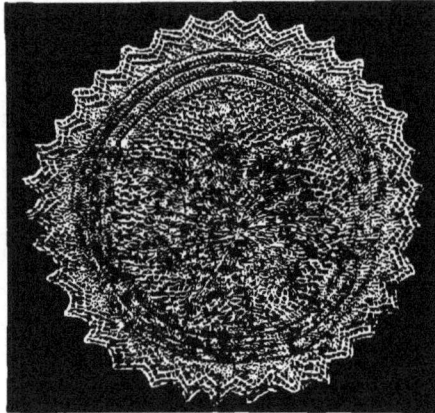

No. 21.—KNITTED LEAF MAT.
(For Description see Page 77.)

Fiftieth row.—O, n, p 1, k 1, o, k 3 to., o, k 3 to., o, k 1, o, k 3 to., o, k 4, p 1, k 4, o, k 3 to., o, n, o, k 1, o, k 3 to., o, n, o, k 1, o, k 3 to., o, k 5, p 1, k 5, o, k 3 to., o, k 1, o, k 3 to., o, k 4, o, k 1, o, k 3 to., o, k 6, p 1, k 6, o k 3 to., o, k 1, o, k 3 to., o, n, o, k 1, o, k 3 to., o, k 6, p 1, k 6, o, k 3 to., o, k 1, o, k 3 to., o, n, o, k 5, n, p 1, n, k 5, o, k 3 to., o, k 1, o k 3 to., o, n, o, k 1, o, k 3 to., o, k 6, p 1, k 6, o, k 3 to., o, k 4 to., o, k 1, o, k 3 to., o, k 5, p 1, k 5, o, k 3 to., o k 1, o, k 3 to., o, k 4 to., o k 1, o, k 3 to., o, k 3 to., o, k 1, o, n, o, k 3 to., o, k 1, o, n, o, k 1.

Fifty-first row.— K 2, p 1, k 14, p 1, k 22, p 1, k 24, p 1, k 25, p 1, k 25, p 1, k 24, p 1, k 21, p 1, k 11.

Fifty-second row.—O, n, p 1, k 1, o, k 4 to., o, k 3, o, n, k 2, n, p 1, n, k 2, n, o, k 3, o, k 3 to., o, k 3, o, n, k 3, n, p 1, n, k 3, n, o, k 3, o, k 3 to. ; o, k 3, o, n, k 6, p 1, k 6, n, o, k 3, o, k 3 to., 3 times ; o, k 3, o, n, k 3, n, p 1, n, k 3, n, o, k 3, o k 3 to., o, k 3, o, n, k 3, p 1, k 3, n, o, k 3, o, k 3 to.

Fifty-third row.—K 2, p 1, k 12, p 1, k 20, p 1, k 23, p 1, k 25, p 1, k 25, p 1, k 23, p 1, k 20, p 1, k 10.

Fifty-fourth row.—O, n, p 1, k 1, o, n, o, k 7, n, p 1, n, k 7, n, o, k 7, n, p 1, n, k 8, o, n, k 9, n, p 1, n, k 10, o, n, k 11, p 1, k 11, n, o, k 10, n, p 1, n, k 9, n, o, k 8, n, p 1, n, k 7, n, o, k 7, n, p 1, n, k 7, n, o, k 1.

Fifty-fifth row.—K 2, p 1, k 12, p 1, k 18, p 1, k 21, p 1, k 24, p 1, k 24, p 1, k 20, p 1, k 18, p 1, k 10.

Fifty-sixth row.—O, n, p 1, k 1, o, k 3 to., k 8, p 1, k 8, o, k 1, o, k 9, p 1, k 9, o, k 1, o, k 9, n, p

1, n, k 9, o, k 1, o, k 10, n, p 1, n, k 10, o, k 1, o, k 9, n, p 1, n, k 9, o, k 1, o, k 9, p 1, k 9, o, k 1, o, k 8, p 1, k 8, o, n.

Fifty-seventh row.—K 2, p 1, k 11, p 1, k 20, p 1, k 22, p 1, k 24, p 1, k 24, p 1, k 20, p 1, k 20, p 1, k 10.

Fifty-eighth row.—O, n, p 1, k 1, o, k 1, o. k 1, n, k 4, n, p 1, n, k 3, n, k 1, o, k 3, o k 1, n, k 4, n, p 1, n, k 4, n, k 1, o, k 3, o, k 1, n, k 5, n, p 1, n, k 5, n, k 1, o, k 3, o, k 1, n, k 6, n, p 1, n, k 6, n, k 1, o, k 3, o, k 1, n, k 5, n, p 1, n, k 5, n, k 1, o. k 3, o, k 1, n, k 4, n, p 1, n, k 4, n, k 1, o, k 3, o, k 1, n, k 3, n, p 1, n, k 3, n, k 1, o, k 2. Knit the first stitch on the next needle onto this needle.

Fifty-ninth row.—K 1, p 1, k 11, p 1, k 18, p 1, k 20, p 1, k 22, p 1, k 22, p 1, k 20, p 1, k 20, p 1, k 18, p 1, k 11.

Sixtieth row.—K 1, p 1, k 1, o, k 3, o k 7, p 1, k 6, o k 1, k 3 to., k 1 o, k 7, p 1, k 7, o, k 1, k 3 to., k 1, o, k 8, p 1, k 8, o k 1, k 3 to., k 1, o, k 9, p 1, k 9, o, k 1, n.

Seventieth row.—Sl 1, p 11, k 1, p 10, p 2 to.

Seventy-first row.—Sl 1, k 1, o k 7, n, p 1, n, k 7, o, k 1, k 3 to., k 1, o, k 8, p 1, k 8, o, k 1, n.

Seventy-second row.—Sl 1, p 10, k 1, p 21, k 1, p 21, k 1, p 10, p 2 to.

Seventy-third row.—Sl 1, k 2, o, k 6, n, p 1, n, k 6, o, k 1, k 3 to., k 1, o, k 8, p 1, k 8, o, k 1, k 3 to., k 1, o, k 6, n, p 1, n, k 6, o, k 1, k 3 to., k 1, o, k 7, p 1, k 7, o, k 1, n.

Seventy-fourth row.—Sl 1, p 9, k 1, p 19, k 1, p 20, k 1, p 20, k 1, p 19, k 1, p 9, p 2 to.

Seventy-fifth row.—Sl 1, k 2, o, k 5, n, p 1, n, k 5, o, k 1, k 3 to., k 1, o, k 7, p 1, k 7, o, k 1, k 3 to., k 1 o, k 6, n, p 1, n, k 6, o, k 1, k 3 to., k 1, o, k 7, p 1, k 7, o, k 1, k 3 to., k 1, o, k 7, p 1, k 7, o, k 1, k 3 to., k 1, o, k 6, p 1, k 6, o, k 1, n.

Seventy-sixth row.—Sl 1, p 8, k 1, p 18, k 1, p 19, k 1, p 19, k 1, p 19, k 1, p 18, k 1, p 17, k 1, p 8, p 2 to.

Seventy-seventh row.—Sl 1, k 1, o, k 5, n, p 1, n, k 4, o, k 1, k 3 to., k 1, o, k 6, p 1, k 6, o, k 1, k 3 to., k 1, o, k 5, n, p 1, n, k 5, o, k 1, k 3 to., k 1, o, k 7, p 1, k 7, o, k 1, k 3 to., k 1; o, k 5, n, p 1, n, k 5, o, k 1, k 3 to., k 1, twice ; o, k 4, n, p 1, n, k 4, o, n.

Seventy-eighth row.—Sl 1, p 6, k 1, p 18, k 1, p 17, k 1, p 18, k 1, p 18, k 1, p 17, k 1, p 16, k 1, p 8, p 2 to.

Seventy-ninth row.—Sl 1, k 2, o, k 4, n, p 1, k 5, o, k 1, k 3 to., k 1, o, k 6, p 1, k 6, o, k 1, k 3 to., k 1, o, k 6, p 1, k 6, o, k 1, k 3 to., k 1, o, k 5, n, p 1, n, k 5, o k 1, k 3 to., k 1, o, k 6, p 1, k 6, o, k 1, k 3 to., k 1, o, k 6, p 1, k 6, o, k 1, k 3 to., k 1, o, k 6, p 1, k 6, o, k 1, n, k 5, o k 1, k 3 to., k 1, o, k 5, p, k 1, x.

Eightieth row.—K 1, p 1, k 11, p 1, k 16 ; p 1, k 17, 4 times ; p 1, k 16, p 1, k 9, o.

Eighty-first row.—K 1, p 1, k 1, o, k 1, k 3 to.' k 1, o, k 3, n, p 1, n, k 3, o, k 1, k 3 to., k 1, o, k 4, n, p 1, n, k 4, o, k 1, k 3 to., k 1, o, k 6, p 1, k 6, o, k 1, k 3 to., k 1, o, k 6, p 1, k 6, o, k 1, k 3 to., k 1, o, k 6, p 1, k 6, o, k 1, n.

Eighty-second row.—Sl 1, p 8, k 1, p 17, k 1, p 17, k 1, p 8, p 2 to.

Eighty-third row.—Sl 1, k 2, o, k 4, n, p 1, n, k 4, o, k 1, k 3 to., k 1, o, k 4, n, p 1, n, k 4, o, k 1, k 3 to., k 1, o, k 4, n, p 1, n, k 4, 0, k 1, k 3 to., k 1, o, k 4, n, p 1, n, k 4, o, k 1, n.

Eighty-fourth row.—Sl 1, p 7, k 1 ; p 15, k 1, 4 times ; k 1, p 14, k 1, p 6.

Eighty-fifth row.—Sl 1, k 1, o, k 4, p 1, k 4 ; o, k 1, k 3 to., k 1, o, k 5, p 1, k 5, 5 times ; o, k 1, k 3 to., k 1, o, k 3, n, p 1, n, k 3, o, k 1, n.

Eighty-sixth row.—Sl 1, p 6, k 1, p 14, k 1 ; p 15, k 1, 4 times ; p 6, p 2 to.

Eighty-seventh row.—Sl 1, k 1 ; o, k 3, n, p 1, n, k 3, o, k 1, k 3 to., k 1, 5 times ; o, k 4, p 1, k 4, o, k 2.

Eighty-eighth row.—Sl 1, p 6 ; k 1, p 13, 6 times ; k 1, p 5, p 2 to.

Eighty-ninth row.—Sl 1; o, k 3, n, p 1, n, k 3, o, k 3 to., 6 times ; o, k 3, n, p 1, n, k 3, o, k 4 to., o, k 1.

Ninetieth row.—K 1, p 1, k 2, k 3 to., k 5; p 1, k 11; 6 times; p 1, k 8.

Ninety-first row.—K 1, p 1, k 3; o, k 3, n, p 1, n, k 2, n, 7 times; o, k 2.

Ninety-second row.—K 1, p 1, k 8, p 1; k 9, p 1, 6 times; k 7.

Ninety-third and Ninety-fourth rows.—Like 92nd row.

Ninety-fifth row.—K 1, p 1, k 6, n; p 1, n, k 5, n, 6 times; p 1, n, k 5. Knit first stitch from next needle onto this needle.

Ninety-sixth row.—P 1, k 7, 8 times.

Ninety-seventh row.—Like 96th row.

Ninety-eighth row.—P 1, n, k 3, n, 8 times.

Ninety-ninth row—P 1, k 5, 8 times.

One Hundredth and One Hundred and First rows.—Like 99th row.

One Hundred and Second row.—P 1, n, k 1, n, 8 times.

One Hundred and Third row.—P 1, k 3, 8 times

One Hundred and Fourth and One Hundred and Fifth rows.—Like 103rd row.

One Hundred and Sixth row.—P 1, k 3 to., 8 times.

One Hundred and Seventh row.—P 1, k 1, 8 times.

One Hundred and Eighth row.—P 2 to., n, 4 times.

One Hundred and Ninth row.—N, 4 times.

One Hundred and Tenth row.—K 1 and slip the other 3 stitches over on this one.

EDGING FOR THIS MAT.

Cast on 7 stitches.

First row.—Sl 1, o, n, o, n, o, n.

Second row.—Make 1 ; by putting the needle *under* the thread to knit the first stitch ; k 1, p 4, k 2.

Third row.—Sl 1, k 1, o, n, o, n, o, n.

Fourth row.—Make 1, k 1, p 4, k 3.

Fifth row.—Sl 1, k 2, o, n, o, n, o, n.

Sixth row.—Make 1, k 1, p 4, k 4.

Seventh row.—Sl 1, k 3, o, n, o, n, o, n.

Eighth row.—Make 1, k 1, p 4, k 3 ; turn.

Ninth row.—Sl 1, k 2, o, n, o, n, o, n.

Tenth row.—K 2, p 4, k 5.

Eleventh row.—Sl 1, k 2, n, o, n, o, n, o, n.

Twelfth row.—K 2, p 4, k 4.

Thirteenth row.—N, o, n, o, n, o, n.

Fourteenth row.—K 2, p 4, k 2.

Fifteenth row.—N, o, n, o, n, o, n.

Sixteenth row.—K 2, p 4, k 1.

Repeat from first row 34 times.

USEFUL AND ORNAMENTAL ARTICLES.

KNITTED SCRAP BAG

No. 1.—Cast on 8 stitches, using 3 needles; join and knit around once plain.

First row.—O, k 1; repeat 7 times more. Knit alternate rows plain.

Third row.—O, k 2; repeat 7 times more.

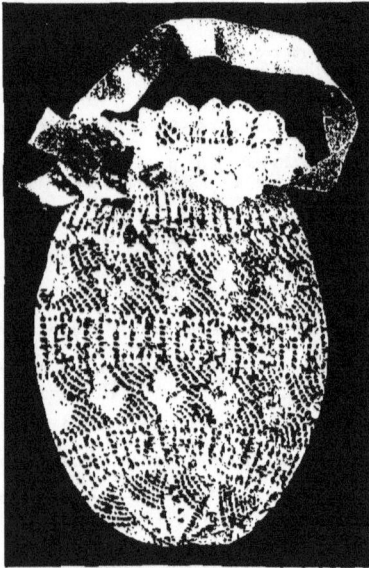

NO. 1.—KNITTED SCRAP BAG

Fifth row.—O, k 3; repeat 7 times more.
Seventh row.—O, k 4; repeat 7 times more
Ninth row.—O, k 5; repeat 7 times more
Eleventh row—O, k 6; repeat 7 times more.
Thirteenth row.—O, k 7; repeat 7 times more.
Fifteenth row—O, k 8; repeat 7 times more
Seventeenth row.—O, k 9; repeat 7 times more.
Nineteenth row.—O, k 10; repeat 7 times more.
Twenty-first row.—O, k 1, o, n, k 8; repeat 7 times more
Twenty-third row.—O, k 1; o and n twice; k 7; repeat 7 times more
Twenty-fifth row.—O, k 1; o and n 3 times; k 6; repeat 7 times more
Twenty-seventh row.—O, k 1; o and n 4 times; k 5; repeat 7 times more.

Twenty-ninth row.—O, k 1; o and n 5 times; k 4; repeat 7 times more.
Thirty-first row.—O, k 1; o and n 6 times; k 3; repeat 7 times more.
Thirty-third row.—O, k 1; o and n 7 times; k 2; repeat 7 times more.
Thirty-fifth row.—O, k 1; o and n 8 times; k 1; repeat 7 times more.
Thirty-seventh row.—O, k 1; o and n 9 times; repeat 7 times more
Thirty-eighth, Thirty-ninth, Fortieth and Forty-first rows.—Plain.
Forty-second row—O and n 7 times, k 2; repeat 9 times more.
Forty-third and Forty-fourth rows.—Plain.
Forty-fifth row.—O, n, k 10, o, n, k 2; repeat 9 times more.
Forty-sixth and Forty-seventh rows—Plain.
Forty-eighth row.—O, n, k 2; o and n 3 times; k 2, o, n, k 2; repeat 9 times more.
Forty-ninth and Fiftieth rows—Plain
Fifty-first row—O, n, k 2, o, n, k 2, o, n, k 2, o, n, k 2; repeat 9 times more
Fifty-second and Fifty-third rows.—Plain.
Fifty-fourth row—O, n, k 2, o, n, k 2; o and n 3 times; k 2; repeat 9 times more
Fifty-fifth and Fifty-sixth rows.—Plain.
Fifty-seventh row.—O, n, k 2, o, n, k 10; repeat 9 times more.
Fifty-eighth and Fifty-ninth rows—Plain
Sixtieth row.—O, n, k 2; * o and n 7 times, k 2 *; repeat from star to star 8 times, then, o and n 6 times more
Sixty-first, Sixty-second, Sixty-third and Sixty-fourth rows.—Plain.
Sixty-fifth row—O and n all the way around. Alternate rows plain now
Sixty-seventh row.—K 1; * o and n 7 times, k 2;

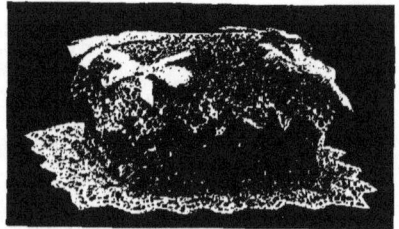

NO. 2.—HAIR-PIN RECEIVER.

* repeat from star to star 8 times, then, o and n 7 times, k 1.
Sixty-ninth row—K 2; * o and n 6 times, k 4,

*; repeat from star to star 8 times, then, o and n 6 times, k 2.

Seventy-first row.—K 3; * o and n 5 times, k 6 *; repeat from star to star 8 times, then, o and n 5 times, k 3.

Seventy-third row.—K 4; * o and n 4 times, k 8 *; repeat from star to star 8 times, then, o and n 4 times, k 4.

Seventy-fifth row.—K 5; * o and n 3 times, k 10 *; repeat from star to star 8 times, then, o and n 3 times, k 5.

Seventy-seventh row.—K 6; * o and n twice, k 12, *; repeat from star to star 8 times, then, o and n twice, k 6.

Seventy-ninth row.—K 7; * o and n once, k 14, *; repeat from star to star 8 times, then, o and n, k 7.

Eighty-first row.—K 6; * o and n twice, k 12 *; repeat from star to star 8 times, then, o and n twice, k 6.

Eighty-third row.—K 5; * o and n 3 times, k 10 *; repeat from star to star 8 times, then, o and n 3 times, k 5.

Eighty-fifth row.—K 4; * o and n 4 times, k 8 *; repeat from star to star 8 times, then, o and n 4 times, k 4.

Eighty-seventh row.—K 3; * o and n 5 times, k 6 *; repeat from star to star 8 times, o and n 5 times, k 3.

Eighty-ninth row.—K 2; * o and n 6 times, k 4 *; repeat from star to star 8 times, o and n 6 times, k 2.

Ninety-first row.—K 1; * o and n 7 times, k 2 *; repeat from star to star 8 times, o and n 7 times, k 1.

Ninety-third row.—O, n all the way across.

Repeat from the thirty-eighth row all over again, then k 4 rows plain; then repeat from the thirty-eighth to the sixty-first row over again; then 8 rows plain; then, o 4 times, n 4 times all the way around. K next row plain, only on every loop k 1, p 1, k 1, p 1; then k 8 rows plain and bind off; then knit enough of the lace to go around the top; run a narrow ribbon through the large holes at the top of the bag to suspend it by and line it with some pretty color of silk.

SHELL LACE FOR TOP OF BAG.

Cast on 13 stitches and knit across plain.

First row.—K 2, o twice, n, k 7, o twice, p 2 to.

Second row.—Thread around needle, p 2 to., k 9, p 1, k 2.

Third row.—K 12, o twice, p 2 to.

Fourth row.—Thread around needle, p 2 to., k 12.

Fifth row.—K 2, o twice, n, o, twice, n, k 6, o twice, p 2 to.

Sixth row.—Thread around needle, p 2 to., k 8, p 1, k 2, p 1, k 2.

Seventh row.—K 14, o twice, p 2 to.

Eighth row.—Thread around needle, p 2 to., k 14.

Ninth row.—K 2, o twice, n, o twice, n, o twice, n, k 6, o twice, p 2 to.

Tenth row.—Thread around needle, p 2 to., k 8, p 1, k 2, p 1, k 2, p 1, k 2.

Eleventh row.—K 17, o twice, p 2 to.

Twelfth row.—Thread around needle, p 2 to., k 17.

Thirteenth row.—K 2, o twice, n, o twice, n, o twice, n, o twice, n, k 7, o twice, p 2 to.

Fourteenth row.—Thread around needle, p 2 to., k 9, p 1, k 2, p 1, k 2, p 1, k 2.

Fifteenth row.—K 21, o twice, p 2 to.

Sixteenth row.—Thread around needle, p 2 to., k 9; bind off all on the right hand needle, k 12. Repeat from beginning.

HAIR-PIN RECEIVER.
(For Illustration see Page 60.)

No. 2.—The foundation of this receiver is a cardboard box about four inches long, two and three-quarters wide, and two-inches high. It is covered at the sides and ends with pale-blue satin ribbon, and the box is then filled with curled hair and overlaid at the top with a piece of scrim. Insertion and edging made of knitting silk are then arranged over the sides and top and about the bottom according to the illustration, and at each corner is sewed a full bow made of picot-edged baby ribbon of a color to match that which covers the box.

Écru cotton or linen thread proves very effective when made into the lace and insertion as in this instance.

To make the Insertion.—Cast on 18 stitches.

First row.— Sl 1, k 1, o twice, p 2 to., k 4; o and n three times; o twice; p 2 to., k 2.

Second, Fourth, Sixth and Eighth rows—Sl 1, k 1, o twice, p 2 to., k 10, o twice, p 2 to., k 2.

Third row.—Sl 1, k 1, o twice, p 2 to., k 3; o and n three times; k 1, o twice, p 2 to., k 2.

Fifth row.—Sl 1, k 1, o twice, p 2 to., k 2; o and n three times; k 2, o twice, p 2 to., k 2.

Seventh row.—Sl 1, k 1, o twice, p 2 to., k 1; o and n 3 times; k 3, o twice, p 2 to., k 2. Repeat from 1st row.

For the Edging.—Cast on 9 stitches.

No. 3.—KNITTED COVER FOR WHISK-BROOM HOLDER.
(For Description see Page 82.)

First row.—O. n crossed, p 1, k 2, o, n, o, k 2.
Second row.—Sl 1, k 6, o twice, p 2 to., k 1.
Third row.—O, n crossed, p 1, k 3, o, n, o, k 2.
Fourth row.—Sl 1, k 7, o twice, p 2 to., k 1.
Fifth row.—O, n crossed, p 1, k 4, o, n, o, k 2.
Sixth row.—Sl 1, k 8, o twice. p 2 to., k 1.
Seventh row.—O, n crossed, p 1, k 5, o, n, o, k 2.
Eighth row.—Sl 1, k 9, o twice, p 2 to., k 1.
Ninth and Eleventh rows.—O, n crossed, p 1, k 10.
Tenth row.—Sl 1, k 1; o and n twice; k 4, o twice, p 2 to., k 1.
Twelfth row.—Sl 1, n; o and n twice; k 3, o twice, p 2 to., k 1.
Thirteenth row.—O, n crossed, p 1, k 9.
Fourteenth row.—Sl 1, n; o and n twice; k 2, o twice, p 2 to., k 1.
Fifteenth row.—O, n crossed, p 1, k 8.
Sixteenth row.—Sl 1, n; o and n twice; k 1, o twice, p 2 to., k 1.
Seventeenth row.—O, n crossed, p 1, k 7.
Eighteenth row.—Sl 1, n, k 4, o twice, p 2 to., k 1.
Repeat.

KNITTED COVER FOR WHISK-BROOM HOLDER.

(For Illustration see Page 81.)

No. 3.—Use fine crochet cotton or coarse thread. Cast on 77 stitches.
First row..—K 3, o 2, ("o 2" means, in every instance, "thread over twice") p 2 to., k 67, o 2, p 2 to., k 1, o, k 2.
Second row.—K 4, o 2, p 2 to., k 67, o 2, p 2 to., k 1, o, k 2.
Third row.—K 4, o 2, p 2 to., k 32, n, o, k 33, o 2, p 2 to., k 2, o, k 2.
Fourth row.—K 5, o 2, p 2 to., k 67, o 2, p 2 to., k 2, o, k 2.
Fifth row.—K 5, o 2, p 2 to., n, k 29, n, o, k 1, o, n, k 29, n, o 2, p 2 to., k 1, o 2, n, o, k 2.
Sixth row.—K 5, p 1, k 1, o 2, p 2 to., k 65, o 2, p 2 to., k 1, o 2, n, o, k 2.
Seventh row.—K 5, p 1, k 1, o 2, p 2 to., n, k 12, n, o 2, n, k 11, n, o, k 3, o, n, k 11, n, o 2, n, k 12, n, o 2, p 2 to., k 7.
Eighth row.—Bind off 4, k 2, o 2, p 2 to., k 15, p 1, k 32, p 1, k 14, o 2, p 2 to., k 7.
Ninth row.—Bind off 4, k 2, o 2, p 2 to., n, k 9, n, o 2, n, n, o 2, n, k 8, n, o, k 1, n, o, k 2, o, n, k 8, n, o 2, n, n, o 2, n, k 9, n, o 2, p 2 to., k 1, o, k 2.
Tenth row.—K 4, o 2, p 2 to., k 12, p 1, k 3, p 1, k 28, p 1, k 3, p 1, k 21, o 2, p 2 to., k 1, o, k 2.
Eleventh row.—K 4, o 2, p 2 to., n, k 10, n, o 2, n, k 9, n, o, k 1, n, o, k 1, o, n, k 1, o, n, k 9, n, o 2, n, k 10, n, o 2, p 2 to., k 2, o, k 2.
Twelfth row.—K 5, o 2, p 2 to., k 13, p 1, k 32, p 1, k 12, o 2, p 2 to., k 2, o, k 2.
Thirteenth row.—K 5, o 2, p 2 to., n, k 5, o, n, n, o 2, n, n, o 2, n, n, o, k 4, n, o, k 1, n, o, k 3, o, n, k 1, o, n, k 4, o, n, n, o 2, n, n, o 2, n, n, o, k 5, n, o 2, p 2 to., k 1, o 2, n, o, k 2.
Fourteenth row.—K 5, p 1, k 1, o 2, p 2 to., k 10, p 1, k 3, p 1, k 28, p 1, k 3, p 1, k 9, o 2, p 2 to., k 1, o 2, n, o, k 2.
Fifteenth row.—K 5, p 1, k 1, o 2, p 2 to., k 7, o,

n, k 1, n, o 2, n, k 1, n, o, k 4, n, o, k 1, n, o, k 1, n, o, k 2, o, n, k 1, n, o, k 1, n, o 2, n, k 1, n, o, k 7, o 2, p 2 to., k 7.
Sixteenth row.—Bind off 4, k 2, o 2, p 2 to., k 12, p 1, k 32, p 1, k 11, o 2, p 2 to., k 7.
Seventeenth row.—Bind off 4, k 2, o 2, p 2 to., n, k 6, o, n, k 4, n, o, k 4, n, o, k 1, n, o, k 1, n, o, k 1, o, n, k 1, o, n, k 1, o, n, k 4, o, n, k 4, n, o, k 6, n, o 2, p 2 to., k 2, o, k 2.
Eighteenth row.—K 4, o 2, p 2 to., k 55, o 2, p 2 to., k 1, o, k 2.
Nineteenth row.—K 4, o 2, p 2 to., n, k 6, o, n, k 2, n, o, k 4, n, o, k 1, n, o, k 1, n, o, k 3, o, n, k 1, o, n, k 1, o, n, k 4, o, n, k 2, n, o, k 6, n, o 2, p 2 to., k 2, o, k 2.
Twentieth row.—K 5, o 2, p 2 to., k 53, o 2, p 2 to., k 2, o, k 2.
Twenty-first row.—K 5, o 2, p 2 to., n, k 6, o, n, n, o, k 4, n, o, k 1, n, o, k 1, n, o, k 1, o, k 2, o, n, k 1, o, n, k 1, o, n, k 4, n, o, n, n, o, k 6, n, o 2, p 2 to., k 1, o 2, n, o, k 2.
Twenty-second row.—K 5, p 1, k 1, o 2, p 2 to., k 51, o 2, p 2 to., k 1, o 2, n, o, k 2.
Twenty-third row.—K 5, p 1, k 1, o 2, p 2 to., k 14, n, o, k 1, n, o, k 1, n, o, k 1, n, o, k 1, o, n, k 1, o, n, k 1, o, n, k 14, o 2, p 2 to., k 7.
Twenty-fourth row.—Bind off 4, k 2, o 2, p 2 to., k 51, o 2, p 2 to., k 7.
Twenty-fifth row.—Bind off 4, k 2, o 2, p 2 to., n, k 11, n, o, k 1, n, o, k 1, n, o, k 1, n, o, k 1, n, o, k 3, o, n, k 1, o, n, k 1, o, n, k 1, o, n, k 11, n, o 2, p 2 to., k 1, o, k 2.
Twenty-sixth row.—K 4, o 2, p 2 to., k 49, o 2, p 2 to., k 1, o, k 2.
Twenty-seventh row.—K 4, o 2, p 2 to., n, k 9, n, o, k 1, n, o, k 1, n, o, k 1, n, o, k 5, o, n, k 1, o, n, k 1, o, n, k 1, o, n, k 9, n, o 2, p 2 to., k 2, o, k 2.
Twenty-eighth row.—K 5, o 2, p 2 to., k 47, o 2, p 2 to., k 2, o, k 2.
Twenty-ninth row.—K 5, o 2, p 2 to., k 9, n, o, k 1, n, o, k 1, n, o, k 1, n, o, k 2, n, o 2, k 3, o, n, k 1, o, n, k 1, o, n, k 9, o 2, p 2 to., k 1, o 2, n, o, k 2.
Thirtieth row.—K 5, p 1, k 1, o 2, p 2 to., k 24, p 1, k 23, o 2, p 2 to., k 1, o 2, n, o, k 2.
Thirty-first row.—K 5, p 1, k 1, o 2, p 2 to., k 8, n, o, k 1, n, o, k 1, n, o, k 1, n, o, k 1, n, o 2, n, n, o 2, n, k 1, o, n, k 1, o, n, k 1, o, n, k 8, o 2, p 2 to., k 7.
Thirty-second row.—Bind off 4, k 2, o 2, p 2 to., k 22, p 1, k 3, p 1, k 21, o 2, p 2 to., k 7.
Thirty-third row.—Bind off 4, k 2, o 2, p 2 to., n, k 5, n, o, k 1, n, o, k 1, n, o, k 1, n, o, k 4, n, o 2, n, k 1, o, n, k 1, o, n, k 1, o, n, k 5, n, o 2, p 2 to., k 1, o, k 2.
Thirty-fourth row.—K 4, o 2, p 2 to., k 23, p 1, k 22, o 2, p 2 to., k 1, o, k 2.
Thirty-fifth row.—K 4, o 2, p 2 to., k 8, o, n, k 1, o, n, k 1, o, n, k 1, o, n, k 2, o 2, n, n, o 2, n, k 2, o, n, k 1, o, n, k 1, o, n, k 1, o, k 8, o 2, p 2 to., k 2, o, k 2.
Thirty-sixth row.—K 5, o 2, p 2 to., k 22, p 1, k 3, p 1, k 21, o 2, p 2 to., k 2, o, k 2.
Thirty-seventh row.—K 5, o 2, p 2 to., n, k 7, o,

n, k 1, o, n, k 1, o, n, k 1, o, n, k 2, n, o 2, n, k 2, n, o, k 1, n, o, k 1, n, o, k 1, n, o, k 7, n, o 2, p 2 to., k 1, o 2, n, o, k 2.

Thirty-eighth row.—K 5, p 1, k 1, o 2, p 2 to., k 13, p 1, k 22, o 2, p 2 to., k 1, o 2, n, o, k 2.

Thirty-ninth row.—K 5, p 1, k 1, o 2, p 2 to., k 9, o, n, k 1, o, n, k 1, o, n, k 1, o, n, k 6, n, o, k 1, n, o, k 1, n, o, k 1, n, o, k 9, o 2, p 2 to., k 7.

Fortieth row.—Bind off 4, k 2, o 2, p 2 to., k 46, o 2, p 2 to., k 7.

Forty-first row.—Bind off 4, k 2, o 2, p 2 to., n, k 8, o, n, k 1, o, n, k 1, o, n, k 1, o, n, k 4, n, o, k 1, n, o, k 1, n, o, k 1, n, o, k 8, n, o 2, p 2 to., k 1, o, k 2.

Forty-second row.—K 4, o 2, p 2 to., k 44, o 2, p 2 to., k 1, o, k 9.

Forty-third row.—K 4, o 2, p 2 to., k 10, o, n, k 1, o, n, k 1, o, n, k 1, o, n, k 2, n, o, k 1, n, o, k 1, n, o, k 1, n, o, k 10, o 2, p 2 to., k 2, o, k 2.

Forty-fourth row.—K 5, o 2, p 2 to., k 44, o 2, p 2 to., k 2, o, k 2.

Forty-fifth row.—K 5, o 2, p 2 to., k 11, o, n, k 1, o, n, k 1, o, n, k 1, o, n, n, bind narrowed stitch over, o, k 1, n, o, k 1, n, o, k 1, n, o, k 11, o 2, p 2 to., k 1, o 2, n, o, k 2.

Forty-sixth row.—K 5, p 1, k 1, o 2, p 2 to., k 43, o 2, p 2 to., k 1, o 2, n, o, k 2.

Forty-seventh row.—K 5, p 1, k 1, o 2, p 2 to., n, k 10, o, n, k 1, o, n, k 1, o, n, k 3, n, o, k 1, n, o, k 1, n, o, k 10, n, o 2, p 2 to., k 7.

Forty-eighth row.—Bind off 4, k 2, o 2, p 2 to., k 41, o 2, p 2 to., k 7.

Forty-ninth row.—Bind off 4, k 2, o 2, p 2 to., k 12, o, n, k 1, o, n, k 1, o, n, k 1, n, o, k 1, n, o, k 1, n, o, k 12, o 2, p 2 to., k 1, o, k 2.

Fiftieth row.—K 4, o 2, p 2 to., k 41, o 2, p 2 to., k 1, o, k 2.

Fifty-first row.—K 4, o 2, p 2 to., k 9, o, n, k 2, o, n, k 1, o, n, k 1, o, k 3 to., o, k 1, n, o, k 1, n, o, k 2, n, o, k 9, o 2, p 2 to., k 2, o, k 2.

Fifty-second row.—K 5, o 2, p 2 to., k 41, o 2, p 2 to., k 2, o, k 2.

Fifty-third row.—K 5, o 2, p 2 to., n, k 8, o, n, k 2, o, n, k 1, o, n, k 3, n, o, k 1, n, o, k 2, n, o, k 8, n, o 2, p 2 to., k 1, o 2, n, o, k 2.

Fifty-fourth row.—K 5, p 1, k 1, o 2, p 2 to., k 39, o 2, p 2 to., k 1, o 2, n, o, k 2.

Fifty-fifth row.—K 5, p 1, k 1, o 2, p 2 to., k 10, o, n, k 2, o, n, k 1, o, n, k 1, n, o, k 1, n, o, k 2, n, o, k 10, o 2, p 2 to., k 7.

Fifty-sixth row.—Bind off 4, k 2, o 2, p 2 to., k 39, o 2, p 2 to., k 7.

Fifty-seventh row.—Bind off 4, k 2, o 2, p 2 to., k 5, n, o 2, n, k 2, o, n, k 2, o, n, k 1, o, k 3 to., o, k 1, n, o, k 2, n, o, k 2, n, o 2, n, k 5, o 2, p 2 to., k 1, o, k 2.

Fifty-eighth row.—K 4, o 2, p 2 to., k 7, p 1, k 24, p 1, k 6, o 2, p 2 to., k 1, o, k 2.

Fifty-ninth row.—K 4, o 2, p 2 to., k 3, n, o 2, n, n, o 2, n, k 1, o. n, k 2, o, n, k 3, n, o, k 2, n, o, k 1, n, o 2, n, n, o 2, n, k 3, o 2, p 2 to., k 2, o, k 2.

Sixtieth row.—K 5, o 2, p 2 to., k 5, p 1, k 3, p 1, k 20, p 1, k 3, p 1, k 4, o 2, p 2 to., k 2, o, k 2.

Sixty-first row.—K 5, o 2, p 2 to., k 5, n, o 2, n,

k 4, o, n, k 2, o, n, k 1, n, o, k 2, n, o, k 4, n, o 2, n, k 5, o 2, p 2 to., k 1, o 2, n, o, k 2.

Sixty-second row.—K 5, p 1, k 1, o 2, p 2 to., k 7, p 1, k 24, p 1, k 6, o 2, p 2 to., k 1, o 2, n, o, k 2.

Sixty-third row.—K 5, p 1, k 1, o 2, p 2 to., n, k 1, n, o 2, n, n, o 2, n, n, o, k 2, n, o, n, k 1, n, o, n, k 2, o, n, o 2, n, n, o 2, n, k 1, n, o 2, p 2 to., k 7.

Sixty-fourth row.—Bind off 4, k 2, o 2, p 2 to., k 4, p 1, k 3, p 1, k 18, p 1, k 3, p 1, k 2, o 2, p 2 to., k 7.

Sixty-fifth row.—Bind off 4, k 2, o 2, p 2 to., k 4, n, o 2, n, k 1, n, o, k 2, n, o, k 1, n, o, k 2, o, n, k 2, o, n, k 1, n, o 2, n, k 4, o 2, p 2 to., k 2, o, n, k 2.

Sixty-sixth row.—K 4, o 2, p 2 to., k 6, p 1, k 22, p 1, k 5, o 2, p 2 to., k 1, o, k 2.

Sixty-seventh row.—K 4, o 2, p 2 to., n, k 6, n, o, n, k 2, o, k 1, n, o, k 1, o, n, k 1, o, n, k 2, o, n, k 6, n, o 2, p 2 to., k 2, o, k 2.

Sixty-eighth row.—K 5, o 2, p 2 to., k 33, o 2, p 2 to., k 2, o, k 2.

Sixty-ninth row.—K 5, o 2, p 2 to., k 6, n, o, k 2, n, o, k 1, n, o, k 3, o, n, k 1, o, n, k 2, o, n, k 6, o 2, p 2 to., k 1, o 2, n, o, k 2.

Seventieth row.—K 5, p 1, k 1, o 2, p 2 to., k 33, o 2, p 2 to., k 1, o 2, n, o, k 2.

Seventy-first row.—K 5, p 1, k 1, o 2, p 2 to., n, k 3, n, o, k 2, n, o, k 1, n, o, k 5, o, n, k 1, o, n, k 2, o, n, k 3, n, o 2, p 2 to., k 7.

Seventy-second row.—Bind off 4, k 2, o 2, p 2 to., k 31, o 2, p 2 to., k 7.

Seventy-third row.—Bind off 4, k 2, o 2, p 2 to., n, k 7, o, n, k 1, o, k 2, n, o 2, k 3, o, n, k 1, o n, k 7, o 2, p 2 to., k 1, o, k 2.

Seventy-fourth row.—K 4, o 2, p 2 to., k 16, p 1, k 15, o 2, p 2 to., k 1, o, k 2.

Seventy-fifth row.—K 4, o 2, p 2 to., n, k 4, n, o, k 1, n, o, k 1, n, o 2, n, n, o 2, n, k 1, o, n, k 1, o, n, k 4, n, o 2, p 2 to., k 2, o, k 2.

Seventy-sixth row.—K 5, o 2, p 2 to., k 13, p 1, k 3, p 1, k 12, o 2, p 2 to., k 2, o, k 2.

Seventy-seventh row.—K 5, o 2, p 2 to., k 4, n, o, k 1, n, o, k 4, n, o 2, n, k 4, o, n, k 1, o, n, k 4, o 2, p 2 to., k 1, o 2, n, o, k 2.

Seventy-eighth row.—K 5, p 1, k 1, o 2, p 2 to., k 15, p 1, k 14, o 2, p 2 to., k 1, o 2, n, o, k 2.

Seventy-ninth row.—K 5, p 1, k 1, o 2, p 2 to., n, k 4, o, n, k 1, o, n, n, o 2, n, n, o 2, n, n, o, k 1, n, o, k 4, n, o 2, p 2 to., k 7.

Eightieth row.—Bind off 4, k 2, o 2, p 2 to., k 12, p 1, k 3, p 1, k 11, o 2, p 2 to., k 8.

Eighty-first row.—Bind off 4, k 2, o 2, p 2 to., n, k 4, o, n, k 1, o, n, k 1, n, o 2, n, k 1, n, o, k 1, n, o, k 4, n, o 2, p 2 to., k 1, o, k 2.

Eighty-second row.—K 4, o 2, p 2 to., k 13, p 1, k 12, o 2, p 2 to., k 2, o, k 2.

Eighty-third row.—K 4, o 2, p 2 to., k 6, o, n, k 1, o, n, k 4, n, o, k 1, n, o, k 6, o 2, p 2 to., k 2, o, k 2.

Eighty-fourth row.—K 5, o 2, p 2 to., k 26, o 2, p 2 to., k 2, o, k 2.

Eighty-fifth row.—K 5, o 2, p 2 to., n, k 5, o, n, k 1, o, n, k 2, n, o, k 1, n, o, k 5, n, o 2, p 2 to., k 1, o 2, n, o, k 2.

Eighty-sixth row.—K 5, p 1, k 1, o 2, p 2 to., k 24, o 2, p 2 to., k 1, o 2, n, o, k 2.

Eighty-seventh row.—K 5, p 1, k 1, o 2, p 2 to., k 7, o, n, k 1, o, n, n, o, k 1, n, o, k 7, o 2, p 2 to., k 7.

Eighty-eighth row.—Bind off 4, k 2, o 2, p 2 to., k 24, o 2, p 2 to., k 7.

Eighty-ninth row.—Bind off 4, k 2, o 2, p 2 to., n, k 6, o, n, k 1, o, n, o, k 1, n, o, k 6, n, o 2, p 2 to., k 1, o, k 2.

Ninetieth row.—K 4, o 2, p 2 to., k 23, o 2, p 2 to., k 1, o, k 2.

Ninety-first row.—K 4, o 2, p 2 to., k 8, o, n, k 3, n, o, k 8, o 2, p 2 to., k 2, o, k 2.

Ninety-second row.—K 5, o 2, p 2 to., k 23, o 2, p 2 to., k 2, o, k 2.

Ninety-third row.—K 5, o 2, p 2 to., n, k 7, o, n, k 1, n, o, k 7, n, o 2, p 2 to., k 1, o 2, n, o, k 2.

Ninety-fourth row.—K 5, p 1, k 1, o 2, p 2 to., k 21, o 2, p 2 to., k 1, o 2, n, o, k 2.

Ninety-fifth row.—K 5, p 1, k 1, o 2, p 2 to., k 9, o, k 3 to., o, k 9, o 2, p 2 to., k 7.

Ninety-sixth row.—Bind off 4, k 2, o 2, p 2 to., k 21, o 2, p 2 to., k 7.

Ninety-seventh row.—Bind off 4, k 2, o 2, p 2 to., n, k 5, n, o, k 3, o, n, k 5, n, o 2, p 2 to., k 1, o, k 2.

Ninety-eighth row.—K 4, o 2, p 2 to., k 19, o 2, p 2 to., k 1, o, k 2.

Ninety-ninth row.—K 4, o 2, p 2 to., k 5, n, o, k 5, o, n, k 5, o 2, p 2 to., k 2, o, k 2.

One Hundredth row.—K 5, o 2, p 2 to., k 19, o 2, p 2 to., k 2, o, k 2.

One Hundred and First row.—K 5, o 2, p 2 to., n, k 2, n, o, k 2, n, o 2, k 3, o, n, k 2, n, o 2, p 2 to., k 1, o 2, n, o, k 2.

One Hundred and Second row.—K 5, p 1, k 1, o 2, p 2 to., k 9, p 1, k 8, o 2, p 2 to., k 1, o 2, n, o, k 2.

One Hundred and Third row.—K 5, p 1, k 1, o 2, p 2 to., k 2, n, o, k 1, n, o 2, n, n, o 2, k 1, o, n, k 2, o 2, p 2 to., k 7.

One Hundred and Fourth row.—Bind off 4, k 2, o 2, p 2 to., k 7, p 1, k 3, p 1, k 6, o 2, p 2 to., k 7.

One Hundred and Fifth row.—Bind off 4, k 2, o 2, p 2 to., n, k 5, n, o 2, n, k 5, n, o 2, p 2 to., k 1, o, k 2.

One Hundred and Sixth row.—K 4, o 2, p 2 to., k 8, p 1, k 7, o 2, p 2 to., k 1, o, k 2.

One Hundred and Seventh row.—K 4, o 2, p 2 to., n, k 2, n, o 2, n, n, o 2, n, k 2, n, o 2, p 2 to., k 2, o, k 2.

One Hundred and Eighth row.—K 5, o 2, p 2 to., k 5, p 1, k 3, p 1, k 4, o 2, p 2 to., k 2, o, k 2.

One Hundred and Ninth row.—K 5, o 2, p 2 to., n, k 3, n, o 2, n, k 3, n, o 2, p 2 to., k 1, o 2, n, o, k 2.

One Hundred and Tenth row.—K 5, p 1, k 1, o 2, p 2 to., k 6, p 1, k 5, o 2, p 2 to., k 1, o 2, n, o, k 2.

One Hundred and Eleventh row.—K 5, p 1, k 1, o 2, p 2 to., n, k 8, n, o 2, p 2 to., k 7.

One Hundred and Twelfth row.—Bind off 4, k 2, o 2, p 2 to., k 10, o 2, p 2 to., k 7.

One Hundred and Thirteenth row.—Bind off 4, k 2, o 2, p 2 to., n, k 6, n, o 2, p 2 to., k 1, o, k 2.

One Hundred and Fourteenth row.—K 4, o 2, p 2 to., k 8, o 2, p 2 to., k 1, o, k 2.

One Hundred and Fifteenth row.—K 4, o 2, p 2 to., n, k 4, n, o 2, p 2 to., k 2, o, k 2.

One Hundred and Sixteenth row.—K 5, o 2, p 2 to., k 6, o 2, p 2 to., k 2, o, k 2.

One Hundred and Seventeenth row.—K 5, o 2, p 2 to., n, k 2, n, o 2, p 2 to., k 1, o 2, n, o, k 2.

One Hundred and Eighteenth row.—K 5, p 1, k 1, o 2, p 2 to., k 4, o 2, p 2 to., k 1, o 2, n, o, k 2.

One Hundred and Nineteenth row.—K 5, p 1, k 1, o 2, p 2 to., n, n, o 2, p 2 to., k 7.

One Hundred and Twentieth row.—Bind off 6, n, o 2, p 2 to., k 7.

No. 4.—CORNER OF KNITTED SHAWL.
(For Description see Page 85.)

One Hundred and Twenty-first row.—Bind off remaining stitches.

To make the holder for the broom: Cut two pieces of cardboard each 5½ inches long, 5 inches wide at its upper edge, and 4 inches at lower edge. Cover the front with plush or velvet in any color preferred, using cambric for lining. To complete the front piece, place the knitted lace over the plush or velvet, fastening it with blind stitches around the edge. Finish with bows of ribbon of the same color as the velvet, or of a contrasting color if preferred, and add ribbon to hang it up by.

DIRECTIONS FOR KNITTED SHAWL.

(For Illustration see Page 84.)

No. 4.—Fine bone needles and Shetland yarn are used in making this shawl. To make a shawl one yard square, cast on 175 stitches and knit once across plain.

First row.—Sl 1, k 1, * make 1, k 1; repeat from * until only 2 stitches remain on the needle; then make 1, k 2.

Second row.—Sl 1, k 1, * k 1, sl 1; repeat from * to the end; always knit the stitch that was made, and slip the one that was knit in the preceding row, and knit the 2 last stitches plain.

Third row.—Sl 1, k 1, * k 2 to; repeat from * to the end, knitting the last stitch plain.

Repeat the three rows until the shawl is square, then bind off.

For the Fringe.—Cut the yarn into 6-inch lengths, and knot three lengths into each stitch all round the shawl.

LADIES' BEDROOM SLIPPERS.

No. 5.—This slipper is made of pink and blue zephyr. Cast on 9 stitches with the pink and knit back and forth once; then continue knitting back and forth, widening once at the end of each row until there are 45 stitches on the needle and 20 ridges. Knit 10 ridges without widening. Now divide the stitches, leaving 22 on each needle, and cast off the odd one at the center. Knit back

No. 5.—LADIES' BEDROOM SLIPPER.

and forth on each needle until each side has 22 ridges, then bind off. For the turn-over, pick up the stitches along the top, using the blue zephyr and beginning each side at the center of the top;

knit 10 ridges, then bind off and sew the backs together over-and-over; sew the upper to the sole and put a blue ribbon bow on the front. Turn the blue portion over as seen in the picture.

DESIGN FOR LADIES' KNITTED UNDER-SKIRT.

No. 6.—Use Germantown yarn, and knit one front-breadth and two back-breadths, and sew

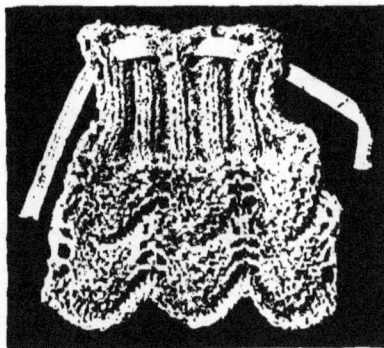

No. 6.—DESIGN FOR LADIES' UNDER-SKIRT.

or crochet them together. For the front-breadth cast on 101 stitches; and for each of the back-breadths cast on 121.

First row.—K plain.
Second row.—Purl.
Third row.—K plain.
Fourth row.—* K 1, th o, k 3, sl 1, n, pass slipped stitched over, k 3, o *; repeat between the stars across the row; at the end, o, k 1.
Fifth row.—Purl.
Sixth row.—Like 4th.
Seventh row.—Purl.
Eighth row.—Like 4th.
Ninth row.—Purl.
Tenth row.—Like 4th.
Eleventh row.—Repeat from 1st row until 15 of the patterns have been knitted; then:
Next row.—K 4, n, * k 8, n *, and repeat between the stars across the row.
Next row.—P 4, p 2 to, * p 7, p 2 to *; repeat between the stars across the row.
Next row.—K plain.

Now, k 2 and p 2 throughout every row until the breadth is as long as desired, then k 3, * o 3 times, k 3 to, k 2, o 3 times, k 3 to *. Repeat between the stars as before.

The 3 loops in the next row will be k 1, p 1, k 1; then knit across plain and bind off.

Run a ribbon through the holes or, if preferred, the holes may be omitted and the skirt-top finished with a belt.

KNITTED TIDY.

No. 7.—Coarse écru or unbleached thread was used for this tidy. Cast on 2 stitches, and use 2 steel needles.

First row.—Knit plain.

Second row.—Th o, k 2.

Third row.—Th o, k 1, o, k 1, o, k 1.

Fourth row.—Th o, k 1, p 3, k 2.

Fifth row.—Th o, k 3, o, k 1, o, k 3.

Sixth row.—Th o, k 2, p 5, k 3.

Seventh row.—Th o, k 5, o, k 1, o, k 5.

Eighth row.—Th o, k 3, p 7, k 4.

Ninth row.—Th o, k 7, o, k 1, o, k 7.

Tenth row. —Th o, k 4, p 9, k 5.

Eleventh row.—Th o, k 9, o, k 1, o, k 9.

Twelfth row.—Th o, k 5, p 11, k 6.

Thirteenth row.—Th o, k 11, o, k 1, o, k 11.

Fourteenth row.—Th o, k 6, p 13, k 7.

Fifteenth row.—Th o, k 7, sl 1, k 1, pass slipped stitch over, k 9, n, k 7.

Sixteenth row.—Th o, k 7, p 11, k 8.

Seventeenth row.—Th o, k 8, sl 1, k 1, pass slipped stitch over, k 7, n, k 8.

Eighteenth row.—Th o, k 8, p 9, k 9.

Nineteenth row.—Th o, k 9, sl 1, k 1, pass slipped stitch over, k 5, n, k 9.

Twentieth row.—Th o, k 9, p 7, k 10.

Twenty-first row.—Th o, k 10, sl 1, k 1, pass slipped stitch over, k 3, n, k 10.

Twenty-second row.—Th o, k 10, p 5, k 11.

Twenty-third row.—Th o, k 11, sl 1, k 1, pass slipped stitch over, k 1, n, k 11.

Twenty-fourth row.—Th o, k 11, p 3, k 12.

Twenty-fifth row.—Th o, k 12, sl 1, n, pass slipped stitch over, k 12.

Twenty-Sixth row.—Th o, k 1, p 24, k the last stitch.

Twenty-seventh row.—Th o, k plain across the needle.

Twenty-eighth row.—Th o, k 1, p all but the last stitch, k 1.

Twenty-ninth row.—Same as last row.

Thirtieth row.—Th o, k the rest plain.

Thirty-first row—Like the twenty-eighth.

Thirty-second, Thirty-third and Thirty-fifth rows.—Like the thirtieth.

Thirty-fourth, Thirty-sixth and Thirty-eighth rows.—Like the twenty-eighth.

Thirty-seventh row.—Th o, k 1, * o, n, o, n, and repeat from * across the needle to the last stitch, which you knit.

Thirty-ninth row.—Th o, k 1, * o, n, o, n, and repeat from * across the needle to the last stitch, which you knit.

Fortieth row.—Th o, p across to the last stitch which is always knit, and therefore will not be mentioned in the following rows.

Forty-first row.—Th o, k 1, * o, n, o, n; repeat from * across the row.

Forty-second row.—Th o, k 1, p across.

Forty-third row.—Th o, k across plain; there will now be 44 stitches on your needle.

Forty-fourth row.—Th o, k 1, p across.

Forty-fifth row.—Th o, k across.

Forty-sixth, Forty-seventh and Forty-ninth rows.—Like forty-fourth row.

Forty-eighth, Fiftieth, Fifty-first and Fifty third rows.—Like forty-fifth row.

Fifty-second row.—Th o, k 1, p across.

Fifty-fourth row.—Like fifty-second row; there will now be 55 stitches on the needle.

Fifty-fifth row.—Th o, k 1, o, k 1, o, k 9, o, k 1, o, k 9, o, k 1, o, k 10, o, k 1, o, k 9, o, k 1, o, k 9, o, k 1, o, k 2.

Fifty-sixth row.—Th o, k 2, p 3, k 9, p 3, k 9, p 3, k 10, p 3, k 9, p 3, k 9, p 3, k 2.

Fifty-seventh row.—Th o, k 3, o, k 1, o, k 11, o, k 1, o, k 11, o, k 1, o, k 12, o, k 1, o, k 11, o, k 1, o, k 11, o, k 1, o, k 4.

NO. 7.—KNITTED TIDY.

Fifty-eighth row.—Th o, k 3, p 5, k 9, p 5, k 9, p 5, k 10, p 5, k 9, p 5, k 9, p 5, k 3.

Fifty-ninth row.—Th o, k 5, o, k 1, o, k 13, o, k 1, o, k 13, o, k 1, o, k 14, o, k 1, o, k 13, o, k 1, o, k 13, o, k 1, o k 6.

Sixtieth row.—Th o, k 4, p 7, k 9, p 7, k 9, p 7, k 10, p 7, k 9, p 7, k 9, p 7, k 4.

Sixty-first row.—Th o, k 7, o, k 1, o, k 15, o, k 1, o, k 15, o, k 1, o, k 16, o, k 1, o, k 15, o, k 1, o, k 15, o, k 1, o, k 8.

Sixty-second row.—Th o, k 5, p 9, k 9, p 9, k 9, p 9, k 10, p 9, k 9, p 9, k 9, p 9, k 5.

Sixty-third row.—Th o, k 9, o, k 1, o, k 17, o, k 1, o, k 17, o, k 1, o, k 18, o, k 1, o, k 17, o, k 1, o, k 17, o, k 1, o, k 10.

Sixty-fourth row.—Th o, k 6, p 11, k 9, p 11, k 9, p 11, k 10, p 11, k 9, p 11, k 9, p 11, k 6.

Sixty-fifth row.—Th o, k 11, o, k 1, o k 19, o, k 1, o, k 19, o, k 1, o, k 20, o, k 1, o, k 19, o, k 1, o, k 19, o, k 1, o, k 12.

Sixty-sixth row.—Th o, k 7, p 13, k 9, p 13, k 9, p 13, k 10, p 13, k 9, p 13, k 9, p 13, k 9, p 13, k 7.

Sixty-seventh row.—Th o, k 7, sl 1, k 1, pass slipped stitch over, k 9, n, k 9, sl 1, k 1, pass slipped stitch over, k 9, n, k 9, sl 1, k 1, pass slipped stitch over, k 9, n, k 10, sl 1, k 1, pass slipped stitch over, k 9, n, k 9, sl 1, k 1, pass slipped stitch over, k 9, n, k 9, sl 1, k 1, pass slipped stitch o, k 9, n, k 8.

Sixty-eighth row.—Th o, k 8, p 11, k 9, p 11, k 9, p 11, k 10, p 11, k 9, p 11, k 9, p 11, k 8.

Sixty-ninth row.—Th o, k 8, sl 1, k 1, passed slipped stitch o, k 7, n, k 9, sl 1, k 1, pass sl stitch o, k 7, n, k 9, sl 1, k 1 pass sl stitch o, k 7, n, k 10, sl 1, k 1, pass sl stitch o, k 7, n, k 9, sl 1, k 1, pass sl stitch o, k 7, n, k 9, sl 1, k 1, pass sl stitch o, k 7, n, k 9.

Seventieth row.—Th o, k 9, p 9, k 9, p 9, k 9, p 9, k 10, p 9, k 9, p 9, k 9, p 9, k 9.

Seventy-first row.—Th o, k 9, sl 1, k 1, pass sl stitch o, k 5, n, k 9, sl 1, k 1, pass sl stitch o, k 5, n, k 9, sl 1, k 1, pass sl stitch o, k 5, n, k 10, sl 1, k 1, pass sl stitch o, k 5, n, k 9, sl 1, k 1, pass sl stitch o, k 5, n, k 9, sl 1, k 1, pass sl stitch o, k 5, n, k 10.

Seventy-second row.—Th o, k 10, p 7, k 9, p 7, k 9, p 7, k 10, p 7, k 9, p 7, k 9, p 7, k 10.

Seventy-third row.—Th o, k 10, sl k, k 1, pass sl stitch over, k 3, n, k 9, sl 1, k 1, pass sl stitch o, k 3, n, k 9, sl 1, k 1, pass sl stitch o, k 3, n, k 10, sl 1, k 1, pass sl stitch o, k 3, n, k 9, sl 1, k 1, pass sl stitch o, k 3, n, k 9, sl 1, k 1, pass sl stitch o, k 3, n, k 11.

Seventy-fourth row.—Th o, k 11, p 5, k 9, p 5, k 9, p 5, k 10, p 5, k 9, p 5, k 9, p 5, k 11.

Seventy-fifth row.—Th o, k 11, sl 1, k 1, pass sl stitch o, k 1, n, k 9, sl 1, k 1, pass sl stitch o k 1, n, k 9, sl 1, k 1, pass sl stitch o, k 1, n, k 10, sl 1. k 1, pass sl stitch o, k 1, n, k 9, sl 1, k 1, pass sl stitch o, k 1, n, k 9, sl 1, k 1, pass sl stitch over, k 1, n, k 12.

Seventy-sixth row.—Th o, k 12, p 3, k 9, p 3, k 9, p 3, k 10, p 3, k 9, p 3, k 9, p 3, k 9, p 3, k 12.

Seventy-seventh row.—Th o, k 12, sl 1, n, pass sl stitch o, k 9, sl 1, n, pass sl stitch, o, k 9, sl 1, n, pass sl stitch o, k 10, sl 1, n, pass sl stitch, o, k 9, sl

1, n, pass sl stitch o, k 9, sl 1 n, pass sl stitch o, k 13.

Seventy-eighth row.—Th o, k 1, p across; you should now have 79 stitches on the needle.

Seventy-ninth and Eighty-second rows.—Th o, k across plain.

Eightieth, Eighty-first and Eighty-third rows.—Th o, k 1, p across.

Eighty-fourth, Eighty-fifth and Eighty-seventh rows.—K 1, n, k across plain.

Eighty-sixth, Eighty-eighth, Ninetieth, Ninety-second and Ninety-fourth rows.—K 1, n, p, across.

Eighty-ninth row.—K 1, n, * o, n, o, n, and repeat from * across the row; k the last stitch plain in this, and all other similar rows where it is left after the narrowing.

Ninety-first and Ninety-third rows.—Same as eighty-ninth row.

Ninety-fifth, Ninety-seventh, One Hundred and Second, and One Hundred and Third rows.—K 1, n, k across plain.

Ninety-sixth, Ninety-eighth, Ninety-ninth, One Hundred and First, Fourth, Sixth and Eighth rows.—K 1, n, p across.

One Hundred and Fifth row.—K 1, n, k across.

One Hundred and Seventh, Ninth and Eleventh rows.—K 1, n, * o, n, and repeat from * across the row.

One Hundred and Tenth, Twelfth and Fourteenth rows.—K 1, n, p across.

One Hundred and Thirteenth and Fifteenth rows.—K 1, n, k across.

One Hundred and Sixteenth, Seventeenth and Nineteenth rows.—K 1, n, p across.

One Hundred and Eighteenth, Twentieth, Twenty-first and Twenty-third rows.—K 1, n, k across.

One Hundred and Twenty-second and Twenty-fourth rows.—K 1, n, p across.

One Hundred and Twenty-fifth, Twenty-seventh and Twenty-ninth rows.—K 1, n, * o, n, and repeat from * across the row.

One Hundred and Twenty-sixth, Twenty-eighth and Thirtieth rows.—K 1, n, p across.

One Hundred and Thirty-first and Thirty-third rows.—K 1, n, k across.

One Hundred and Thirty-second, Thirty-fourth and Thirty-fifth rows.—K 1, n, p across.

One Hundred and Thirty-sixth, Thirty-eighth and Thirty-ninth rows.—K 1, n, k across.

One Hundred and Thirty-seventh, Fortieth and Forty-second rows.—K 1, n, p across.

One Hundred and Forty-first row.—K 1, n, k across.

One Hundred and Forty-third, Forty-fifth and Forty-seventh rows.—K 1, n, * o, n, and repeat from * across the row.

One Hundred and Forty-fourth, Forty-sixth, Forty-eighth, Fiftieth, Fifty-second and Fifty-third rows.—K 1, n, p across.

One Hundred and Forty-ninth, Fifty-first and Fifty-fourth rows.—K 1, n, k across plain.

One Hundred and Fifty-fifth row.—K 1, n, p across.

One Hundred and Fifty-sixth and Fifty-seventh rows.—K 1, n, k across plain.

One Hundred and Fifty-eighth, Sixtieth and Sixty-second rows.—K 1, n, p across.

One Hundred and Fifty-ninth and Sixty-first rows.—K 1, n, k across plain.

Now bind off the stitches on the needle tightly.

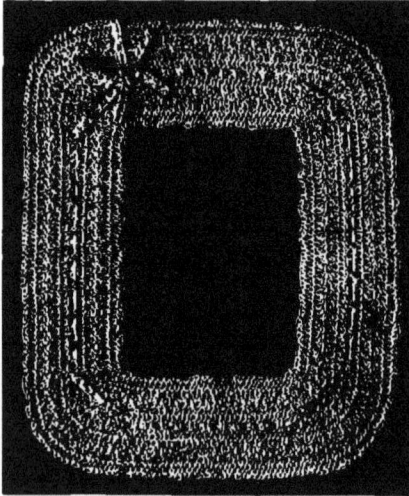

No. 8.—KNITTED PICTURE-FRAME COVER.

This completes the first block. Knit 3 more like this, then sew the four together, joining the leaves in the center, and sewing over in each loop. If done neatly, the effect will be as if it were knit on 5 needles. The direction may seem very long, but the work is extremely easy and quickly done, as the different rows are so nearly alike.

The edging around the tidy is made as follows.

Cast on 32 stitches and knit across plain.

First row.—K 3, o twice, p 2 to, k 4, n, o, k 1, o, n, k 4, o twice, p 2 to., k 1, p 2, k 1, o, k 1, o, k 1, p 2, k 2, o twice, k 2.

Second row.—K 3, p 1, k 4, p 5, k 3, o twice, p 2 to., k 13, o twice, p 2 to., k 3.

Third row.—K 3, o twice, p 2 to., k 3, n, o, k 3, o, n, k 3, o twice, p 2 to., k 1, p 2, k 2, o, k 1, o, k 2, p 2, k 6.

Fourth row.—K 8, p 7, k 3, o twice, p 2 to., k 13, o twice, p 2 to., k 3.

Fifth row.—K 3, o twice, p 2 to., k 2, n, o, k 5, o, n, k 2, o twice, k 1, p 2, k 3, o, k 1, o k 3, p 2, k 2, o twice, n, o twice, k 2.

Sixth row.—K 3, p 1, k 2, p 1, k 4, p 9, k 3, o twice, p 2 to., k 13, o twice, p 2 to., k 3.

Seventh row.—K 3, o twice, p 2 to., k 1, n, o, k 7, o, n, k 1, o twice, p 2 to., k 1, p 2, k 4, o, k 1, o, k 4, p 2, k 9.

Eighth row.—K 11, p 11, k 3, o twice, p 2 to., k 13, o twice, p 2 to., k 3.

Ninth row.—K 3, o twice, p 2 to., n, o, k 9, o, n, o twice, p 2 to., k 1, p 2, sl 1, k 1, pass slipped stitch over, k 7, n, p 2, k 2, o twice, n, o twice, n, o twice, n, k 1.

Tenth row.—K 3, p 1, k 2, p 1, k 2, p 1, k 4, p 9, k 3, o twice, p 2 to., k 13, o twice, p 2 to., k 3.

Eleventh row.—K 3, o twice, p 2 to., k 2, o, n, k 5, n, o, k 2, o twice, p 2 to, k 1, p 2, sl 1, k 1, pass slipped stitch over, k 5, n, p 2, k 12.

Twelfth row.—K 3, n, k 9, p 7 k 3, o twice, p 2 to., k 13, o twice, p 2 to, k 3.

Thirteenth row.—K 3, o twice, p 2 to., k 3, o, n, k 3, n, o, k 3, o twice, p 2 to., k 1, p 2, slip 1, k 1, pass slipped over, k 3, n, p 2, k 2, o twice, n, o twice, n, o twice, n, k 1.

Fourteenth row.—K 3, p 1, k 2, p 1, k 2, p 1, k 2, p 1, k 4, p 5, k 3, o twice, p 2 to., k 13, o twice, p 2 to., k 3.

Fifteenth row.—K 3, o twice, p 2 to., k 4, o, n, k 1, n, o, k 4, o twice, p 2 to., k 1, p 2, slip 1, k 1, pass slipped stitch over, k 1, n, p 2, k 15.

Sixteenth row.—Bind off 10, k 6, p 3, k 3, o twice, p 2 to., k 13, o twice, p 2 to., k 3.

Seventeenth row.—K 3, o twice, p 2 to., k 5, o, slip 1, n, pass slipped stitch over, o, k 5, o twice, p 2 to., k 1, p 2, slip 1, n, pass slipped stitch over, p 2, k 5.

Eighteenth row.—K 8, make 1 stitch by picking up a thread and knitting it, thus making 9 stitches; then k 3 more, making 12 stitches on the right-hand needle, o twice, p 2 to., k 13, o twice, p 2 to., k 3, and repeat from first row.

KNITTED PICTURE-FRAME COVER.

No. 8.—The foundation of this frame is cut from thick cardboard and should be about 10 inches long and 8½ wide. An opening suitable for a cabinet picture leaves the frame about 2½ inches wide. Cover with dark-blue plush, laying one

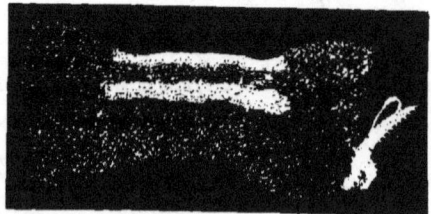

No. 9.—KNITTED HOLDER.

(For Description see Page 89.)

thickness of wadding between plush and cardboard. Do not cut and make the foundation until after the cover is knitted.

The cover is made as follows: Cast on 26 stitches.

First row.—Thread o 2 ("o 2" means "thread over twice"), p 2 to., o, p 2 to., k 1, k 3 to.; k 1 p 1 and k 1 in the next stitch; o 2, p 2 to., n, o, n, o 2, p 2 to., k 1, k 3 to.: k 1, p 1, and k 1 in next stitch; o 2, p 2 to., o, p 2 to.

Second row.—O 2, p 2 to., o, p 2 to., k 2, o, n, k, 1, o 2, p 2 to., k 2; p 1 and k 1 in next st., o 2, p 2 to., k 2, o, n, k 1, o 2, p 2 to., o, p 2 to.; drop last stitch.

Third row.—O 2, p 2 to., o, p 2 to., k 5, o 2, p 2 to., k 4, o 2, p 2 to., k 5, o 2, p 2 to., o, p 2 to.; drop last stitch.

Fourth row.—O 2, p 2 to., o, p 2 to., k 1, k 3 to.; k 1 p 1 and k 1 in next stitch; o 2, p 2 to., k 4, o 2, p 2 to., k 1, k 3 to.; k 1, p 1 and k 1 in next stitch; o 2, p 2 to., o, p 2 to.

Fifth row.—O 2, p 2 to., o, p 2 to., k 2, o, n, k 1, o 2, p 2 to., k 4, o 2, p 2 to., k 2, o, n, k 1, o 2, p 2 to., o, p 2 to.

Sixth row.—O 2, p 2 to., o, p 2 to., k 5, o 2, p 2 to., k 4, o 2, p 2 to., k 5, o 2, p 2 to., o, p 2 to.

Repeat 12 times for ends, and 17 times for sides of frame.

For the Corners.—After knitting 6th row knit as follows:

First row.—O 2, p 2 to., o, p 2 to., k 1, k 3 to.; k 1, p 1 and k 1 in next stitch; o 2, p 2 to., k 13, leave 2; turn.

Second row.—Sl 1, k 2; o, n, 5 times; o 2, p 2 to., k 2, o, n, k 1, o 2, p 2 to., o, p 2 to.; drop last stitch.

Third row.—O 2, p 2 to., o, p 2 to., k 5, o 2, p 2 to., k 11; leave 4.

Fourth row.—Sl 1, k 10, o 2, p 2 to., k 1, k 3 to., k 1, p 1 and k 1 in next stitch; o 2, p 2 to., o, p 2 to.; drop last stitch.

Fifth row.—O 2, p 2 to., o, p 2 to., k 2, o, n, k 1, o 2, p 2 to., k 9, leave 6.

Sixth row.—Sl 1, k 2; o, n, 3 times; o 2, p 2 to., k 5, o 2, p 2 to., o, p 2 to.

Seventh row.—O 2, p 2 to., o, p 2 to., k 1, k 3 to.; k 1, p 1 and k 1 in next stitch; o 2, p 2 to., k 7, leave 8.

Eighth row.—Sl 1, k 6, o 2, p 2 to., k 2, o, n, k 1, o 2, p 2 to., o, p 2 to.

Ninth row.—O 2, p 2 to., o, p 2 to., k 5, o 2, p 2 to., k 5, leave 10.

Tenth row.—Sl 1, k 2, o, n, o 2, p 2 to., k 1, k 3 to.; k 1, p 1 and k 1 in next stitch; o 2, p 2 to., o, p 2 to.

Eleventh row.—O 2, p 2 to., o, p 2 to., k 2, o, n, k 1, o 2, p 2 to., k 3, leave 12.

Twelfth row.—Sl 1, k 2, o 2, p 2 to., k 5, o 2, p 2 to., o, p 2 to.

Thirteenth row.—O 2, p 2 to., o, p 2 to., k 1, k 3 to.; k 1, p 1 and k 1 in next stitch; o 2, p 2 to., k 1, leave 14.

Fourteenth row.—Sl 1, k 4, o, n, k 1, o 2, p 2 to., o, p 2 to.

Fifteenth row.—O 2, p 2 to., o, p 2 to., k 6, leave 16.

Sixteenth row.—Sl 1, k 1, k 3 to.; k 1, p 1, k 1 in next stitch; o 2, p 2 to., o, p 2 to.

Seventeenth row.—O 2, p 2 to., o, p 2 to., k 2, o, n, k 1, o 2, p 2 to., k 15.

Eighteenth row.—Sl 1, k 14, o 2, p 2 to., k 5, o 2, p 2 to., o, p 2 to.

Make three points for each corner, and then repeat pattern from first row again. Join together and draw baby ribbon in center eyelets, crossing the corners, as shown in cut, and finish with loops where the lace is joined. Lay the cover on the frame, and fasten in place with invisible stitches.

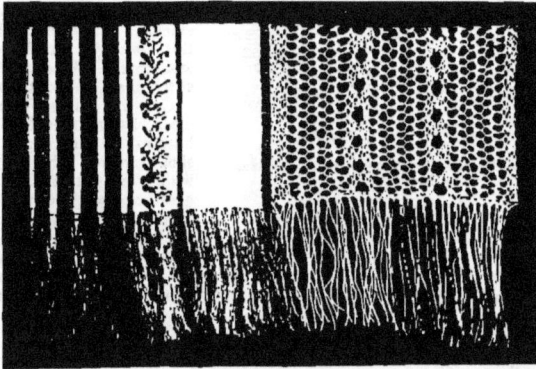

No. 10.—SECTION OF PICTURE THROW.

KNITTED HOLDER.

(For Illustration see Page 86)

No. 9.— Knit on 2 needles, using red and white, or any other colors preferred, in cotton or wool.

Cast on 45 stitches of red, and knit 20 rows.

Twenty-first row.—K 10 r; k 5 w, k 5 r, 5 w, 5 r, 5 w, 10 r.

Twenty-second row.—K 10 r; p 5 w, 5 r, 5 w, 5 r, 5 w; k 10 red. Continue like 21st and 22nd rows, alternately, until you have 40 rows of stripes. Now k 20 red rows, and bind off. Fold together and tie one end with a tiny bow of baby ribbon. When knitting the stripes, draw the threads tightly across each time, to give the ridged appearance represented in the engraving.

PICTURE THROW.

No. 10.—To make this dainty and pretty throw, which is composed of three knitted stripes and two ribbon stripes, 2¾ yards of ribbon 2½ inches wide, in any pretty shade, and No. 30 thread will be required. The knitted pattern consists of only 6 rows, that are repeated until the length required is obtained. Cast on 32 stitches and knit across plain.

First row.—Sl 1, k 2, th o twice, p 2 to., th o, p 2 to., th o, p 2 to., n, th o twice, n, th o twice, p 2 to., th o, p 2 to., th o, p 2 to., n, th o twice, n, th o twice, p 2 to., th o, p 2 to., th o, p 2 to., k 3.

Second row.—Sl 1, k 2, th o twice, p 2 to., th o,

No. 11.—KNITTED EMERY-CUSHION AND NEEDLE-BOOK, COMBINED.
(STRAWBERRY DESIGN.)

p 2 to., th o, p 2 to., k 2, p 1, k 1, th o twice, p 2 to., th o, p 2 to., th o, p 2 to., k 2, p 1, k 1, th o twice, p 2 to., th o, p 2 to., th o, p 2 to., k 3.

Third row.—Sl 1, k 2, th o twice, p 2 to., th o, p 2 to., th o, p 2 to., k 4, th o twice, p 2 to., th o, p 2 to., th o, p 2 to., k 4, th o twice, p 2 to., th o, p 2 to., th o, p 2 to., k 3.

Fourth and Fifth rows.—Like 3rd.

Both ends can be finished with fringe, or one of them with tassels. The fringe is drawn in with a crochet hook, and can be of any length desired. Fringe the ribbon to match.

KNITTED EMERY-CUSHION AND NEEDLE-BOOK, COMBINED.
(STRAWBERRY DESIGN.)

NOS. 11, 12 AND 13.— The emery-cushion here illustrated is made of strawberry-red knitting silk, and the leaves may be of green felt, cloth or velvet.

Make the Cushion-Cover as follows : Use 4 very fine knitting needles, and cast 10 stitches onto 2 of the needles, and 12 on the 3rd.

Knit round with the 4th needle until you have a sufficient depth (say an inch and a half), in the

same way as you knit a stocking; then narrow at each end of every alternate round until you have 2 stitches left on each of the 2 needles, and 4 on the 3rd one, on which there were originally 12. Pass a needle and thread through all these loops or stitches so as to secure them from dropping or raveling. Take out the knitting needles, turn the work on the wrong side, restore the 4 loops to one needle and 4 to another, and then cast off. This prevents the strawberry from being pointed at the top.

In narrowing, the following method is recommended : At the beginning of the rows take one stitch on the needle, knit the next, and pass the 1st stitch over the 2nd ; at the end of each row take two stitches together. This produces corresponding lines of contraction.

The emery-cushion must be cut from cloth by the diagram seen at No. 12, three sections being necessary. Turn the edges and over-hand together; fill with the emery. Now slip the knitted cover over this and draw up the end with a needle and thread. The seeds are made by a stitch like a "back-stitch," with yellow silk.

Cut the leaves from green velvet or cloth, shaping them like No. 13; and nicely button-hole the edges with green silk a shade or two lighter. Cut the leaves in which the needles are to be stuck from green or black cloth, making them a little smaller than the velvet ones. Make a bow with ends, of green ribbon half an inch wide, and sew where the leaves join. Sew the berry to the middle leaf, just behind the bow, and you have something useful as well as ornamental.

KNITTED CATCH-ALL FOR TOILET-TABLE.
(For Illustration see Page 91.)

NO. 14.—The catch-all as here pictured is knitted

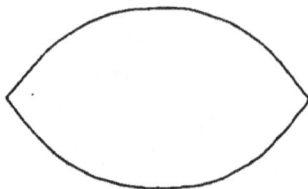

No. 12.—SECTION OF BERRY (FULL SIZE).

No. 13.—SHAPE OF LEAVES (QUARTER SIZE).

with knitting cotton No. 18, and 4 steel needles No. 16.

Make a slip-knot in the cotton, leaving the loose end quite long; then in the loop cast on 7 stitches thus : Use two needles and, working with the loose end of the cotton, k 1 stitch, then purl 1 in the first loop, until there are 7 in all ; then pass 2 onto each of 2 needles, and leave 3 on the 3rd; then draw up the slip-knot closely, and knit first and every alternate round to the thirty-seventh, plain.

Second round.—* Th o, k 1, and repeat from * for entire round.

Fourth round.—* Th o, k 2, and repeat from * to end of round.

Sixth round.—* Th o, k 3, and repeat from * to the end of round.

Eighth round.—* Th o, k 4, and repeat from *.

Tenth round.—* Th o, k 5, and repeat from *

Twelfth round.—* Th o, k 6, and repeat from *.

Fourteenth round.—* Th o, k 7, and repeat from *.

Sixteenth round.—* Th o, k 8, and repeat from *.

Eighteenth round.—* Th o, k 9, and repeat from *.

Twentieth round.—* Th o, k 1, o, sl and b, k 7, and repeat from *.

Twenty-second round.—* Th o, k 3, o, sl and b, and repeat from *.

Twenty-fourth round.—* Th o, k 5, o, sl and b, k 5, and repeat from *.

Twenty-sixth round.—* Th o, k 7, o, sl and b, k 4 and repeat from *.

Twenty-eighth round.—* Th o, k 9, o, sl and b, k 3, and repeat from *.

Thirtieth round.—* Th o, k 11, o, sl and b, k 2, and repeat from *.

Thirty-second round.—* Th o, k 13, o, sl and b, k 1, and repeat from *.

Thirty-fourth round.—* Th o, k 15, o, sl and b, and repeat from *.

Thirty-sixth round.—* O, n, and repeat from *.

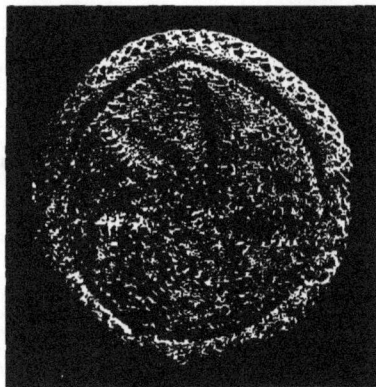

NO. 14.—KNITTED CATCH-ALL FOR TOILET-TABLE.

(For Description see Page 90.)

Thirty-seventh, Thirty-eighth, Thirty-ninth, Fortieth and Forty-first rounds.—Purl.

Forty-second, Forty-third, Forty-fourth, Forty-fifth and Forty-sixth rounds.—Knit.

Forty-seventh Forty-ninth, Fifty-first, Fifty-third

and Fifty-fifth rounds.—O, n, and repeat for the entire round. Knit the five even rounds between the last rounds.

Fifty-seventh, Fifty-eighth, Fifty-ninth, Sixtieth and Sixty-first rounds.—Knit.

Sixty-second, Sixty-third, Sixty-fourth, Sixty-fifth

NO. 15.—HAIR-PIN CUSHION IN KNITTING AND CROCHET.

and Sixty-sixth rounds.—Purl; then bind off.

HAIR-PIN CUSHION IN KNITTING AND CROCHET.

No. 15.—This cushion is made of three colors of single zephyr or Germantown yarn and with two coarse steel needles. Cast on 36 stitches and knit in patent knitting thus:

First row.—* Throw thread forward, slip 1, k 2 to., and repeat from * for all the row.

Second row.—Work back in the same way to within 3 stitches of the end; do not knit these; turn. The three stitches will be on the right hand needle after turning, and are to be considered as the first three of the third row; they produce the narrowing necessary.

Third row.—Work back in patent knitting for the rest of the row; turn.

Fourth row.—Knit to within 6 stitches of the end; turn.

Fifth row.—Knit across the row.

Sixth row.—Knit to within 9 stitches of the end; turn.

Seventh row.—Knit across the row.

Eighth row.—Knit to within 12 stitches of the end; turn.

Ninth row.—Knit across the row.

Tenth row.—Knit to within 15 stitches of the end; turn.

Eleventh row.—Knit across the row.

Twelfth row.—Knit to within 18 stitches of the end.

Thirteenth row.—Knit across the row.

Fourteenth row.—Knit entirely across the row; turn.

Fifteenth row.—Join on the black wool and work 2 rows entirely across. Join on the third color and knit entirely across; turn. Now repeat from the second row until there are 12 points (alternating) of the two colors, with the black between. Bind off the stitches, using black for the last 2 rows, and sew together over and over; draw the small end together as closely as possible with needle and wool, and fasten securely. Fill with curled hair and draw down with a strong thread or the wool to fit the circular piece which is made as follows: Make a ring of about 3 ch.; work twice around this in single crochet, widening often enough to keep the circle flat; then once around in double crochet. Join to edges of opening with over-and-over stitch, and sew through the center.

KNITTED SASH-CURTAIN.

NOS. 16, 17 AND 18.—To be dainty in effect to the close-by observer, knitted sash curtains should be made of moderately fine crochet cotton. To be effective when viewed from a distance, they should be knitted of coarse crochet cotton. It is ad-visable for the knitter to experiment with cottons of various sizes before she begins her work in earnest, in order to ascertain whether or not the design as given, will develop to the width desired. When worked in coarse cotton the design seen at figure No. 17 will work out to fit an ordinary-sized window. Any handsome insertion knitted with coarse cotton may be joined in strips to form such a curtain. If an edge is desired, several of the edgings given on previous pages will be pretty for the purpose. Use very coarse needles. Knit two strips of the required length, and lace through the edge with cord finished with tassels; or sew crocheted rings to the edge and lace through them. This pattern may be greatly varied by binding off one-third at a time, and thus forming a serrated edge, shortest in the center; or, reverse the sides and let the longer edges meet in the center, as taste may dictate.

To knit the design illustrated, begin as follows:

Cast on 53 stitches, and knit across plain, twice.

First row.—Knit 3, o, n, k 3, o, k 1, o, k 5, o, n, k 1, o, n, k 2, o, n, k 3, o, k 1, o, k 5, o, n, k 1, o, n, k 2, o, n, k 3, o, k 1, o, k 5, o, n, k 1.

NO. 16.—KNITTED SASH-CURTAIN FOR A DOOR.

Second row.—K 3, o, n, k 1, n, o, k 3, o, n, k 3, o, n, k 1, o, n, k 2, o, n, k 1, n, o, k 3, o, n, k 3, o, n, k 1, o, n, k 2, o, n, k 1, n, o, k 3, o, n, k 3, o, n, k 1.

Third row.—K.3, o, n twice, o, k 5, o, n, k 2, o, n, k 1, o. n, k 2, o, n twice, o, k 5, o, n, k 2, o, n, k 1, o, n, k 2, o, n twice, o, k 5, o, n, k 2, o, n, k 1.

Fourth row.—K 3, o, k 3 together, o, n, k 3, n, o, n, k 1, o, n, k 1, o, n, k 2, o, k 3 together, o, n, k 3, n, o, n, k 1, o, n, k 1, o, n, k 2, o, k 3 together, o, n, k 3, n, o, n, k 1, o, n, k 1.

Fifth row.—K 3, o, n, k 1, o, n, k 1, n, o, k 3, o, n, k 1, o, n, k 2, o, n, k 1, n, o, n, k 1, n, o, k 3, o, n, k 1, o, n, k 2, o, n, k 1, o, n, k 1, n, o, k 3, o, n, k 1.

Sixth row.—K 3, o, n, k 2, o, slip 1, n, pass slipped stitch over the narrowed one, o, k 4, o, n, k 1, o, n, k 2, o, n, k 2, o, slip 1, n, pass slipped stitch over the narrowed one, o, k 4, o, n, k 1, o, n, k 2, o, n, k 2, o, slip 1, n, pass slipped stitch over the narrowed one, o, k 4, o, n, k 1. Repeat from first row.

KNITTED CORNER FOR A HANDKERCHIEF.

(For Illustration see Page 94.)

No. 19.—Having learned to knit a corner in one pattern, anyone can form a corner in any pattern. The pattern here given is very pretty for other uses.

To begin Corner.—In beginning the pattern 22 stitches are cast on to commence a point, see directions further on and there must be 22 stitches on the needle (after completing a point) when the corner is begun. Then work as follows:

First row of Corner.—Sl 1, k 2, th o twice, n, k

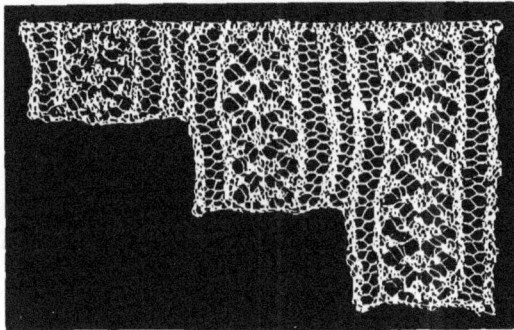

No. 17.—DESIGN FOR KNITTED SASH-CURTAIN.

10, th o twice, n, th o twice, n, th o twice, n, k 1.
Second row.—K 3, p 1, k 2, p 1, k 2, p 1, k 12, p

i, k 2; this will leave one on left-hand needle; turn,
Third row.—Sl 1, k 24.
Fourth row.—K 24; this will now leave 2 on

No. 18.—KNITTED SASH-CURTAIN FOR A WINDOW.
(For Description see Page 92.)

left hand needle, there will be one more left on the left-hand needle each time in the following rows.

Fifth row.—Sl 1, th o twice, n, th o twice, n, k 12, th o twice, n, th o twice, n, th o twice, n, k 1.

Sixth row.—K 3, p 1, k 2, p 1, k 2, p 1, k 14, p 1, k 2, p 1.

Seventh row.—Sl 1, k 27.

Eighth row.—K 3, n, * k 1, n, repeat 6 times more from * ; k 1.

Ninth row.—Sl 1, k 1, * th o twice, n, and repeat 7 times more from * ; k 1.

Tenth row.—K 3, p 1, * k 2, p 1; repeat 6 times morefrom * ; k 1.

Eleventh row.—Sl 1, k 25.

Twelfth row.—K 3, n, * k 1, n, *; repeat 7 times between the stars.

Thirteenth row.—Sl 1, * th o twice, n, *; repeat 8 times between the stars, k 1.

Fourteenth row.—K 3, p 1, * k 2, p 1 *; repeat 7 times between the stars.

Fifteenth row.—Sl 1, k 24.

Sixteenth row.—K 3, n, * k 1, n * ; repeat 6 times between the stars, k 1.

Seventeenth row.—Sl 1, k 1, * th o twice,

n *; repeat 7 times between the stars, k 1.

Eighteenth row.—K 3, p 1, * k 2, p 1 *; repeat 6 times between the stars, k 1.

Nineteenth row.—Sl 1, k 22.

Twentieth row.—Bind off 9, k 12.

Twenty-first row.—Sl 1, k 5, * th o twice, n *; repeat 3 times between the stars, k 1.

Twenty-second row.—K 3, p 1, * k 2, p 1 *; repeat twice between the stars, k 5.

Twenty-third row.—Sl 1, k 14.

Twenty-fourth row.—K 14.

Twenty-fifth row.—Sl 1, k 6, * th o twice, n *; repeat 3 times between the stars, k 1.

Twenty-sixth row.—K 3, p 1, * k 2, p 1 *; repeat twice between the stars, k 6.

Twenty-seventh row.—Sl 1, k 15.

Twenty-eighth row.—K 3, n, * k 1, n *; repeat 3 times between stars, k 1.

Twenty-ninth row.—Sl 1, k 1, * th o twice, n *; repeat 4 times between the stars, k 1.

Thirtieth row.—K 3, p 1, * k 2, p 1 *; repeat 3 times between the stars.

Thirty-first row.—Sl 1, k 12.

Thirty-second row.—K 3, n, * k 1, n *; repeat twice between the stars, k 1.

Thirty-third row.—Sl 1, k 1, * th o twice, n *; repeat 3 times between the stars, k 1.

Thirty-fourth row.—K 3, p 1, * k 2, p 1 *; repeat twice between the stars, k 1.

Thirty-fifth row.—Sl 1, k 10.

Thirty-sixth row.—Bind off 9, k 4, make one by catching under the loops which are between the two needles, k 10, make another, k 2, make another, k 2.

Thirty-seventh row.—Sl 1, k 21.

Thirty-eighth row.—K 22. This finishes half of corner.

Thirty-ninth row.—Sl 1, k 14, * th o twice, n *; repeat 3 times between the stars, k 1.

Fortieth row.—K 3, p 1, * k 2, p 1 *; repeat twice between the stars, k 3.

Forty-first row.—Sl 1, k 12.

Forty-second row.—K 12.

Forty-third row.—Sl 1, k 4, * th o twice, n *; repeat 3 times between the stars, k 1.

Forty-fourth row.—K 3, p 1, * k 2, p 1 *; repeat twice between the stars, k 5.

Forty-fifth row.—Sl 1, k 14.

Forty-sixth row.—K 3, n, * k 1, n *; repeat 3 times between the stars, k 2.

Forty-seventh row.—Sl 1, * th o twice, n *; repeat 5 times between the stars, k 1.

Forty-eighth row.—K 3, p 1, * k 2, p 1 *; repeat 4 times between the stars, k 2.

Forty-ninth row.—Sl 1, k 17.

Fiftieth row.—K 3, n, * k 1, n *; repeat 4 times between the stars, k 2.

Fifty-first row.—Sl 1, * th o twice, n *; repeat 6 times between the stars, k 1.

Fifty-second row.—K 3, p 1, * k 2, p 1 *; repeat 5 times between the stars, k 2.

Fifty-third row.—Sl 1, k 20.

Fifty-fourth row.—Bind off 9, k 12.

Fifty-fifth row.—Sl 1, k 5, * th o twice, n *; repeat 3 times between the stars, k 1.

Fifty-sixth row.—K 3, p 1, * k 2, p 1 *; repeat twice between the stars, k 7.

Fifty-seventh row.—Sl 1, k 16.

Fifty-eighth row.—K 18.

Fifty-ninth row.—Sl 1, k 10, * th o twice, n *; repeat 3 times between the stars, k 1.

Sixtieth row.—K 3, p 1, * k 2, p 1 *; repeat twice between the stars, k 12.

Sixty-first row.—Sl 1, k 21.

Sixty-second row.—K 3, n, * k 1, n *; repeat 5 times between the stars, k 1.

Sixty-third row.—Sl 1, k 1, * th o twice, n *; repeat 7 times between the stars, k 1.

Sixty-fourth row.—K 3, p 1, * k 2, p 1 *; repeat 6 times between the stars, k 3.

Sixty-fifth row.—Sl 1, k 24.

Sixty-sixth row.—K 3, n, * k 1, n *; repeat 6 times between the stars, k 3.

Sixty-seventh row.—Sl 1, k 1, * th o twice, n *; repeat 8 times between the stars, k 1.

Sixty-eighth row.—K 3, p 1, * k 2, p 1 *; repeat 7 times between the stars, k 3.

Sixty-ninth row.—Sl 1, k 27.

Seventieth row.—Bind off 9, k 15, pick up 1, k 2, pick up 1, k 2.

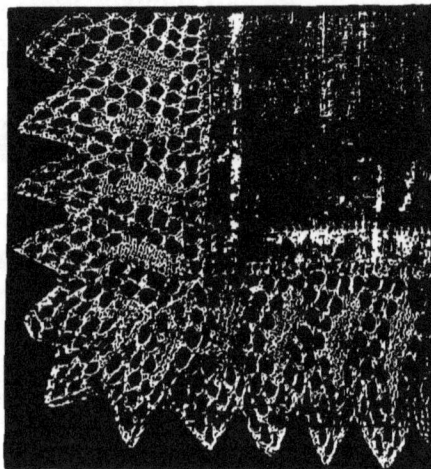

No. 19.—KNITTED CORNER FOR A HANDKERCHIEF.
(For Description see Page 93.)

FOR THE LACE.

Now begin the first point beyond the corner. There are 22 stitches on the needle.

First row.—K 3, th o twice, n, k 10, th o twice, n, th o twice, n, th o twice, n, k 1.

Second row.—K 3, p 1, k 2, p 1, k 2, p 1, k 12, p 1, k 3.

Third and Fourth rows.—Plain.

Fifth row.—K 3, th o twice, n, th o twice, n, k 12, th o twice, n, th o twice, n, th o twice, n, k 1.

Sixth row.—K 3, p 1, k 2, p 1, k 2, p 1, k 14, p 1, k 2, p 1, k 3.

Seventh row.—Plain.

Eighth row.—K 3, n, * k 1, n, and repeat 7 times more from * ; k 2.

Ninth row.—K 3, * th o twice, n, and repeat 8 times more from * ; k 1.

Tenth row.—K 3, p 1, * k 2, p 1, and repeat 7 times more from * ; k 3.

Eleventh row.—Plain.

Twelfth row.—K 3 ; then n, k 1, and repeat across the row, knitting the last 2 plain.

Thirteenth row.—K 3, * th o twice, n, and repeat 8 times more from * ; k 1.

Fourteenth row.—K 3, p 1, * k 2, p 1, and repeat 7 times more from * ; k 3.

Fifteenth row.—Plain.

Sixteenth row.—Bind off 9 stitches or until there are 21 stitches left on the left-hand needle. Knit these plain and repeat from the first row.

FANCY WRISTER.

No. 20.—This wrister is made of silk. Cast on enough stitches to make the desired width, and knit with 2 needles.

First row.—K 4, o twice, p 2 to., k all but the

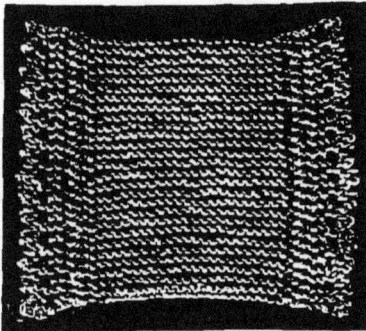

No. 20.—FANCY WRISTER.

last 6 ; then o twice, p 2 to., k 2, o twice, k 2.

Second row.—K 3, p 1, k 2, o twice, p 2 to., k all but 6, o twice, p 2 to., k 2, o twice, k 2.

Third row.—K 3, p 1, k 2, o twice, p 2 to., k all but 8, o twice, p 2 to., k 6.

Fourth row.—Bind off 2 stitches, k 3, o twice, p

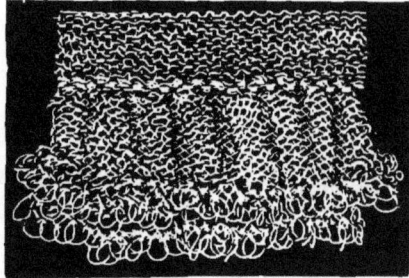

No. 21.—KNITTED NECK-RUCHING.

2 to., k all but 6 stitches, o twice, p 2 to., k 2, o twice, k 2 ; and repeat from 2nd row until the work is large enough to fit the wrist snugly, then bind off and sew together.

KNITTED NECK-RUCHING.

No. 21.—This ruching may be made of either silk, crochet cotton or thread, fine cotton being used for the one pictured. Cast on 20 stitches.

First row.—Th o twice, p 2 to, k 9, o, n, p 5, o, p 2 to., drop the last stitch.

Second row.—Th o twice, p 2 to., k 7, p 9, o, p 2 to., drop the last stitch. Repeat the 1st and 2nd rows twice more.

Third row.—Th o twice, p 2 to., p 9, o, n, k 5, o twice, p 2 to., drop the last stitch.

Fourth row.—Th o twice, p 2 to., p 7, k 9, o twice, p 2 to., drop the last stitch. Repeat the last 2 rows twice more; then repeat the 4 rows in the order given, until the work is long enough. The pattern will generally have to be repeated 50 times for half a yard of ruching. Lay the knitted strip over the needle and use the bars through the middle for stitches. Knit 2 bars or stitches together, and repeat until all are used up; then continue to knit plain until you have the width desired for a band.

A double ruche may be made by making another ruche like the last, except that you make it a very few stitches narrower, and then, after knitting a few rows of the band, join it to the single ruche, being careful to have it come on the right side, and knitting through the bars and the stitches already on the needle at the same time, knitting two of the bars together as directed above. If knit of silk, the effect will be prettier and more lace-like if the silk is put over the needle three times at the beginning of each row instead of only twice.

KNITTED PITCHER-PURSE.

No. 22.—Purses of this description are knitted of silk on fine steel needles, and may be of one color or two, to suit the taste of the maker. Four needles are used. Work the top of the pitcher thus:

Cast 21 stitches on first needle and 18 on each of the other two

First round.—On 1st needle k 1, p 1, sl and b, k 14, k 2 to., and p 1. The rest of the round is k 1, p 1.

Continue like first round until there are only 4 stitches left on the 1st needle. This forms the spout of the pitcher. Of course, it will be seen that there are 12 stitches instead of 14 in the second round between the narrowings and in each following round there remain two less each time until there are none left.

Now take enough stitches from the other two needles upon the first to make them all even, and begin neck.

First round.—Open work, thus: P 2 to. all the way round.

Second round.—Over, and k 1 all round.

Third round.—Knit plain, knitting the loop as one stitch.

Fourth round.—Knit plain.

These four rounds form the pattern. Repeat them until you have knit the pattern 6 times. Then, o and k 1, all round.

Next round.—Knit plain, knitting loop as in first round. You have now twice as many stitches as before.

Next round.—P all round; continue to k plain and p, alternately until you have 4 rounds of each. Then increase as before (over k 1). Now k plain, and p alternately as before the increase until you have 4 rounds of each.

Knit the open work again as before until you have made the pattern 4 times.

Now p round, and k round alternately 4 times. Then, k 2 to., entirely round. This brings you to the bottom of the pitcher. Now p round and k round 4 times. Then k 2 to., k 1 and repeat all round. K 3 rounds plain; then k 2 to., k 1 and repeat all round; continue narrowing in this way with 3 rounds between until there are 5 on each needle; then knit all together and fasten off.

For the Handle.—On each of 3 needles cast 3 stitches. K 1 round, and p 1 round alternately until you have a strip 4 inches long; sew in place exactly opposite the spout. Take a small ring and crochet or button-hole round, and then slip over the handle before sewing to the pitcher. This can be slipped over the top, thus closing the mouth of the purse. If preferred, a purse ring may be used.

KNITTED BAG.

(For Illustration see Page 97.)

No. 23.—This bag may be made of either No. 12 knitting cotton, or No. 16 Madonna crochet cotton. Cast onto each of three needles 30 stitches.

First, Second and Third rounds.—K 1, o, k 3, sl 1, n, pass the slipped stitch over, k 3, o, and repeat from beginning. Knit 2 rounds plain.

Sixth round.—K 1, o, n, and repeat from *.

Purl the next 2 rounds.

Knit the next round, and make 1 extra stitch at the end of the third needle. K 1 round plain.

Eleventh round.—Sl 1, n, pass the slipped stitch over, o twice, and repeat from the beginning; at the end, k 1.

Twelfth round.—K 2 and purl the second half of the 2 put-overs; repeat for the entire round.

Thirteenth round.—K plain, narrowing once on each needle.

NO. 22.—KNITTED PITCHER-PURSE.

There should now be 83 stitches; arrange 32 stitches on each of 2 needles, and 24 on the third.

Fourteenth round.—Knit plain.

Fifteenth round.—* P 3, o, n, k 3, and repeat from *.

Sixteenth round.—P 3, o, k 1, n, k 2, and repeat from the beginning of the round.

Seventeenth round.—P 3, o, k 2, n, k 1, and repeat from the beginning of round.

Eighteenth round.—P 3, o, k 3, n and repeat from the beginning of round.

Nineteenth round.—* P 3, k 3, n, o (to make 1 stitch), and repeat from *.

Twentieth round.—P 3, k 2, n, k 1, o; and repeat from beginning of round.

Twenty-first round.—P 3, k 1, n, k 2, o, and repeat from beginning of round.

Twenty-second round.—P 3, n, k 3, o, and repeat from beginning of round.

These last eight rounds form a pattern which is to be repeated 7 times, or more, if you desire the bag longer.

Knit 8 rounds plain, then narrow until there are 8 stitches on each of 2 needles, and 6 stitches on the third.

Then in the next round, k 1, o, and repeat for the entire round. Next few rounds narrow until there is but 1 stitch on each needle, then bind off tightly. Draw narrow ribbon through the open spaces at the top, and tie a bow with long loops and ends at the bottom (see picture.)

LONG TIDY FOR PATENT ROCKER.
(For Illustration see Page 98.)

No. 24.—Cast on 139 stitches, knit across twice plain.

First row.—Sl 1, k 2; o and n across the needle, k last 2 stitches.

Second, Third and Fourth rows.—Plain.

Fifth row.—Like 1st.

Sixth, Seventh and Eighth rows.—Plain.

Ninth row.—Sl 1, k 2; o and n 11 times; k 6, n, o, k 1, o, n, * k 7, n, o, k 1, o, n; repeat 5 times more from *, k 7; o and n 11 times; k 2.

Tenth row.—Sl 1, k 31, p 3, * k 9, p 3; repeat 5 times more from *, k 32.

Eleventh row.—Sl 1, k 29, n, o, k 3, o, n, * k 5, n, o, k 3, o, n; repeat 5 times more from *, k 30.

Twelfth row.—Sl 1, k 30, p 5, * k 7, p 5; repeat 5 times more from *, k 31.

Thirteenth row.—Sl 1, k 2; o and n 11 times; k 4, n, o, k 5, o, n, * k 3, n, o, k 5, o, n; repeat 5 times more from *, k 5; o and n 11 times; k 2.

Fourteenth row.—Sl 1, k 29, p 7, * k 5, p 7; repeat 5 times more from *, k 30.

Fifteenth row.—Sl 1, k 29, o, n, k 3, n, o, * k 5, o, n, k 3, n, o; repeat 5 times more from *, k 30.

Sixteenth row.—Sl 1, k 29, p 5, * k 7, p 5; repeat 5 times more from *, k 32.

Seventeenth row.—Sl 1, k 2; o and n 11 times; k 6, o, n, k 1, n, o, * k 7, o, n, k 1, n, o, repeat 5 times more from *, k 7; o and n 11 times; k 2.

Eighteenth row.—Sl 1, k 30, p 3, * k 9, p 3, repeat 5 times more from *, k 33.

Nineteenth row.—Sl 1, k 31, o, k 3 together, o, * k 9, o, k 3 together, o, repeat 5 times more from *, k 32.

Twentieth row.—All plain.

Twenty-first row.—Sl 1, k 2; o and n 11 times; plain to border; o and n 11 times; k 2.

Twenty-second, Twenty-third and Twenty-fourth rows.—Plain.

Twenty-fifth row.—Sl 1, k 2; o and n across needle, k last 2.

Twenty-sixth, Twenty-seventh and Twenty-eighth rows.—Plain.

Twenty-ninth row.—Like 25th.

Thirtieth, Thirty-first and Thirty-second rows.—All plain.

Thirty-third row.—Sl 1, k 2, o, n, o, n, k 14, o, n, o, n, plain to border, o, n, o, n, k 14, o, n, o, n, k 2.

Thirty-fourth, Thirty-fifth and Thirty-sixth rows.—Plain.

This completes the border for the end. Now knit 1 row as follows:

Sl 1, k 2, o, n, o, n, k 14, o, n, o, n, knit plain to border, o, n, o, n, k 14, o, n, o, n, k 2. Now knit 3 rows plain and commence center pattern.

CENTER PATTERN FOR TIDY.

First row.—Sl 1, k 2, o, n, o, n, k 4, n, o, k 1, o, n, k 5, o, n, o, n, k 7, n, o, k 1, o, n, * k 9, n, o, k 1, o, n, repeat 4 times more from *, k 8, o, n, o, n, k 4, n, o, k 1, o, n, k 5, o, n, o, n, k 2.

Second row.—Sl 1, k 11, p 3, k 18, p 3, * k 11, p 3, repeat 4 times more from * k 18, p 3, k 12.

Third row.—Sl 1, k 9, n, o, k 3, o, n, k 14, n, o, k 3, o, n, * k 7, n, o, k 3, o, n, repeat 4 times more from *, k 14, n, o, k 3, o, n, k 10.

Fourth row.—Sl 1, k 10, p 5, k 16, p 5, * k 9, p 5, repeat 4 times more from *, k 16, p 5, k 11.

Fifth row.—Sl 1, k 2, o, n, o, n, k 2, n, o, k 5, o, n, k 3, o, n, o, n, k 5, n, o, k 5, o, n, * k 5, n, o, k 5, o, n, repeat 4 times more from *, k 6, o, n, o, n, k 2, n, o, k 5, o, n, k 3, o, n, o, n, k 2.

Sixth row.—Sl 1, k 9, p 7, k 14, p 7, * k 7, p 7, repeat 4 times more from *, k 14, p 7, k 10.

Seventh row.—Sl 1, k 9, o, n, k 3, n, o, k 12, n, o,

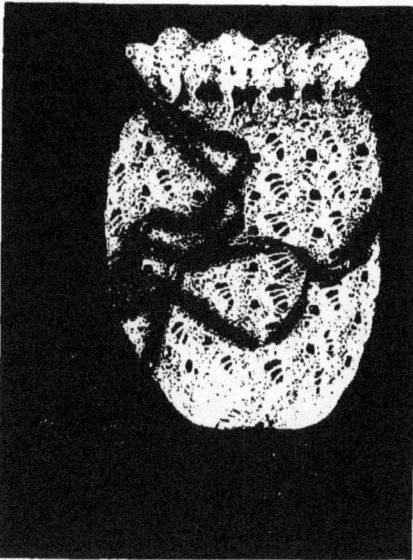

No. 23.—KNITTED BAG.
(For Description see Page 96.)

k 7, o, n, * k 3, n, o, k 7, o, n, repeat 4 times more from *, k 12, o, n, k 3, n, o, k 10.

Eighth row.—Sl 1, k 10, p 5, k 14, p 9, * k 5, p 9, repeat 4 times more from *, k 14, p 5, k 11.

Ninth row.—Sl 1, k 2, o, n, o, n, k 4, o, n, k 1, n, o, k 5, o, n, o, n, k 5, * o, n, k 5, n, o, k 5, repeat 4 times from *, k 6, o, n, o, n, k 4, o, n, k 1, n, o, k 5, o, n, o, n, k 2.

Tenth row.—Sl 1, k 11, p 3, k 16, p 7, * k 7, p 7, repeat 4 times from *, k 16, p 3, k 12.

Eleventh row.—Sl 1, k 11, o, k 3 together, o, k 16, o, n, k 3, n, o, * k 7, o, n, k 3, n, o, repeat 4 times more from *, k 16, o, k 3 together, o, k 12.

Twelfth row.—Sl 1, k 31, p 5, * k 9, p 5, repeat 4 times more from *, k 32.

Thirteenth row.—Sl 1, k 2, o, n, o, n, k 14, o, n, o, n, k 7, o, n, k 1, n, o, * k 9, o, n, k 1, n, o, repeat 4 times more from *, k 8, o, n, o, n, k 14, o, n, o, n, k 2.

Fourteenth row.—Sl 1, k 32, p 3, * k 11, p 3, repeat 4 times more from *, k 33.

Fifteenth row.—Sl 1, k 32, o, k 3 together, o, * k 11, o, k 3 together, o, repeat 4 times more from *, k 33.

Sixteenth row.—All plain.

Seventeenth row.—Sl 1, k 2, o, n, o, n, k 4, n, o, k 1, o, n, k 5, o, n, o, n, k 14, n, o, k 1, o, n, * k 9, n, o, k 1, o, n, repeat 3 times more from *, k 15, o, n, o, n, k 4, n, o, k 1, o, n, k 5, o, n, o, n, k 2.

Eighteenth row.—Sl 1, k 11, p 3, k 25, p 3, * k 11, p 3, repeat 3 times more from *, k 25, p 3, k 12.

Nineteenth row.—Sl 1, k 9, n, o, k 3, o, n, k 21, n, o, k 3, o, n, * k 7, n, o, k 3, o, n, repeat 3 times more from *, k 21, n, o, k 3, o, n, k 10.

Twentieth row.—Sl 1, k 10, p 5, k 23, p 5, * k 9, p 5, repeat 3 times more from *, k 23, p 5, k 11.

Twenty-first row.—Sl 1, k 2, o, n, o, n, k 2, n, o, k 5, o, n, k 3, o, n, o, n, k 12, n, o, k 5, o, n, * k 5, n, o, n, k 5, o, n, repeat 3 times more from *, k 13, o, n, o, n, k 2, n, o, k 5, o, n, k 3, o, n, o, n, k 2.

Twenty-second row.—Sl 1, k 9, p 7, k 21, p 7, * k 7, p 7, repeat 3 times more from *, k 21, p 7, k 10.

Twenty-third row.—Sl 1, k 9, o, n, k 3, n, o, k 19, n, o, k 7, o, n, * k 3, n, o, k 7, o, n, repeat 3 times more from *, k 19, o, n, k 3, n, o, k 10.

Twenty-fourth row.—Sl 1, k 10, p 5, k 21, p 9, * k 5, p 9, repeat 3 times more from *, k 21, p 7, k 11.

Twenty-fifth row.—Sl 1, k 2, o, n, o, n, k 4, o, n, k 1, n, o, k 5, o, n, o, n, k 12, o, n, k 5, n, o, * k 5,

o, n, k 5, n, o, repeat 3 times more from *, k 13, o, n, o, n, k 4, o, n, k 1, n, o, k 5, o, n, o, n, k 2.

Twenty-sixth row.—Sl 1, k 11, p 3, k 23, p 7, * k 7, p 7, repeat 3 times more from *, k 23, p 3, k 12.

Twenty-seventh row.—Sl 1, k 11, o, k 3 together, o, k 23, o, n, k 3, n, o, * k 7, o, n, k 3, n, o, repeat 3 times more from *, k 23, o, k 3 together, o, k 12.

Twenty-eighth row.—Sl 1, k 38, p 5, * k 9, p 5, repeat 3 times more from *, k 39.

Twenty-ninth row.—Sl 1, k 2, o, n, o, n, k 14, o, n, o, n, k 14, o, n, k 1, n, o, * k 9, o, n, k 1, n, o, repeat 3 times more from *, k 15, o, n, o, n, k 14, o, n, o, n, k 2.

Thirtieth row.—Sl 1, k 39, p 3, * k 11, p 3, repeat 3 times more from *, k 40.

Thirty-first row.—Sl 1, k 39, o, k 3 together, o, * k 11, o, k 3 together, repeat 3 times more from *, k 40.

Thirty-second row.— Knit all plain.

These 32 rows complete the pattern, and are to be repeated until you have 21 diamonds in the side borders, but in last repetitions use only first part, as that leaves a prettier corner. Then repeat the 36 rows of border for end and bind off loosely. This tidy is made of No. 30 thread, which makes it fine and nice, and yet not too fine to be serviceable.

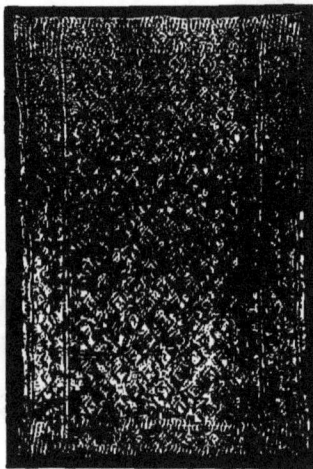

No. 24.—Long Tidy for Patent Rocker.
(For Description see Page 97.)

KNITTED WRISTER.
(For Illustration see Page 99.)

No. 25.—Single zephyr in two colors that contrast nicely, and four knitting needles of a size suitable for the zephyr, are needed in making these wristers.

Cast on any number of stitches divisible by 10, as 10 stitches form the pattern. 110 stitches make a wrister of average size.

First round.—K 1, th o, k 3, sl 1, n, pass the slipped stitch over the narrowed one, k 3, th o (always be sure to put the thread over the needle before knitting the first stitch on the next needle so that the extra stitch will be on the needle last used every time). Repeat entirely around. Every row is alike. Make stripes any desired width. Five rounds is a pretty width. Make the wrister as long as desired, and bind off. The colors used in the wrister illustrated are orange and black.

KNITTED FASCINATOR.

No. 26.—The fascinator here pictured is very pretty in shape and is made of white Germantown wool, Saxony yarn and lavender knitting silk, and is completed with bows of lavender ribbon as shown in the engraving. The knitting silk is used to finish the edges of the two rows of shells that are crocheted with the Saxony around the fascinator as a border.

The top or head portion of the fascinator is knitted all in one piece. The tabs, which are knitted separately, may be tied loosely or caught together with a bow of ribbon or a pin. Saxony yarn may be used for the entire fascinator, if desired.

To Begin the Fascinator.—Cast on 64 stitches. Knit back and forth so that five consecutive rows will appear purled and five similar rows will appear plain. This will form two broad ribs of knitting. Work in this manner until there are fifteen of these ribs. Then knit or purl, as the case may be, 24 stitches. Next, cast off 16, dropping the 1st, 6th, 11th and 16th stitches. Then knit or purl the remaining 24 stitches. Continue to knit as before until each tab is 44 ribs long. Cast off the stitches, dropping the 5th, 10th, 15th and 20th. Now pull or slip all of the dropped stitches the full length of the work, being careful to keep the cross loops even. Fold the work and crochet the wide end together for the top of the fascinator and lay it in plaits to fit the head.

To Make the Border : First row.—Make 4 double crochets in the middle of each rib.

Second row.—Fasten between 2 groups of double crochets with a single crochet; then make 8 treble crochets between the next two groups, and fasten

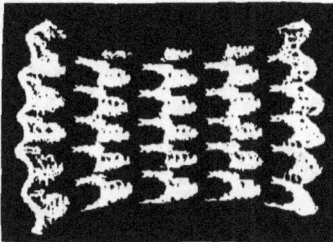

NO. 25.—KNITTED WRISTER
(For Description see Page 98.)

with a single crochet between the following 2 groups; repeat around the fascinator.

Third row.—Groups of 4 doubles in the middles of the first groups.

Fourth row.—Like second row, arranging scollops to come between those of the first row.

For the Edge.—Fasten the silk in a single crochet, 3 chain, 1 single between the 1st and 2nd trebles of a shell. Repeat for the next spaces 6 times more;

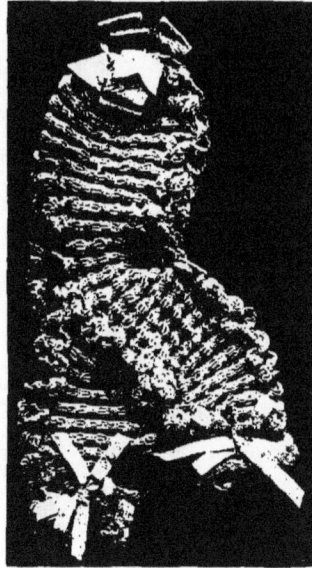

NO. 26.—KNITTED FASCINATOR.

then 3 chain, 1 single over the single underneath. Repeat in this way for all the scollops.

Fasten the bow of wide ribbon over the plaits in the top of the fascinator. Take the narrow ribbon, pass it up through the first and last spaces in the fourth rib from the bottom of each tab, and tie it in two double bow-knots as seen in the picture.

If made of Saxony yarn or silk, the knitter must cast on more stitches and allow more rows to a rib in order to make the fascinator large enough. By casting on in Germantown wool and then in Saxony or silk and measuring the latter stitches with those of the Germantown, the knitter can ascertain for herself the number of stitches required.

KNITTED SHAWL.
(For Illustration see Page 100.)

NOS. 27 AND 28.—Half a pound of Saxony wool will be required for this shawl. Knit with double thread, very loosely. Cast on 4 stitches.

First row.—Purl.

Second row.—Th o, k, l, th o, k 3; then put the

first of the last three knit ones over the other two.

Third row.—Purl.

Fourth row.—Same as second, except at the

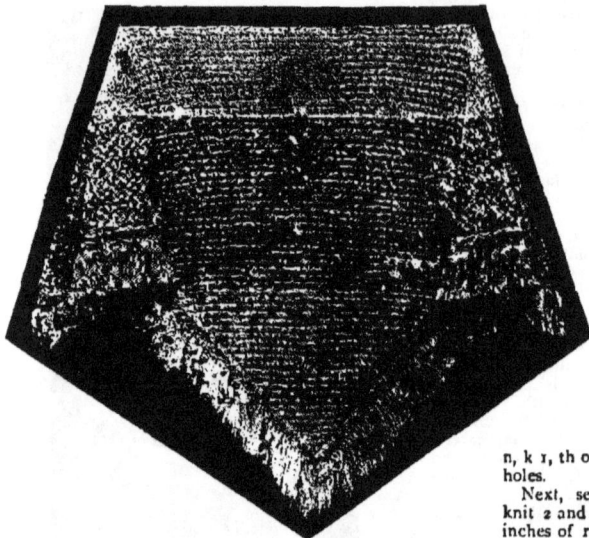

NO. 27.—KNITTED SHAWL.

end where you throw thread over and knit 1.

Fifth row.—Purl.

Sixth row.—Same as second row but end with o, k 2, pass stitch over.

Seventh row.—Purl.

Eighth row.—Same as second; end same as fourth row.

Ninth row.—Purl.

Tenth row.—Same as second row.

When of the required size bind off, holding right side towards you. Then turn, take up and knit each stitch along one edge. Then holding right side towards you again, knit one row of pattern, (same as in body of shawl), then purl on wrong side, then another row of pattern, then bind off. For the other side, hold right side of shawl toward you, take up and knit each stitch; at the end break off worsted. Now, still holding right side towards you, tie on the worsted and bind off; turn and holding wrong side towards you, take up and knit each stitch and finish same as other side with one row of pattern; then purl one row; next, knit another row of pattern and then bind off. Widen two or three stitches at the corner to make the border lie flat and draw together with needle and wool. Put in fringe across the two sides as seen in the picture.

KNITTED BED-SOCKS.
(For Illustration see Page 104.)

No. 29.—Cast 120 stitches on small ivory or rubber needles, using Germantown yarn. Knit back and forth 14 times, or until you have 7 ribs on each side.

Fifteenth row.—Knit 57 rows plain, narrow next 2 (58th and 59th), knit 2 plain, narrow next 2; knit the rest plain. Seam back, narrowing each side of the 2 center stitches in each row. (These 2 stitches are not ribbed, but knit plain.) When there are 3 rows, reverse and knit 2 plain rows and seam 1 row for right rib. Repeat until there are 5 right and 5 reverse ribs. There will now be 60 stitches on the needle.

Now knit 1 row plain and seam 1 row.

Next row.—K 1, th o, n, k 1, th o, n, and so on, making a row of holes.

Next, seam 1 row, knit 1 row plain; knit 2 and seam 2 until you have about 4 inches of ribbing; then bind off.

Crochet a border at the top as follows:

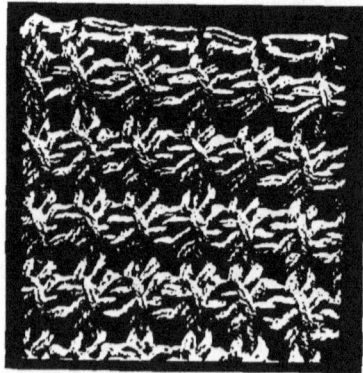

NO. 28.—DETAIL OF KNITTED SHAWL.
(For Description see Page 99.)

1 s. c. in a stitch, skip 2 stitches, 7 d. c. in the next, 1 s. c. in the 3rd stitch beyond. Repeat all across the top. *Next row.*—1 s. c. in each stitch of last row. There should be 10 scollops.

When the scollops are completed, sew the sock together.

KNITTED MAT.

No. 30.—Use two colors of Germantown yarn, and two steel needles, No. 14. Cast on 21 stitches.

First row.—Insert the needle in first stitch, wind the yarn around the first three fingers of the left hand for loop of fringe; knit 3 stitches; turn and knit back.

Third row.—Wind yarn as before and knit 6 stitches; turn and knit back.

Work like these four rows, back and forth, knitting 3 more stitches each time after winding the yarn than were knitted in the preceding row, until you have knit the 21 stitches cast on; turn and knit back. This completes one section.

Now join the other color and knit the same as in the first and all following rows to form the section.

Alternate these two sections until you have an even and necessary number of each, and the work lies flatly. Bind off and join the two edges, running a thread through the stitches at the center to close the hole, and fasten tightly. Press with a warm iron on the wrong side, and cut open the fringe.

Serviceable table-mats may be knitted in this manner with knitting cotton. Made of fine cotton or linen thread, with a lace edge knitted on instead of the fringe, mats like this are pretty for cushion-covers or doileys.

RUSSIAN HOUSE-SHOE.
(For Illustration see Page 102.)

No. 31.—The comfortable and cosy-looking slip-

No. 29.—KNITTED BED-SOCK.
(For Description see Page 100.)

pers, knit in various ways, which have been in popular favor for so long a time are supplanted to a certain extent at present by the Russian

house-shoe, which covers the ankle as well as the foot, and will, therefore, be appreciated by the many who experience disagreeable effects in chang-

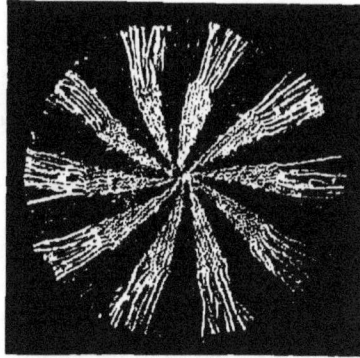

No. 30.—KNITTED MAT.

ing from a high shoe to a slipper, be the latter ever so warm. As the shoe top is ribbed and made without an opening, it is quite as easy to adjust as the slipper and once on, stays in place much better. The shoes are finished with fleece-lined soles, just as the slippers are.

The shoe illustrated and described is made in two shades of brown, although colors, of course, in other cases will be matters of individual choice. For this pair of shoes two skeins of dark-brown Germantown yarn and half a skein of light-brown were used, and they were knit upon two coarse steel needles.

Begin the shoe at its lower edge thus:

Cast upon one needle 160 stitches of the dark-brown, then knit back and forth in garter style, six times.

After knitting back and forth plain six times, as directed, begin to seam at the center of the part you are knitting, the same as you would at the back of a stocking, except that you seam two stitches instead of one. Narrow on both sides of this seam every time across, and knit back and forth in this manner 46 times. Now continue to knit in the same way with the light-brown 4 times across, then 4 times more with the dark-brown. (The cut shows the foot knitted of one color, but the variation directed is prettier.) This finishes the foot of the shoe.

Now with the light-brown begin to rib, by seaming 2 stitches and knitting 2 alternately without narrowing, until half of the original amount of light-brown yarn is used; then bind off. This ribbed portion forms the upper or ankle part of the shoe.

The directions given will make a shoe 7 inches high, and 10 inches long from heel to toe when doubled flat; and one that will fit a No. 5 sole.

In knitting the plain or garter stitch, which forms

No. 31.—Russian House-Shoe.
(For Description see Page 101.)

the lower part of the shoe, a better edge will be given the back if the first stitch each time across is slipped off with the thread forward, as in seaming; then throw the thread back and proceed with the knitting as usual. This will form a regular chain stitch along the edge, which holds the shape better and makes a smoother, firmer edge to join for the back of the shoe.

When the ribbed portion has been bound off, the shoe is sewed firmly together up the back, and also, wrong side out, to the edge of the sole and firmly turned up.

A bow of ribbon or a full rosette of worsted or ribbon may be added to the front, if desired.

The upper edge may be finished with a shell or fancy stitch, but if this is made at all full it will be more liable to catch upon the skirts than if finished plain.

For elderly ladies, for invalids or for nurses, these shoes will be found especially comfortable and convenient. As bath shoes they cannot be excelled. Made in dainty colors they are particularly attractive for children's wear.

Knitted Spool-Bag.

No. 32.—With ordinary knitting silk and medium-sized steel needles, cast on enough stitches to make the bag as large around as you wish it to be, and add 12 more stitches for the edge.

First row.—K 2, * o, n; * repeat between stars until 12 stitches are left; then k 3, o twice, n, o twice, n, k 5.

Second row.—K 7, p 1, k 2, p 1, knit plain to end.

Third row.—Knit plain.

Fourth row.—K 14; * o, n, * and repeat between stars to end.

Fifth row.—Knit plain until 14 stitches are left, then k 3, o twice, n, o twice, n, o twice, n, k 5.

Sixth row.—K 7, p 1, k 2, p 1, k 2, p 1, k 3; k rest plain.

Seventh row.—K 2; * o, n, * and repeat between stars until 17 stitches remain; k rest plain.

Eighth row.—Sl and bind 5; k plain to end.

This completes one point of the edging. Repeat until the strip is long enough for the bag, and crochet it together across the lower edge and up the side. If preferred, two pieces may be knitted and crocheted together to form the bag. Run a cord or ribbon in the row of holes nearest the beginning of the edging for a drawing string.

A clever knitter can vary the design of the bag in many ways, using any fancy pattern for the bag portion, and any edging that pleases her for the top. Lined, such a bag will serve as a button-holder.

Knitted Bed-Slipper.

(For Illustration see Page 103.)

No. 33.—Cast on stitches enough so that by stretching them slightly they can be made to reach from the heel to the toes. Knit on large steel needles or wooden ones; the latter are the best. The materials required are single zephyr, ribbon and rubber cord. Knit the first row plain. Next make a row of holes across the work made by

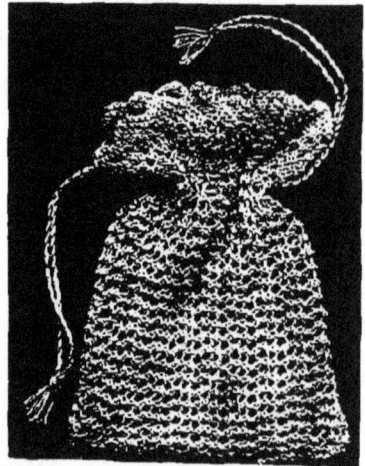

No. 32.—Knitted Spool-Bag.

putting over the thread and narrowing alternately. Next, make 26 ribs or row of holes, one plain row, and bind off. Sew up at the heel. Sew the row half way, then turn back the corners, and sew together across the bias edge. Crochet a row of scallops around edge and points, as follows: 1 s. c., skip 1 stitch, 1 d. c. in next, 3-ch., 1 s. c. in top of d. c. (making picot); repeat d. c. and picot twice more; skip 1 stitch, 1 s. c. in next, etc. Run the rubber cord around the row of holes in the top and tie under the points in front. Finish with a bow of ribbon.

KNITTED LAMP-SHADE.

No. 34.—Use unbleached linen thread, crochet cotton or a delicate shade of knitting silk. Cast on 50 stitches and knit across plain.

First, Third and Fifth rows.—Knit plain.

Second and Fourth rows.—Purl. This completes one rib.

Sixth, Eighth and Tenth rows.—Knit plain.

Seventh and Ninth rows.—Purl. This completes the second rib; continue knitting these 2 ribs as directed until the strip is long enough to reach around the bottom of the lamp-shade; then bind off in the following manner. Knit 5, drop the 6th and pull it all the way through; pull the 5th stitch rather loosely so it will reach across the vacant space, k 5, drop the next stitch as before, and continue across the strip; then bind off. Dropping the stitches widens the strip greatly. Finish the lower edge with a heavy fringe, knotted in. At the top finish the edge with a heading, thus:

First row.—Make 1 d. c. with 3 ch. between in about every other stitch.

Second row.—Make 7 ch., * 3 d. c. with 7 ch. between, in the first space, 7 ch., and repeat from * in all the spaces.

Run ribbon through the holes at the top, and tie in long loops and ends. If desired, ribbon may be run through the spaces where the stitches are dropped. This knitted shade fits a common porcelain globe, but it can be made larger or smaller, as desired.

KNITTED HOLDER.
(For Illustration see Page 101.)

No. 35.—This holder is made of two shades

No. 33.—KNITTED BED-SLIPPER.
(For Description see Page 102.)

of corn-yellow zephyr and is knitted on steel needles.

Cast on 50 stitches with the lightest shade, then k 1, and p 1 back and forth until there are 13 rows; then join the dark zephyr, k 5, join on the light, k

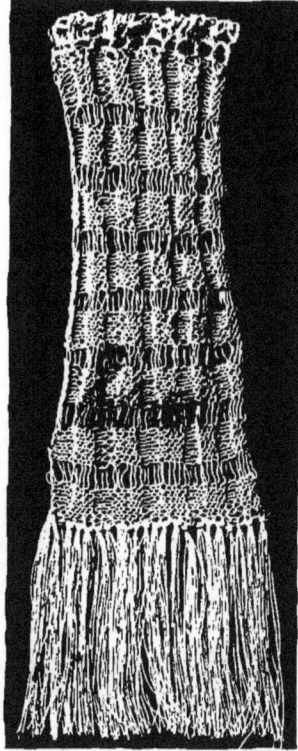

No. 34.—SECTION OF KNITTED LAMP-SHADE.

5, carry the dark along the back of the work, and k 5 with the light; then carry the light along and repeat until there are 10 kernels or until the stitches are all worked up. Be careful to always carry the wool along on the same side.

Next row.—As the light shade was the last one used, start back with the dark and k 5; then k 5 with the light, and repeat until there are 17 ridges; then join on the light and k 1 and p 1 until there are 4 rows; then, 4 more rows, narrowing in each row until there are 7 sts. Bind off. Gather up each end, and sew the edges of the light portion together; finish the end having 13 plain rows with a green bow having 5 ends which are caught down as shown in the picture.

SLUMBER SOCKS.

No. 36.—A skein of white Saxony and one of colored will be needed in making these socks. With No. 2 ivory needles, or steel ones of corresponding size cast on 54 stitches with the colored yarn.

First row.—Knit.
Second row.—Purl.
Third row.—Knit.
Fourth row.—Purl.
Fifth row.—Knit.
Join in white and knit as follows:
Sixth row.—Knit.
Seventh row.—Purl.
Eighth row.—Knit.
Ninth row.—Purl; then with the color work thus:
Tenth row.—Knit.
Eleventh row.—Knit.
Twelfth row.—Purl.
Thirteenth row.—Knit.
Fourteenth row.—Purl.
Fifteenth row.—Knit. Continue until there are 18 ribs of color and the same number of white; then, with the color:
Next row.—Knit.
Next row.—Purl.
Next row.—Knit.
Next row.—Purl.
Next row.—Knit, narrowing every 4th stitch.
Next row.—Purl; next knit, next purl, next knit, narrowing every 3rd stitch; next row purl, next knit, next purl, next knit, narrowing every 2nd stitch; next purl, next knit, next purl, next knit,

fine steel needles (No. 18) take up 104 stitches on side with white, taking three in colored and two in white ribs, knitting them as you take them up.

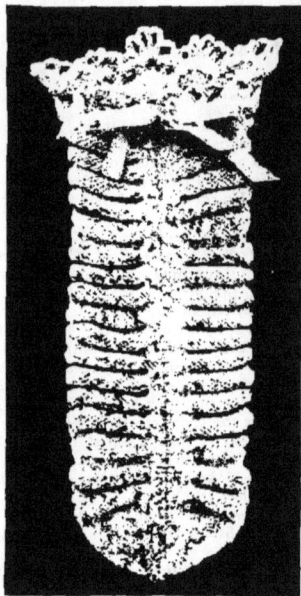

No. 36.—SLUMBER SOCK.

Next row.—Purl, next knit, next purl, next knit three white stitches, then three with color across the needle; purl back with both colors; knit back with both colors to form blocks, leaving the stitches on the needle; take up the same number stitches on other side with white, knitting same as other side; and when you begin to make blocks begin so as to alternate the colors. Narrowing every other row at the toe will make it of better shape. Now with the two needles together bind off with the third needle. Crochet any kind of border preferred, making spaces through which to run ribbon.

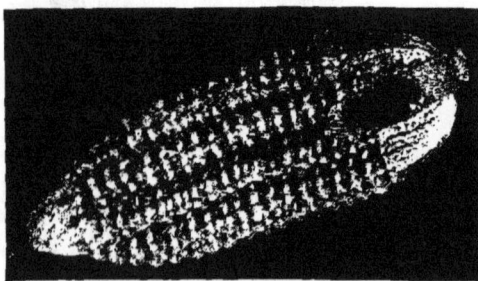

No. 35.—KNITTED HOLDER.
(For Description see Page 102.)

narrowing every 2nd stitch; next purl, next knit, narrowing every stitch; then bind off. Now with

KNITTED BOOK-MARK.
(For Illustration see Page 105.)

No. 37.—This useful article is knitted with knitting silk in two colors. Red and white, or blue and ecru would make a pretty combination. One must be careful to keep all the threads carried from one point to another, on the wrong side. As far as possible the letters *w* and *r* will be used in these directions to indicate white and red.

Cast on 21 stitches with white silk.

Knit 2 rows plain.

Third row.—K 1; o and n, 10 times. K 6 rows plain.

Tenth row.—K 8. Join red silk; 1 red, 2 white, 2 red, 8 white.

Eleventh row.—K 7 w; purl 1 r, 2 w, 1 r, 2 w, 1 r; k 7 w.

Twelfth row.—K 7 w, 1 r, 2 w, 1 r, 2 w, 1 r, 7 w.

Thirteenth row.—Like 11th.

Fourteenth row.—K 8 w, 2 r, 2 w, 1 r, 8 w.

Forty-fifth row.—Like 39th.

Forty-sixth row.—Like 34.

Forty-seventh row.—Like 15th.

Forty-eighth row.—Like 16th.

Forty-ninth row.—Like 15th.

Fiftieth row.—Like 20th.

Fifty-first row.—K 7 w; p 1 w, 5 r, 1 w; k 7 w.

Fifty-second row.—K 7 w, 1 r, 2 w, 1 r, 2 w, 1 r, 7 w.

Fifty-third row.—K 7 w; p 1 r, 1 w, 1 r, 1 w, 1 r, 1 w, 1 r; k 7 w.

Fifty-fourth row.—K 7 w, 1 r, 5 w, 1 r, 7 w.

Fifty-fifth row.—K 7 w; p 1 w, 1 r, 3 w, 1 r, 1 w; k 7 w.

Fifty-sixth row.—Like 16th.

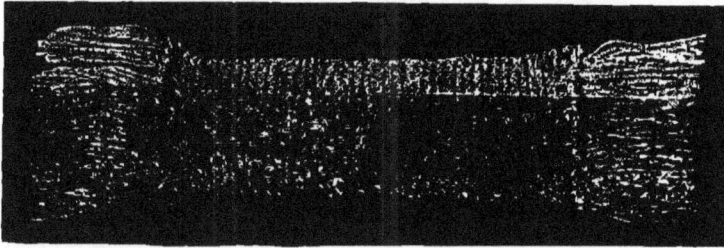

No. 37.—KNITTED BOOK-MARK.
(For Description see Page 104.)

Fifteenth row.—K 7; p 7; k 7 with white.

Sixteenth row.—K across plain with white.

Seventeenth row.—Like 15th.

Eighteenth row.—K 9 w, 3 r, 9 w.

Nineteenth row.—K 7 w; p 1 w, 1 r, 3 w, 1 r, 1 w; k 7 w.

Twentieth row.—K 7 w, 1 r, 5 w, 1 r, 7 w.

Twenty-first row.—K 7 w; p 1 r, 5 w, 1 r; k 7 w.

Twenty-second row.—K 8 w, 1 r, 3 w, 1 r, 8 w.

Twenty-third row.—K 7 w; p 2 w, 3 r, 2 w; k 7 w.

Twenty-fourth row.—Like 16th.

Twenty-fifth row.—Like 15th.

Twenty-sixth row.—Like 16th.

Twenty-seventh row.—K 7 w; p 1 r, 6 w; k 7 w.

Twenty-eighth row.—K 8 w, 6 r, 7 w.

Twenty-ninth row.—K 7 w; p 6 w, 1 r; k 7 w.

Thirtieth row.—K 7 w, 1 r, 13 w.

Thirty-first row.—Like 29th.

Thirty-second row.—Like 30th.

Thirty-third row.—K 7 w; p 6 r, 1 w; k 7 w.

Thirty-fourth row.—K 13 w, 1 r, 7 w.

Thirty-fifth row.—Like 15th.

Thirty-sixth row.—Like 16th.

Thirty-seventh row.—Like 15th.

Thirty-eighth row.—Like 34th.

Thirty-ninth row.—K 7 w; p 1 w, 1 r, 5 w; k 7 w.

Fortieth row.—K 10 w, 4 r, 7 w.

Forty-first row.—K 7 w; p 4 w, 2 r, 1 w; k 7 w.

Forty-second row.—Like 30th.

Forty-third row.—Like 41st.

Forty-fourth row.—Like 40th.

Fifty-seventh row.—Like 15th.

Fifty-eighth row.—Like 16th.

Fifty-ninth row.—K 7 w; p 1 r, 5 w, 1 r; k 7 w.

Sixtieth row.—K 8 w, 5 r, 8 w.

Sixty-first row.—K 7 w, p 1 r, 6 w; k 7 w.

Sixty-second row.—K 11 w, 2 r, 8 w.

Sixty-third row.—K 7 w; p 3 w, 2 r, 2 w; k 7 w.

Sixty-fourth row.—K 8 w, 1 r, 12 w.

Sixty-fifth row.—K 7 w; p 1 w, 6 r; k 7 w.

Sixty-sixth row.—Like 34th.

Sixth-seventh row.—Like 15th.

Sixty-eighth row.—Like 16th.

Sixty-ninth row.—Like 15th.

Seventieth row.—Like 50th.

Seventy-first row.—Like 51st.

Seventy-second row.—Like 50th.

Seventy-third row.—Like 15th.

Seventy-fourth row.—Like 16th.

Seventy-fifth row.—Like 15th.

Seventy-sixth row.—K 7 w, 1 r, 5 w, 1 r, 7 w.

Seventy-seventh row.—K 7 w, p 7 r, k 7 w.

Seventy-eighth row.—K 10 w, 1 r, 2 w, 1 r, 7 w.

Seventy-ninth row.—K 7 w; p 1 r, 2 w, 1 r, 3 w, k 7 w.

Eightieth row.—Like 78th.

Eighty-first row.—K 7 w, p 1 w, 2 r, 1 w, 3 r, k 7 w.

Eighty-second row.—K 7 w, 1 r, 13 w.

Eighty-third row.—Like 15th.

Knit five rows plain, then knit 1; o and n ten times; then knit 2 rows plain, and bind off. Tie fringe in the spaces at each end.

KNITTED YOKE FOR CORSET-COVER.

FIGURES NOS. 38 AND 39.—Cast on 37 stitches. To shape front end of yoke:

First row.—Sl 1, k 1, o twice, p 2 to., n, o twice, n, o twice, p 2 to., k 1; o and n 11 times; k 1, leave 3; turn.

Second row.—Sl 1, k 23, o twice, p 2 to., k 2, p 1, k 1, o twice, p 2 to., k 2.

Third row.—Sl 1, k 1, o twice, p 2 to., k 4, o

Ninth row.—Sl 1, k 1, o twice, p 2 to., n, o twice, n, o twice, p 2 to., k 1; o and n 5 times; k 1, leave 15.

Tenth row.—Sl 1, k 11, o twice, p 2 to., k 2, p 1, k 1, o twice, p 2 to., k 2.

Eleventh row.—Sl 1, k 1, o twice, p 2 to., k 4, o twice, p 2 to., k 9, leave 18.

Twelfth row.—Sl 1, k 8, o twice, p 2 to., k 4, o twice, p 2 to., k 2.

Thirteenth row.—Sl 1, k 1, o twice, p 2 to., n, o

FIGURE NO. 38.—(FRONT.)

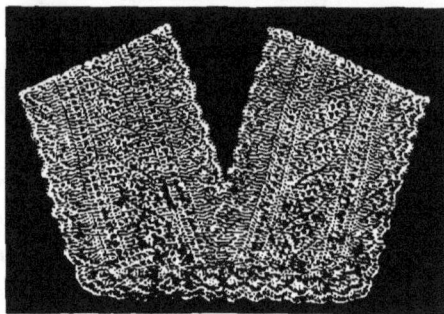

FIGURE NO. 39.—(BACK.)
FIGURES NOS. 38 AND 39.—KNITTED YOKE FOR CORSET-COVER.

twice, p 2 to., k 21, leave 6.

Fourth row.—Sl 1, k 20, o twice, p 2 to., k 4, o twice, p 2 to., k 2.

Fifth row.—Sl 1, k 1, o twice, p 2 to., n, o twice, n, o twice, p 2 to., k 1; o and n 8 times; k 1, leave 9.

Sixth row.—Sl 1, k 17, o twice, p 2 to., k 2, p 1, k 1, o twice, p 2 to., k 2.

Seventh row.—Sl 1, k 1, o twice, p 2 to., k 4, o twice, p 2 to., k 15, leave 12.

Eighth row.—Sl 1, k 14, o twice, p 2 to., k 4, o twice, p 2 to., k 2.

twice, n, o twice, p 2 to., k 1, o, n, o, n, k 1, leave 21.

Fourteenth row.—Sl 1, k 5, o twice, p 2 to., k 2, p 1, k 1, o twice, p 2 to., k 2.

Fifteenth row.—Sl 1, k 1, o twice, p 2 to., k 4, o twice, p 2 to., k 3, leave 24.

Sixteenth row.—Sl 1, k 2, o twice, p 2 to., k 4, o twice, p 2 to., k 2.

Seventeenth row.—Sl 1, k 1, o twice, p 2 to., n, o twice, n, o twice, p 2 to., k 1; o and n 8 times; o twice, p 2 to., n, o twice, n, o twice, p 2 to., k 2.

Eighteenth row.—Sl 1, k 1, o twice, p 2 to., k 2,

p 1, k 1, o twice, p 2 to., k 17, o twice, p 2 to., k 2,
p 1, k 1, o twice, p 2 to., k 2.

Nineteenth row.—Sl 1, k 1, o twice, p 2 to., k 4,
o twice, p 2 to., k 17, o twice, p 2 to., k 4, o twice,
p 2 to., k 2.

Twentieth row.—Like 19th.

The pattern begins now and is as follows:

First row.—Sl 1, k 1, o twice, p 2 to., n, o twice, n,
o twice, p 2 to., k 1; o and n 3 times; n, o, k 2; o, n, 3.
times; o twice, p 2 to., n, o twice, n, o twice, p 2 to., k 2.

Second row.—Sl 1, k 1, o twice, p 2 to., k 2, p 1,
k 1, o twice, p 2 to., k 17, o twice, p 2 to., k 2, p 1,
k 1, o twice, p 2 to., k 2.

Third row.—Sl 1, k 1, o twice, p 2 to., k 4, o
twice, p 2 to., k 6, n, o, k 1, o, n, k 6, o twice, p 2
to., k 4, o twice, p 2 to., k 2.

Fourth row.—Sl 1, k 1, o twice, p 2 to., k 4, o twice,
p 2 to., k 17, o twice, p 2 to., k 4, o twice, p 2 to., k 2.

Fifth row.—Sl 1, k 1, o twice, p 2 to., n, o twice, n,
o twice, p 2 to., k 1, o, n, n, o, k 3, o, n, k 1, o, n,
o, n, o twice, p 2 to., n, o twice, n, o twice, p 2 to., k 2.

Sixth row.—Like 2nd.

Seventh row.—Sl 1, k 1, o twice, p 2 to., k 4, o
twice, p 2 to., k 4, n, o, k 5, o, n, k 4, o twice, p 2
to., k 4, o twice, p 2 to., k 2.

Eighth row.—Like 4th.

Ninth row.—Sl 1, k 1, o twice, p 2 to., n, o
twice, n, o twice, p 2 to., k 1, o, n, n, o, k 2, n, o
twice, k 3, o, n, k 1, o, n, o twice, p 2 to., n, o
twice, n, o twice, p 2 to., k 2.

Tenth row.—Sl 1, k 1, o twice, p 2 to., k 2, p 1,
k 1, o twice, p 2 to., k 9, p 1, k 8, o twice, p 2 to.,
k 2, p 1, k 1, o twice, p 2 to., k 2.

Eleventh row.—Sl 1, k 1, o twice, p 2 to., k 4, o
twice, p 2 to., k 2, n, o, k 1, n, o twice, n, n, o
twice, n, k 1, o, n, k 2, o twice, p 2 to., k 4, o twice,
p 2 to., k 2.

Twelfth row.—Sl 1, k 1, o twice, p 2 to., k 4, o
twice, p 2 to., k 7, p 1, k 3, p 1, k 6, o twice, p 2
to., k 4, o twice, p 2 to., k 2.

Thirteenth row.—Sl 1, k 1, o twice, p 2 to., n, o
twice, n, o twice, p 2 to., k 1, n, o, k 4, n, o twice,
n, k 4, o, n, k 1, o twice, p 2 to., n, o twice, n, o
twice, p 2 to., k 2.

Fourteenth row.—Like 10th.

Fifteenth row.—Sl 1, k 1, o twice, p 2 to., k 4, o
twice, p 2 to., k 3, o, n, n, o twice, n, n, o twice, n,
n, o, k 3, o twice, p 2 to., k 4, o twice, p 2 to., k 2.

Sixteenth row.—Like 12th.

Seventeenth row.—Sl 1, k 1, o twice, p 2 to., n, o
twice, n, o twice, p 2 to., k 1, o, n, k 1, o, n, k 1, n,
o twice, n, k 1, n, o, k 2, o, n, o twice, p 2 to., n, o
twice, n, o twice, p 2 to., k 2.

Eighteenth row.—Like 10th.

Nineteenth row.—Sl 1, k 1, o twice, p 2 to., k 4,
o twice, p 2 to., k 5, o, n, k 4, n, o, k 5, o twice, p
2 to., k 4, o twice, p 2 to., k 2.

Twentieth row.—Sl 1, k 1, o twice, p 2 to., k 4, o
twice, p 2 to., k 18, o twice, p 2 to., k 4, o twice, p
2 to., k 2.

Twenty-first row.—Sl 1, k 1, o twice, p 2 to., n,
o twice, n, o twice, p 2 to., k 1, o, n, o, n, k 1, o, n,
k 2, n, o, k 2, o, n, o, n, o twice, p 2 to., n, o twice,
n, o twice, p 2 to., k 2.

Twenty-second row.—Sl 1, k 1, o twice, p 2 to., k
2, p 1, k 1, o twice, p 2 to., k 18, o twice, p 2 to.,
k 2, p 1, k 1, o twice, p 2 to., k 2.

Twenty-third row.—Sl 1, k 1, o twice, p 2 to., k
4, o twice, p 2 to., k 7, o, n, n, o, k 7, o twice, p 2
to., k 4, o twice, p 2 to., k 2.

Twenty-fourth row.—Sl 1, k 1, o twice, p 2 to.,
k 4, o twice, p 2 to., k 8, n, k 8, o twice, p 2 to., k
4, o twice, p 2 to., k 2.

Repeat these 24 rows 8 times more; then, to
shape the back end of yoke, work as follows:

First row.—Sl 1. k 1, o twice, p 2 to., n, o twice,
n, o twice, p 2 to., k 1, o, n 10 times, k 3, leave 3;
turn.

Second row.—Sl 1, k 23, o twice, p 2 to., k 3, p 1,
k 1, o twice, p 2 to., k 2.

Third row.—Sl 1, k 1, o twice, p 2 to., k 4, o
twice, p 2 to., k 21, leave 6.

Fourth row.—Sl 1, k 20, o twice, p 2 to., k 4, o
twice, p 2 to., k 2.

Fifth row.—Sl 1, k 1, o twice, p 2 to., n, o twice.
n, o twice, p 2 to., k 1, o, n 8 times, k 1, leave 9.

Sixth row.—Sl 1, k 17, o twice, p 2 to., k 2, p 1,
k 1, o twice, p 2 to., k 2.

Seventh row.—Sl 1, k 1, o twice, p 2 to., k 4, o
twice, p 2 to., k 15, leave 12.

Eighth row.—Sl 1, k 14, o twice, p 2 to., k 4, o
twice, p 2 to., k 2.

Ninth row.—Sl 1, k 1, o twice, p 2 to., n, o twice,
n, o twice, p 2 to., k 1; o, n 5 times; k 1, leave 15.

Tenth row.—Sl 1, k 11, o twice, p 2 to., k 2, p 1,
k 1, o twice, p 2 to., k 2.

Eleventh row.—Sl 1, k 1, o twice, p 2 to., k 4, o
twice, p 2 to., k 9, leave 18.

Twelfth row.—Sl 1, k 8, o twice, p 2 to., k 4, o
twice, p 2 to., k 2.

Thirteenth row.—Sl 1, k 1, o twice, p 2 to., n, o
twice, n, o twice, p 2 to., k 1, o, n, k 3, leave 21.

Fourteenth row.—Sl 1, k 5, o twice, p 2 to., k 2,
p 1, k 1, o twice, p 2 to., k 3.

Fifteenth row.—Sl 1, k 1, o twice, p 2 to., k 4, o
twice, p 2 to., k 3, leave 24.

Sixteenth row.—Sl 1, k 8, o twice, p 2 to., k 2.

Seventeenth row.—Sl 1, k 1, o twice, p 2 to., k 6,
leave 27.

Eighteenth row.—Sl 1, k 5, o twice, p 2 to., k 2.

Nineteenth row.—Sl 1, k 6, leave 30.

Twentieth row.—Sl 1, k 6.

Twenty-first row.—Bind off 37. This is for one
side. Make another piece just like it.

For the Edge.—Cast on 11 stitches.

First row.—Sl 1, k 2, n, o, k 1, o, n, k 1, o, k 2.

Second row.—O, n, rest plain; all even rows same.

Third row.—Sl 1, k 1, n, o, k 3, o, n, k 1, o, k 2.

Fifth row.—Sl 1, n, o, k 5, o, n, k 1, o, k 2.

Seventh row.—Sl 1, k 2, o, n, k 1, n, o, n, k 1, o,
n, k 1.

Ninth row.—Sl 1, k 3, o, k 3 to., o, n, k 1, o, n,
k 1.

Eleventh row.—Sl 1, k 5, n, k 1, o, n, k 1. Repeat.

Knit two pieces the length of the longest side of
the yoke, which is the inside, and one piece to go
around the whole work; sew on, and run baby
ribbon through the eyelets.

KNITTED INITIALS AND NUMERALS.

INITIALS.

In the following directions, w will stand for "white" and d for "dark." The directions given are for knitting in an initial when working round and round. If the article to be marked is knitted back and forth, then every other row must be purled instead of knitted and the directions for the row must be read backwards or from the end of the row toward the beginning.

These initials may be knitted into stockings, socks, mittens or any article that is made with knitting-needles, and for which an initial is required as a mark of identification.

FIGURE No. 1.—A.—(19 stitches wide.)

First row.—1 w, 2 d, 2 w, 4 d, 3 w, 3 d, 1 w, 2 d, 1 w.

Second row.—1 d, 2 w, 3 d, 3 w, 1 d, 1 w, 1 d, 3 w, 1 d, 2 w, 1 d.

Third row.—1 w, 1 d, 2 w, 2 d, 2 w, 1 d, 5 w, 1 d, 2 w, 1 d, 1 w.

Fourth row.—4 w, 1 d, 8 w, 1 d, 5 w.

Fifth row.—5 w, 2 d, 3 w, 1 d, 3 w, 1 d, 4 w.

Sixth row.—5 w, 9 d, 5 w.

Seventh row.—3 w, 1 d, 1

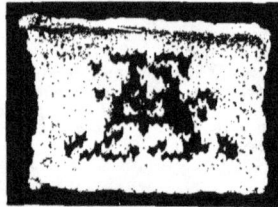

FIGURE No. 1.

Thirteenth row.—5 w, 1 d, 1 w, 3 d, 1 w, 1 d, 7 w.

Fourteenth row.—5 w, 1 d, 4 w, 2 d, 3 w, 1 d, 3 w.

Fifteenth row.—5 w, 4 d, 1 w, 4 d, 5 w.

FIGURE No. 2.—B.—(13 stitches wide.)

First row.—2 w, 6 d, 1 w, 3 d, 1 w.

Second row.—1 w, 2 d, 4 w, 3 d, 2 w, 1 d.

Third row.—3 d, 1 w, 3 d, 1 w, 1 d, 4 w.

Fourth row.—3 d, 2 w, 1 d,

FIGURE No. 2.

FIGURE No. 3.

FIGURE No. 4.

w, 3 d, 2 w, 1 d, 2 w, 1 d, 5 w.

Eighth row.—2 w, 1 d, 1 w, 4 d, 1 w, 1 d, 1 w, 1 d, 1 w, 1 d, 5 w.

Ninth row.—3 w, 1 d, 2 w, 3 d, 1 w, 1 d, 1 w, 1 d, 2 w, 3 w.

Tenth row.—6 w, 1 d, 3 w, 3 d, 6 w.

Eleventh row.—6 w, 2 d, 3 w, 1 d, 7 w.

Twelfth row.—7 w, 1 d, 3 w, 1 d, 7 w.

FIGURE No. 5.

FIGURE No. 6.

FIGURES Nos. 1 TO 6.—KNITTED INITIALS.

1 w, 3 d, 3 w.

Fifth row.—3 d, 1 w, 1 d, 2 w, 3 d, 3 w.

Sixth row.—3 d, 2 w, 1 d, 1 w, 3 d, 3 w.

Seventh row.—1 w, 2 d, 3 w, 4 d, 1 w, 1 d, 1 w.

Eighth row.—2 w, 4 d, 1 w, 3 d, 2 w, 1 d.

Ninth row.—1 w, 2 d, 3 w, 4 d, 1 w, 1 d, 1 w.

Tenth row.—3 d, 2 w, 1 d, 1 w, 3 d, 3 w.

Eleventh row.—3 d, 1 w, 1 d, 2 w, 3 d, 3 w.
Twelfth row.—3 d, 2 w, 1 d, 1 w, 3 d, 3 w.
Thirteenth row.—3 d, 4 w, 3 d, 3 w.
Fourteenth row.—1 w, 2 d, 3 w, 4 d, 2 w, 1 d.
Fifteenth row.—2 w, 7 d, 1 w, 3 d.

FIGURE NO. 3.—C.—(13 stitches wide.)
First row.—2 w, 6 d, 2 w, 1 d, 1 w, 1 d.
Second row.—1 w, 9 d, 1 w, 1 d, 1 w.
Third row.—2 d, 5 w, 4 d, 2 w.
Fourth row.—2 d, 5 w, 3 d, 3 w.
Fifth and Sixth rows.—Like 4th.
Seventh row.—1 w, 1 d, 3 w, 1 d, 1 w, 3 d, 1 w, 1 d, 1 w.
Eighth row.—4 w, 1 d, 1 w, 5 d, 1 w, 1 d.
Ninth row.—5 w, 1 d, 1 w, 3 d, 1 w, 1 d, 1 w.
Tenth row.—1 d, 6 w, 3 d, 3 w.
Eleventh row.—Like 10th.
Twelfth row.—2 d, 5 w, 3 d, 3 w.
Thirteenth row.—3 d, 4 w, 3 d, 1 w, 1 d, 1 w.
Fourteenth row.—2 w, 2 d, 2 w, 3 d, 1 w, 2 d, 1 w.
Fifteenth row.—2 w, 8 d, 1 w, 1 d, 1 w.

FIGURE NO. 4.—D.—(13 stitches wide.)
First row.—2 w, 6 d, 1 w, 3 d, 1 w.
Second row.—1 w, 3 d, 2 w, 4 d, 2 w, 1 d.
Third row.—1 w, 2 d, 4 w, 3 d, 1 w, 1 d, 1 w.
Fourth row.—3 d, 2 w, 1 d, 1 w, 3 d, 3 w.
Fifth row.—Like 4th.
Sixth row.—3 d, 1 w, 1 d, 2 w, 3 d, 3 w.
Seventh row.—3 d, 2 w, 1 d, 1 w, 3 d, 1 w, 1 d, 1 w.
Eighth row.—3 d, 3 w, 5 d, 1 w, 1 d.
Ninth row.—Like 7th.
Tenth row.—3 d, 1 w, 1 d, 2 w, 3 d, 3 w.
Eleventh row.—3 d, 2 w, 1 d, 1 w, 3 d, 3 w.
Twelfth row.—3 d, 2 w, 1 d, 1 w, 3 d, 3 w.
Thirteenth row.—1 w, 2 d, 4 w, 3 d, 1 w, 1 d, 1 w.
Fourteenth row.—1 w, 2 d, 4 w, 3 d, 2 w, 1 d.
Fifteenth row.—2 w, 6 d, 1 w, 3 d, 1 w.

FIGURE NO. 5.—E.—(14 stitches wide.)
First row.—1 d, 1 w, 7 d, 1 w, 3 d, 1 w.
Second row.—1 w, 1 d, 5 w, 4 d, 2 w, 1 d.
Third row.—3 d, 5 w, 3 d, 1 w, 1 d, 1 w.
Fourth row.—1 w, 1 d, 3 w, 1 d, 2 w, 3 d, 3 w.
Fifth row.—1 d, 5 w, 1 d, 1 w, 3 d, 3 w.
Sixth row.—4 w, 2 d, 2 w, 3 d, 3 w.
Seventh row.—3 w, 1 d, 2 w, 1 d, 1 w, 3 d, 1 w, 1 d, 1 w.
Eighth row.—2 w, 1 d, 1 w, 1 d, 1 w, 6 d, 1 w, 1 d.
Ninth row.—3 w, 1 d, 1 w, 2 d, 1 w, 3 d, 1 w, 1 d, 1 w.
Tenth row.—5 w, 1 d, 2 w, 3 d, 3 w.
Eleventh row.—1 d, 5 w, 1 d, 1 w, 3 d, 1 w.
Twelfth row.—1 w, 1 d, 3 w, 1 d, 2 w, 3 d, 3 w.
Thirteenth row.—3 d, 5 w, 3 d, 1 w, 1 d, 1 w.
Fourteenth row.—1 w, 1 d, 6 w, 3 d, 2 w, 1 d.
Fifteenth row.—1 d, 1 w, 7 d, 1 w, 3 d, 1 w.

FIGURE NO. 6.—F.—(14 stitches wide.)
First row.—6 w, 3 d, 1 w, 3 d, 1 w.
Second row.—5 w, 1 d, 2 w, 3 d, 2 w, 1 d.

Third row.—6 w, 1 d, 1 w, 3 d, 1 w, 1 d, 1 w.
Fourth row.—8 w, 3 d, 3 w.
Fifth row.—5 w, 1 d, 2 w, 3 d, 3 w.
Sixth row.—4 w, 3 d, 1 w, 3 d, 3 w.
Seventh row.—3 w, 1 d, 1 w, 1 d, 2 w, 3 d, 1 w, 1 d, 1 w.
Eighth row.—2 w, 1 d, 1 w, 1 d, 1 w, 6 d, 1 w, 1 d.
Ninth row.—3 w, 1 d, 1 w, 1 d, 2 w, 3 d, 1 w, 1 d, 1 w.
Tenth row.—4 w, 3 d, 1 w, 3 d, 3 w.
Eleventh row.—1 d, 4 w, 1 d, 2 w, 3 d, 3 w.
Twelfth row.—1 w, 1 d, 6 w, 3 d, 3 w.
Thirteenth row.—3 d, 5 w, 3 d, 1 w, 1 d, 1 w.
Fourteenth row.—3 d, 5 w, 3 d, 2 w, 1 d.
Fifteenth row.—1 d, 1 w, 7 d, 1 w, 3 d, 1 w.

FIGURE NO. 7.—G.—(16 stitches wide.)
First row.—2 w, 2 d, 1 w, 5 d, 2 w, 1 d, 3 w.
Second row.—3 w, 3 d, 3 w, 2 d, 5 w.
Third row.—3 w, 3 d, 4 w, 3 d, 3 w.
Fourth row.—3 w, 3 d, 4 w, 2 d, 4 w.
Fifth row.—Like 3rd.
Sixth row.—1 w, 1 d, 1 w, 3 d, 1 w, 1 d, 2 w, 3 d, 3 w.
Seventh row.—1 d, 2 w, 3 d, 2 w, 1 d, 1 w, 3 d, 1 w, 1 d, 1 w.
Eighth row.—1 w, 3 d, 1 w, 3 d, 2 w, 4 d, 1 w, 1 d.
Ninth row.—10 w, 3 d, 1 w, 1 d, 1 w.
Tenth row.—7 w, 1 d, 2 w, 3 d, 3 w.
Eleventh row.—6 w, 1 d, 1 w, 1 d, 1 w, 3 d, 3 w.
Twelfth row.—4 w, 1 d, 2 w, 1 d, 2 w, 3 d, 3 w.
Thirteenth row.—3 w, 3 d, 4 w, 3 d, 3 w.
Fourteenth row.—4 w, 1 d, 4 w, 2 d, 2 w, 1 d, 2 w.
Fifteenth row.—3 w, 1 d, 1 w, 5 d, 2 w, 1 d, 3 w.

FIGURE NO. 8.—H.—(17 stitches wide.)
First row.—1 w, 3 d, 1 w, 3 d, 1 w, 3 d, 1 w, 3 d, 1 w.
Second row.—1 d, 2 w, 3 d, 2 w, 1 d, 2 w, 3 d, 2 w, 1 d.
Third row.—1 w, 1 d, 1 w, 3 d, 1 w, 1 d, 1 w, 1 d, 1 w, 3 d, 1 w, 1 d, 1 w, 1 d, 1 w.
Fourth row.—3 w, 3 d, 2 w, 1 d, 2 w, 3 d, 3 w.
Fifth row.—3 w, 3 d, 5 w, 3 d, 3 w.
Sixth row.—Like 5th.
Seventh row.—1 w, 1 d, 1 w, 4 d, 3 w, 4 d, 1 w, 1 d.
Eighth row.—1 d, 1 w, 4 d, 1 w, 3 d, 1 w, 4 d, 1 w, 1 d.
Ninth row.—1 w, 1 d, 1 w, 4 d, 3 w, 4 d, 1 w, 1 d.
Tenth row.—3 w, 3 d, 5 w, 3 d, 3 w.
Eleventh row.—Like 10th.
Twelfth row.—3 w, 3 d, 2 w, 1 d, 2 w, 3 d, 3 w.
Thirteenth row.—1 w, 1 d, 1 w, 3 d, 1 w, 1 d, 1 w, 1 d, 1 w, 3 d, 1 w, 1 d, 1 w.
Fourteenth row.—1 d, 2 w, 3 d, 2 w, 1 d, 2 w, 3 d, 2 w, 1 d.
Fifteenth row.—1 w, 3 d, 1 w, 3 d, 1 w, 3 d, 1 w, 3 d, 1 w.

FIGURE NO. 9.—I.—(9 stitches wide.)
First row.—1 w, 3 d, 1 w, 3 d, 1 w.
Second row.—1 d, 2 w, 3 d, 2 w, 1 d.

Third row.—1 w, 1 d, 1 w, 3 d, 1 w, 1 d, 1 w.
Fourth row.—3 w, 3 d, 3 w.
Fifth, Sixth and Seventh rows.—Like 4th.
Eighth row.—1 w, 1 d, 1 w, 3 d, 1 w, 1 d, 1 w.
Ninth row.—1 d, 1 w, 5 d, 1 w, 1 d.
Tenth row.—Like 8th.
Eleventh row.—Like 4th.
Twelfth row.—Like 4th.
Thirteenth row.—Like 8th.
Fourteenth row.—Like 2n'.
Fifteenth row.—1 w, 3 d, 1 w, 3 d, 1 w.

FIGURE NO. 10.—J.—(13 stitches wide.)
First row.—3 w, 1 d, 1 w, 6 d, 1 w, 1 d.
Second row.—3 w, 4 d, 4 w, 1 d, 1 w.
Third row.—3 w, 3 d, 4 w, 1 d, 1 w, 1 d.
Fourth row.—3 w, 3 d, 5 w, 1 d, 1 w.
Fifth row.—3 w, 3 d, 6 w, 1 d.
Sixth row.—3 w, 3 d, 7 w.
Seventh row.—1 w, 1 d, 1 w, 3 d, 1 w, 1 d, 5 w.
Eighth row.—1 d, 1 w, 5 d, 1 w, 1 d, 4 w.
Ninth row.—1 w, 1 d, 1 w, 3 d, 1 w, 1 d, 5 w.
Tenth row.—3 w, 3 d, 7 w.
Eleventh and Twelfth rows.—Like 10th.
Thirteenth row.—Like 9th.
Fourteenth row.—1 d, 2 w, 3 d, 2 w, 1 d, 4 w.
Fifteenth row.—1 w, 3 d, 1 w, 3 d, 5 w.

FIGURE NO. 11.—K.—(16 stitches wide.)
First row.—1 w, 2 d, 1 w, 2 d, 3 w, 2 d, 1 w, 3 d, 1 w.
Second row.—1 d, 1 w, 3 d, 1 w, 1 d, 1 w, 1 d, 1 w, 3 d, 2 w, 1 d.
Third row.—3 w, 3 d, 4 w, 3 d, 3 w.
Fourth row.—3 w, 3 d, 4 w, 3 d, 3 w.
Fifth row.—2 w, 1 d, 1 w, 3 d, 3 w, 3 d, 3 w.
Sixth row.—5 w, 3 d, 2 w, 3 d, 3 w.
Seventh row.—6 w, 3 d, 1 w, 3 d, 1 w, 1 d, 1 w.
Eighth row.—7 w, 7 d, 1 w, 1 d.
Ninth row.—8 w, 1 d, 1 w, 3 d, 1 w, 1 d, 1 w.
Tenth row.—7 w, 1 d, 2 w, 3 d, 3 w.
Eleventh row.—6 w, 1 d, 3 w, 3 d, 3 w.
Twelfth row.—5 w, 1 d, 4 w, 3 d, 3 w.
Thirteenth row.—4 w, 1 d, 3 w, 1 d, 1 w, 3 d, 1 w, 1 d, 1 w.
Fourteenth row.—1 w, 1 d, 1 w, 1 d, 1 w, 1 d, 1 w, 3 d, 2 w, 1 d.
Fifteenth row.—2 w, 1 d, 1 w, 1 d, 3 w. 3 d, 1 w, 3 d, 1 w,

FIGURE NO. 12.—L.—(13 stitches wide.)
First row.—1 d, 1 w, 6 d, 1 w, 3 d, 1 w.
Second row.—1 w, 1 d, 5 w, 3 d, 2 w, 1 d.
Third row.—3 d, 4 w, 3 d, 1 w, 1 d, 1 w.
Fourth row.—1 w, 1 d, 5 w, 1 d, 1 w, 1 d, 3 w.
Fifth row.—1 d, 6 w, 1 d, 1 w, 1 d, 3 w.
Sixth row.—7 w, 1 d, 1 w, 1 d, 3 w.
Seventh row.—7 w, 1 d, 1 w, 1 d, 1 w, 1 d, 1 w.
Eighth row.—6 w, 2 d, 1 w, 2 d, 1 w, 1 d.
Ninth row.—3 w, 1 d, 1 w, 1 d, 1 w, 1 d, 1 w, 1 d, 1 w, 1 d.
Tenth row.—4 w, 1 d, 2 w, 1 d, 1 w, 1 d, 3 w.
Eleventh row.—5 w, 1 d, 1 w, 1 d, 1 w, 1 d, 3 w.
Twelfth row.—7 w, 1 d, 1 w, 1 d, 3 w.

Thirteenth row.—5 w, 1 d, 1 w, 1 d, 1 w, 1 d, 1 w, 1 d, 1 w.
Fourteenth row.—4 w, 1 d, 2 w, 1 d, 1 w, 1 d, 2 w, 1 d.
Fifteenth row.—5 w, 3 d, 1 w, 3 d, 1 w.

FIGURE NO. 13.—M.—(19 stitches wide.)
First row.—1 w, 3 d, 1 w, 3 d, 2 w, 1 d, 2 w, 2 d, 1 w, 2 d, 1 w.
Second row.—1 d, 2 w, 3 d, 2 w, 1 d, 1 w, 1 d, 1 w, 1 d, 2 w, 1 d, 2 w, 1 d.
Third row.—1 w, 1 d, 1 w, 3 d, 1 w, 1 d, 2 w, 1 d, 2 w, 1 d, 1 w, 1 d, 1 w, 1 d, 1 w.
Fourth row.—3 w, 3 d, 3 w, 3 d, 3 w, 1 d, 3 w.
Fifth row.—Like 4th.
Sixth row.—3 w, 3 d, 1 w, 1 d, 1 w, 3 d, 1 w, 1 d, 1 w. 1 d, 3 w.
Seventh row.—1 w, 1 d, 2 w, 2 d, 2 w, 1 d, 1 w, 3 d, 2 w, 1 d, 1 w, 1 d, 1 w.
Eighth row.—1 d, 1 w, 4 d, 2 w, 1 d, 1 w, 3 d, 2 w, 2 d, 1 w, 1 d.
Ninth row.—1 w, 1 d, 1 w, 3 d, 2 w, 1 d, 1 w, 3 d, 2 w, 1 d, 1 w, 1 d, 1 w.
Tenth row.—3 w, 1 d, 1 w, 1 d, 3 w, 2 d, 2 w, 1 d, 3 w.
Eleventh and Twelfth rows.—Like 10th.
Thirteenth row.—1 w, 1 d, 1 w, 4 d, 5 w, 4 d, 1 w, 1 d, 1 w.
Fourteenth row.—1 d, 2 w, 4 d, 1 w, 1 d, 3 w, 4 d, 2 w, 1 d.
Fifteenth row.—1 w, 3 d, 1 w, 3 d, 3 w, 2 d, 1 w, 1 d, 1 w, 2 d, 1 w.

FIGURE NO. 14.—N.—(16 stitches wide.)
First row.—3 w, 1 d, 1 w, 1 d, 4 w, 2 d, 1 w, 2 d, 1 w.
Second row.—3 w, 3 d, 3 w, 1 d, 2 w, 1 d, 2 w, 1 d.
Third row.—3 w, 4 d, 3 w, 1 d, 1 w, 1 d, 1 w, 1 d, 1 w.
Fourth row.—3 w, 4 d, 5 w, 1 d, 3 w.
Fifth row.—3 w, 1 d, 1 w, 3 d, 4 w, 1 d, 3 w.
Sixth row.—Like 5th.
Seventh row.—1 w, 1 d, 1 w, 1 d, 2 w, 3 d, 3 w, 1 d, 1 w, 1 d, 1 w.
Eighth row.—1 d, 1 w, 2 d, 3 w, 2 d, 3 w, 2 d, 1 w, 1 d.
Ninth row.—1 w, 1 d, 1 w, 1 d, 3 w, 2 d, 3 w, 1 d, 1 w, 1 d, 1 w.
Tenth row.—3 w, 1 d, 3 w, 3 d, 2 w, 1 d, 3 w.
Eleventh row.—3 w, 1 d, 4 w, 3 d, 1 w, 1 d, 3 w.
Twelfth row.—Like 11th.
Thirteenth row.—1 w, 1 d, 1 w, 1 d, 5 w, 4 d, 1 w, 1 d, 1 w.
Fourteenth row.—1 d, 2 w, 1 d, 2 w, 1 d, 2 w, 4 d, 2 w, 1 d.
Fifteenth row.—1 w, 2 d, 1 w, 2 d, 5 w, 1 d, 1 w, 2 d, 1 w.

FIGURE NO. 15.—O.—(17 stitches wide.)
First row.—K 2 w, 1 d, 2 w, 6 d, 2 w, 1 d, 3 w.
Second row.—1 w, 1 d, 2 w, 1 d, 5 w, 2 d, 1 w, 2 d, 2 w.
Third row.—2 w, 3 d, 6 w, 3 d, 3 w.
Fourth row.—3 w, 2 d, 1 w, 1 d, 2 w, 1 d, 1 w, 2 d, 4 w.
Fifth row.—2 w, 3 d, 2 w, 2 d, 2 w, 3 d, 3 w.
Sixth row.—2 w, 3 d, 1 w, 1 d, 2 w, 1 d, 1 w, 3 d, 3 w.

Seventh row.—1 d, 1 w, 3 d, 1 w, 1 d, 2 w, 1 d, 1 w, 3 d, 1 w, 1 d, 1 w.

Eighth row.—1 w, 4 d, 6 w, 4 d, 1 w, 1 d.

Eleventh row.—2 w, 3 d, 2 w, 2 d, 2 w, 3 d, 3 w.

Twelfth row.—Like 10th.

FIGURE No. 7.

FIGURE No. 8.

FIGURE No. 9.

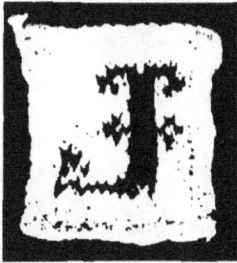

FIGURE No. 10.

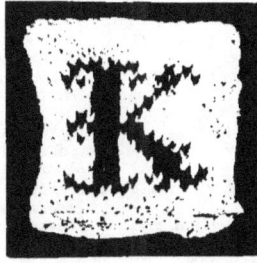

FIGURE No. 11.

FIGURE No. 12.

FIGURE No. 13.

FIGURE No. 14.

FIGURE No. 15.

FIGURES NOS. 7 TO 15.—KNITTED INITIALS.

Ninth row.—1 d, 1 w, 3 d, 1 w, 1 d, 2 w, 1 d, 1 w, 3 d, 1 w, 1 d, 1 w.

Tenth row.—2 w, 3 d, 1 w, 1 d, 2 w, 1 d, 1 w, 3 d, 3 w.

Thirteenth row.—Like 3rd.

Fourteenth row.—1 w, 1 d, 2 w, 2 d, 4 w, 2 d, 2 w, 1 d, 2 w.

Fifteenth row.—Like 1st.

FIGURE No. 16.—P.—(13 stitches wide.)
First row.—5 w, 3 d, 1 w, 3d, 1 w.
Second row.—4 w, 1 d, 2 w, 3d, 2 w, 1 d.
Third row.—5 w, 1 d, 1 w, 3 d, 1 w, 1 d, 1 w.
Fourth row.—7 w, 3 d, 3 w.
Fifth and Sixth rows.—Like 4th.
Seventh row.—7 w, 3 d, 1 w, 1 d, 1 w.
Eighth row.—2 w, 9 d, 1 w, 1 d.
Ninth row.—1 w, 2 d, 4 w, 3 d, 1 w, 1 d, 1 w.
Tenth row.—3 d, 1 w, 1 d, 2 w, 3 d, 3 w.
Eleventh row.—4 d, 1 w, 1 d, 1 w, 3 d, 3 w.
Twelfth row.—3 d, 1 w, 1 d, 2 w, 3 d, 3 w.
Thirteenth row.—3 d, 4 w, 3 d, 1 w, 1 d, 1 w.
Fourteenth row.—1 w, 3 d, 2 w, 4 d, 2 w, 1 d.
Fifteenth row.—3 w, 5 d, 1 w, 3 d, 1 w.

FIGURE No. 17.—Q.—(17 stitches wide.)
First row.—2 w, 3 d, 1 w, 6 d, 2 w, 1 d, 2 w.
Second row.—1 w, 5 d, 5 w, 2 d, 2 w, 1 d, 1 w.
Third row.—1 d, 3 w, 5 d, 3 w, 3 d, 2 w.
Fourth row.—4 w, 2 d, 6 w, 2 d, 3 w.
Fifth row.—3 w, 3 d, 1 w, 1 d, 2 w, 1 d, 1 w, 3 d, 2 w.
Sixth row.—3 w, 4 d, 2 w, 1 d, 2 w, 3 d, 2 w.
Seventh row.—1 w, 1 d, 1 w, 3 d, 1 w, 1 d, 2 w, 1 d, 1 w, 3 d, 1 w, 1 d.
Eighth row.—2 w, 5 d, 4 w, 5 d, 1 w.
Ninth row.—1 w, 1 d, 1 w, 3 d, 1 w, 1 d, 2 w, 1 d, 1 w, 3 d, 1 w, 1 d.
Tenth row.—3 w, 3 d, 2 w, 2 d, 2 w, 3 d, 2 w.
Eleventh row.—3 w, 3 d, 1 w, 1 d, 2 w, 1 d, 1 w, 3 d, 2 w.
Twelfth row.—4 w, 2 d, 6 w, 2 d, 3 w.
Thirteenth row.—3 w, 3 d, 6 w, 2 d, 3 w.
Fourteenth row.—2 w, 1 d, 2 w, 2 d, 4 w, 2 d, 2 w, 1 d, 1 w.
Fifteenth row.—3 w, 1 d, 2 w, 6 d, 2 w, 1 d, 2 w.

FIGURE No. 18.—R.—(16 stitches wide.)
First row.—1 w, 3 d, 1 w, 1 d, 2 w, 3 d, 1 w, 3 d, 1 w.
Second row.—1 d, 1 w, 4 d, 1 w, 1 d, 2 w, 3 d, 2 w, 1 d.
Third row.—3 w, 3 d, 2 w, 1 d, 1 w, 3 d, 3 w.
Fourth, Fifth and Sixth rows.—Like 3rd.
Seventh row.—4 w, 2 d, 4 w, 3 d, 1 w, 1 d, 1 w.
Eighth row.—5 w, 9 d, 1 w, 1 d.
Ninth row.—4 w, 2 d, 3 w, 4 d, 1 w, 1 d, 1 w.
Tenth row.—3 w, 3 d, 1 w, 1 d, 2 w, 3 d, 3 w.
Eleventh row.—3 w, 3 d, 4 w, 3 d, 3 w.
Twelfth row.—Like 11th.
Thirteenth row.—3 w, 3 d, 4 w, 3 d, 1 w, 1 d, 1 w.
Fourteenth row.—4 w, 2 d, 4 w, 3d, 2 w, 1 d.
Fifteenth row.—5 w, 5 d, 1 w, 4 d, 1 w.

FIGURE No. 19.—S.—(12 stitches wide.)
First row.—3 w, 7 d, 1 w, 1 d.
Second row.—1 w, 2 d, 7 w, 1 d, 1 w.
Third row.—2 d, 3 w, 1 d, 3 w, 3 d.
Fourth row.—2 d, 2 w, 1 d, 1 w, 1 d, 3 w, 1 d, 1 w.
Fifth row.—3 d, 2 w, 1 d, 5 w, 1 d.
Sixth row.—4 d, 1 w, 1 d, 6 w.
Seventh row.—2 w, 6 d, 4 w.
Eighth row.—2 w, 8 d, 2 w.
Ninth row.—4 w, 6 d, 2 w.
Tenth row.—5 w, 1 d, 1 w, 4 d, 1 w.
Eleventh row.—1 d, 4 w, 1 d, 3 w, 3 d.

Twelfth row.—1 w, 1 d, 2 w, 1 d, 1 w, 1 d, 3 w, 2 d.
Thirteenth row.—3 d, 2 w, 1 d, 4 w, 2 d.
Fourteenth row.—1 w, 1 d, 7 w, 2 d, 1 w.
Fifteenth row.—1 d, 1 w, 7 d, 3 w.

FIGURE No. 20.—T.—(13 stitches wide.)
First row.—3 w, 3 d, 1 w, 3 d, 3 w.
Second row.—2 w, 2 d, 1 w, 3 d, 1 w, 2 d, 2 w.
Third row.—3 w, 3 d, 1 w, 3 d, 1 w, 1 d, 3 w.
Fourth row.—5 w, 3 d, 5 w.
Fifth row.—Like 4th.
Sixth row.—1 w, 1 d, 3 w, 3 d, 3 w, 1 d, 1 w.
Seventh row.—Like 6th.
Eighth row.—2 w, 1 d, 3 w, 3 d, 2 w, 1 d, 2 w.
Ninth row.—1 w, 2 d, 2 w, 3 d, 2 w, 2 d, 1 w.
Tenth row.—1 d, 2 w, 1 d, 1 w, 3 d, 1 w, 1 d, 2 w, 1 d.
Eleventh row.—Like 10th.
Twelfth row.—2 d, 3 w, 3 d, 3 w, 2 d.
Thirteenth row.—3 d, 2 w, 3 d, 2 w, 3d.
Fourteenth row.—13 d.
Fifteenth row.—Like 14th.

FIGURE No. 21.—U.—(16 stitches wide.)
First row.—4 w, 7 d, 1 w, 1 d, 3 w.
Second row.—3 w, 1 d, 5 w, 4 d, 3 w.
Third row.—3 w, 1 d, 6 w, 3 d, 3 w.
Fourth, Fifth and Sixth rows.—Like 3rd.
Seventh row.—1 w, 1 d, 1 w, 1 d, 2 w, 2 d, 2 w, 3 d, 1 w, 1 d, 1 w.
Eighth row.—1 d, 1 w, 2 d, 1 w, 1 d, 2 w, 1 d, 1 w, 4 d, 1 w, 1 d.
Ninth row.—1 w, 1 d, 1 w, 1 d, 2 w, 2 d, 2 w, 3 d, 1 w, 1 d, 1 w.
Tenth row.—3 w, 1 d, 6 w, 3 d, 3 w.
Eleventh and Twelfth rows.—Like tenth.
Thirteenth row.—1 w, 1 d, 1 w, 1 d, 1 w, 1 d, 2 w, 1 d, 1 w, 3 d, 1 w, 1 d, 1 w.
Fourteenth row.—1 d, 2 w, 1 d, 6 w, 3 d, 2 w, 1 d.
Fifteenth row.—1 w, 2 d, 1 w, 2 d, 2 w, 3 d, 1 w, 3 d, 1 w.

FIGURE No. 22.—V.—(16 stitches wide.)
First row.—5 w, 3 d, 1 w, 3 d, 4 w.
Second row.—4 w, 1 d, 2 w, 1 d, 2 w, 3 d, 3 w.
Third row.—5 w, 1 d, 1 w, 3d, 1 w, 1 d, 4 w.
Fourth row.—6 w, 1 d, 1 w, 3 d, 5 w.
Fifth and Sixth rows.—Like fourth.
Seventh row.—6 w, 2 d, 2 w, 3 d, 4 w.
Eighth row.—5 w, 2 d, 1 w, 1 w, 2 d, 4 w.
Ninth row.—3 w, 1 d, 1 w, 1 d, 4 w, 2 d, 1 w, 1 d, 2 w.
Tenth row.—4 w, 1 d, 2 w, 1 d, 2 w, 3 d, 3 w.
Eleventh row.—4 w, 1 d, 5 w, 3 d, 3 w.
Twelfth row.—Like tenth.
Thirteenth row.—1 w, 1 d, 1 w, 1 d, 1 w, 1 d, 5 w, 3 d, 2 w.
Fourteenth row.—1 d, 1 w, 2 d, 2 w, 1 d, 4 w, 3 d, 2 w.
Fifteenth row.—1 w, 5 d, 3 w, 3 d, 1 w, 3 d.

FIGURE No. 23.—W.—(23 stitches wide.)
First row.—5 w, 2 d, 1 w, 2 d, 3 w, 2 d, 1 w, 2 d, 5 w.
Second row.—4 w, 1 d, 2 w, 1 d, 2 w, 1 d, 1 w, 1 d, 2 w, 1 d, 2 w, 1 d, 4 w.
Third row.—5 w, 1 d, 1 w, 1 d, 1 w, 1 d, 3 w, 1 d, 1 w, 1 d, 1 w, 1 d, 5 w.

Fourth row.—7 w, 2 d, 2 w, 1 d, 2 w, 3 d, 6 w.
Fifth row.—6 w, 3 d, 5 w, 3 d, 6 w.
Sixth row.—6 w, 3 d, 2 w, 1 d, 2 w, 3 d, 6 w.
Seventh row.—3 w, 1 d, 1 w, 5 d, 3 w, 1 d, 1 w, 3 d, 1 w, 1 d, 3 w.
Eighth row.—2 w, 1 d, 1 w, 2 d, 1 w, 3 d, 1 w, 1 d, 1 w, 1 d, 1 w, 2 d, 1 w, 1 d, 1 w, 1 d, 2 w.
Ninth row.—3 w, 1 d, 1 w, 1 d, 1 w, 4 d, 2 w, 1 d, 2 w, 3 d, 1 w, 1 d, 2 w.
Tenth row.—4 w, 1 d, 3 w, 3 d, 1 w, 1 d, 3 w, 3 d, 4 w.

Fourth row.—4 w, 3 d, 2 w, 1 d, 2 w, 1 d, 4 w.
Fifth row.—5 w, 2 d, 4 w, 1 d, 5 w.
Sixth row.—6 w, 3 d, 1 w, 1 d, 6 w.
Seventh row.—4 w, 1 d, 1 w, 4 d, 2 w, 1 d, 4 w.
Eighth row.—3 w, 1 d, 1 w, 1 d, 1 w, 3 d, 1 w, 1 d, 1 w, 1 d, 3 w.
Ninth row.—4 w, 1 d, 2 w, 3 d, 2 w, 1 d, 4 w.
Tenth row.—6 w, 1 d, 1 w, 3 d, 6 w.
Eleventh row.—5 w, 1 d, 2 w, 3 d, 6 w.
Twelfth row.—4 w, 1 d, 4 w, 3 d, 5 w.

FIGURE No. 16.

FIGURE No. 17.

FIGURE No. 18.

FIGURE No. 19.

FIGURE No. 20.

FIGURE No. 21.

FIGURES NOS. 16 TO 21.—KNITTED INITIALS.

Eleventh and Twelfth rows. — Like tenth.
Thirteenth row.—1 w, 1 d, 1 w, 1 d, 1 w, 1 d, 3 w, 3 d, 3 w, 1 d, 1 w, 3 d, 1 w, 1 d, 1 w.
Fourteenth row.—1 d, 1 w, 1 d, 2 w, 1 d, 2 w, 3 d, 2 w, 1 d, 2 w, 3 d, 2 w, 1 d.
Fifteenth row.—1 w, 2 d, 1 w, 2 d, 2 w, 2 d, 1 w, 2 d, 3 w, 2 d, 1 w, 3 d, 1 w.

FIGURE No. 24.—N.—(17 stitches wide.)
First row.—1 w, 3 d, 1 w, 3 d, 3 w, 2 d, 1 w, 2 d, 1 w.
Second row.—1 d, 2 w, 3 d, 4 w, 1 d, 2 w, 1 d, 2 w, 1 d.
Third row.—1 w, 1 d, 1 w, 3 d, 5 w, 1 d, 5 w.

Thirteenth row.—1 w, 1 d, 1 w, 1 d, 4 w, 1 d, 1 w, 3 d, 1 w, 1 d, 2 w.
Fourteenth row.—1 d, 2 w, 1 d, 1 w, 1 d, 1 w, 1 d, 2 w, 3 d, 2 w, 1 d, 2 w.
Fifteenth row.—1 w, 2 d, 1 w, 1 d, 3 w, 3 d, 1 w, 3 d, 2 w.

FIGURE No. 25.—Y.—(19 stitches wide.)
First row.—3 w, 1 d, 2 w, 3 d, 1 w, 3 d, 6 w.
Second row.—2 w, 1 d, 2 w, 1 d, 2 w, 3 d, 2 w, 1 d, 2 w, 1 d, 2 w.
Third row.—3 w, 2 d, 1 w, 1 d, 1 w, 3 d, 1 w, 1 d, 1 w, 2 d, 3 w.
Fourth row.—8 w, 3 d, 8 w.

Fifth and Sixth rows.—Like fourth.
Seventh row.—5 w, 1 d, 2 w, 3 d, 2 w, 1 d, 5 w.

Second row.—1 w, 1 d, 6 w, 3 d, 1 w.
Third row.—3 d, 5 w, 3 d, 1 w.

FIGURE No. 22.

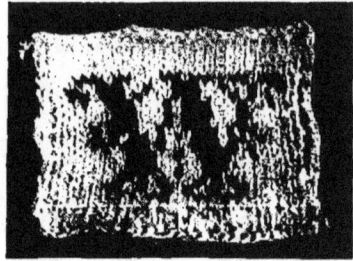

FIGURE No. 23.

FIGURE No. 24.

FIGURE No. 25.

Eighth row.—4 w, 1 d, 1 w, 1 d, 1 w, 3 d, 1 w, 1 d, 1 w, 1 d, 4 w.
Ninth row.—5 w, 9 d, 5 w.
Tenth row.—6 w, 1 d, 3 w, 3 d, 6 w.
Eleventh row.—5 w, 1 d, 5 w, 3 d, 5 w.
Twelfth row.—4 w, 1 d, 7 w, 3 d, 4 w.
Thirteenth row.—1 w, 1 d, 1 w, 1 d, 1 w, 1 d, 5 w, 1 d, 1 w, 3 d, 1 w, 1 d, 1 w.
Fourteenth row.—1 d, 2 w, 1 d, 2 w, 1 d, 3 w, 1 d, 2 w, 3 d, 2 w, 1 d.
Fifteenth row.—1 w, 2 d, 1 w, 2 d, 5 w, 3 d, 1 w, 3 d, 1 w.

FIGURE No. 26. — Z. — (12 stitches wide.)
First row.—1 d, 1 w, 8 d, 1 w, 1 d.

FIGURE No. 26.

FIGURES NOS. 22 TO 26.—KNITTED INITIALS.

Fourth row.—1 w, 1 d, 5 w, 3 d, 2 w.
Fifth row.—1 d, 2 w, 1 d, 2 w, 3 d, 3 w.
Sixth row.—Like fifth.
Seventh row.—1 w, 2 d, 2 w, 3 d, 3 w, 1 d.
Eighth row.—1 w, 1 d, 2 w, 3 d, 3 w, 1 d, 1 w.
Ninth row.—1 d, 3 w, 3 d, 2 w, 2 d, 1 w.
Tenth row.—1 d, 2 w, 3 d, 2 w, 1 d, 2 w, 1 d.
Eleventh row.—2 w, 3 d, 3 w, 1 d, 2 w, 1 d.
Twelfth row.—2 w, 3 d, 2 w, 1 d, 2 w, 1 d, 1 w.
Thirteenth row.—1 w, 3 d, 5 w, 3 d.
Fourteenth row.—4 d, 6 w, 1 d, 1 w.
Fifteenth row.—1 d, 1 w, 8 d, 1 w, 1 d.

NUMERALS.

In the following directions, w will stand for "white" and d for "dark." The directions given are for knitting in a numeral when working round and round. If the article to be marked is knitted back and forth, then every other row must be purled instead of knitted, and the directions for the row must be read backwards or from the end of the row toward the beginning.

These numbers may be knitted into stockings, socks, mittens or any article that is made with knitting-needles, and for which a number is required as a mark of indentification.

FIGURE NO. 1.—1.—(10 stitches wide.)
First and Second rounds.—8 d, and 2 w.
Third round.—2 w, 4 d, 4 w; knit 7 more rounds likethird.
Eleventh and Twelfth rounds.—2 w, 4 d, 2 w, 2 d.

Seventh and Eighth rounds.—4 w, 4 d, 6 w.
Ninth and Tenth rounds.—2 w, 4 d, 8 w.
Eleventh, Twelfth, Thirteenth and Fourteenth rounds.—2 w, 4 d, 4 w, 4 d.
Fifteenth and Sixteenth rounds.—4 w, 8 d, 2 w.

FIGURE NO. 1.

FIGURE NO. 2.

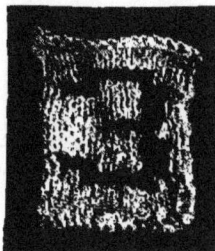

FIGURE NO. 3.

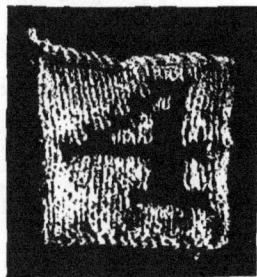

FIGURE NO. 4.

FIGURE NO. 5.

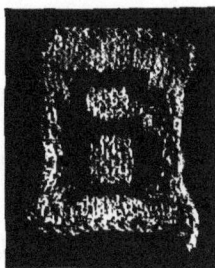

FIGURE NO. 6.

FIGURES NOS. 1 TO 6.—KNITTED NUMERALS.

Thirteenth and Fourteenth rounds.—2 w, 6 d, 2 w.
Fifteenth and Sixteenth rounds.—2 w, 4 d, 4 w.

FIGURE NO. 2.—2.—(14 stitches wide.)
First and Second rounds.—2 w, 10 d, 2 w.
Third and Fourth rounds.—2 d, 2 w, 6 d, 4 w.
Fifth and Sixth rounds.—6 w, 2 d, 6 w.

FIGURE NO. 3.—3.—(12 stitches wide.)
First and Second rounds.—2 w, 8 d, 2 w.
Third and Fourth rounds.—4 d, 4 w, 4 d.
Fifth, Sixth and Seventh rounds.—4 d, 8 w.
Eighth and Ninth rounds.—2 w, 6 d, 4 w.
Tenth, Eleventh and Twelfth rounds. — Like Fifth.

Thirteenth and Fourteenth rounds.—Like third.
Fifteenth and Sixteenth rounds.—Like the first round.

FIGURE No. 4.—4.—(14 stitches wide.)
First and Second rounds.—8 d, 6 w.
Third, Fourth, Fifth and Sixth rounds.—2 w, 4 d, 8 w.
Seventh and Eighth rounds.—14 d.
Ninth and Tenth rounds.—2 w, 4 d, 4 w, 2 d, 2 w.

FIGURE No. 7. — 7. — (12 stitches wide.)
First and Second rounds.—4 w, 6 d, 2 w.
Third, Fourth, Fifth and Sixth rounds.—4 w, 4 d, 4 w.
Seventh, Eighth, Ninth and Tenth rounds.—2 w, 4 d, 6 w.
Eleventh and Twelfth rounds.—2 w, 2 d, 8 w.
Thirteenth and Fourteenth round.—2 w, 4 d, 2 w, 4 d.
Fifteenth and Sixteenth rounds.—10 d, 2 w.

FIGURE No. 7.

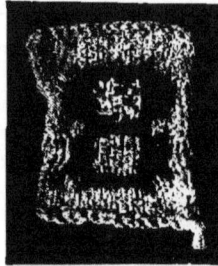

FIGURE No. 8.

FIGURE No. 9.

Eleventh and Twelfth rounds.—2 w, 4 d, 2 w, 2 d, 4 w.
Thirteenth and Fourteenth rounds.—2 w, 2 d, 2 w, 2 d, 6 w.
Fifteenth and Sixteenth rounds.—2 w, 4 d, 8 w.

FIGURE No. 5.—5. — (12 stitches wide.)
First and Second rounds.—2 w, 8 d, 2 w.
Third and Fourth rounds.—4 d, 4 w, 4 d.
Fifth and Sixth rounds.—4 d, 8 w.
Seventh and Eighth rounds.—4 d, 4 w, 2 d, 2 w.
Ninth and Tenth rounds.—2 w, 8 d, 2 w.
Eleventh and Twelfth rounds.—8 w, 2 d, 2 w.
Thirteenth and Fourteenth rounds.—4 w, 6 d, 2 w.
Fifteenth and Sixteenth rounds.—2 w, 3 d, 3 w, 2 d, 2 w.

FIGURE No. 6.—6.—(12 stitches wide.)
First and Second rounds.—2 w, 8 d, 2 w.
Third, Fourth, Fifth, Sixth, Seventh and Eighth rounds.—4 d, 4 w, 4 d.
Ninth and Tenth rounds.—2 w, 10 d.
Eleventh and Twelfth rounds.—8 w, 4 d.
Thirteenth and Fourteenth rounds.—4 d, 4 w, 2 d, 2 w.
Fifteenth and Sixteenth rounds.—Like first.

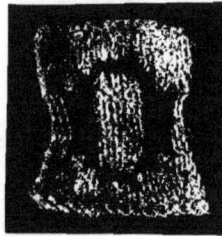

FIGURE No. 10.

FIGURES NOS. 7 TO 10.—KNITTED NUMERALS.

2 w, 2 d, 4 w, 4 d.
Fifth and Sixth rounds.—4 d, 8 w.
Seventh and Eighth rounds.—10 d, 2 w.
Ninth, Tenth, Eleventh, Twelfth, Thirteenth and Fourteenth rounds.—4 d, 4 w, 4 d.
Fifteenth and Sixteenth rounds.—2 w, 8 d, 2 w.

FIGURE No. 10.—10.—(12 stitches wide.)
First and Second rounds.—4 w, 4 d, 4 w.
Third and Fourth rounds.—2 w, 2 d, 4 w, 2 d, 2 w.
Fifth, Sixth, Seventh, Eighth, Ninth, Tenth, Eleventh and Twelfth rounds.—All alike, thus: 4 d, 4 w, 4 d.
Thirteenth and Fourteenth rounds.—Like third.
Fifteenth and Sixteenth rounds.—Like first.

FIGURE No. 8. — 8.—(12 stitches wide.)
First and Second rounds.—2 w, 8 d, 2 w.
Third, Fourth, Fifth, Sixth and Seventh rounds.—4 d, 4 w, 4 d.
Eighth and Ninth rounds.—Like first.
Tenth, Eleventh, Twelfth, Thirteenth and Fourteenth rounds.—Like Third.
Fifteenth and Sixteenth rounds.—Like first.

FIGURE No. 9. — 9.—(12 stitches wide.)
First and Second rounds.—2 w, 8 d, 2 w.
Third and Fourth rounds.—

PRETTY ARTICLES FOR LITTLE FOLKS.

CHILD'S KNITTED POINT LACE COLLAR.

No. 1.—This collar is made in sections. Use Barbours' linen thread. Cast on 26 stitches.
"Fagot" means o twice, p 2 to.
First row.—O, n, k 1, fagot, k 1, k 3 to.; p 1 and

hereafter be given as "edge." The terms between the stars form the stripe. Knit the edge, then the stripe as directed in the following rows.
Seventh row.—Edge, k 1, o, k 1, o, k 1, edge.
Eighth row.—Edge, k 5, edge.
Ninth and Tenth rows.—Like 8th.

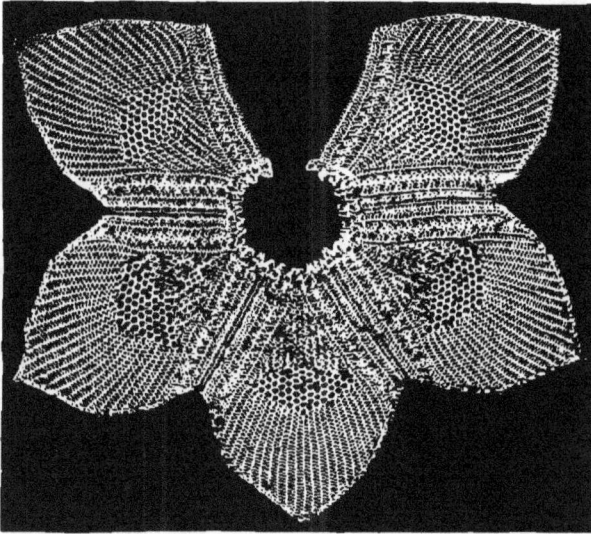

No. 1.—Child's Knitted Point Lace Collar.

k 1 in next st.; fagot, * k 2, * fagot, k 1, k 3 to.; k 1, p 1 and k 1 in next stitch, fagot, k 3.
Second row.—O, n, k 1, fagot, k 2, o, n, k 1, fagot, * k 2, * fagot, k 2, o, n, k 1, fagot, k 3.
Third row.—O, n, k 1, fagot, k 5, fagot, * k 1, o, k 1, * fagot, k 5, fagot, k 3.
Fourth row.—O, n, k 1, fagot, k 1, k 3 to.; k 1, p 1 and k 1 in next st., fagot, * k 3, * fagot, k 1, k 3 to.; k 1, p 1 and k 1 in next st., fagot, k 3.
Fifth row.—O, n, k 1, fagot, k 2, o, n, k 1, fagot * k 3, * fagot, k 2, o, n, k 1, fagot, k 3.
Sixth row.—O, n, k 1, fagot, k 5, fagot, * k 3, * fagot, k 5, fagot, k 3.
The pattern of outside stripe is completed in these six rows, and is to be repeated, and will

Eleventh row.—Edge, k 2, o, k 1, o, k 2, edge
Twelfth row.—Edge, k 7, edge.
Thirteenth and Fourteenth rows.—Like 12th.
Fifteenth row.—K 1, o, n, o, k 1, o, n, o, k 1, edge.
Sixteenth row.—Edge, k 9, edge.
Seventeenth and Eighteenth rows.—Like 16th.
Nineteenth row.—Edge, k 2, o, n, o, k 1, o, n, o, k 2, edge.
Twentieth row.—Edge, k 11.
Twenty-first and Twenty-second rows.—Like 20th.
Twenty-third row.—Edge, k 1, o, n, o, n, o, k 1, o, n, o, n, o, k 1, edge.
Twenty-fourth row.—Edge, k 13.
Twenty-fifth and Twenty-sixth rows.—Like 24th.

Twenty-seventh row.—Edge, k 2, o, n, o, n, o, k 1, o, n, o, n, o, k 2, edge.

Twenty-eighth row.—Edge, k 15.

Twenty-ninth and Thirtieth rows.—Like 28th.

Thirty-first row.—Edge, k 1; o and n 3 times; o, k 1; o and n 3 times; o, k 1, edge.

Thirty-second row.—Edge, k 17, edge.

Thirty-third and Thirty-fourth rows.—Like 32d.

Thirty-fifth row.—Edge, k 2; o and n, 3 times; o, k 1; o and n 3 times, o, k 2, edge.

Thirty-sixth row.—Edge, k 19, edge.

Thirty-seventh and Thirty-eighth rows.—Like 36th.

Thirty-ninth row.—Edge, k 1; o and n 4 times; o, k 1; o and n, 4 times; o, k 1, edge.

Fortieth row.—Edge, k 21.

Forty-first and Forty-second rows.—Like 40th.

Forty-third row.—Edge, k 2; o and n 4 times; o, k 1; o and n 4 times; o, k 2, edge.

Forty-fourth row.—Edge, k 23, edge.

Forty-fifth and Forty-sixth rows.—Like 44th.

Forty-seventh row.—Edge, k 1; o and n 4 times; o, k 2, o twice, n, k 1; o and n 4 times; o, k 1, edge.

Forty-eighth row.—Edge, k 13, p 1, k 12, edge.

Forty-ninth row.—Edge, k 9, n, o twice, n, n, o twice, n, k 9, edge.

Fiftieth row.—Edge, k 11, p 1, k 3, p 1, k 10, edge.

Fifty-first row.—Edge, k 2, o, n, o, n, o, k 1; n, o twice, n, 3 times; k 1, o, n, o, n, o, k 2, edge.

Fifty-second row.—Edge, k 10, p 1, k 3, p 1, k 3, p 1, k 9, edge.

Fifty-third row.—Edge, k 6; n o twice, n 4 times; k 6, edge.

Fifty-fourth row.—Edge, k 8, p 1; k 3, p 1, 3 times; k 7, edge.

Fifty-fifth row.—Edge, k 1, o, n, o, k 1; n, o twice, n 5 times; k 1, o, n, o, k 1, edge.

Fifty-sixth row.—Edge, k 7, p 1; k 3, p 1, 4 times; k 6, edge.

Fifty-seventh row.—Edge, k 3; n, o twice, n, 6 times; k 3, edge.

Fifty-eighth row.—Edge, k 5, p 1; k 3, p 1, 5 times; k 4, edge.

Fifty-ninth row.—Edge, k 1, o; n, o twice, n, 7 times; o, k 1, edge.

Sixtieth row.—Edge, k 4, p 1; k 3, p 1, 6 times; k 3, edge.

Sixty-first row.—Edge; n, o twice, n 8 times; edge.

Sixty-second row.—Edge, k 2, p 1; k 3, p 1, 7 times; k 1, edge.

Sixty-third row.—Edge, o twice, p 1, k 1; n, o twice, n, 7 times; k 1, o twice, p 1, edge.

Sixty-fourth row.—Edge, o twice; p 2 to.; k 3, p 1, 7 times; k 2, o twice, p 2 to.; edge.

Sixty-fifth row.—Edge, o 2, p 2 to., (o 2, p 2 to., is now called "fagot;" "o 2" means o twice , o 2, p 1, k 2; n, o 2, n, 6 times; k 2, o 2, p 1, fagot, edge.

Sixty-sixth row.—Edge, fagot twice, k 4, p 1, k 3, p 1, 5 times, k 3, fagot twice, edge.

Sixty-seventh row.—Edge, fagot 3 times, o 2, p 1, k 1; n, o 2, n, 5 times, k 1, o 2, p 1, fagot 3 times, edge.

Sixty-eighth row.—Edge, fagot 4 times, k 3, p 1, 5 times; k 2, fagot 4 times, edge.

Sixty-ninth row.—Edge, fagot 4 times, o 2, p 1, k 2; n, o 2, n, 4 times; k 2, o 2, p 1, fagot 4 times, edge.

Seventieth row.—Edge, fagot 5 times, k 4, p 1; k 3, p 1, 3 times; k 3, fagot 5 times, edge.

Seventy-first row.—Edge, fagot 6 times, o 2, p 1, k 1, n, o 2, n 3 times; k 1, o 2, p 1, fagot 6 times, edge.

Seventy-second row.—Edge, fagot 7 times; k 3, p 1, 3 times; k 2, fagot 7 times, edge.

Seventy-third row.—Edge, fagot 7 times, o 2, p 1, k 2, n, o 2, n twice, k 2, o 2, p 1, fagot 7 times, edge.

Seventy-fourth row.—Edge, fagot 8 times, k 4, p 1, k 3, p 1, k 3, fagot 8 times, edge.

Seventy-fifth row.—Edge, fagot 9 times, o, p 1, k 1, n, o 2, n, k 1, o 2, p 1, fagot 9 times, edge.

The edge stripe is now discontinued, and these stitches are knitted plain as the point is decreased, as follows:

First row.—O, n, n, k 6, fagot 12 times, k 1, p 1, fagot 12 times, k 10.

Second row.—O, n, n, k 6, fagot 25 times, k 9.

Third row.—O, n, n, k 5, fagot 25 times, k 9.

Fourth row.—O, n, n, k 5, fagot 25 times, k 8.

Fifth row.—O, n, n, k 4, fagot 25 times, k 8.

Sixth row.—O, n, n, k 4, fagot 25 times, k 7.

Seventh row.—O, n, n, k 3, fagot 25 times, k 7.

Eighth row.—O, n, n, k 3, fagot 25 times, k 6.

Ninth row.—O, n, n, k 2, fagot 25 times, k 6.

Tenth row.—O, n, n, k 2, fagot 25 times, k 5.

Eleventh row.—O, n, n, k 1, fagot 25 times, k 5.

Twelfth row.—O, n, n, k 1, fagot 25 times, k 4.

Thirteenth row.—O, n, n, fagot 25 times, k 4.

Fourteenth row.—O, n, n, fagot 25 times, k 3.

Fifteenth row.—O, n, n, k 1, fagot 24 times, k 3.

Sixteenth row.—O, n, n, k 1, fagot 23 times, k 4.

Seventeenth row.—O, n, n, fagot 23 times, k 4.

Eighteenth row.—O, n, n, fagot 23 times, k 3.

Nineteenth row.—O, n, n, k 1, fagot 22 times, k 3.

Twentieth row.—O, n, n, k 1, fagot 21 times, k 4.

Twenty-first row.—O, n, n, fagot 21 times, k 3.

Twenty-second row.—O, n, n, fagot 21 times, k 3.

Twenty-third row.—O, n, n, k 1, fagot 20 times, k 3.

Twenty-fourth row.—O, n, n, k 1, fagot 19 times, k 3.

Twenty-fifth row.—O, n, n, fagot 19 times, k 4.

Twenty-sixth row.—O, n, n, fagot 19 times, k 3.

Twenty-seventh row.—O, n, n, k 1, fagot 18 times, k 3.

Twenty-eighth row.—O, n, n, k 1, fagot 17 times, k 4.

Twenty-ninth row.—O, n, n, fagot 17 times, k 4.

Thirtieth row.—O, n, n, fagot 17 times, k 3.

Thirty-first row.—O, n, n, k 1, fagot 16 times, k 3.

Thirty-second row.—O, n, n, k 1, fagot 15 times, k 4.

Thirty-third row.—O, n, n, fagot 15 times, k 4.

Thirty-fourth row.—O, n, n, fagot 15 times, k 3.

Thirty-fifth row.—O, n, n, k 1, fagot 14 times, k 3.

Thirty-sixth row.—O, n, n, k 1, fagot 13 times, k 4.

Thirty-seventh row.—O, n, n, fagot 13 times, k 4.
Thirty-eighth row.—O, n, n, fagot 13 times, k 3.
Thirty-ninth row.—O, n, n, k 1, fagot 12 times, k 3.
Fortieth row.—O, n, n, k 1, fagot 11 times, k 4.
Forty-first row.—O, n, n, fagot 11 times, k 4.
Forty-second row.—O, n, n, fagot 11 times, k 3.
Forty-third row.—O, n, n, k 1, fagot 10 times, k 3.
Forty-fourth row.—O, n, n, k 1, fagot 9 times, k 4.
Forty-fifth row.—O, n, n, fagot 9 times, k 4.
Forty-sixth row.—O, n, n, fagot 9 times, k 3.
Forty-seventh row.—O, n, n, k 1, fagot 8 times, k 3.
Forty-eighth row.—O, n, n, k 1, fagot 7 times, k 4.
Forty-ninth row.—O, n, n, fagot 7 times, k 4.
Fiftieth row.—O, n, n, fagot 7 times, k 3.
Fifty-first row.—O, n, n, k 1, fagot 6 times, k 3.
Fifty-second row.—O, n, n, k 1, fagot 5 times, k 4.
Fifty-third row.—O, n, n, fagot 5 times, k 4.
Fifty-fourth row.—O, n, n, fagot 5 times, k 3.
Fifty-fifth row.—O, n, n, k 1, fagot 4 times, k 3.
Fifty-sixth row.—O, n, n, k 1, fagot 3 times, k 4.
Fifty-seventh row.—O, n, n, fagot 3 times, k 4.
Fifty-eighth row.—O, n, n, fagot 3 times, k 3.
Fifty-ninth row.—O, n, n, k 1, fagot twice, k 3.
Sixtieth row.—O, n, n, k 1, fagot once, k 4.
Sixty-first row.—O, n, n, fagot once, k 4.
Sixty-second row.—O, n, n, fagot once, k 3.
Sixty-third row.—O, n, n, k 4.
Sixty-fourth row.—O, n, n, k 3.
Sixty-fifth row.—O, n, n, n.
Sixty-sixth row.—O, n, n.
Bind over 2, draw thread through and fasten

No. 2.—Infants' Bib

blindly. Five of these points are required and are joined with over hand stitches, or they can be laced loosely together with linen thread and baby ribbon, loops and ends being left at the lower edge. The neck is finished with a narrow lace knitted as follows: Cast on 4 stitches.
First row.—Sl 1, k 1, o, k 2.
Second row.—Knit 5.
Third row.—Sl 1, k 2, o, k 2.
Fourth row.—Knit 6.
Fifth row.—Sl 1, k 1, o twice, n, o, k 2.
Sixth row.—Knit 5, p 1, k 2.
Seventh row.—Sl 1, k 5, o, k 2.
Eighth row.—Bind off 5, k 3.

INFANTS' BIB.

No. 2.—This bib may be knitted with thread, linen or knitting cotton. As shown it is made of twilled lace-thread No. 60, and two steel needles No. 18.

Cast on 14 stitches, and knit across plain, twice.
First row.—K 2, o, n, o, n, o, n, o, n, o, n, o twice, k 2.
Second row.—K 3, p 1, k 12.
Third row.—K 3, o, n, o, n, o, n, o, n, k 5.
Fourth row.—Bind off 2, k 13.

Repeat from first row until there are 50 scollops or large holes. Knit across twice plain, and bind off. Without breaking the thread, pick up the stitches across the selvedge; there will now be 100 stitches. Knit in plain garter stitch a piece about the depth of the lace.
First row.—K 4, p 92, k 4.
Second row.—K 4, * o, n * ; repeat between stars until the last 4 stitches, which k plain.
Third row.—K 4, p all but the last 4, which k plain.
Fourth row.—K 5, * o, n * ; repeat between stars until the last 3, which you knit.

Fifth row.—K 4, p all but last 4 ; k these plain.
Sixth row.—Knit plain.
Seventh row.—K 4, p 92, k 4.
It must be remembered that the first four and

No. 3.—Infants' Knitted Hood.

the last four stitches are knit plain in every row. They will not be alluded to again ; the pattern between them only will be given.

Eighth row.—* O, k 1, o, k 3 * ; repeat between the stars.

Ninth row.—Purl.

Tenth row.—* K 3, o, sl 1, k 2 to., pass sl stitch over, o, * repeat between stars across the work.

Eleventh row.—Purl.

Twelfth row.—* O, sl 1, k 2 to., pass sl stitch over, o, k 3 * ; repeat between stars.

Thirteenth row.—Purl.

Fourteenth row.—* N, n, k 2 * ; repeat between stars until the stitches are reduced to 10c.

Repeat from second to seventh row. Then knit in plain garter stitch until the bib is the required length ; knit 33, bind off 34 for the neck, k 33.

Knit these 33, remembering to narrow every row at the neck side until there are 15 stitches on the needle : knit across 10 times, and bind off. Knit the other 33 stitches in the same manner, and bind off.

For the narrow lace, cast on 10 stitches and knit 60 scollops, the same as for the bottom ; bind off, and sew to the neck and across the end of the tabs. Tape may be sewed to the tabs to tie around the neck.

INFANTS' KNITTED HOOD.

No. 3.—This hood is made of blue and white Saxony on rather coarse steel needles.

Cast on 20 stitches and knit back and forth plain until there are 8 ribs, then in each of the next 6 ribs widen 1 stitch in each rib ; this will make 26 stitches after completing the 14th rib ; widen 2 stitches in the next rib, then knit plain for 23 ribs ; then for the next 3 ribs narrow once, then once in each of the next 2 ribs ; this will leave 20 stitches, the same as the number cast on. Now pick up 44 stitches down each side, one in each rib, and knit 9 ribs plain ; then knit plain in the next rib until within 30 stitches of the end ; turn, slip the 1st stitch, then work back to within 31 stitches of the other end ; turn again, slip the 1st stitch and knit the rest, knitting 1 stitch of those set aside ; turn again, slip 1 stitch, knit to end of those just knit, and 1 of those set aside, work in this way until there are 4 ribs, then work back and forth plain until there are 24 ribs more. Now join on the blue, cast on 12 more stitches at each end, and knit 24 more ribs of the blue, and cast off. Pick up the stitches across the bottom of the hood, and knit 12 ribs, also of the blue ; cast off the stitches and sew the ends to the edge of the border where the 12 stitches were cast on. Turn the front border over about half its width, and sew a ribbon tie to each corner as seen in the picture.

INFANTS' CARRIAGE SOCKS, ANGORA LINED.

No. 4.—This sock can be made of either silk or

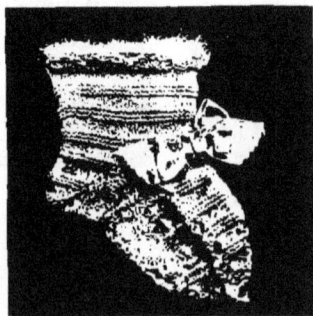

No. 4.—Infants' Carriage Sock, Angora Lined.

Saxony. If done in silk, use Saxony needles and knit rather loosely. Cast on 66 stitches.

Knit 6 rounds plain, * seam 1 round, k 1 round, repeat between stars till there are 3 seamed rounds ; now repeat from the beginning till there are 3 seamed stripes; k 6 rounds plain. Divide the stitches, leaving 34 stitches on one needle and at each of the remaining two needles for the heel, 16 stitches. Seam across on these two needles all but one stitch, seam back all but one stitch, seam back and leave 2 stitches, seam back, leave 2 stitches, seam back, leave 3 stitches, seam back, leave 3 stitches. Knit back and leave 4 stitches; now alternate plain and seam, leaving each time one more stitch without knitting than was left in previous round, till you have 7 rounds of plain knitting; then make a seamed stripe as at first. Next, 7 rounds of plain knitting, alternate stripes, till you have but 8 stitches left; now knit back and forth, taking up one stitch each time till you have taken them all up, taking care to keep your plain and seamed stripes as at first. The rest of the knitting on these two heel needles is plain. Knit 5 stitches plain at the beginning and end of the front needle and between those stitches the stripes must be kept the same as they were in the leg until the sock is finished. K 38 rounds before narrowing, then k 9, narrow all way round; 3 rounds plain, k 8, narrow all way round, 3 rounds plain, k 7, narrow all way round, 3 rounds plain, k 6, narrow, 3 rounds plain, k 5, narrow, 3 rounds plain, k 4, narrow, 3 rounds plain, k 3, narrow, 2 rounds plain, k 2, narrow, 1 round plain, k 1, narrow, bind off. Finish the top and around the seamed stripes in foot, with shell stitches in crochet.

For the Angora Lining.—Cast on 36 stitches, use coarse needles, and knit loosely. When you have knit enough for the leg, make the heel in the same way you did the sock heel. In toeing off narrow in center of each needle twice around plain, till you have but nine stitches; then bind off. Finish sock with a bow of ribbon.

CHILD'S KNITTED OPEN-WORK CAP.

No. 5.—Cast on 39 stitches. To make the direc-

tions more simple "x" will stand for 'o twice, p 2 to., o, p 2 to., o, p 2 to."

First row.—K 9; x, k 4, twice; x, k 3.
Second row.—Sl 1, k 2; x, k 4, twice; x, k 9.
Third row.—K 9; x, k 4, twice; x, k 2.
Fourth row.—Sl 1, k 1; x, k 4, twice; x, k 9.
Fifth row.—K 9; x, k 4, twice; x, k 1.
Sixth row.—Sl 1; x, k 4, twice; x, k 9.
Seventh row.—K 9; x, k 4, 3 times.
Eighth row.—Sl 1, k 3; x, k 4, twice; x, k 9.
Ninth and Tenth rows.—Like 1st and 2nd rows.
Eleventh row.—K 9, x, k 4.
Twelfth row.—Sl 1, k 3, x, k 9.
Thirteenth row.—K 9, x, k 1.
Fourteenth row.—Sl 1, x, k 9.
Fifteenth row.—K 9, x, k 2.
Sixteenth row.—Sl 1, k 1, x, k 9.
Seventeenth row.—K 2, sl and b 6, x, n, o twice, n, x, k 1.
Eighteenth row.—Sl 1, x, k 2, p 1, x, k 1, x, k 1, o 6 times, k 2.
Nineteenth row.—K 3, p 1, k 1, p 1, k 1, p 1, k 1; x, k 4, twice.
Twentieth row.—Sl 1, k 3, x, k 4, x, k 9.
Twenty-first row.—K 9, x, k 4, x, k 1.
Twenty-second row.—Sl 1, x, k 4, x; make 1 by knitting a stitch into the stitch under the next stitch to be knit; k 9.

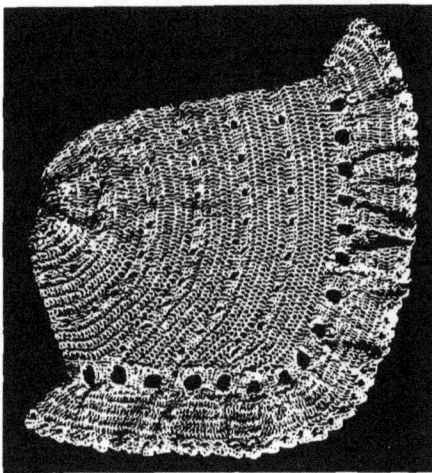
No. 5.—CHILD'S KNITTED OPEN-WORK CAP.

Twenty-third row.—K 10, x, k 4, x, n, o twice, n, x, k 1.
Twenty-fourth row.—Sl 1, x, k 2, p 1, k 1, x, k 4, x, k 1, make 1, k 9.
Twenty-fifth row.—K 11; x, k 4, twice; x, k 2.
Twenty-sixth row.—Sl 1, k 1; x, k 4, twice; x, k 2, make 1, k 9.
Twenty-seventh row.—K 12; x, k 4, twice; x, k 3.
Twenty-eighth row.—Sl 1, k 2; x, k 4, twice; x, k 3, make 1, k 9.
Twenty-ninth row.—K 2, sl and b 6; k 4, x, 3 times; k 2.
Thirtieth row.—Sl 1, k 1; x, k 4, 3 times; make 1, k 1, o 6 times, k 2.
Thirty-first row.—K 3, p 1, k 1, p 1, k 1, p 1, k 6, x, n, o twice, n, x, k 4, x, k 3.

Thirty-second row.—Sl 1. k 2, x, k 4, x, k 2, p 1, k 1, x, k 4, o twice, p 1, k 9.

Thirty-third row.—K 9, o twice, p 2 to.; k 4, x, 3 times; k 2.

Thirty-fourth row.—Sl 1, k 1; x, k 4, 3 times; o twice. p 2 to., make 1, k 9.

Thirty-fifth row.—K 10, o twice, p 2 to.; k 4, x, 3 times; k 1.

Thirty-sixth row.—Sl 1; x, k 4, 3 times; o twice, p 2 to., o, p 1, k 9.

Thirty-seventh row.—K 9, o twice, p 2 to., o, p 2 to., n, o twice, n, x, k 4.

Thirty-eighth row.—Sl 1, k 3, x, k 2, p 1, k 1, o twice, o, p 2 to., make 1, k 9.

Thirty-ninth row.—K 10, o twice, p 2 to., o, p 2 to.; k 4, x, twice; k 1.

Fortieth row.—Sl 1; x, k 4, twice; o twice, p 2 to., o, p 2 to., o, p 1, k 9.

Forty-first row.—K 9; x, k 4, twice; x, n, o twice, n, x, k 4.

Forty-second row.—Sl 1, k 3, x, k 2, p 1, k 1; x, k 4, twice; x, make 1, k 9.

Forty-third row.—K 2, sl and b 6, k 1; x, k 4, 4 times.

Forty-fourth row.—Sl 1, k 3; x, k 4, 3 times; x, k 1, make 1, k 1, o 6 times, k 2.

Forty-fifth row.—K 3, p 1, k 1, p 1, k 1, p 1, k 3; x, k 4, 3 times; x, k 1.

Forty-sixth row.—Sl 1; x, k 4, 3 times; x, k 2, make 1, k 9.

Forty-seventh row.—K 12, x, k 4, x, n, o twice, n, x, k 4.

Forty-eighth row.—Sl 1, k 3, x, k 2, p 1, k 1, x, k 4, x, k 3. make 1, k 9.

Forty-ninth row.—K 13, x, k 1.

Fiftieth row.—Sl 1, x, k 4, make 1, k 9.

Fifty-first row.—K 14, x, k 4.

Fifty-second row.—Sl 1, k 3, x, k 4, o twice, p 1, k 9.

Fifty-third row.—K 9, o twice, p 2 to., k 4, x, k 1.

Fifty-fourth row.—Sl 1, x, k 4, o twice, p 2 to., make 1, k 9.

Fifty-fifth row.—K 10, o twice, p 2 to., k 4, x, n, o twice, n, x, k 1.

Fifty-sixth row.—Sl 1, x, k 2, p 1, k 1, x, k 4, o twice, p 2 to., o, p 1, k 9.

Fifty-seventh row.—K 2, sl and b 6, o twice, p 2 to., o, p 2 to., n, o twice, n; x, k 4, twice.

Fifty-eighth row.—Sl 1, k 3, x, k 4, x, k 2, p 1, k 1, o twice, p 2 to., o, p 2 to., m 1, k 1, o 6 times, k 2.

Fifty-ninth row.—K 3, p 1, k 1, p 1, k 1, p 1, k 2, o twice, p 2 to., o, p 2 to.; k 4, x, twice; k 1.

Sixtieth row.—Sl 1; x, k 4, twice; o twice, p 2 to., o, p 2 to., o, p 1, k 9.

Sixty-first row.—K 9; x, k 4, 4 times; x, k 2.

Sixty-second row.—Sl 1, k 1; x, k 4, 4 times; x, k 9.

Sixty-third row.—K 9; x, k 4, 4 times; x, k 1.

Sixty-fourth row.—Sl 1; x, k 4, 4 times; x, m 1, k 9.

Sixty-fifth row.—K 10; x, k 4, 4 times.

Sixty-sixth row.—Sl 1, k 3; x, k 4, 3 times; x, k 1, m 1, k 9.

Sixty-seventh row.—K 11; x, k 4, 3 times; x, k 1.

Sixty-eighth row.—Sl 1; x, k 4, 3 times; x, k 2, make 1, k 9.

Sixty-ninth row.—K 12; x, k 4, 3 times.

Seventieth row.—Sl 1, k 3; x, k 4, twice; x, k 3, make 1, k 9.

Seventy-first row.—K 2, sl and b 6, k 4, x; n, o twice, n, x, twice; k 4, x, k 2.

Seventy-second row.—Sl 1, k 1, x, k 4; x, k 2, p 1, k 1, twice; x, k 4, make 1, k 1, o 6 times, k 2.

Seventy-third row.—K 3, p 1, k 1, p 1, k 1, p 1, k 6; x, k 4, twice; x, k 1.

Seventy-fourth row.—Sl 1; x, k 4, 3 times; o twice, p 1, k 9.

Seventy-fifth row.—K 9, o twice, p 2 to.; k 4, x, 3 times; k 4.

Seventy-sixth row.—Sl 1, k 3; x, k 4, 3 times; o twice, p 2 to., make 1, k 9.

Seventy-seventh row.—K 10, o twice, p 2 to.; k 4, x, 3 times; k 2.

Seventy-eighth row.—Sl 1, k 1; x, k 4, 3 times; o twice, p 2 to., o, p 1, k 9.

Seventy-ninth row.—K 9, o twice, p 2 to., o, p 2 to., n, o twice, n; x, k 4, twice; x, n, o twice, n, twice; x, k 4.

Eightieth row.—Sl 1, k 3; x, k 2, p 1, k 1, twice; x, k 4, twice; x, k 2, p 1, k 1, o twice, p 2 to., o, p 2 to., make 1, k 9.

Eighty-first row.—K 9.

Eighty-second row.—Sl 1, k 8.

Eighty-third row.—K 10.

Eighty-fourth row.—Sl 1, k 9.

Eighty-fifth row.—K 2, sl and b 6, k 1, o twice, p 2 to., o, p 2 to., k 3.

Eighty-sixth row.—Sl 1, k 2, o twice, p 2 to., o, p 2 to., o, p 1, k 1, o 6 times, k 2.

Eighty-seventh row.—K 3, p 1, k 1, p 1, k 1, p 1, k 1.

Eighty-eighth row.—Sl 1, k 8.

Eighty-ninth row.—K 9, x, k 1.

Ninetieth row.—Sl 1, x, k 9.

Ninety-first row.—K 9, x, k 4.

Ninety-second row.—Sl 1, k 3, x, k 9.

Ninety-third row.—K 9.

Ninety-fourth row.—Sl 1, k 8.

Ninety-fifth row.—K 9, x, k 1.

Ninety-sixth row.—Sl 1, x, k 9.

Ninety-seventh row.—K 9.

Ninety-eighth row.—Sl 1, k 8.

Ninety-ninth row.—K 2, sl and b 6; x, k 4, 5 times; x, k 1, o 6 times, k 2.

One Hundredth row.—Sl 1, k 3; x, k 4, 4 times; x, k 1, o 6 times, k 2.

One Hundred and First row.—K 3, p 1, k 1, p 1, k 1, p 1, k 1, x, k 1.

One Hundred and Second row.—Sl 1, x, k 9.

One Hundred and Third row.—K 9, x, k 4.

One Hundred and Fourth row.—Sl 1, k 3, x, k 9.

One Hundred and Fifth row.—K 9, x, k 4, x, k 1.

One Hundred and Sixth row.—Sl 1, x, k 4, x, k 9.

One Hundred and Seventh row.—K 9; x, k, 4, twice.

One Hundred and Eighth row.—Sl 1, k 3, x, k 4, x, k 9.

One Hundred and Ninth row.—K 9, x, k 1.

One Hundred and Tenth row.—Sl 1, x, k 9.

One Hundred and Eleventh row.—K 2, sl and b 6, x, k 4.

One Hundred and Twelfth row.—Sl 1, k 3; x, k 1, o 6 times, k 2.

One Hundred and Thirteenth row.—K 3, p 1, k 1, p 1, k 1, p 1, k 1, x, k 1.

One Hundred and Fourteenth row.—Sl 1, x, k 9.

One Hundred and Fifteenth row.—K 9; x, n, o twice, n, twice; x, k 1.

One Hundred and Sixteenth row.—Sl 1; x, k 2, p 1, k 1, twice; x, k 9.

One Hundred and Seventeenth row.—K 9; x, k 4, 3 times.

One Hundred and Eighteenth row.—Sl 1, k 3; x, k 4, twice; x, k 9.

One Hundred and Nineteenth row.—K 9; x, k 4, twice; x, k 1.

One Hundred and Twentieth row.—Sl 1; x, k 4, twice; x, k 9.

One Hundred and Twenty-first row.—K 9; x, k 4, twice; x, n, o twice, n, x, k 1.

One Hundred and Twenty-second row.—Sl 1, x, k 2, p 1, k 1; x, k 4, twice; x, k 9.

One Hundred and Twenty-third row.—K 9; x, k 4, 5 times; x, k 2.

One Hundred and Twenty-fourth row.—Sl 1, k 1; x, k 4, 5 times; x, k 9.

One Hundred and Twenty-fifth row.—K 2, sl and b 6, x, k 1.

One Hundred and Twenty-sixth row.—Sl 1, x, k 1, o 6 times, k 2.

One Hundred and Twenty-seventh row.—K 3, p 1, k 1, p 1, k 1, p 1, k 1, x, k 4, x, k 1.

One Hundred and Twenty-eighth row.—Sl 1, x, k 4, x, k 9.

One Hundred and Twenty-ninth row.—K 9.

One Hundred and Thirtieth row.—Sl 1, k 8.

One Hundred and Thirty-first row.—K 9; x, k 4, twice; x, k 1.

One Hundred and Thirty-second row.—Sl 1; x, k 4, twice; x, k 9.

One Hundred and Thirty-third row.—K 9; x, k 4, 3 times; x, k 1.

One Hundred and Thirty-fourth row.—Sl 1; x, k 4, 3 times; x, k 9.

One Hundred and Thirty-fifth row.—K 9; x, k 4, 4 times; x, k 1.

One Hundred and Thirty-sixth row.—Sl 1; x, k 4, 4 times; x, k 9.

One Hundred and Thirty-seventh row.—K 9; x, n, o twice, n, twice; x, k 4, 3 times; x, k 1.

One Hundred and Thirty-eighth row.—Sl 1; x, k 4, 3 times; x, k 2, p 1, k 1, twice; x, k 9.

One Hundred and Thirty-ninth row.—K 2, sl and b 6; x, k 4, 5 times; x, k 3.

One Hundred and Fortieth row.—Sl 1, k 2; x, k 4, 5 times; x, k 1, o 6 times, k 2.

One Hundred and Forty-first row.—K 3, p.1, k 1, p 1, k 1, p 1, k 1; x, k 4, 5 times; x, k 1.

One Hundred and Forty-second row.—Sl 1; x, k 4, 5 times; x, k 9.

One Hundred and Forty-third row.—K 9, x, k 1.

One Hundred and Forty-fourth row.—Sl 1, x, k 9.

One Hundred and Forty-fifth row.—K 9; x, k 4, twice; x, n, o twice, n 3 times; x, k 2.

One Hundred and Forty-sixth row.—Sl 1, k 1, x, k 2, p 1, k 1, 3 times; x, k 4, twice; x, k 9.

One Hundred and Forty-seventh row.—K 9; x, k 4, 4 times; x, k 1.

One Hundred and Forty-eighth row.—Sl 1; x, k 4, 4 times; x, k 9.

One Hundred and Forty-ninth row.—K 9; x, k 4, 3 times; x, k 1.

One Hundred and Fiftieth row.—Sl 1; x, k 4, 3 times; x, k 9.

One Hundred and Fifty-first row.—K 2, sl and b 6; x, k 4, twice.

One Hundred and Fifty-second row.—Sl 1, k 3, x, k 4, x, k 1, o 6 times, k 2.

One Hundred and Fifty-third row.—K 3, p 1, k 1, p 1, k 1, p 1, k 1, x, k 4, x, k 1.

One Hundred and Fifty-fourth row.—Sl 1, x, k 4, x, k 9.

One Hundred and Fifty-fifth row.—K 9; x, n, o twice, n, twice; x, k 1.

One Hundred and Fifty-sixth row.—Sl 1; x, k 2, p 1, k 1, twice; x, k 9.

One Hundred and Fifty-seventh row.—K 9, x, k 1.

One Hundred and Fifty-eighth row.—Sl 1, x, k 9.

One Hundred and Fifty-ninth row.—K 9.

One Hundred and Sixtieth row.—Sl 1, k 8.

One Hundred and Sixty-first row.—K 9; x, k 4, 6 times.

One Hundred and Sixty-second row.—Sl 1, k 3; x, k 4, 5 times; x, k 9.

One Hundred and Sixty-third row.—K 2, sl and b 6, x, k 4.

One Hundred and Sixty-fourth row.—Sl 1, k 3, x, k 1, o 6 times, k 2.

One Hundred and Sixty-fifth row.—K 3, p 1, k 1, p 1, k 1, p 1, k 1; x, k 4, twice.

One Hundred and Sixty-sixth row.—Sl 1, k 3, x, k 4, x, k 9.

One Hundred and Sixty-seventh row.—K 9; x, k 4, 3 times.

One Hundred and Sixty-eighth row.—Sl 1, k 3; x, k 4, twice; x, k 9.

One Hundred and Sixty-ninth row.—K 9; x, k 4, 4 times.

One Hundred and Seventieth row.—Sl 1, k 3; x, k 4, 3 times; x, k 9.

One Hundred and Seventy-first row.—K 9; x, k 4, 5 times.

One Hundred and Seventy-second row.—Sl 1, k 3; x, k 4, 4 times; x, k 9.

One Hundred and Seventy-third row.—K 9; x, k 4, 5 times; x, k 1.

One Hundred and Seventy-fourth row.—Sl 1; x, k 4, 5 times; x, k 9.

One Hundred and Seventy-fifth row.—K 2, sl and b 6; x, n, o twice, n, 3 times; x, k 4, twice; x, k 2.

One Hundred and Seventy-sixth row.—Sl 1, k 1; x, k 4, twice; x, k 2, p 1, k 1, 3 times; k 1, o 6 times, k 2.

One Hundred and Seventy-seventh row.—K 3, p 1, k 1, p 1, k 1, p 1, k 1; x, k 4, 3 times; x, n, o twice, n, x, k 4.

One Hundred and Seventy-eighth row.—Sl 1, k 3, x, k 2, p 1, k 1; x, k 4, 3 times; x, k 9.

One Hundred and Seventy-ninth row.—K 9; x, k 4, 5 times; x, k 1.

One Hundred and Eightieth row.—Sl 1; x, k 4, 5 times; x, k 9.

One Hundred and Eighty-first row.—K 9; x, k 4, 5 times; x, k 3.

One Hundred and Eighty-second row.—Sl 1, k 2; x, k 4, 5 times; x, k 9.

One Hundred and Eighty-third row.—K 9; x, k 4, 5 times.

One Hundred and Eighty-fourth row.—Sl 1, k 3; x, k 4, 4 times; x, k 9.

One Hundred and Eighty-fifth row.—K 9; x, k 4, 4 times; x, n, o twice, n, x, k 1.

One Hundred and Eighty-sixth row.—Sl 1, x; k 2, p 1, k 1; x, k 4, 4 times; x, k 9.

One Hundred and Eighty-seventh row.—K 2, sl and b 6; x, k 4, 4 times.

One Hundred and Eighty-eighth row.—Sl 1, k 3, x, k 4, 3 times; x, k 1, o 6 times; k 2.

One Hundred and Eighty-ninth row.—K 3, p 1, k 1, p 1, k 1, p 1, k 1; x, n, o twice, n, 5 times; x, k 1.

One Hundred and Ninetieth row.—Sl 1; x, k 2, p 1, k 1, 4 times; x, k 9.

One Hundred and Ninety-first row.—K 9; x, k 4, 6 times.

One Hundred and Ninety-second row.—Sl 1, k 3; x, k 4, 5 times; x, k 9.

One Hundred and Ninety-third row.—K 9; x, k 4, 5 times; x, k 1.

One Hundred and Ninety-fourth row.—Sl 1; x, k 4, 5 times; x, k 9.

One Hundred and Ninety-fifth row.—K 9; x, k 4, 5 times; x, k 2.

One Hundred and Ninety-sixth row.—Sl 1, k 1; x, k 4, 5 times; x, k 9.

One Hundred and Ninety-seventh row.—K 9; x, k 4, 5 times; x, k 3.

One Hundred and Ninety-eighth row.—Sl 1, k 2; x, k 4, 5 times; x, k 9.

One Hundred and Ninety-ninth row.—K 2, sl and b 6; x, k 4, 5 times.

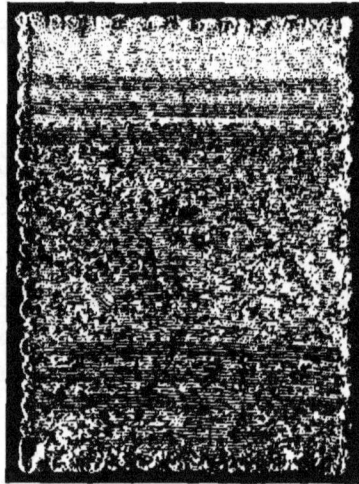

No. 6.—KNITTED BABY BLANKET.

(For Description see Page 125.)

Two Hundredth row.—Sl 1, k 3; x, k 4, 4 times; x, k 1, o 6 times, k 2.

Two Hundred and First row.—K 2, p 1, k 1, p 1, k 1, p 1, k 1; x, k 4, 4 times; x, k 1.

Two Hundred and Second row.—Sl 1; x, k 4, 4 times; x, k 9.

Two Hundred and Third row.—K 9; x, k 4, 5 times; x, k 2.

Two Hundred and Fourth row.—Sl 1, k 1; x, k 4, 5 times; x, k 9.

Two Hundred and Fifth row.—K 9; x, n, o twice, n, 5 times; x, k 1.

Two Hundred and Sixth row.—Sl 1; x, k 2, p 1, k 1, 5 times; x, k 9.

Two Hundred and Seventh row.—K 9; x, k 4, 5 times.

Two Hundred and Eighth row.—Sl 1, k 3; x, k 4, 4 times; x, k 9.

Two Hundred and Ninth row.—K 9; x, k 4, 5 times; x, k 1.

Two Hundred and Tenth row.—Sl 1; x, k 4, 5 times; x, k 9.

Two Hundred and Eleventh row.—K 9; x, k 4, 6 times.

Two Hundred and Twelfth row.—Sl 1, k 3; x, k 4, 5 times; x, k 9.

Repeat 211th and 212th rows, but at the beginning of the 211th row k 2, sl and b 6, rest same as 211th row. Knit back same as 212th row; at the end k 1, o 6 times, k 2. Now begin and knit *back* this way: Knit row 211, then 212; knit row 209, then 210; knit row 207, then 208; knit 205, then 206.

Be careful to *narrow* where the directions say "m 1." In knitting the holes in the edges, *reverse* the directions, for instance in the 201st row knit k 2, sl and b 6 instead of k 3, p 1, k 1, p 1, k 1, p 1, k 1, etc.

Cast on 11 stitches for the border.

First row.—K 2, x, k 1, o 3 times, k 2.

Second row.—K 3, p 1, k 2, x, k 2.

Third row.—K 2, x, k 6.

Fourth row.—K 6, x, k 2.

Fifth and Sixth rows.—Like 3rd and 4th rows.

Seventh row.—Like 3rd row.

Eighth row.—Sl and b 3, k 2, x, k 2. Repeat from 1st row 105 times. Join the parts neatly with a needle and thread.

This little cap is very pretty knitted either of silk or fine linen thread, and can be worn as it is, or lined.

KNITTED BABY BLANKET.
(For Illustration see Page 121.)

No. 6.—This little blanket is knitted on two rather coarse needles with pink and white Germantown wool. White Saxony is used to finish the border.

Begin with the white and cast on 115 stitches. Knit 32 rows of plain knitting, then join on the pink and make 8 rows, then 8 rows of white, 8 of pink, 8 of white, 8 of pink, then 128 of white, 8 of pink, 8 of white, 8 of pink, 8 of white, 8 of pink, and finish with 32 rows of white.

For the Border.—Crochet with the pink a shell of 7 d. c., fasten down with a s. c.; then another shell, being careful to make the shells so that they will lie perfectly flatly, and arrange to have one come in each corner. Finish the edge with picots made of white Saxony thus: Make a * s. c. between the first shell and s. c. (which fastens it down) 3 ch., 1 s. c. between the s. c. and next shell; then 1 s. c. between every d. c. in the shell, with 3 ch. between, and repeat from * for all the edge.

The blanket from which our illustration was made is twenty-eight inches wide by thirty-six inches long. These dimensions, however, may be varied to suit the size of the crib or carriage in which the blanket is to be used.

KNITTED BALL.

No. 7.—Cast on 30 stitches and knit across plain. Turn and knit all but last 7 stitches; leave them on the needle, pass the yarn between the needles, turn and knit back, leaving the last 7 stitches at the end; turn back and knit all but 6; turn again and knit all but 6; then, knitting as before, leave 5

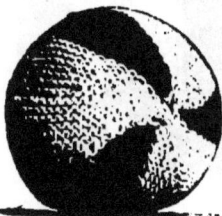

No. 7.—KNITTED BALL.

at each end, then 4, then 3, then 2, then 1; then knit all.

Be careful to make no mistake and you will then begin each gore at the same end. Knit 9 gores,

slip and bind loosely the last gore, and sew the two edges together after filling the ball with cotton.

INFANTS' BIB.

No. 8.—Use linen thread No. 30, or knitting silk,

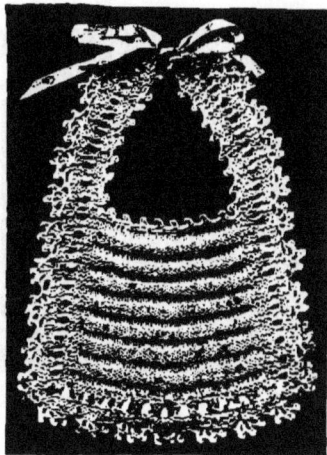

No. 8.—INFANTS' BIB.

in making this bib. Cast on 55 stitches, and knit across and back five times.

Sixth row.—K 3, o twice, n, o twice, n, o twice, n, and so on till there are but 2 stitches, which knit plain.

Seventh row.—Knit plain, dropping one of the th o-loops and knitting only one; the "thread over twice" is simply to make the holes larger, but only one of them is to be knitted. All of these loops are knitted the same way.

Eighth and Ninth rows.—Plain.

Tenth row.—K 3, o twice, n, knit to within 4 stitches, o twice, n, k 2.

Eleventh row.—Knit across plain.

Twelfth row.— Knit plain, n once at center, turn.

Thirteenth row.—K 7, purl all but 7, which k plain.

Fourteenth row—K 3, o twice, n, k all plain but 4, then, o twice, n, k 2.

Fifteenth row.—K 7, purl all but 7, which k plain.

Sixteenth row.—Knit plain.

Seventeenth row.—Plain.

Eighteenth row.—K 3, o twice, n, k 2, purl all but 7, k 3, o twice, n, k 2.

Nineteenth row.—Plain.

Twentieth row.—K 7, purl all but 7, which k plain.

Twenty-first row—Plain.

Twenty-second row.—K 3, o twice, n, k plain all but 4, then o twice, n, k 2.

Twenty-third row.—K 7, purl all but 7, which k plain.

Twenty-fourth row.— Knit plain, n at center.

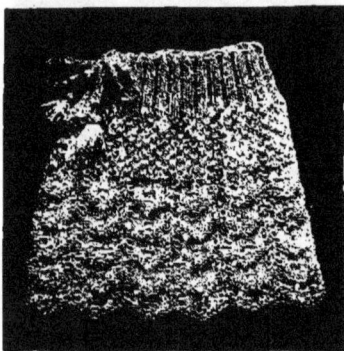

No. 9.—CHILD'S KNITTED PETTICOAT.

Twenty-fifth row.—K 7, purl all but 7, which k plain.

Twenty-sixth row.—K 3, o twice, n, k plain all but 4, then o twice, n, k 2.

Twenty-seventh row.—Knit plain.

Twenty-eighth row.—K 7, purl all but 7, which k plain.

Twenty-ninth row.—Knit plain.

Thirtieth row.—K 3, o twice, n, k 2, purl all but 7, k 3, o twice, n, k 2.

Thirty-first row.—Plain.

Thirty-second row.—Plain.

Thirty-third row.—K 7, purl all but 7, which k plain.

Thirty-fourth row.—K 3, o twice, n, k plain all but 4 ; narrow at center o twice, n, k 2.

Repeat twice more from 14th row and then from 14th to 26th row. K 3, o twice, n, k 2, slip and bind off all but 6, of which, k 2, o twice, n, k 2. Knit this way back and forth on both sides till long enough to go around the neck. Make the holes same as on the sides of bib every 4th row. When long enough bind off.

Finish the neck and edge with crochet scollops made as follows:

For the Neck.—3 s. c., in 3 stitches of edge, a p. of 3 ch, skip 1 stitch of edge, 3 s. c. in next 3 and repeat.

For the Outside.—In one stitch of bib make 4 tr. c. with picots thus: 1 tr. c., ch. 3, catch with s. c. in

top of tr. c. repeat 3 times more, ch. 1, skip 2 stitches of bib, sl stitch, in next stitch, ch. 1, repeat around. Run baby ribbon through the holes and tie at the back.

CHILD'S KNITTED PETTICOAT.

No. 9.—This petticoat is made of Germantown wool, on two needles, in two sections, which are sewed together. The colors selected are blue and white. Cast on 101 stitches with the blue wool, knit back and forth twice, then join on the white wool.

Third row.—P 2, th o, * k 4, sl off 2 st. from the left-hand needle, then put them back on the needle so that the first one slipped off will now be the second one on the needle and come in front of the other, then k 3 st. together; this will give a crossed effect from left to right; k 4, th o twice, p 2, th o and repeat from * across the row, but at the end make half the point instead of the whole point, and finish with th o twice, p 2.

Fourth row.—K 2, p 7, * k 2, p 11 and repeat from * across the row, ending with k 2.

Continue third and fourth rows until there are 3 holes or 6 rows; then join on the blue and knit back and forth 6 rows; join on the white again and work the 6 rows the same as the first stripe of white; continue working in this way until there are 5 stripes of white and 6 of blue, but in the last blue

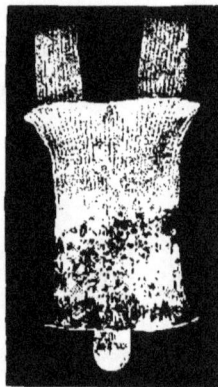

No. 10.—INFANTS' KNITTED BAND, WITH SHOULDER STRAPS.

(For Description see Page 127.)

stripe after the 5th stripe of white, make only 2 rows of blue; then join on the white and work thus: P 1; then k 2, p 2 across the row, but narrow about 12 times to bring the stitches down to 86.

Next row.—P the k and k the p st. so as to form small blocks; then in the next 2 rows work so that the purled blocks will come over the knit ones and the knit ones over the purled ones. Work in this way for 24 rows, which will make 6 rows of the purled and 6 of the knit blocks. Finish in rib fashion (k 2, p 2), making 18 rows; then at the top work across thus: th o, n, across the row and bind off. Make the other half exactly the same, except that after you finish the block pattern you only knit half across then back and forth for the 18 rows: then cast on 6 extra stitches for the underlap and finish the other half of the stitches. Fasten the under-lap under the opposite side at the bottom of the placket, and sew the two halves together. Make a cord and run through the holes, and finish each end of the cord with a tassel.

A ladies' skirt can be made in the same way by casting on more stitches. Add 13 stitches for every extra point.

INFANTS' KNIT-
TED BAND
WITH SHOULDER
STRAPS.

(For Illustration see
Page 136.)

No. 10.—This little band is made of very fine white Saxony yarn and with fine needles. It is made in 2 pieces and sewed together, and the shoulder straps and pinning piece at the lower edge of the front are also knitted separately and sewed on. Cast on 134 st. for each half, and k 2, purl 2, across the row; turn, and knit back so that a rib will be formed by purling the stitches which were knitted and knitting those which were purled in the previous row. Make 125 rows, and bind off. Sew the two sections together over-and-over.

For the Shoulder Strap.—Cast on 38 stitches and knit in rib fashion for 135 rows, and bind off. Sew each strap to the top of the band with about 7 ribs under the arm between the outer edges of the strap.

(These straps may be made as short or as long as required.)

For the Pinning Piece at the Lower Edge.—Cast on 30 sts., k 1 and p 1, back and forth for 21 rows: then narrow at each edge to round the work off for about 15 rows, and finish securely. Sew the piece to the bottom of the band at the center of the front. The edges of the band and the edge of the small piece may be finished in button-hole or cross-stitch with the working yarn, or with embroidery silk.

If coarser wool is used fewer stitches must be cast on, and not so many rows made. The band here illustrated measures about seven inches and a half in length, and four and a half in width.

KNITTED BIB.

No. 11.—To make the knitted bib illustrated at picture No. 11, use needles of medium size and No. 12 knitting cotton. A finer number may be used, but the bib will then be lighter and consequently not as useful.

Cast on 48 stitches.

First row.—* Knit 3, purl 3 across the row.

Second row.— Knit 3, purl 3 across the row.

Third row.— Knit 3, purl 3 across the row.

These three rows form one row of squares.

No. 11.—KNITTED BIB.

Now reverse the block, beginning each row with purl 3, and make 3 rows; then repeat from * till 24 rows of checks are made. Next, knit 12, bind off 24, knit 12.

These two groups of 12 stitches form the beginnings of the pieces which go around the neck. These are knitted back and forth in garter stitch for 40 rows.

Bind off, leaving the thread at the inner corner, each side, and with it crochet a cord about six inches long. Finish the cord with a small tassel made of the knitting cotton.

To finish the edge, crochet a chain of 3, first

catching with a single stitch to edge of bib, chain of 3, catch again, etc. From the inner corner around to the inner corner on the other side make

No. 12.—KNITTED SOCK FOR INFANT.

a second row of chains of 3, catching with single crochets into the preceding loop.

KNITTED SOCK FOR INFANT.

No. 12.—White Saxony, with any other pretty tint, and four needles of proper size, are required in making this little sock.

With the colored wool cast on 52 sts., and knit four rows as follows: knit 1, purl 1.

With white wool knit one row plain, purl the next.

Next row.—Sl 1, k 1; then o, n, across the needle.

Next row.—Purl.

With the colored wool now knit 6 rows plain. Repeat these two stripes alternately until there are four white stripes. Then, with the colored wool knit 17 sts.; with the 3rd needle knit 18 sts. for the instep, leaving the remaining 17 for the left side. Knit four stripes of each, same as before directed; then use only the colored wool for the foot. Knit across the toe, pick up 16 sts. of left side of instep, knit the 17 stitches; turn and knit to center of toe. With 3rd needle knit the remaining stitches on toe, pick up 16 on the right side and knit the 17 stitches on that side. Now knit 12 plain rows; there should be 42 sts. on each needle. Decrease every alternate row as follows:

First needle.—Sl 1, k 1, slip and bind, knit all but three, n, k 1.

Second needle.—Knit 1, slip and bind, knit all but three, n, k 1.

So continue until there are but 30 sts. on the needle; then bind off and sew up on the wrong side.

Finish the upper edge with a simple crochet edge in any design desired.

CARRIAGE LEGGINGS FOR INFANTS.

No. 13.—Use medium-sized bone needles and Germantown wool. Cast on 46 stitches.

First and Second rows.—Plain.

Third row.—K 1, make 1, k 22, make 1, k 22, make 1, k 1.

Fourth row.—K 1, make 1, knit across plain to within 1 stitch, then make 1, k 1.

Fifth row.—K 25 plain, make 1, k 1, make 1, k 25 plain.

Sixth row.—Plain.

Seventh row.—K 25, make 1, k 3, make 1, k 25.

Eighth row.—Plain.

Ninth row.—K 25, make 1, k 5, make 1, k 25.

Tenth row.—Plain.

Eleventh row.—K 25, make 1, k 7, make 1, k 25.

Eighteenth row.—K 33, n, turn, leave rest of stitches on needle.

Nineteenth row.—K 8, n, turn, leave rest of stitches on needle.

Twentieth row.—K 8, n (in narrowing always

No. 13.—CARRIAGE LEGGING FOR INFANTS.

take one of the stitches left on needle), turn.

Twenty-first row.—K 8, n, turn.

Twenty-second row.—K 8, n, turn.

Seventeenth row.—K 4, make 1, k 4, turn.

Eighteenth row.—Now the patent-knitting begins as follows: * th o, slip one stitch, inserting the needle as if for purling, knit 1, * repeat 4 times more between stars, but instead of knitting the last stitch narrow it with one of the stitches left on needle.

Nineteenth row.—* Th o, slip the knitted stitch, inserting the needle as if for purling and knit the th o, and slipped stitch together; repeat 4 times more between the stars. Knit back and forth like last row until you have 11 stitches left at each side of the narrowing. (32 stitches in all must now be on needle.)

Next row.—Leave 11 stitches on the right-hand needle; patent-knitting to the 11th stitch of the left-hand, then * th o, slip 1 stitch, inserting the needle as if for purling and k 1, * repeat twice more between stars, k 5 plain, turn.

Next row.—K 5 plain, patent-knitting to 11th stitch, * th o, slip 1, inserting the needle as if for purling, and k 1; * repeat twice more between stars, k 5 plain.

Next row.—K 5, patent-knitting to within 5 stitches which are to be knitted plain. Knit 60 more rows same as last, but at the beginning and end of the 8th, 20th and 35th of these rows make 1 stitch; this will form 6 stitches which are to widen the leg. After the 60 rows are knitted th o, n, then knit across plain (but the th o, and slipped stitch from the patent-knitting should be knitted together) this leaves 37 stitches on the needle.

Next and all other rows are knitted as follows: th o; then knit across, n at the end of needle, drop last loop. Repeat till all stitches are used up and break off the wool. Fasten the wool in the first loop where the narrowing begins; pick up every loop and knit it, there should be 38 stitches on the needle.

Next row.—Knit 8, then patent-knitting same as in 18th row, to within 8 stitches which are to be knitted plain; knit 27 more rows as follows: K 8,

patent-knitting as in 19th row to within 8 stitches which are to be knitted plain. Knit last row plain across, but knit the th o, and slip stitch from the patent-knitting together, and then bind off.

Finish the top with crocheted shells. Fold the work together so that the corresponding stitches will come together and sew them neatly with over-and-over stitches. Insert a cord in the loops, sew a tassel to each end and tie in front.

INFANTS' KNITTED BONNET.

No. 14.—This little bonnet is made in three sections, but if nicely sewed together has the appearance of being made all in one.

For the Front Piece.—Cast on 75 stitches.

First row.—Sl 1, k 3, o, n, o, n, o twice, p 2 to., n, o twice, n, o twice, p 2 to., k 2, n, o, k 1, o, n, k 2, o twice, p 2 to., k 2, o, k 2, sl 1, n, bind 1 over, k 2, o, k 1, o, k 2, sl 1, n, bind 1 o, k 2, o, k 2, o twice, p 2 to., k 2, n, o, k 1, o, n, k 2, o twice, p 2 to., n, o twice, n, o twice, p 2 to., k 1, o, n, o, k 1, o twice, p 2 to., o, p 2 to.

Second row.—O twice, p 2 to., o, p 2 to., o, p 2 to., k 5, o twice, p 2 to., k 2, p 1, k 1, o twice, p 2 to., k 3, p 3, k 3, o twice, p 2 to., k 3, p 13, k 3, o twice, p 2 to., k 3, p 3, k 3, o twice, p 2 to., k 2, p 1, k 1, o twice, p 2 to., k 8.

Third row.—Sl 1, k 7, o twice, p 2 to., k 4, o twice, p 2 to., k 1, o, n, k 3, o, n, k 1, o twice, p 2 to., k 3, o, k 1, sl 1, n, bind 1 o, k 1, o, k 3, o, k 1, sl 1, n, bind 1 o, k 1, o, k 3, o twice, p 2 to., k 1, n, o, k 3, o, n, k 1, o twice, p 2 to., k 4, o twice, p 2 to., k 5, o twice, p 5 to., o, p 2 to., drop last stitch.

Fourth row.—O twice, p 2 to., o, p 2 to., o, p 2 to., k 5, o twice, p 2 to., k 4, o twice, p 2 to., k 2, p 5, k 2, o twice, p 2 to., k 4, p 11, k 4, o twice, p 2 to., k 2, p 5, k 2, o twice, p 2 to., k 4, o twice, p 2 to., k 8.

Fifth row.—Sl 1, k 3, o, n, o, n, o twice, p 2 to., n, o twice, n, o twice, p 2 to., n, o, k 5, o, n, o twice,

No. 14—INFANTS' KNITTED BONNET.

p 2 to., k 4, o, sl 1, n, bind 1 o, o, k 5, o, sl 1, n, bind 1 o, o, k 4, o twice, p 2 to., n, o, k 5, o, n, o twice, p 2 to., o twice, n, o twice, p 2 to., k 1, o, n, k 1, o, k 1, o twice, p 2 to., o, p 2 to., o, p 2 to., drop last stitch.

Sixth row.—O twice, p 2 to., o, p 2 to., o, p 2 to., k 6, o twice, p 2 to., k 2, p 1, k 1, o twice, p 2 to., k 1, p 7, k 1, o twice, p 2 to., k 5, p 9, k 5, o twice, p 2 to., k 1, p 7, k 1, o twice, p 2 to., k 2, p 1, k 1, o twice, p 2 to., k 8.

Seventh row.—Sl 1, k 7, o twice, p 2 to., k 4, o twice, p 2 to., k 1, o, k 2, sl 1, n, bind 1 over, k 2, o, k 1, o twice, p 2 to., k 3, n, o, k 1, o, k 2, sl 1, n, bind 1 o, k 2, o, k 1, o, n, k 3, o twice, p 2 to., k 1, o, k 2, sl 1, n, b 1 o, k 2, o, k 1, o twice, p 2 to., k 4, o twice, p 2 to., k 6, o twice, p 2 to., o, p 2 to., o, p 2 to., drop last stitch.

Eighth row.—O twice, p 2 to., o, p 2 to., o, p 2 to., k 6, o twice, p 2 to., k 4, o twice, p 2 to., k 2, p 5, k 2, o twice, p 2 to., k 4, p 11, k 4, o twice, p 2 to., k 2, p 5, k 2, o twice, p 2 to., k 4, o twice, p 2 to., k 8.

Ninth row.—Sl 1, k 3, o, n, o, n, o twice, p 2 to., n, o twice, n, o twice, p 2 to., k 2, o, k 1, sl 1, n, bind 1 over, k 1, o, k 2, o twice, p 2 to., k 2, n, o, k 3, o, k 1, sl 1, n, bind 1 over, k 1, o, k 3, o, k 2, o twice, p 2 to., k 2, o, k 1, sl 1, n, bind 1 over, k 1, o, k 2, o twice, p 2 to., n, o twice, n, o twice, p 2 to., k 1, o, n, k 2, o, k 1, o twice, p 2 to., o, p 2 to., o, p 2 to., drop last stitch.

Tenth row.—O twice, p 2 to., o, p 2 to., o, p 2 to., k 7, o twice, p 2 to., k 2, p 1, k 1, o twice, p 2 to., k 3, k 3, o twice, p 2 to., k 3, p 13, k 3, o twice, p 2 to., k 3, p 3, k 3, o twice, p 2 to., k 2, p 1, k 1, o twice, p 2 to., k 8.

Eleventh row.—Sl 1, k 7, o twice, p 2 to., k 4, o twice, p 2 to., k 3, o, sl 1, n, bind 1 over, o, k 3, o twice, p 2 to., k 1, n, o, k 5, o, sl 1, n, bind 1 over, o, k 5, o, n, k 1, o twice, p 2 to., k 3, o, sl 1, n, bind 1 over, k 1, o, k 3, o twice, p 2 to., k 4, o twice, p 2 to., k 6, o twice, p 2 to., o, p 2 to., o, p 2 to., drop last stitch.

Twelfth row.—Bind off 3, k 9, o twice, p 2 to., k 4, o twice, p 2 to., k 9, o twice, p 2 to., k 2, p 15, k 2, o twice, p 2 to., k 9, o twice, p 2 to., k 4, o twice, p 2 to., k 8. Repeat from 1st row until you have 22 scollops.

For Crown-Piece.—Cast on 11 stitches.

First row.—O, k 11.

Second row.—O, k 12.

Third row.—O, k 4, n, o, k 1, o, n, k 4.

Fourth row.—O, k 5, p 3, k 6.

Fifth row.—O, k 4, n, o, k 3, o, n, k 4.

Sixth row.—O, k 5, p 5, k 6.

Seventh row.—O, k 4, n, o, k 5, o, n, k 4.

Eighth row.—O, k 5, p 7, k 6.

Ninth row.—O, k 1, n, o, k 2, o, n, o, k 1. sl 1, n, bind 1 over, k 2, o, n, o, k 1, o, n, k 1.

Tenth row.—O, k 2, p 3, k 2, p 5, k 2, p 3, k 3.

Eleventh row.—O, k 1, n, o, k 3, o, n, o, k 1, sl 1, n, bind 1 over, k 1, o, n, o, k 3, o, n, k 1.

Twelfth row.—O, k 2, p 5, k 2, p 3, k 2, p 5, k 3.

Thirteenth row.—O, k 1, n, o, k 5, o, n, o, sl 1, n, bind 1 over, o, n, o, k 5, o, n, k 1.

Fourteenth row.—O, k 2, p 7, k 5, p 7, k 3. You should now have 25 sts.

Fifteenth row.—Sl 1, k 2, o, k 2, sl 1, n, bind 1 over, k 2, o, n, o, k 1, o, n, o, k 2, sl 1, n, bind 1 over, k 2, o, k 3.

Sixteenth row.—Sl 1, k 3, p 5, k 2, p 3, k 2, p 5, k 4.

Seventeenth row.—Sl 1, k 3, o, k 1, sl 1, n, bind 1 over, k 1, o, n, o, k 3, o, n, o, k 1, sl 1, n, bind 1 over, k 1, o, k 4.

Eighteenth row.—Sl 1, k 4, p 3, k 2, p 5, k 2, p 3, k 5.

Nineteenth row.—Sl 1, k 4, o, sl 1, n, bind 1 over, o, n, o, k 5, o, n, o, sl 1, n, bind 1 over, o, k 5.

Twentieth row.—Sl 1, k 8, p 7, k 9.

Twenty-first row.—Sl 1, k 3, n, o, k 1, o, n, o, k 2, sl 1, n, bind 1 over, k 2, o, n, o, k 1, o, n, k 4.

Twenty-second row.—Sl 1, k 4, p 3, k 2, p 5, k 2, p 3, k 5.

Twenty-third row.—Sl 1, k 2, n, o, k 3, o, n, o, k 1, sl 1, n, bind 1 over, k 1, o, n, o, k 3, o, n, k 3, p 5, k 4.

Twenty-fourth row.—Sl 1, k 3, p 5, k 2, p 3, k 2, p 5, k 4.

Twenty-fifth row.—Sl 1, k 1, n, o, k 5, o, n, o, sl 1, n, bind 1 over, o, n, o, k 5, o, n, k 2.

Twenty-sixth row.—Sl 1, k 2, p 7, k 5, p 7, k 3. Repeat from 15th row to 26th, twice. Then decrease as follows :

First row—Sl 1, k 2, o, k 2, sl 1, n, bind 1 over, k 2, o, n, o, k 1, o, n, o, k 2, sl 1, n, bind 1 over, k 2, o, k 1, n.

Second row.—Sl 1, k 2, p 5, k 2, p 3, k 2, p 5, k 2, n.

Third row.—Sl 1, k 2, o, k 1, sl 1, n, bind 1 over, k 1, o, n, o, k 3, o, n, o, k 1, sl 1, n, bind 1 over, k 1, o, k 1, n.

Fourth row.—Sl 1, k 2, p 3, k 2, p 5, k 2, p 3, k 2, n.

Fifth row.—Sl 1, k 2, o, sl 1, n, bind 1 over, o, n, o, k 5, o, n, o, sl 1, n, bind 1 over, o, k 1, n.

Sixth row.—Sl 1, k 5, p 7, k 5, n.

Seventh row.—Sl 1, k 5, o, k 2, sl 1, n, bind 1 over, k 2, o, k 4, n.

Eighth row.—Sl 1, k 5, p 5, k 5, n.

Ninth row.—Sl 1, k 5, o, k 1, sl 1, n, bind 1 over, k 1, o, k 4, n.

Tenth row.—Sl 1, k 5, p 3, k 5, n.

Eleventh row.—Sl 1, k 5, o, sl 1, n, bind 1 over, o, k 4, n.

Twelfth row.—Sl 1, k 10, n.

Thirteenth row.—Sl 1, k 9, n.

Fourteenth row.—Sl 1, k 8, n.

Fifteenth row.—Bind off 10. This completes the crown. Sew the front-piece to it, holding it quite full over the top, to obtain the proper shape. Sew narrow lace across the ends, thus completing the neck. The following are the directions for this lace :

Narrow Lace for Neck of Bonnet.—Cast on 11 stitches.

First row.—Sl 1, k 1, o, n, o, k 1, o twice, p 2 to., o, p 2 to., o, p 2 to.

Second row.—O twice, p 2 to., o, p 2 to., o, p 2 to., k 6.

Third row.—Sl 1, k 5, o twice, p 2 to., o, p 2 to., o, p 2 to., drop last stitch.

Fourth row.—Like 2nd.

Fifth row.—Sl 1, k 1, o, n, k 1, o, k 1, o twice, p 2 to., o, p 2 to., o, p 2 to., drop last stitch.

Sixth row.—O twice, p 2 to., o, p 2 to., o, p 2 to., k 7.

Seventh row.—Sl 1, k 6, o twice, p 2 to., o, p 2 to., o, p 2 to., drop last stitch.

Eighth row.—Like 6th.

Ninth row.—Sl 1, k 1, o, n, k 2, o, k 1, o twice, p 2 to., o, p 2 to., o, p 2 to., drop last stitch.

Tenth row.—O twice, p 2 to., o, p 2 to., o, p 2 to., k 8.

Eleventh row.—Sl 1, k 7, o twice, p 2 to., o, p 2 to., o, p 2 to , drop last stitch.

Twelfth row.—Bind off 3, k 10. Repeat until you have 18 scollops.

This is also a very pretty narrow lace for trimming children's clothes.

INFANTS' BOOTEE. (SUITABLE FOR A BABE OF SEVEN MONTHS.)

No. 15.—Cast on 54 stitches, if to be made in Saxony; if in silk, 60 stitches. * K 4 rounds plain, 4 rounds seamed; repeat till there are 3 seamed rounds, with a seamed round at the top; now, k 2, seam 1 all the way round till you have made 20 rounds. Divide the stitches leaving 28 stitches on one needle and on each of the remaining two needles, for the heel, leave 13 stitches.

For the heel, knit plain back and forth on the latter two needles as follows: Knit plain all but 1 stitch, turn, and knit back all but 1 stitch; alternate these rows, leaving each time one more stitch without knitting than you did the time before

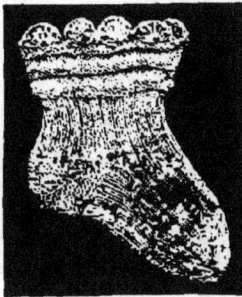

NO. 15.—INFANTS' BOOTEE.

till you have but 6 knitting stitches; now knit back and forth taking up one of the left over stitches each time, till you have taken up all of them again.

Next knit 30 rounds plain; now knit 7, narrow 1 all the way round; k 3 rounds plain; k 6, narrow all the way round; k 3 rounds plain; k 5, narrow all

NO. 16.—BABY'S KNITTED SACK.

the way round; k 3 rounds plain, k 4, narrow all the way round, k 2 rounds plain, narrow, k 1 round plain, narrow and bind off; finish top of bootee in crochet shell design; add a bow of ribbon if desired. The advantage of this bootee is in the heel, which is very easy to make.

BABY'S KNITTED SACK.

No. 16.—This comfortable sack is knitted with white woollen yarn. It is worked in plain knitting, with an open-work border at the bottom and sleeves, and a row of holes at the neck, through which a ribbon is drawn. The work begins at the lower edge, the back and fronts being knitted in one piece up to the arm-holes. Cast on 128 stitches, and knit to and fro, the 1st row in plain knitting.

Second row.—Narrow 1 stitch (to do which, slip 1, knit the next, and pull the slipped stitch over it), knit 3, * thread over, k 1, thread over, knit 3, narrow 3 (for which knit 3 stitches together), knit 3; repeat from * 12 times; then thread over, k 1, thread over, knit 3, knit 2 together.

Third to Fifteenth rows.—Knit as in the 1st and 2nd by turns, but for the point at the middle (the jacket can be open at the back or front, as preferred), narrow 2 at the middle of the 13th and 15th rows, in a direct line above the narrowing in the middle pattern of the preceding row.

Sixteenth to Eighteenth rows.—Plain throughout, but in the 16th row narrow 2 above the narrowing in every pattern of the preceding row.

Nineteenth row.—Slip 1, then by turns thread over and purl 2 together.

Twentieth and Twenty-first rows.—Plain throughout.

Twenty-second row.—Cast off the first 3, knit 15 out of the next stitch for a widening, knit 1 plain and 1 crossed, knit 17, widen again as previously, knit 11, narrow 2, knit 11, widen 1, knit 17, widen 1, knit the remainder.

Twenty-third row.—Cast off the first 3, then knit the rest plain.

Twenty-fourth and Twenty-fifth rows.—Like the

No. 17.—Design for Knitted Petticoat for Little Girls.

preceding 2 by turns, but omit casting off the first 3, and instead slip the first stitch of every row. From the 46th row upward the front and back are knit apart. To form the armhole, knit to and fro on the back on the first 26 and last 26 stitches of the row in 52 rows of plain knitting; in the last 18 rows of these, for the shoulder, knit 2 stitches together in every second row at 3 stitches from the end on the shoulder side; after completing the 97th row set the stitches aside. Resume the stitches that were left between the first and last 26, and knit 48 rows of plain knitting, widening as heretofore above the widenings in the preceding rows, and narrowing at the middle; in the 61st, 66th, 72d, 78th, 84th and 90th rows, make one more widening, taking it out of the next stitch toward the middle next the usual widening. In the last 2 rows cast off the first 16 stitches, for the shoulders, and join these to the edge stitches of the last 18 rows of the back.

Next take up the edge stitches along the side edges, and add them to the rest. Work 1 row of plain knitting.

Second row.—Plain knitting at the sides, and on the neck stitches a row of holes as in the 19th row of the border.

Third and Fifth rows.—Plain throughout; if

the jacket is to be open at the back in the European fashion; then, in the first of these rows work 5 button-holes in the back at intervals of 7 stitches, for each of which thread over and knit 2 together; join the edge stitches of these last 5 rows on both sides to the stitches cast off in the 22nd and 23d rows.

Begin the sleeves at the lower edge with 38 stitches, and knit 19 rows like the first 19 of the jacket; then knit 77 rows in plain knitting, but in the 45th, 55th, 65th and 75th widen at the beginning. Join the sleeves from the wrong side, and sew them into the arm-holes. The 20 rows at the bottom are turned up for a cuff.

DESIGN FOR KNITTED PETTICOAT FOR LITTLE GIRLS.

FIGURE NO. 17.—This design is fluted and intended to be sewed to a flannel yoke, fitted to the hips. The length may be varied by the number of stitches cast on, or by the depth of the yoke.

Cast 64 stitches of double woollen thread, Saxony yarn, or single Zephyr, on coarse knitting needles for the design shown, and knit across plain.

First row.—K 57, o, n, k 3, o, k 2.

Second row.—K 8, p 53, k 4.

Third row.—K 57, o, n, k 4, o, k 2.

Fourth row.—K 9, p 53, k 4.

Fifth row.—K 57, o, n, k 5, o, k 2.

Sixth row.—K 10, p 53, turn, k 4.

Seventh row.—K 57, o, n, k 6, o, k 2.

Eighth row.—K 11, p 53, k 4.

Ninth row.—K 57, o, n, k 7, o, k 2.

Tenth row.—K 12, p 53, k 4, turn.

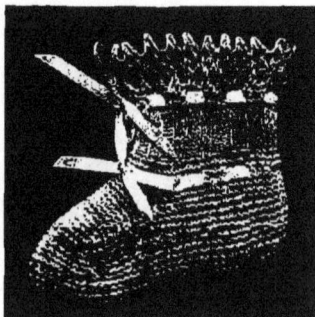

No. 18.—Infants' Knitted Sock.
(For Description see Page 133.)

Eleventh row.—K 57, o, n, k 8, o, k 2.

Twelfth row.—Sl and b 6, p 53, k 4.

This design has neither right nor wrong side.

INFANTS' KNITTED SOCK.

(For Illustration see Page 132.)

No. 18.—This little sock is made of pink and white Saxony. Cast on 80 stitches, turn, and make one rib which consists of 2 rows; in the next rib, widen at each end and also at the center of the work. Make one plain rib without widening; in the next rib widen once at the center of the work or toe, then make 6 ribs without widening. In the next rib k 43 st., then leave the rest on the other needle; join on the white wool and with another needle work back 16 sts., now on these 16 sts., leaving the others unworked, make 3 ribs with the white, then join on the pink and make 2 ribs, then with the white make 3 ribs, then one rib with the pink. Now join these 9 ribs on each edge to 9 sts. on the two needles, sewing them over and over with a needle and wool, and passing through each stitch. Slip each stitch off the needle as sewed. Now pass all the stitches onto one needle and make 4 ribs with the pink. Next, k 2, * th o twice, n, k 2, and repeat 13 times more from *, th o twice, n, k 2, k back plain dropping the second half of the 2 put-overs, make 2 more ribs, then k 2, * purl 3, k 3, and repeat 9 times more from last *; this forms the ankle ribs; work back purling the knitted and knitting the purled stitches; make 13 rows, then knit one row, and p 1; now make one rib-row then k 2, * th o twice, n, k 2, and repeat 14 times more from *; k back plain, dropping the second half of the 2 put-overs; make 1 more rib-row and bind off.

For the Border at Top of Sock.—Cast on 4 sts.

First row.—K 1, th o twice, n, th o twice, k 1.

Second and Fourth rows.—Knit back plain, dropping the second half of the 2 put-overs.

Third row.—K 2, th o twice, n, th o twice, k 1.

Fifth row.—K 3, th o twice, n, th o twice, k 1.

Sixth row.—Bind off 3, dropping the second half of the 2 put-overs and leaving 3 on the left-hand needle which knit plain. Repeat from first row until the strip is long enough to go across the top of the sock, and sew it on over and over. Sew up the sock at the back. Run a thread across the toe-portion for a short distance, and draw it in to shape the toe. Run very narrow ribbon through the 2 rows of holes and tie in a pretty bow.

BABY'S KNITTED SOCK.

No. 19.—Silk, Saxony, zephyr, or any wool preferred may be used. White Saxony for the leg and pink for the foot, were chosen in this instance.

Four steel needles will be required. With the white, cast 18 stitches on each of three needles. K 2, p 1 for 10 rounds; then knit the fancy part thus:

First round.— K 1, o, k 2 to., o, k 1, sl and b. Repeat all around.

Next round.— Knit plain.

Repeat these two rounds alternately until the leg is as long as desired. Then knit 4 rounds like top. Now on one needle put 2 stitches from the next needle, so that there will be 2 plain stitches on each end. There will be 20 in all. Leave the two needles, without knitting until you have knit back and forth on the one with 20 stitches for 15 rows (k 2, p 1). Of course, every alternate row must be reversed (p 2, k 1). Slip the first stitch each time. Now leave this needle, and with the pink knit on the other two back and forth for 15 rows, slipping the 1st stitch each time. Now, k 10, sl and b, k 3, k 2 to., sl and b, k 3, k 2 to., k 10.

Next row.—Knit plain; next row, narrow as before.

When all except one are narrowed between the two groups of 10 at each end of needle, knit to middle of needle, fold the work together wrong side out, and bind off like any heel. (K 1 from each needle together and draw the preceding stitch over the one that was left between the 10.) Continue to knit from each needle and bind off until

No. 19.—BABY'S KNITTED SOCK.

none are left but the binding stitch. Turn the work right side out and pick up stitches each side of heel. Knit across back and forth, taking up a stitch each time across from the strip of white to

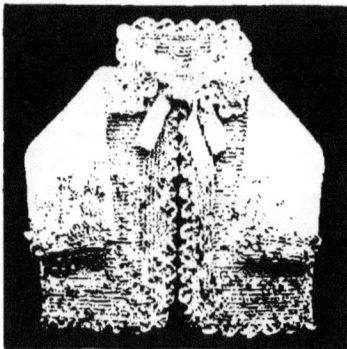

No. 20.—BABY'S KNITTED SACK.

o join the instep to the bottom of foot; draw the last stitch knitted over the stitch picked up. Widen two stitches on each side when first joining the instep. When the bottom piece is as long as the white instep-piece, knit all three needles, using the pink, and purling alternate rounds, until the foot is as long as desired, before narrowing. Take from each of the two needles upon the instep needle enough stitches to make the number on that equal to that of the other two. Beginning at the first end of instep needle (k 1, sl and b), knit to all but three at the other end; then k 2 to., k 1.

Second needle.—K 1, sl and bind, knit all the stitches from that needle, and all off the next but three; then k 2 to., k 1; this completes the first narrowing round. Next round plain. Continue to narrow in same manner, with one round between, until but 5 or 6 are left, when narrow all off and fasten.

For the Roll at Top of Slipper Part. —With the pink, take up the stitches all around the top of slipper part, k and p alternately for 6 rounds, then bind off, and with the pink material and a sewing needle catch down to the slipper to form the roll. Form a roll at the top of the leg in same manner. Run ribbon around ankle and tie in front.

BABY'S KNITTED SACK.

No. 20.—This little sack is made of pink and white Saxony, and is formed in one section and joined under the arms and along the sleeves. Cast on 67 stitches with the white wool for the lower edge of the back, and knit back and forth until there are 35 ridges. (Two rows of knitting make a ridge.) Now at each side of this center-piece cast on 26 sts. and knit until there are 20 more ridges. Now knit back 50 sts. at one side, take another needle and bind off 23 sts. Knit off the remaining sts. on the needle. Knit at each side 5 ridges, then cast on 7 sts. at each side and knit 16 ridges; then bind off 31 sts. for each sleeve. Knit 35 ridges for each front and bind off across the bottom. Pick up the stitches across the bottom of each sleeve, and with the pink knit 6 ridges. Sew up the garment under the arms and along the sleeves.

Now with the pink yarn pick up the sts. across the bottom and knit across once. Now knit 2, th o twice, n; then knit plain until within 3 sts. from the end; th o twice, n, k 1. In knitting back knit 3, p 1, then knit plain until within 2 sts. of the end; then p 1, k 1; knit in this way until there are 6 ridges, then bind off. Pick up the sts. along each front beginning at the bottom and knit back plain. Now k 1, th o, n, and knit plain to the top of the sack. Knit back plain to within 2 of the end, then p 1, k 1. Knit in this way until there are 6 ridges and overhand the slanting corners of the border together.

Now pick up the sts. across the neck and border

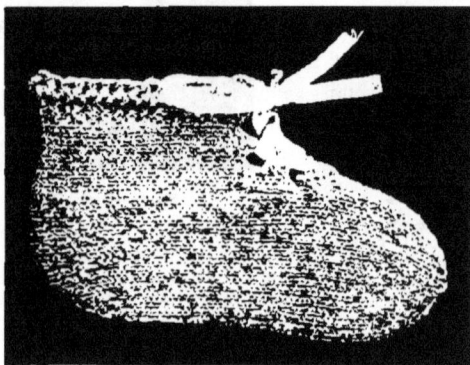

No. 21.—INFANTS' LACED SHOE.
(For Description see Page 135.)

and knit one ridge plain, then k 7 sts., th o twice, n, * k 5, th o twice, narrow and repeat from * across the work. In working back drop the last half of every put-over thread. Now knit one more plain ridge, then k 2, th o twice, n; then knit plain to within 3 sts. of the end, th o twice, n, k 1. In knitting back k 3, p 1, and knit plain until within 2 sts. of the end; then p 1, k 1. Knit in this way until there are 6 ridges. Finish the edge of the sack with a crocheted scollop of 1 s. c., * skip 1 st., make a shell of 1 s. c. and 3 d. c. in the next one, 2 ch., skip 2, 1 s. c. in the next. and repeat from * for all the edges of the sack, collar and sleeve. Run ribbon through the holes and tie in a pretty bow.

INFANTS' LACED SHOE.

(For Illustration see Page 134.)

No. 21.—Use Saxony and cast on 45 stitches.

First row.—Th o twice, p 2 to., k 2; p to within 4 stitches from the end, then k 2, o twice, p 2 to.

Second row.—Th o twice, p 2 to., k to the center stitch, widen 2 stitches by knitting the loop at each side of the center stitch; k to within 2 of the end, then o twice, p 2 to. Repeat these 2 rows 5 times more.

Twelfth row.—Th o twice, p 2 to., k 2, p 49, k 2, o twice, p 2 to.

Thirteenth row.—Th o twice, p 2 to., k 53, o twice, p 2 to.; repeat the last 2 rows 10 times more.

Thirty-fourth row.—Th o twice, p 2 to., k 2, p 49, k 2, o twice, p 2 to.

Thirty-fifth row.—Th o twice, p 2 to., k 2, o twice, n, n, k 41, n, n, o twice, k 2, o twice, p 2 to.

Thirty-sixth row.—Th o twice, p 2 to., k 2, p 1, k 1, p 1, k 1, p 41, k 1, p 1, k 1, p 1, k 2, o twice, p 2 to.

Thirty-seventh row.—Bind off 6, k 2, o twice, n, n, k 33, n, n, o twice, k 8.

Thirty-eighth row.—Bind off 6, k 2, p 39, k 3.

No. 22.—KNITTED WASH-RAG FOR AN INFANT.

Thirty-ninth row.—K 2, n, k 37, n, k 2.
Fortieth row.—K 2, p 39, k 2.
Forty-first row.—K 2, n, k 35, n, k 2.
Forty-second row.—K 2, p 37, k 2.

Forty-third row.—K 2, o twice, n, n, k 29, n, n, o twice, k 2.
Forty-fourth row.—K 3, p 35, k 3.
Forty-fifth row.—K 2, n, k 33, n, k 2.
Forty-sixth row.—K 2, p 35, k 2.
Forty-seventh row.—K 2, n, k 31, n, k 2. Slip

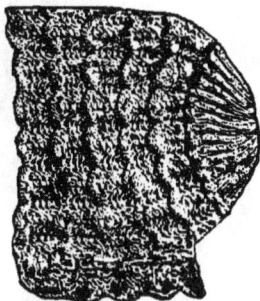

No. 23.—INFANTS' KNITTED SILK CAP.

the stitches onto 3 needles, 12 on each of 2 needles, and 13 on the third. Narrow the edge stitches together on the third needle, thus leaving 12 stitches on each of the three needles.

K 14 rounds plain, then narrow for the toe by narrowing once at the end of each needle in 1 round, then 1 round plain, and repeat the last 2 rounds until but 6 stitches are left on each needle; then k 2 to., until all are gone. Lace the shoe with baby ribbon and tie in a dainty bow.

The shoe is extremely pretty when knit in coarse silk, but care must be taken that the number of stitches given, when cast on in silk, make the sock the same size as in the wool; if they do not, cast on enough more to make it the right size. A good plan is to knit a small piece of each and thus see what the difference, if any, there may be.

KNITTED WASH-RAG FOR AN INFANT.

No. 22.—Dexter's cotton was used for this wash-rag. Cast on 52 stitches and knit back and forth plain until there are 4 ridges; 2 rows of knitting form a ridge. Next row, k 1, th o, n, and repeat to end of row, knitting the last stitch plain. Knit back plain and then make 3 more ridges, then another row of holes, then 27 ridges, a row of holes, 3 more ridges, a row of holes, then 3 more ridges and bind off. Crochet a scollop along each top and bottom edge, thus: Fasten the cotton in the edge, and make 6 s. c.; then fasten down with a s. c., making the scollop lie perfectly flat, and repeat.

INFANTS' KNITTED SILK CAP.

No. 23.—In knitting this cap use two needles

of ordinary size. About one ball and a half of knitting silk will be needed. Cast on 141 stitches.

First row.—Sl 1, p across.

Second row. — Sl 1, k across.

Third row.—Sl 1, p across.

Fourth row.—Sl 1, p across.

Fifth row.—Sl and b, k 3, th o, p 1, th o, * k 3, sl 1, n and b, k 3, th o, p 1, th o; repeat from * 12 times, then sl and b.

Sixth row. — Sl 1, p 4 (purl the thread thrown over in last row same as stitches), * k 1, p 9; repeat from * to end of row.

Repeat fifth and sixth

No. 21.

narrowing in between the narrowing of last row.

Now cut off your silk, leaving a long thread; thread this into a darning needle and pass the thread through the stitches to draw the work together as tightly as possible. If the hole left is too large to look well, darn it with a lace stitch. Then sew the edges of the ribbed part and one of the patterns together, thus forming the crown of the cap. Now cast on 101 stitches, and knit as follows :

First row.—Sl 1, p across.

Second row. — Sl 1, k across.

Third row.—Sl 1, p across.

No. 25.

No. 26.

rows 4 times. Then repeat the whole pattern 4 times. In the last purled row, in the last pattern, narrow 13 times at equal distances apart. In the next row * k 2, p 2, repeat from * across the row.

Continue to knit the knitted stitches and purl the purled stitches until you have knit about three-quarters of an inch.

Then narrow again by purling every two purled stitches together across the row. Knit again until you have knit about half an inch.

Then narrow by knitting every two knitted stitches together across the row. Then knit plain for half an inch. Then knit across plain, narrowing at every tenth and eleventh stitch. Then purl across,

No. 27.

Nos. 24. 25. 26 AND 27.—INFANTS' SOCKS.

(For Descriptions see Pages 136 and 137.)

Fourth row.—Sl 1, p across.

Fifth row.—Sl and b, k 3, th o, p 1, th o, * k 3, sl 1, n and b, k 3, th o, p 1, th o; repeat from * 8 times, then sl and b.

Sixth row.—Sl 1, p 4, * k 1, p 9; repeat from * to end of row.

Then bind off.

Now sew the section (fulling it a little) across the neck of the cap for a curtain, sewing the ends to first pattern around the face of the cap.

INFANTS' SOCK.

NO. 24.—Use three-thread Saxony and No. 24 needles. Cast on 61 stitches. K 1, over, k 1, * sl 1, narrow, pass sl st over, knit 1, over, k 1, over, knit 1, * continue between stars to end of row, always knitting the two last stitches on needle together. Purl back; continue these two rows until you have 18 rows of holes, knit 1 row, purl 1 row; then knit row for ribbon: Knit first stitch over, narrow to end of row; purl back; knit 1 row, purl 1 row, then continue fancy pattern until you have 2 rows of holes. Slip 22 stitches off on another needle, knit off 17 and make one stitch at end of needle, leaving 22 stitches on left hand needle; knit back and forth on the 18 stitches, which form the instep, in this way:

First row.—Knit 3, purl 3, across the row.

Second row.—Work back knitting the purled stitches and purling the knitted ones to keep the pattern.

Third row.—Like first.

Fourth row.—Like second.

Fifth row.—Now reverse the pattern so that knitted stitches will come over the purled ones and the purled stitches over the knitted ones. Knit for four rows as before. This will form the block pattern. Alternate these blocks till there are 10 rows of blocks; then knit across and back 3 times plain; fasten wool. Then on another needle knit off the 22 stitches on right hand needle; pick up stitches along the side of instep, knit across instep, pick up stitches on the other side of instep, and knit off the 22 stitches on left hand needle. Knit back and forth plain on these 3 needles, narrowing every other time at the toe-end of the side needles until you have 8 ridges of knitting on right side of work; then narrow every alternate row at heel-end of needles. On the instep needle narrow every time in center of needle until there are only 2 stitches left; then slip one on each side needle. knit a row plain, bind off, sew up back of leg and stretch over sock last. Run a ribbon in and out as seen in the picture and tie it in a bow in front.

INFANTS' SOCK.

(For Illustration see Page 186.)

No. 25.—Use three-thread Saxony and No. 24 knitting needles. Cast on 65 stitches with color, and knit across plain. Then knit 1, th o, knit 2, * slip 1, narrow pass slipped stitch over, knit 2, over, knit 1, over, knit 2, * and continue between stars to end of row always knitting the two last stitches on needle together, purl back plain; continue these two rows until you have 5 rows of holes; then fasten in white wool and continue the work with the white until you have 13 rows of holes; then knit 2 rows, purl 1 row, knit 1 row. Then make the ribbon row: slip first stitch; over twice; and continue to over twice and narrow, to end of row; purl back, purl 1 row, knit 2 rows, purl 1 row, knit 1 row, purl 1 row narrowing the last row at each end of needle; slip off 23 stitches on a third needle; with color knit off the next 17 stitches and make one stitch at end of needle, leaving 23 on left hand needle; knit back the 18 stitches and across and back again; then fasten in white and make 3 rows as before, then

3 rows with color; continue knitting that way until there are 5 stripes of color and 5 of white; then with color knit three rows and fasten end. Next with color knit off the 23 stitches on right hand needle, pick up the stitches along the side of instep, knit across instep, pick up the 24 stitches on the other side of instep, and knit off the 23 stitches on left-hand needle; knit back and forth plain on these three needles, narrowing every other alternate row at the toe-end of the side needles until you have 8 ridges of knitting on right side of work; then narrow every alternate row at heel-end of needles. On the instep needle narrow every time in center of needle until there are only 2 stitches left on instep-needle; then slip one on each side needle, knit a row plain, bind off, sew up back of leg and stretch sock over sock last. Run a ribbon in and out as seen in picture and tie in a bow in front.

INFANTS' SOCK.

(For Illustration see Page 186.)

No. 26.—Use three-thread Saxony and No. 24 knitting needles. Cast on 61 stitches with color, knit a row, purl a row, knit a row; then commence fancy pattern thus: fasten in white worsted. Slip 1, over, knit 3, * slip 1, knit 2 together, pass slipped stitch over this last stitch, knit 3, over, knit 1, over, knit 3 *; continue the pattern between stars to end of row and purl back; repeat these two rows until you have 4 holes. Then fasten in color again and purl across, knit back, repeat once more; fasten on white wool and continue fancy pattern as above until there are 4 holes, fasten on color; purl across, knit back, repeat once more; fasten on white and continue fancy pattern until there are 9 holes; then make the row for the ribbon. Commence by slipping first stitch, then over, narrow to end of row, purl back. Continue fancy pattern till there are 4 holes and purl back. Slip 22 stitches on another needle, knit off the next 17 with color for instep and make 1 stitch on end of needle, leaving 22 stitches on left hand needle, then, with a fourth needle. knit back and forth on the 18 stitches. Fasten in the color, make a stripe of four rows of purl stitches, then with the white wool make a stripe of four rows of plain; continue in this way until you have 5 stripes of color and 5 of white; then fasten in color and knit 6 rows plain, break worsted and fasten end; then with color knit off the 22 stitches on right hand needle, pick up stitches along the side of instep, knit across instep, pick up stitches on the other side of instep and knit off the 22 stitches on left hand needle; knit back and forth plain on these 3 needles, narrowing every alternate row at the toe-end of the side needles until you have eight ridges of knitting on right side of work; then narrow every alternate row at heel-end of needles. On the instep needle narrow every time in center of needle until there are only 2 stitches left; then slip one on each side needle, knit a row plain, bind off, sew up back of leg, and stretch over sock last. Run narrow ribbon in and out through the holes and tie a bow in front.

INFANT'S SOCK.

(For Illustration see Page 136.)

No. 27.—Single zephyr or heavy Saxony yarn, white and colored, and four steel needles are needed in making these socks. With the colored wool on 98 stitches, sl 1, k 1, *, drop 4, k 3, repeat from *, there will now be 42 stitches on the needle. Knit one row plain. Then with the white wool sl 1, knit across throwing the thread around the needle twice, knit one plain row. These last two rows make one rib which must always be counted on the right side. Make 1 rib of color, 1 white, 1 color, 16 white. In knitting the 15th make a row of eyelets thus: k 1, n, o, all the way across. With the color make 2 ribs; now divide the stitches on three needles; on the middle 14 make the instep, thus: 5 white ribs, 2 colored ribs, 3 white, 2 colored. After the 8th and 11th ribs narrow at the beginning and end of the needle.

With the color knit the 14 stitches, pick up the 12 stitches on the right side of instep adding one stitch after the 4th, 8th and 12th. With another needle knit the 10 stitches across the toe, pick up the stitches on left side adding 3 as on right side; knit the 14 stitches. There are now 68 stitches on the needles with which to make the foot which is 12 ribs deep. Widen at the end of the first needle and the beginning of the third until there are 76 stitches; make 1 rib without widening,

then transfer one stitch from the first needle and one from the third to the second, and narrow at the beginning and end of this needle in every right side row. In the last three ribs narrow for the heel by knitting together the 4th and 5th stitches from the beginning and end of the row; narrow three times in the middle of the last row. Bind off and sew together on the wrong side. Run a ribbon through the eyelets.

All the widening and narrowing (except the last) is made in a right side, and all the made stitches must be knit off crossed.

NO. 28.—INFANTS' KNITTED SOCK.

INFANTS' KNITTED SOCK.

No. 28.—Pale-pink Saxony yarn and cream-white knitting silk were used for this sock, although, if preferred, two shades of Saxony may be used instead.

Cast on 61 stitches with the silk, and knit 3 rows plain; then k 2 rows plain with the wool.

Sixth row.—K 1, th o, k 3, slip 1, n, pass slipped stitch over, k 3, o, and repeat 5 times more; then k 1.

Seventh, Ninth and Eleventh rows.—Purl.

Eighth and Tenth rows.—Like sixth row.

Twelfth, Thirteenth and Fourteenth rows. —Use the silk, and knit plain.

Fifteenth row.—Purl.

Sixteenth, Seventeenth, Eighteenth, Nineteenth and Twentieth rows.—Use wool and k plain.

Twenty-first row.—Purl.

Twenty-second row.—Use silk, k plain.

Twenty-third row.—Purl.

NO. 29.—DESIGN FOR BABY AFGHAN IN RAILROAD BLOCK STITCH.

(For Description see Page 139.)

Twenty-fourth, Twenty-sixth, Twenty-eighth and Thirtieth rows.—Like sixth row.

Twenty-fifth, Twenty-seventh, Twenty-ninth and Thirty-first rows.—Purl.

Next five rows.—Use wool, k plain.

Next row.—K 2, o, n, * k 4, o, n, and repeat 8 times more from *; k 3.

Next row.—Purl; next, k 5 rows plain, then p 1 row. Now, with the silk k 1 row, p 1 row, k 1 row, p 1 row, k 1 row, p 1 row. Next with the wool knit 38 stitches, turn and knit back 15 stitches, then knit 4 times more across the 15 stitches (making 3 ribs). Next, with the silk, k 1 row, p 1 row, k 1 row, p 1 row.

Next with the wool knit six rows plain.

Then with the silk work like the last stripe of silk; next, another wool stripe like the former; then the silk the same as before, except that you narrow once at each side in the last row. Now make another wool stripe; then a silk stripe the same as before, except that you narrow at each side in all the plain or knit rows. Now take the wool and pick up the stitches along the right side of the instep; knit the stitches across the toe; pick up the stitches on the left side and knit the remaining stitches on the left needle.

Knit plain until there are 6 ribs, then in the next row narrow at each end (the heel) and three times at the toe, thus: once in the middle and at each side, leaving 5 stitches between. Narrow in the same way after the 8th, 10th and 11th ribs, and after the 12th rib bind off. Sew up the sock

at the back and across the bottom, and make a silk cord finished with tassels, and run it through the holes at the ankle, tying in a pretty bow.

To shape the socks nicely, it is a good plan to draw them over a last, dip in clear water, and dry them on the last. They will prove of perfect shape when removed from the last.

DESIGN FOR BABY AFGHAN IN RAILROAD BLOCK STITCH.

No. 29.—Cast 42 stitches on one needle and knit across plain.

Then, k 6, p 5, k 5, p 5, k 5, p 5, k 5, p 6.

Work back and forth for 5 rows; then, p 6, k 5, p 5, k 5, p 5, k 5, p 5, k 6, for 5 rounds.

Now reverse the work so that the little squares will be smooth and rough alternately. When the strip is long enough, bind off, dropping every fifth stitch. Pull the work, thus ravelling the dropped stitches to the end of the strip. Narrow ribbon, if fancied, may be run through the ravelled-stitch rows.

No. 30.—DESIGN FOR BABY AFGHAN IN RAILROAD STITCH.

No. 31.—BABY'S BED-SHOE.

DESIGN FOR BABY AFGHAN IN RAILROAD STITCH.

No. 30.—This is knit just like No. 29, in squares, but every other stitch is dropped and ravelled out. A bright lining of silk or opera flannel shows through the open work and contrasts with the color of the afghan.

BABY'S BED-SHOE.

No. 31.—Use white Germantown wool and 2 bone needles in making this shoe.

Cast on 60 stitches. Knit the first 12 rows plain. (Once across the needle is a row.)

Thirteenth row.—K 27, n, k 2, n, k 27.
Fourteenth row.—K 26, n, k 2, n, k 26.

Continue narrowing every row each side of the

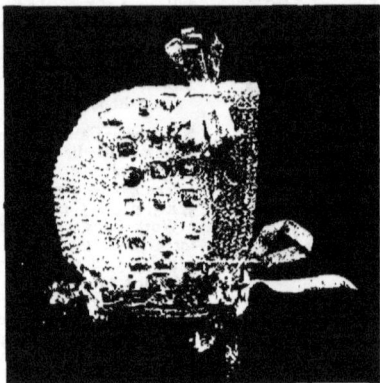

No. 32.—Dolls' Knitted Hood.

two center stitches, until there are only 32 stitches left on the needle. This will be the 25th row. Then knit 14 rows plain, which brings you to the 39th row.

Fortieth row.—Purl.
Forty-first row.—Plain.
Forty-second row.—Plain.
Forty-third row.—Purl.

Continue to knit 2 rows plain and purl 1 row, until there are 19 ribs on the right side of the work.

To vary the size, make a chain with a crochet needle the length of the shoe or foot, always having an even number of stitches on the needle and leaving the two center stitches plain. For an adult it would be best to leave four or six in the center, between the narrowings. About 20 rows plain to begin the work would form the sole.

Dolls' Knitted Hood.

No. 32.—This little hood is made of blue and white Saxony. Cast on 22 sts. with the white, and knit back and forth until there are 24 ridges, 2 rows to a ridge. Cast on 23 sts. at each side of this piece, and knit 3 ridges; then make a row of holes thus: th o twice, n, k 2, and repeat across the row. In knitting back, drop the second half of the 2 put-overs. Make 3 ridges, then a row of holes, 3 ridges, a row of holes, then 6 ridges; join

on the blue and cast on 6 sts. at each end of the needle; turn, work back and forth until there are 9 ridges of the blue and cast off. Sew the sides to the center-back, letting the 6 added sts. at each end come below the hood. Now, across the back at the bottom pick up the sts. and knit across, making a row of holes the same as described for the upper part of hood. Join on the blue and make 6 ridges. Sew the part that was just made to the edge of the blue which was added. Run ribbon through the holes at the back and tie a bow at the center, and also through the 3 rows of holes in front of the hood. Turn back the blue piece at the front, make a full bow for the top of the hood, and sew a string at each corner.

By adding more stitches to the number here cast on the hood can be made of suitable size for an infant or even a larger child.

Child's Knitted Slipper.

No. 33.—This slipper is made of blue and white single zephyr. It is knitted in a straight strip that is long enough after it is joined to go entirely around the sole to be used. In joining the *two ends* are not sewed together but are attached as follows: Turn the corner of one end down so that the end-edge will be even with the lower edge. This will make a bias fold, which extends along the foot from the toe to the top of the instep. Then bring the remaining end around and join it to the edge, which now crosses the strip from top to bottom beyond the bias fold, and join the two at this point. This will shape the slipper and make it ready for the sole. In sewing on the latter the point must be turned under and held a little full to shape it nicely. The design is in honeycomb pattern with 2 stitches to a square, and is made as follows:

Cast on 14 sts. with the blue, and knit across plain.

For the Squares.—Slip off 2 blue sts., inserting

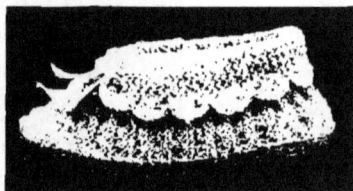

No. 33.—Child's Knitted Slipper.

the needle in each as for purling. Next, with the white, k 2, slip 2 blue sts. as before, k 2, and so on across the row. In working back sl 2 blue sts. and p 2 white ones alternately. Work back and forth in same order once more. Now with the blue knit back and forth plain 4 times, then repeat the squares with the blue and white as before. Repeat in this way until the strip is 30 squares long for a No. 4 slipper, or sufficiently long to go around the sole to be used. Join the slipper as previously directed and sew it to the sole.

For the Turn-over Top.—Cast on 10 stitches and knit back and forth until there are 48 ribs (2 rows to a rib), or until the strip is long enough to go around the top of the slipper, just meeting in front. Crochet a little scollop with the white up each end and along the lower edge, making 4 s. c. to each scollop, and catch down with a s. c. Crochet a row of holes along the top of the slipper of 1 d. c. in each square; sew the turn-over portion to the top of this (see picture), run ribbon through the holes and tie in a bow in front.

INFANTS' KNITTED SOCKS.

No. 34.—These dainty little socks are made of white Saxony and pink silk. Blue and white may be used, if preferred.

For the Foot-Portion.—Cast on 32 stitches, using rather fine needles; make one rib (which consists of 2 plain rows); in the next rib widen 1 st. at the toe-end, widen once at the toe-end in the next rib, then make 10 ribs without widening; in the fourteenth rib also widen again at the toe-end, making 35 stitches in all; take off 16 sts. from the back on a thread, and work the remaining 19 plain; work 4 ribs on the 19 sts., then widen once at the toe-end in the next rib;

No. 34.—INFANTS' KNITTED SOCK.

next make 6 ribs without widening; in the next rib narrow once at the toe-end; in the next rib cast on 16 sts. and widen once; then make 10

ribs without widening, and narrow once in each of the next 2 ribs; next bind off the stitches.

Pick up 46 stitches across the top of the foot

No. 35.—DOLLS' KNITTED SACK.

(For Description see Page 142.)

portion just knitted; then k 3, n, * th o twice, n, and repeat 7 times more from *; k 4, n, ** th o twice, n, repeat 8 times more from **; then k 2, knit back plain dropping the second half of the put-overs. Next work back and forth until there are 11 more ribs, widening once in the first, then in every other rib so that there will be 52 sts.; then k 4, * th o twice, n, k 1, and repeat 13 times more from *; then th o twice, n, k 4.

Next row, p; then k one row, and purl one row. Next row, k 6, * th o twice, n, k 1, and repeat 12 times more from *; then, th o twice, n, k rest plain. Next row, p; then k one row, and p one row. Next row, k 5, then make the holes the same as before, then p; k and p the next 3 rows. Next row, k the same as the first row of holes; then make the 3 rows of p, k and p; next k 3, then make the holes. Next, k back and forth until there are 3 ribs, being careful to always drop the second half of the put-overs after making the holes. Now make one more rib thus: Widen once in the first st. by knitting and purling in the same st. K 5, widen, k 8, w, k 8, widen and so on across the row; then bind off the stitches to make a fine edge.

Sew up the sock across the toe along the bottom and up the back; then across the top use the pink silk and crochet 1 d. c. in each stitch, except at the widening, where you make 2 in one stitch to emphasize the point. Run narrow ribbon through the holes and tie in a bow. If preferred, a cord of silk or Saxony finished with tassels of the same may be used.

DOLLS' KNITTED SACK.
(For Illustration see Page 141.)

No. 35.—This little sack is made of blue and white Saxony and is formed in one section and joined under the arms. Cast on 56 sts. with the white wool for the lower edge of the back, and knit back and forth until there are 28 ridges (2 rows of knitting make a ridge). Now at each side of this center-piece cast on 33 sts. and knit un-

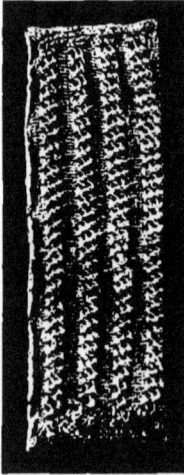

NO. 36.—DESIGN FOR KNITTED PETTI-
COAT FOR LITTLE GIRL.

til there are 9 more ridges; then knit back 49 sts., bind off 22 sts., and knit off the remaining sts. on the needle. Knit 8 ridges at each side; then cast on 11 sts. and knit 9 ridges; then bind off 35 sts. for each sleeve; knit 28 ridges for each front, and bind off across the bottom. Make 8 ridges of the blue across the bottom of each sleeve. Sew up the garment under the arms and along the sleeves. Pick up the sts. across the neck and make 3 ridges with the white ; leave the sts. on a thread. Now with the blue wool pick up the sts. across the bottom and make 8 ridges. Pick up the sts. along each front and make 8 ridges. Use the blue and pick up the sts. along the front edge of the neck and knit those that were left on the string, then pick up those along the other end in the blue border, knit 2, th o twice, n, and repeat across the row. Knit back and drop the second half of the

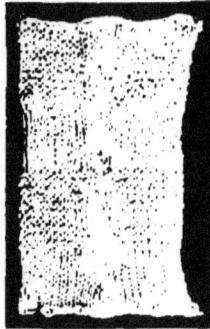

NO. 37.—CABLE STITCH DESIGN FOR BABY
AFGHAN.

CABLE-STITCH DESIGN FOR A BABY AFGHAN.

No. 37.—An afghan of this design may be made

2 put-overs. Knit 8 ridges and bind off. Run a ribbon through the holes at the neck.

This sack may be made large enough for an infant by casting on more stitches, of course, preserving a number divisible by two.

DESIGN FOR KNITTED PETTICOAT FOR LITTLE GIRL.

No. 36.—A selvedge at the top and a firm hem at the bottom, in double-stitch, render this petticoat strong and durable. The length may be varied by the number of stitches cast on.

Cast 74 stitches of double woollen thread, Saxony yarn or single zeyhyr, on coarse knitting needles and knit across plain.

First row.—Sl 1, p 1, for 6 stitches, p 56, sl 1, p 1 for 12 stitches.

Second row.—Sl 1, k 1 for 12 stitches, k 56, sl 1, k 1 for 6 stitches; repeat back and forth, making 7 rows in all.

Eighth row.—Sl 1, k 1 for 12 stitches, over, narrow 28 times, sl 1, k 1 for 6 stitches.

Ninth row.—Sl 1, p 1 for 6 stitches, p 56, sl 1, p 1 for 12 stitches.

Tenth row.—Like 8th.

Eleventh row.—Like 9th.

Twelfth row.—Like 8th.

This makes the open work. Continue as from the 1st row. When every other stitch is slipped, carrying the thread across to the next stitch in alternating, and knitting the slipped stitch and slipping the knitted stitch make a double-stitch in the selvedge and hem.

NO. 38.—TUFTED BORDER FOR BABY
AFGHAN.
(For Description see Page 148.)

of Saxony, split zephyr or any soft yarn and on bone or shell needles. Cast 26 stitches on one needle and knit across plain; knit 10 stitches plain, purl 6, knit 10 plain. Knit back plain and repeat for 10 rows. Then pick up 3 stitches of the 6 middle ones on an extra needle and leave them, knitting the remaining 13 stitches plain. Knit the 10 side stitches plain, but purl the 6 middle ones, knitting the 3 on the extra needle first. This gives the cable twist. Always knit the extra stitches on the right side. When the side rows are 20 in number, knit 15 others plain on the right side and purled on the wrong side. This makes the rough and smooth squares on each side of the cable twist. Knit 3 stitches on an extra needle every 10 rows, and proceed as above described.

TUFTED BORDER FOR BABY AFGHAN.

(For Illustration see Page 142).

No. 38.—Use Saxony, split zephyr or any soft yarn. Cast 5 stitches on one knitting needle and knit across plain. Then throw the thread in loops over the end of the forefinger three times and knit five stitches. Then purl the next row. This border edges baby afghans very prettily in place of fringe or a crocheted edge.

INFANTS' SOCKS.

No. 39.—Two or three thread Saxony yarn, knitting silk, and four steel knitting needles of suitable size are required in making these socks. With a double thread knit on 60 stitches as follows:

First to Eighth rows.—Sl 1, k 1, *, o, n, k 2, repeat from *.
Ninth to Twelfth rows.—Sl 1, knit plain.
Thirteenth row.—Sl 1, purl.
Fourteenth row.—With yarn sl 1, k 1, * with silk, k 2, with yarn, k 2; repeat from *.
Fifteenth row.—With wool, sl 1, p 1, * with silk, p 2, with wool p 2, repeat from *.
Sixteenth row.—Sl 1, knit.
Seventeenth, Nineteenth, Twenty-first, Twenty-third and Twenty-fifth rows.—Sl 1, purl.
Eighteenth and Twenty-second rows.—Sl 1, k 2, *, p 3, k 3, repeat from *.
Twentieth and Twenty-fourth rows.—Sl 1, p 3, *, k 3, p 3, repeat from *.
Twenty-sixth and Twenty-seventh rows. — Same as 14th and 15th.
Twenty-eighth row.—Sl 1, knit.
Twenty-ninth row.—Sl 1, purl.
Thirtieth to Thirty-fourth rows.—Sl 1, knit.

Thirty-fifth row.—Sl 1, k 2, *, p 3, k 3, repeat from *.
Thirty-sixth row.—Sl 1, knit.
Repeat these two rows twice.
Forty-first row.—Sl 1, p 2, *, k 3, p 3, repeat from *.
Forty-second row.—Sl 1, knit.
Repeat these two rows twice.
Forty-seventh row.—Sl 1, purl.
Forty-eighth row.—Sl 1, k 1, * o twice, n, k 1, repeat from *.
Forty-ninth row.—Sl 1, purl, purling the o twice as one stitch.
Fiftieth row.—Sl 1, knit.
Fifty-first row.—Sl 1, k 2, *, p 3, k 3, repeat from *.
Fifty-second row.—Sl 1, knit.
Repeat these 2 rows twice.
Fifty-seventh row. — Sl 1, p 2, *, k 3, p 3, repeat from *.
Fifty-eighth row.—Sl 1, k 39, turn the work and on 20 stitches knit the instep, purl with a third needle. Knit the pattern of checks until there are 7 rows, counting from the row of eyelets; then 15

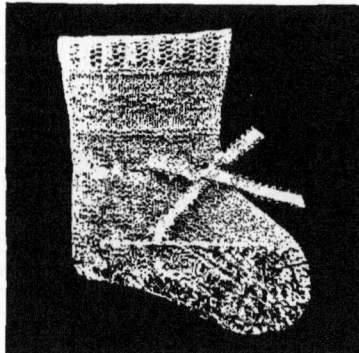

NO. 39.—INFANTS' SOCK.

rows plain; in the 10th, 12th and 14th, sl 1, k 2, n, knit all but 5, sl and b, k 3. With the needles on the right side having on it 20 stitches, pick up the stitches on the instep, making one stitch after the 4th, 8th, 12th and 16th; with another needle knit the 14 stitches across the toe; pick up the stitch on left side of instep making four stitches to correspond with the other side, knit the 20 stitches. Transfer three stitches from the first and three stitches from the third needle to the second; this will make 20 stitches on the toe-needle. Now knit back and forth on these three needles for the foot, following the check pattern on the 21st stitch at the beginning and end of the row until the sole is reached. When there are 6 ridges on the right side, n at the end of the row until the sole is reache l. When there are 6 ridges on the right side, n at the end of the row; on the toe-needle k 1, sl and b, knit all but three, n, k 1, sl and b at the beginning of the third needle. Narrow thus in every alternate row till all the stitches on the toe-needle are narrowed off. When there are 11 ridges on the right side make the sole by purling 4 wrong side rows. In last three

NO. 40.—INFANTS' SOCK.
(For Description see Page 144.)

knit rows sl 1, k 2, n, knit all but 5, sl and b, k 3. Bind off, sew up, and finish with baby ribbon.

INFANTS' SOCK.

(For Illustration see Page 145.)

No. 40.—This little sock is knitted with white Saxony wool in plain knitting with steel needles.

Begin at the middle of the sole, casting on 24 stitches; knit 24 rows in plain knitting to and fro on two needles; in the 2nd, 4th, 6th and 8th of the 24 rows, to form the heel, widen by knitting 2 stitches out of the 3rd stitch from the beginning, one stitch plain and one crossed; also for the toe, widen in the same manner at the close of every even row at the 3rd stitch from the last. In the 25th row knit off 22 stitches on a separate needle, and leave them aside while knitting 32 rows on the remaining 18 stitches without widening or narrowing. At the end of the last row, and in connection with it, cast on 22 new stitches, and on the 40 stitches knit 24 rows, which will correspond with the first 24 in the first half, and in which, therefore, narrow wherever there is a widening in the first half (for narrowing, simply knit 2 stitches together); cast off the 24 stitches that remain at the end of the last row. Take up the 22 stitches last cast on, and also the 16 edge stitches toward the top of the 32 rows knitted for the front of the foot, on separate needles, and on the latter work 20 rows for the upper part of the front; at the close of every row knit off the last stitch together with the next stitch of the 22 on the needle at the side. After completing the 20th row, knit up the remaining stitches at the side to the middle of the back, then on all the stitches taken together knit a row of holes through which a ribbon is to be drawn; for this, by turns knit 2 stitches together and put the wool over; each thread-over answers for a stitch in the next row. Next 40 rows in plain knitting for the top, and then knit for the open-work edge as follows:

First row.—A row of holes like that described.

Second row.—Purled throughout.

Repeat these two rows three times, then cast off the stitches, and join the back edges down to the toe, fulling the toe a trifle.

BABY'S COMBINATION SHOE AND LEGGING.

No. 41.—Cast on 55 stitches, using zephyr or Germantown wool.

First row.—Sl 1 th o, k 1, sl 1, n, pass slipped stitch over. Now * k 1, o, k 1, o, k 1, sl 1, n, pass sl st. o. Repeat from * as far as you can; there will be 2 stitches left over at the end; k 1, th o, k last one. These last 2 stitches, with the first, will form a full scollop.

Second row.—Seam across, and thus alternate: 1 row of figure and 1 row of purling or seaming. Knit 4 times across with each color (that is, 2 figures and 2 seams); knit 3 colored patterns and 2 white ones; then knit with white 1 row of the figure, 1 seamed row, 1 plain and 1 seamed row.

Fifth row.—K 1, th o, n, k 1, th o, n; this makes a row of holes. Seam the next row and knit the next.

Commence ribbing, thus: 1 row plain, 1 seam, 1 plain, which makes 1 rib. Knit 10 ribs and 1 reverse rib; narrow 2 stitches every 6th row, that is, on the last row of every reverse rib, until there are 38 stitches; narrow 1 on the last needle.

Divide into 3 parts, thus: 12 stitches on the middle needle and 13 on each side. Knit up the middle part for 2 ribs, that is, 2 right and 2 reverse ribs; bind off for instep, and break off the thread.

Put the 13 stitches on the needle, holding the right side toward you. Then begin with the color. Knit 13 stitches on side of instep and 11 for toe, making 32 on the needle. Knit 2 ribs and 1 reverse rib. In the next reverse rib and the right rib, narrow 6 at the toe, that is, once on the end of each needle for 6 times across. Narrow at the heel once in each rib. Bind off. Take up the 11 cast on for toe, and knit 5 ribs, 3 reverse and 2 right. Take up 8 on the instep and knit the other 13 stitches, 2 ribs and 1 reverse; then on next reverse rib narrow 6 at the toe, and one on each rib at the heel, and bind off and sew up.

No. 41.—BABY'S COMBINATION SHOE AND LEGGING.

NO. 42.—KNITTED ORANGE.

KNITTED ORANGE.

No. 42.—Fine, orange-colored Saxony and four fine steel needles are used for making this pretty little ornament or ball.

Cast 48 stitches on each of three needles, k 1, and p 1 for 40 rounds; then bind off, gather up each end and stuff the orange with cotton and fasten securely. Sew a full bunch of loops of narrow green ribbon with a piece of cord formed in a loop to the top (either end).

MITTENS AND GLOVES FOR ADULTS AND CHILDREN.

LADIES' FANCY MITTENS. (SIZE 6¼.)

No. 1.—The materials required for a pair of mittens like the illustration are: 1½ oz. Saxony wool or, 1½ oz. medium knitting silk and 4 fine needles.

These directions are correct for any material making 12 stitches to an inch of work. Any sized mittens may be knit by the directions by changing the stitches to a greater or less number to the inch, as required.

Cast on loosely 74 stitches, or any even number. Knit 5 rounds plain, then one round of o, n. Knit 5 more rounds plain. Turn the edge up inside, and with each stitch on the needles

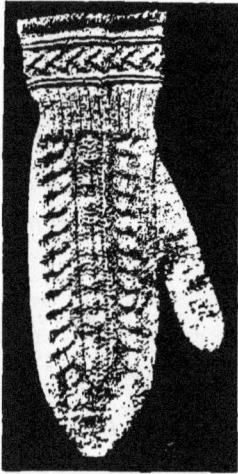

No. 1.—LADIES' FANCY MITTEN. (SIZE 6¼.)

knit 1 corresponding loop on the edge, thus forming a hem. Make a stitch at the end of this round, as the fancy wrist pattern calls for a number of stitches divisible by 5. Knit 2 rounds plain, purl 1 round, knit 2 rounds plain, purl 1 round, knit 3 rounds plain. Then knit 4 rounds as follows. O, k 3, n, and repeat.

Fifth round.—Plain.

Sixth round.—O, sl and b 1, k 3; repeat.

Seventh round.—K 1, o, sl and b 1, k 2; repeat.

Eighth round.—K 2, o, sl and b 1, k 1; repeat.

Ninth round.—K 3, o, sl and b 1; repeat. K 3 rounds plain, p 1 round, k 2 rounds plain, p 1 round, k 3 rounds plain.

Next round.—Knit 2, purl 1 all round; repeat this round till the wrist is as long as desired. In the first round of ribbed work, purl the last two stitches of the round together.

To Shape the Hand of the Mitten.—In the first round make one stitch on each needle; commence the widening for the thumb in the middle of one needle; also begin the fancy stripe. (To make the fancy stripe, see below.) Widen the thumb by purling and knitting a stitch out of one stitch, and purl next stitch. The purled stitches must be purled in each row, one just above the other, and wherever the widening should be made widen between the purled stitches; at the beginning purl and knit a stitch out of the first purled stitch, knit to the second purled stitch and knit and purl a stitch out of it. Knit 3 rounds plain, except that you must purl the purled stitches, and widen again in the 4th round; continue to widen the thumb every 4th round till there are 25 stitches gained. Take them off on a cord and leave for the thumb; cast on 8 stitches in their place; these 8 must be all narrowed off in the usual thumb and hand gores.

After finishing the hand gore knit till the fancy stripe is the required length, then narrow thus : Narrow at each end of each needle in one round, knit two rounds plain. Repeat the last three rounds till one stitch is left, draw through the yarn and fasten. Pick up the 8 thumb stitches. Narrow off these 8 stitches in the usual thumb gore. Knit plain till two inches long and narrow off.

For Fancy Stripe in Back of Mitten.—This stripe is 29 inches wide, and is commenced in the first round of the hand—7 stitches from the purling at the side of the widenings for the thumb—to the *right* for a right-hand, and to the *left* side for a left-hand mitten. The strip should run straight up the back of the mitten.

First round.—Slip and bind, k 6, o, k 2, o, k 3, slip 1, n, and pass the slipped stitch over the narrowed one, k 3, o, k 2, o, k 6, n.

Second round.—Sl and b, k 5, o, k 15, o, k 5, n.

Third round.—Sl and b, k 4, o, k 4, o, k 3, sl 1, n, pass the slipped stitch over, k 3, o, k 4, o, k 4, n.

Fourth round.—Sl and b, k 3, o, k 19, o, k 3, n.

Fifth round.—Sl and b, k 2, o, k 6, o, k 3, sl 1, n, pass slipped stitch over, k 3, o, k 6, o, k 2, n.

Sixth round.—Sl and b 1, k 1, o, k 23, o, k 1, n.

Seventh round.—Sl and b, o, k 8, o, k 3, sl 1, n, pass slipped stitch over, k 3, o, k 8, o, n.

Eighth round.—Knit plain. Repeat these eight rounds twelve times, and end the fancy strip in six rounds by the following directions:

First round.—K 8, n, o, k 1, o, k 2, sl 1, n, and and pass slipped st. over, k 2, o, k 1, o, sl and b, k 8.

Second, Fourth and Sixth rounds.—Plain.

Third round.—K 12, o, k 1, sl 1, n, pass slipped stitch over, k 1, o, k 12.

Fifth round.—K 13, o, sl 1, n, pass slipped stitch over, o, k 13.

LADIES' KNITTED GLOVES. (SIZE 6½.)

No. 2.—The materials required for a pair of gloves are: 2 skeins of Saxony wool, or 2 oz. medium silk, and fine steel needles. A glove or mitten of any size, knit from any yarn, may be made from these directions by changing the number of stitches as required. In the directions 12 stitches are used for one inch of knitting. Cast, rather loosely, 72 stitches, or any other number divisible by 6 on 3 needles, 24 on each.

First, Second, Third and Fourth rounds.—Knit 4, p 2; repeat all round.

Fifth round.—O, slip 1, knit 3 and draw the slipped stitch over the 3 knitted ones, p 2; repeat around.

Repeat these 5 rows alternately till the wrist is as long as desired.

To Knit the Hand of the Glove: First round.—Knit plain, making 1 stitch in 2 places on each needle.

Second round.—Commence the thumb widenings on one of the needles by purling and knitting a stitch out of one stitch, then purl 1 out of next stitch; knit rest and 3 more rounds plain except the purled stitches, which must be purled in each row, one just above the other, and wherever the widening is made widen between the purled stitches as in the following row; purl and knit a stitch out of the first purled stitch, knit one and knit and purl a stitch out of next purled stitch; widen in this manner every 4th round till there are 25 stitches gained for the thumb.

For a glove with fancy rib like sample, commence the ribs at the third thumb-widening, 13 stitches to the left of purled stitches for a left-hand mitten, and 13 stitches to the right of purled stitches for a right-hand mitten.

First row.—P 1, o, sl 1, k 2, and draw slipped stitch over the 2 knitted ones, p 1, k 1 plain stitch between the ribs, and knit 2 more ribs as before. This row and the widenings for the thumb always come in the same round till the thumb stitches are taken off on a cord.

Second, Third and Fourth rounds.—P 1, k 3, p 1, knitting 1 plain stitch between the ribs.

Fifth round.—Widen the thumb as usual, * k 12 stitches, p 1, o, sl 1, k 2 and draw sl stitch over the 2 knitted ones, p 1, k 2 plain stitches, work 2 more ribs with 2 plain stitches between. Knit 3 rows thus: P 1, k 3, p 1, k 2 plain, etc. Knit plain

rest of the way.* Repeat between stars, gaining 1 plain stitch between the ribs every fourth time the pattern is repeated till 5 stitches are gained between the ribs. Slip the 25 stitches gained for thumb on a cord and leave for the thumb; then cast on 8 stitches in their place. These 8 stitches are all to be narrowed off to form the hand and thumb gores.

To Knit the Gore.—Begin at the first of the 8 stitches.

First round.—Sl 1, k 1, bind the slipped stitch over the knitted one, k 4, n, knit rest of the round plain.

Second and Third rounds.—Knit plain.

Fourth round.—Slip and bind one, knit 2, narrow over the stitches previously narrowed in first round; knit rest of round plain.

Fifth and Sixth rounds.—Knit plain around.

Seventh round.—Sl and b 1 and n over the last narrowings, knit rest of the round plain.

Eighth and Ninth rounds.—Knit plain around.

Tenth round.—Narrow at the same place, knit rest of round plain. This finishes the gore of the hand.

Knit plain till the space is ¾ of an inch deep from the thumb-hole. Fold the hand lengthwise even with the *left* side of the 8 stitches looped on at the thumb-hole, for the *left*-hand glove, or with the *right* side for the *right*-hand. The fold on one edge will be half way of the forefinger; on the other edge it will be on the outside of the hand at the little finger. Be careful that the folds are even, one-half the stitches being on each side of the hand. Take the stitch on the outside fold of the hand and 9 stitches on each side of it, 19 stitches in all, off on a cord, and leave for the little finger; then cast on 4 stitches in their place, knit 7 rounds plain. Take the 4 stitches which were last looped on, and 8 stitches on each side of them, 20 in all, on a cord and leave for the ring finger, looping 4 new stitches on in their place. Knit 3 rounds plain. Take the last 4 stitches looped on and 10 stitches on each side of them, 24 stitches in all, on a cord and leave for the middle finger; loop on 4 new stitches in their place. The 28 stitches on the needles are for the fore-finger; knit plain till the finger is 2½ inches long and narrow off. Take the stitches left for the middle finger and pick up the 4 at the base of the fore-finger on the needles and knit plain till the finger is 2¾ inches long and narrow off.

Take the stitches left for the ring finger and the

NO. 2.—LADIES' KNITTED GLOVE.
(SIZE 6½.)

4 stitches at the base of the middle finger, 24 in all, and knit plain till the finger is 2½ inches long, then narrow off.

Take the stitches left for the little finger and pick up with them the 4 stitches at the base of the

No. 3.—Mitten Knitted in Puff Stitch. (Suitable for a Boy of 8 Years.)

ring finger, 23 stitches in all, knit plain till 2 inches long and narrow off.

Take up the stitches left for the thumb and the 8 across the hand, which will be narrowed off for the thumb gore. Narrow the gore off as directed for the *hand* gore, knit the rest plain till 2 inches long and narrow off thus :

Start at one of the needles, k 1, narrow, knit to within 3 stitches of end of needle, narrow, k 1. Narrow other 2 needles the same. Next round, plain ; repeat these 2 rounds till but 4 stitches are left. Then narrow continuously till but 1 stitch is left ; break thread and secure neatly. Finish all fingers the same way.

A plain mitten is well shaped by following the directions for a plain glove till the hand gore is finished ; then knit plain till the space is 3 inches deep from the thumb-hole. Narrow off as directed for glove.

A pretty fancy mitten may be knitted by continuing 4 rows of the fancy work, like the wrist pattern, up the entire length of the mitten back, the first rib of the pattern being 6 stitches from the purled stitch that is at the widenings for the thumb.

This pattern is quite easy, yet is very handsome and showy for the work required.

MITTENS KNITTED IN PUFF STITCH. (SUITABLE FOR A BOY OF 8 YEARS.)

No. 3—The materials needed are: 1 skein of Saxony wool and 4 fine steel needles. Cast very loosely 22 stitches on each of the three needles —66 in all—and knit seven rounds plain.

Eighth round.—O, n, k 1, all round.

The fancy pattern is now commenced as follows:

First, Second, Third and Fourth rounds.—K 1, p 2; repeat around.

Fifth, Sixth and Seventh rounds.—Knit plain.

Eighth round.—Turn up the edge inside and with each stitch on the needles knit one corresponding loop from the edge, thus forming a hem. Repeat the last seven rounds five times, or as many times as desired.

To Knit the Close Wrist.—K 2, purl 1, till the ribbed work is one inch deep.

The entire mitten is now knitted in puffed stitch thus: Knit 3 rounds plain, then 4 rounds thus: k 1, p 2. This pattern is so small that with a little care it will not interfere with the shape of the mitten.

To Shape the Hand and Widen for the Thumb.— Widen the thumb at the beginning of one needle by purling and knitting a stitch out of the first stitch, then purl 1 stitch. The purled stitches must be purled in each row, one just above the other, and wherever the widening should be made widen between the purled stitches at the beginning; purl and knit a stitch out of the first purl stitch, knit to the second purl stitch (keeping the pattern as in the mitten) and knit and purl a stitch out of it. Work three rounds without widening but always purling the purled stitches, and widen again in the 4th round; continue to widen the thumb every 4th round till there are 23 stitches gained. Slip these 23 stitches on a cord and leave for the thumb, and cast or loop on 8 more stitches in their place. Narrow these stitches off for the usual hand gore or gusset, then knit in the fancy pattern for the rest of the mitten till the latter is 2½ inches deep from the thumb-hole. Then narrow off once at each end of each needle in one round, and knit two rounds without narrowing. Repeat the three rounds till but four or five stitches are left on each needle; then narrow continuously till one is left; draw the thread through and fasten. Take up all the thumb stitches; also pick up the 8 cast-on stitches. Narrow off the 8 stitches in a thumb gore. Knit till the thumb is 1¾ inches deep; narrow off like the hand and fasten.

To adapt these directions to coarser yarn for boy's wear, cast on a number of stitches and knit plain several times across; then count the number of stitches in an inch of work and substitute that number of stitches for each 12 stitches in the directions, as the directions call for 12 for each inch of work.

The pattern is also handsome for gentlemen's silk mittens. For size 7½, cast on with medium silk 84 stitches; continue the thumb widenings until there are 33 stitches; take them on a cord to use for the thumb, and loop on 12 stitches in their

place. Knit till 3 inches deep from thumb-hole.
Narrow off. Knit thumb 2¼ inches long and narrow off.

LADIES' BICYCLE MITTENS, WITH CLOSE WRIST.
(SIZE 6½.)

No. 4.—The materials required for a pair of

No. 4.—LADIES' BICYCLE MITTEN, WITH CLOSE WRIST.
(SIZE 6½.)

mittens like the illustration are: 2 skeins of Saxony yarn, or 2 ounces of knitting silk and fine steel needles.

Gloves of any size or material may be knitted from these directions by using more or less stitches as required. In these directions 12 stitches are allowed for one inch of knitting.

Cast on loosely 72 stitches on three needles. Knit 5 rounds plain.

Sixth round.—O, n, all around. Knit 5 more rounds plain. Turn the edge up inside and with each stitch on the needles knit 1 corresponding loop from the edge, thus forming a hem. Knit 3 rounds plain. The ribbed work may be knit on any number of stitches divisible by 3 and can be knitted in two styles, as follows :

Bring yarn to the front between the stitches, slip 1 same as for purling, k 2 together. Repeat around.

Next round.—P 2 to., bringing the yarn to the front over the needles. In doing so, put the yarn back *between* the stitches, slip 1 same as for purling; repeat around. In this round, at the end of needles, pass the yarn over and around the needle.

The k 2, and p 2 to. are always a *stitch* and a *loop* after the 1st round. If the loop is not in its place on the needle it will be found lying like a long thread across the back or front of stitch, and is easily picked up. Plain ribbing, k 2, p 1, may be substituted for these ribs, if desired. Knit the wrist 3 or 4 inches long.

To Shape the Hand : First round.—Knit plain, making 1 stitch in two places on each needle.

Second round.—Commence the thumb widening in middle of one needle by purling and knitting a stitch out of one stitch, then p next stitch, knit rest of round plain. The purled stitches must be purled in each row, one just above the other and wherever the widening should be made widen between the purled stitches. At the beginning purl and knit a stitch out of purled stitch, knit to the second purled stitch and knit and purl a stitch out of it.

Knit 3 rounds plain except the purled stitches, which must be purled, and widen again at the sixth round; continue to widen the thumb every fourth round until there are 25 stitches gained. Then slip them on a cord and leave them for the thumb. Cast on 8 stitches in their place. These 8 stitches are narrowed off for the hand and thumb gores by following directions. Both gores are knit alike. Knit 2 rounds plain.

Third round.—N the first two of the 8 cast-on stitches, k 4, n ; knit rest of round plain. Knit 2 rounds plain.

Sixth round.—N over the first narrowing in third round, k 2, n; rest of the round plain. Knit two rounds plain.

Ninth round.—N, n, over narrowings in 6th round, knit rest of the round plain. Knit 2 rounds plain.

Twelfth round.—N the two narrowings in 9th round together; k rest of the round plain. This

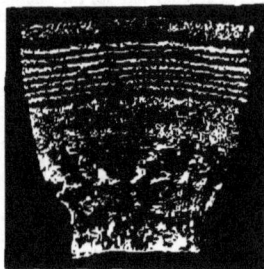

No. 5.—GAUNTLET TO BICYCLE MITTEN.
(For Description see Page 149.)

finishes the hand gore. Knit plain till the space from the thumb-hole is 1⅛ inch deep.

Fold the mitten lengthwise even with the *left side* of the thumb-hole for the *left* hand, or even with the *right side* of the thumb-hole for the right-hand mitten. Take off on a cord 11 stitches on each side of the fold, 22 stitches in all, and leave them for the forefinger. Cast on 4 stitches in their place.

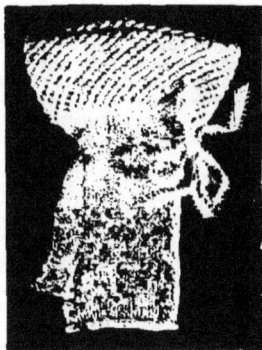

No. 6.—MITT FOR LITTLE GIRL FROM FOUR TO SIX YEARS OF AGE.

Knit plain till the space from the finger-hole is 1¼ inch deep, then commence to narrow.

First round.—Knit 1 at corner of the needle, n, knit to within 3 stitches, n, k 1. Repeat for the other two needles the same. Knit 2 rounds plain. Repeat these 3 rounds alternately, till but 3 or 4 stitches are left on a needle. Narrow continuously till 1 stitch is left; draw thread through and darn the end of mitten.

Put the 26 stitches for the forefinger on the needles. Knit plain till 2½ inches long. Narrow off as directed for other part of the mitten.

Put the 25 stitches for the thumb on the needles and pick up with them 8 of the cast-on stitches for the thumb gore across the hand. The thumb gore is knit and narrowed like the hand gore. Then knit the rest of the thumb plain till it is two inches long and narrow off as directed for the other parts of the mitten.

GAUNTLET TO LADIES' BICYCLE MITTEN.
(SIZE 6½.)
(For Illustration see Page 148.)

No. 5.—Cast 30 stitches on each of three needles, 90 stitches in all. Form a hem, by knitting 6 rounds plain, then o, n, once around; knit 6 more rounds plain, then, turn the edge up inside and knit one loop from the edge with each corresponding stitch on the needles.

Knit 2 rounds plain and purl 1 round; this makes a corded pattern. Repeat these three rounds to the desired length. Sometimes the whole cuff is knitted in corded work. In the sample the pattern

is repeated 7 times. Then knit plain till the gauntlet is as deep as desired; 3 inches will make a nice length. Then commence the close ribbed work; knit 2, p 1, p 2 together, reducing the number of stitches to 24 on each needle. Next and all following rounds: Knit 2, purl 2 continuously till the wrist is 1¼ inch deep or as long as desired and bind off. Both gauntlet and close wrist may be knitted of any depth desired.

MITTS FOR LITTLE GIRL FROM FOUR TO SIX YEARS OF AGE.

No. 6.—Cast 15 stitches of split zephyr on each of three needles and knit around plain. Then k 2, p 2 for two rounds; then * o and n for one round; next, k plain for one round *. Continue between stars alternately, until the open-work gauntlet is a little more than half a finger deep.

Now begin the wrist thus: Knit plain one round; k plain, narrowing at every 8th st.; k plain; k plain, narrowing at every 8th st.; k plain; k plain, narrowing at every 8th st.; k plain for 5 rounds.

Knit plain and th over and narrow at every 4th st., which will form the holes to run the ribbon through at the wrist. Knit plain for two rounds, and in the third round th over once in the middle of one needle, which begins the widening for the thumb. K 2 rounds plain; k plain, but th over on each side of the one hole; k 2 rounds plain. Knit 1 round plain, and th over on each side of the 2

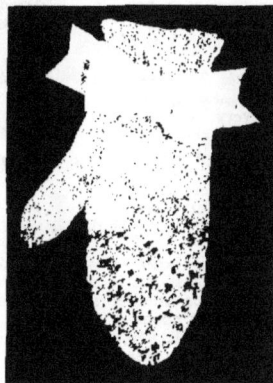

No. 7.—CHILD'S SILK MITTEN.
(For Description see Page 150.)

holes; this makes the gore for the thumb. Continue thus to widen, allowing 2 rounds between the round that makes the holes, till 16 stitches have been added, besides the first hole. Knit 7 plain rounds and then cast 12 stitches on an extra needle and knit around the thumb piece. Narrow at each end of the needle with the new stitches on it until 4 are left. Knit 3 plain rounds; k 2, p 2 for six rounds. Bind off, and the thumb is finished. Pick up the 12 stitches at the base of the thumb and knit around plain for the hand part of the mitt. Narrow on each end of the needle with the new stitches on it, at every other round until 6 stitches have been narrowed off. Then knit plain for one inch, and purl 2, k 2 for 6 rounds and bind off. Turn the gauntlet under, like a hem, and sew it to place with blind stitches. Run a narrow ribbon through the holes and tie it in a neat bow. A cord and tassels of zephyr may be used at the wrist of the mitt instead of ribbon, if preferred.

CHILD'S SILK MITTENS.
(SUITABLE FOR A CHILD OF THREE OR FOUR YEARS.)
(For Illustration see Page 149.)

No. 7.—Two fifty-yard spools of knitting silk will make a pair of mittens of this size. Worked out in Saxony the mitten will be large enough for a child of seven years.

Cast on 54 stitches (18 stitches on each of 3 needles), k 2 and seam or purl 1 all the way round; k 24 of these rounds.

To Begin the Thumb.—K 5, seam 1, k 2, seam 1, k rest plain; in every 4th round widen at the right of the first, and at the left of last stitch between the 2 seam stitches, until there are 18 stitches between the seam stitches. Cast off on a silk thread the 18 made stitches.

To Make Thumb Gusset.—Cast on 5 stitches on the right-hand needle, k 1 round plain, narrow in center of 5 cast-on stitches every round for 3 rounds, k 26 rounds plain.

To Narrow Off.—K 7, n, repeat all round; k 3 rounds plain; k 6, n, repeat all round; 3 rounds plain; k 5, n, repeat all round; 3 rounds plain; k 4, n, repeat all round; 3 rounds plain; k 3, n, repeat all round; 2 rounds plain; k 2, n, repeat all round, 1 round plain; k 1, n, repeat all round.

Next round.—N twice on each needle; next round bind off, leaving a length of thread to fasten stitches.

To Make Thumb.—Fasten silk to the right of stitches, take up stitches on two needles, k round to gusset and take up on a third needle 5 stitches

at base of 5 cast-on stitches, also 1 stitch on each side of these 5; this makes the work close; narrow once every time you reach the cast-on stitches till there are but 3 stitches left; add 2 stitches from each of the other needles to these 3 stitches; you now have 7 stitches on each needle; k 13 rounds plain. Now narrow in center of each needle every other time round, until there are but 6 stitches on each needle, then narrow every round until there are but 2 stitches on each needle, and bind off. A tiny bow of ribbon is an addition to the mittens.

To Make Mittens One Size Larger.—Add 3 stitches to each needle, and narrow off in same manner as directed for above size, only knit a few more rounds before you narrow.

KNITTED GARDENING OR CYCLING GLOVES.

No. 8.—For knitting these gloves four medium-sized steel needles are required, and Dexter cotton No. 10. Wool or silk can also be used according to the purpose for which they are intended. One advantage in these gloves is the introduction of gussets between the fingers, thus giving plenty of freedom in using the hand.

Cast 15 stitches on each of the first two needles, and 18 st. on the 3rd needle.

First round.—Knit 3, purl 3, repeat all round.

The succeeding 19 rounds are a repetition of the 1st round.

Twenty-first to Thirty-seventh round.—Knit plain. If a long wrist is desired, knit more plain rounds here.

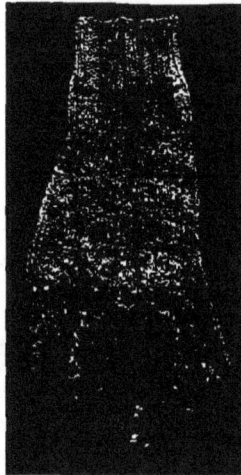

NO. 8.—KNITTED GARDENING OR CYCLING GLOVE.

Thirty-seventh round.— Knit plain, except in the middle of the first needle (which is the beginning of the thumb) where you make a stitch by knitting one stitch and purling one out of one stitch. Follow this method wherever a stitch has to be made.

Thirty-eighth round.—Knit plain, except that you purl each knit and purled stitch made in last round.

In the following rounds the directions for the thumb are only given; the rest of the rounds are always knitted plain, and all the purl stitches should be directly above each other as the widening is made between them.

Thirty-ninth round.—Purl and knit a stitch in the first purled stitch of last round, and knit and purl another stitch in the stitch next to it.

Fortieth round.—P 1 over first p stitch, k 2, p 1; rest plain.

Forty-first round.—P and k a stitch in the first

purl stitch of preceding row, k 2, k and p a stitch in the second purl stitch of preceding row.

Forty-second round.—P in 1st p stitch of preceding row, k 4, p in second p stitch of preceding row.

Forty-third round.—P and k a stitch in 1st p stitch of preceding row, k 4, k and p a stitch in second p stitch of preceding row.

Continue knitting in this manner always knitting one round plain except at the thumb where you purl the first purl stitch of last row, knit to the second purl stitch and purl it also. Knit plain except at the thumb where you purl and knit a stitch out of the first purl stitch, then knit to the second purl stitch and knit and purl a stitch out of it; repeat these two rounds to the 70th round except the 51st, 52nd, 53rd, 56th, 57th, 58, 61st, 62nd, 63rd, 66th, 67th and 68th rounds are not widened and are knitted plain except at the thumb where you purl the purled stitches.

Seventieth round.—K plain to the middle of the thumb. Take a coarse needle and a short piece of coarse thread and run through all the stitches except those of the thumb, taking out the two knitting needles and leaving the thumb on two of the needles. Knit plain to the last stitch on the left side of the thumb needle. Knit the last stitch onto a third needle and cast 10 stitches on this needle. This makes the foundation of a gusset for the thumb.

Join the three needles together by drawing the cotton close where the 1st stitch on the 1st needle joins the loop stitches. Knit the thumb now like a stocking. Knit one round plain.

The 2nd and succeeding rounds are knit plain, with the exception of the thumb gusset (the 10 cast-on stitches). Narrow now on both sides of this gusset at every round, until there are only two stitches left of the gusset, then narrow once at the point of the gusset and in every following round at the same place until there are 20 stitches in all left on the three needles. Knit plain rounds until the thumb is long enough, which can be ascertained by slipping on over the hand. It must be very nearly as long as the thumb of the hand before beginning to narrow it off. When the narrowing begins, take two together every time, until all are knit off and the last stitch is drawn through the end. Leave a short piece of cotton to finish the end, which should be done by drawing it to the wrong side with a coarse needle and darning through a few stitches to prevent ravelling. The fingers

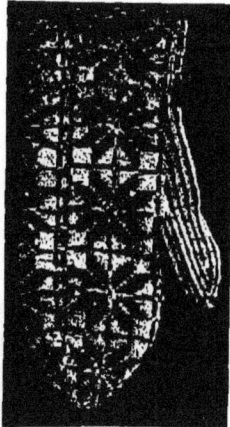

No. 9.—BOYS' DOUBLE KNITTED MITTEN.
(For Description see Page 152.)

are all narrowed and finished in the same manner.

Next take the stitches which have been held in place by the cord on two needles. Take the knitting cotton about 4 inches from the end and pick up every loop around the gusset of the thumb gore with another needle, knitting them in picking them up. There will be 14 of these stitches to join to the body of the hand. This is a continuation of the thumb gore, which must be narrowed on each side at every round until there is only one stitch left of the gore, which is left to form a part of the body of the hand. Knit 8 rounds plain. Take off 14 st. (7 stitches on each side nearest the thumb) for the 1st finger.

Slip all the remaining stitches on a cord as before. After knitting around plain to the last stitch, take this on a 3rd needle and cast on 10 stitches as before in making the thumb gusset. These added stitches form the gusset. The first round is knit plain. The 2nd and succeeding rounds are plain except the gusset, which must be narrowed on each side until it is 6 st. wide and there are 20 st. in all on the needles. Then knit plain rounds, measure and finish as for the thumb.

For the 2nd finger take off 6 stitches on each side next the 1st finger, leaving the remaining stitches on the cord. Take up all the loops around the gusset of the 1st finger, slipping a knitting needle through them as before explained. Knit plain around to the other side of the finger. After the last stitch on the 3rd needle cast on 10 stitches, as before described. Begin narrowing the gusset on the side of the 1st finger in the 1st round, but knit once plain across the cast-on stitches on the other side. Knit plain rounds except the narrowing on each side of the gussets until each of these is 4 st. wide and there are 20 st. in all on the needles, when knit plain rounds, measure and finish.

The 3rd finger is formed exactly like the 2nd, except that one more stitch is narrowed from the gusset next the little finger, and 19 st. in all left on the needles.

There are 10 stitches left for the little finger. The stitches of the last gusset, 12 in number, are drawn through in loops and slipped on a needle as before.

In knitting otherwise plain rounds, narrow on each side of the gusset until it is 6 stitches wide and there are 16 stitches left on the needles. Knit plain rounds, measure and narrow off as for the other finger ends.

BOYS' DOUBLE KNITTED MITTENS.

(For Illustration see Page 151.)

No. 9.—Three ounces each of brown and red zephyr and four knitting needles will be required

NO. 10.—MEN'S KNITTED HAND SHIELD.

(For Description see Page 153.)

to make a pair of mitttens like these. Cast 26 stitches on each of three needles, making 78 in all. Tie on the other thread. In giving directions it will be necessary to mention but one needle, as the details for knitting off each needle are alike in each round.

First round.—Knit 1 brown, 5 red, 1 brown, 5 red, 1 brown, 5 red, 1 brown, 5 red, 1 brown, 1 red.

Second round.—Knit 1 brown, 5 red, 2 brown 4 red, 1 brown, 4 red, 1 brown, 4 red, 2 brown, 5 red, 1 brown, 1 red.

Third round.—Knit 1 brown, 5 red, 3 brown, 3 red, 1 brown, 3 red, 3 brown, 5 red, 1 brown, 1 red.

Fourth round.—Knit 1 brown, 5 red, 4 brown, 2 red, 1 brown, 2 red, 4 brown, 5 red, 1 brown, 1 red.

Fifth round.—Knit 1 brown, 5 red, 5 brown, 1 red, 1 brown, 1 red, 5 brown, 5 red, 1 brown, 1 red.

Sixth round.—Knit 1 red, 5 brown, 1 red, 5 brown, 1 red, 5 brown, 1 red, 5 brown, 1 red, 1 brown.

Seventh round.—Knit 1 brown, 1 red, 5 brown, 1 red, 4 brown, 1 red, 4 brown, 1 red, 5 brown, 1 red, 1 brown, 1 red.

Eighth round.—Knit 1 brown, 2 red, 5 brown, 1 red, 3 brown, 1 red, 3 brown, 1 red, 5 brown, 2 red, 1 brown, 1 red.

Ninth round.—Knit 1 brown, 3 red, 5 brown, 1 red, 2 brown, 1 red, 2 brown, 1 red, 5 brown, 3 red, 1 brown, 1 red.

Tenth round—Knit 1 brown, 4 red, 5 brown, 1 red, 1 brown, 1 red, 1 brown, 1 red, 5 brown, 4 red, 1 brown, 1 red.

Eleventh round.—Knit 1 brown, 5 red, 5 brown, 3 red, 5 brown, 5 red, 1 brown, 1 red.

Twelfth round.—Knit 1 red, 5 brown, 6 red, 1 brown, 6 red, 5 brown, 1 red, 1 brown.

Thirteenth round.—Knit 1 brown, 5 red, 5 brown, 3 red, 5 brown, 5 red, 1 brown, 1 red.

Fourteenth round.—Knit 1 brown, 4 red, 5 brown, 1 red, 1 brown, 1 red, 1 brown, 1 red, 5 brown, 4 red, 1 brown, 1 red.

Fifteenth round.—Knit 1 brown, 3 red, 5 brown, 1 red, 2 brown, 1 red, 2 brown, 1 red, 5 brown, 3 red, 1 brown, 1 red.

Sixteenth round.—Knit 1 brown, 2 red, 5 brown, 1 red, 3 brown, 1 red, 3 brown, 1 red, 5 brown, 2 red, 1 brown, 1 red.

Seventeenth round.—Knit 1 brown, 1 red, 5 brown, 1 red, 4 brown, 1 red, 4 brown, 1 red, 5 brown, 1 red, 1 brown, 1 red.

Eighteenth round.—Knit 1 red, 5 brown, 1 red, 5 brown, 1 red, 5 brown, 1 red, 5 brown, 1 red, 1 brown.

Nineteenth round.—Knit 1 brown, 5 red, 5 brown, 1 red, 1 brown, 1 red, 5 brown, 5 red, 1 brown, 1 red.

Twentieth round.—Knit 1 brown, 5 red, 4 brown, 2 red, 1 brown, 2 red, 4 brown, 5 red, 1 brown, 1 red.

Twenty-first round.—Knit 1 brown, 5 red, 3 brown, 3 red, 1 brown, 3 red, 3 brown, 5 red, 1 brown, 1 red.

Twenty-second round.—Knit 1 brown, 5 red, 2 brown, 4 red, 1 brown, 4 red, 2 brown, 5 red, 1 brown, 1 red.

Twenty-third round.—Knit 1 brown, 5 red, 1 brown, 5 red, 1 brown, 5 red, 1 brown, 5 red, 1 brown, 1 red.

Twenty-fourth round.—Knit 1 red, 5 brown, 1

NO. 11.—MITTEN KNITTED ON TWO NEEDLES.

(For Description see Page 153.)

red, 5 brown, 1 red, 5 brown, 1 red, 5 brown, 1 red, 1 brown. Repeat for the rest of round.

This finishes one star and bar. Now widen one stitch on the end of the needle for the thumb; continue to widen on each side of this stitch every fourth round until you knit one star and a half more; take off the stitches for the thumb on a thread, cast on 10 stitches for the gusset of the thumb and narrow one stitch of cast-on stitches every round until all are off.

For Second Star.—Repeat from first to twenty-fourth round and so on until you have 4 stars; begin to narrow off the mitten at the beginning of the fifth star and narrow every other round on every needle until the work is finished. Make the thumb alternately red and brown all the way through.

MEN'S KNITTED HAND SHIELD.

(For Illustration see Page 152.)

No. 10.—This shield is for protecting the back of the hand when a whole glove is inconvenient to wear. The size illustrated is for the average hand. Being intended only for usefulness the shield is usually knitted of coarse yarn or thread. In these directions 8 stitches will represent 1 inch of knitting, and Scotch knitting yarn is used.

Shields of any size and of any material may be knitted by the following rule: Measure the exact size of the glove required. Knit a short piece and count the number of stitches in an inch of the work and substitute that number for the 8 stitches given in the directions; the number must be divisible by 4.

56 stitches were cast on in the pattern given. K 2, p 2, continuously, till the wrist is as long as desired.

Now the plain knitting begins, and in the first round also begins the widening for the thumb. Take one rib from the wrist to start the thumb. Widen by purling and knitting a stitch out of one stitch, then knit the 2 stitches of the rib, widen again by knitting and purling a stitch out of next stitch. The purled stitches must be purled in each row, one just above the other, and wherever the widening should be made widen between the purled stitches; at the beginning purl and knit a stitch out of the first purled stitch, then knit to the other purled stitch and knit and purl a stitch out of it. Knit 4 rounds plain, except that you purl the purled stitches; in the 5th round knit to within 16 stitches of the thumb, bind off 14 stitches, k 2, p 1, k 1 out of first purled stitch, k 4, and k 1, p 1, out of second purled stitch, knit plain to end of row; turn, sl 1, purl back on wrong side except the purled stitches, which are to be knitted; turn, knit across and purl back in the manner just described till the ribbing

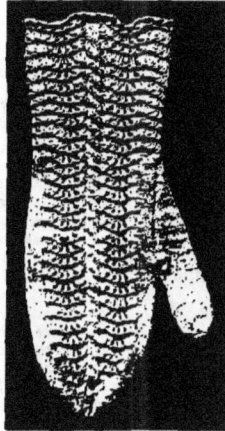

No. 12.—MITTEN IN PRINCESS FEATHER PATTERN FOR A GIRL OF 10 YEARS.

(For Description see Page 154.)

begins. The thumb widening is to be continued in every 5th row till 22 stitches are gained between the two purled stitches; take them off on a cord for the thumb; there must be 2 stitches in front of the purling; knit the 2 remaining stitches, cast on 5 stitches. Continue to knit back and forth till the space from the thumb hole is one inch deep. Then knit across to within 20 stitches on side of shield opposite the thumb, take off 18 stitches on a cord for the little finger, and cast on 3 new ones in their place. Knit the 2 remaining stitches. Cast on 14 stitches. Even the stitches on the 3 needles, and knit around the whole hand; and rib the same as around the wrist. There should now be 52 stitches. If not add to or decrease the number to 52. Continue the ribbing till it is 1 inch deep, bind off on the *wrong side* and fasten.

Take the 22 stitches on the cord, the 5 cast-on stitches across the hand and one loop, making 28 stitches, on the needles for the thumb. Knit in ribbed work till 1 inch long, bind off and fasten the wool.

Take the 21 stitches for the little finger and 3 extra loops on the inside, to make up 24 stitches. Knit in the ribbed stitch till one inch deep; bind off on the wrong side and fasten.

It would be an improvement to *knit* the first and last 2 stitches of *each row*, whether the row is knitted or purled; this would prevent the edge from turning over or drawing back.

Into the opening of this shield may be sewn a leather or chamois palm, or even one of kid, if desired.

MITTENS KNITTED ON TWO NEEDLES.

(For Illustration see Page 156.)

No. 11.—Mittens knitted in this way are very elastic and fit better than those knitted on four needles. They are very nice when made of silk, though Saxony yarn is generally chosen for them. To make any required size, cast on stitches enough to reach from the wrist to the end of the little finger, and, knitting plain, widen until as long as the middle finger.

For misses' mittens, cast on 40 stitches and knit across plain, making 1 next to the last stitch.

Next row.—Plain. Continue knitting plain, widening 1 next to the last stitch of each alternate row; this leaves one end straight and the other sloping. When you have 52 stitches, knit 4 rows plain.

Next, narrow in alternate rows on the sloping end until you have 40 stitches. You have now half the mitten; knit the other half exactly like first; bind off. Fold together so that the points are even, and sew neatly around the points and half-way down the straight side. Leave two-thirds of the other half open for the thumb, and join the remainder.

For the Thumb.—Cast on 2 stitches; · knit as before and widen every row until you have 7, then cast on 10 more ; widen 1 at the end of each row until you have 26. Then make 2 rows without widening at the end where you cast on the 10 stitches (which is to be the end of the thumb), but widen in each row on the other end. Now narrow every alternate row at the end of the thumb, and widen at the other end, until you have narrowed as many stitches as you widened at that end.

You have half the thumb. Knit the other half like it, narrowing at the lower end as many times as you widened in the other half, thus forming a point. Bind off 10 stitches, then knit the remaining 7, narrowing 2 in each row until 3 are left; bind off. Fold together and sew down to widest part of point. Place the point at the bottom of the opening left in the seam of the mitten, and sew in.

For the Wrist.—Pick up the stitches around the top of the mitten and divide by 8; if there are more than can be evenly divided by 8, narrow off the odd ones and purl 3 rounds. Then knit as follows:

First round.—P 2, o, k 4, n ; repeat all round.
Second round.—P 2, k 1, o, k 3, n, and repeat.
Third round.—P 2, k 2, o, k 2, n ; repeat.
Fourth round.—P 2, k 3, o, k 1, n ; repeat.
Fifth round.—P 2, k 4. o, n ; repeat.

The 5 rounds form the fancy pattern. Repeat from 1st round as many times as desired. Then make 3 rounds thus : K 1, p 1, and bind off loosely.

MITTENS IN PRINCESS FEATHER PATTERN FOR A GIRL OF 10 YEARS.

(For Illustration see Page 155.)

No. 12.—The materials required for a pair of mittens are: One skein of Saxony yarn or one ounce of medium knitting silk and three fine steel needles.

Twelve stitches are calculated for each inch of knitting. This pattern is also handsome when used in knitting a ladies' glove. When increasing the size of glove, 10 stitches are needed for each plume or pattern added.

Cast 22 stitches on each of the three fine needles —66 in all. Knit one round plain.

Second round.—O, n, all round.
Third round.—Knit plain.

Turn the edge up inside and with each stitch on the needles knit one corresponding loop from the edge, forming a very narrow fancy hem. Knit one round plain, narrowing the last two stitches together. The first 6 stitches in each round form a twist which runs straight down the middle of the mitten back, with one plume on each side.

For Fancy Wrist.—*First round.*—Purl 1, slip the 2 next stitches on an extra needle, k 2, knit the 2 on the extra needle, purl 1, n 3 together; * o, k 1, three times, o, n, n 3 together, n, repeat from *. At the last narrowing, in each round, always k 3 together instead of 2.

Second round.—P 1, k 4; purl the rest of the round.

Third, Fourth, Fifth and Sixth rounds.—P 1, k 4, p 1; knit plain around.

Repeat these six rounds till the wrist is as long as desired.

Fancy Mitten Back.—*First round of the Hand.*— (In this round the thumb is also commenced; see below.) P 1, k 4, p 1, k 10 plain. Then rearrange the stitches so that 26—10 each side of the 6 stitches forming the twist—will be on one needle at the back of the hand. On these the fancy pattern will ·be continued. thus:

First, Second, Third and Fourth rounds.—K 10, p 1, k 4, p 1, k 10.
Fifth round.—N, n, o, k 1, o, k 1, o, k 1, o, k 3 together, p 1, slip 2 on extra needle, k 2, k the 2 on the extra needle, p 1, k 3 together, o, k 1, o, k 1, o, k 1, o, n, n.
Sixth round.—P 11, k 4, p 11. Repeat these six rounds alternately until the number of stitches on this needle are reduced to 20 by the narrowings at the tip of the mitten, when the fancy stripe should be discontinued.

To Widen the Thumb.—*First round.*—Commence the thumb widenings 5 stitches to the right of the fancy strip, for the left hand, or to the left for a right hand mitten by purling one stitch and knitting one stitch out of 6th stitch from fancy pattern, k 1, knit one and purl one out of next stitch. The purled stitches must be purled in each row, one just above the other, and wherever the widening should be made widen between the purl stitches at the beginning ; purl and knit a stitch out of the first purl stitch ; knit to the other purl stitch and knit and purl a stitch out of it.

Knit 3 rounds plain, except that you purl the purled stitches and widen again in the 4th round. Continue to widen the thumb every 4th round till there are 23 stitches gained. Slip them on a cord and leave for thumb ; then cast on 6 new ones in their place. These 6 stitches are to be all narrowed off both in the hand and thumb to form the usual hand and thumb gores, thus : N, k 2, slip and bind 1; knit twice across the 4 remaining stitches. In the next row, n, n, knit twice across the two remaining stitches. In the next row, narrow those two stitches together, finishing the gore; this last being the *seventh* round of which the gore has formed a part. After the gore is finished knit the hand, continuing the pattern on back, till the hand is 2¼ inches deep from the thumb-hole. Then begin to narrow off.

To Narrow the Mitten or Thumb.—K 1, n at each end of each needle, knitting other stitches plain, except the fancy back, which is continued to the required length as directed above.

Second and Third rounds.—Knit 2 rounds plain, except the fancy back. Repeat last three rounds alternately till but 4 or 5 stitches are left on a needle; then narrow continuously till but 1 stitch is left. Draw the thread through and fasten.

Put the stitches for the thumb on the needles, pick up the 6 cast on stitches and narrow off the 6 stitches in the gore as usual. Knit plain till the thumb is 1¾ inches deep from the thumb-hole. Narrow off and fasten.

STOCKINGS AND SOCKS FOR ADULTS AND CHILDREN.

GENTLEMEN'S KNITTED SOCKS.

No. 1.—Use knitting pins, No. 15. Four ounces of German Fingering wool will be required for one pair of socks.

Cast on 80 stitches, 21 on one pin, 23 on each of the others. Rib by knitting 2 and purling 2, until

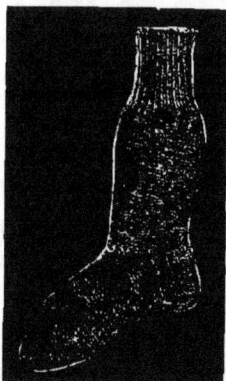

NO. 2.—GENTLEMEN'S KNITTED SOCK

you have 4¼ inches. Now begin to knit plain, making one stitch the seam stitch. Knit until you have 7 inches done including the ribbed part. Now narrow on each side of the seam stitch for the ankle. This is done by knitting to within last 3 stitches of seam; then, slip 1, and knit 1, draw the slipped stitch over the knitted one, knit one, purl the seam stitch, knit 1, knit 2 together, knit rest plain. Repeat this 5 times, doing 5 rounds between each narrowing. Now knit plain until the leg measures 10½ inches. Divide stitches for heel; have 17 stitches on each side of seam; knit and purl the stitches until the heel measures 3 inches. Always slip first stitch whether it be knitted or purled. Now knit across, knit 20 stitches, knit 2 together, knit 1, turn; purl 5, purl 2 together, purl 1, turn; knit 5, knit 2 together, knit 1; repeat these two rows until you have only 7 stitches left. Now pick up side stitches, do 3 plain rounds, then narrow.

First Pin of Heel.—Knit 1, knit 2 together, knit rest plain.

Second Pin.—Knit to within the last 3 stitches, slip 1, knit 1, pass the slipped stitch over the knitted one, knit 1; do 2 plain rounds between each nar-

rowing. There should be 6 narrowings. Next knit plain until you have 8 inches. Now divide stitches for toe, half on front pin, one-quarter on each of the others. The front must lie flatly on the sole of foot.

Front Pin.—Knit 1, knit 2 together, knit to within the 3 last stitches, slip 1, knit 1, pass the slipped stitch over the knitted one; knit 1.

Second Pin—Knit 1, knit 2 together, knit the rest plain.

Third Pin.—Knit to within the 3 last stitches, slip 1, knit 1, pass the slipped stitch over the knitted one; do 2 plain rounds between each narrowing. Repeat until you have only 24 stitches left on pins, or until foot measures 10 inches; cast off and sew up.

LADIES' PLAIN KNITTED STOCKINGS, WITH DOUBLE HEELS.

No. 2.—With Spanish knitting yarn cast 100 stitches on 4 medium-sized needles and k 4 rounds plain. Then, o twice, p 2 to., all around. Knit four more rounds plain. For the next round, knit each stitch on the needles together with the corresponding stitch originally cast on, thus: put needle in stitch on needle, then in the corresponding loop cast on, and knit them together; pick up every loop in that way. Then p 2, k 2, for 40 rounds. Now knit 5 inches plain. At the first row of the plain knitting make the seam stitch which must be purled to the end of the heel. After five inches of the plain knitting is done, the narrowing begins. Narrow at each side of the seam stitch every 8th round for 10 times. Then knit for 5 inches plain.

NO. 2.—LADIES' PLAIN KNITTED STOCKING, WITH DOUBLE HEEL.

Now divide the stitches so that one-half of the stitches will be on one needle for the heel. Keep the seam stitch in the center of that needle; knit across and purl back as follows: K 1, slip 1 across the needle, turn; in the next row the stitches are reversed thus: slip the knitted stitch (put needle in same as for purling) and purl the slipped stitch. Continue to thus alternate until there are 18 loops on each side. Then sl 1, k, 1, for 24 stitches, n, k 1, turn, sl 1, p 1, for 9 stitches, n, p 1, (repeat k 1, sl 1 till the heel is finished) * sl 1, knit across, and knit the stitch following the last narrowing with the next of the stitches left on needle together, k 1, turn, sl 1, purl across and purl the stitch following the last narrowing together with the next of the stitches left on needle, purl 1; repeat from * until the stitches on both sides of the needle are used up. Pick up all the loops on the left hand side, knit across and pick up the loops on right hand side. Narrow one stitch on each side every other round just where the heel begins for 14 times. Then knit plain for 3½ inches. Now the narrowing for the toe begins as follows: Knit one and narrow, at the beginning of each needle, every other round till 6 stitches are left. Bind off and secure thread on the wrong side.

PURITAN STOCKING.

No. 3.—This plain stocking is perfect in shape, and, if preferred may be ornamented with fancy knitting or embroidery or ribbed work, as the knitter may choose. The same directions may be used for all kinds of full or three-quarter length hose by adapting the number of stitches to the size of yarn and needles used in knitting. The mode of shaping remains the same, whether bicycle, golf or fine silk hose are knitted.

These directions are especially prepared for the finest silk and needles, and are correct for a ladies' No 8½ stocking, which may be either full or three-quarter length as desired, the latter being often preferred by invalids.

To find the number of stitches necessary to be used with coarser yarn: cast on stitches and knit plain about six or seven times across. Count the number of stitches in an inch. In these directions there were 13 stitches in an inch of knitting. A full-sized stocking should be 12½ inches around the top. Multiply the number of stitches in an inch of knitting by 12½ and you will have the number of stitches necessary for commencing the stocking; but in case of ribbed work, the number should always be divisible by 5. In fancy patterns the number should be divisible by some number cor-

No. 3.—PURITAN STOCKINGS.

responding to the number in the repeat of the pattern, which number is usually given in the directions for all fancy patterns.

To knit the Puritan stocking with silk and No. 19 needles work as follows: Cast on, with double yarn, 160 stitches, 55 on each of two needles and 50 on the third.

First round.—Knit 3, seam 2; continue around the stocking, and repeat this round until the ribbed work is 2 inches deep. Now commence the seam which runs straight through the back of the stocking leg, by knitting 27 on one of the needles having 55 stitches; then, seam 1, * knit around plain, seaming the seam stitch. Repeat from * till the narrowings are reached. This plain space between the ribbed top and the narrowings in the back of the leg, forms all the difference between a long and a short or three-quarter length stocking. Knit this plain space 13 inches long for a full length and 6 inches long for a three-quarter or invalids length of stocking.

To Narrow in the Back of Leg.—First, Second, Third, Fourth and Fifth round.—Narrow once each side and next to seam; finish the round plain; now knit around plain, seaming the seam stitch. Repeat these 6 rounds 26 times more; then, knit plain, always seaming the seam stitch till the leg is long enough to set the heel. The leg should be 16 inches long for a three-quarter, and 23 inches for a full-length stocking, and 4 inches wide at the heel when folded together flatly.

To Knit the Heel.—On the needle having the seam stitch at the center, take 4 stitches more than half the number around the stocking (or in a coarse stocking, just half) for the heel. In this stocking, leave 49 stitches on the front of stocking; these stitches are not to be used till the heel is finished. Take the 57 stitches at the back of the leg and work as follows:

First row.—Knit 28, seam 1, knit 28.

Second row.—Slip 1, purl 27, knit 1, purl 28.

Third row.—Slip 1, knit 27, seam 1, knit 28. Repeat the last two rows till the heel is 2¼ inches long, then narrow off.

To Narrow off Heel.—First row.—Knit 12, n, knit till within two of seam, n, seam 1, narrow, knit till 14 are left, n, knit 12. Commence to narrow in right side of work.

Second row.—Purl to seam stitch, knit seam stitch,

purl remainder of stitches. Repeat these two rows till but 12 stitches are left at each side ot the seam stitch. Seam 12 stitches. Fold the right sides of the heel flat together so that the stitches on the two needles lie evenly together; knit 1, knit two stitches, one from each needle, together, and bind the first stitch knit over them. Continue to do thus till but one stitch is left and the heel is fully bound off.

To Set the Foot.—Keep the stitch left on the needle after binding off the heel still on the needle, pick up the loop at the back side of the edge of the heel next to this stitch and knit it. Take up three more loops in the same way. Take up one loop directly in front of the last back loop knit, and knit it; then, pick up and knit four more back loops, then one loop on the front. Continue to do thus till all the loops on that side of the heel have been used; then knit 8 of those stitches onto the needle with the loops just taken up on the side of the heel—there should now be 48 stitches on the needle at that side of the heel. Knit 33 stitches plain for the top, or instep of the foot, on another needle. Leave 8 stitches to be put on the next needle, knit one loop between those stitches and the side of heel; pick up the loops with the same needle in the same way as on the other side of the heel. There should now be 48 stitches on the two heel, or bottom-of-foot needles, and 33 on the instep needle.

To Narrow at the Instep.—*First round.*—Knit across the instep needle plain. Knit 8 on the heel needle, slip and bind once, knit plain till 10 are left on the opposite heel-needle. Narrow, knit 8 plain.

Second round.—Like first.

Third round.—Knit plain.

Repeat these three rounds till there are 33 stitches on each needle. Now knit plain till the foot is 7½ inches long—then narrow off the toe.

To Narrow off the Toe.—*First round.*—Begin at the instep needle, knit 1, narrow, knit till three are left on needle, narrow, knit 1; knit the other two needles in the same way. Knit two rounds plain. Repeat these three rounds till but 5 stitches are left on each needle. Then narrow continuously till but one is left. Draw through and darn the toe.

FANCY STOCKING TOP.

No. 4.—Cast on 160 stitches, 55 on each of two needles and 50 on a third. Knit five rounds plain.

Sixth round.—O, n, repeat all round.

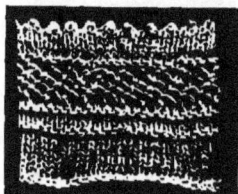

NO. 4.—FANCY STOCKING TOP.

Knit five more rounds plain. In the next round turn up the edge of the work inside, and with *each stitch* on the needles knit *one loop* from the edge, where the work was commenced, thus forming a perfect hem. Purl one round, knit 2 rounds plain. Purl one round.

Next round.—O twice, purl 2 together and repeat around. Repeat this last round enough times to make the fancy stripe as wide as desired. In the design shown it was repeated 8 times. When the stripe is wide enough, purl one round, knit 2 rounds, purl one round.

The rest of a stocking with this top may be knitted according to the directions for the Puritan stocking; and it may also be ornamented with a fancy stripe on the front, if an elaborate effect is desired. This pattern may be knit on any number of stitches divisible by two.

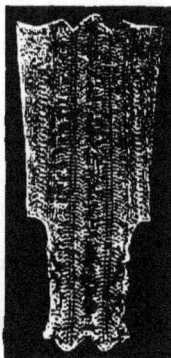

NO. 5.—FANCY FRONT AND INSTEP OF STOCKING.

FANCY FRONT AND INSTEP OF STOCKING.

(JACOB'S LADDER PATTERN.)

No. 5.—This pattern is 41 stitches wide, and may be knitted on the 20 stitches at each side of the center stitch in the front of any shaped stocking. The stripe may be commenced about 8 inches above the heel and runs straight down the front and over the instep of the stocking, reaching to within 3 inches of the toe. In a stocking knitted by the Puritan pattern, the stripe should be begun in the next round after the 11th narrowing in the back of the leg, stitches being knit on each side between the seam and fancy stripe.

First round.—Purl 2, n, n, n, o, k 1, o, k 1, o, k 1, o, k 1, o, k 1, o, n, n, n, p 1, k 1, p 1, n, n, n, o, k 1 five times, o, n, n, n, purl 2.

Second round.—Purl 2, k 17, p 1, k 1, p 1, k 17, p 2. Repeat these two rounds through the whole fancy stripe, taking care to keep the work straight by always seaming the same stitches. When two inches of the fancy stripe have been knitted the clockings, which end at the heel, should be begun. In this design two plain stitches are knit between the fancy stripe and clockings; but in any case these narrow, straight rows of fancy work should come just above where the heel joins the instep of the stocking at the side. These clockings are 6 stitches wide and knit in band stitch. Commence the one on the right side of the leg 8 stitches before knitting the fancy stripe.

First round.—(P 1, slip 1, o, k 3, draw the slipped stitch over the 3 knit stitches p 1,) knit 2, knit the fancy stripe, knit 2; then, knit the directions in parenthesis for the clocking on the left side of the leg.

Second and Third rounds.—P 1, k 4, p 14; repeat these three rows on each side of the leg two stitches from the fancy stripe till the stitches are taken off for the heel, when they are discontinued and the fancy stripe alone is continued on the instep or top of the foot.

A very dainty bicycle stocking may be knitted by adding these narrow clockings alone, without other fancy work, to the plain Puritan stocking, the effect being particularly satisfactory, when the stocking is knit with coarser yarn and larger needles.

DOUBLE HEEL FOR HOSE.

No. 6.—This heel is knitted with two needles which make two separate heels joined only by the edge stitches. This kind

NO. 6.—DOUBLE HEEL FOR HOSE.

of a heel will wear twice as long as a single heel. The method, by a little care, can be adapted to any shaped heel and any number of stitches. The directions are correct for a lady's silk or fine cotton hose No. 8½, or, in coarser wool for gentlemen's golf or bicycle stockings. The single heel on which the double heel is set up or begun is set the same as a single heel usually is, and has 39 stitches—a seam stitch at the middle with 19 stitches on each side of it.

To Set the Double Heel:—Knit 1, make 1 by knitting the slanting loop at the side of the stitch, and repeat across the heel. There should now be 78 stitches on the needle—2 seam stitches with 38 stitches on the each side. Make one after the last stitch to fill out the 78 stitches. In working off the knit stitches be careful to pass the needle through so as to bring them in regular shape.

First row.—Sl 1, k 1, * bring yarn to the front between the needles, slip 1, put the yarn back, k 1 and repeat from * 18 times. Seam 1 by bringing the yarn to the front between the needles, slip 1, seam 1, slip 1, and put the thread back, k 1. Repeat the details between the stars for other side of the heel.

Second row.—Follow the directions for the first row exactly. The stitches that are knitted should be slipped, and the slipped ones knitted. Repeat these two rows alternately 30 times or until long enough to narrow off. Begin to narrow off on the right side of the heel, thus:

First row.—Knit the first 18 stitches like the rest of the heel, then narrow as follows: Bring the yarn to the front, slip 1, take the next stitch off on an extra needle or a hair pin, slip the next stitch, put the yarn back, put back the stitch from the extra pin on to the left needle, narrow. Always narrow like this in 1st, 3rd, 5th, 7th and 9th rows, and knit 12 stitches like rest of heel. Narrow, slip 1, seam 1, n, knit 12 like rest of heel, n, k 18.

Second row.—K 18 like rest of heel, narrowing by bringing yarn to the front, slip 1, yarn back, narrow the stitches which were slipped side by side in first row. Always narrow like this in 2nd, 4th, 6th, 8th and 10th rows and knit 12 in the heel stitch; narrow, yarn to the front, slip 1, seam 1, narrow, knit 12 in the heel stitch, narrow, knit 18 in the heel stich.

Third row.—Like first row, except that there are

NO. 7.—DOUBLE TOE FOR HOSE.

8 instead of 12 stitches between narrowings.

Fourth row.—Like second row, except that there are 8 instead of 12 stitches between narrowings.

Fifth row.—Like first row, except that there are but 4 stitches between narrowings.

Sixth row.—Like second row, except that there are but 4 stitches between narrowings.

Seventh row.—Like first row, but the narrowings come together with no stitches between them.

Eighth row.—Like second row, but the narrowings come together with no stitches between them.

Ninth row.—Like first row, with but one narrowing on each side.

Tenth row.—Like second row, with but one narrowing on each side.

Separate the stitches, putting the stitches of the under side or lining on one pair of needles, and the outside stitches on another pair, half of the stitches of each part being on one needle and half on another; fold the needles of the outside together and narrow or knit the first stitch on each needle together. Narrow the next two together and slip the stitch resulting from the first narrowing over it. Continue to do thus till the stitches are all bound off. Then fasten the yarn. Then bind off the lining or under side of the heel the same as the outside; draw the thread through the last stitch but do not break it off, as it will be needed to take up the foot stitches.

DOUBLE TOE FOR HOSE.
(For Illustration see Page 158.)

No. 7.—This toe is knitted with four needles, and makes two entirely separate toes, joined only where the rows meet. For this reason it is better to commence making the extra stitches needed for the double part at the corner of the needle which crosses the sole of the foot. The foot may have any number of stitches around it before setting in the double toe.

To begin the Toe:—* Knit 1, make 1 by knitting the slanting loop at the side of the stitch; repeat around the stocking from *. There should be twice as many stitches, less one, as there were on the foot before beginning the toe; the full number being uneven. If there is an even number, drop one of the made stiches.

First row.—K 1, yarn to the front between the needles, slip 1, put the yarn back; repeat around the foot.

Second row.—Slip 1, k 1, and repeat around the foot, knitting the slip stitch and slipping the knit stitch in first row. Repeat these rows alternately to the narrowings.

To Narrow off the Toe:—Knit one double or three single stitches at each end of the needle. Next to these stitches narrow according to the directions for the different rows, making a narrowing very near each end of each needle; narrow in two rounds, then knit 4 rounds like rest of toe without narrowing. Always begin narrowing in a round that is knitted like the first one. Repeat these six rounds—two narrowed and then four

No. 8.—ELASTIC HOSE FOR AN INVALID (RAILROAD STITCH)

like rest of toe—alternately, until there are only stitches enough for one narrowing on each needle. Separate the stitches of lining and outside and put the lining stitches on a cord until needed. Narrow off the stitches of the outside until but one remains; draw the yarn through it, and fasten. Narrow the lining in the same way.

To Narrow In:—First round.—Take 4 stitches, the first of which is a slip stich. Bring yarn to the front, slip 1, take next stitch off on an extra needle or a hair pin; slip 1, put the stitch on the extra pin back on the left needle, put yarn back, narrow; knit like the rest of the toe to the next narrowing.

Second round. — Just back of the narrowings in first round will be found two slip stitches side by side; knit them together at each narrowing in first round and knit the other parts of the round like the rest of toe.

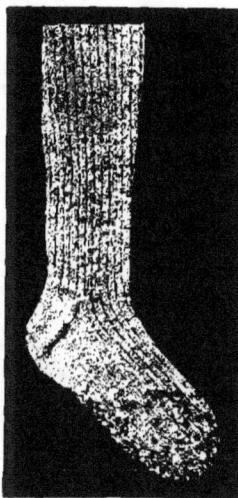

No. 9.—GERMAN STOCKING.

ELASTIC HOSE FOR AN INVALID (RAILROAD STITCH).

No. 8.—Cast 78 stitches on three medium-sized knitting needles, with split zephyr or thread of corresponding size, and knit once around plain. Knit 3, purl 3 for 9 rounds. Then, knit plain for 3 fingers and a half in length. Now drop every other stitch and knit the 34 remaining ones plain, narrowing one stitch on the end of every needle till only 6 are left. Knit these together and bind off. Secure the thread, with sewing thread and needle, by a few stitches on the wrong side. Pull the work, thus ravelling the dropped stitches to the end where the ribbed stitches will form a border. This elastic stocking is admirable for an invalid, as it draws on and off easily. It shapes itself to the heel.

GERMAN STOCKING.

No. 9.—This stocking is knitted with German wool and medium-sized steel needles. The leg and top of the foot are in ribbed knitting, the heel in double knitting and the toe and sole in plain knitting. Cast 97 stitches on 3 needles, 32 on each of 2 and 33 on the third. Work 140 rounds for the leg, knitting 2 and purling 2; the odd stitch is for the seam which must be in the middle of one of the needles between 2 plain stitches; be careful to keep the seam stitch at the middle of the back with a knitted stitch at each side of it. In the sixtieth round begin to narrow thus: When you reach the 3rd stitch from the center or purled stitch you will have 2 purled and one k stitch;

No. 10.—HALF-HOSE FOR A BOY OF SEVEN OR EIGHT YEARS. (MADE WITH DOUBLE HEEL.)

(For Description see Page 161.)

now slip the first purled stitch as if for purling, purl the next, and pass the slipped stitch over, k 1, purl the center or seam, k 1, slip 1 purled stitch, purl 1 and pass the purled st. over; then continue to k and p for the entire round; make 8 more rounds without narrowing, but at the center of the back there will be but 1 purl, instead of 2, just before and after the seam where the narrowing was last made. In the sixty-eighth row, when you reach the 2 knit stitches in front of the 1 purled stitch at the right of the seam, work thus : K 1; slip 1, k 1, (the purled stitch of last row) pass slipped stitch over, k 1, purl the center or seam stitch, k 1; slip 1, k 1, pass slipped stitch over, k 1, then purl and knit for remainder of round. In the next round there will be 3 stitches to k just before and after the center or seam stitch; make 8 more rounds without narrowing, then, in the next round, narrow thus: when you reach the third stitch from the center or seam (the 3 k stitches) slip 1, k 1, pass slip stitch over, k 1, purl the seam, slip 1, k 1, pass slipped stitch over, k 1, and continue to p and k for remainder of round. Make 9 more rounds, (p and k); then when you reach the third stitch from seam, slip 1, k 1, pass slipped stitch over, purl the seam or center stitch, k 1, slip 1, k 1, pass slipped stitch over, then purl and knit in regular order; there will now be only 1 purl stitch

at the right and left of the seam with the 2 knit stitches between. Make 9 rounds without narrowing, then narrow as in last narrowing; be very careful to keep the ribs regular. Make 9 rounds without narrowing, but at the right and left of the center or seam there will be 4 k stitches in each of the 9 rounds. In the next round narrow as usual; there will now be 3 k stitches at each side of the center or seam in the next 9 rounds, which are made without narrowing; in the next round narrow again; this will leave the 2 k stitches at the right and left of the center or seam. Make 9 more rounds, then narrow again which will leave 1 purl st. at each side of the 2 k stitches. Make 4 rounds without narrowing.

Next, make the heel thus: Put 35 stitches having the center or seam stitch in the middle on one needle and knit back and forth for 24 rows in this manner; always purl the stitches on the inside of the heel.

First row.—Slip 1, k 1 and repeat across the row.

Second row.—Slip 2 stitches, p 1, sl. 1 and repeat across the row. Repeat the first and second rows being careful to k or p the stitches that were slipped in the former row and slip the knit and purled ones. When there are 25 stitches on each side of the seam leave off with a purled row and in the next row, which is the right side, knit until you knit 1 stitch beyond the center or seam; then, k 2 to., 1 plain and turn. Slip 1, p 4, p 2 to., then p 1, turn. Slip 1, k 5, k 2 to., k 1, turn. Slip 1, p 6, p 2 to., p 1, turn. Slip 1, k 7, k 2 to., k 1, and so continue

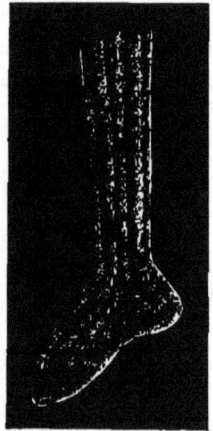

No. 11.—RIBBED SOCK FOR BOY TEN YEARS OLD.

(For Description see Page 161.)

always knitting 1 stitch more in each row until all are knit.

Pick up the 25 stitches on the left side of heel, knitting each as it is picked up. Knit across the instep and pick up 25 stitches on the right side.

In the next 78 rounds work the 46 stitches on

the top of the foot in ribbed knitting, and the stitches for the gussets and sole in plain knitting.

To form the Gussets.—Narrow in each of the next 8 rounds on the second and third stitch next to the ribbed knitting across the top, then in every other round until there are 12 rounds in all that are narrowed.

Knit 36 more rounds and then make the toe thus: k 2 to., k 7, and repeat for the round. Knit 7 rounds plain, then in the eighth narrow again, but k 6 stitches between each narrowing instead of 7; knit 6 rounds then narrow in the seventh again leaving 5 stitches between each narrowing and so on until all the stitches are used up.

HALF-HOSE FOR BOY OF SEVEN OR EIGHT YEARS. (MADE WITH DOUBLE HEEL.)

(For Illustration see Page 160.)

No. 10.—Cast 30 stitches on each of three needles and knit once around plain. Then knit 2, purl 2 for a little over half a finger's length. Then knit plain, purling one stitch in the middle of one needle, for the seam, until the sock is as long as desired.

Then divide the stitches so that 36 will be on one needle, for the heel. Knit 1, slip 1 across, and back again, knitting the slipped stitch and slipping the knitted one. Alternate this way, back and forth, knitting the outside plain, and purling the inside rows till the piece is over half a finger's length. Then evenly divide with 18 stitches on each needle, knit them together and bind off. Pick up every stitch down the selvedge or side of the heel; knit across the instep and pick up the selvedge stitches up the other side. Knit plain, narrowing one stitch every other round just where the picked up stitches on each side of heel begin. This will form the gusset at each side and reduce the foot to the proper size, which will be 26 stitches on each of the three needles.

Knit the foot as long as desired, and narrow one stitch at the end of each needle every other round. Narrow at each end of each needle, leaving just one stitch at the end of needle, which will leave two stitches between each narrow. When the foot is narrowed down to 4 stitches on each needle, take

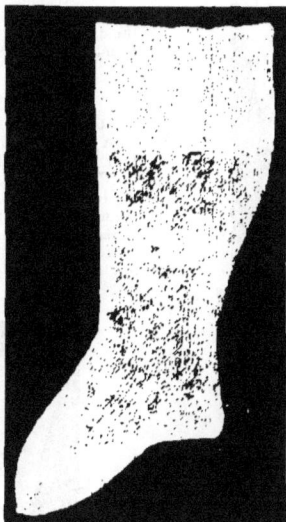

NO. 12.—CHILD'S PLAIN STOCKING.

six on each of two needles, knit them together and bind off. Pass the end of the thread through to the wrong side and secure it by a few stitches in sewing.

RIBBED SOCKS FOR BOY 10 YEARS OLD.

(For Illustration see Page 160.)

No. 11.—Four ounces of 3-ply yarn will be needed for one pair of socks; use No. 14 pins.

Cast on 48 stitches, 16 on each needle. Rib by knitting 3 plain, and purling 3, until the leg is 10¼ inches long. Now divide for heel, putting 25 stitches onto one needle. Knit and purl these 25 stitches (always slipping the first) until you have a flap 3 inches long. From this time you cease to rib on sole of foot. Knit 14 plain, knit 2 together, k 1, turn and p 5, p 2 to., purl 1, turn and repeat these 2 rows (always slipping the first stitch) until you have only 7 stitches left. Now take up side stitches. Knit 4 plain rounds, always ribbing the front. On first needle of heel knit 1, knit 2 together, knit rest plain. On second needle knit to within the last 3 stitches, slip 1, knit 1, pass the slipped one over the knitted one, knit 1, knit 2 plain rounds between each narrowing. There must be 5 narrowings. Knit until foot measures 6 inches.

For the Toe.—You now cease to rib. Front needle: knit 1, knit 2 together, knit to within the last 3 stitches, knit 2 together, knit 1. Second needle: knit 1, knit 2 together, knit rest of stitches. Third needle: knit to within last 3 stitches, then knit 2 together, knit 1. Knit 2 plain rounds between each narrowing; there should be 8 narrowings. Cast off and sew up.

CHILD'S PLAIN STOCKING.

No. 12.—This well proportioned stocking is designed for a child from 2 to 4 years, but may be adapted to a larger size by casting on an additional number of stitches.

Cast on any number of stitches, according to the size desired, say from 60 to 80, using four needles, and knit once around plain. Then knit 2, p 2 for to rounds; knit plain, leaving one purl stitch in the middle of one needle for the seam, for 12 rounds. Yarn over once on each side of the seam

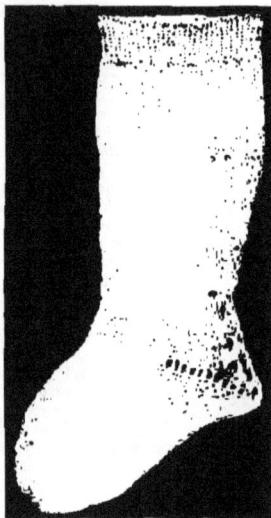

No. 13.—Baby's First Sock.

stitch of the 13th round. Knit 3 rounds, then yarn over once each side of the seam stitch and continue thus until 6 stitches are made, which widens the stocking to fit the calf of the leg. Knit plain forty or a hundred rounds, according to the size and length required. Then narrow to fit the limb where it tapers to the ankle by narrowing once on each side of the seam stitch every 5 rounds. Knit the ankle as long as desired and proceed with the heel by dividing the stitches so that one half, with seam stitch in the middle of the needle, will be on one needle. For a child knit the heel from one to two inches deep; for a grown person, four inches is a good depth for the heel. Next divide the stitches evenly on two needles, fold and knit the two divisions together; then bind off. Pick up the stitches down the selvedge of the heel until there are as many stitches made as there are rows in the heel. Knit across the instep to the other selvedge, forming stitches up the side of the heel, and continue to knit plain. Narrow every other round on each side where the heel starts until the foot measures the same as the ankle. When the foot is long enough, from 2 to 3 inches, narrow at each end of each needle every other round until only 2 stitches are left on each. Bind off, pass thread through and secure with a few neat stitches.

Another way to narrow and finish off the toe is as follows: Narrow, knit 8 all round; knit 8 rounds without narrowing; narrow, knit 7, all round; knit 7 rounds without narrowing; narrow, knit 6 all round; knit 6 rounds without narrowing; narrow, knit 5 all round; knit 5 rounds without narrowing; narrow, knit 4 all round; knit 4 rounds without narrowing; narrow, knit 3 all round; knit 3 rounds without narrowing; narrow, knit 2 all round. Then bind off, draw the end of the thread through to the wrong side and secure it. This makes a tapering toe that suits a long, slender foot.

This stocking may be made as much longer as is desired by knitting more rows between the top and the calf; an extra number of stitches would have to be made if the stocking is to extend above the knee.

Baby's First Sock.

No. 13.—This sock is made of fine white Saxony. Cast on 54 stitches, seam 1, knit 1, for 12 rounds, knit 38 rounds plain, mark one stitch for the center, * bind off a stitch to the right and narrow to the left of center stitch, knit 6 rounds plain, repeat from * till you have narrowed and bound off 6 times, knit 15 rounds plain.

Now divide the stitches leaving 28 stitches on one needle and 13 stitches on each needle at each

No. 14.—Ribbed Knee-Cap for Boy of Seven Years.
(For Description see Page 163.)

side of the center stitch, for the heel. Then knit back and forth on these two needles, as follows: Knit plain all but 1 stitch, turn, and seam back all but 1 stitch; alternate these rows, leaving each time one more stitch without knitting than you did the time before, till you have but 6 knitting stitches. Now knit and seam, taking up one of the left over stitches each time, till you have taken up all of them again.

K 30 rounds plain; now k 7, narrow all the way round; k 3 rounds plain; k 6, narrow all the way round; k 3 rounds plain; k 5, narrow all the way round; k 3 rounds plain; k 4, narrow all the way round; k 3 rounds plain; k 3, narrow all the way round; k 2 rounds, plain; k 2, narrow all the way round; 1 round plain; k 1, narrow all the way round; bind off. This sock can be knit of No. 300 knitting silk and will be quite large enough for a baby's first sock, if knit on Saxony needles.

RIBBED KNEE-CAP FOR BOY OF SEVEN YEARS.
(For Illustration see Page 163.)

No. 14. — Cast 25 stitches on each of 3 coarse knitting needles, using double woolen yarn. Knit once around plain. Then knit 2, purl 2 for 3 or 4 inches. Divide the stitches so that 30 will be on one needle. Work for 4 rows, 2 plain and 2 purl, back and forth, as for a heel. Then purl 2 and knit 2 for 20 stitches, joining the 20th stitch to the one next it, as for narrowing when turning a heel.

Knit back, and purl 2 and knit 2 for 10 stitches, joining the 10th stitch to the one next it. Knit back for 10 stitches and narrow again. Knit back the other way for 10 stitches and narrow. Knit back to the first narrowed stitch and pick up the 4 selvedge stitches. Knit around to the other selvedge, pick up the 4 stitches and knit the balance of the cap as long as desired, narrowing every other round at the sides just where the selvage stitches were picked up. This narrows it in shape like the heel of a stocking. The ribbing, 2 plain, and 2 purl stitches must be observed in turning the cap, as this makes it fit closely.

A knee cap may be turned to fit the knee, like the heel of a stocking, by other ways. Any knitter who can turn a heel can turn a knee-cap.

Any kind of yarn used for knitting stockings, socks or mittens can be used in knitting knee-caps.

CHILD'S FIRST SOCK.

No. 15.—This pretty sock is a dainty little thing for a child just promoted to its first shoe. The pattern is knitted in fine thread, but the same directions can be used for silk, if the latter is preferred. A correct estimate for the size of a sock when knitted may be made from the following: 21 stitches measure an inch in width, and 20 rows half an inch in depth.

To begin knitting the sock, cast onto one needle 90 stitches; knit off 30 stitches onto a second needle, and 30 onto the third needle; join and knit 1 round plain. Care must be taken to commence every new needle from the back of the last one knitted off; if this is not carefully observed, there will be a loose stitch on every needle, which impairs the work. Knit 30 rounds of 2 plain stitches, and 1 purl stitch alternately made.

Thirty-second row.— Knit 10, * make 1, knit 3, slip 1, knit 2 together, draw the slipped stitch over the knitted ones, knit 3, make 1, knit 1, and repeat from * 6 times more; after this repetition knit 9 instead of 10, and purl the last stitch for the seam stitch. The latter is kept in the whole length of the leg.

Thirty-third round.— Knit plain; then repeat these 2 rounds 30 times; this brings you to the heel; divide for it, and knit to the end of the second open-work stripe—that is, the *three* stitches knitted plain after the slip-and-drawn-over stitch; turn, knit 3, purl the stitches to the *middle* of the 2nd stripe after the seam stitch, knit the 3 plain ones of this stripe after the drawn-over stitch. These 3 stitches on each side of the heel must be knitted in each row. Knit 28 more little rows, keeping the seam stitch. In the next row decrease the 1st stitch on each side the seam stitch, knitting one plain between the decreased stitch and the seam stitch; next row plain; repeat these 2 little rows ; times more; in the next row knit to the 3 center stitches, knit these 3 as one, then with another needle knit off the stitches together from each needle, and cast off as you knit them.

To Knit the Foot.—The thread is at the center of the heel. Take up 26 stitches on the heel to the first open stitch of the little stripe, which must be

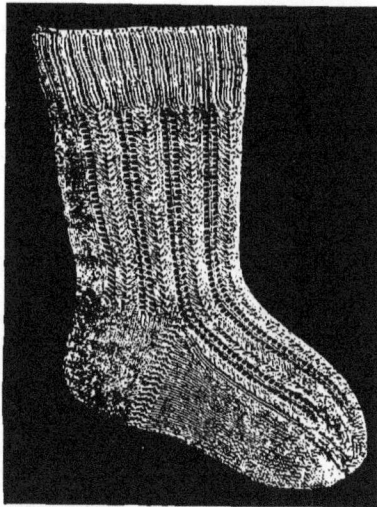

No. 15.—CHILD'S FIRST SOCK.

carefully kept; then make 1, knit 1, make 1, * knit 3, slip 1, knit 2 together, draw over, knit 3, make 1, knit 1, make 1, repeat from * twice more; then knit 2, and take these up on the heel, then take up 24 more stitches. Next row knit plain.

Third row.—K 22, k 2 together, k 2, m 1, k 1, * m 1, k 3, slip 1, knit 2 together, and draw over; k 3, m 1, k 1; repeat from * twice, then make 1, k 2. k 2 together; knit the rest plain to the middle of the heel.

Fourth row.—Plain.

Fifth row.—K 18, k 2 together, k 1, k 2 together, k 2, then make 1, k 1, * m 1, k 3, slip 1, k 2 together and draw over, k 3, m 1, k 1, repeat from * twice more. The last time make 1, k 2, k 2 together, k 1, k 2 together, knit to the center of heel, which completes the row.

Sixth row.—Knit plain.

Seventh row.—K 17, k 2 together, k 1, k 2 together, k 2, then make 1, k 1, * m 1, k 3, slip 1, k 2 together, draw over, k 3, m 1, knit from * twice more; then make 1, k 2, k 2 together, k 1, k 2 together, knit the remainder of the row.

Eighth row.—Knit plain.

Ninth row.—K 16, k 2 together, k 1, k 2 together, k 2, then make 1, k 1, * m 1, k 3, slip 1, k 2 together, draw over, k 3, m 1, k 1, repeat from * twice more; then make 1, k 2, k 2 together, k 1, k 2 together; knit the rest plain.

Tenth row.—Plain.

Eleventh row.—K 18, k 2 together, k 2, then make 1, k 1, m 1, k 3, slip 1, k 2 together, draw over, k 3, m 1, k 1; repeat from * twice more, then make 1, k 2, k 2 together, knit the rest plain.

Twelfth row.—Knit plain; repeat these last 2 rounds 23 times more, which brings you to the toe.

To Knit the Toe.—K 14, k 2 together, k 2, k 2 together, k 34, k 2 together, k 2, k 2 together. Knit to the end of the round. The 34 stitches knitted plain should bring you to the last increased stitch of the stripe. The decreasings in this row are for the shaping of the toe; there must be 2 stitches between each decreasing on each side of the foot.

Next two rows: Knit plain; repeat the first row of the toe, making two decreasings on each side of the 2 stitches knit plain; then a plain row; repeat these 2 rows until you have only 32 stitches left on the needles; place half the stitches, *i.e.,* from the center of the 2 knit plain to the corresponding stitch on the other side of the foot, onto one needle, and the remaining stitches on the 2nd needle. With a 3rd needle knit the 1st stitch on

each needle together; then knit the 2nd stitch on each needle together; draw the 1st stitch knitted over the 2nd, and so cast off. Run the end in neatly through the stitches to fasten off.

FANCY STOCKINGS FOR A CHILD FROM SIX MONTHS TO ONE YEAR OLD.

No. 16.—Cast 20 stitches on each of 3 knitting needles of medium size (60 in all), of split zephyr silk or Drexel cotton.

Knit once around plain. Then knit 3, purl 3 for 6 rounds. Then knit 2 rounds plain and purl 7 rounds. Knit 7 rounds plain. Purl 7 rounds and knit 3 rounds. Then begin the fancy stitches:

Over, narrow, knit 2; over, n, knit 2 for 7 rounds. Then knit the over stitch; then over, narrow, knit 2 for 7 rounds.

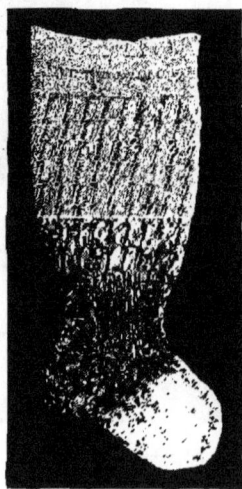

No. 16.—FANCY STOCKING FOR CHILD FROM SIX MONTHS TO ONE YEAR OLD.

Knit the over stitch; over, narrow, knit 2 for 7 rounds till the stocking measures over half a finger's length. Then knit plain, leaving one purl stitch in the middle of the needle for the seam. Narrow one on each side of the seam stitch every 5 rounds till the ankle is small enough and knit 10 plain rounds.

Divide the stitches so that exactly one-half will be on one needle for the heel. Knit across plain, and purl back, continuing thus across and back again till the heel is as long as required.

Now on the heel needles knit 16 and narrow, turn, purl 8 and narrow, k back 8 and n, continue thus till the cap is formed, or the heel turned. Then take the thread and the empty needle and pick up the stitches down the selvedge edge of the heel until there are as many stitches made as there are rows in the heel. Knit across the instep to the other selvedge, forming stitches up the side of the heel, and pick them up; then continue to knit plain, narrowing every other round, on each side, where the heel starts until the foot measures the same as the ankle. When the foot is long enough narrow at each end of each needle, every other round, until only two stitches are left on each. Bind off, pass the thread through to the wrong side and secure with a few neat stitches.

CHILDS' STOCKING. (SUITABLE FOR A CHILD ABOUT TWO YEARS OLD.)

(For Illustration see Page 165.)

No. 17.—This stocking is made of white Saxony with any preferred shade for the stripes. Pale blue or pale pink and white is the prettiest combination. Use needles rather coarser than for making

Saxony fancy-work. The stockings may also be made of silk or cotton, if desired. Cast 24 stitches on each of 3 needles, holding the left-hand thread very loosely so that the stocking will stretch easily over the knee.

First round.—Knit 2, and purl 2 alternately, being careful to have the 1st two stitches on each needle knitted and the last two purled. Repeat this for 11 rounds.

Twelfth round.—Put the end of the striping color up through the inside of the stocking and knit 2 with both the colored and white yarn. Drop the white, then purl 2 and knit 2 with the color for 5 rounds.

Seventeenth round.—Knit 2 with both threads, purl 2 with white, and continue with the white; knit 2 and repeat for 5 rounds.

Twenty-second round. — Knit 2 with both threads, and continue with the colored, knitting 2 and purling 2 for five rounds.

Twenty-seventh round. — Knit 2 with both threads, purl 2 with white, and continue with white for 2 rounds.

Twenty-ninth round. — Knit 1, throw thread round needle twice, knit 2 together, p 1, knit 1, throw thread round needle twice, knit 2 together, purl 1, knit 1, throw thread round needle twice, purl 1, and continue the same all the way around.

Thirtieth round.—* Knit 1, knit 1 on loop, purl 1 on loop, purl 1 and repeat from * once around.

Thirty-first and Thirty-second rounds.—Knit 2 and purl 2 alternately.

Thirty-third round.—Knit 2 together; then purl 1, knit 1 all the way round; but do not narrow except the 1st two stitches on 1st needle.

Thirty-fourth round. — Purl 1, knit 1; repeat, taking care each round to purl the stitch that was knit in the round before and knit the one that was purled, which forms a beaded stripe. Repeat this 20 times more around.

Fifty-fifth round.—Knit 1, widen 1 by picking up a loop; then purl 2, knit 2, and repeat for 2 rounds.

Fifty-seventh round.—* Knit 1, throw thread round needle twice, knit 2 together, purl 1, and repeat from * all the way around.

Fifty-eighth round.—* Knit 1, knit 1 on loop, purl 1 on loop, purl 1, and repeat from * all the way round.

Fifty-ninth round.—* Knit 2 and purl 2, and repeat from * 65 times around, or about 4 inches.

For the Heel.—Take half the stitches, 36, on one needle, beginning with two that are knit plain, and ending with two that are purled. Leave the other half on two needles and knit with two needles back and forth across one half for the heel. Purl those on the wrong side which are knit plain on the right side and vice versa, and *knit* the 1st stitch each time instead of slipping it off. Knit 12 times on each side, which is 24 times across.

Next round.—Knit and purl as before 23 stitches, slip the 24th, knit the next one and pass the slipped one over it.

Next round.—Turn and knit back the same as if you had knitted clear across; knit 11 stitches, slip the 12th, knit the 13th and pass slipped stitch over it.

Next round.—Turn and knit back 11 stitches, slip 12th, knit 13th, pass slipped stitch over, turn again and repeat, till all the stitches at the sides are narrowed off.

Next round. — Take up loops down left side of heel, knitting 2 and putting thread over needle. When you come to the corner of instep needle knit the purled stitches together, and the plain ones plain all the way across. Take up the selvedge stitches on right side of heel same as on the left throwing thread over at every 3rd stitch. Knit together the plain stitches and the purled ones, thereby narrowing half of them and place them on each of the heel-needles. Knit loops down sides of heel.

Next round.—Knit plain across instep, slip 1st stitch from heel-needle, knit 2nd and pass slipped stitch over. Knit plain till the end of 2nd heel needle, then knit 2 stitches together. Repeat till there are 13 stitches on each side of heel. Then slip stitches so there will be the same number on each needle. Knit plain till the foot measures 3 inches from the heel. Knit one stitch at corner of needle, narrow, knit 12, narrow, knit 1. Repeat on each needle. Knit plain twice aroun l, knit 1, narrow, knit 10, narrow, knit 1. Repeat on next 2 needles. Knit 2 rounds plain, and narrow on each needle as before. Then narrow in the same way till only 2 are left and break off thread. Knit each stitch, draw thread through and fasten with worsted needle.

CHILD'S SHELL STOCKING.

(For Illustration see Page 166.)

No. 18.—This stocking, as pictured, was made of linen thread No. 90, with 4 steel needles No. 20, and is for a child a year and a half old.

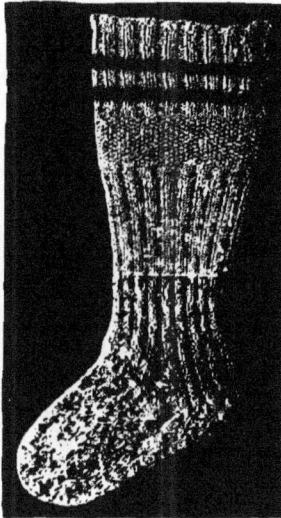

No. 17.—CHILD'S STOCKING. (SUITABLE FOR A CHILD ABOUT TWO YEARS OLD.)
(For Description see Page 164.)

FANCY AND PRACTICAL KNITTING.

Cast 50 stitches onto each of 3 needles and knit 1 round plain. For forty-five rounds k 2 and p 2. Then knit 5 rounds plain, purling 1 stitch in the middle of one of the needles for a seam stitch. This stitch must be purled in every following round, and all rounds will start from this stitch for the entire length of the leg and heel.

Fifty-first round.—K 1, * o, n, and repeat from * for the round.

Fifty-second round.—Knit plain, but purl the seam stitch as before directed.

Fifty-third round.—K 2, * o, n, and repeat from * until the stitch before the seam stitch, which you k without narrowing; then p the seam stitch; this will make 151 stitches on the needle.

Fifty-fourth round.—K plain, p the seam stitch.

Fifty-fifth round.—K 32, p 2, * k 5, p 2; repeat 11 times more from *, k 32, p 1.

Fifty-sixth round.—K 32, p 2, * k 1, o, k 1, o, k 1, o, k 1, o, k 1, p 2; repeat 11 times more from *; k 32, p 1.

Fifty-seventh round.—K 32, p 2, * k 9, p 2, and repeat 11 times more from *; k 32, p 1.

Fifty-eighth round.—K 32, p 2, * sl and bind, k 5, n, p 2, and repeat 11 times more from *; k 32, p 1.

Fifty-ninth row.—K 32, p 2, * sl and b, k 3, n, p 2, and repeat 11 times more from *; k 32, p 1. This makes 1 shell in length, and 12 in width; continue the shells by repeating from the fifty-sixth round.

There is a decrease of 2 stitches by narrowing at the right of the seam stitch, with 1 plain stitch between; and at the left, slip and bind, knitting 1 stitch between, which will make 3 plain stitches at each side of the seam stitches in each of the following rounds:

Seventy-fifth, Eighty-first, Eighty-seventh, Ninety-third, Ninety-ninth, One Hundred and Fifth, Eleventh, Seventeenth, Twenty-third, Twenty-ninth, Thirty-fifth, Forty-first, Forty-seventh, Fifty-third, Fifty-ninth, Sixty-fifth, Seventy-first, Seventy-seventh, Eighty-third, Eighty-ninth, Ninety-fifth; Two Hundred and First, Seventh, Thirteenth, Nineteenth, Twenty-fifth, Thirty-first, Thirty-seventh and Two Hundred and Forty-third rounds.

Knit 40 rounds more and set the heel by slipping 3 rows of shells and 1 of the outer plain stitches onto the seam needle at each side of the seam; knit out the heel needle, purling the 2 plain stitches between the shells, and knitting the 5 shell stitches plain.

Knit back on the heel, slip the first stitch, p the plain stitches; knit the purled stitches every time across on the inside of the heel.

Knit the rows across on the out or right side of

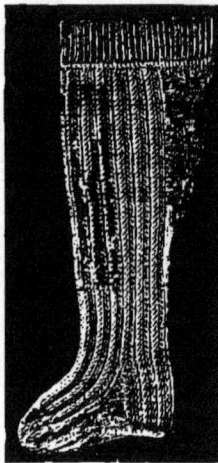

NO. 18.—CHILD'S SHELL STOCKING.
(For Description see Page 165.)

the work in the usual manner until there are 9 rows of shells; then p across, and k the seam stitch. On the right side of the work k plain to the third stitch from seam, then n, k 1, p 1, k 1, sl and b, knit the rest plain.

Next row.—Purl across, k the seam stitch, and continue these 2 rounds 7 times more.

Next, purl to the seam stitch, bind the heel off leaving the last stitch on the needle, turn the heel right side out, pick up 34 stitches on the heel at the right side of the foot, knit off 1 purl, 1 shell, and 2 p onto this needle from the instep; knit in the usual manner for the next 4 shells and the 2 purl stitches between them on the instep needle; then knit the remaining shell and 1 purl onto another needle, and pick up on this last needle 35 stitches on the heel at the left side of the foot.

Second round.—Commence at the bottom of the foot, make 1 extra stitch every 5th stitch where the stitches were picked up; then purl 2, make the shells across, p 2, k 4, and make 1 every fifth stitch on the other side of the heel where the stitches were picked up.

Third round.—K 39, n, k 1, p 2, make shells across to the other side of the heel, p 2, k 1, sl and bind, k 39. Continue narrowing in every round on the right side of the foot, and sl and bind on the left side until there are 48 stitches across the bottom of the foot between the sl and bind and narrowing, when the foot will be small enough.

Make the foot 9 rows of shells in length from the narrowing, and then begin the toeing-off on the under side of the foot, as follows:

* N, k 7, and repeat from * for the round; there will be 4 stitches left between the last narrowing and the first. Knit 7 plain rounds.

* N, k 6, and repeat from * for the entire round. Knit 6 rounds plain.

* N, k 5, and repeat from * for the entire round. Knit 5 rounds plain.

* N, k 4, repeat from * for the round. K 4 rounds plain.

* N, k 3, repeat for the round. Knit 3 rounds plain.

* N, k 2, repeat for the round. Knit 2 rounds plain.

* N, k 1, repeat for the round. Knit 1 round plain.

* Narrow for the entire round. K 1 round plain.

Break off the thread, leaving a length of 8 or 10 inches; * n, pull stitch through, and repeat from *; then thread a needle, run through the stitches; draw the thread up tightly and fasten neatly.

SWEATERS AND STOCKINGS FOR GOLF, CYCLING, ETC, FOR ADULTS AND YOUNG FOLKS.

SUGGESTIONS CONCERNING THE MAKING OF SWEATERS.

To make sweaters larger or smaller than the ones described in this article, add or decrease 8 stitches for every inch increase or decrease beyond or under the breast measures given.

The quantities here given are for the yarns used in the sweaters illustrated. Finer or coarser yarns may be used, but in this event the knitter must use her own judgment as to the quantity of yarn she will require and the number of stitches to be cast on.

The "fancy pattern" used in making these sweaters is the ordinary block pattern, made thus:

First row.—K 2, p 2.

Second row.—Work back, knitting the purled stitches and purling the knitted ones.

Third row.—Same as first row except that you purl the two knitted stitches and knit the two purled ones to form the block.

Fourth row.—Like second.

Any fancy stitch preferred to the one described may be used, but care must be taken to keep the ribs as we have directed.

"Rib" means: K 1, p 1 across; work back on wrong side, knitting the purled stitches and purling the knitted ones to keep the pattern.

The sailor collars may be ribbed throughout, if preferred. They may also, in most instances, be knitted upon the sweater by taking up the required number of stitches around the neck edge and then knitting down to their lower edges and binding off there.

The shoulders of the sweaters may be bound together instead of being sewed, if preferred; or, if the worker is accustomed to knitting garments, she may knit the fronts and backs in one piece, begin-

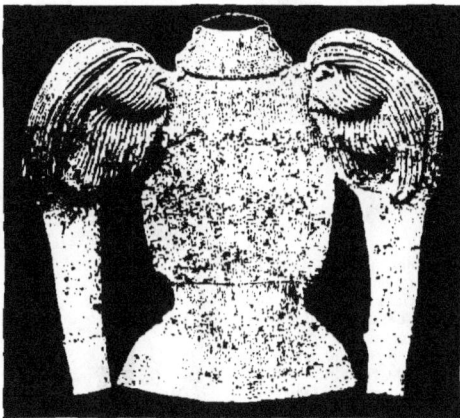

NO. 1.—LADIES' AND MISSES' SWEATER.

ning either the front or back at the lower edge and finishing the other half at the corresponding lower edge.

All of the sweaters here described are begun at the lower edge.

LADIES' AND MISSES' SWEATERS. (34 INCHES BUST MEASURE.)

NOS. 1 AND 2.—These sweaters are both knitted by the following instructions as the two are exactly alike except the sleeves. The difference is clearly illustrated by the engravings. The wrists are simply turned back like cuffs. Directions for each style of sleeve will be given. Illustration No. 2 shows the sweater as worn, while No. 1 shows its shape before such adjustment.

Fourteen ounces of white knitting worsted, 16 buttons, fine ivory needles, No. 12 steel knitting needles and fine steel knitting needles are required in making each of these sweaters. The upper part of the sleeve is knitted with the ivory needles; the lower part of the sleeve, the neck and the close part about the waist with the fine steel knitting needles, and the rest of the sweater with No. 12 knitting needles.

To Make the Front Body Portion.—Cast on 116 stitches; work in fancy stitch for 1¾ inch. Now rib for five rows. * Next, k 1, p 1, k 3 together, rib across to within 5 stitches, k 3 together, p 1, k 1, *; repeat between stars every third row for four times more; then rib for 4 rows more, 4 rows fancy. Now rib with the fine needles for 2¾ inches. Then with the No. 12 needles make 4 rows of fancy pattern. Rib for 11 inches; then, 8 rows of fancy pattern, making button-holes in the second row, as follows: Work 2, sl and bind 2, work 4, sl and bind 2, work 4, sl and bind 2, work across to within 18 stitches of the other end; then make 3 more button-holes, as follows: Sl and bind 2, work 4, sl

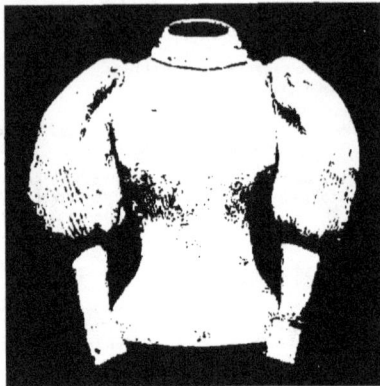

No. 2.—Ladies' and Misses' Sweater.
(For Description see Page 167.)

and bind 2, work 4, sl and bind 2, work 2; turn work back and put thread over twice wherever two stitches were bound off in previous row. When the 8 rows of fancy pattern are made, use the fine needles, bind off 14 stitches, rib across to within 14, and bind them off; this will form the shoulder edges; rib back and forth with the remaining stitches for 4¼ inches, to form the collar, making four button-holes by the method just described along each edge, making them two stitches back of the edge and three-fourths of an inch apart; then knit 8 fancy rows, and in the fourth row of it at each edge make a 5th button-hole. Bind off loosely.

To Make the Back Body Portion.—Knit exactly like front and sew buttons to the shoulder and collar edges to correspond with the button-holes in front portion, sewing the three upper ones at each edge on the inside of the collar portion, so that when the collar is turned over the buttons will be on the outside. Make an underlap (in ribbing) about 3 inches long and 1¼ wide, and sew under the button side of the shoulder closing, after the manner of an ordinary underlap. Lay the right sides of the portions together with the side and lower edges even, and sew them together from the lower edges for the depth of 15½ inches. Also lap the shoulder edges of the front body-portion over those of the back body-portion and tack the parts together at the arm's-eye edges only. Finish the

edges of the button-holes with over-and-over stitches to make them strong.

To Make the Sleeve of No. 1.—Cast 120 stitches on the ivory needles and rib very loosely for sixteen inches. Knit four rows fancy pattern. With the fine needles work back and forth thus: * K 1, n, rib across to within 3 stitches, narrow, p 1, turn, rib back ; * repeat between stars till 30 stitches are narrowed off on each side. Rib for 8 inches more and bind off. Sew the lower part of the sleeve together to the fancy pattern, and from there sew it up for 2½ inches more. Lay the top of the sleeve in a box-plait and four side plaits at each side turning from the box-plait. Sew the sleeve in, placing the center of the box-plait at the shoulder seam and the seam of the sleeve at the underarm seam.

To Make the Sleeve of No. 2.—Use the ivory needles and cast on 150 stitches. Rib very loosely for 17 inches; next, make 4 rows of fancy knitting. Now use the fine needles and rib one row, narrowing every tenth stitch by knitting two stitches together.

Next row.—* K 1, n, rib across to within three stitches, n, p 1, turn, rib back, *; repeat between stars ; rib thus till 35 stitches are narrowed off on each side; then knit for six inches more, and bind off. Sew the lower part of the sleeve together as

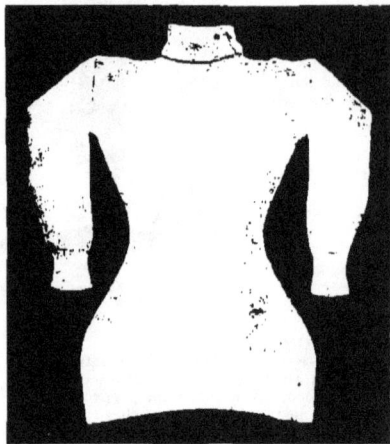

No. 3.—Ladies' Sweater with Close Sleeves and Hip Gores. (Also Suitable for an Undervest.)
(For Description see Page 169.)

far as the fancy pattern ; also sew it together from the fancy pattern for eight inches more. Plait and sew in the sleeve as in the other sweater.

LADIES' SWEATER, WITH CLOSE SLEEVES AND HIP GORES. (32 INCHES, BUST MEASURE.)

(For Illustration see Page 121.)

No. 3.—One pound and a quarter of brown German knitting worsted, seven buttons, fine steel needles for the wrists and neck, and medium-sized steel needles for the rest of the garment are required in making this sweater. Made in fine yarn and without the collar this sweater is also suitable for an undervest. The hip gores may be enlarged or altogether omitted, according to the requirements of the figure.

To Make the Front Body Portion.—Cast on 140 stitches; work 3 inches fancy pattern; rib for 2½ inches. * Rib 6 inches, knit 3 together to narrow; rib across to within 9 stitches, knit 3 together, rib 6 stitches, * repeat between the stars in every 6th row until 11 narrowings in all have been made. Then rib for 3 inches more. * Rib 6 stitches, widen 2 stitches, rib across to within 6 stitches, widen 2 stitches, rib 6 stitches, * repeat between stars every 5th row until 12 widenings in all have been made. Rib for 6½ inches. Now rib 8 stitches at the right side of the work and right-hand side of needle and then, to make 3 button-holes, continue to work as follows: Sl and bind 2, rib 8, sl and bind 2, rib 8, sl and bind 2, rib rest of stitches, turn; rib back and put thread over twice wherever two stitches were bound off in previous row. Rib for four more rows; then at the right-hand side bind off 33 stitches; rib to within 33 stitches on left side and bind latter off.

To Make the Back Body Portion.—Cast on 140 stitches. Knit exactly as front body portion with the exception of the button-holes, and sew the right shoulder edges neatly together on the wrong side.

To Make the Collar.—Using the stitches remaining and fine needles, begin at the right hand side of front portion; rib across to the corresponding edge of the back; turn, and rib back.

Next row.—Rib 4 stitches, make a button-hole in the front edge of the collar portion as before, rib for one inch, make another button-hole in this edge. Rib for one and a half inch; rib across to within 6 stitches and make another button-hole in the opposite edge. Rib for one-fourth of an inch more and make another button-hole in the same edge. Make 6 rows fancy pattern. Bind off.

To Make the Gores.—Cast on 41 stitches. Knit 3 inches fancy pattern, rib 2½ inches. Rib 4 stitches, knit 3 together, to narrow, rib across to within 7 stitches, knit 3 together, rib 4 stitches. Narrow this way every 6th row at the side till all the stitches are narrowed off. Then sew the gores in neatly on the wrong side with over-and-over stitches. Count from each shoulder edge of the front and back down, 53 stitches and sew the parts together below these stitches with the lower edges even. The arm's-eyes are thus formed.

To Make the Sleeves.—Take up the 106 stitches around each arm's-eye on three medium-sized steel knitting needles, and knit the sleeve like a stocking. Make the seam stitch in line with the under-arm seam; it is purled in one round and knitted in the next one. Rib for 4 inches, and then rib to within 7 stitches of seam stitch. Knit 3 to., rib 4 stitches, make seam stitch, rib 4, knit 3 to.; this forms the first narrowing. Make 3 more similar narrowings 5 rounds apart. Rib for 7 inches, make 5 more narrowings as before, 5 rounds apart. Then rib for 1½ inch. Now use the fine steel needles and rib for 2½ inches; work 6 rows of fancy pattern. Bind off loosely. Finish the edges of the button-holes with over-and-over stitches to make them strong. Sew on buttons to correspond with the button-holes. Knit an underlap about an inch and a half wide and 5 inches long, and sew it to the back portion under left shoulder-edge.

No. 4.—YOUTHS' SWEATER, WITH "TURTLE-NECK" COLLAR.

YOUTHS' SWEATER WITH "TURTLE-NECK" COLLAR. (BREAST MEASURE, 32 INCHES.)

No. 4.—Thirteen ounces of fine white knitting worsted will be needed in making this sweater. Fine steel knitting needles are used for the wrists and neck and medium-sized steel knitting needles for the rest of the sweater.

To Make the Front Body Portion.—Cast on 170 stitches and work in fancy pattern for 3¼ inches. Rib for 20¼ inches; then make 6 rows of the fancy pattern or, if preferred, the six rows may be ribbed like the previous portion. Now bind off 35 stitches, rib 100, and bind off the other 35 stitches.

To Make the Back Body Portion.—Work exactly as front portion. Then sew the corresponding

inches; then work six rounds of fancy pattern and bind off. Turn the collar over on the outside, as illustrated.

To Make the Sleeves.—Count from the shoulder

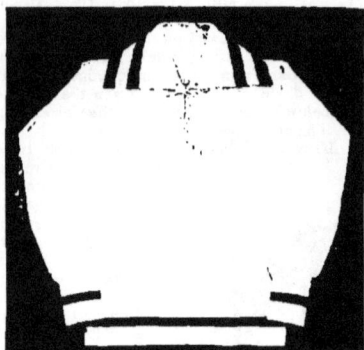

No. 5.

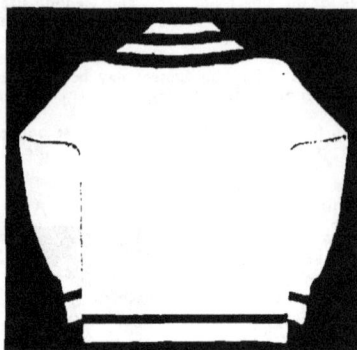

No. 6.

FIGURES NOS. 5 AND 6.—MEN'S SHORT SWEATER, WITH HUNTING COLLAR.

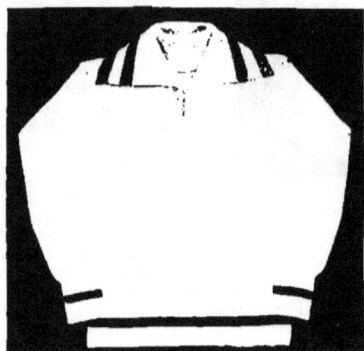

No. 8.

No. 9.

NO. 7.—SWEATER SHOWING "TURTLE-NECK" CHEST PROTECTOR ADJUSTED.

NOS. 8 AND 9.—TURTLE-NECK CHEST PROTECTOR.

(For Descriptions of Nos. 5, 6, 7, 8 and 9, see Pages 171 and 172.)

bound-off stitches, which form the shoulder edges, together on the wrong side.

For the Collar.—Use the fine needles and rib with the remaining stitches from the front and back portion all round like a stocking for 5½

seam 65 stitches down each side of the front and back body portions for the arm's-eyes, and sew the portions below these 120 stitches together on the wrong side. Then take up the 120 stitches around each arm's-eye on three medium-sized steel needles and knit the sleeves like a stocking, making the seam stitch in line with the under-arm seam, purling it in one round and knitting it in the next one. Rib for 2 inches; then, to narrow, work thus: Knit 3 together at each side of the seam stitch when within two stitches of it every sixth round for five times. Rib 4½ inches more, narrow as before at each side of the seam stitch every sixth round for five times; then rib for 1¼ inch. Now use the fine needles and rib for 3½ inches, to form the wrist, and bind off.

MEN'S SHORT SWEATER, WITH HUNTING COLLAR.
(BREAST MEASURE, 40 INCHES.)

(For Illustrations see Page 170.)

NOS. 5, 6 AND 7.—Navy-blue and white knitting

for seven inches; then, 8 rows fancy pattern; and bind off. Knit the other side on its 95 stitches in the same way.

To Make the Back Body Portion.—Knit exactly like the front portion except that the stitches are not divided to form an opening. Lay the right sides of the portions together so that the shoulder and side edges will come even, and sew the shoulder edges from the arm's-eye edges to within 3 inches of the neck-edge together, and turn the three-inch pieces left on the front portion inside the sweater to form the front neck-edges and tack them invisibly to position. Now count down from the shoulder seam each from the front and back body portion for the arm's-eye, and sew the portions below those 120 stitches together.

To Make the Sleeve.—Take up 120 stitches

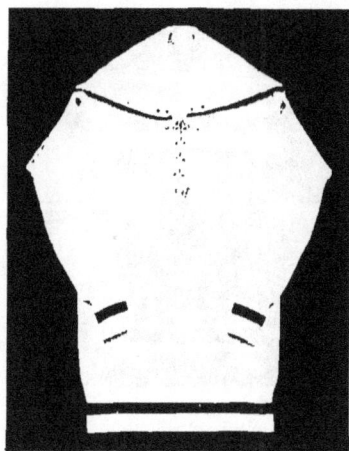

No. 10.

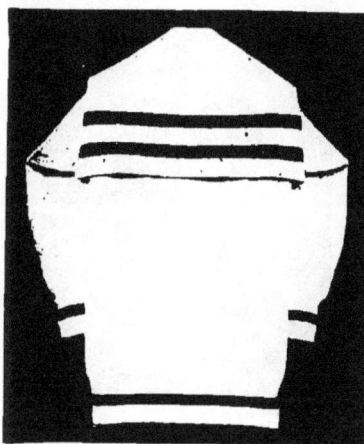

No. 11.

NOS. 10 AND 11.—YOUTHS' SWEATER WITH DEEP SAILOR-COLLAR. (TO BE WORN WITH OR WITHOUT 'TURTLE-NECK' CHEST PROTECTOR.)

(For Descriptions of Nos. 10 and 11, see Page 172.)

worsted was used for this sweater. 14 ounces of the white and about one ounce of the blue will be needed. Fine steel knitting needles were used for the wrists, and medium-sized steel needles for the rest of the sweater.

For the Front Body Portion.—Cast on 190 stitches; work in fancy pattern, 1½ inch white, ¾ inch blue, 1½ inch white. Rib for 11¼ inches. Divide the stitches in two parts so that there will be 95 stitches on one needle; this is to form the opening. Rib back and forth on one of the needles

around the arm's-eye on three medium-sized steel needles and knit the sleeve like a stocking, making the seam stitch in line with the under-arm seam, purling it in one round and knitting it in the next one. Rib 4 inches, k 3 to. at each side when within two stitches of the seam stitch, every sixth round, for 3 times; rib 8 inches and narrow as before at each side of the seam stitch every sixth round for four times; rib 1¼ inch. Now use the fine needles and rib 1½ inch white, 10 rounds blue, 1½ inch white.

To Make the Collar.—The collar is knitted in one straight piece and in sewing it on the ends must be even with the ends of the opening in the front portion. Measure the collar after a few rows are knitted to make sure of the required size about the neck. Cast on 190 stitches; knit fancy or plain, as preferred, about 1 inch blue, the same of white, another blue stripe and 4 inches white; bind off. Sew on the collar. Underface the edges of the opening from the neck edge to a little below the opening with strong braid and have eyelets put in; also have two eyelets put in each side of the collar three-fourths of an inch apart. The latter are only to be used if it is desired to draw the collar close to the neck. Close the sweater with a lacing cord as shown in the picture.

At No. 7 the sweater is shown adjusted over the steel knitting needles for the body portion and three fine needles for the collar. Six ounces of worsted will be needed. Care must be taken in knitting the collar to make it just large enough to slip over the head.

For the Front Portion.—Cast on 180 stitches. Work the fancy pattern for 1½ inch. Now rib for 12 inches. Cast off 45 stitches, k 90, cast off 45.

For the Back Portion.—Knit exactly like front portion. Then lay the right sides of the portions evenly together and join by sewing the cast-off stitches on the shoulder edges together with over-and-over stitches; also sew the side-edges together from the lower edges far enough up to form arm's-eyes of the size required.

For the Neck.—(See No. 9.) Knit with the rest of stitches all around like a stocking with the

No. 12.

No. 13.

NOS. 12 AND 13.—BOYS' SWEATER, WITH DEEP SAILOR COLLAR. (BREAST MEASURE, 24 INCHES.)

(For Descriptions of Nos. 12 and 13, see Page 174.)

turtle-neck chest protector illustrated at No. 8 on page 170.

"TURTLE-NECK" CHEST PROTECTOR.

(For Illustrations see Page 170.)

NOS. 8 AND 9.—This chest protector is to be worn with sweaters having sailor or open collars, as such sweaters require this extra portion in cooler weather. If the collar portion is omitted the "turtle" may be worn as an ordinary chest protector. It may be left adjustable or sewed to the arms' eyes as preferred. The model was 40 inches breast measure.

Use German knitting worsted and medium-sized three finer needles for 6½ to 7 inches, including one inch of the fancy pattern for the edge. Bind off loosely, and turn the neck-portion over as illustrated at No. 8.

YOUTHS' SWEATER, WITH DEEP SAILOR COLLAR. (BREAST MEASURE, 30 INCHES.)

(For Illustrations see Page 171.)

NOS. 10 AND 11.—This sweater was made of white and blue knitting worsted, the stripes being made of blue. Thirteen ounces of white and about one ounce of blue will be needed. Fine knitting needles were used for the wrists and medium-sized needles for the rest of the sweater.

To Make the Front Body Portion.—Cast on 160 stitches and work in fancy pattern for 1¼ inch with white, 6 rows blue, 1 inch white. Now rib for 12½ inches. Then divide the stitches so that ½ of them will be on one needle; this is to form the opening in the front. Now work only with 80 stitches. Rib for ¾ inch, then narrow thus: Rib to within 6 stitches of end of needle nearest the arm's-eye edge, k 3 to., rib the other 3 stitches, turn, rib back; repeat the last-two rows twice more,

To Make the Sleeve.—Take up 125 stitches around the arm's-eye on three medium-sized steel knitting needles and rib the sleeve like a stocking, making the seam stitch in line with the under-arm seam, purling it in one round and knitting it in the next one. Rib for 2½ inches, then narrow thus: K 3 to. when within 3 stitches of the seam stitch at each side of it every sixth round, for five times. Rib for 4¾ inches, narrow as before at each side of the seam-stitch every sixth round, for five times; rib for

No. 14.—Boys' Sweater, with Removable Shield.

No. 15.—Knitted Sweater for a Boy.

(For Descriptions of Nos. 14 and 15, see Page 174.)

then rib for 4½ inches more. Now the narrowing along the neck edge is made as follows: Rib for 3½ inches and narrow in every row thus: Rib 4 stitches, k 2 to., rib across, turn, rib back to within 6 stitches, narrow, rib 4 stitches, repeat last 2 rows till 22 stitches are narrowed off, then bind off. Knit the other side of the front the same way.

To Make the Back Body Portion.—Cast on 160 stitches and knit the stripes same as in front portion. Then rib for 18 inches. Now rib for 4 inches more, narrowing 2 stitches at each side thus: Rib 4 stitches, k 3 to., rib across to within 7 stitches, k 3, rib 4 stitches, turn, rib back without narrowing; repeat these last two rows till there are 58 stitches on each side narrowed off. When the four inches are finished measure the front and back, and if the back is not long enough add a few rows, then bind off. Sew the front and back portions together from the lower edge for 16¼ inches at each side. Join the shoulder edges with over-and-over stitches; the arm's-eyes will now be formed.

No. 16.—Sweater for Infants from Six to Twelve Months Old.

(For Description of No. 16, see Page 175.)

1¼ inch. Now with the fine needles rib for 1¼ inch white, ¾ inch red, 1¼ inch white, and bind off.

To Make the Sailor-Collar.—Cast on 170 stitches, work in fancy pattern 1¼ inch white, ¾ inch blue, 1¼ inch white, ¾ inch blue, 8 inches white. Bind off and sew the collar to the neck; the ends must be even with the ends of the opening of front portion. If preferred, the collar may be made in rib stitch on the sweater by taking up the stitches around the neck edge and then knitting downward, reversing the order of the measurements and stripes as given above. Underface the edges of the opening from the neck edge to a little below the opening with strong braid and have eyelets put in; also have two eyelets put in each side of the collar about three-quarters of an inch apart to be used if the collar is desired close around the neck. Rib an underlap about 5½ inches long and 1½ inch wide, and sew one long edge a little back of the opening and the lower edge to position. Close the sweater with a lacing cord, as seen in the picture.

BOYS' SWEATER, WITH DEEP SAILOR COLLAR.
(BREAST MEASURE, 24 INCHES.)
(For Illustrations see Page 172.)

NOS. 12 AND 13.—This sweater was made of red and white knitting worsted, the stripes being made of the white. 9½ ounces of red and about one ounce of white will be needed. Fine knitting needles were used for the wrists and medium-sized needles for the rest of the sweater.

To Make the Front Body Portion.—Cast on 130 stitches, and work in fancy pattern 12 rows red, 6 rows white, 12 red, 4 white, 6 red. Now rib for 9 inches; then divide the stitches so that one half of them will be on one needle; this is to form the opening; work only with the 65 stitches; rib for one inch on one of the needles, then narrow one stitch in each of the following six rows at the end of the needle nearest the arm's-eye edge. Rib without narrowing for 3¼ inches; then rib for 3¾ inches more, narrowing one stitch every row at the end of the needle nearest the neck edge thus : Rib 4 stitches, narrow, rib across, turn, rib back to within 6 stitches, narrow, rib 4 stitches; repeat these last two rows till 17 stitches are narrowed off; then bind off. Knit the other side the same way.

To Make the Back Body Portion.—Cast on 130 stitches and knit the stripes the same as in the front portion; then rib for 13½ inches. Now rib for 3¾ inches, narrowing two stitches at each side thus: Rib 4 stitches, k 3 to., rib across to within 7 stitches, k 3 to., rib 4 stitches, turn, rib back without narrowing; repeat these last two rows till there are 40 stitches narrowed off on each side. When the 3¾ inches are finished, measure the front and back and, if the back is not long enough, add a few rows, then bind off. Sew the shoulder edges neatly together on the wrong side with over-and-over stitches. Sew the front and back portions together from the lower edge for 12½ inches at each side ; the arm's-eyes will now be formed.

To Make the Sleeves.—Take up about 90 stitches around each arm's-eye on three medium-sized steel knitting needles; knit the sleeve like a stocking, making the seam stitch in line with the under-arm seam, purling it in one round and knitting it in the next one. Rib for two inches, then narrow thus : Knit 3 together when within 3 stitches of the seam stitch at each side, narrow every sixth round, for five times. Rib 2½ inches, narrow as before at each side of the seam stitch every sixth round, for 5 times. Rib one inch more. Then with the fine needles, rib three-fourths of an inch red, 4 rows white, three-fourths of an inch red, 6 rows white, three-fourths of an inch red and bind off.

To Make the Sailor Collar.—Cast on 140 stitches. Work in fancy pattern 1½ inch red, 1 inch white, 1¼ inch red, ½ inch white. 1½ inch red, 4 rows white, and about 4½ inches red; bind off and sew the collar to the neck; the ends must be even with the ends of the opening in the front portion. If preferred the collar may be made in rib stitch on the sweater by taking up the stitches around the neck edge and then knitting downward. reversing the order of the measurements and stripes as given above.

Underface the edges of the opening from the neck edge to a little below the opening with strong braid, and have eyelets put in; also have two eyelets put in each side of the collar about three-fourths of an inch apart to be used if the collar is desired close around the neck. Close the sweater with a lacing cord as shown in the picture.

BOYS' SWEATER, WITH REMOVABLE SHIELD.
(SUITABLE FOR A BOY OF 8 YEARS.)
(For Illustration see Page 172.)

NO. 11.—The sweater here illustrated was made of red German knitting worsted, with white wool for the stripes and shield. Of the red 9½ ounces will be needed; of the white about one ounce. Fine steel needles were used for the wrist, and medium-sized steel needles for the rest of the sweater.

To Make the Front Body Portion.—With the red cast on 140 stitches; work the fancy pattern for 6 rows: then 4 rows white, 6 rows red, 4 rows white, and 4 rows red. Now with the red rib 13 inches. Divide the stitches in two parts so that there will be 70 stitches on each needle. (This is to form the opening.) Rib back and forth on one of the needles having 70 stitches for 7 inches, and narrow every other row at the end of the needle where the division was made, till there are 32 stitches left; bind off when the required length is reached. Work the other side the same way.

To Make the Back Body Portion.—Cast on 140 stitches, work same as front, omitting opening, until it is six rows shorter than the front portion. Then rib 32 stitches and cast off 76. Next knit 6 rows with each of the needles having 32 stitches, and bind off. Sew the shoulder edges neatly together on the wrong side. Count from this seam 45 stitches each down the front and back body portion for the arm's-eyes, and sew the portions together below these 90 stitches, with the lower edges evenly together.

To Make the Sleeves.—Take up the 90 stitches around each arm's-eye on three medium-sized steel needles, and knit the sleeve like a stocking. Make the seam stitch in line with the under-arm seam; this stitch is purled in one round and knitted in the next one. Knit for 4½ inches, then narrow one stitch at each side of the seam stitch two stitches from it, for three times. Then knit for 4½ inches; narrow again as before, three times. Then work for 4 inches. Now use the fine steel needles. Rib 8 rounds red, 8 white, 8 red, 8 white, 6 red, and then 6 of fancy pattern, also in red.

To Make the Sailor-Collar.—Cast on 130 stitches and knit fancy pattern, 8 rows red, 4 rows white, 6 red, 4 white. Then work for 6 inches. Work 40 stitches, cast off 50. Work on one of the needles with the 40 stitches back and forth, narrowing one stitch at the end of the needle nearest the cast off stitches every row for 6 times. Then work for 4 inches. Then narrow at the side you narrowed before, every other row, till there are but 10 stitches left. Now measure the collar from the center of the back to the center of the front with its center at that of the back, and if it is not long enough add sufficient rows. Knit the other side the same way, and sew on the collar with over-and-over stitches.

To Make the Shield.—Cast on 40 stitches with the white worsted and work in fancy pattern for 44 rows, narrowing every fourth row at each end of the needle. Bind off the rest of stitches and secure the shield to the sweater with hooks and loops.

To Make the Pocket.—Cast on 20 stitches; work 4 rows fancy; rib 14 rows. Then * k 1, n, rib across the needle to within 3 stitches, n, k 1.

Next row.—Plain. Repeat from * till there is but one stitch left and sew the pocket to the left side as seen in the picture. Arrange a lanyard around the neck beneath the collar and slip the whistle in the pocket.

KNITTED SWEATER FOR A BOY.

(For Illustration see Page 173.)

No. 15.—This sweater is for a boy from ten to twelve years of age, and is knit from four-threaded German knitting wool. One ounce of white and 12 ounces of crimson yarn are required. Six No. 13 steel needles, and four very fine ones are required in knitting the sweater.

A deep crimson and white makes a pleasing combination.

To Make the Body.—With the crimson wool cast 192 stitches on four of the coarse needles; join, and knit 1, purl 1, the entire way around. (The garment is thus knit in ribs, the entire work being done by knitting 1 and purling 1. This must be kept in mind as the work will be spoken of as ribbing.) With the crimson rib 14 rows; join on the white wool and rib 7 rows; join on crimson wool and rib 7 rows; then 7 more rows of white and 105 rows of crimson. Take off 96 stitches on another needle, and with the remaining 96 stitches rib 60 rows. Take up the other 96 stitches and rib 60 rows on them.

Now join the two sides and knit entirely around twice. On the third round narrow four times, once on each side of each shoulder seam; knit 3 rows, and narrow as before. Continue to do this until

there are but 120 stitches left, then rib 18 rows and join on the white wool; rib alternately 5 rounds white and 5 rounds red till there are 8 stripes in all, the red being last, and bind off as loosely as possible. This completes the body and rolling collar.

To Make the Sleeves.—Take up 12 stitches on each side of the shoulder seam, and knit across once, then take up one stitch at the end of each row, until there are 88 stitches on the needles. Take up the remaining 32 stitches at the under side of the arm's-eye, and rib entirely around. Rib 75 rows, then narrow twice directly under the arm; rib 3 rows and then narrow twice again at the same place. Continue to do this until there are but 88 stitches left on the needles. Rib 7 rows, then, with the fine needles, rib 36 rows for the wrist. Bind off loosely. This finishes one sleeve, and the other is ribbed in a like manner. Thread a darning needle with the crimson wool, and darn in at the shoulder seams and where the sleeves join the body. These are the weak places. Be sure to leave the ends of the wool loose, so they will not draw when the garment is put on.

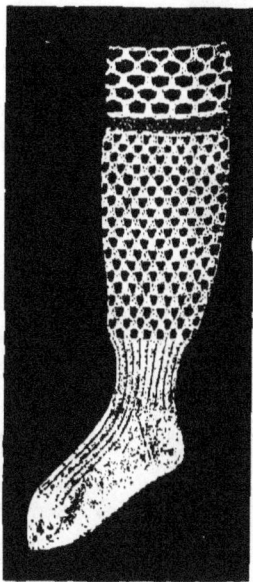

No. 17.—FANCY CYCLING OR GOLF STOCKING FOR LADIES OR GENTLEMEN.

(For Description see Page 176.)

SWEATER FOR INFANTS FROM SIX TO TWELVE MONTHS OLD.

(For Illustration see Page 173.)

No. 16.—Use 4½ ounces of the German knitting worsted, fine steel needles for the neck and wrists, and medium-sized needles for the rest of the sweater.

To Make the Front Body Portion.—Cast on 100 stitches. Knit 3¾ inches in fancy pattern. Then rib for 9 inches. Now make 2 button-holes in the next row thus: rib 4, sl and bind 2, rib 3, sl and bind 2, rib to end of needle, turn. Rib back and put thread over needle twice wherever 2 stitches have been bound off in last row, and rib for two rows more. Now use the fine needles, bind off 15 stitches, rib to within 15 stitches and bind off the latter off.

To Make the Back Body Portion.—Work exactly as for front, except that you omit the button-holes.

For the Collar.—Work with the fine needles on all the remaining stitches, thus: Begin to rib on right-hand side of front portion, rib to correspond··

ing side of back portion, turn. Rib back on wrong side; this will form an opening on the left shoulder. Rib back and forth for 3 inches, making one but-

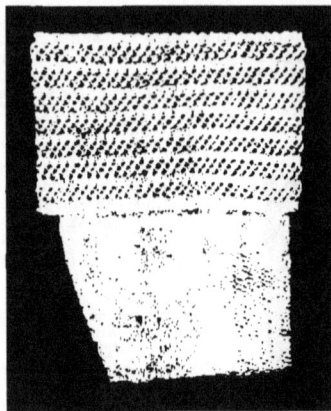

No 18.—BICYCLE HOSE, WITH FANCY TOP AND FRONT STRIPE.

(For Description see Page 177.)

ton-hole at the 6th row 4 stitches back of the edge; make 2 more button-holes ¾ inch apart. Work 6 rows of fancy pattern, making another button-hole at the second row, and bind off. Turn the collar over on the outside so that the first and fourth and the second and third button-holes will evenly meet, and tack them thus with over-and-over stitches. Sew buttons to the opposite edge of the opening to correspond with the button-holes in the front edge, and tack the arm's-eye edges of the shoulder opening together. Count from the shoulder edge down 35 stitches from the front and 35 stitches from back body portion for the arm's-eye, and sew the portions below these 70 stitches together with their lower edges even.

To Make the Sleeve.—Take up the 70 stitches around the arm's-eye on three medium-sized needles and knit the sleeve like a stocking. Make the seam stitch in line with the under-arm seam, purling it in one round and knitting it in the next one. Rib for 1¾ inch. * Then rib to within 6 stitches of the seam stitch, knit 3 together, rib 3 stitches, make the seam stitch, rib 3 stitches, and knit 3 together*; rib 4 rows and repeat once more between stars. Rib for 3 inches, then narrow again every fifth round for three times as before. Rib for 1¾ inch more. Now, with the fine needles, rib for 2½ inches and bind off. Knit an underlap about 2½ inches long and 1½ inch wide, and sew it to the left shoulder edge of the back portion.

STOCKINGS.

The golf and cycling stockings illustrated on preceding and following pages, though designed for games and wheeling, may be used for other or ordinary purposes. In stockings having fancy tops worked with two or more colors, care must be taken to always have the thread you are working with above the one previously used, and also to leave the threads which are carried along the wrong side of the work quite loose in order to keep the work from drawing. Any top preferred may be used with any of the stockings described, but the stitches of the tops and legs must be the same in number.

FANCY CYCLING OR GOLF STOCKING FOR LADIES OR GENTLEMEN.

(For Illustration see Page 175.)

No. 17.—Spanish yarn in Havana Brown and écru are used for this stocking.

With the brown yarn cast 90 stitches on 4 medium-sized needles. P 1, k 1 for 3 inches. 10 stitches must be gained or "made" in the last row so that there will be 100 stitches on the four needles. P 1, k 1 for 9 rounds. Knit 7 rounds plain. P 1, k 1 for 9 rounds. Now begin knitting with the two colors. With the écru, k 1 round, p 2 rounds. Next knit * 6 brown rounds; k 1 écru round. * P 8 stitches with écru. Now knit the fancy stitches, which are made the same way throughout the stocking. The stitches which pull up other stitches to form the fancy pattern (see following directions) must be very loose so the work will not appear drawn. Work as follows: the thread must be in front

No. 19.—TOP FOR BICYCLE STOCKING

(For Description see Page 177.)

of the needle; slip next stitch from left to right-hand needle with needle inserted same as for purling. Then pick up in the last row of the écru stripe below, the stitch which is below the stitch just slipped from left-hand needle. Now slip the stitch just picked up and the next stitch which was slipped from needle onto the left hand needle, and purl those two stitches very loosely together; make out of next écru stitch another fancy stitch in the same way; repeat from second * all around; p 1 round écru; repeat 4 times more from first *. In the following rows work the fancy stitches in the 4th and 5th stitch of the 8 écru purled stitches below. (See illustration.)

Then knit 1 round brown; in this round two stitches must be gained; there will now be 102 stitches on the needles. With the brown p 1, k 1 for 8 rounds. This finishes the top.

With the écru, k 1 round and p 2 rounds. With the brown **k 5 rounds; with the écru, k 1 round, * p 4 stitches, make the 2 fancy stitches as before; repeat from single * all round; p 1 round. With the brown, k 5 rounds; with the écru, k 1 round p 2 stitches; make the fancy stitches in the second and third of the four écru purl stitches below, * purl 4 stitch-es, make the fancy stitches and repeat from last * all around; purl 1 round and repeat from ** for the rest of the leg por-tion, always making the fancy stitches in the second and third of the four écru purled stitches below. After the fourth écru stripe is finished begin to narrow 6 stitches in the 5 brown rounds as fol-lows: The stitches above the second and third of the four purled stitches below indicate or form the center of the stocking. In the first, third and fifth fol-lowing brown rounds narrow

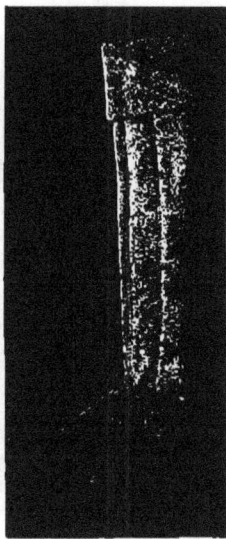

No. 20.—GENTLEMEN'S CYCLING STOCK-ING, WITH THIN FOOT.

(For Description see Page 178.)

at each side of these two center stitches. The next time the fancy stitch is made, skip the 4 écru purl stitches below the narrows and work the fancy

stitches in the next four écru purl stitches below. Narrow 6 stitches the same way at the tenth, fif-teenth and nineteenth brown stripes; one narrow-ing must be exactly above the other. Knit rest of stocking with écru. When the last narrowing is made, p 2, k 2 for 3½ inches. Or, if preferred, the fancy stitches may be continued to the heel. Divide the stitches so that 36 stitches will be on one needle for the heel, and keep the center of the stocking in the middle of that needle. Knit across, turn, * sl 1, k 1, purl across to within 2 stitches, k 1, p 1, turn, sl 1, knit across and repeat from * till there are 16 loops on each side. Knit across 21 stitches, n, k 1, turn, sl 1, purl back on wrong side 7 stitches, n, p 1, turn, * knit across to the stitch succeeding the last nar-rowing, n, k 1, turn, purl back to stitch succeeding the last narrowing, n, p 1, turn, repeat from *till the remaining stitches on each side of needle are all used. Pick up the loops on left hand side, p 2, k 2 across the instep; knit in this way on instep till the narrowing for the toe begins. The sole is to be

No. 21.—FOOTLESS GOLF OR BICYCLE STOCKING.

(For Description see Page 179.)

knitted plain; then pick up the loops on the right-hand side and narrow one stitch every other round for seven times just where the heel begins. Then work for 3½ inches. Divide the stitches so that the stitches for the instep are on two needles and the stitches for the sole are on two. Then, narrow every other round at the beginning of the first and end of the second needle for the instep, and at the beginning of the first and end of second needle for the sole; always have two plain stitches between the narrows. Narrow this way till there are 6 stitches left. Bind off and secure thread on wrong side.

BICYCLE HOSE, WITH FANCY TOP AND FRONT STRIPE.

(For Illustration see Page 176.)

No. 18.—Cast 40 stitches on each of three medium sized steel knitting needles, using thread of corre-sponding size.

Knit the first round plain; then knit 2, purl 2 for 5 rounds.

Then, over, narrow, over, narrow all of one round. Knit the next round plain. Continue to thus alternate for 6 rounds. Knit 3 rounds plain. Then, over and narrow, and knit plain, alternately, for 6 rounds; knit plain for 3 rounds till 6 open stripes have been finished. Now, knit 10

No. 22.—GOLF STOCKING.
(For Description see Page 180.)

rounds plain. The work must now be turned on the needles, wrong side out, to begin the plain part of the stocking. The wrong side will now be the right side. Knit 2 plain rounds, purling 1 stitch in the middle of one needle for the seam. Knit plain and narrow 1 stitch on each side of the seam, every 4 rounds, till 10 stitches have been narrowed off. Knit plain for 3 inches, then begin to narrow every 4 rounds on each side of the seam stitch and thus narrow till 12 stitches are narrowed off.

Divide the stitches, so that by exact measurement 20 stitches will come directly in front, measured from the seam stitch. These 20 stitches will form the pin-checked stripe down the front; knit plain, purl the seam stitch, and when the 20 stitches are in hand work across them thus: Knit 1, purl 1; reverse in the next round by purling the knitted stitch and knitting the purled stitch. Alternate thus on every round across the fancy portion. Continue to narrow every 4 rounds till 12 more stitches have been narrowed off.

Knit 8 inches from where the narrows stop, being careful to knit 1, purl 1 as directed, for the stripe.

When the stocking, exclusive of the top or turned over part, measures 17 inches, divide the stitches so that one-half will be on one needle, for the heel. Knit plain on the right and purl on the wrong side till 3 inches are knitted. Then divide the stitches

evenly on 2 needles, knit them together and bind off. Pick up the selvedge stitches down the side of the heel, knit plain across the instep, and pick up the other selvedge stitches. Knit plain, narrowing one stitch on each side just where the heel begins, every other round till the instep measures one-half inch less than the ankle.

Knit plain for 4 inches and narrow 1 stitch on each end of each needle, every other round till only 6 stitches are left. Knit these together and bind off, securing the thread on the wrong side.

The size of the foot may be increased by narrowing off fewer stitches on each side of the heel.

The length of the foot may be increased by knitting a longer section between the narrows at the heel and the narrows for the toe.

TOP FOR BICYCLE STOCKING.
(For Illustration see Page 176.)

No. 19.—This top may be knitted in any contrasting color desired. The embroidery is done in regular cross-stitch such as used on canvas. Each row of knitted stitches corresponds to the squares in canvas (see picture), thus making the work very easy. Any pretty cross-stitch pattern may be used.

Brown and green yarn was chosen for the combination in the top illustrated which was knitted as follows: Cast on 106 stitches with the brown, and k 2, p 2 for six rounds. Then with the green k 2, p 2 for two rounds. Then k 2, p 2 for two rounds with brown; k 2, p 2 for two rounds with green. Then knit 17 rounds with the brown, 2 rounds with green, 2 rounds with brown, 2 rounds with green. Then knit 15 rounds brown. This finishes the top, which should be turned over on the stocking about half an inch above the last green round.

No. 23.—BICYCLE HOSE, WITH DOUBLE KNEE.
(For Description see Page 180.)

GENTLEMEN'S CYCLING STOCKING, WITH THIN FOOT.
(For Illustration see Page 177.)

No. 25.—This stocking is much liked by the masculine sex generally, as it takes up so much less room in the boot. The materials required are: 6 ounces coarse knitting worsted for the leg, 2 ounces 4-ply wool for the foot; four needles, No. 13; four, No. 15.

Cast 69 stitches with the coarse wool on No. 13 needles, 23 on each needle. Knit 5, purl 5, knitting and purling 1 over the other each round to form a diagonal stripe. When the top is finished, turn the work inside out, and begin on the needle you have just finished. Knit 1 plain round; in this round you narrow 3 times, once on each needle.

To Knit Leg.—First back needle: knit 18, purl 3. Second back needle: knit 18, purl 3. Front needle: knit 9, purl 3, knit 9, purl 3.

Next round.—First back needle: knit 18, purl 1, knit 1, purl 1. Second back needle: knit 18, purl 1, knit 1, purl 1. Front needle: knit 9, purl 1, knit 1, purl 1, knit 9, purl 1, knit 1, purl 1. Repeat these 2 rounds until the leg (including top) measures 8¼ inches. Now narrow for ankle. First back needle: knit 15, knit 2 together, knit 1; do the rib. Second back needle: knit 1, knit 2 together, knit 15. There must be 9 narrowings, and 6 plain rounds between each narrowing; then knit as before until leg measures 23 inches.

Now divide for heel, having 25 stitches on the back needle; make the middle stitch the seam stitch. Knit and purl these 25 stitches (always slipping the first) until flap measures 3½ inches. Knit 14, knit 2 together, knit 1. Turn, slip first stitch, purl 4, purl 2 together, purl 1. Turn, and repeat until only 7 stitches are left. Now join on the wool for the foot and take No. 15 needles. Pick up 24 or 25 stitches on each side of the heel. Do 4 plain rounds. First back needle: knit 1, slip 1, knit 1, pass the slipped stitch over the knitted one; knit rest plain. Second needle: knit to within the last 3 stitches, knit 2 together, knit 1. There should be 5 narrowings and 2 plain rounds between each. Now knit as before (keeping the pattern on front needle) until foot measures 8 inches, then narrow for toe. Front needle: knit 1, slip 1, knit 1, pass the slipped stitch over the knitted one; knit plain to within the last 3 stitches, knit 2 together, knit 1. First back needle: knit 1, slip 1, knit 1, pass the slipped stitch over the knitted one, knit rest plain. Second back needle: knit to within the last 3 stitches, knit 2 together, knit 1, knit 2 plain rounds between each narrowing, and narrow until there are only 25 stitches left. Cast off, and sew up. Turn

the top down on outside as seen in the picture.

FOOTLESS GOLF OR BICYCLE STOCKING.

(For Illustration see Page 177.)

No. 21.—Footless stockings may be worn over a thin pair of cotton hose by those who find wool stockings uncomfortable. The one illustrated is made of black, old-rose and mixed gray wool. For the old-rose any other color preferred may be used, green being a popular color.

To Make the Top.—Cast 128 stitches on three needles, using black yarn. P 1 and k 1 for 6 rounds; then alternate 2 rounds of old-rose (or any preferred color) and 2 rounds of black, 3 times. (See picture.) Next, * p 1 and k 1 for 31 stitches with the black; then 1 st. of old-rose, which must be a plain stitch, and repeat from * all around. Next round, * p 1 and k 1 for 27 stitches with black; then 5 stitches of old-rose and repeat from * all around. P 1 and k 1 in the same way in every round, being careful to add 2 stitches of the old-rose in every round at each side of the old-rose square until you have 29 old-rose stitches with 3 black stitches between each old-rose square. Now decrease the colored stitches and increase the black ones by knitting in every round 2 stitches less of old-rose at each side of the square, until there is only 1 old-rose stitch left. Then alternate again two rounds of old-rose and two of black, 3 times, as at beginning. Break off the old-rose thread and knit rest of the top black, thus: K 1, p 1 for 12 rounds; then narrow every 5th stitch until there are just 100 stitches on the three needles. Now

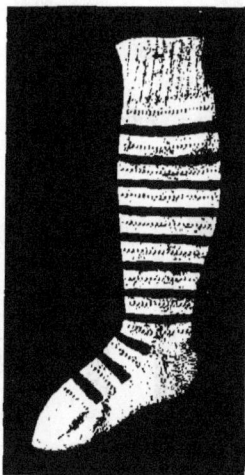

No. 24.—CYCLE OR GOLF STOCKING FOR LADIES OR GENTLEMEN.

(For Description see Page 181.)

turn the work inside out and proceed to knit the leg portion in the manner described below. The part just knitted forms the turn-over shown at the top of the stocking. It will be wrong side out while the leg proper is being knitted, but turns over right side out when the work is completed, as may be seen in the picture.

To Make the Leg.—With the black yarn now k 4, p 1 for 6 rounds, and then break off the black and knit the rest of the stocking in mixed gray, thus: K 4, p 1 for 8 inches. Ascertain the center of the stocking and narrow every 6 rounds at each side of this center for 9 times. Knit for 5 inches and then narrow once at the center of the front and back of the stocking. Now divide the stitches on two needles so that the stitches from the center of the back on each side to the center of the front will be on one needle. Knit across on one of the two needles and then * p back and k across, p back and k across, p back; now k 1, k 3 to., knit across to within 4 stitches, then k 3 to., k 1; repeat from* 4 times more. The n knit across and p back for 12 rows and bind off. Knit the other side to correspond, and join the ends by sewing over-and-over. If preferred, the two ends may be joined by "binding-off," as in a heel. If the opening is desired larger, a few more rows may be added at the ends.

GOLF STOCKING.
(For Illustration see Page 178.)

No. 22.—Cast 110 stitches on three medium-sized needles, with yarn as heavy as single zephyr, and knit one round plain. Then knit 5, purl 5, for 5 rounds. Reverse, and purl 5, knit 5, for 5 rounds. This forms the "plaid" or "checkerboard" design. Continue to knit the squares for 9 inches, and then narrow one stitch on each side of the middle stitch of one of the needles, purling this stitch for the seam. Continue to knit in squares as before described, then narrow again one stitch on each side of the purled seam-stitch every sixth round, and so on till 30 stitches have been narrowed off. This will leave 80 stitches. Continue to knit in squares until the hose measures 22 inches in length, and then divide the stitches so that one-half in even number will be on one needle, with the seam stitch in the middle. Knit plain across and purl back on this needle for 2½ inches. This makes the heel, which is closed as follows: Purl across to the seam stitch; then fold the right sides of the heel flatly together; now k 1; then k 2 stitches (one from each needle) together and bind the stitch previously knit over

them. Continue to do this until but one stitch is left. Pick up the selvedge stitches down one side of the heel. Knit across the instep and pick up the selvedge stitches along the other side of the heel. Knit plain, and narrow one stitch in every other round, just where the heel begins on each side, until you have again 80 stitches on the three needles. Knit plain till the foot measures 6 inches, and then begin the narrows for the toe by narrowing one stitch at the beginning and end of each needle in every other round, as follows: K 1, n, knit across the needle, except last 3 stitches, then n, k 1. Knit the alternate rounds plain and work in this way until you have 6 stitches left; knit them together and bind off, securing the end of the thread on the wrong side.

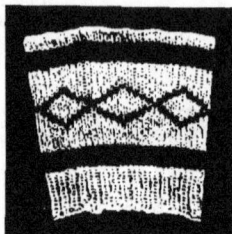

BICYCLE HOSE, WITH DOUBLE KNEE.
(For Illustration see Page 178.)

No. 23.—Cast 130 stitches on three medium-sized steel knitting needles and knit around plain. Knit 3, purl 3 for 5 rounds, and then begin to knit double for the knee as follows: knit 1, slip 1, for 1 round; in the next round the stitches are reversed thus: slip the knitted stitch and knit the slipped stitch. Continue thus to alternate for 1½ inch, when 1 stitch on each side of the middle stitch on one needle must be narrowed every 4 rounds till 10 stitches have been narrowed off.

Continue to knit 1, slip 1, and reverse as before for 5½ inches, when begin to purl 4, knit 4 and thus work for 5 inches. Then narrow one on each side of the center stitch (which must now be purled for the seam) every 5 rounds for 5 inches, or until 32 stitches have been narrowed off.

This brings the leg to the size for the ankle—88 stitches. Continue to purl 4, knit 4, for 6 inches, and then divide the stitches so that one-half will be

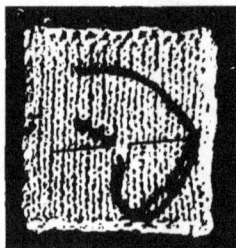

No. 25.—TOP FOR BICYCLE STOCKING.

Nos. 26 AND 27.—DETAILS FOR EMBROIDERING TOP.

(For Descriptions see Pages 181 and 182.)

on one needle for the heel. Knit plain across on this needle and purl back on the wrong side for 2½ inches and purl to center of needle. Fold the right side of the heel flatly together so that the stitches on the two needles are even; then k 1, k 2 stitches (1 from each needle) together and bind the stitch previously knitted over them; continue till but one stitch is left. Pick up the selvedge stitches and knit across plain, then pick up the other selvedge stitches. Then knit plain, narrowing 1 stitch, every other round on each side just where the heel begins, till there are as many stitches as just before beginning the heel. Knit plain till the foot measures 6 inches from the inside of the heel; then narrow at the beginning and end of each needle as follows: K 1, n, k plain across the needle, except 3 stitches; then, n, k 1. Repeat every other round, knitting the alternate rounds plain, until there are 6 stitches left; bind off these, securing the thread on the wrong side.

Cycle or Golf Stocking for Ladies or Gentlemen.

(For Illustration see Page 181.)

No. 24.—The stocking here illustrated is made of Spanish yarn in black and gray; four medium steel needles were used. The following directions provide for two lengths so that the stocking may be made to wear above or below the knee.

For the shorter stocking cast on 94 stitches with the gray yarn and p 1, k 1 for 2½ inches. Then knit 1 round plain; in this round 6 stitches must be gained, so that there will be 100 stitches on the four needles. For the longer stocking cast 100 stitches on four needles and knit one round plain. The remainder of the directions will be for either length. * O twice, p 2 to., k 3, all round. Next round plain. Repeat from * for four inches. * Next 7 rounds plain. Then o twice, p 2 to. all round. Then 7 rounds plain. Now begin to knit with black yarn. Knit 1 round plain, purl for 6 rounds, repeat from last * till the heel is reached. If a long stocking is desired, the narrowing begins at the center of the fourth black stripe; if a short stocking, at the center of the third stripe. Ascertain the center of the stocking, leaving two stitches between the narrowings, which will indicate the center, and narrow every 7th round at each side of this center for 11 times. Then knit until there are 8 stripes in all for the longer stocking, or 7 for the shorter stocking.

Then begin the heel at the top of the plain gray knitting. Now divide the stitches so that there will be 38 stitches on one needle for the heel. Keep the center stitches in the middle of that needle and purl on the right side and knit back on

the wrong side of work until there are 18 loops on each side; then purl across 22 stitches, n, k 1, turn, sl 1, k 7, n, k 1, turn, * sl 1, purl across and purl together the stitch following with the next of the stitches left on needle, p 1, turn, sl 1, k back, and knit together the stitch following the last narrowing with the next stitch; k 1 and repeat from * until all the stitches on both sides of the needle are used. Pick up every loop on left-hand side. Discontinue the work here, but do not break off the yarn; fasten another thread at the first loop on the right hand side of the heel, and pick up every loop; knit across the gusset to the last loop on left-hand needle, and break off this thread; now work with the thread which was left at the first loop on the left-hand side, beginning thus: Purl across on wrong side, turn and sl 1, n, knit across the two needles for the sole to within three stitches; n, k 1, narrow in this way every other round for 12 times. When there are seven rows knitted on the two sole needles, begin to knit on the two instep needles with the black yarn; knit across the two instep needles, turn, * sl 1, k back on the wrong side, turn, sl 1, p across on right side, turn, repeat from * for seven rows in all; break off the black yarn, leaving about seven inches. Knit the other two black stripes the same way *; now knit all around the foot on the four needles for 15 rows with the gray, being careful to keep the open pattern on the two instep needles between the seven rows. Then with the gray purl on wrong side with the two needles for the sole. Knit across and purl back that way for seven rows. Then with the black purl on right side and knit on wrong side of work for seven rows on the two instep needles, as before; repeat once more from *; knit the rest all in gray. Knit around on four needles for 15 rounds, making the open pattern between the seven rows only on the two instep needles. Now the narrowing begins at the first of the two instep needles, thus: K 2, n, knit across the two instep needles to within four stitches of the end of second instep needle, n, k 2. First sole needle: k 2, n, knit across the two sole needles to within 4 stitches from the end of second sole needle, n, k 2. Narrow this way every other round till 6 stitches are left. Bind off and secure the thread on the wrong side. If the shorter stocking has been knitted, turn the plain part and three-fourths of an inch of the fancy top inside the stocking, and tack it to place at short intervals.

Top for Bicycle Stocking.

(For Illustration see Page 180.)

No. 25.—The design here illustrated was made of

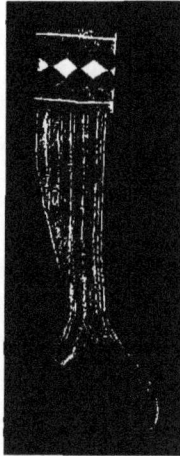

No. 28.—Ladies' Bicycle Stocking, with Fancy Top.

(For Description see Page 182.)

brown and red wool as follows: Cast on 80 stitches with brown wool. P 1, k 1 for 12 rounds. Now, k 6 rounds with the red wool. Next k 25 rounds with the brown, then 6 rounds with the red, 20 rounds with brown wool. This top can be used for any bicycle stocking and should be turned over about half an inch above the upper red rounds. The decoration is worked in brown in a fancy stitch. Details of the latter are seen at Nos. 26 and 27, which make the method of working perfectly clear.

LADIES' BICYCLE STOCKING, WITH FANCY TOP.
(For Illustration see Page 181.)

No. 28.—This stocking is made of Spanish yarn in gray, white and black.
To Make the Top. — Cast 96 stitches on 4 medium-sized knitting needles. Knit 40 rounds in gray, 2 rounds in white, 15 rounds in gray, 2 rounds in white, and 7 rounds in gray. Now the squares begin and are knitted in two colors, as follows :
First round.—Knit 15 stitches with the gray, 1 with the black and repeat all the way round.
Second round.—K 13 gray, 3 black, and repeat all round, increasing the black squares 1 stitch at each side the same as in the previous rows. At the 8th round there will be 15 black stitches and 1 gray.
Ninth round.—Black.
Tenth round. — Decrease the black squares 1 stitch on each side in every round; k 15 black, 1 white.
Eleventh round.—K 13 black, 3 white, all round; knit the same until the 17th round is reached; then k 15 white, 1 black.
Eighteenth round.—K 3 black, 13 white. Decrease the white and increase the black as before until the 24th round is reached.
Twenty-fourth round. — K 15 black, 1 white.
Twenty-fifth round. — Black.
Twenty-sixth round. — K 15 black, 1 gray.
Twenty-seventh round.—K 13 black, 3 gray ; decrease as before until there is but 1 black stitch; this finishes the squares. Then k 7 rounds gray, 2 rounds white, 15 rounds gray, 2 rounds white; break off the white; 12 rounds gray. Then bind off very loosely. Fold the work with the wrong sides together at the center (seventh row) between the two white stripes at the top and bottom. When the work is carefully folded, sew the cast-on stitches together with the corresponding bound-off stitches on the right side of the work with over-and-over stitches. Use an embroidery needle for the purpose. Take up 96 stitches out of the other side of stitches just sewed together, thus : Put the needle in each stitch and knit each as it is taken up until

you have 96 stitches. Now begin to knit the stocking. Be very careful to continue the knitting beyond the 40 rounds of plain gray knitting; this brings the top wrong side out but it will be turned over when the stocking is finished. K 1 round plain. P 1, k 1 for two inches. Then the pattern begins, and 14 stitches have also to be gained in order to preserve the uniformity of the pattern. Make 3 of these stitches on each of two needles and 4 of them on each of the other two needles. 110 stitches must now be on the needles.* K 1 (which will be the seam stitch) p 2, k 5, p 2; repeat from * all round. Knit that way for 5½ inches. Then the narrowings begin and if done according to the directions will add to the appearance of the stocking. The narrowings must be made at each side of the seam stitch, beginning at the right side as follows: N, p 2, knit the seam stitch, p 2, n; (the p 2, seam, p 2, must always be between the narrowings). Then narrow every 5th round till there are 6 narrowings on each side; now narrow every 4th round till there are 5 narrowings on each side; next narrow every 3rd round till there are 9 narrowings on each side; there must be 20 narrowings in all at each side, and 70 stitches on the needles. Now work for four inches. Take 35 stitches on one needle for the heel; the seam stitch must be in the center; knit back and forth on this needle, but keep the pattern same as before till you have 15 loops on each side. Then knit once across plain and purl back, k 21 stitches across, n, k 1, turn, slip 1, purl back 9 stitches, n, p 1, turn; there should be 7 stitches between the two narrowings just made; * slip 1, knit across to the stitch following the narrowing, and knit this stitch together with the next of the stitches left on needle; turn, slip 1, purl back to the stitch purled after the narrowing, and purl this stitch together with the next of the stitches left on the needle; repeat from * till all the stitches at each side of the needle are used. Pick up all the loops on the left-hand side and knit across the instep, keeping the pattern; then pick up the loops on the right-hand side. The pattern on the instep must be continued to the narrowing of the toe, while the sole is knitted plain. Narrow every other round just where the heel begins on each side for seven times; then work for 3½ inches. Now the narrowing for the toe begins at the first of the two instep needles, thus: K 1, n, k across to within 3 stitches of the second instep needle, n, k 1. First needle for sole: k 1, n, knit across and also to within 3 stitches of end of second needle for the sole, then n, k 1. Narrow this way every 3rd round until there are 6 stitches left

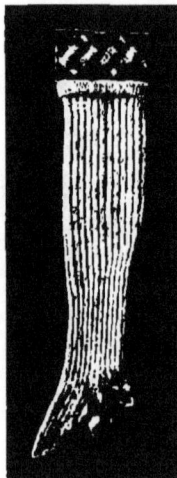

No. 29.—LADIES' FOOTLESS GOLF OR
BICYCLE STOCKING.

(For Description see Page 184.)

on each of two needles; bind off with a crochet needle by taking 2 stitches, (one from each needle) thread over and pull through the 2 stitches. Secure the thread on the wrong side.

LADIES' FOOTLESS GOLF OR BICYCLE STOCKING.
(For Illustration see Page 184.)

No. 29.—This stocking is made of brown knitting yarn, with a top of gray bordered with brown and with the decoration in green and red.

Any fancy stocking may be changed to the "footless" style by following or applying the principle of the directions given below the double star seen later on. The ribs at the instep may be knitted plain.

Cast 120 stitches on 4 needles with the brown; knit one round plain; p 1, k 1 for 22 rounds. For the next (24th) round knit each stitch on the needles together with the corresponding stitches originally cast on thus: Put the needle in the stitch on needle, then in the loop cast on and knit them together; then knit 3 rounds plain. Then, with the gray, knit 3 rounds. Now begin the decoration.

First round.—K 10 stitches with the gray yarn, 1 stitch with the red, 3 stitches with the gray, 1 stitch with the green, 9 stitches with the gray. Repeat all round.

Second round.—9 gray, 3 red, 1 gray, 3 green, 8 gray. Repeat.

Third round.—8 gray, 5 red, 4 green, 7 gray.

Fourth round.—7 gray, 7 red, 4 green, 6 gray.

Fifth round.—8 gray, 7 red, 2 green, 7 gray.

Sixth round.—9 gray, 7 red, 8 gray.

Seventh round.—4 gray, 1 red, 3 gray, 2 green, 7 red, 3 gray, 1 green, 3 gray.

Eighth round.—3 gray, 3 red, 1 gray, 4 green, 7 red, 1 gray, 3 green, 2 gray.

Ninth round.—2 gray, 4 red, 6 green, 6 red, 5 green, 1 gray.

Tenth round.—1 gray, 4 red, 7 green, 1 gray, 4 red, 7 green.

Eleventh round.—2 gray, 2 red, 7 green, 3 gray, 2 red, 7 green, 1 gray.

Twelfth round.—3 gray, 7 green, 5 gray, 7 green, 2 gray.

Thirteenth round.—2 gray, 7 green, 2 red, 3 gray, 7 green, 2 red, 1 gray.

Fourteenth round.—1 gray, 7 green, 4 red, 1 gray, 7 green, 4 red.

Fifteenth round.—2 gray, 5 green, 6 red, 6 green, 4 red, 1 gray.

Sixteenth round.—3 gray, 3 green, 1 gray, 7 red, 4 green, 1 gray, 3 red, 2 gray.

Seventeenth round.—4 gray, 1 green, 3 gray, 7 red, 2 green, 3 gray, 1 red, 3 gray.

Eighteenth round.—9 gray, 7 red, 8 gray.

Nineteenth round.—8 gray, 2 green, 7 red, 7 gray.

Twentieth round.—7 gray, 4 green, 7 red, 6 gray.

Twenty-first round.—8 gray, 4 green, 5 red, 7 gray.

Twenty-second round.—9 gray, 3 green, 1 gray, 3 red, 8 gray.

Twenty-third round.—10 gray, 1 green, 3 gray, 1 red, 9 gray. Knit 3 rounds plain with the gray. This finishes the decoration.

The rest of the stocking is knitted with the brown yarn. Knit 3 rounds plain. Purl 1, k 1 for 2 inches. Now turn the stocking inside out and proceed to knit the leg portion in the manner described below. The part just knitted forms the turn-over shown at the top of the stocking and it will be wrong side out while the leg portion is being knitted, but turns over right side out when the work is completed, as seen in the picture.

Purl for three rounds, knit 15 rounds plain; then p 1, k 4 all around; knit this way for 7½ inches. The narrowings begin at the center rib of the back of the stocking and end at the center rib in the front of the stocking. Make the first or center-back narrowing as follows: On one of the needles which begins, p 1, k 4, purl the purled stitch, k 1, sl. 1, k 1, pass slipped stitch over and k 1. This completes the first narrowing and the rib now consists of 1 purled stitch and 3 plain ones only.

All the narrowings are made the same way. * Knit 5 rounds. In the sixth round knit to the rib preceding the narrowed center rib, and narrow that rib as before; then knit to the rib following the narrowed center rib and narrow it; also repeat from *, always narrowing in every 6th round at each side of the previous narrowing until all the ribs, including the front center one, are narrowed. Then knit for four inches.

** Divide the stitches so that one half will be on one needle for the heel part; keep the center-back rib, (or center stitch in other stockings,) in the middle of that needle and knit only on this needle, same as for a heel; knit across on right side, and purl back on wrong side, till there are nine loops on each side. Stop working on this needle but do not break off the thread. Fasten a new thread at the top loop on left hand-side, and with another needle pick up the 9 loops on left-hand side, then p 1, k 3 across the two instep needles; with the second front needle pick up the nine loops on right-hand side. (The nine stitches just picked up on each side must be kept on the two instep

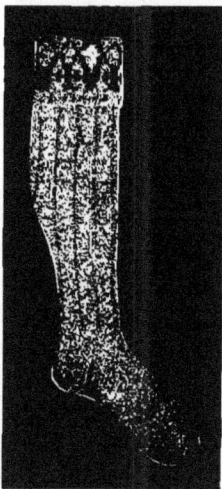

No. 30.—MEN'S GOLF OR BICYCLE STOCKING.
(For Description see Page 184.)

needles.) Proceed with the work now only on the two instep needles ; knit across and purl back thus : * Knit the nine picked up stitches plain ; p 1, k 3 across to the 9 picked up stitches which are to be knitted plain ; turn, slip 1 stitch, p 8 ; k 1, p 3 across to the 9 picked up stitches which must be purled ; repeat from * until 12 loops on each side are knitted. Then narrow in working across at the beginning of the first instep needle and at the end of the second instep needle, thus : * n, knit 7, then, p 1, k 3 across to the 9 plain stitches, knit 7, n, turn.

Next row.—Work back on wrong side, keeping the pattern, and repeat from * till there are only 4 ribs left, and bind off *very loosely.* Two stitches will be short after each narrowing, so care must be taken to keep the ribs as all through the preceding portion of the stocking. Now divide the stitches from the heel part on two needles, and pick up with the thread left before the 12 loops on left-hand side below the narrowing of part for the front of foot ; then purl across on wrong side of work and pick up the 12 loops on right-hand side. Knit across and purl back till there are five loops on each side. Now divide the stitches you are working with in three parts ; knit the first part, bind off the second part and knit the third part. Sl 1, purl back on the part where the thread is left (or to the side where the stitches have been bound off), turn, * n, knit across, turn ; sl 1, purl back and repeat from * till there are 12 stitches left. Now knit the corresponding part. * K across, narrow at the end of needle, turn ; sl 1, purl back and repeat from * till there are twelve stitches left. Now fold the right sides of the two parts just knitted together ; k 1, then knit two stitches (one from each needle) together and bind the stitch previously knitted over them ; continue till all the stitches are bound off. Work very loosely in single crochet twice around the lower edges to give extra strength.

No. 31.—BICYCLE HOSE, WITH SIMULATED LACING.
(For Description see Page 185.)

MEN'S GOLF OR BICYCLE STOCKING.

(For Illustration see Page 183.)

No. 30.—Coarse mixed yarn and fine brown yarn were used for the foundation of this stocking, while plain black and red were used for the decoration of the top. The foot is made of the fine brown wool.

To Make the Top.—Cast 100 stitches on 4 medium-sized knitting needles. P 2, k 2 for 6 rounds.

Seventh round.—Plain.

Eighth and Ninth rounds.—K 1 stitch with the black yarn, 7 with the brown, 3 with the red, 7 with the brown, 2 with the black.

Tenth and Eleventh rounds.—K 2 black, 5 brown, 5 red, 5 brown, 3 black.

Twelfth and Thirteenth rounds.—K 3 black, 2 brown, 2 red, 1 brown, 3 red, 1 brown, 2 red, 2 brown, 4 black.

Fourteenth and Fifteenth rounds.—K 3 black, 1 brown, 11 red, 1 brown, 4 black.

Sixteenth and Seventeenth rounds.—K 3 black, 2 brown, 2 red, 1 brown, 3 red, 1 brown, 2 red, 2 brown, 3 black, 1 brown.

Eighteenth and Nineteenth rounds.—K 3 black, 5 brown, 3 red, 5 brown, 3 black, 1 brown.

Twentieth and Twenty-first rounds.—K 1 brown, 3 black, 3 brown, 5 red, 3 brown, 3 black, 2 brown.

Twenty-second, Twenty-third and Twenty-fourth rounds.—K 2 brown, 3 black, 1 brown, 2 red, 3 brown 2 red, 1 brown, 3 black, 3 brown.

Twenty-fifth and Twenty-sixth rounds.—K 3 brown, 3 black, 1 red, 5 brown, 1 red, 3 black, 4 brown.

Twenty-seventh and Twenty-eighth rounds.—K 4 brown, 2 red, 1 black, 5 brown, 1 black, 2 red, 5 brown.

Twenty-ninth and Thirtieth rounds.—K 2 brown, 3 red, 1 brown, 2 black, 3 brown, 2 black, 1 brown, 3 red, 3 brown.

Thirty-first and Thirty-second rounds.—K 1 brown, 3 red, 3 brown, 2 black, 1 brown, 2 black, 3 brown, 3 red, 2 brown.

Thirty-third and Thirty-fourth rounds.—K 3 red, 5 brown, 3 black, 5 brown, 3 red, 1 brown.

Thirty-fifth round.—K 2 red, 7 brown, 1 black, 7 brown 3 red.

Thirty-sixth and Thirty-seventh rounds.—K 1 red, 8 brown, 1 black, 8 brown, 2 red. This ends the decoration.

Now begin with the mixed brown. Knit 10 rounds plain, but in the tenth round narrow 24 stitches, so that there will be 76 stitches on the four needles.

Now, *turn the work inside out* and proceed to knit the leg portion in the manner described below. The part just knitted forms the turn-over shown at the top of the stocking. It will be wrong side out while the leg portion is being knitted, but turns over right side out when the work is completed, as seen in the picture.

To Make the Leg.—K 4 (these 4 stitches form the seam and center of the stocking) ; * p 2, k 6 ; repeat all round from *. When 2½ inches are knitted, make 1 stitch between the 2nd and 3rd of the 4 stitches which formed the seam, to widen the leg ; after this make 1 more stitch every 8th round till there are 4 stitches gained ; there will now be 8 stitches for the center instead of 4. Then work 8

rounds. Now the narrowing begins at the center of the seam and all the other narrows *must be kept in the center*, one above the other. K 3 stitches, n, k 3. narrow in this way every other round till the 8 stitches are used. There will now be 4 purled stitches; narrow them the same way till they are used. There will now be 12 plain stitches; narrow them off in the same way till there are 3 stitches left; these will now form the center rib; this ends the narrowing. Work for 5½ inches, to where the heel begins. Divide the stitches so that 25 will be on one needle for the heel. Keep the three seam stitches in the middle of needle, and knit plain on the right side and purl on the wrong side until there are seven loops at each side. The rest of the heel and foot beyond the ribbing are to be knitted of the finer yarn. Fasten the thread and knit across and purl back as before till there are in all 17 loops on each side. Then knit across 18 stitches, n, k 1, turn, sl 1, purl back 9 stitches, n, p 1, turn, * sl 1, k across, knitting the stitch following the last narrowing together with the next of the stitches left on needle; k 1, turn, sl 1, purl back and knit the stitch following the last narrowing together with the next stitch, purl 1; repeat from * until all the stitches on each side of the needle are used; break off the thread. Fasten the thread at the first loop at the right side in the heel, and pick up the loops on the right-hand side; knit across the gusset and pick up the loops on the left hand side; * purl back on the wrong side, turn, sl 1, n, knit across the two sole needles to within 3 stitches, n, k 1; * turn, and repeat these two rows six times Purl back and knit across on the two sole needles until 50 rows are knitted. Now, with the brown mixed yarn begin the knitting on the two instep needles; work back and forth, keeping the ribs as before until you have exactly the same length as the sole part of the foot; break off the mixed yarn and knit plain all round

No. 32.—BICYCLE STOCKING IN DOUBLE STITCH..
(For Description see Page 186.)

with the plain brown yarn on the 4 needles for 3½ inches more. Now, the narrowing begins at the first of the two instep needles. K 1, n, knit across to within 3 stitches of the second instep needle, n, k 1. First sole needle: k 1, n, knit across; also knit across second sole needle to within 3 st. of the end, n, k 1. Narrow this way every other round until 6 stitches are left. Bind off with a crochet needle by taking 2 stitches (one from each needle) catch thread and pull through the 2 stitches. Secure the thread on wrong side.

BICYCLE HOSE, WITH SIMULATED LACING.
(For Illustration see Page 184.)

No. 31.—Cast 110 stitches on three medium-sized knitting needles with knitting silk or woollen yarn, and knit one round plain.

K 3, p 3 for 8 rounds; o, n, the next round. Then knit plain 1 round. O, n, another round, and knit another round plain, which will finish the edge.

Knit plain, but purl the middle stitch on one needle for the seam. When one inch is knitted, throw the thread over, to widen one stitch on each side of the seam. Knit the th o stitches plain in the next round. Continue thus to widen until 8 stitches have been added.

Knit plain, except the seam stitch, which must be purled the full length of the hose. When 5 inches have been knit, begin to narrow one stitch on each side of the seam stitch every 6th round until 28 stitches have been narrowed off.

This will shape the hose to fit the ankle. Knit plain, and when directly opposite the seam stitch by exact measure, throw the thread over, narrow, and in the next round knit these stitches plain. This will form the first eyelet in the diamonds down the front.

Knit plain until the eyelet is reached; then, th o, and knit

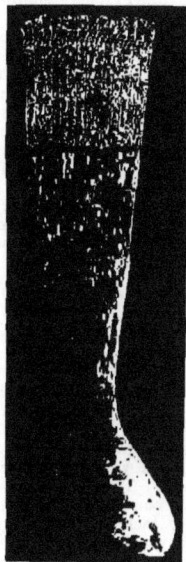

No. 33.—RIBBED BICYCLE STOCKING.
(For Description see Page 186.)

the stitch preceding the put-over in last row and the put-over together, to narrow. O and knit the next two stitches together to form second eyelet in this round. Knit the next row plain.

Be careful to narrow so that the eyelets at the left-hand side of the work will correspond with and be exactly opposite those of the right side. After you have five eyelets on each side knit plain, including first put-over from last row; then, th o, n, k plain, th o and knit stitch preceding the last put-over and the put-over together.

This completes the first diamond. Proceed with the remaining three as with the first. In the meantime the narrows on each side of the seam stitch must be continued till, in all, 28 stitches have been narrowed off, to shape the hose to the ankle. When four diamonds are knit, finish the last one with a single eyelet at the end like the first one made. Knit plain till the hose measures 15 inches. Divide the stitches so that one half, with the seam stitch in the middle, will be all on one needle, to form the heel. Knit across plain. Purl back across, and so continue till the heel measures 2½ inches. Then purl to center of needle. Fold the right sides of the heel flatly together so that the stitches on two needles lie even. Knit 1; k 2 (one from each needle) together, and bind the stitch previously knitted over them; continue till but 1 stitch is left.

Turn the heel and pick up the selvedge stitches down the side. Knit across plain and pick up the selvedge stitches on the opposite side of the heel. Knit plain, and narrow one stitch on each side every other round, just where the heel begins, until you have as many stitches as there were just before beginning the heel. Knit plain till the foot measures 6 inches from the inside of the heel. Then narrow at the beginning and end of each needle as follows: K 1, n, k plain across the needle except three stitches; then n, k 1. Repeat every other round, knitting the alternate rounds plain until there are six stitches left. Bind off these stitches and secure end of thread on wrong side.

BICYCLE STOCKING IN DOUBLE STITCH.
(For Illustration see Page 185.)

No. 32.—Cast 116 stitches of knitting silk on three knitting needles of suitable size, and knit one round plain. If woollen yarn is used, cast on fewer stitches according to the size desired, keeping the number even. K 1, p 1 for 10 rounds to form the ribbed edge. Then * sl 1, k 1, pass the left-hand needle through the slipped stitch from left to right and knit it*. Repeat between stars for the round. This is the "double" stitch. Knit the next round plain. Alternate the rounds in this way for 7 inches. Then begin to shape the hose by narrowing one stitch on each side of the middle stitch of one of the needles. Knit 6 rounds, double and plain alternately, and narrow again. Continue to narrow one stitch on each side of the middle stitch until 20 stitches have been narrowed off. The middle stitch is the seam. Continue to knit in alternate double and plain rounds until the leg measures 17 inches long. Divide the stitches so that one-half will be all on the needle with the seam stitch in the middle, and knit the heel on this needle in double stitch across, and purl stitch back on the wrong side, thus alternately, for 2

inches. Knit the second third of the stitches in the center of the needle plain, and knit the last stitch together with the first one on the needle holding the last third of the stitches. Turn and purl back, knitting the end stitch of the second third together with the first of the one-third stitches on the other needle. Knit across and narrow the same way. Purl back and narrow, and so on until every stitch is knit and the cap of the heel turned. Then pick up the selvedge stitches down the side of the heel, knit across plain and pick up the selvedge stitches on the opposite side. Knit plain and narrow one stitch on each side just where the heel begins every other round, until there are as many stitches as there were just before beginning the heel. When the foot measures (inside the heel) 6 inches, narrow at the beginning and end of each needle as follows: K 1, n, k plain across the needle, except three stitches, then n, k 1. Repeat every other round, knitting the alternate rounds plain. Work in this way till six stitches are left. Bind off last six stitches and secure the end of thread on the wrong side.

Twice the time is required to knit a stocking in this double stitch as in plain style, but "double stitch" will wear twice as long as the plain.

RIBBED BICYCLE STOCKING.
(For Illustration see Page 185.)

No. 33.—Cast 40 stitches of silk, woollen or cotton, on each of three medium-sized knitting needles. Knit once around plain. K 3, p 1, for 10 rounds.* Then th o, k 2 to., all around; next round plain; repeat from * 3 times. Then, k 3, p 1 for 7 inches. Knit 3, p 1 all around to the middle of one needle, when narrow 1 stitch on each side of a purled (center) stitch in the middle of the needle. Continue to k 3, p 1, and narrow one stitch each side of the seam stitch every 5 rounds for 7 inches. (The uneven numbers in the ribbed stitches will come straight when the narrowing has been finished.) Knit 3, p 1 for 6 inches, and then divide the stitches so that one half will be on one needle, for the heel. Keep the center stitch in the middle of that needle and knit plain on the right side and purl on the wrong, back and forth, until 2½ inches have been knitted. Then purl to center of needle. Fold the right sides of the heel flat so that the stitches on the two needles lie evenly together. Knit 1; k 2 stitches (one from each needle) together, and bind the stitch previously knitted over them; continue until but one stitch is left. Pick up the selvedge stitches of the heel, knit across plain and pick up the opposite selvedge stitches. Knit plain, narrowing one stitch on each side just where the heel begins every other round until there are as many stitches as there were just before beginning the heel. Knit plain 6 inches and begin the toe by narrowing at the beginning and end of each needle, as follows: K 1, n, k plain across the needle except 3 stitches; then n, k 1. Repeat every other round, knitting the alternate rounds plain and working until six stitches are left. Bind these off and secure the end of thread on the wrong side.